McGraw-Hill

Handbook
of English

Canadian Edition

Harry Shaw, formerly Director, Workshops in
Composition, New York University, and
Lecturer in English, Columbia University

McGraw-Hill Company of Canada Limited
Toronto • Montreal • New York • London • Sydney
Mexico • Panama • Johannesburg • Dusseldorf

ACKNOWLEDGMENTS

We wish to thank these authors, publishers, and other holders of copyright for permission to use the following excerpts from copyright materials:

The excerpt from *This Green World* by Rutherford Platt, reprinted by permission of Dodd, Mead & Company and Rutherford Platt. The excerpts from "Why a Classic Is a Classic" and other essays from *Literary Taste: How to Form It* by Arnold Bennett, reprinted by permission of Doubleday & Co., Inc. The excerpt from "Liberty for What?" by Alexander Miklejohn from *Harper's Magazine*, reprinted by permission of Alexander Miklejohn and Harper's Magazine, Inc. The excerpts from *The Bases of Speech* by G. S. Gray and C. M. Wise, *On Various Kinds of Thinking* by James Harvey Robinson, and from "Comfort" by Aldous Huxley, reprinted by permission of Harper and Row Publishers. The excerpts from "Loyalty and Freedom" by Archibald MacLeish, reprinted by permission of Houghton Mifflin Co. The excerpts from "Education for Freedom" by Robert Maynard Hutchins, reprinted by permission of the Louisiana State University Press. The dictionary excerpts from *Webster's Seventh New Collegiate Dictionary* and *Webster's Third New International Dictionary*, reprinted by permission of G. & C. Merriam Co., Publishers of the Merriam-Webster Dictionaries. The excerpt from *The Sea Around Us* by Rachel L. Carson, copyright © 1950, 1951, 1960 by Rachel L. Carson, reprinted by permission of the Oxford University Press, Inc. The excerpt from "Faith in Science" by I. I. Rabi in the *Atlantic Monthly*, January 1951, reprinted by permission of I. I. Rabi. The excerpts from *A Mencken Chrestomathy* (1949) by H. L. Mencken and the excerpt from *The American College Dictionary*, reprinted by permission of Random House, Inc. The excerpt from "The Uses of the Moon" by Arthur C. Clarke, copyright © 1961 by Harper & Brothers, Publishers, reprinted by permission of the author and his agents, Scott Meredith Literary Agency, Inc., 580 Fifth Avenue, New York, New York 10036. The excerpt from "How to Find Time to Read" by Louis Shores, reprinted by permission of Louis Shores. The excerpts from *How to Read a Book* by Mortimer J. Adler, "Why Men Fight" by Will Durant, *The Secret of Santa Vittoria* by Robert Crichton, and "The Organization Man" by William H. Whyte, reprinted by permission of Simon & Schuster, Inc. The excerpt from *The Grapes of Wrath* by John Steinbeck, reprinted by permission of The Viking Press, Inc. Dictionary excerpt from *Webster's New World Dictionary*, reprinted by permission of The World Publishing Company. Dictionary excerpt from *Concise Oxford Dictionary:* reprinted by permission of Oxford at the Clarendon Press

FOREWORD

The *McGraw-Hill Handbook of English*, Second Edition, is designed to help you discover, develop, and refine the skills you need to meet the speaking and writing demands of a lifetime. Its fundamental objective is to provide training in correct, clear, effective, and appropriate writing and rewriting. To this end, the book now in your hands describes English as it is employed by careful, accurate speakers and writers — and by others not always either careful or accurate. It states the facts about usage of the English language that educated people should know, whether or not they wish to adopt and follow them in part or in whole.

Throughout, the *McGraw-Hill Handbook of English* tries to make clear distinctions between *grammar* and *usage*, that is, between (1) a systematic description of words and their structures, patterns, and relationships in, say, a sentence, and (2) the ways in which Canadians actually use their language in various situations. The handbook takes the position that the writing of students is normally and rightly expected to be different from informal speech, but it also recognizes that the style of one's writing and speech should be appropriate to each occasion and modified as needed by differing purposes.

This handbook is not rigid and inflexible in its prescriptive rules concerning usage, but neither does it advocate a laissez-faire attitude of "anything goes." A student, or any user of English, can be so intimidated by "rules" or "correct grammar" that he is unable to express himself with the ease, naturalness, and effectiveness which should be his right and his heritage. Conversely, every student should realize that, in certain clearly defined circumstances, "bad grammar" or poor usage — using *ain't,* misspelling a word, saying *went* when *gone* is indicated, or writing an ill-advised fragmentary sentence — can cost a social opportunity, a job, a promotion, or even a potential friend.

This handbook is filled with specific recommendations and definite suggestions. If some consider them to be "rules and regulations," such may be the needs of students seeking definite answers. Much about language is *descriptive* (the answer, for example, to the question, "Do good writers split infinitives?" °), but the application of this information must be sometimes *prescriptive* (the answer to "Should *students* split infinitives?" °). Improvement in thinking and writing involves replacing bad habits with good; learning composition — or any intellectual or social activity — is necessarily negative in part.

Such a "middle-of-the-road" approach may appear reactionary to some and overly liberal to others. Staying in the middle of the road is

° The answer to both questions is "Yes, sometimes."

indeed fatal on a highway, but not, perhaps, on the highway to better speech and composition. In short, the credo of this edition of the *McGraw-Hill Handbook of English* is that expressed by Theodore M. Bernstein of *The New York Times* in his excellent book, *Watch Your Language:*

> To be sure, the English language is a changing and growing thing. All its users have, of course, a perceptible effect upon it. But in changing and growing it needs no contrived help from chitchat columnists or advertising writers or comic strip artists or television speakers. It will evolve nicely by itself. If anything, it requires protection from influences that try to push it too fast. There is need, not for those who would halt its progress altogether, but for those who can keep a gentle foot on the brake and a guiding hand on the steering wheel. . . .

This new edition offers a thorough reworking of the previous edition. Addition, deletion, emendation, and expansion are evident in every part of the book and all of its extensive exercises.

The principal changes in the second edition occur in three major areas: (1) Substantial recognition is given to the findings and recommendations of modern linguists. The handbook does not claim to be in the avant-garde of linguistic theory. But it does incorporate several modern insights concerning the structure of the English language into an eclectic approach combining, hopefully, the most usable and teachable elements of both "traditional" and "scientific" grammatical terminology and practice.

(2) Actual usage on both formal and informal levels has been carefully evaluated and, in certain constructions, has been modified and liberalized. The handbook recognizes that some prescriptive usage is outmoded, inconsistent, and illogical; it avoids, therefore, recommending once-hallowed absurdities in ways of speaking and writing. Nevertheless, it attempts never to waver from those principles of good usage which are based on clarity, social usefulness, good judgment, and common sense.

(3) Major additions have been made to (a) the treatment of the longer paper and the paragraph; this expanded treatment is in line with the increased emphasis upon the study of rhetoric as a sensible, workable approach to composition; and (b) special purposes and problems in writing—the last-named constituting a completely new section in this edition.

The author believes that the writing needs of most students are best served by genuinely solid work, under teacher supervision, in thinking, planning, writing, and rewriting. Learning to think clearly and to write correctly and appropriately are worthwhile intellectual pursuits that are valuable not alone in composition classes but in all intellectual endeavors.

In short, this edition of the *McGraw-Hill Handbook of English* has been thoroughly revised and updated. But it would be far less helpful than hopefully it is without the thoughts, suggestions, and contributions of others. My indebtedness is greatest to Virginia Shaffer, formerly head of the English Department, Forest Park High School, Baltimore, now Coordinator of the Writing Program, Johns Hopkins University. As coauthor of the previous edition, Miss Shaffer has made contributions which continue into the present volume. Responsibility for this edition belongs wholly to the undersigned, but hearty thanks are due to this able, dedicated teacher whose imprint and influence fortunately persist. The roll call of others who have aided all along the line is too lengthy for listing here, including, as it does, former students, teachers who have used the previous edition, and colleagues in various schools and universities. Among these, mention must be made at least of Philip Burnham, St. Paul's School, Concord, New Hampshire; Ruskin Kerr, Long Lots Junior High School, Westport, Connecticut; Dr. Hans J. Gottlieb, formerly of Washington Square College, New York University; Robert Morris, Kent School, Kent, Connecticut; Margaret Casey, Bethesda-Chevy Chase High School, Maryland; Dudley C. Enos, George Washington High School, Denver, Colorado; Mary Ellen Bridges, Central High School, Tulsa, Oklahoma. I would also like to express my gratitude to Benno Curtis and Ann Perry, who have performed many editorial and secretarial chores with loyalty and intelligence.

Harry Shaw

CONTENTS

GRAMMAR

USAGE

PUNCTUATION AND MECHANICS

DICTION

THE SENTENCE

THE PARAGRAPH

THE LONGER PAPER

SPECIAL PURPOSES AND PROBLEMS

GRAMMAR—
WHAT IT IS AND WHY

"Why study grammar again? I've been swallowing it for years. By now, I know all the grammar I'll ever need. If not, I'll never learn. Besides, grammar is dull and dry. It's not worth studying."

Do such remarks express your feelings about grammar? They do reflect common student attitudes. Furthermore, these opinions are neither silly nor illogical.

First, you *have* been studying grammar for years. In fact, the first school you attended may have been called "grammar" school. You may be brimful of grammar study. And it is possible that you now have a masterful command of English grammar.

If so, you are indeed lucky. But you might heed a small warning. Like many other words, "grammar" no longer means the same thing to everyone. You are probably tired of hearing that this is an era of quick and constant change. But you had better be aware that, in schools, not only attitudes toward grammar but basic ideas of what grammar is are vigorously argued. Definitions and principles that may be settled in your mind are being called into serious question.

Then again you may consider yourself one of those who didn't and can't learn grammar.

Was it that you had grammar stuffed into you the way a python is force-fed at a zoo, so that now you are curled up in a verbally listless and lifeless cage? Perhaps you had to memorize endless lists of "rules" and then write sentences "applying" them. Maybe everything you said or wrote was put under a microscope to find each mistake or error. Possibly you were bombarded with terms like "subjunctive," "genitive," "ellipsis," "phonemes," "substantive," to name just a few of a host of words whose meaning or practical value you could never quite grasp? Were you required to draw lines for diagrams and then force words and phrases to fit into spaces or ride on slanted lines until you began to think of a sentence as a stick-man flat on his back with his arms and legs going every-which-way?

Without denying the good reasons anyone may have to feel antagonistic to grammar, you may have trouble in school if your attitude does not change. Certain requirements apply to those who possess the advantage of an education, the very first of which is the character of the language one uses. Regardless of the accents and idioms retained from your geographical or social background, the language you speak and write will be subjected to certain standards wherever you go. It will simply have to look and sound "grammatical"; otherwise you may find yourself being snubbed socially or rejected for a job without really knowing why.

In short, do not confuse a right to complain with an excuse for ignorance.

Boys do not stop looking at girls because they must smile at an occasional witch. If a way could be found to make grammar as exciting as a girl on the beach, English teachers could hope to be millionaires. Grammar, however, can be interesting, even exciting, if you see it for what it is and, more important, understand what it can do for you.

Actually, because grammar can resemble a science, some people enjoy observing it, gathering facts, and classifying results just as do scientists in fields other than language. A linguist draws conclusions from his observations as does the chemist, the botanist, or the physicist. Most students, however, are content with an understanding of basic principles evolved from the conclusions of linguists. Often they are content with much less than this. Medical students do not ordinarily enjoy the study of anatomy, as such, but a knowledge of anatomy is necessary for both physician and surgeon. Many football players dislike drill in fundamentals, but games are won by players who have mastered blocking and tackling and are lost by those who have not. A study of anatomy, of football fundamentals, of grammar, is but a means to an end. Thus considered, none of these endeavors can be considered "dull" or "dry."

Grammar is ordinarily understood as a statement, or series of statements, of the way a language works; English grammar is "the English way of saying things." That is, grammar discusses the forms of words, their use in phrases, clauses, and sentences, their tenses, cases, and other changes in form. The word *grammar*, which comes from a Greek word *gramma* ("letter," "written symbol"), now means the basic structure of an entire given language.

The preceding paragraph defines grammar as the scientific, systematic *description* of a language. When grammar deals with the evolution of words and compares present with former usage, it is called "historical." When the grammar of one language, say that of English, is compared with the grammar of another, say Spanish, it is called "comparative."

Besides these types of scientific, analytical grammar — wholly unconcerned with what is "correct" or "incorrect," "right" or "wrong" — we should consider *prescriptive* grammar. This is the application of so-called "rules" as guides to expression, as statements of how people *should* speak and write. Much prescriptive grammar is out-of-date, illogical, and inconsistent. And yet a certain amount of prescription is needed if our speaking and writing are to conform to principles extended from descriptive grammar. For example, descriptive grammar reveals that most speakers and writers use the objective form after a preposition: *between him and me*. It is prescriptive grammar which suggests that *between he and I* is "incorrect" and that the use of such an expression may cost you embarrassment *or* money *or* a job. Prescriptive grammar which forbids ever ending a sentence with a preposition is absurd; prescriptive grammar which advises that you use common sense and reasoned judgment in splitting infinitives is practical and sensible.

It is true that *what* we have to say is more interesting than a study of the language itself. Yet grammar can also be "worth studying" if only because, properly understood, it can help us to express our ideas clearly and effectively. Obscurity and weakness in writing and sloppiness of sentence structure are often traceable to an inadequate understanding of grammar. You do not need to know the principle of the combustion engine in order to drive an automobile, but you must know where to insert the ignition key, how to start the motor, how to work an automatic or manual shift, steer, and apply brakes. Some drivers are so proficient in these operations that they perform them "without thinking."

Skilled speakers and writers are not always consciously aware of grammar. A professional writer might find it difficult to define an adjective, but if the phrase "a night when the wind blew" came to mind, he might "instinctively" change it to the shorter and possibly more effective "windy night." If you do not know what a clause and a phrase are, you will find it difficult to follow your instructor's suggestion to "reduce predication." But only a little knowledge of grammar will enable you to change the sentence "Diphtheria, which used to be a deadly disease, is now rare" to the more direct "Diphtheria, once a deadly disease, is now rare." Every good writer has a working knowledge of words and their ways.

Certain differences between speech and writing are both clear and important. What many educated people might consider acceptable in informal speech they would frown upon if it appeared in writing. (Also, some words and expressions used in formal writing might sound stuffy and pretentious in ordinary speech.) An attitude of "anything goes" in speech does not apply in most writing situations—and *writing* is the subject matter of the book you hold in your hand. (See Section 117.)

The grammar section of this book is concerned with conveying a clear and working understanding of how to write effective sentences. You simply cannot put pen to paper with certainty and confidence if you do not have a sure sense of the sentence.

When you begin to write sentences, you become impressed with a basic difference between speaking and writing. Writing is a more formal mode of communicating than speaking. In ordinary conversation you can rely on vocal intonations, surrounding circumstances, what the hearer knows of you and the subject of the discussion, and the opportunity to explain and clarify in response to specific questions if your meaning is not immediately clear.

However, a written text is usually read at another time, in another place, by a reader who is by himself or at least in a state of relative quiet. All the easy-going give-and-take that makes talking a pleasant pastime may be supplied by your reader as his eyes run calmly over your page. But can you be sure?

You can be sure only if you know *how to* write. The words "how to" involve the mastery of practical guidelines and principles that have been evolving and developing since the day man came upon a way to translate spoken sounds into visual symbols in a relatively simple system which we call the *alphabet*. Our word for alphabet comes, as you probably know, from the first two *letters* of the Greek alphabet. Grammar can be looked at as a further elaboration of any language's system of writing.

Grammar is elaborate because the art of writing is more complicated than that of speaking. The alphabet is a simplified code for the sounds the voice can make.

The letters and the sounds they represent blend together to make the written words (composed of letters) and the spoken words (composed of sounds) of the English language. The proper arrangement of these words, whether written or spoken, is the fundamental device which grammar uses to make meaning possible.

Reading is the art or technique of receiving meaning from a page. Writing is the art or technique of putting meaning on a page. And grammar is what makes both reading and writing possible.

Because man was not conscious of *grammar* until he began to write, are we then to say that there was no such thing? At least there was a solid basis for grammar. Because language, before writing, was a system or structure of vocal sound arrangements, men could communicate meanings by spoken words. The structure or system by which sounds are arranged into significant units, or words, and these words are related into larger units of meaning —like statements, questions, or outcries—makes writing possible.

If you consider that man has been on the earth from four to ten million years, according to current guesses, and that he has been working with the alphabet system of writing for around five thousand years, the fact that you may have difficulty understanding language systems should not be surprising. Recall also that man discovered how to mass produce alphabetic writing by means of printing only a little over five hundred years ago: a book like the one you are reading now is a relatively new development. The idea that everybody should learn how to read and write has been current for less than two hundred years.

That everyone should be able to read and write is now one of the central assumptions of our economic, political, and social system. Try to get a decent job, cast an intelligent vote, run for public office, or move up to a higher social level and you will see how essential it is to read and write in a modern industrial democracy such as ours.

You *must* be literate. You will be judged by the literate character of your speaking and your writing; and literate writing, among many other things, is grammatical. This book attempts to present an approach to English grammar that will give you a clear and coherent sense of how English sentences are written.

Sentences are composed of words. Grammar breaks down or, better, classifies words as "parts of speech." They are grouped according to the purpose they serve, or how they convey meaning *as words:*

Naming words	nouns and pronouns
Asserting words	verbs
Modifying words	adjectives and adverbs
Joining words	conjunctions and prepositions
Exclamatory words	interjections

But words work together to convey meaning. Grammar is also concerned with explaining how the parts of speech can be grouped together in sentences. Structures involving groups of words, that is, *phrases* and *clauses,* are essential to mature sentence construction, so that we must see how parts of speech are placed with one another to produce these structures.

Finally, words take on basic functions in the sentence, which is the central unit of meaning in all writing. How the parts of speech function in the sentence as a whole is really what grammar is all about.

1. NOUNS

1a. DEFINITION

A *noun* (derived from the Latin word *nomen,* meaning "name") designates or names a person, place, or thing; a quality, idea, or action; an event or point in time.

> *Albert* met his *sister's* best *friend,* a pretty *girl.* (Persons)
> They were standing at the *corner* of *Maple* and *Third* in the downtown *section* of *Uranium City.* (Places)
> Albert was carrying his *coat, necktie,* and *umbrella.* (Things)
> They were on their way to the *Homecoming Dance,* which

was held every *fall*, usually in *November* before the *game* with Central. (Events and points in time)

Her *pride* suffered because of her *forgetfulness*, but Albert's *courtesy* to her made *happiness* return. (Qualities)

The family *honor* had been preserved. (General idea)

The definition of a noun given above has certain weaknesses. It is circular, *noun* and *name* being two forms of the same word. The definition really states that "a name is the name of a person, place, or thing, etc." Also, no matter how many subdivisions are added to the definition, some nouns do not easily fit into it. The real markers, or characteristics, of nouns may be summarized as follows:

1. Nouns are usually preceded by such words as *the, a, an, my, your, his, her, some, each, every, their, this, that.*

2. Certain nouns have characteristic endings — *al, tion, ness, ment, ure, dom, ism, ance,* for example — which distinguish them from corresponding verbs or adjectives: *arrive, arrival; refine, refinement; depart, departure; soft, softness; real, realism; rely, reliance; wise, wisdom.*

3. Nouns and identically spelled verbs may sometimes be differentiated by accent. The first member in each of these pairs of words is a noun, the second a verb: *per'mit, permit'; rec'ord, record'; sur'vey, survey'; sub'ject, subject'.*

4. Nouns are found in set positions, such as before a verb (a *lion* roars), after a verb (wash the *car)*, or after a preposition (working for *money)*.

5. Nouns may be singular or plural in *number*. The plural of most English nouns is obtained by adding *-s* or *-es* to the singular form: boys, trees, fields, beaches, peaches. Some nouns have only one form for both the singular and the plural: deer, sheep, moose. Some nouns have irregular plurals: oxen, mice, wives.

6. Nouns have four genders: *masculine* (man, boy), *feminine* (girl, woman), and *neuter* (chalk, dirt). When a noun may be either masculine or feminine, it has a *common* gender (teacher, companion, friend).

7. Nouns have three *cases*: subject case, object case, and possessive. In English, nouns have a common form for both the subject and the object case. An apostrophe is used to designate a noun in the possessive case: Joe's, ship's, neighbor's.

1b. KINDS OF NOUNS

Nouns are classified in many ways.

A *common* noun is a name given to all the members of a class: *dozen, child, farm, road, city, boxes, boy, structure.* Common nouns can be recognized as such because they do *not* begin with a capital letter.

A *proper* noun names a particular member of a class; it *does* begin with a capital: *Rover, Michael, Sunny Acres, Don Valley Parkway, Toronto, Jack Dempsey, Eiffel Tower.*

An *abstract* noun is the name of a quality or general idea that cannot be felt by the senses: *faith, intelligence, grace, happiness, courage, fear.*

Concrete nouns name material (tangible) things that can be perceived by one or more of the senses: *fire, aroma, book, hamburger, stone, rose, record, candy.*

A *collective* noun names a group of individuals. Although it refers to more than one, it is singular in form: *pair, committee, squad, team, senate, species, crowd, army, crew, assembly.*

Can you name a noun that can fit in three or more classes or compose a sentence using all five classes?

EXERCISE 1

Write down all of the nouns in the following sentences. Be prepared to discuss in class the classification (common, proper, concrete, abstract, or collective) of each noun.

1. They saw a marvelous performance at the theater.
2. That is a delightful perfume which you are wearing.
3. All generalizations are false.
4. Your son told me that he wants to be an astronaut someday.
5. Which lawn mower do you prefer?
6. Snoopy has become a national hero; Linus is also popular.
7. The policeman opened up the hydrant and we then had a good time splashing around in the water.
8. I shall never forget what's-his-name; he was quite a fellow.
9. Stephen Leacock was born with the gift of laughter and a sense that the world was mad.
10. Autumn is my favorite season, although I am also very fond of summer; spring and winter have never appealed to me.

2. PRONOUNS

2a. DEFINITION

A *pronoun* (from the Latin *pro* and *nomen*, meaning "for a name") is difficult to define because this part of speech includes groups of quite different words. In general, however, a pronoun is a word that can be replaced by a noun in a particular context. Pronouns can function like nouns as subjects and objects; many pronouns also have plural forms and a genitive (possessive) case formed with *s*. A pronoun, then, acts in the place of, or on behalf of, a noun.

2b. KINDS OF PRONOUNS

Pronouns are ordinarily classified as *personal, relative, demonstrative, interrogative, reflexive, intensive, indefinite,* and *reciprocal.*

Personal pronouns refer to an individual or individuals. Of all pronouns, this group causes the greatest difficulty. Personal pronouns have thirty case forms, some of which include all genders and some with special forms for masculine, feminine, and neuter. Personal pronouns also bear the labels of first person, second person, third person. First person pronouns indicate the speaker or writer, either singular or plural. Second person pronouns indicate the person or persons spoken to, with identical forms for singular and plural. Gender (or sex) is the same for all first and second person pronouns. Third person pronouns indicate the person or persons spoken of or written about. Third person pronouns involve considerations of number and gender, as shown in this table:

		Singular	
Nominative (Subject Case)		*Genitive* (or Possessive)	*Objective* (Object Case)
1st person	I	my, mine	me
2nd person	you	your, yours	you

(masculine)	he	his	him
(feminine)	she	her, hers	her
(neuter)	it	its	it

		Plural	
1st person	we	our, ours	us
2nd person	you	your, yours	you
3rd person			
(all genders)	they	their, theirs	them

Relative pronouns relate or connect the clauses they introduce to independent clauses (see Section 8). Specifically, a relative pronoun connects an adjective clause to an antecedent (the noun or pronoun to which a pronoun refers or for which it is substituted).

> The man *who* wants to become Prime Minister must campaign vigorously.
> The used car *which* you sold to me last weekend broke down.
> The novel *that* I read has since become a best-seller.

Each of these relative pronouns has an antecedent ("man," "car," and "novel"), and each introduces a subordinate clause.

The same forms — *who, whose, whom, which, that* — serve for gender or number; their having gender or being singular or plural depends upon their antecedents. The choice of a relative pronoun is also largely determined by its antecedent. *Who, whose,* and *whom* are used to refer to persons. *Which* is used to refer to inanimate objects, animals, and groups of persons. *That* may refer to either things or persons.

Who, which, and *that* are frequently used relative pronouns; *whoever, whenever, whichever,* and *whatever* are less often used. *Whosoever, whichsoever,* and *whatsoever* have gone almost entirely out of current use.

Demonstrative pronouns point out and identify nouns or other pronouns. The important demonstrative pronouns are *this* and *that* (singular), *these* and *those* (plural), and *such* (singular or plural).

> *This* is the man I told you about in my letter.
> *That* is the school which I attended for six years.
> *These* are the missing articles.

Those are the ideals which we all admire.

Such a newspaper and *such* magazines are worth reading.

An *interrogative* pronoun *(who, whom, whose, which, what,* occasionally *whoever, whichever, whatever)* introduces a question.

Who has asked you to the dance?

Whom did they expect to play in the finals?

Which of the crab grass experts did he recommend?

What can I say, dear, after I say I'm sorry?

Whose Corvette has the best chance of winning the race?

Whatever do you mean by that remark?

A *reflexive pronoun* is used to refer to the subject of a sentence or clause. It is a compound of one of the personal pronouns plus *self* or *selves: myself, yourself, himself, herself, itself, ourselves, yourselves, themselves.*

Did you burn *yourself?*

He gave *himself* a present for his birthday.

They appointed *themselves* to the committee.

An *intensive pronoun* is used to draw particular attention to a noun. Intensives take the same forms as reflexives.

We must give the same rights to the men *themselves.*

The doctor *himself* examined the x-rays.

Indefinite pronouns are less specific in reference and exact in meaning than other pronouns. It is often difficult or impossible to pin down a precise antecedent for an indefinite pronoun. Among the more frequently used are *all, another, any, anyone, anything, everybody, everyone, everything, few, many, nobody, none, one, several, some, each.* The pronoun *one* and its compound forms, and compound forms built on the element *-body* form the possessive in the same way as nouns (anybody's, everyone's).

A *reciprocal pronoun* completes an interchange of action involved in the predicate. This interchange can be seen in the following sentences which exhibit the only reciprocal pronouns in English:

The two teams complimented *each other.*

The opposing lines scowled at *one another.*

EXERCISE 2

Certain pronouns are italicized in the sentences below. On a separate sheet, classify each as one of the eight kinds of pronouns.

1. That battered chemistry book is *yours*.
2. *Which* of the sailboats crossed the finish line first?
3. *All* of the sea gulls hovered above the pier, waiting for scraps of fish.
4. *Whom* did you vote for, Mr. Peepers?
· 5. Mother, I want to do it *myself!*
6. Do you know what *it* means to be "Miss Canada"?
7. As for the flamingos, *theirs* is not to reason why; theirs is but to do or fly.
8. *Few* of us remember streetcars on Yonge Street.
9. The passengers on the flight were friendly to *one another*.
10. *This* is a gross error of judgment, Colonel Arnold.

EXERCISE 3

On a separate sheet of paper substitute a noun for each of the pronouns in these sentences:

1. Please give the hamburger patties to her.
2. That is the building referred to in the catalogue.
3. Be kind to one another.
4. Edgar Blossom himself attended the concert.
5. Lamar Gene Gumbody asked them to roll back the carpet.
6. Those in the top balcony can listen to the music on the radio.
7. Anybody can see that the game is lost.
8. For whom are you preparing the dessert?
9. My friend and she have had a violent argument.
10. Nearly everybody left the theater before the play was finished.

3. VERBS AND VERBALS

3a. DEFINITION

A verb is a word which, through the addition of various endings or internal changes, specifies actions or events which take place in time. In greater detail, a verb may be defined as any member of a class of words (parts of speech) that typically expresses action, state, or a relation between two things, that functions as the main element of a predicate and that, when inflected, exhibits changes indicating tense, tone, voice, mood, and agreement with its subject or object.

The Johnsons *moved* to their new home last week.

I *shall be* ready when you *arrive*.

Jack *worked* all summer on various community projects.

A *verbal* is a verb form that cannot serve as a predicate. The three kinds of verbals are *participles, gerunds,* and *infinitives.* Each of these three kinds of verbals is discussed in Section 3g.

3b. KINDS OF VERBS

Verbs may be classified as *transitive, intransitive,* or *linking.*

A *transitive* verb is regularly followed by a noun or pronoun (the object) which completes the action specified by the verb.

John *hit* the *ball.*

Tony *has* a part-time *job* on weekends.

The farmer *planted* three *rows* of corn near his house.

A transitive verb shows the relationship existing between the noun or pronoun (the subject) which performs the action specified by the verb and the noun which follows it (the object). In a sentence like "John hit the ball," *hit* expresses the nature of the relationship between *John* and *ball.*

An *intransitive* verb does not need to be followed by a noun or pronoun to make complete sense in the sentence in which it appears.

The fullback *ran* directly through the center of the line.

Anderson *walked* slowly down the street.

Many verbs can be used in *either* a *transitive* or *intransitive* sense.

We *read* the *news* with great care. (transitive)

We *read* until late at night. (intransitive)

I *won* the first *set.* (transitive)

I *won* easily. (intransitive)

A *linking,* or *copula,* verb shows the relationship between the subject and the noun which follows it. The noun which follows it is sometimes called the *predicate noun.* Frequently, a linking verb expresses the relationship existing between the subject and an adjective following it. The adjective which follows it is sometimes called the *predicate adjective.* Linking verbs are illustrated and further discussed in Section 16.

3c. CHARACTERISTICS OF VERBS

Verbs have certain characteristics.

1. English verbs have a base form. The base form of a verb is called the *infinitive* form. It is sometimes preceded by the word *to.*

   to run, to walk, to cook, to evaporate

2. Verbs in English have *three principal forms* in addition to the base form. (See Section 15.) These forms have certain inflectional endings.

Present Tense—The present tense of English verbs is the same as the base form.

   to run, run; to walk, walk; to hide, hide

Past Tense—The past tense of English verbs varies, depending upon whether the verb is *regular* or *irregular.* In regular verbs, the past tense is formed by adding the ending *-ed* to the base form.

   walk, walked; invent, invented; originate, originated

The past tense of irregular verbs differs from word to word and must be learned individually. Most past tense forms of irregular verbs are familiar to native speakers of English.

   throw, threw; tear, tore; say, said; go, went

Past Participle—The past participle of regular verbs is identical to the past tense.

   organize, organized, *organized;* arrange, arranged, *arranged;*
   conduct, conducted, *conducted;* solve, solved, *solved*

The past participle of irregular verbs differs from word to word and must be learned individually. It is always the form which makes sense with the verb *have:* have *gone,* have *written,* have *torn.*

   run, *run;* sing, *sung;* draw, *drawn;* do, *done*

English verbs also have a *present participial* form which is obtained by adding *-ing* to the base form.

    have, having; go, going; rain, raining; speak, speaking

3. Verbs in English have one other characteristic inflectional ending. When a verb in the present tense follows either the words *he, she,* or *it,* or a noun which may be substituted for *he, she,* or *it,* the letter *-s* (or *-es* with some verbs) is added to the base form.

    sing, sings; run, runs; go, goes; laugh, laughs

4. In the present tense, an English verb changes its inflectional ending when the subject changes from singular to plural.

    A bird *sings.* Birds *sing.* Joe *goes.* Bill and Joe *go.*
    Sara *plays* the piano. The girls *play* the piano.

5. Certain *prefixes and suffixes* are used with verbs. The prefixes *en-* and *be-* are often used with verbs.

    *en*force, *en*able, *en*title, *en*tangle, *en*tail, *be*come, *be*friend, *be*head, *be*stir, *be*moan

The suffixes *-(i)fy, -ate,* and *-ize* commonly signal verbs.

    testi*fy,* veri*fy,* clari*fy,* codi*fy,* segreg*ate,* supplic*ate,* oper*ate,* domestic*ate,* civil*ize,* colon*ize,* urban*ize,* symbol*ize*

6. *Verb markers,* or *auxiliaries,* frequently signal verbs. The most common auxiliaries in English are *be* (and all its forms), *have, do, can, could, shall, should, will, would, may, might, must,* and *ought.* (See Section 16.)

3d. VOICE

Transitive verbs are classified as to *voice.*

A verb is in the *active voice* when the noun or pronoun which names the performer of the action specified by the verb is the actual subject of the verb.

    We *built* a large house in the country.

    The engineers *have developed* new types of electrical refrigerators.

    The Great Coalition *helped* bring about Confederation.

A verb is in the *passive voice* when its grammatical subject is not the actual performer of the activity specified by the verb. When verbs appear in the passive voice, the noun which names the actual performer of the action appears either in a prepositional phrase at the end of the sentence or is not specifically named at all. The noun which names the actual performer of the action of passive verbs can always be determined by converting the verb to the active voice.

The criminal was apprehended by the police. (passive)

The police apprehended the criminal. (active)
The firm was run by one man. (passive)

One man ran the firm. (active)
The money was found in the subway. (passive)

(The man) found the money in the subway. (active)

NOTE: The passive voice always consists of some form of the verb *be* followed by the past participle form of the verb.

3e. MOOD

The *mood* of a verb stipulates the manner in which the writer or speaker thinks of the action. (See Section 18.)

3f. TENSE

Verbs have *tense*. Tense indicates the time of the action or state of existence expressed by the verb. Tense can be thought of as either *simple* or *progressive*. The *simple tenses* designate actions which are either occurring now, have occurred in the past, or will occur in the future. The *progressive tenses* designate continuing action in either present or past time. (See Section 17.)

3g. VERBALS

A *participle* is a word which functions either as a verb or as an adjective. The present participle always ends in -*ing* (*laughing, throwing*). The past participle is the third principal part of a verb (*laughed, thrown*). The perfect participle consists of *having* or *having been* plus the past participle (*having laughed, having been thrown*). Some past participles end in *-ed;* others in *-n;* still others change the vowel (*sung*); some change their form completely (*sought*). The participle can take an object and be modified by an adverb. When it does, the group of words forms a *participial phrase.* (See Section 7.)

A *gerund* is a verbal noun. Gerunds have the same form as present or perfect participles, but are used as nouns instead of adjectives.

> *Studying* is hard work.
>
> *Saying* that studying is hard work is easy.

A gerund may take an object and be modified by an adverb or adjective.

> *Completing* the *project* was the goal of the committee.
>
> *Ending the famine* was *difficult.*
>
> *Eating well* is *desirable.*

An *infinitive* is the form of the verb usually preceded by *to.* An infinitive may be used as a noun, an adjective, or an adverb.

> His greatest fear is *to forget* his lines in the play. (noun)
>
> John had three weeks *to spend* on his vacation. (adjective)
>
> Harvey was disappointed *to have failed* his examination. (adverb)

Sometimes the word *to* is omitted from the infinitive.

> Let him *sail* with you.
>
> Will they make him *resign?*
>
> Help me *decorate* the gymnasium.

The infinitive may take an object and be modified by an adverb or an adverbial phrase or clause.

> *To find the missing lens* we searched for twenty minutes.
>
> Daisy and Tanya struggled *to swim faster.*
>
> The debris began *to accumulate along the highway.*
>
> Desmond plans *to wait until we call him.*

EXERCISE 4

On a separate sheet of paper write a complete sentence for each of the following verbs. Each must be transitive—use any tense form that you prefer.

expedite	deter
harass	allow

rattle	pursue
throw	slap
submerge	congratulate

EXERCISE 5

On a separate sheet of paper write a complete sentence for each of the following verbs. Each must be *intransitive*. Use any tense form that you prefer.

incorporate	publicize
read	swim
laugh	cough
write	insinuate
race	bounce

EXERCISE 6

The italicized verbs in these sentences are active. On a separate sheet, rewrite the sentences to make each of them passive. (Slight changes of wording may be necessary to make the revised sentences read smoothly.)

1. Howard *read* the newspaper.
2. The musicians *carried* their instruments to the theater.
3. The arrow *split* the apple.
4. Mickey Mantle *hit* his 500th home run on May 14, 1967.
5. Desmond *took* the St. Bernard for a walk on University Avenue.
6. The Crees *captured* Fort Pitt.
7. Gloria *drove* the diesel truck through the restaurant window.
8. Charlie Johnson *threw* twenty-five touchdown passes.
9. Tony *drank* the cough syrup reluctantly.
10. The airline strike *inconvenienced* thousands of travelers.

EXERCISE 7

The italicized verbs in these sentences are passive. On a separate sheet, rewrite the sentences to make each of them active.

1. The picture window was *shattered* by the softball.
2. The robins were *blown* all the way to Manitoba by the hurricane.
3. "The Littlest Hobo" is *loved* by millions of young television viewers.
4. The groundhog was *chased* by Taffy across the field.
5. We were *seen* by the spectators who then cheered us wildly.
6. The Maverley brothers' crops were *consumed* by locusts.

7. I was *given* complete directions by the provincial police.
8. Esmerelda is *considered* to be a beauty by her parents.
9. The weather report was hastily *revised* by the bureau after the tidal wave.
10. Were you *asked* to participate by the officials?

EXERCISE 8

On a separate sheet of paper, make a list of verbals from the following sentences. After each verbal, write an identifying letter: P—participle; G—gerund; I—infinitive.

1. A smiling face is better than a discontented one; to smile is one way to win friends.
2. Dewey liked to swim and dance with me, but I always felt that he would rather read than do either.
3. The man buying his ticket is a local merchant going to Montreal.
4. Having written with more than usual care, I was surprised when the teacher said that my writing was illegible.
5. As it flowed down the gray rock wall, the swiftly falling water seemed to have lost its liquid quality; it looked like a smooth and solidified pillar of green.
6. Jim's tackling and running are excellent, but I don't believe that he will ever learn to punt or catch passes.
7. To know more about a subject than other people know is a worthy ambition; not to make a parade of one's learning is an even more worthy ambition.
8. Bathing, shaving, and dressing are necessary preliminaries to eating breakfast.
9. The game already having been won, we decided to leave soon after the intermission.
10. Spoken words are naturally kept in mind with much more difficulty than those one reads, but a well-trained person can retain amazing amounts of conversation that he has heard.

4. ADJECTIVES AND ADVERBS

Certain words and groups of words are used within a sentence to specify, qualify, or otherwise determine the meaning of another word. This relationship is known grammatically as *modification*. A modifier does not *change* or *alter* the meaning of the word it modifies. The purpose of the modifier is to make the meaning of the word more exact and specific within the sentence or in the overall context. The parts of speech whose basic functions are to modify *by themselves* are *adjectives* and *adverbs*.

Full definitions of an adjective and adverb are supplied in Section 19. Look there for statements about the characteristics of these *modifying* parts of speech.

EXERCISE 9

In one column on your paper, list each word (including verbals) used as an adjective in this paragraph. In another column, list the noun that each adjective modifies. (Do not list the articles *the* or *a(n)*.) If necessary, check Section 19 before completing this exercise.

> Across a sea that was now turquoise, now emerald, we could watch the Venezuelan coastline with the purple Andes in the background. Flying fish stood a moment on their tails, flew a little distance, and dived back into the sea. The air was still. The fresh odor of the sea mingled with the heavy smell of sweat from the stevedores' bodies. In a few moments a dozen small boats had reached the side of our ship, and their brown-skinned occupants were slipping into the clear water to find the money that the passengers had thrown down for them.

EXERCISE 10

In one column on your paper, list each word (including verbals) used as an adverb in the following paragraph. In another column, list the word that each adverb modifies. If necessary, check Section 19 before completing this exercise.

> Have you read *The Ancient Mariner?* Many very interesting stories are told about the author of the poem, Samuel Coleridge. Among them are some particularly good tales of the poet's love for talking. One day Coleridge met Lamb walking rapidly to work and stopped to talk to him. Lamb, who was hurrying to reach his job on time, moved away; but Coleridge quickly grabbed the button of his listener's coat and insisted upon finishing his story. For a few minutes Lamb waited patiently, but Coleridge was apparently preparing for a long talk. Pres-

ently Lamb took a knife from his pocket and carefully cut off the button that Coleridge was holding. That evening Lamb, returning from work, saw Coleridge still holding the button and still talking vigorously.

5. CONJUNCTIONS

Conjunction is the traditional term for a limited group of words that introduce and tie together clauses and that join series of words and phrases. Because many words which function as conjunctions also have other functions, particularly adverbial uses, identifying them as a specific part of speech is sometimes difficult.

A full definition of the conjunction and a detailed list of the meanings and purposes of all commonly used conjunctions appear in Section 20.

EXERCISE 11

On your paper, identify each of the conjunctions in the sentences below according to its classification (coordinating, subordinating, or correlative). If necessary, check Section 20 before completing this exercise.

1. *After* we lit the fire, we sat back and waited for the steaks.
2. *Neither* time *nor* energy was wasted at Batoche.
3. We danced *and* laughed until sunrise.
4. Elwood cannot decide *whether or* not to study chemistry.
5. *Unless* you season the hamburgers properly, they will taste awful.
6. McGill and Trent are excellent colleges, *although* my sister prefers McMaster.
7. *Inasmuch as* Santa Fe and Taos both plan to celebrate authentic Southwestern art, Parker Plotz plans to visit New Mexico soon.
8. Jan will let you know *when* the tide goes out.
9. *Not only* Taffy *but* Tasha chases woodchucks all over the meadow.
10. Hackbart Philbin seldom loses a debate *unless* an opponent has the sense to challenge his source material.

6. PREPOSITIONS

6a. DEFINITION

A preposition is a linking word used before a noun or pronoun to show its relationship to some other word in the sentence. Note the literal meaning of the word: *pre—* "before," plus *position.* The following list contains all of the prepositions commonly used in English:

about	beside	in	since
above	besides	inside	through
across	between	into	throughout
after	beyond	like	till
against	but	near	to
along	by	notwithstanding	toward
alongside	concerning	of	under
amid	despite	off	underneath
among	down	on	until
around	during	onto	unto
at	ere	outside	up
before	except	over	upon
behind	excepting	per	with
below	for	regarding	within
beneath	from	save	without

6b. USES OF THE PREPOSITION

All prepositions (1) require an object and (2) relate to other words by modifying (modification).

Nouns, pronouns, gerund and prepositional phrases, and noun clauses can and do serve as the objects of prepositions placed before them.

> The deer ran *into* the *forest.* (Noun)
> I did it *for him.* (Pronoun)
> He took great interest *in running the contest.* (Gerund phrase)
> The column advanced *to within a mile* of town. (Prepositional phrase)
> You can quote *from whatever source serves your case.* (Noun clause)

The preposition and its object are called a *prepositional phrase*. When such a phrase modifies a noun, it acts like an adjective and thus is called *adjectival*. When it modifies a verb, it acts like an adverb and thus is called *adverbial*.

Adjectival Prepositional Phrases:
> The road *to the left* leads nowhere. (Modifies "road")
> He bought the horse *with the brown spots*. (Modifies "horse")

Adverbial Prepositional Phrases:
> He left *for the airport.* (Modifies "left")
> *In the morning* I will ask for a raise. (Modifies "will ask")

6c. SIMPLE AND COMPOUND PREPOSITIONS

There are two kinds of prepositions, *simple* and *compound*. Note these examples of simple prepositions:
> the knock *at* the door (knock-door)
> the house *by* the river (house-river)
> presents *for* children (presents-children)
> a letter *from* home (letter-home)
> a cat *in* the hat (cat-hat)
> a handful *of* dust (handful-dust)
> the face *on* the floor (face-floor)
> going *to* Dawson City (going-Dawson City)

Now consider these examples of compound prepositions:
> the room *across from* the library (room-library)
> places *apart from* the commonwealth (places-commonwealth)
> results *due to* circumstances (results-circumstances)

Many of the problems involved in using prepositions correctly concern idiomatic usage. (See Section 46.)

EXERCISE 12

On your paper, copy the following sentences, inserting prepositions in the blank spaces. You may use simple or compound prepositions, but do not use the same one twice. Indicate the function (use) of each prepositional phrase.

1. ＿＿ the discovery, Harvey went out and celebrated.
2. We plan to borrow the power-mower ＿＿ Dick and Karen.
3. Wilcox made his way ＿＿ the wind, rain, and hail.
4. Chichi sat ＿＿ her favorite football player.

5. The professor sought the answer ＿＿ the pages of his notes.
6. ＿＿ you and me, I prefer the Edmonton Eskimos.
7. The leaflets were distributed ＿＿ the student demonstrators.
8. We always walk in the forest ＿＿ sunset.
9. ＿＿ our late start, we had a successful trip.
10. For many reasons, he was a man ＿＿ a country.

7. PHRASES

7a. DEFINITION

A *phrase* is a group of two or more grammatically related words which do not contain a subject and predicate and which usually serve as a single part of speech.

7b. FORMS OF THE PHRASE

A *prepositional phrase* is a group of words which begins with a preposition and ends with a noun or pronoun. For example:

on the table	*by* the chair
at the corner	*for* me
from you	*in* the morning newspaper
of interest	*to* the lighthouse

A *participial phrase* includes a participle together with its modifiers:

> *Straightening his tie,* Pierre welcomed his guests.
> *Leaving before sunrise,* we reached Windsor that night.
> The village, *ravaged by the tornado,* was like a ghost town.

Note that each participle (straightening, leaving, ravaged) introduces a phrase, and each phrase, as a unit, then modifies a noun or pronoun (Pierre, we, village). These are participial phrases functioning as adjectives.

A *gerund* phrase contains a gerund and may also include one or more modifiers and other closely related words:

> We lost the game by *failing to score enough points.* (Gerund phrase as object of preposition *by*)

Lying to your friend is a serious mistake. (Gerund phrase as subject of sentence)

My teacher urges *sending in applications on time.* (Gerund phrase as object of verb *urges*)

My ultimate goal is *winning the history prize.* (Gerund phrase as predicate nominative)

A gerund phrase can be introduced by a preposition. Such constructions are sometimes referred to as *prepositional-gerund* phrases: *After graduating from high school,* I hope to go to college.

An *infinitive phrase* contains an infinitive; the unit can serve as a noun or as a modifier:

The soldiers plan *to attack soon.* ("Soon" modifies "to attack." The phrase serves as the object of "plan.")

We intended *to call them.* ("Them" is the object of "to call." The phrase serves as the object of "intended.")

To attend Canada College is Herbie's great desire. (An infinitive phrase is used as the subject of the sentence.)

The plumber insists there is a method *to solve the leak.* (An infinitive phrase modifies *method.*)

Hazel claims that she is too tired *to attend the dance.* (An infinitive phrase modifies *tired.*)

Michael Cassio's decision is *to visit his school board.* (An infinitive phrase acts as a predicate nominative.)

The *absolute* phrase, an odd construction, usually consists of a noun followed and modified by a participle or participial phrase. The unit is a phrase because it cannot stand alone as a sentence (it is without a subject and predicate); it is absolute because it modifies no single word in the sentence of which it is a part, but the absolute phrase does have a thought relationship to the sentence or some word or phrase in it.

My work completed, I left for home.

Sue left the party, *her foot hurting badly.*

Nightfall coming, many of the birds in the forest began to sing.

7c. USES OF THE PHRASE

A phrase normally fulfills the function of a noun, adjective, verb, or adverb. Phrases containing adjectives modifying nouns, or containing adverbs modifying verbs, are labeled according to their stronger words, that is, noun phrases or verb phrases.

A phrase can be used as a noun is used; that is, as subject, object, etc. These are *noun phrases:*

> *After tomorrow* will be too late.
> *In the garage* is where the bicycle should be.
> *Playing in the school orchestra* was his main ambition.

Prepositional phrases usually serve as adjectives or adverbs. Let's use the examples in Section 7b within complete sentences:

> The book is *on the table*. (Where is the book?)
> We met them *at the corner*. (Where did we meet them?)
> The gift *from you* meant the most to him. (Which gift?)
> The teachers' strike is *of interest*. (Is the teachers' strike worth caring about?)
> Taffy slept *by the chair*. (Where did Taffy sleep?)
> The spectators cheered *for me*. (For whom did they cheer?)
> He replied *in the morning newspaper*. (Where did he reply?)

When a phrase modifies a noun or pronoun, we call it an *adjective phrase.* Consider these examples:

> Many *of the strikers* went back to work. (Many)
> Relatives *from Chicago* visited us for a week. (Relatives)
> Dozens of magazines *in the waiting room* are ten years old. (magazines)

But when a phrase modifies a verb, an adjective, or another adverb, it is an *adverb phrase.* For example:

> Shirley sings *with enthusiasm*. (how)
> We prefer to study the problem *before trying to solve it*. (when)
> Al collects butterflies *for his biology class*. (why)
> Doctor O'Leary searched *for years* before finding the cure. (to what extent)

In the above sentences, adverb phrases modify verbs.

In the sentences which follow, adverb phrases modify adjectives:

> Nathan Hale was true *to his promise*. (true)
> That coffee is good *to the last drop*. (good)
> Alfred claims that children are unpredictable *in the extreme*. (unpredictable)

Adverb phrases modify adverbs. For example:

> Premier Fuzzle smiled coyly *for a reason*. (coyly)
> My friend George parked the car far *in back*. (far)
> We dropped the ice cream slowly *into the punch*. (slowly)

EXERCISE 13

On your paper copy each of the italicized phrases in the following sentences. After each phrase, (1) list the word (or words) it modifies, (2) state what form (kind) of phrase it is, (3) indicate its use as what part of speech.

1. *Enjoying myself fully* is what I plan to do next summer.
2. We plan to meet you in Toronto *at the convention.*
3. My grandfather, *crippled by arthritis,* was still able to smile good-naturedly whenever we entered the room.
4. *To be with you an hour a day,* that is why I took the course.
5. The legionnaires fought the invaders *to the last man.*
6. Mallard dropped the litter *into the basket.*
7. Most *of the swallows* have returned to Capistrano.
8. Marcia plays tennis *with a passion.*
9. The student remained in the library *for two hours.*
10. Louise walked calmly *into the supermarket.*

EXERCISE 14

On a sheet of paper write down all of the phrases in the following sentences. Opposite each phrase, supply the three items of information called for in Exercise 13.

1. Having been unanimously elected president, I expressed my gratitude for the honor bestowed upon me.
2. To get experience and not to make money was his goal in seeking a summer job.
3. Through the night the huge four-engined jet roared on to its destination.
4. Your teacher has no objection to your turning in well-written themes.
5. Having reached the age of 18, I have no desire ever to fall in love again.
6. A motion was made to close the nominations, no other names being proposed.
7. To get along well with people, you must learn to share their interests.
8. Smith being pretty well battered, the coach sent in Jones to replace him at tackle.
9. In the spring, according to the poet, a young man's fancy lightly turns to thoughts of love.
10. Seen from a distance, the night train, creeping up the mountain grade, looked like an animated glowworm.

8. CLAUSES

8a. DEFINITION

A *clause* is a group of words having a subject and a predicate and forming part of a sentence. By means of a conjunction or of an implied connection, a clause is related to the remainder of the sentence in which it appears. ("The boy and girl danced slowly around the room to increasing applause" is a *sentence,* not really a clause.) Clauses are of two kinds: *independent* (or *main* or *principal)* and *dependent (subordinate).*

8b. KINDS OF CLAUSES

Independent clauses assert the central act of predication in a sentence. The subject and especially the predicate in such a clause are the sentence elements to which everything else in the sentence is related.

When two or more clauses in the same sentence are not subordinated in any way, they must be coordinated. This structure results in a *compound* sentence, which has more than one main clause. The unsubordinated clauses in a compound sentence are called *coordinate clauses* and are usually joined by a coordinate or correlative conjunction. (See Section 5.)

> *Tom went to the movies,* but *Jim went to the circus.*
>
> Not only *will he make a contribution himself,* but *he will also ask his friends.*

Dependent clauses, grammatical structures that function within sentences, also include within themselves a predicate. They are introduced by a subordinating conjunction that specifies the relationship of the dependent clause to the main clause.

> *That Einstein formulated the theory of relativity* is a commonly known fact. (This is a noun clause acting as the subject and is introduced by the subordinating word "that.")
>
> The elephant, *which had a long ivory tusk,* thundered

toward us. (A relative clause, introduced by a subordinating relative pronoun, includes the predicate "had.")

When Terry drives, traffic scatters. (An adverbial clause introduced by the subordinating adverb "when" includes the verb "drives.")

After the game was over, the team shook hands with the opposition; then the players headed for the showers. (An adverbial clause introduced by a subordinating adverb includes the verb "was." Note also that two coordinate clauses are joined by the conjunctive adverb "then.")

A special kind of dependent clause is the *elliptical* clause. Such a construction is called "elliptical" because its subject and frequently its predicate are omitted and can be understood (inferred) from the independent (main) clause.

Although I was ill, I insisted on going to the game.

Although ill, I insisted on going to the game. (Elliptical clause)

While she was knitting, Ann looked at television.

While knitting, Ann looked at television.

Trouble—and sometimes laughter—arise when omitted, understood parts are *not* those of the independent clause.

When six years old, my mother married for the second time.

8c. USES OF CLAUSES

Coordinate clauses are used to construct compound and compound-complex sentences. (See these terms in the Glossary, Section 10.)

David took the dog for a walk, and *Sally put the cat out.* (Compound)

While the hot water was running, *Jim took his shower;* but *I got there to find only cold water left.* (Compound-complex; the coordinate clauses are in italics.)

Dependent clauses can function like *nouns* within the sentence. Noun clauses usually are introduced by *that, what, who, which, where, when, how, why.*

Who came to the party is no concern of yours. (Subject)

Jim wished *that he could ride a horse.* (Object)

We judge a man by *what he does.* (Object of preposition)

The doctor came to the conclusion *that he was out of danger.* (Appositive)

29

One serious problem is *that there is no running water.* (Predicate complement)

Dependent clauses can act like *adjectives.* Adjectival clauses are usually introduced by a relative pronoun, *who, which, that,* or by a subordinating conjunction, *when, where, why.* The relative pronoun is sometimes left out. Clauses introduced by relative pronouns or adjectives are also called *relative clauses.*

The bat *which you have used* has been broken. (Adjectival clause modifying "bat")

He knows the reason *why I could not come.* (Adjectival clause modifying "reason")

The job has been given to the man *whom you recommended.* (Adjectival clause modifying "man")

She is a girl *I never could stand.* (Adjectival clause modifying "girl"; the relative pronoun *whom* is left out)

Dependent clauses can modify like *adverbs.* Such clauses can express nine important relationships with certain subordinating conjunctions:

Time: *when, before, while, since*

When a boy rows a boat, he must keep control of the oars. (Adverbial clause modifies "must keep")

Place: *where, wherever*

After finding the book *where I had left it,* I hurried back into the house. (Adverbial clause modifies gerund "finding")

Manner: *as, as if*

He kicked the can *as if it were a ball.* (Adverbial clause modifies verb "kicked")

Condition: *if, so, unless, provided that*

Unless you make the payment, service will be cut off. (Adverbial clause modifies verb "will be cut off")

Cause: *because, as, since*

The train, three hours late *because the locomotive had broken down,* was full of angry passengers. (Adverbial clause modifies adjective "late")

Purpose: *in order that, so that*

The girls worked hard all day *so that the gym would be ready for the dance.* (Adverbial clause modifies verb "worked")

Result: *that, so that, so . . . that*

> We were *so* hungry *that we ate stale crackers.* (Adverbial clause modifies adjective "hungry")

Degree or comparison: *than, as much as, as . . . as, just as*

> John climbed farther *than you did.* (Adverbial clause modifies adverb "farther")

Concession: *though, although*

> *Although he did not score,* he made the best play of the game. (Adverbial clause modifies verb "made")

EXERCISE 15

Number your paper from 1 to 15. Read the following clauses carefully and decide which are *independent* and which are *dependent.* If a clause is independent, write **I** next to its number. If it is dependent, write **D.**

1. the moon is blue
2. when the sun shone brightly
3. from his vantage point he realized
4. although the bluebirds have returned
5. from a distant hill he approached
6. after the train arrived
7. Andy Panda sat on the veranda
8. what is new is news
9. from Toronto we returned to Montreal
10. inasmuch as Beverly asked your permission
11. the man with the hat was smiling
12. when we were young
13. while you cried
14. not on your life
15. within the pages of this book are serious thoughts

EXERCISE 16

On a sheet of paper indicate the kind of dependent clause italicized in each of these sentences. List the function (use) of each.

1. The Smith family goes to the beach *whenever it is possible.*
2. Competing with a person *who is a better player* will help your tennis.

3. *Because I hate pizza* I ordered a filet mignon.
4. The children play in the streets *wherever there is no traffic.*
5. Fishing for trout is *what I plan to do in Ontario.*
6. Did David tell Santa Claus *what he wanted for Christmas?*
7. Sergeant Clancy is the policeman *who protected the demonstrators.*
8. We shall keep the puppies *until the owners come to take them away.*
9. You should decide *when you should return the used books to Hiram.*
10. This garden, *which was ravaged by the hurricane,* will grow back.

EXERCISE 17

On a sheet of paper copy the following sentences, leaving a blank space between each two lines. Underline each clause in each sentence. Above each underlined clause indicate by these abbreviations its function in the sentence: *Ind.* — independent; *N* — noun; *Adj.* — adjective; *Adv.* — adverb.

1. Among other kinds of men we can single out these two: those who think and those who act.
2. The people of that section have been marketing a great quantity of vegetables in the city this summer.
3. He jumped up and down, he shouted and yelled; and yet, for some strange reason, no one paid him the slightest attention.
4. I recommend a visit to Chicago, but when you go, remember that your impressions will be determined by where you get off the train.
5. Whenever my high school friends assembled, we listened to the new records in anyone's collection.
6. I have often heard it said that people are funny, and I am sorry to have to admit that the statement is true.
7. As it was getting late, we began looking for a place where we might land and camp for the night.
8. Not all people in the library are scholars: across the table from me a boy is enjoying himself looking at the cartoons in a magazine; sitting farther away in a quiet corner are a boy and a girl having a library date.
9. The men who have been working in the experiment station are trying to develop a plant that will grow in any kind of soil.
10. The highlight of my childhood summers was a visit to Grandfather's farm; letting a boy do everything under the sun, it seemed, was Grandfather's idea of showing me a good time.

9. SENTENCES

9a. DEFINITION

It is difficult to define a sentence satisfactorily. Traditionally, a sentence is defined as "a group of words containing a subject and predicate and expressing a complete thought." However, some "sentences" accepted as such by knowledgeable persons do not contain both an expressed subject and predicate. Furthermore, what exactly is a "complete thought"? Frequently, the "completeness" of a thought depends upon what statements precede or follow it. (See Section 61a.)

All that accurately and fairly can be said is that *a sentence is a stretch of prose (or poetry, for that matter) which a capable writer punctuates by beginning with a capital and ending with a terminal mark* (see Section 21) *and which an educated reader will recognize and accept as a "sentence."* (Perhaps you can do better with a definition of your own!) Despite the difficulty of understanding what a sentence is, the material in Sections 9b to 9d should clarify many problems about the patterns and kinds of English sentences. (See also Section 120.)

9b. KINDS OF SENTENCES

A sentence can be classified according to its structure or according to the character of the statement it makes.

Structurally, a sentence can be *simple, compound, complex* or *compound-complex.* In meaning and intent, a sentence can be *declarative, interrogative, imperative,* and *exclamatory.*

A *simple* sentence includes only one act of predication. All simple sentences are basic sentence patterns. (See Section 9c.) It may have more than one subject, or more than one predicate, but all are unified into a single act of predication; that is, all of the subjects must perform all of the actions in the predicates.

S.   P.

The *mule-skinner fell* in the well.

Coordinate subject   P.

The *mule-skinner* and his *mule fell* in the well.

Subject   Coordinate predicate

The *mule-skinner*   *fell* and *got soaked* in the well.

Coordinate subject

The *mule-skinner* and his *mule*

Coordinate predicate

fell and *got soaked* in the well.

A *compound* sentence includes two or more coordinate main clauses. A compound sentence is actually made up of two sentence patterns joined by a coordinate conjunction, a correlative conjunction, a comma, or a semicolon. (See Section 9c.)

Coordinating conjunction:

 The applesauce was warm and sweet, *but* the sweet potatoes were burned to a crisp.

Correlative conjunction:

 Not only is he a candidate for a scholarship, *but* he is *also* holding down a part-time job.

Comma:

 The thunder struck, rain began to fall.

Semicolon:

 I pulled guard duty today; tomorrow it will be someone else's turn.

Within a *complex* sentence there are one main clause and one or more dependent, or subordinate, clauses. Usually the subordinate clause modifies the main clause or some element in it. (See Section 8.) A complex sentence contains only one sentence pattern (see Section 9c), except when the clause functions as an integral part of the pattern, as is the case in the first example below.

Noun clause in act of predication of independent clause:

That the sun will rise is indisputable. (Subject)

Modifying like an adverb:

When she arrives, Alice will take charge. (Modifies verb "will take")

Modifying like an adjective:

The municipal government *which has serious financial problems,* will ask for a tax increase. (Modifies noun "municipal government")

Compound-complex sentences include two or more coordinate independent clauses, along with one or more dependent clauses.

Dependent

When the legislature passed a sales tax

Independent

many people complained; but the premier agreed to use most of the money for better schools.

A *declarative* sentence makes an assertion, either by stating a fact or expressing an opinion. This assertion can be negative.

Two and two equal four.

That candidate will surely be elected.

George isn't coming.

Dessert may not be served.

An *interrogative* sentence asks a direct question.

Is four really the sum of two and two?

Do you think he will be elected?

George isn't coming?

Why will dessert not be served?

An *imperative* sentence expresses a request, entreaty, or command.

Don't be shy.

Forward, march.

Fill out the application blank and mail it immediately.

Buy savings bonds now.

An *exclamatory* sentence expresses strong, intense emotion.

Let's get going!

What a game!

Oh, if only you had telephoned!

9c. SENTENCE PATTERNS

A sentence is composed of a series of words. This series can convey meaning in English only because certain of those words are *structurally related to one another in such a way* that they express an act of predication. The patterns indicate the order in which English places these basic structural relationships.

The sentence patterns indicate the basic kinds of words which sentences contain. In other words, the patterns specify the types of words which must be present in a statement before it may be called a "sentence."

In English, there are seven basic predication patterns:

Pattern 1.

Subject	*Predicate*
People	talk.
Horses	jump.
Fires	burn.
We	sing.

This is the simplest predication pattern in English. It consists only of a noun or pronoun subject and a predicate. In this most basic pattern, the verb used in the predicate is called *intransitive,* that is, it asserts an action that does not carry across to an object. (See Section 3.) In Pattern 1 sentences, an action, a state, or a quality is expressed of a subject by a predicate.

Pattern 2.

Subject	*Predicate*	*Direct Object*
Boys	play	baseball.
Birds	build	nests.
Gentlemen	prefer	blondes.
You	need	me.

This is probably the most common predication pattern in English. In it, the action of a verb functioning as the predicate carries across to a noun or pronoun called its object. This kind of verb is called *transitive,* and the word functioning as the direct object answers the question "What?" or "Whom?"

Note that in the first two examples above, the verbs *play* and *build* may be classified as either transitive or intransitive, depending on the functions with which they are patterned. Both verbs can appear in Pattern 1 sentences: *Bill plays. Contractors build.*

In a Pattern 2 sentence, the predicate shows the relationship existing between the noun or pronoun subject and the noun or pronoun direct object.

Pattern 3.

Subject	Predicate	Indirect Object	Direct Object
Jim	gives	Joan	presents.
Mary	wrote	him	letters.
Sue	baked	Ted	pies.

Note that in Pattern 3 sentences the relationship between the noun or pronoun subject and the noun or pronoun indirect object is different from the relationship between the subject and the direct object. The latter answers the question "What?" or "Whom?" The former answers the question *"To* or *for* whom?" The indirect object tells *to* or *for whom* about the action of the predicate. This relationship is always patterned with a direct object that is either expressed or implied, and the indirect object is placed somewhere between the predicate and the direct object.

Pattern 4.

Subject	Linking Verb	Predicate Noun
Jay	is	a pilot.
He	was	the foreman.
Jan	will be	a nurse.
I	am	he.

In this pattern, special predication problems arise. First, notice that the verb does not assert any specific action. The linking verb merely serves to identify or classify the subject. In other words, it links the subject with the noun which follows the verb. In this pattern, the subject and the noun following the linking verb refer to one and the same person. "Jay" and "pilot," in other words, are merely two ways of looking at the same person. In one case he is referred to as

"Jay"; in the other, he is designated as "pilot." "Pilot" is the classification into which "Jay" is placed.

Notice that if we look at the first two words of the pattern, *Jay is,* a question arises, Jay is what? It may be that we simply want to say that a man named Jay in fact exists. If this is our intention, we have a Pattern 1 (Subject—Predicate) sentence and can leave it at that: *Jay is.*

But if we wish to affirm beyond the simple fact that Jay exists, we can complete a Pattern 4 predication with a noun. This noun is called a *predicate noun* or a *predicate complement,* and the verb in the pattern is described as a *linking* (or *copulative*) *verb.*

NOTE: Observe that the predicate noun in the first three examples is preceded by a definite or indefinite article. These articles are also called noun markers or determiners (see Section 1) and frequently signal nouns. These markers were omitted from the first three patterns in order to focus attention upon the bare essentials of these patterns. In a Pattern 4 sentence, however, an article is almost always used before the predicate noun. Articles and other noun markers appear frequently in the other patterns also (see Section 9d). Note that in the fourth example, the pronoun stands without a marker.

Pattern 5.

Subject	Linking Verb	Predicate Adj.
Dogs	are	mean.
Ginger	is	beautiful.
Roses	smell	delightful.
It	seems	fine.

In this pattern, a linking verb is followed by an adjective, which roughly answers the question "What sort of quality does the subject possess?" In Pattern 5 sentences, the predicate adjective describes or indicates a quality that the subject has.

Note that in this pattern verbs other than *to be* can function as the link between the subject and the *predicate adjective*; linking verbs such as *become, appear, seem, taste, grow,* etc., can work this way. These verbs generally express how things look or how we sense them. Note the following examples:

Margaret became *angry*.
The car seemed *fast*.
Aunt Rose looked *young*.
Pomegranates taste *tart*.
The idea sounded *good*.
Her face grew *purple*.
The sky continued *cloudy*.

Note that in each of these sentences the adjective following the verb describes the subject. Note also that the sentences contain several noun markers.

It is important to remember that a predicate adjective always provides a description of the subject, not the predicate verb. Confusion often arises because those words that *modify* verbs, called *adverbs*, often appear in the same pattern position as predicate adjectives.

Apples grow *quickly*.
Aunt Rose looked *away*.
Sam appeared *immediately*.

To determine whether the word in this position is an adjective or an adverb, try it in the typical noun-modifying position, before the noun modified:

Red apples   Quickly apples
Young Aunt Rose   Away Aunt Rose

It is clear that "quickly" and "away" are related to verbs in these sentences rather than to subject-nouns. (See Section 4.) Adverbs are never essential parts of basic sentence patterns.

Confusion about Pattern 5 can also arise when verbs appear in forms that use the verb *to be* as an auxiliary:

Subject	*Predicate*
Celia	is singing.
Alison	was praying.

These are actually sentences employing Pattern 1 with the verb *to be* used as an auxiliary in forming a certain *tense*. (See Section 17.) Generally, a verb ending in *-ing* after a form of the verb *to be* is a form of the progressive tense. If the *-ing* word is asserting an *action* rather than a quality or description, you have a Pattern 1 predication. Further, the verb form may be modified by a word that looks like an adjective:

Subject	*Predicate*
William	has been working hard.

Here simply place "hard" before "William" in the noun-modifying position: *Hard William has been working.* This doesn't make sense in the same way. It seems clear that "hard" is an adverb modifying "has been working." There is no substitute for common sense or good judgment in deciding a problem like this.

Pattern 6.

Subject	*Predicate*	*Direct Obj.*	*Obj. Complement*
Louise	named	her fish	Percy.
John	called	his friend	a fool.
They	elected	him	president.
Jill	considered	Sam	her friend.

In this pattern, a predicate is followed by a direct object. In addition, another noun, called an *object complement*, follows the direct object and serves to complete the meaning of the predicate. There is a relationship between the direct object and its complement that resembles the relationship between the subject and the predicate noun in Pattern 4. That is, the linking verb *to be* is implied:

> her fish (is) Percy
> his friend (is) a fool
> he (is) president
> Sam (is) her friend

The object complement, in other words, serves to identify or classify the direct object.

Note that we could take a series of words like "Louise named her fish" and make a complete sentence which would be Predication Pattern 2. However, verbs that express actions such as naming or electing raise a natural question about their direct objects. In the examples, note that the object complement answers the question "What?" Since the answer to the question is an integral part of the act of naming or choosing specified by the verbs, the object complement has a place in the predication pattern. Since the object complement completes a meaning relevant to the direct object, it is called the object complement.

NOTE: The sentences in the examples contain noun markers before some of the direct objects and object complements. (See Section 1.)

40

Pattern 7.

Subject	Predicate	Direct Obj.	Adj. Complement
Mr. Anderson	painted	the house	green.
Marie	thought	her boyfriend	handsome.
Joe	considered	the problem	difficult.
Ted	made	the garden	beautiful.

As in Pattern 6, a predicate is followed by a direct object. In this pattern, however, the direct object is followed by a complement which is an adjective. The relationship between the direct object and the *adjective complement* is similar to the relationship between the subject and the predicate adjective in a Pattern 5 sentence. In other words, the verb *to be* may be understood between the direct object and the adjective complement: the house (is) green, her boyfriend (is) handsome, etc.

To make certain that the complement is an adjective, check by placing it before the word it complements (in the regular adjective-modifying position) and decide whether it applies in a sense in tune with the sentence. For example, "difficult problem" and "beautiful garden" make sense and therefore the words are obviously adjective complements.

9d. EXPANDING SENTENCE PATTERNS

In the preceding section, the basic sentence patterns were illustrated by using only the minimum necessary words, except where noted. This was purposely done in order to focus your attention on the basic underlying structure of the various patterns. In actual speaking and writing, of course, such "bare-bones" sentences are rare. In actual practice, speakers and writers use several kinds of modifiers to expand the basic structures.

There are many types of modifiers which serve to expand the basic elements of any pattern. The following are worth noting:

1. Definite and indefinite articles and other noun markers. Articles attach themselves to and signal nouns. (See Section 1.) Rare is the sentence without articles or noun markers.

The boys built *a* boat.   (Pattern 2)
My brother lost *his* comb.   (Pattern 2)

2. Single word adjectives and adverbs frequently modify the elements of the basic patterns.

The *energetic* boys *quickly* built a boat. (Pattern 2)
She is an *accomplished* nurse. (Pattern 4)
They elected a *capable* man premier. (Pattern 6)
He works *well*. (Pattern 1)

3. Phrases of various kinds (see Section 7) frequently modify the basic words in patterns.

In the morning, they left *for Regina*. (Pattern 1)
Hoping to win the girl, Tom entered the race. (Pattern 2)
Victoria, *a truly beautiful city*, is a popular place for tourists. (Pattern 4)
To get there on time, Tony told the driver *to speed it up*. (Pattern 2)
He gave his mother a present *by staying out of trouble*. (Pattern 3)

4. Clauses of various kinds (see Section 8) frequently modify basic words in patterns.

Because he had failed twice already, John lost his desire to try again. (Pattern 2)
Athens, *which enjoys a temperate climate*, is the capital of Greece.   (Pattern 4)
He always fought *for what he believed in*. (Pattern 1)

In order to identify easily the basic patterns in expanded sentences, you must be able to distinguish modifying phrases and clauses. This is a relatively simple matter. Familiarity with prepositions, for example, will enable you to spot the phrases which they introduce. Similarly, a knowledge of the infinitive signal word *to*, the relative pronouns, the *-ing* forms of the participle and gerund, and the subordinating conjunctions will permit you to identify, respectively, infinitive phrases, adjective clauses, participial and gerund phrases, and adverb clauses.

When attempting to identify sentence patterns, be on your guard to avoid confusing dependent clauses with basic patterns. Since dependent clauses contain predications (subjects and predicates), they might be confused with the basic patterns. Keep in mind that there is no pattern which makes provision for relative pronouns or subordinating conjunctions. Since both of these types of signal words are intimately connected with the predications which they introduce, they can never stand alone nor fulfill the structural requirements of the basic patterns.

When infinitive and gerund phrases or noun clauses, however, serve as either subjects or objects, they may be considered as integral parts of basic patterns. Note the following examples:

> *To forgive* is divine. (Pattern 5)
> The team tried *to win*. (Pattern 2)
> *Developing new territories* was the marketing manager's main responsibility. (Pattern 4)
> They tried *growing hybrid plants*. (Pattern 2)
> *That he won* was obvious. (Pattern 5)
> He knew *what to do*. (Pattern 2)

It is also worth noting that any essential part of a sentence pattern may be compounded through the use of a correlative conjunction. Compound subjects, predicates, and complements are considered as single units as far as the patterns are concerned.

9e. VARIATIONS FROM THE BASIC PATTERNS

In the preceding section, the basic patterns of English sentences were discussed. You will note, however, that only sentences which constitute *direct statements* were included in the basic patterns. But there are a few other types of sentences in English. The following variations are common. A knowledge of them will help to provide an excellent working definition of the English sentence.

The Passive Variation. Sentences employing a verb in the passive voice (see Section 3d) are common in English. Such sentences are usually developed from Pattern 2 sentences. Take, for example, the following Pattern 2 sentences:

Subject	Predicate	Direct Object
John	hit	the ball.
Captain Kidd	hid	the treasure.
Mr. Owens	built	a house.
The sergeant	scolded	the men.

The passive variation is formed by moving the direct object into the subject position and by making the subject into the object of a preposition in a prepositional phrase. The verb also changes to the passive voice, which is always made up of a form of the verb *to be* followed by the past participle:

Subject	Predicate	(Prep. Phrase)
The ball	was hit	(by John).
The treasure	was hidden	(by Captain Kidd).
A house	was built	(by Mr. Owens).
The men	were scolded	(by the sergeant).

Note that the prepositional phrases appear in parentheses. This is to indicate that the phrase is optional. In some passive sentences, the prepositional phrase is omitted.

Pattern 6 and Pattern 7 sentences can also be changed into the passive voice. Note the changes which occur in the following examples:

Pattern 6: Louise named her fish Percy.
  The fish was named Percy (by Louise).
Pattern 7: Mr. Anderson painted his house green.
  The house was painted green (by Mr. Anderson).

Note that when a Pattern 2 sentence is changed into the passive, it may be considered a Pattern 1 sentence. When Patterns 6 and 7 are changed, the revisions may be considered as Patterns 4 and 5, respectively.

The Question Variation. Sentences which ask questions are, of course, common in English or any other language. The question variation follows certain set patterns in English. These can be summarized as follows:

1. If in an affirmative :statement a verb has one or more auxiliaries, the first auxiliary is switched so that it comes before the subject. Here are some examples:

Affirmative: The game was won.
  The arrest will be made.
  The deer was shot.
  The house could have been repainted.
  The guest has eaten.
Questions: Was the game won?
  Will the arrest be made?
  Was the deer shot?
  Could the house have been repainted?
  Has the guest eaten?

2. If the affirmative statement contains no auxiliary, some form of the verb *do* is placed in front of the subject. Here are some examples:

Affirmative: The boy runs fast.
Sara likes music.
Jane danced well.
Bill helps his friends.
Joe flew an airplane.
Sam likes mathematics.

Questions: Does the boy run fast?
Does Sara like music?
Did Jane dance well?
Does Bill help his friends?
Did Joe fly an airplane?
Does Sam like mathematics?

These same rules apply when questions begin with common question words like *where, when, why,* and *how*.

The Imperative Variation. The imperative mood in English also constitutes another basic variation. This variation may appear in any of the seven basic patterns. The imperative is commonly viewed as having the subject "you" understood or implied. Here is an example of the imperative variation in each of the seven basic patterns:

Begin! (Pattern 1)
Begin the game! (Pattern 2)
Give him a chance. (Pattern 3)
Be a doctor. (Pattern 4)
Remain silent. (Pattern 5)
Name the dog Spot. (Pattern 6)
Color his face red. (Pattern 7)

EXERCISE 18

On your paper, number each of these sentences and indicate whether it is simple, compound, complex, or compound-complex.

1. Although few of the actors knew their lines, the rehearsal went well.
2. I want all of you to return to your rooms immediately.
3. Do the best you can; however, do not be discouraged by difficulties which will surely occur.
4. Get me to the church on time.

5. When I first read *The Brothers Karamazov,* my favorite character was Ivan; but now I prefer Dimitri, who seems more believable.
6. Fish have to swim; birds have to fly.
7. During the 1920's, F. Scott Fitzgerald was an enormously popular novelist.
8. When the girls play field hockey, you yourself had better protect your shins; they are lethal competitors.
9. I lost my heart in Montreal but not to a girl.
10. Dripping water in Wyoming's Fossil Mountain Ice Cave is transformed into sparkling columns of ice, and where water drops have splashed and frozen, the floor glitters as if it were covered with diamonds.

EXERCISE 19

On your paper, number each of the following sentences and indicate its meaning and intent: declarative, imperative, interrogative, or exclamatory. Supply a suitable end stop (see Section 21) for each sentence.

1. Do me a favor and sit down for a moment
2. It will cost $765.00 to repair a dented fender
3. That sum is highway robbery
4. All I want for Christmas is my two front teeth
5. When do you expect me to get all of this ironing done, Melvin
6. Drop those guns, Sheriff Murtz, or I'll have to ventilate you
7. Contact lenses can cause problems until one gets used to them
8. You want another popsicle
9. What a magnificent sunset
10. Identifying sentences builds character

EXERCISE 20

Make two columns on your paper. Head one Subject and the other Predicate. From the following sentences, select those words which are fulfilling those functions and write them in the proper columns.

1. Jane laughed.
2. Mother baked.
3. The dog howled.
4. Father sang.
5. The car stalled.
6. Jody cried.
7. The candle melted.
8. Burr cooks.
9. The cat ran.
10. The fog lifted.

EXERCISE 21

Number your paper from 1 to 10. Arrange the following jumbled series of words into sentences. Write "Subject" and "Predicate" over the words acting in those functions.

1. awoke she early
2. rare Rover meat ate the
3. the well Myron in fell
4. bought a farm Walter
5. the movie Johnny frightened

6. wore clown the a sign
7. his blew horn Dennis
8. flew the ladybug home
9. a kite flew Ike
10. his Christmas ate Jack pie

EXERCISE 22

Determine the sentence patterns in the following expanded sentences. Number a sheet of paper from one to twenty. Next to each number, write the code for the pattern, following this example:

Mary bought her brother a tiny pup.
Answer: Subject — Predicate — Indirect Object — Direct Object

1. Because they had to leave before sunrise, the men assembled their equipment the night before.
2. When the whistle blew, Frank sat down.
3. Unable to hold onto the cookie jar, Tim dropped it on the floor.
4. He had always been the best worker in the firm.
5. Frances, seeing that it was too early to get up, fell asleep for another few minutes.
6. The Queen awarded the hero the Commonwealth's highest decoration.
7. Although Fred had attempted to change her mind, Marie still thought him an extraordinary fool.
8. We pay our bills on the first of the month.
9. Mrs. Simpson considered the former convict honest.
10. When Andy came home, the house was a mess.
11. The woman knew a good bargain when she saw one.
12. Several men had applied for the job without success.
13. The cool water tasted wonderful.
14. Virtue is its own reward.
15. Having looked all over town and having been convinced that a good used car could not be found for fifty dollars, the men, disillusioned but not completely hopeless, went home.
16. If we look hard enough, we might find a nice gift.
17. The passengers considered the day perfect for flying.

18. Many hours of work produced a beautiful garden.
19. Locating the street seemed hopeless.
20. We will meet you later.

EXERCISE 23

Change each of the following sentences into a passive, an imperative, and at least one type of question.

1. Bill sold apples.
2. The truck will deliver the furniture.
3. The children love my aunt.
4. Sam conducted the orchestra.
5. The boys have built a new clubhouse.

EXERCISE 24

The following paragraph includes sentences with Pattern 1 predications only. Number your paper from 1 to 10. Extract the patterns from the sentences (there may be more than one pattern to a sentence) and write them after the number. Identify the words functioning as subject and predicate.

We drove to the store. While Mother waited, we shopped. The aisles were crowded and the shelves were stacked with cans. I walked slowly, pushing the cart. The apples glistened with drops of water, but the lettuce was wilted. The checker smiled as Jane paid.

EXERCISE 25

Number your paper from 1 to 10. Write ten sentences, five including Pattern 1 and five including Pattern 2. Label those words in each sentence which are functioning as subject, predicate, and direct object.

EXERCISE 26

Number your paper from 1 to 5. Write five sentences illustrating Pattern 3. Label those words in each sentence which are functioning as subject, predicate, indirect object, direct object.

EXERCISE 27

Number your paper from 1 to 10. Write five sentences illustrating Pattern 4 and five sentences illustrating Pattern 5.

Label those words in each sentence which are functioning as subject, predicate, predicate complement. Make sure to distinguish between the predicate noun and the predicate adjective.

EXERCISE 28

Number your paper from 1 to 10. Write five sentences illustrating Pattern 6 and five sentences illustrating Pattern 7. Label those words in each sentence which are functioning as subject, predicate, direct object, and object complement. Be sure to distinguish clearly between the noun and adjective complement.

10. GLOSSARY OF GRAMMATICAL TERMS

The following list defines briefly and sometimes illustrates those elements of grammar for which you will have greatest need. Refer to this glossary when you are in doubt about the meaning of a grammatical term. Most of the items listed in this quick-reference guide are treated fully at appropriate places within the text itself.

Absolute expression. An absolute phrase or expression usually consists of a noun or pronoun followed by a participle modifying it. The participle is usually expressed; it may be understood. The expression is "absolute" because it modifies no special word in the sentence; yet it does not stand alone as a sentence.

> *Two hours having elapsed,* we again set out on our journey.
> *The tire being flat,* we decided to pump it up.
> The little boat hugged the shore, *its sails flapping in the wind.*

Active voice. The form of an action-expressing verb which tells that the subject does or performs the action. See *Voice* below.

Agreement. Correspondence or sameness in number, gender, and person — between subject and predicate, and between pronoun and antecedent. Subjects and predicates *agree* in number (both are singular or both are plural):

> *Martha is* my cousin. (Subject and predicate are singular.)
> *Martha and Sue are* my cousins. (Subject and predicate are plural.)

Pronouns agree with their antecedents in having the same gender, person, and number:

> A *woman* hopes to retain *her* youthful appearance.
> Many *women* retain *their* youthful appearance.
> Gary is one of those *boys who* are always well-mannered.

Antecedent (meaning, literally, *going before*). The substantive (noun or pronoun) to which a pronoun refers, or for which it is substituted. See Section 13.

> If *John* tries it, *he* will like it.
> *I* should have done it *myself*.
> *Neither* of the birds built *its* nest.

Although by definition the antecedent is placed before the pronoun, it is sometimes illogically, yet clearly, placed after:

> When *she* finally arrived, *Mother* explained why she was late.

Appositive. A substantive, usually a noun, added to or following another substantive to identify or explain it. The appositive signifies the same thing, and the second substantive is said to be in *apposition.*

> More hardy than wheat are these grains—*rye, oats,* and *barley. (Rye, oats,* and *barley* are in apposition with *grains.)*
> One important product, *coffee,* this country has to import. *(Coffee* is in apposition with *product.)*

An appositive agrees in number and case with the substantive to which it refers and is set off by commas if its relationship is loose (nonrestrictive) and is used without punctuation if the relationship is close (restrictive). See Section 25o.

Auxiliary. A verb used to "help" another verb in the formation of tenses, voice, mood, and certain precise ideas. *Be (am, is, are, was, were, been), have (has, had), do (does), can, could, may, might, shall, should, will, would, must, ought, let, dare, need, used* are examples. See Section 16.

> He *has* gone away for a visit.
> We *should have been* working with the stevedores on the dock.
> *Will* you please turn on the light?

Case. A term referring to the forms that nouns or pronouns have (nominative, possessive, objective) to indicate their relation to other words in the sentence. See Section 14.

Clause. A group of words containing a subject and predicate and forming part of a sentence. A one-word *imperative,* with the understood subject *you,* can serve as an independent clause. See Section 8.

> When the cheering stopped, *Wilson was sad.* (independent)
> This is the present *that I bought.* (dependent adjective clause)
> *Wherever we travel,* we shall have fun. (dependent adverb clause)
> Boswell insisted *that he tried to do it.* (dependent noun clause)

Comparison. The change in form of an *adjective* or *adverb* to indicate greater or smaller degrees of quantity, quality, or manner. Comparison is discussed and explained in some detail in Section 19e.

> Positive: The *small* boy ran *swiftly.*
> Comparative: The *smaller* boy ran *more swiftly.*
> Superlative: The *smallest* boy ran *most swiftly.*

Complement. A word or expression used to *complete* the idea indicated or implied by a verb. A *predicate complement* (sometimes called *subjective complement)* may be a noun, a pronoun, or an adjective which follows a linking verb and describes or identifies the subject of the linking verb.

> Mr. Jones is a *salesman.*
> Jane is *cheerful.*
> The club members are elderly.

An *object (objective) complement* may be a noun or adjective which follows the direct object of a verb and completes the necessary meaning:

> They called the dog *Jerry.*
> We dyed the dress *blue.*

Note that the verb is transitive in a sentence or clause containing an object complement.

Complex sentence. A sentence containing one independent clause and one or more dependent clauses. See Section 9.

> Although they try, the Expos cannot win a pennant.
> If they offer you the job, accept it.

Compound sentence. A sentence containing two or more clauses which could stand as complete sentences. See Section 9.

> The sun is bright and the sky is clear.

Compound-complex sentence. A sentence containing two or more independent clauses and one or more dependent clauses. See Section 9.

> You can send candy, and you can send flowers, but you must certainly send something to Mother because she expects a gift.

Conjugation. The inflectional changes in the form or uses of a verb to show tense, mood, voice, number, and person. See these terms in this glossary and see also Sections 3, 17, 18.

Conjunction. A part of speech which serves as a linking or joining word to connect words or groups of words like phrases, dependent clauses, independent clauses, or sentences: *and, or, if, when, nevertheless, moreover,* etc. See Section 5.

Conjunctive adverb. A certain kind of adverb which can also be used as a conjunction coordinating two independent clauses: *also, furthermore, nevertheless, besides, however, therefore, thus, so, consequently, hence, likewise, still, then, moreover,* etc. See Section 22b.

> The library is open on Saturday; *however,* it will be closed on Sunday.

Context. This is not specifically a grammatical term, but it is often used in discussions of grammar and composition. The word means the parts of a piece of writing or of speech which precede or follow a given word or passage with which they are directly connected.

Declension. The inflectional changes in the form or use of a noun or pronoun to indicate case, number, and person. "To decline" means to give these grammatical changes.

Determiner. A determiner may be an article (a, an, the); a possessive (my, your, her, its, their, his, own); a demonstrative (this, that, these, those). Determiners commonly, and always in basic sentence patterns, occur with nouns, but not with *all* nouns. Determiners do not appear with proper nouns, for example, nor do *a* and *an* occur with such nouns as *courage* and *oxygen*. In general, a determiner is any member of a subclass of adjectival words that limits the noun it modifies and that usually is placed before descriptive adjectives.

Direct address. The noun or pronoun showing to whom speech is addressed (also called the *vocative*):

> *Barnaby*, are you there?
> After you mow the grass, *Fred*, take out the garbage.

Ellipsis (elliptical clause). The omission of a word or words from a clause or sentence. The omitted words are not needed because they are understood from other words or from context. An elliptical clause is occasionally an independent clause; usually it is a dependent clause with its subject and part of its predicate omitted, since these are clearly understood from the main clause. See Section 8. In the following examples, the words shown in brackets are often omitted in speaking and writing.

> Some drove to Keswick, others [drove] to Wasaga Beach.
> While [we were] swimming in the pool, we agreed to attend a movie later.
> She was fifteen years of age; her sister, [was] ten [years of age].

Expletive. Frequently when a writer is at a loss about beginning a sentence or independent clause, he resorts to an *expletive*—a word or words not needed for the sense but used merely to fill out a sentence. The most common expletives are *it* and *there;* the most common expletive phrases are *there is, there are, there was, there were*. Usually, *there is* no weaker or more ineffective way to begin a sentence; occasionally, however, expletives are desirable or even necessary, but as a general principle they should be avoided whenever *there is* a better, more effective way of beginning a statement. (See Section 58.)

> *It* was Alice whom we saw.
> *It* is a truism that men love freedom.
> *There* are four hundred people present.

Finite verb. A verb form or verb phrase that serves as a predicate; it has number and person. Opposed to the finite verb is the non-finite verb form, which cannot serve as a predicate. Non-finite forms are participles, gerunds, and infinitives. See Section 3g.

> He *walked* to school.
> I *have finished* the job.

Gender. The classification of nouns or pronouns according to sex. The four genders are masculine, feminine, neuter, and common (either masculine or feminine): *boy, girl, it, individual.* In modern English nearly all traces of grammatical gender, as these are indicated by endings, have disappeared: *poetess* is an obsolete word, *actress* is still in good use. Gender, when indicated, is clear from the noun or pronoun, and no one pays any attention to endings as such: *actor, actress, he, she, it.*

Gerund. A verbal noun ending in *ing*, that is, a noun formed from and based on a verb. A gerund has the same form as the present or perfect participle: "Your *speaking* is appreciated"; "Your *having spoken* to us is greatly appreciated." See also Section 3g.

Grammar. The science dealing with words and their relationships to one another. *Rhetoric* deals with the art of expressive speech and writing and with the principles of clear, effective writing. *Grammar,* a descriptive statement of the way language works, includes a discussion of the forms of words, their use in phrases, clauses, and sentences, their tenses, cases, or other changes in form according to their relationships with one another.

Idiom (idiomatic usage). The manner of expression characteristic of a language or a level of usage within that language. (See Section 46.)

Impersonal construction. A method of phrasing in which neither a personal pronoun nor a noun naming a person is stated as the actor. The passive voice is used, or words like *it* or *there.*

> *It* is difficult to say.
> *It* is snowing.
> *It* remains to be seen.

Indirect object. A noun or pronoun preceding the direct object of a verb and before which the word *to* or *for* is understood. When such an object follows the direct object, the preposition *to* or *for* is used.

> Will you lend *him* your notes until Thursday?
> (Will you lend your notes *to him* until Thursday?)
> Yesterday I sent *her* a letter.
> (Yesterday I sent a letter *to her.*)

Indirect question. Restatement by one person of a direct question asked by another.

> Direct: Where will you stay?
> Indirect: Peggy asked where I would stay.

Indirect quotation. Restatement by one person in his own words of the words written or spoken by someone else.

> Direct: Jim wrote, "I'll be there on Sunday."
> Indirect: Jim wrote that he will be here on Sunday.

Infinitive. A verb form which is the first of the three principal parts of a verb; the infinitive has the function of a verb (as part of the predicate), but it is also commonly used as a verbal or in a verbal phrase, like a noun, adjective, or adverb. In these last three uses—as verbal—it is usually preceded by the sign of the infinitive, the word *to*. See Section 3g.

> to run, to jump, to laugh, to dream, to think, to explain

Inflection. A change in the form of a word to show a change in use or meaning. *Comparison* is the inflection of adjectives and adverbs; *declension* is the inflection of nouns and pronouns; and *conjugation* is the inflection of verbs.

> Examples: I, me, mine; we, us, ours; he, him, his; have, has, had; loud, louder, loudest; beautiful, more beautiful, most beautiful; sing, sang, sung.

Intensifier. This is a word or element used to strengthen, increase, or enforce meaning. *Certainly, awful*, and *abominably* are examples of intensifiers.

Interjection. A part of speech—an exclamatory word—expressing strong feeling or surprise, which has little connection with the remainder of the sentence.

> *Oh*, that's what you mean.
> *Gosh!* What fun that will be.

Intransitive verb. A verb that does not require a direct object to complete its meaning; the meaning ends with itself and the verb therefore may have adverbial modifiers but not an object. See Section 3b.

> The fearful shepherd *trembled* as he *spoke*.
> The mountain *roared* and issued forth a mouse.

Irregular verb. Sometimes called *strong* verbs, irregular verbs do not follow a regular system, or pattern, in forming their principal parts. Instead, the principal parts are usually formed by a change in the vowel: *see, saw, seen; drive, drove, driven; choose, chose, chosen; lose, lost, lost.* Your dictionary is your guide. See Section 15 also.

Juncture. This word has several meanings, all of which involve the act or state of "joining" or "connecting." In linguistics, the term has a somewhat specialized meaning relating to the fact that words as we speak them are not usually separated to the extent that they are in writing. Our words tend to flow together without the pauses which, in writing, are shown by spaces. If we speak the sentence, "The person who can do this well deserves praise," we would need briefly to interrupt our flow of sound after either *this* or *well* in order to be fully understood.

Linking verb (also called a *joining verb*, a *copula*, a *copulative verb*, or *coupling verb*). A verb which does not express action but only a state of being or a static condition. It serves to link the subject with another noun (predicate noun) or pronoun (predicate pronoun) or with an adjective (predicate adjective). These words following the linking verb are called predicate complements or subjective complements. Common linking verbs are the forms of *to be, look, seem, smell, sound, appear, feel, become, grow, prove, turn, remain, stand*, etc. See Section 16.

> The other man *was* his uncle.
> That *seems* reasonable.
> That dress *looks* pretty.

Modify. To describe or limit. Adjectives are used with nouns or pronouns, and adverbs are used with verbs, adjectives, or other adverbs to describe, limit, or make meaning more definite in some other closely related way. Descriptive: *gray* skies, *tall* buildings. Limiting: *six* envelopes, the *only* man.

Mood. A characteristic of verbs, revealing how action or expression is thought of: as a fact *(indicative mood),* as a possibility or something desired *(subjunctive mood),* or as a command or request *(imperative mood).* Other kinds of expression are possible through use of certain auxiliary verbs. See Section 18.

> He *is* my cousin. (Indicative)
> I wish I *were* with you. (Subjunctive)
> *Drop* that cupcake. (Imperative)

Morpheme. Any word or part of a word not further divisible into smaller meaningful elements: *boy, -ish* in *boyish, ad-* in *advice.*

Morphology. The patterns of word formation in a language, including derivation and inflection. *Morphology* and *syntax* together form a basic division of grammar.

Non-finite verb. A verb form which cannot serve as predicate, since it shows neither person nor grammatical number. Non-finite verb forms—the verbals—are *gerunds, participles, infinitives.* See Section 3g.

Number. The change in the form of a noun, pronoun, or verb to show whether one or more than one is indicated. The formation of the plural of *nouns* is discussed in Section 1a; the few *pronouns* that have plural forms are listed in Section 2b.

Plurals of *verbs* are relatively simple. Main verbs have the same form for singular and plural except in the third person singular, present tense, which ends in *s (sees, moves, thinks,* etc.) or occasionally *es (goes).*

Of the verb *to be:* in the present tense, *am* (1st person) and *is* (3rd person) are singular, *are* is 2nd person singular and 1st, 2nd, 3rd person plural; in the past tense, *was* is 1st and 3rd person singular, *were* is 2nd person singular and 1st, 2nd, 3rd person plural.

Of the verb *to have: has* is the third person singular, present tense form. Of the verb *to do, does* is the third person singular, present tense form.

Use your dictionary when you are in doubt concerning the singular or plural form of a noun, pronoun, or verb.

Object. The noun, pronoun, or noun clause following a preposition or following a transitive verb.

He is in the *room.*
The carpenters built a *house.*
He said *that he would go.*

A *simple object* is the noun or pronoun or noun clause alone. A *complete object* is a simple object together with its modifiers. A *compound object* consists of two or more nouns or pronouns or noun clauses.

Object complement. A word—usually a noun or adjective—used after a direct object of certain verbs to complete the meaning. See *Complement,* also.

We have elected John *treasurer.*

Participle. A verb form having the function either of a verb used as part of the predicate or of an adjective. See Section 3g. The three forms are *present participle, past participle, perfect participle.*

The player *swinging* the bat is Henry Bubble.
I have *finished* my essay.
Having finished my essay, I turned it in.

Parts of speech. The classifications to one of which every word must belong: *noun, pronoun, adjective, verb, adverb, preposition, conjunction, interjection.*

Passive voice. The form of an action-expressing verb which tells that the subject does not act but is acted upon. Literally and actually, the subject is *passive.* See *Voice,* below.

Person. The change in the form of a pronoun or verb—sometimes, merely a change in use as with verbs—to indicate whether the "person" used is the person speaking (*first person*), the person spoken to (*second person*), or the person or thing spoken about (*third person*): *I* read, *you* read, *he* reads, *we* read, *you* read, *they* read, *it* plays.

Phoneme. A class, or family, of closely related sounds regarded as a single sound. (These speech sounds are called *phones.*) For example, by contrast of the phoneme *p* with other phonemes, *nip* differs from *pip* and *tip.* Linguists differ in their analysis of the sounds of our language but are generally agreed that some 50 phonemes exist in the English language. No wonder many expressions are difficult to pronounce, since a phoneme is, by definition, the "simplest possible significant classification of sound."

Phonetics. The science of speech sounds and their production.

Phrase. A group of related words not containing a subject and a predicate, and serving as a single part of speech. See Section 7.

Pitch. The combination of *pitch, stress,* and *juncture* (see entry) forms what is know as *intonation,* an important item in any analysis of spoken language. In linguistic terms, intonation means "the significant speech pattern or patterns resulting from pitch sequences and pauses (juncture)." *Pitch* is closely connected with *stress;* the latter, which refers to loudness, may be primary, secondary, tertiary, or weak (neutral). One linguist (Paul Roberts) uses the sentence "The White House is a white house" to indicate the different emphases given *White House* and *white house.*

Pitch is usually numbered from 1 to 4 (low to high or high to low, depending upon what linguist is speaking or writing). Pitch signals help in distinguishing spoken questions from statements just as question marks and periods do in writing.

Plural. A classification of nouns, pronouns, subjects, and predicates to indicate two or more units or members. Note that a subject with two or more singulars joined by *and* becomes plural. See Section 12 and *Number,* above.

Predicate. The verb or verb phrase in a sentence which makes a statement—an assertion, an action, a condition, a state of being—about the subject. A *simple predicate* is a verb or a verb phrase alone, without an object or modifiers; a *complete predicate* consists of the verb with its object and all its modifiers; a *compound predicate* consists of two or more verbs or verb phrases. See Section 9.

Shakespeare *wrote* plays. (Simple predicate)

Al Balding *drove the ball nearly 300 yards.* (Complete predicate)

I *wrote* the letter yesterday *and mailed* it first thing this morning.(Compound predicate)

Predicate adjective. An adjective used in the predicate after a linking or joining or coupling verb; this adjective modifies or qualifies the subject.

> Today seems *warmer* than yesterday.
> The players appear *ready* for the match.

Predicate complement, also called *subjective complement.* A *predicate noun* or *pronoun,* or a *predicate adjective.*

Principal parts. The three parts of a verb *(present infinitive, past tense,* and *past participle)* from which all other forms and uses of verbs (tense, mood, tone, voice) can be expressed, sometimes without but most frequently with the necessary auxiliary verbs. In learning the principal parts of unfamiliar verbs, consult your dictionary. See Section 15.

Reference. A word used with pronouns and their antecedents to indicate the relationship between them. The pronoun *refers* to the antecedent, the antecedent is indicated or *referred* to by the pronoun.

Regular verbs. Also called weak verbs, these are the most common verbs in English because they usually form their past tense and past participle by adding *d, ed,* or *t* to the present infinitive form: *move, moved, moved; walk, walked, walked; mean, meant, meant.* See Section 15.

Rhetoric. The art or science of literary uses of language. *Rhetoric* is concerned with the effectiveness and general appeal of communication and with methods of achieving literary quality and vigor. It is only loosely connected with correctness or with specific details of mechanics, spelling, and grammar, as such.

Root. In linguistics, the base of a word is a *root,* a morpheme to which may be added prefixes and suffixes. An approximate synonym for *base* and *root* in this sense is *stem;* all mean the part of a word to which suffixes and prefixes are added or in which phonetic changes are made. Thus we say that *love* is the root (stem or base) of the word *loveliness, form* of the word *reform,* and so on.

Sign of the infinitive. The word *to* accompanying the infinitive form of the verb: *to* go, *to* see, *to* arrive. "I plan *to* go." "I hope *to* arrive next week." In certain expressions, especially with certain auxiliary verbs, the *to* is not used: "He can *go.*" "I do *see.*"

Simple sentence. A sentence containing one subject (simple or compound) and one predicate (simple or compound). See Section 9.

> Anthony was a handsome baby.
> Sunshine and lollipops are Mallard's wants for his birthday.

Singular. The number classification of nouns, pronouns, subjects, and predicates to indicate *one: boy, student, woman, I, he, she, it, is, has, was, goes, studies.* See *Number* above.

Subject. The person or thing (noun, pronoun, noun phrase, noun clause) about which a statement or assertion is made in a sentence or clause. A *simple subject* is the noun or pronoun alone. A *complete subject* is a simple subject together with its modifiers. A *compound subject* consists of two or more nouns, pronouns, noun phrases, noun clauses. See Section 9.

Substantive. An inclusive term for noun, pronoun, verbal noun (gerund, infinitive), or a phrase or a clause used like a noun. The practical value of the word *substantive* is that it saves repeating all the words which are included in this definition. The following italicized words are examples of substantives:

> The *porridge* was ten days old.
> *We* shall return in September.
> *From Vancouver to Halifax* is a great distance.
> Don't you realize *that Santa Claus will be here tomorrow?*

Syllable. In phonetics, a *syllable* is a segment of speech uttered with one impulse of air pressure from the lungs. In writing, *syllable* refers to a character or set of characters (letters of the alphabet) representing one sound. In general, *syllable* refers to the smallest amount or unit of speech or writing.

Syntax. For all practical purposes, not a very useful word. Compare these two dictionary definitions of *syntax:*

"Sentence structure; the due arrangement of word forms to show their mutual relations in the sentence; that part of grammar which treats of the expression of predicative, qualifying, and other word relations, according to established usage in the language under study."

— *Webster's New Collegiate Dictionary*

"Sentence-construction, the grammatical arrangement of words in speech or writing, set of rules governing this."

— *Concise Oxford Dictionary*

Let's use, then, the words *grammar* and *grammatical*.

Tense. The time of the action or the state of being expressed by the verb: *present, past, future, present perfect, past perfect, future perfect.* The first three of these six are sometimes named the *simple* or *primary* tenses; the last three are sometimes named the *compound* or *secondary* or *perfect* tenses. See Section 17.

Tone. A word used in this handbook to distinguish a characteristic of tenses of verbs, indicating within any one tense or time limit *emphasis* or *progress* or *simple* time. See Section 17.

Transitive verb. A verb accompanied or followed by a direct object which completes its meaning. See Section 3.

She *shook* the plum tree.
Buford *helps* the distressed.

Verb phrase. A verb together with an auxiliary or auxiliaries, or with its object or its modifiers: *is going, was finished, shall have taken, will have been taken, studied the assignments, flows slowly, whispers nonsense to himself.* Distinguish between a *verb phrase* and a *verbal* (participle, infinitive, gerund).

She *has known* many people in her time.
Clym's letter *was rewritten* several times.

Verbals. The verb forms — *participles, gerunds, infinitives.* One or more of these serve at times as adjectives, adverbs, nouns, parts of the predicate — but *never* as a predicate alone. See Section 3g.

Skiing is delightful. (Gerund used as a noun)
To succeed is exhilarating. (Infinitive used as a noun)

The *quaking* house may collapse. (Participle used as an adjective)

Sandy was glad *to have come*. (Infinitive used as an adverb)

Voice. The change in the form or use of a verb—a transitive verb only—to indicate whether the subject is the performer of the action *(active voice)* or is acted upon *(passive voice)*. In the formation of the passive voice, some form of the auxiliary verb *to be* is used with the past participle. See Section 3.

Bellweather *shot* the cougar. (Active voice)

The trout *was caught* by Grandma Frickert. (Passive voice)

Word order. An English sentence does not consist of a string of words in free relationship to each other but of groups of words arranged in patterns. Words in an English sentence have meaning because of their position. That is, they have one meaning in one position, another meaning in another position, and no meaning in still another position. Some linguists maintain that the basis of English grammar is word order. Certainly the order of words and of other locutions is a fundamental part of grammar and is basic in sentence construction. In addition, word order contributes to many effects of style, especially emphasis.

USAGE

11. LEVELS OF USAGE

In today's society, few people fail to acknowledge the importance of using what is generally called "good English." Will Rogers, the late American humorist, was never more amusing than when he remarked, "A lot of people who don't say *ain't*, ain't eatin'." Nevertheless, it is important that we choose those expressions and grammatical forms that will convey to hearers and readers exactly the ideas and emotional tones we wish to present.

11a. CHOOSE AN APPROPRIATE LEVEL OF USAGE.

The controlling guide to usage should always be the test of appropriateness: How can I most suitably express what I have in mind so that it will be most effectively communicated to a specific reader (or listener)? In one set of circumstances, it might be appropriate to say, for instance, "Scram" or "Beat it" or "Get lost" or "Go chase yourself" or "Blow." In another situation it would be more appropriate to say "Please leave" or "Au revoir" or "Godspeed." The appropriateness of a given level of usage depends upon the situation involved.

11b. DISTINGUISH AMONG VARIOUS LEVELS OF USAGE.

Within English and all other living languages are varieties of usage associated with geographical concerns (regional dialects), social status, educational background, relationships involving style, and such special forms of communication as technical language, profanity, and slang.

In a broad sense, a primary distinction may be made between informal and formal usage. Actually, the problem of levels of usage is more involved than this; at least five levels may be mentioned. It is often difficult to tell, however, precisely where one level ends and another begins.

1. *Carefully Selected Written English.* Precisely prepared and painstakingly edited books and magazines exhibit this level of usage. In addition, the writing of many educated men and women in all parts of the country falls into this category, which is largely (but not exclusively) the usage described and recommended in this handbook.

2. *General Written English.* Most newspapers, radio and television scripts, business letters and reports, and several widely circulated magazines employ this second level of usage. It does not involve all the niceties and dogmatic rules of choice written English, but it is generally acceptable and represents the writing level which all serious students should try to attain in written work.

3. *Choice Spoken English.* This is the language heard in serious or formal addresses and talks and in the conversation of many educated people who normally apply the requirements of carefully selected written English to the spoken variety. It is neither so "correct" nor so inflexible as the two earlier varieties mentioned, because oral English is nearly always freer and less constrained than is written English.

4. *General Spoken English.* Most fairly well educated people employ this level in ordinary conversation. It is somewhat more easygoing than level No. 3, employs more newer and shorter forms (slang, contractions), and is sometimes referred to as "colloquial."

5. *Substandard English.* This is a term used to characterize illiterate or vulgar expressions. Such expressions, associated with the uneducated, appear also in the speech of many educated persons who "know better" but choose to express themselves in ways sometimes considered uncouth. One who speaks Vulgate (common) English is not necessarily vulgar any more than one who chooses to use Carefully

Selected Written English or Choice Spoken English is necessarily affected or snobbish.

The distinctions just made are somewhat arbitrary; they can be precisely labeled at their centers but they run together at their extremes. Further, most expressions are identical on all levels. One who says or writes "I spoke slowly" is using an expression which has no distinct level of usage.

It is difficult to label constructions apart from their contexts, but the five levels mentioned may be illustrated:

Carefully Selected Written English:	I shall not speak.
General Written English:	I will not speak.
Choice Spoken:	I'll not speak.
General Spoken:	I'm not going to speak.
Substandard:	I ain't gonna say nothing.

In addition to being modified by the general distinction between formal and informal usage, our language is encased in many rules about grammatical structure and word choice that are themselves modified by considerations of time, place, and situation. In general, word usage and grammatical structure should be in *current, national,* and *reputable* use. These matters are discussed in Sections 37-39.

Although attitudes toward usage have become less rigid in recent years, many occasions arise for everyone in which a knowledge of acceptable, reputable English is either desirable or essential. You may not wish or need to use "correct" English at all times, but you should at least know what preferred usage directs when you are conversing with other educated, socially responsible people and when you are writing business letters, class papers, minutes of club meetings, and all compositions designed to be read by others.

EXERCISE 1

Each of the following sentences contains an error in usage, an acknowledged violation of reputable, acceptable language practice. Make necessary corrections in each sentence. If any of the sentences give you trouble, study carefully Sections 12-20, which follow.

1. I do not like them clothes as much as I do these.
2. She don't have to go unless she wants to.

3. This here model is difficult to build.
4. Mary and I we went to the party.
5. She is an intelligent person but she cannot learn me anything.
6. Just between you and I, the meat was badly cooked and served.
7. Every boy and girl in the class were shocked by the severity of the examination.
8. What I want to know is who did he give it to?
9. She just wanted to lay down and rest awhile.
10. The test was difficult for all of we students.

EXERCISE 2

Follow the instructions for Exercise 1.

1. After his illness, Bruce was unable to sleep good.
2. If I was you, I would not say anything at all.
3. There is hundreds of people in the hall right now.
4. As soon as I was served, I set down and started eating.
5. Jack knew it was them who stole the car.
6. Helen is not even gonna give Herb a chance to apologize.
7. We can't hardly expect any more help from the coaches.
8. Bill is not certain why Beulah give him a date for the dance.
9. Betty and me were sorry to hear of your accident.
10. This outline, together with the charts, provide a clear idea of our plan.

EXERCISE 3

Follow the instructions for Exercise 1.

1. He asked me to do like he told me.
2. My opinion, like my presence here, are taken too much for granted.
3. Before the party, I made the discovery that the boys had broken into the refrigerator and drank most of the cokes.
4. Bill looked as if he was about to die from hunger.
5. Either you or Dolly dances better than her.
6. Everybody working on a holiday will have their pay doubled.
7. If we talk soft enough, we may be able to get close enough to take a picture.
8. Who do you take me to be anyway?
9. You should of told me about your problem before this.
10. The cause for all the noise and confusion were not clear to Ned and me.

12. SUBJECT AND VERB AGREEMENT

Grammatical agreement means *oneness* or *unison* or *concord* or *harmony* of parts of a sentence. Thus when a subject agrees with its verb, both subject and the verb in the predicate are alike in having the same *person* (first, second, third) and *number* (singular or plural).

12a. A VERB MUST AGREE WITH ITS SUBJECT IN PERSON AND NUMBER.

Look for the person or thing about which the verb makes a statement. When you find it, you have the subject. A subject is always either a noun, a word or group of words used as a noun, or a pronoun.

> Our *football team* [subject] *plays* [verb] eight games each year.

In the preceding sentence, the subject and the verb are easy to find, but in some sentences the subject comes after the verb or is separated from the verb by other words. Before you try to make the verb agree with the subject, be sure that you have the *real* subject.

Few problems in agreement arise because English verbs (except *to be*) have the same form for singular and plural and for all persons except the third person singular present tense. Most nouns and verbs form their plurals in directly opposite ways; that is, most nouns form plurals by adding *s* or *es* and most verbs add an *s* in the third person singular. Remember that used as subjects, *I* and *we* are the forms for the first person; *you*, for the second person; *he, she, it*, and *they*, for the third person.

> The first concert helps us to pay for new clarinets for the orchestra. (The noun *concert* is third person singular. The verb *helps* is also third person singular.)
>
> The seniors invite the juniors to the first soccer game. (*Seniors* is third person plural. The verb *invite* is also third person plural.)
>
> I invite a different girl for each dance. (*I* is first person singular. The verb *invite* is also first person singular.)

NOTE: *Don't* means *do not*. It is used correctly with plural subjects and with *I* and *you* as singular subjects. Be careful not to use it with a third person singular subject like *he, the chair, the motor, Charles*. With such subjects use *doesn't*.

Substandard: He *don't* play golf.

Right: He *doesn't* play golf.

The meat *doesn't* need curing.

Jim *doesn't* appear to be working well.

12b. *THERE* AND *HERE* ARE NOT SUBJECTS.

After *there* and *here* we usually find the verb first and then the subject.

Substandard: There *is* dances every Friday evening at the new gym.

Right: There *are* dances every Friday evening at the new gym.

Substandard: Here *is* the tickets for the play.

Right: Here *are* the tickets for the play.

12c. A PREPOSITIONAL PHRASE THAT FOLLOWS THE SUBJECT DOES NOT AFFECT THE NUMBER OF THE VERB.

Phrases such as *of the men, in the various groups, to my cousins* are called prepositional phrases. The important words in a prepositional phrase are a preposition *(to, for, from, with, by, in, between, of, near* are some common ones) and a noun or pronoun which is the object of the preposition. Do not make the verb agree with the object of a preposition.

Substandard: Personnel managers from the Pearce Company *interviews* boys in our senior class every year. (The word *Company* is the object of the preposition *from*. *Managers* is the subject.)

Right: Personnel managers from the Pearce Company *interview* boys in our senior class every year.

Substandard: One of the members *preside* at each meeting.

Right: One of the members *presides* at each meeting.

12d. SINGULAR PRONOUNS REQUIRE SINGULAR VERBS.

These pronouns are singular: *another, anybody, anyone, anything, each, either, everybody, everyone, everything, many a one, neither, nobody, no one, one, somebody, someone.*

Substandard: Each of the girls *cook* some dish well.
Right: Each of the girls *cooks* some dish well.
Substandard: Everyone in the Hawaiian Islands *were* concerned about the danger of invasion.
Right: Everyone in the Hawaiian Islands *was* concerned about the danger of invasion.
Substandard: Neither of the Senators *show* any uncertainty.
Right: Neither of the Senators *shows* any uncertainty.
Substandard: Either of the twins *like* to go swimming in the nearby lake.
Right: Either of the twins *likes* to go swimming in the nearby lake.

Neither & Either are singular pronouns

NOTE: Certain nouns or pronouns are considered singular or plural according to the singular or plural number of the key word in a modifying phrase. Examples are *none, some, all, half, what,* and *which.*

Some of my *allowance has* been spent.
Some of our *athletes have* been awarded letters.
No ice is left; *all* of *it has* melted.
No girls are left on the frozen pond; *all* of *them have* gone inside to get warm.
Half of this *dress is* to be completed by Saturday.
Half of the *dresses* in the store *are* imported from England.
Which [one] of the cars *is* reserved for the guest speaker?
Which [ones] of the cars *are* reserved for the town officials?

None (literally *no one,* but frequently meaning *not any*) may be followed by either a singular or a plural verb. Studies of the use of *none* have revealed that it is as often followed by a plural as by a singular verb, especially when the phrase which modifies *none* contains a plural noun.

None [no one] of the players on our team *is* likely to make varsity.
None [not any] of the players on our team *have* failed to pass their examinations.

70

12e. ✓WORDS JOINED TO A SUBJECT BY *WITH*, *TOGETHER WITH*, *IN ADDITION TO*, *AS WELL AS*, AND *INCLUDING* DO NOT AFFECT THE VERB✓

Our allies, as well as the enemy, *were* suffering.
My whole equipment, including fishing rods, tackle, and knapsack, *was* lost on the trip.

12f. A COLLECTIVE NOUN USUALLY TAKES A SINGULAR VERB. IF, HOWEVER, THE INDIVIDUALS OF THE GROUP ARE CONSIDERED, THE VERB IS PLURAL.

Common collective nouns are *army, assembly, clergy, committee, company, couple, crew, crowd, family, flock, group, herd, jury, mob, multitude, orchestra, pair, personnel, squad, team, union.* Most of these nouns also have plural forms: *army, armies; assembly, assemblies; company, companies; crowd, crowds; team, teams;* etc.

Without the *s*, they are considered singular and take a singular verb and singular pronouns when the collection of individuals is thought of as a unit, as a whole; they are considered plural and take a plural verb and plural pronouns when the members of the group are thought of as individuals, acting separately.

The jury [a unit] *is* going to reach a verdict before six o'clock.
The jury [members] *have* ordered their suppers and are going to eat them in the jury room.
The committee *has* appointed a new chairman.
The committee *have* been unwilling to charge for personal expenses.
The couple at the head table *is* named Johnson.
The couple *were* assigned simple tasks during the service.
Our platoon *marches* very well.
The family *disagree* on the question of my dates.

12g. FOR NOUNS PLURAL IN FORM BUT SINGULAR IN MEANING, USE A SINGULAR VERB.

Calisthenics *is* included in our physical fitness program.
Mumps *is* a contagious disease.

Although authorities differ in their opinions about the number of some of these nouns, the following are usually considered to be singular: *physics, economics, news, politics, ethics, measles.* Consult your dictionary for guidance.

Subjects plural in form, which describe a quantity or number, require a singular verb when the subject is regarded as a unit.

> Ten miles *is* too far to walk.
> Two from five *leaves* three.
> Five dollars *was* the price of the book.
> Two-thirds of a gallon *does* not seem enough.

A title of a book, play, film, painting, musical composition, or other such work is singular.

> *Pride and Prejudice* is my favorite novel.
> *The Frogs* is a play by Aristophanes.

12h. BE CAREFUL OF THE PLURALS OF NOUNS OF FOREIGN ORIGIN.

Singular	*Plural*
datum	data
phenomenon	phenomena
genus	genera
synopsis	synopses
alumnus	alumni

> Synopses of two stories *were* submitted.
> The alumni *were* in favor of building the stadium.

NOTE: *Data* is correctly used as a plural, though many now use it as a singular.

12i. FORMS OF *TO BE* AGREE WITH THE SUBJECT, NOT WITH THE PREDICATE NOUN OR PRONOUN.

In some constructions, between two nouns or pronouns comes some form of the verb *to be: am, is, are, was, were, have been, has been.* The noun or pronoun coming first is considered the subject.

> The hardest part of the job *is* the bending and lifting.
> Bending and lifting *are* the hardest part of the job.

12j. A COMPOUND SUBJECT JOINED BY *AND* REQUIRES A PLURAL VERB.

> French and biology *are* my favorite subjects.
> Television and radio *have* revolutionized social habits.
> On the landing field *stand* a jet and a small helicopter.

NOTES:

1. When the two nouns or pronouns form a single thought or have a closely related meaning or mean one thing or one person, a singular verb is used.

> The secretary and treasurer of our club *is* named Benno Curtis.
> Bread and peanut butter *is* my favorite snack.
> My comrade and friend *was* with me.

2. If two or more singular subjects are joined by *and* with the first noun preceded by *every* or *each*, the verb is singular.

> Every boy and girl in the auditorium *applauds* the principal when he appears on the stage.
> Each boy and girl *has* received a letter from the dean.

12k. IF TWO SUBJECTS ARE JOINED BY *OR*, *EITHER . . . OR*, *NEITHER . . . NOR*, THE VERB AGREES WITH THE SUBJECT NEARER IT.

> Neither the student president nor his friends *want* to see Jack elected.
> Either new athletic fields or a swimming pool *is* to be provided in the spring.
> Either they or I *am* at fault.
> Either some of her classmates or Bill *is* willing to volunteer.
> Either Bill or some of her classmates *are* willing to volunteer.

12l. A RELATIVE PRONOUN (WHO, WHICH, THAT) IS SINGULAR OR PLURAL ACCORDING TO THE WORD TO WHICH THE PRONOUN REFERS. WHEN THE PRONOUN FUNCTIONS AS A SUBJECT, THE VERB MUST AGREE WITH IT IN NUMBER.

The only way to tell whether a relative pronoun is singular or plural is to examine the part of the sentence that precedes it and decide which word in the sentence the pronoun refers to. This word is called the *antecedent* of the pronoun. If the antecedent is singular, the pronoun will be singular, and the verb that goes with it must be singular.

Our team is the only one of the bowling groups which *has* kept rigidly to the schedule. (*Which* is the subject of the relative clause. It refers to *one* and is therefore singular.)

Monieka is one of the six mission stations that *are* supported by our church. (*That* is the subject of the relative clause. It refers to *stations* and is plural.)

Jerry is the only one of the golfers who *has* maintained a consistently good score. (*Who* refers to *one*.)

EXERCISE 4

Write on your paper the number of each sentence. Beside it write the subject of each incorrect verb and the correct form of that verb. Be prepared to explain in class why you have made the correction. If the sentence is correct, write C after its number.

1. For men who want to join clubs there is the Elks, Kiwanis, and Rotary.
2. The real meaning of success for many boys are making more and more money.
3. Semantics is a good thing for a boy to interest himself in, and so is athletics.
4. The loss of three fingers and an ear were the price Snitkin had to pay for his curiosity.
5. Fifteen dollars were all the Old Stone Peers could collect for playing at the dance.
6. Either you or I are going to have to push the car out of the ditch.
7. Except for a few scattered cousins, the seven aunts was all the family Wesley had.
8. The tastiest part of most school lunches are the spaghetti and meatballs.
9. Your letter, together with your check, was received yesterday.
10. Everybody, students and instructors alike, are glad that school is opening.
11. Delaney insisted that champagnes from a non-vintage year was not to be considered.
12. Whoever finds Thomas Aquinas a dull and uninteresting writer are, I fear, devoid of intellectual curiosity and humorless.

13. Each of the girls in the drama club is an aspiring television star.
14. Measles, for adults, are often a serious disease.
15. Tipley smilingly disagreed when someone remarked that *The Dynasts* were great literature.
16. *Westward the Worms* are one of the finest novels ever to come from Shillingbreek's typewriter.
17. For Mallard twenty miles of hiking over rugged terrain were no challenge.
18. Beside the cottage stands a pine tree, a willow, and a maple.
19. What we feared was that there was in literal fact flying saucers over Shawbridge.
20. Neither Gilbert nor Sullivan were very easy to get along with.

EXERCISE 5

1. Appleby was discharged because the spelling on the memoranda he wrote to his boss was so bad.
2. Cursing and imprecation are not going to help us find our way out of the jungle, Dawson.
3. Important in a person's development is the schools he has attended.
4. The senior class is having their pictures taken at five-minute intervals this afternoon.
5. In the States, Rudolfo, shooting laundrymen or their families are against the law.
6. The fatheadedness of my two assistants were simply indescribable.
7. Each of the school regulations have a definite purpose.
8. Mallard is one of the most sophisticated men that has ever lived in this community.
9. It was one of the roads that leads to Calgary, and that was all that mattered.
10. The superintendent, with two members of the board of vestrymen, inspects the heating plant every fall.
11. There is a Holt Renfrew, a T. Eaton, a Woolworth, and two large banks in town.
12. Violet is a good student who has no trouble at examination time.
13. You forget, Scott, that your mother and I am aging fast.
14. Hernandez was one of those clumsy and inartistic matadors that sometimes wangles an engagement in the off season.
15. Jay soon realized that politics were not for him.
16. Martin and Myrtle meets each other after every class.
17. There was certain moments when little Edson feared he could bear the pain no longer.

18. The plans for the celebration of St. Patrick's Day was kept a closely guarded secret.
19. It seems that either he or I have to make all the decisions.
20. I told him that eight dollars was too little for a day's work.

13. PRONOUNS AND ANTECEDENTS

Our writing would be dull if we repeated nouns again and again. Consequently, we use a pronoun (*pro-* means "for") instead of repeating the noun.

13a. A PRONOUN SHOULD AGREE WITH ITS ANTECEDENT IN GENDER, NUMBER, AND PERSON.

The meaning of the pronoun will not be clear unless it has the same gender, number, and person as the noun for which it stands. This noun is called the *antecedent,* the relationship of which to the pronoun itself must be unmistakably clear if your reader is not to be misled or confused.

Orlon is an important synthetic material. *It* is said to be better than nylon. (*It* refers to *orlon,* the antecedent. Both *orlon* and *it* are neuter gender, singular number, third person.)

The woman put on *her* gloves. (Singular antecedent, feminine.)

The women put on *their* gloves. (Plural antecedent, feminine.)

Pronouns do not necessarily agree with their antecedents in case. In the sentences above, *woman* and *women* are nominative, *her* and *their* are possessive. See Section 14.

13b. SINGULAR PRONOUNS REFER TO SINGULAR ANTECEDENTS.

The words *each, either, neither, somebody, anyone, anybody, everybody,* and *nobody* are singular, and in formal

English a pronoun referring to any one of these words should be singular (*he, his, him, she, her, it*).

In colloquial English, the rule stated above has been relaxed somewhat. People who wish their language to sound informal and casual sometimes use *their* to refer to *everybody*. When the sense of *everybody, anyone*, etc., is *many* or *all*, the plural personal pronoun referring to these indefinite pronouns is frequently found in both formal and informal English: "Everybody is expected to do *their* share of the work." Such use is preferable to the somewhat artificial and even awkward "Everybody is expected to do *his* or *her* share of the work." Notice, however, that a singular, not a plural verb form is used.

Informal: Everybody took *their* heavy coat to camp.

Formal: Everybody took *his* heavy coat to camp.

Informal: Each of the boxers was accompanied by *their* manager.

Formal: Each of the boxers was accompanied by *his* manager.

Informal: Anyone can try *their* luck at this game.

Formal: Anyone can try *his* luck at this game.

13c. A COLLECTIVE NOUN USED AS AN ANTECEDENT TAKES A SINGULAR PRONOUN IF THE GROUP IS THOUGHT OF AS A UNIT AND A PLURAL PRONOUN IF IT IS THOUGHT OF IN TERMS OF ITS INDIVIDUAL MEMBERS.

The crowd of boys took off *their* hats. (The crowd acted as individuals.)

The crowd shouted *its* overwhelming approval. (The crowd acted as a unit.)

NOTE: Once you decide whether a collective noun is to be singular or plural, stick to your decision. If you use it as the subject with a singular verb, make sure that all pronouns referring to it are singular; and if you use it with a plural verb, make sure that all pronouns are plural.

Doubtful: The family *was* discussing *their* problems.

Right: The family *was* discussing *its* problems.

Right: The family *were* discussing *their* problems.

13d. A NOUN OR AN INDEFINITE PRONOUN USED AS AN ANTECEDENT TAKES A PRONOUN IN THE THIRD PERSON.

All nouns and indefinite pronouns are in the third person except when they are used in direct address or in apposition with a pronoun of the first or second person. Aside from these two uses, all nouns and indefinite pronouns require a third-person pronoun. A phrase such as *of us, of you* coming between the pronoun and its antecedent does not affect the person of the pronoun.

Informal: If a man wants to succeed, *you* must work hard.
Right: If a man wants to succeed, *he* must work hard.
Informal: Neither of you has finished *your* lunch.
Right: Neither of you has finished *his* lunch.

13e. WHEN THE ANTECEDENT IS A SINGULAR NOUN OF COMMON GENDER, THE MASCULINE PRONOUN SHOULD BE USED UNLESS IT IS CLEAR THAT THE NOUN REFERS TO A GIRL OR A WOMAN.

Right: Each member of the dramatic club indicated *his* choice of a play for the annual production.
Right: Each member of the girls' glee club was asked to name *her* favorite Christmas carol.

13f. A PRONOUN AGREES WITH THE NEARER OF TWO ANTECEDENTS.

Occasionally, two antecedents, different in gender or number, occur in a sentence. With two antecedents and only one pronoun, the pronoun referring to the nearer antecedent should be used.

He loves everybody and everything *which* is connected with his work.

He loves everything or everybody *who* is connected with his work.

In this cool room, neither the gardenia nor the roses will lose *their* freshness.

13g. *WHO* REFERS TO PERSONS, *WHICH* REFERS TO THINGS, AND *THAT* REFERS TO PERSONS OR THINGS.

The man *who* told me the story is your doctor.

The book *which* you lent me contains some very exciting stories.

The woman flier *that* took her plane on a round-the-world trip has been awarded a medal.

13h. *WHAT* SHOULD NOT BE USED TO REFER TO AN EXPRESSED ANTECEDENT.

Substandard: The book *what* you sent me as a graduation present arrived yesterday.

Right: The book *that* you sent me arrived yesterday.

Right: I heard *what* you said.

13i. THE ANTECEDENT OF A PRONOUN SHOULD BE EXPRESSED, NOT MERELY IMPLIED.

The relation of a pronoun to its antecedent must be clear and unmistakable, except for indefinite pronouns. The reference word should be placed close to its antecedent in order that no intervening words may cause confusion. A *relative* pronoun must be in the same sentence as its antecedent, but *personal* or *demonstrative* pronouns may be placed some distance away, frequently in other sentences, if there is no intervening noun or pronoun to cause confusion.

Implied reference occurs when the antecedent of a pronoun is not actually expressed but must be inferred from the context. One of the most common forms of implied reference is the use of the pronouns *it, this, that, which* to refer to an entire preceding statement rather than to some noun or pronoun in that statement.

You, as a writer, must decide whether such words refer to an implied antecedent or whether their antecedent occurs in a preceding or even following statement. Frequent use of implied reference is found in the work of many reputable writers, and when confusion is not possible, the use may be effective.

Faults in the implied reference of *it, which, this, that, these, those,* etc., may be corrected by (1) summing up the idea of the preceding statement in a noun which acts as the antecedent; (2) rephrasing the sentence so as to eliminate the pronoun or to give it a clear and appropriate antecedent.

Doubtful: I worked for the Post Office last Christmas vacation and enjoyed *it* very much.

Improved: I was employed by the Post Office last Christmas vacation and enjoyed the work very much.

Doubtful: Wednesday morning I was ill but *it* became steadily better during the day.

Improved: Wednesday morning I was ill but felt steadily better during the day.

Doubtful: You will have a lot of hiring and firing to do, and *this* takes a great deal of diplomacy.

Improved: You will have a lot of hiring and firing to do, a task that demands a great deal of diplomacy.

Doubtful: At the beach we saw the lavish fireworks display. *This* concluded our celebration.

Improved: When we saw the lavish fireworks display at the beach, we concluded our celebration.

Doubtful: Strewn over the floor was everything from broken bottles to rusted rotor heads. *That* solved the mystery.

Improved: Strewn over the floor was everything from broken bottles to rusted rotor heads. That mess solved the mystery.

Doubtful: He was in bad shape, *which* was made obvious by his persistent bleeding.

Improved: He was in bad shape, a condition which was made obvious by his persistent bleeding.

13j. AVOID THE INDEFINITE USE OF *IT* AND *THEY*.

It as a third person singular pronoun, neuter, should usually have an appropriate antecedent. Also, when *it* is used impersonally and acceptably (*it* seems, *it* is possible, *it* is raining, etc.), do not use another *it* in the same sentence to refer to a definite antecedent. See Section 13k.

They, their, theirs, them, as plural forms of the third person personal pronoun, should have definite antecedents: plural nouns or other pronouns in the plural. Otherwise, do not use these pronouns.

Indefinite: In this article, *it* shows that war is horrible.

Better: This article shows that war is horrible.

Indefinite: *They* have good roads in Alberta.

Better: Alberta has good roads.

Vague: *They* say that Argentina is a wealthy nation.

Better: Economists say that Argentina is a wealthy nation.

NOTE: *It* is sometimes used impersonally to introduce an idea.

It will be clear tomorrow.

It was Churchill who made the "Their Finest Hour" speech.

It is necessary, it is true, it is certain, it is likely, it is imperative are correct.

13k. DO NOT USE IMPERSONAL *IT* AND THE PRONOUN *IT* IN THE SAME SENTENCE.

Vague: We can send the refrigerator today, or we can keep it in the factory for a few days if *it* is necessary.

Better: We can send the refrigerator today, or we can keep *it* for a few days.

NOTE: In informal English, *it* sometimes refers to an idea instead of a single antecedent.

Informal: He was nervous, but he tried not to show it.

Formal: He was nervous, but he tried not to show uneasiness.

13l. IN FORMAL WRITING AVOID THE USE OF *YOU* TO MEAN PEOPLE IN GENERAL.

In colloquial or informal speech, expressions such as "You can see how important money is" or "Dancing makes you graceful" are permissible. Formal English requires the use of *one* or *anyone* in these statements.

Anyone can see how important money is.

Dancing makes one graceful.

81

13m. ✓AVOID THE USE OF *SAME* IN PLACE OF A PERSONAL PRONOUN. ✓

Wrong: Please fill out the blank and return same to us.
Right: Please fill out the blank and return it to us.

13n. AVOID DOUBLE REFERENCE FOR A PRONOUN.

Double reference occurs when two antecedents are possible for a single pronoun. The pronoun reference is therefore ambiguous; instead, the antecedent should be clear and definite.

Ambiguous reference can be corrected by (1) repeating the antecedent, (2) using a synonym for the antecedent, (3) changing the wording of the sentence so that the antecedent of each pronoun is unmistakable.

Dubious: When a father hands over the car to his son, *he* is not always sure it is in good condition.

Better: A father is not always sure the car is in good condition when he hands it over to his son.

Dubious: The actor told Bob that *he* should move upstage. (Who should move: *Bob?* The *actor?*)

Better: The actor said, "I shall move upstage." (The *actor* will move.)

The actor told Bob of his intention to move upstage. (The *actor* will move.)

The actor advised Bob to move upstage. *(Bob* should move.)

The actor told Bob that he, as a supporting player, should move upstage. *(Bob* should move.)

EXERCISE 6

Write on your paper the number of each sentence. Then write the correct form of any pronoun which is substandard or doubtful. Beside the correct form of the pronoun, write the antecedent of the pronoun which you have corrected. If a verb requires change, make this alteration also. If an indefinite pronoun must be removed, rewrite the entire sentence. If a sentence is correct, write "C" next to its number.

1. Both Silversmith and his partner Botts knew how to handle himself in a fist fight.
2. You can tell when you have a fish on your line because you can feel them struggle.
3. In the advertisement it explained why Twodekay is popular with youngsters.
4. If every member of the class does their best, we should finish *Giants in the Earth* by April.
5. When a student doesn't have a car, they must take a bus or hitchhike to town.
6. A blonde wig can be carefully curled and which can be an expensive hairdo.
7. You know very well that the Smithfield Grange always has their suppers on Friday nights.
8. No one wanted to go back to work because they are watching the pigeons.
9. My aunt is an archeology professor. This is an unusual position for a woman.
10. Coach Redblood instructed the team doctors to stand by with their novocain.
11. The Finch family was an industrious group that never tired of their work.
12. When I look into your deep purple eyes, Minerva, I get that old thrill.
13. The teacher promised that each child would have a chance to make their speech.
14. That company has a particularly good retirement policy for their employees.
15. They say that falling in love is wonderful.
16. Never touch a high-voltage wire without throwing the switch; they may kill you.
17. A girl likes to go steady with a boy that they can feel proud of.
18. I want you to unbuckle those galoshes for the children and then tell them to put them away when they are out of them.
19. Marsha's glance gave Marvin that sinking feeling.
20. Bill attended a party occasionally, but he always left before they started dancing.

EXERCISE 7

Follow the directions for Exercise 6.

1. We tried to explain to Grandfather that a man of sixty-five would only make a spectacle of themselves in ballet.
2. If a person on our campus wants to know the latest news, they simply find Myrtle and ask her.

3. As soon as the customers left the tables, the waiters cleaned them.
4. Everyone should outline his research paper before writing it, not afterward.
5. Neither the hot sun nor the gentle rains will have their usual effect on the tourists this year.
6. When you play with matches you often get burned.
7. As each man reached headquarters, they gave the adjutant the information they had gathered.
8. Neither Jay nor his brother was permitted to own a car until they got licenses.
9. Every grocer that raises every price will be boycotted.
10. The sergeant discovered, too late, that one of his men had neglected to brush their teeth.
11. Even someone like Daisy has his problems.
12. In that particular discotheque it was difficult to hear every note of the music.
13. If you've never watched a dickcissel gobbling up their suet, you've missed one of Nature's loveliest sights.
14. Either the lecture or the slides will have their special appeal for the audience.
15. Lolly's mother is a liontamer. That is a tricky business.
16. Never fell a eucalyptus tree in a high wind; they may fall the wrong way and hurt someone.
17. When you find the scissors, will you please give it to me?
18. Selma took the children from the buses and sent them to the zoo.
19. In the notice it says that parking fees will be increased fifteen dollars a year.
20. Rex is one person that I always enjoy seeing at the library.

14. CASE OF PRONOUNS

Case is a grammatical term referring to one of the forms that a noun or pronoun takes to indicate its relation to other words. The three cases in English — subjective or nominative, possessive or genitive, objective or accusative — appear in the singular and plural.

The following principles for use of nominative and objective cases rarely apply to nouns but are a guide for use of pronoun forms.

Learn the different forms of personal, relative, and interrogative pronouns.

PERSONAL PRONOUNS
Singular

	NOMINATIVE	*POSSESSIVE*	*OBJECTIVE*
1st person	I	my, mine	me
2nd person	you	your, yours	you
3rd person			
(masculine)	he	his	him
(feminine)	she	her, hers	her
(neuter)	it	its	it

Plural

1st person	we	our, ours	us
2nd person	you	your, yours	you
3rd person			
(all genders)	they	their, theirs	them

RELATIVE AND INTERROGATIVE
Singular and Plural

who	whose	whom

When there are two possessive forms of the personal pronoun, the first one given in the list above is followed by the noun it qualifies as a possessive adjective; the second is used alone, as a possessive pronoun.

My book is on the desk; *yours* is on the shelf.
The book on the desk is *mine.*
His appointment is in the morning; *hers* is in the afternoon.

No change in form occurs in the use of *that* and *which.*

14a. THE SUBJECT OF A VERB IS IN THE NOMINATIVE CASE.

If the subject is a noun, improper usage is unlikely. Even those who use substandard English will have difficulty making grammatical errors. Nominative pronoun forms are *I, you, he, she, it, we, you, they*.

> Sarah and *I* have eaten too much candy.
> When Ned comes, *he* and *I* are going to build a fire.
> *We* boys can do a better job without your help.

14b. THE PRONOUN FOLLOWING ANY PART OF THE VERB *BE (AM, IS, ARE, WAS, WERE, BEEN, BE)* AND REFERRING TO THE SUBJECT IS IN THE NOMINATIVE CASE. IT IS CALLED A *PREDICATE NOMINATIVE.*

> The officers of the class are *Carol, Alfred*, and *I*.
> It was *they* who telephoned last night.
> Do you think it could have been *she* who sang on the radio?

The foregoing principle applies to the first person pronoun, plural, *we, us*, and to the second and third person pronouns, singular and plural, *she, her, he, him, they, them*. Controversy exists over "This is *I*" or "It is *I*" versus "This is *me*" or "It is *me*." In one opinion poll among competent judges, 59 percent labeled the *me* use acceptable. Studies have shown that *both* "It is *I*" and "It is *me*" are avoided by careful speakers and writers in favor of "This is Jones" or "This is he" or a simple "Yes" to the question, "Is this Jones?"

14c. THE OBJECT OF A VERB OR A PREPOSITION IS IN THE OBJECTIVE CASE: *ME, YOU, HIM, HER, IT, US, THEM.*

Watch particularly the second member of a compound object. Both members must be in the same case.

> Mother met *Hilda* and *me* at the airport. (*Hilda* and *me* are objects of the verb *met*.)
> Mrs. Fulton had invited *her* and *me* to a party. (*Her* and *me* are objects of the verb *invited*.)
> Between *Jack* and *him* there has always been a good understanding. (*Jack* and *him* are objects of the preposition *between*.)
> All the plans for the party were made by *Fred* and *her*. (*Fred* and *her* are objects of the preposition *by*.)

14d. THE INDIRECT OBJECT IS IN THE OBJECTIVE CASE.

The indirect object is the noun or pronoun before which *to* or *for* is understood.

Uncle Fred sent *me* a bracelet from India. *(Bracelet* is the direct object; *me* is the object of *to* understood.)

Save *me* a piece of that cake. *(Me* is the object of *for* understood; *piece* is the direct object.)

14e. AN ELLIPTICAL CLAUSE OF COMPARISON, PRECEDED BY *THAN* OR *AS*, REQUIRES THE CASE CALLED FOR BY THE EXPANDED COMPARISON.

An elliptical clause is one with a word or more missing; the omitted word or words are understood from other parts of the sentence. If you supply the missing word or words, you should have little trouble about the correct case form.

My sister is taller than *I. (Than* introduces the elliptical clause *I am. I* is the subject of the verb *am* understood.)

Tom is just as good an actor as *she. (She* is subject of *is* understood.)

Nobody cares more about your happiness than *he. (He* is subject of *does* understood.)

I like Jan better than *her. (Her* is object of *like* understood.)

This television program pleased you much more than *me.* *(Me* is object of *pleased* understood.)

14f. THE SUBJECT OF AN INFINITIVE IS IN THE OBJECTIVE CASE.

Infinitives are certain verb forms preceded by an expressed or implied *to:* to study, to sleep, to eat.

I wanted *him* to run for class secretary. (The whole group of words is the object of *wanted; him* is the subject of *to run.)*

Lee expected *me* to wait for her.

Jack asked *me* to go to the dance.

The music teacher let *Gordon and me* sing a duet. (A verb used after *let* is an infinitive although it is used without *to. Gordon and me* are subjects of the infinitive *to sing.)*

14g. THE OBJECT OF AN INFINITIVE, GERUND, OR PARTICIPLE IS IN THE OBJECTIVE CASE.

The librarian wants to see *us*. (*Us* is the object of the infinitive *to see.*)

Finding *you* here is a surprise. (*You* is the object of the gerund *finding.*)

Having recognized *him* instantly, I hurried across the street. (*Him* is the object of the participle *having recognized.*)

14h. THE OBJECTIVE COMPLEMENT OF THE INFINITIVE *TO BE* IS IN THE OBJECTIVE CASE WHEN THE SUBJECT OF THE INFINITIVE IS EXPRESSED.

This construction may cause some trouble because it requires an objective case after a linking verb. It may help to remember that the objective case will occur after *to be* only when two conditions prevail: (1) The sentence must use the infinitive form of the verb *to be;* (2) the subject of that infinitive must be expressed. Notice the difference in these examples:

I thought you were *he*. (Here, the form *were* is not an infinitive.)

I took you to be *him*. (In this sentence, *you* is the subject of the infinitive *to be*. The subject of an infinitive is in the objective case. Then the objective case must follow.)

Aunt Jane took Lucy to be *me*.

The construction is an awkward one and can be avoided.

14i. AN APPOSITIVE MUST BE IN THE SAME CASE AS THE NOUN OR PRONOUN WHICH IT IDENTIFIES OR EXPLAINS.

The principal wants us all—Albert, Roland, and me—to run for the office. (*Albert, Roland, me* are in apposition with *us* and must be in the same objective case.)

We, you and I, are the only persons here not wearing hats. (Nominative.)

14j. THE POSSESSIVE CASE OF A NOUN OR PRONOUN SHOULD BE USED BEFORE A GERUND.

The possessive case with a gerund is usually clear, whereas the objective case with a gerund may not be. Here are some examples of possessives with gerunds.

I do not approve of *his* playing football. (*Playing* is the gerund. It is the object of the preposition *of.*)

My teachers were not sure of *my* winning the prize. (*Winning* is the gerund.)

His singing could be improved. (*Singing* is the gerund.)

NOTE: Be sure to distinguish between gerund and participle. The latter is used as an adjective and does not have a possessive case preceding it.

We saw him standing on the corner. (*Standing* is a participle modifying *him.*)

14k. *WHO* AND *WHOEVER* ARE USED AS SUBJECTS OF VERBS OR PREDICATE PRONOUNS; *WHOM* AND *WHOMEVER* ARE USED AS OBJECTS OF VERBS AND PREPOSITIONS.

Many grammatical errors arise from misunderstanding the pronoun forms *who* or *whom* and *whoever* or *whomever.* This discussion supplements and expands that given above, Sections 14a-j.

1. The following sentences illustrate proper use of *who* and *whoever,* nominative forms serving as subjects of the verbs in the dependent clauses:

I demand the opportunity for *whoever* wishes it. (*Whoever* is the subject of the verb *wishes;* the whole dependent clause is the object of the preposition *for.*)

The question of *who* can seize the opportunity must be answered. (*Who* is the subject of *can seize;* the whole dependent clause is the object of the preposition *of.*)

I cannot tell *who* is *who* in the present student council, but I can tell *who* was *who* in last year's council. (Each *who* before *is* and *was* is the subject; each *who* after *is* and *was* is a predicate pronoun.)

In other words, subject of a verb takes precedence over object of a preposition or verb, when pronoun case forms are in question.

2. The following sentences illustrate proper use of *whom* and *whomever,* objective forms serving as objects in the dependent clauses:

This is the interesting girl *whom* I met at the sorority tea. (Direct object of *met.*)

Bring *whomever* you like. (Direct object of *like;* the dependent clause is the object of *bring.*)

The statement began, "To *whom* it may concern." (Direct object of *concern;* the dependent clause is the object of the preposition *To.*)

The new father offered a cigar to *whomever* he met that morning. (Direct object of *met;* the dependent clause is the object of the preposition *to.*)

3. The nominative and objective cases are frequently confused because of intervening words. The case of a pronoun depends upon its use in the sentence and must not be influenced by words which come between the pronoun and its antecedent.

He asked us *who* we supposed would be elected. (Check by omitting *we supposed.*)

Who do you imagine would ever do such a thing? (Check by omitting *do you imagine.*)

I danced with the boy *whom* no one would have dreamed I could like. (Check by omitting *no one would have dreamed.*)

4. Whenever you are in doubt about *who* or *whom,* substitute *he* or *him* and see which makes sense:

Who/whom are you speaking to? (To *who/whom* are you speaking?)

He/him are you speaking to? (To *he/him* are you speaking?)

This is the kind of leader *who/whom* we admire.

. . . we admire *who/whom.*

. . . we admire *he/him.*

NOTE: Current-usage studies indicate that the distinction between *who* and *whom* is breaking down, partly because keeping them straight is difficult and partly because many people start a sentence or clause with *who,* not knowing how they are going to end. One dictionary says of *whom:* "the objective case of *who;* in colloquial usage, now often replaced by *who*" (*Webster's New World Dictionary*), i.e., in informal English *who* may replace *whom* when it stands before a verb or preposition of which it is the object. Precise speakers and writers probably will still observe the conventional distinctions of *who* vs. *whom: who* only as subject, *whom* only as object.

EXERCISE 8

Write on your paper the number of each sentence and beside it write the appropriate pronoun or noun forms from the choices provided. Be prepared to explain in class why you have made each choice.

1. Let Scott and *(I, myself, me)* wire your chicken house.
2. Give the flowers to *(whoever, whomever)* comes to the door and mention *(who, whom)* sent them.
3. Fire over the head of *(whoever, whomever)* crosses the river, Dawson; Guthrie and *(I, myself, me)* will try to get at the position from the rear.
4. That is the opinion *(who, which)* is held by a man *(who, which)* ought to know.
5. *(He, Him)* and *(I, me)* often shoot ducks together.
6. Don't you realize that Mallard is richer than you and *(I, me)?*
7. The speaker said that the future of civilization depended largely on *(we, us)* plumbers.
8. Between you and *(I, me)*, Harold, this new basketball coach doesn't know what he's talking about.
9. For *(they, them)* who have to work for a living *(he, him)* and Delaney have the deepest compassion.
10. I thought it was *(they, them)* who felt that basketball knew no better coach than *(him, he)*.

EXERCISE 9

Follow the directions for Exercise 8.

1. *(He, Him)* and the cobra get along better now, thanks to *(their, them)* discovering a mutual interest in music.
2. "It isn't a question of *(my, me)* remaining a bachelor," thought Mallard, "only of *(who, whom)* I should marry."
3. At *(who, whom)* did the lady smile, Westergong—you or *(I, me)?*
4. Just between you and *(I, me)*, what's the chance of the *(team, team's)* winning next week?

5. Among *(we, us)* six who received the unfair penalty, five were wholly innocent.
6. I hurt *(myself, me)* as much as I did *(her, herself)*.
7. What puzzled Harry and *(I, myself, me)* was not so much the presence of *(she, her)* and Clifford in the house as *(their, them)* being permitted to sit at the same table with those of *(we, us)* who were of better blood.
8. Of *(who, whom)* are you speaking, Martin or *(I, me)?*
9. Mr. Throop wandered through the forest with his dog beside *(him, himself)*.
10. *(We, Us)* Canadians are rightly proud of *(Nancy Greene, Nancy Greene's)* winning the Olympic Gold Medal in 1968.

EXERCISE 10

Follow the directions for Exercise 8.

1. The new matron is a woman *(who, whom)* we're quite sure will be able to control the boys.
2. Jay's wife isn't fond of *(his, him)* working late at night.
3. Jacques and *(I, myself, me)* are very good friends, but he has never approved of *(me, my)* playing the banjo.
4. *(We, Us)* three—you, Jay, and *(I, myself, me)*—have been elected to the dishwashing detail.
5. Those boys will get *(themselves, theirselves)* in trouble if they keep on dynamiting power plants.
6. Last night Mallard introduced his new girlfriend to *(us, we)* boys.
7. Just *(who, whom)* do you think you are?
8. *(Martin, Martin's)* carrying on disturbed Myrtle as well as *(I, me)*.
9. Do you think *(she, her)* and Louinda really ought to go alone?
10. The Canadian Legion boys certainly had *(themselves, theirselves)* a time at the convention while I was in Vancouver.

15. PRINCIPAL PARTS OF VERBS

In every language, verbs have principal parts, sometimes three, as in German, sometimes five, as in French, Spanish, and Italian. The English verb has three principal parts: *pres-*

ent tense (present infinitive), *past tense,* and *past participle.*
Example: *eat, ate, eaten.* An excellent way to recall the principal parts of a verb is to substitute those of any verb for the following:

I *eat* today.	I *walk* today.
I *ate* yesterday.	I *walked* yesterday.
I *have eaten* every day this month.	I *have walked* every day this week.

The present participle, a necessary verb form considered almost important enough to be included in the principal parts of English verbs, is formed by adding *ing* to the present infinitive form. This "fourth" part, if in any way irregular, is given in your dictionary. Examples: *eating, walking, working, starting, doing, finding.* The present participial form has constant use both as part of the predicate and as adjective.

The *past* and the *past participle* of many English verbs are formed by adding -*d*, -*ed*, or -*t* to the present. These are called *regular,* or *weak,* verbs.

Present	Past	Past Participle
save	saved	saved
talk	talked	talked
ask	asked	asked
mean	meant	meant
spend	spent	spent
wish	wished	wished

There are, however, other verbs, which do not follow this pattern. These are called *irregular,* or *strong,* verbs, and they form the past tense and past participle in several ways. Although it is impossible to establish a rule for these changes, groups of these words do often fall into a special pattern. One group has a vowel change in the past tense, and in some cases in the past participle as well.

Present	Past	Past Participle
drink	drank	drunk
sing	sang	sung
cling	clung	clung
fight	fought	fought
sit	sat	sat
shoot	shot	shot
come	came	come
run	ran	run
find	found	found

Some verbs in this group, in addition to the vowel change, add -*n* to the past participle.

Present	Past	Past Participle
grow	grew	grown
break	broke	broken
fly	flew	flown
freeze	froze	frozen
drive	drove	driven
write	wrote	written
eat	ate	eaten
ride	rode	ridden
fall	fell	fallen

Another group changes its form completely in the past tense and past participle.

Present	Past	Past Participle
bring	brought	brought
think	thought	thought
buy	bought	bought
stand	stood	stood
go	went	gone
do	did	done
lie	lay	lain
catch	caught	caught
wind	wound	wound

A few verbs change the last consonant, but not the vowel.

Present	Past	Past Participle
make	made	made
have	had	had
build	built	built

A few others have the same form for all three principal parts.

Present	Past	Past Participle
cut	cut	cut
burst	burst	burst
hurt	hurt	hurt
set	set	set
spread	spread	spread
cast	cast	cast
put	put	put

If you are uncertain about the correct verb form, consult your dictionary.

Following is a list of 50 troublesome verbs. Study them; put them into the three expressions suggested in the first paragraph of p. 93.

bear	bore	borne (born, *given birth to*)
begin	began	begun
bid	bid	bid (*as in an auction*)
bid	bade	bidden (*as in a command*)
bite	bit	bitten (bit)
blow	blew	blown
break	broke	broken
burst	burst	burst
catch	caught	caught
choose	chose	chosen
come	came	come
dig	dug	dug
dive	dived	dived
do	did	done
drag	dragged	dragged
draw	drew	drawn
drink	drank	drunk
drown	drowned	drowned
eat	ate	eaten
fall	fell	fallen
fly	flew	flown
forget	forgot	forgotten (forgot)
freeze	froze	frozen
get	got	got (gotten)
go	went	gone
hang	hung	hung (*object*)
hang	hanged	hanged (*person*)
know	knew	known
lay	laid	laid
lead	led	led
lend	lent	lent
lie	lay	lain (*recline*)
lie	lied	lied (*falsehood*)
lose	lost	lost
pay	paid	paid
raise	raised	raised
ride	rode	ridden
rise	rose	risen
run	ran	run
set	set	set

sing	sang	sung
sit	sat	sat
speak	spoke	spoken
swim	swam	swum
take	took	taken
tear	tore	torn
wake	waked (woke)	waked (woke)
wear	wore	worn
wring	wrung	wrung
write	wrote	written

15a. DO NOT CONFUSE THE PAST TENSE AND THE PAST PARTICIPLE.

The past participle, the third principal part, makes a compound tense of the verb only when it is accompanied by some part of *have* or *be*.

The past form, or the second principal part, of a verb is used without an auxiliary.

Present	*Past*	*Past Participle*
see	saw	seen
do	did	done

Substandard: I *seen* the flames reach the top of the building.

Right: I *saw* the flames reach the top of the building.

Substandard: The fireman *done* something very brave.

Right: The fireman *did* something very brave.

Seen and *done* are past participles and form tenses only with the aid of some part of the verb *have* or *be*.

Substandard: I *have saw* several ice hockey games.

Right: I *have seen* several ice hockey games.

Substandard: Herbert was praised because he *had did* a good job on the assignment.

Substandard: I *done* it myself.

Right: I *did* it myself.

Be careful not to write *of* for *have*.

Substandard: I could *of gone* to the game.

Right: I could *have gone* to the game last week.

Right: I could'*ve* gone to the game.

96

15b. DO NOT CONFUSE AN IRREGULAR VERB WITH A REGULAR VERB.

For centuries, most strong and weak verbs in English have kept the principal parts that they now have. Only in a few isolated instances has a strong or irregular verb changed to weak or regular (*help, holp, holpen* to *help, helped, helped*) or a weak verb added an alternative strong-verb ending (*prove, proved, proved* or *proven*).

Confusion or carelessness may cause you to add regular-verb endings to irregular verbs or to treat an occasional regular verb like an irregular verb.

Substandard: He *drawed* a bucket of water from the well.
Right: He *drew* a bucket of water from the well.
Substandard: Last night the wind *blowed* at thirty miles an hour.
Right: Last night the wind *blew* at thirty miles an hour.
Substandard: I *throwed* it to him fast.
Right: I *threw* it to him fast.

EXERCISE 11

Write on your paper the number of each sentence and next to it place the correct form of the verb which appears in parentheses. When in doubt about the correct form, restudy Section 15 or consult your dictionary.

1. Martin missed his appointment because he had (lie) in bed until 8:30.
2. Jenny (arise) every day at dawn and walked ten miles.
3. He was glad that he had not (drown).
4. Hugh feared that he and his friends would be (throw) out of the theater.
5. After eating for an hour and a half, the glutton realized that he (begin) to lose his appetite.
6. Barbara stuck her head out and nearly got it (shoot) off.
7. The phone had (ring) several times before Myrtle answered it.
8. The presence of Colonel Hogben (lend) an air of dignity to the meeting.
9. As the passengers threw coins into the water, young boys (dive) for the money.
10. So far Doris had (bear) the slipshod service patiently.

EXERCISE 12

Follow the directions for Exercise 11.

1. Throckmorton had apparently (drink) both bottles.
2. Marvin did not look like someone who had (swim) the Channel, and he hadn't.
3. The day the water mains (burst), we irrigated our tomatoes.
4. It was Euclid; he had (take) the plane from the hangar.
5. Had he only (dive) a little more to the left he would have hit the water.
6. The sailor caught the line and was (drag) onto the lobster boat.
7. Just then someone (begin) to pull rabbits out of the hat.
8. His father's spirits (sink) when Marvin declined the offer.
9. I fear, Dawson, that you have (draw) the shorter straw.
10. Who knows how long this jet has (fly) in the wrong direction?

EXERCISE 13

Follow the directions for Exercise 11.

1. Because he had other fish to fry, he (know) the little perch would survive.
2. Why buy new overalls, Harry, when a patch may be (sew) on your old ones?
3. Simpson declared that he'd rather be (hang) than miss the opening of the deer season.
4. Sophocles had (prove) to his own satisfaction that hemlock tastes awful.
5. Gladys (speed) across the lawn, the gorilla drawing ever closer.
6. It was good to hear the old familiar songs being (sing).
7. If he said his hen (lay) sixteen eggs in three days, he lied.
8. For the next two days little Munster was (bind) hand and foot.
9. When the grand old lady entered the room, we all (rise) from our chairs.
10. Marcellus (bid) his friends a sad farewell and crawled away.

16. LINKING AND AUXILIARY VERBS

Most verbs assert action but a few express a static condition or state of being (no action). Most, not all, of these "inactive" verbs are *linking* (or *joining* or *copulative*) verbs.

They serve the purpose of coming between, or *coupling,* two substantives or a substantive and an adjective. The substantive following the linking verb is a *predicate noun* or *predicate pronoun* (never a direct object). Nouns cause no trouble; pronouns may present problems. An adjective following the linking verb is a *predicate adjective,* for it modifies the subject, not the predicate.

The most common linking verb is *to be,* in its various forms of number, person, tense, and mood. Other common linking verbs are *appear, become, feel, grow, look, prove, remain, seem, smell, sound, stand, taste, turn.* Except for forms of *to be,* these other linking verbs are followed by adjectives — rarely, if ever, by pronouns or nouns as predicate substantives. When these verbs are followed by nouns or pronouns as direct objects, they are not linking verbs but imply or express action. They are linking verbs if you can substitute some form of *to be* for them, especially *is, are, was, were.* Of course, some verbs not expressing action, such as *endure, exist, lie, sit, wait,* are not considered linking verbs. In the following examples, the linking verbs are in italics; the words linked are in small capitals.

> This HAMBURGER *is* THIN.
>
> PETER JONES *is* my ROOMMATE.
>
> That PLAY *was* GOOD.
>
> The new AUDITORIUM *is* MULTI-LEVEL.
>
> The DIRECTOR *will be* FAMOUS tomorrow.
>
> The STUDENT *seems (is)* SHY today; next week HE may *turn (grow, become, be)* BOLDER.
>
> Their SUSPICION *became (seemed, grew, was)* HEAVIER as fresh evidence was turned up.
>
> Those SHARKS *appear (look, seem, are)* COFFEE-COLORED.

16a. DISTINGUISH BETWEEN A LINKING VERB AND ONE THAT EXPRESSES ACTION.

Note the difference between verb words when they assert action of the subject and when they do not state action but serve merely as links.

> The sky *looks* cloudy this morning. (Linking)
>
> Bill *looks* at Mary as though he hates her. (Action)
>
> The coffee *tasted* too sweet. (Linking)

Betty gingerly *tasted* the soup. (Action)

The team did not *feel* unhappy about its defeat. (Linking)

If you cannot see in the dark, try to *feel* your way along. (Action)

16b. USE THE CORRECT AUXILIARY VERB.

An auxiliary verb "helps out" a main verb. That is, it aids in forming the tenses and tones (see Section 17), mood (see Section 18), and voice (see page 104) of the main verb. An auxiliary verb has little meaning of its own, but it changes the meaning of the main verb, which provides the central or key meaning of the verb phrase. In these sentences, the italicized form is an auxiliary verb; the form in small capitals is the main verb.

Mary *has* LEFT the city.

The machine parts *will be* SHIPPED early this afternoon.

As we *were* LEAVING, we *were* STOPPED by a guard.

I *did* MAIL the letters this morning.

The meanings of the commonly used auxiliary verbs are contained in your dictionary. These verbs and their uses may be summarized as follows:

1. *to be* — used in all tenses in forming the progressive tone and the passive voice

2. *to have* — used in the present perfect, past perfect, and future perfect tenses; also in the perfect infinitive and the perfect participle

3. *to do* — used to express emphasis (emphatic tone) in the present and past tenses
— used to avoid repetition of a verb or full verb expression: "John slept as soundly as I *did*." "We shall start out when they *do*."

4. *shall* — used as the precise auxiliary for the first person, future and future perfect tenses
— used in the second and third persons to express command or determination: "You *shall* be more prompt in the future."

5. *will* — used as the precise auxiliary for the second and third persons, future and future perfect tenses
— used in all three persons to express willingness or consent: "I *will* take the examination."

—used in the first person to indicate determination or resolution: "We *will* pay the bill immediately."

6. *should*—used as a kind of "past" tense of *shall*, in the first person, but weaker in emphasis: "I *should* not scold the little boy." "I *should* hope for the best."

—used frequently in a conditional meaning: "If I *should* make other plans, I shall let you know." "If Jay *should* want soda, we can provide some."

—used in all three persons to express duty or propriety or necessity: "You *should* organize your work." "She *should* be quite proud of him."

—used in all three persons to express expectation: "We *should* be flying over Edmonton now." "The letter *should* reach her on Monday."

7. *would*—used as a kind of "past" tense of *will*, in the second and third persons, but less strong in meaning: "You *would* scarcely bother about them."

NOTE: If the verb in the independent clause is in the past tense, use *would* to express futurity in the dependent clause; if the verb in the independent clause is in the present tense, use *will* in the dependent clause: "John *told* me he *would* write." "John *tells* me he *will* write."

—used frequently in a conditional meaning, or after a conditional clause: "If you *would* agree, they would be pleased." "If the traffic were heavy, he *would* take another route." "If I could, I *would*."

—used to express determination: "He *would* try, no matter how difficult the undertaking appeared to be."

—used in all three persons to express repeated or habitual action: "Last winter we *would* play ice hockey every day."

—used infrequently to express wish or desire: "*Would* that we all had done otherwise!"

8. *may*—used to express permission: "*May* I have your name?" "You *may* keep the book." "If I *may* say so, that color scheme is terrible."

—used to express probability or a wish: "It *may* hurt a little." "*May* your trip be a pleasant one!"

9. *might*—used as a kind of "past" tense of *may* to express the same ideas of possibility or probability in a weaker manner: "You *might* be interested in astrology."

10. *can*—used to express ability or power or the idea of "being able to": "I *can* meet him at 7 o'clock." "My daddy *can* fix anything."

11. *could*—used as a kind of "past" tense of *can* to express the same ideas in a weaker manner: "Finney *could* not haul in the heavy anchor."

12. *must*—used to express obligation or compulsion: "Every girl *must* help in the camp kitchen." "You *must* list your expenses."
—used to express reasonable certainty: "Jim was here promptly at seven o'clock, so he *must* have set his alarm clock." "I hear thunder, so there *must* be a storm coming."

13. *ought*—used to express duty or obligation, one of the few auxiliary verbs followed by the sign of the infinitive *(to)* with the main verb: "You *ought* to learn French, son." "Everyone *ought* to keep his shoes shined."
NOTE: *Have* and *had* are never used before *ought* or *must.*
     Wrong: I *had ought* to start studying.
     Right: I *ought to have started* studying long ago.

14. *let*—used to express the ideas of "allowing" or "permitting," "suggesting," "ordering": "*Let* me follow him." "*Let's* have a picnic." "*Let* me think a minute." "*Let* her finish her milk."

15. *need*—used to express necessity or obligation: "I *need* not give her my pin." "They *need* only to speak up and speak out."
NOTE: As auxiliary verb, third person singular form is also *need:* "He *need* not take my advice."

16. *used*—in the past tense only, *used* expresses custom or habitual action: "I *used* to cry a lot when I was a child." "It *used* to rain every day in Kensington."

17. *dare*—used, usually with *say*, to express probability: "I *dare* say that's true." "I *dare* say the choice will be difficult to make."

EXERCISE 14

Write on your paper the number of each sentence. After the number, write *linking* or *action* to describe the function of each italicized verb.

1. As a good chef Henry *tasted* the unsavory mess wryly.
2. The moon, riding high above clouds, *appeared* ghostly.
3. Gardeners *have* never *seen* flowers grow so rapidly.
4. If the crowd *turns* surly, we shall turn around rapidly and head for the hills.
5. The child *looked* ashamed of himself after the third spanking.
6. Throw the meat away; it *smells*.
7. You have learned to pick up your feet; you *are becoming* graceful.
8. When you get high marks, you certainly *feel* good.
9. On a hot day a glass of lemonade *smells* good and *tastes* better.
10. When a man has a pretty wife, he feels sure that he *is* fortunate.

EXERCISE 15

Write on your paper the number of each sentence. After the number, write *linking* or *action* to describe the function of each italicized verb. If the verb has an auxiliary, indicate the purpose that the auxiliary serves or the meaning that it expresses.

1. Eloise should *keep* a diary; I could certainly *profit* by reading it.
2. You may *catch* the fish, but can you *cook* it?
3. Jim used to think he *was* an expert sailor; now he *is* not so sure.
4. One ought to saw tree branches carefully; otherwise, he may *find* himself out on a limb.
5. Have you *tried* sky diving? It might *amuse* you.
6. I will never *allow* a girl of mine to be without memories.
7. Let no one *forget* the fight; it will *do* us all harm.
8. Must we *go*? We have not *been* here long.
9. When I *was* a lad, Father would *assign* us new chores every other day.
10. We should have *served* the fried chicken; in fact, we might have served it if our cook had not *dropped* it into the sand.

17. TENSE AND TONE

Tense indicates the time of the action or time of the static condition (state of being) expressed by a verb. The three divisions of time—past, present, future—are shown in

17a TENSE AND TONE

English by six tenses. The three primary, or simple, tenses are the *present* tense, the *past* tense, the *future* tense. The three secondary, or compound, tenses are the *present perfect*, the *past perfect*, the *future perfect*.

Within some tenses, verbs also have certain *tones* which express precisely what the writer wishes to say: *simple* tone (I read); *progressive* tone (I am reading); and *emphatic* tone (I do read).

17a. USE THE CORRECT TENSE TO EXPRESS PRECISE TIME.

The following brief table and comments on each tense should help you to use the precise tenses needed to convey your ideas:

Active Voice

Present	I hear (am hearing)
Past	I heard (was hearing)
Future	I shall hear (shall be hearing)
Present perfect	I have heard (have been hearing)
Past perfect	I had heard (had been hearing)
Future perfect	I shall have heard (shall have been hearing)

Passive Voice

Present	I am heard (am being heard)
Past	I was heard (was being heard)
Future	I shall be heard
Present perfect	I have been heard
Past perfect	I had been heard
Future perfect	I shall have been heard

Verbals (Nonfinite Verb Forms)

Present infinitive	to hear (to be hearing)
Perfect infinitive	to have heard (to have been hearing)
Present participle	hearing
Past participle	heard
Perfect participle	having heard (having been hearing)
Present gerund	hearing
Perfect gerund	having heard (having been hearing)

1. *Present tense* indicates that the action or condition is going on or exists now:

He *eats* a big breakfast every morning.

The scores *are* posted.

2. *Past tense* indicates that an action or condition took place or existed at some definite time in the past:

Yesterday she *baked* a chocolate cake.

They *were* married on Saturday.

3. *Future tense* indicates that an action will take place, or that a certain condition will exist, in the future:

We *shall move* to Saskatchewan next week.

The cruise ship *will be sailing* at midnight.

The future may be stated by the present tense accompanied by an adverb (or adverbial phrase) of time. Such constructions as the following are common:

I am going downtown later on today.

This Friday the plane takes off for Newfoundland.

4. *Present perfect tense* indicates that an action or condition was begun in the past and has just been completed or is still going on. The time is past but it is connected with the present. The present perfect tense *presupposes* some relationship with the present:

We *have lived* in Halifax for fifteen years.

The water *has been* too cold for swimming.

I *have* long *been* a friend of Senator Twitchell.

We *have waited* here long enough.

5. *Past perfect tense* indicates that an action or condition was completed at a time now past. It indicates action "two steps back." That is, the past perfect tense presupposes some relationship with an action or condition expressed in the past tense:

The market place was crowded because a new shipment *had arrived* early that morning.

He was employed by the Browne Company. He *had worked* there for a fortnight.

6. *Future perfect tense* indicates that an action or condition will be completed at a future time:

By the time you arrive, I *shall have finished* lunch.

The ice *will have broken* up before the ship reaches this harbor.

The three secondary, or compound, tenses always indicate *completed* action, whether it be in the present (present perfect tense), in the past (past perfect tense), or in the future (future perfect tense).

17b. USE THE CORRECT TONE TO EXPRESS PRECISE MEANING.

The *simple* tone is a concise statement of a "snapshot" or instantaneous action of a verb: I *walk* (present tense), I *walked* (past tense), I *shall walk* (future tense), I *have walked* (present perfect tense), I *had walked* (past perfect tense), I *shall have walked* (future perfect tense).

The *progressive* tone forms in each of the six tenses are built by using proper tense forms of the verb *to be* followed by the present participle of the main verb: I *am walking, was walking, shall be walking, have been walking, had been walking, shall have been walking.*

The *emphatic* tone forms are formed by the verb *to do* and the present infinitive of the main verb. The emphatic tone is used only in present and past tenses: I *do walk*, I *did walk*.

17c. WATCH CAREFULLY THE SEQUENCE OF TENSES.

When only one verb is used in a sentence, it should express the precise time involved. When two or more verbs appear in a sentence, they should be consistent in tense. Most importantly, remember that the tense of a verb in a subordinate clause depends on the tense of the verb in the main clause.

1. The present tense is used in a dependent clause to express a general truth:

> At that time, many sailors could not understand that the earth *is* round.

The present tense is used alone to express a "timeless" truth.

> Man *does not live* by bread alone.

Do not allow the tense of a verb to be attracted into the past when it should be present: "Last summer we visited a village in Lapland; the people of that community were hardy and resourceful." It is conceivable that the community no longer exists, or that its people have since become weakened, but is that what is meant?

Passages in some short stories and novels are written in the present tense, although the action occurred in time which is past. This use of what is called the *historical present* sometimes makes narrative more vivid, but it quickly becomes monotonous.

2. Use a present infinitive except when the infinitive represents action completed before the time of the governing verb:

I made a note to *talk* [not *to have talked*] with you about it.

The coach is happy *to have made* Jerry a member of the team.

3. A present participle indicates action at the time expressed by the verb; a past participle indicates action before that of the verb:

Eating in so many restaurants, he *is* introduced to some exotic foods.

Having been a benched player himself, he *felt* sympathy for Bob.

4. When narration in the past tense is interrupted for reference to a preceding event, use the past perfect tense:

Last week they *fixed* the pipes which *had been frozen* all winter.

She *confided* that she *had been* in love for over a month.

As a summary, these two formulas for the sequence of tenses may be helpful to you:

PAST←————————PRESENT——→FUTURE
PAST PERFECT←——PAST————→FUTURE

EXERCISE 16

On your paper write the number of each sentence below. Opposite the number, write any verb which appears in the wrong tense and then write the correct form.

1. Some historians think that Napoleon's chief hope in conquering Italy was that he may win the admiration and love of Josephine.

2. I ought to have paid this utilities bill before the discount period ends.

3. After Cortez subdued the Aztecs, all Mexico will be quickly explored.

4. By the time the new hay crop was ready, the barns are almost empty.

5. When the Expos lost, Borpmann felt that life is no longer worth living.

6. When the plumbers laid the pipe line on the surface, they forgot that water became solid at below-freezing temperatures.
7. Carstairs believes that the principal effect of *Hamlet* was catharsis.
8. After we went a half-dozen miles, we ran out of gas.
9. Unfortunately I had not had time to have played the entire concerto.
10. When the teacher explained that all bodies are subject to the law of gravity, my visiting brother, a former paratrooper, yells "Amen."

EXERCISE 17

Follow the directions for Exercise 16.

1. Last week I was just too tired to have pruned the peaches.
2. By the time we reached Montreal, we were too low on money to have stayed at the Ritz Carlton Hotel.
3. After he had pacified the usher, Wesley leads his seven aunts down the aisle.
4. Modern historians have concluded that Troy had been besieged for commercial rather than personal reasons.
5. When Sweeney sees the grade on his term paper, he screamed like a wounded panther.
6. When I stopped at the teacher's desk, as he requested, he says to me, "Where's your term paper?"
7. Harvey circled until he saw an opening; then he grabs the giraffe by the ears.
8. Violet wanted desperately to have received an A in history.
9. Having opened the manuscript, the editor lunges for his blue pencil.
10. After my parents lived on a farm for ten years, they moved into town.

EXERCISE 18

Follow the directions for Exercise 16.

1. If you had a bit of common sense, Flinders, you will stay off roller skates.
2. We analyzed "The Turn of the Screw" to determine whether it was a psychological study or a ghost story.
3. A straight and narrow path is one that had no primroses on it.
4. After his girl takes a poker to him, my buddy stayed away for a week.
5. If we could find out who released the spiders, we can take the proper steps.

6. On steak fries, Professor White used to remind us that man is a carnivorous animal.
7. Snitkin explained patiently that amperes were coulombs per second.
8. If the tobacco seed bed was not burned over before the seeds are planted, the weeds will sprout.
9. Had the distance from the pool to the house not been so great, Gladys might have escaped from the gorilla.
10. This is my parents' anniversary; they had been married for twenty-one years.

18. MOOD

Mood, literally, is a state or temper of mind; *mode,* literally, is a prevailing fashion or manner. In grammar, the *mood* or *mode* of a verb indicates the state of mind or the manner in which a statement is made: a fact, a request or command, a condition or probability. English has commonly three moods: *indicative, imperative,* and *subjunctive.* Other "states of mind" or "prevailing manners"—such as willingness, duty, propriety, necessity, expectation, permission, ability, obligation, compulsion, custom—are expressed by auxiliary verbs.

18a. USE THE INDICATIVE MOOD TO EXPRESS A FACT OR TO ASK A QUESTION OF FACT.

Who *designed* the house? (Question of fact)
Wetherill *made* the blueprints. (Statement of fact)
The construction *is* faulty. (Statement of fact)

18b. USE THE IMPERATIVE MOOD TO EXPRESS A COMMAND, A POLITE OR STRONG REQUEST, AN ORDER.

Shut the door. (Command)
Come and *bring* a friend. (Polite request)
Please *be* there on time! (Strong request)
Come home at once! (Order)

18c. LEARN TO RECOGNIZE THE SUBJUNCTIVE FORMS.

Present Indicative		*Present Subjunctive*	
I am	we are	(if) I be	(if) we be
you are	you are	(if) you be	(if) you be
he is	they are	(if) he be	(if) they be

Past Indicative		*Past Subjunctive*	
I was	we were	(if) I were	(if) we were
you were	you were	(if) you were	(if) you were
he was	they were	(if) he were	(if) they were

Present Indicative		*Present Subjunctive*	
I come	we come	(if) I come	(if) we come
you come	you come	(if) you come	(if) you come
he comes	they come	(if) he come	(if) they come

NOTES:

1. Distinctive subjunctive verb forms in current English have disappeared or are disappearing in favor of more commonly used indicative verb forms.

Former use: If it *be* possible, I shall come.
A student, if he *write* well, will receive a high grade.

Current use: If it *is* possible, I shall come.
A student, if he *writes* well, will receive a high grade.

2. Our language still retains a number of subjunctive forms in sayings handed down from times when this mood was more widely used: *Heaven forbid, Thy Kingdom come, if need be, he need not speak, suffice it to say, come what may,* etc. Also, careful speakers and writers employ the subjunctive mood to express the precise manner in which they make their statements, when the indicative mood would not serve effectively.

18d. USE THE SUBJUNCTIVE *WERE* TO EXPRESS A CONDITION WHICH IS HYPOTHETICAL, IMPROBABLE, OR IMPOSSIBLE.

If I *were* you, I'd refuse to let her use my car.
If we *were* at home, we could consult our unabridged dictionary for the derivation of the word.

(I am not you. We are not at home. Hence the statements in the preceding examples are contrary to fact.)

CAUTION: Not every clause that begins with *if* requires a subjunctive.

>If he *was* out late last night, he is probably still asleep. (The speaker thinks he may have been out late.)

>If she *was* there, I didn't see her. (The speaker is willing to accept the fact that she was there even though he did not see her.)

18e. USE THE SUBJUNCTIVE *WERE* AFTER *AS THOUGH* OR *AS IF* TO EXPRESS DOUBT OR UNCERTAINTY.

>He talks as if he *were* the only intelligent person in the group.
>She looked as though she *were* completely exhausted.

NOTE: Do not use the subjunctive after *though* when it is not preceded by *as*.

>Even though he *is* deaf, he doesn't have to shout.
>Though he *can*, he won't.

18f. USE THE SUBJUNCTIVE IN *THAT* CLAUSES EXPRESSING NECESSITY OR A PARLIAMENTARY MOTION.

>I move that the committee *be appointed* by the president.
>It is essential that he *appear* at the meeting.
>It is expected that every man *pay* his own way.
>The committee insisted that he *tell* the whole story.
>I suggest that the topic *be considered* at our next meeting.
>The motion is that the chairman *be authorized* to proceed.

18g. IN PARALLEL CONSTRUCTIONS, DO NOT SHIFT THE MOOD OF VERBS.

>Substandard: If I *were* in your position and *was* offered a trip to Europe, I'd certainly go.
>Right: If I *were* in your position and *were* offered a trip to Europe, I'd certainly go.

111

Substandard: If Lee *were* to resign and Dee *was* elected, we should have better leadership.

Right: If Lee *were* to resign and Dee *were* elected, we should have better leadership.

EXERCISE 19

Number each of the following sentences on your paper. Opposite each number write the form of the italicized verb which you prefer and indicate whether it is indicative or subjunctive.

1. If she were that intelligent and *(was, were)* modest also, she would be a remarkable person.
2. Charlemagne sometimes wondered if Alcuin *(was, were)* pulling his leg.
3. I think Jerry tries not to be concerned, but he *(is, be)*.
4. Gladys feared that the gorilla *(was, were)* only a step or two behind.
5. Myrtle couldn't save herself even if she *(was, were)* given an oar to pull with.
6. *(Were, Was)* he really an honest man, he wouldn't have agreed with the professor.
7. The regulations require that a coed *(is, be)* in her dormitory by ten on week nights.
8. *(Is, Be)* Shillingbreek's new novel worth reading?
9. Sometimes I wish that my father *(was, were)* as avant-garde as Martin's.
10. Glory *(is, be)* to God for dappled things.

EXERCISE 20

Follow the directions for Exercise 19.

1. If that *(is, be)* he, as I believe, let him in.
2. Be sure the tent is secure, Dawson, lest it *(washes, wash)* away in the monsoon.
3. If I *(was, were)* tardy seven times, as my instructor says, I certainly didn't know it.
4. I move that the treasurer *(explains, explain)* how he became rich enough to buy a race horse.
5. How my little brother wishes he *(was, were)* a sky diver!
6. I don't care if the business *(fails, fail)*, Muldoon, if we still have each other.
7. Violet sometimes acts as if she *(was, were)* the only intelligent girl in the school.

8. If McHenry be not worthy of promotion, who *(is, be)?*
9. I fear that I *(was, were)* responsible for the hysteria.
10. Tipley smilingly insisted that the infinitive *(is, be)* split.

19. ADJECTIVES AND ADVERBS

Ordinarily we experience little difficulty in determining when an adjective *or* adverb should be used. *Adjectives* "go with" nouns and pronouns; *adverbs* "go with" verbs, adjectives, and other adverbs. And yet we commonly misuse adjectives and adverbs, for three main reasons: (1) after linking verbs, an adjective is used if reference is to the subject, an adverb if reference is to the verb itself; (2) idiomatic usage often violates the distinction between adjectives and adverbs; (3) some adjectives and adverbs have identical or similar forms. Keep in mind the following basic distinctions.

An *adjective* modifies a noun or pronoun by describing, limiting, or otherwise making meaning more nearly exact. An adjective may indicate quality or quantity, may identify or set limits. Consequently, adjectives are of three general types: descriptive (a *yellow* dress, a *broad* horizon, a *tired* businessman); limiting (the *third* phase, her *given* name, *several* weeks); proper (a *Canadian* policy, a *Florida* orange).

Some adjectives — indeed most — have endings which mark them as adjectives. The more important of these include:

    -able (-ible): workable, combustible, serviceable
    -al: partial, radial, experimental, optional
    -ary: auxiliary, beneficiary, primary, arbitrary
    -en: golden, smitten, hidden, rotten
    -ful: sinful, rueful, scornful, dutiful
    -ic: artistic, pessimistic, altruistic, rustic
    -ish: slavish, peevish, reddish, babyish
    -ive: restive, festive, corrosive, explosive
    -less: faultless, guileless, fearless, mindless
    -ous: marvelous, viscous, luscious, amorous
    -some: lonesome, fearsome, awesome, handsome
    -y: sticky, risky, funny, catty, dreamy

An adjective may modify a noun directly ("the *violet* shadows lengthening along the sand") or indirectly ("the prisoner, *wan* and *shabby*, was led gently from the stand"). In sentences such as "The seat felt *hard*" and "The path is *treacherous*," each adjective is related to the subject, the word it modifies, by a linking verb. (A linking verb has little meaning of its own; it serves primarily as a connection between subject and predicate noun or predicate adjective.) In the sentences above, *hard* and *treacherous* are called *predicate adjectives* or *complements*.

An *adverb* modifies a verb, adjective, or other adverb by describing or limiting to make meaning more precise. Adverbs generally tell *how, when, where, why, how often,* and *how much.* In "The high cliff loomed *forbiddingly* above him," the adverb modifies the verb *loomed* and tells *how.* In "We are *nearly* ready for supper," the adverb modifies the adjective *ready.* In "Close the hatch *very* quickly," the adverb modifies the adverb *quickly.*

Adverbs have the following characteristics:

1. Adverbs are commonly, but not always, distinguished from corresponding adjectives by the suffix *-ly: true, truly; poor, poorly; sharp, sharply.*

2. Certain adverbs are distinguished from corresponding nouns by the suffixes *-wise* and *-ways: sideways, lengthwise, clockwise, counterclockwise.*

3. Certain adverbs are distinguished from corresponding prepositions in not being connected to a following noun:

Adverb: He fell *down.*
Preposition: He fell *down* the staircase.

4. Like adjectives, but unlike nouns and verbs, adverbs may be preceded by words of the *very* group (intensifiers):

It was the *least expensively* furnished house.
We must see him *right now.*

19a. DO NOT USE AN ADJECTIVE TO MODIFY A VERB.

The form of a word does not always reveal whether it is an adjective or adverb. Most words ending in *-ly* are adverbs, but *holy, sickly, motherly, unruly* are adjectives. Also, some adjectives and adverbs have the same form: *quick, little,* *early, fast, kindly.* Finally, a few adverbs have two forms quite different in meaning: *late, lately; sharp, sharply.*

Wrong: He spends his money too *rapid. (Rapidly,* an adverb, should modify the verb *spends; rapid* is an adjective.)

The dog barks *loud* when he spies the cat. (Use *loudly.*)

She spoke to him *motherly.* (in *a motherly way*)

The officer spoke sharp to me. *(sharply)*

19b. DO NOT USE AN ADJECTIVE TO MODIFY ANOTHER ADJECTIVE.

Wrong: Sam is a *real* good basketball coach. (Use *really,* an adverb.)

That is an *awful* big hat you're wearing. (Use *awfully.*)

The sailor made his knot *plenty* tight. (Use *very,* or *quite,* or *exceedingly.*)

19c. AFTER SUCH VERBS AS *APPEAR, BE, BECOME, FEEL, LOOK, SEEM, SMELL, TASTE,* THE MODIFIER SHOULD BE AN ADJECTIVE IF IT REFERS TO THE SUBJECT, AN ADVERB IF IT DESCRIBES OR DEFINES THE VERB.

Correct: This pastry tastes *good.* (Adjective)

The sunshine felt *wonderful.* (Adjective)

Carol appeared *happy* when he came. (Adjective)

She looked at him *tenderly.* (Adverb)

Fred feels *keenly* that he was cheated. (Adverb)

Joe speaks *deliberately* when addressing a class. (Adverb)

19d. BE ACCURATE IN USING WORDS THAT MAY BE EITHER ADJECTIVES OR ADVERBS.

Correct: Sue's father, the *late* mayor, had a small estate. (Adjective)

Sue has been studying French *lately.* (Adverb)

115

Skippy is a *little* beagle. (Adjective)
Put the lamp a *little* farther back. (Adverb)
Grandfather was a *kindly* man. (Adjective)
He treated all of us *kindly*. (Adverb)

19e. BE ACCURATE IN THE USE OF COMPARATIVES AND SUPERLATIVES.

Most adjectives and adverbs change their forms to show a greater or smaller *degree* of the quality they express. This change of form is called *comparison*. The three degrees of comparison are: *positive, comparative,* and *superlative.*

Positive Degree	Comparative Degree	Superlative Degree
happy (adj.)	happier	happiest
soon (adv.)	sooner	soonest

In comparisons that indicate *less* of a quality, the words *less* and *least* are used with all adjectives and adverbs that can be compared.

Positive	Comparative	Superlative
ill	less ill	least ill
afraid	less afraid	least afraid
honest	less honest	least honest

This construction, however, can be avoided if it seems awkward.

Formal: She is less ill than she was this morning.
Better: She is not so ill.
She is better.

Most adjectives and adverbs of one syllable form the comparative degree by adding *-er* and the superlative degree by adding *-est.*

Positive	Comparative	Superlative
tall	taller	tallest
cheap	cheaper	cheapest
tough	tougher	toughest

Although adjectives of two syllables usually add *-er* for the comparative and *-est* for the superlative, there are times when such adjectives have two forms for both comparative and superlative.

Positive	Comparative	Superlative
sturdy	sturdier	sturdiest
manly	manlier	manliest
portly	more portly	most portly
	or	or
	portlier	portliest
rotten	more rotten	most rotten
	or	or
	rottener	rottenest

Adverbs that end in *-ly* and adjectives of more than two syllables usually form the comparative and superlative by prefixing *more* and *most*.

Positive	Comparative	Superlative
beautifully	more beautifully	most beautifully
rapidly	more rapidly	most rapidly
nearly	more nearly	most nearly
dutiful (adj.)	more dutiful	most dutiful
efficient (adj.)	more efficient	most efficient

Some adjectives and adverbs form their changes irregularly.

good (adj.)	better	best
bad (adj.)	worse	worst
badly (adv.)	worse	worst
well (adv.)	better	best

1. The comparative is used for comparing two persons or objects or actions; the superlative is used for comparing more than two.

I bought two new outfits. Which do you think is *more suitable?*

Which of your brothers is the *better* sportsman?

Caribbean water is *greener* than Atlantic water.

Susan's was the *most artistic* of all the flower arrangements.

In informal English, the superlative is often used when only two things are compared.

2. Avoid double comparatives and superlatives; that is, when *-er* or *-est* has been added to form the comparative or superlative, do not use *more* or *most* before the word.

Wrong: She is more prettier than her sister.

Right: She is prettier than her sister.

3. Choose the comparative form with care. Do not confuse the comparative of an adjective with that of an adverb.

117

Wrong: She carries trays steadier than Trudy does.
Right: She carries trays more steadily than Trudy does.

4. A few adjectives like *parallel, unique, square, round,* and *equal* are logically incapable of comparison because their meaning is absolute. Two lines, actions, or ideas are parallel or they are not. They cannot logically be more parallel. However, these words have somewhat lost their superlative force and in informal English are often compared. Even good writers use adverbs like *entirely* or *quite* before them.

5. Avoid including the subject compared if the subject is part of a group with which it is being compared. Use *else* or *other* in such cases.

Illogical: Our boat is larger than any in the fleet.
Better: Our boat is larger than any *other* in the fleet.
Illogical: Mary is smarter than anyone in her class.
Better: Mary is smarter than anyone *else* in her class.

EXERCISE 21

On your paper number each of the following sentences. Next to the number write the word or phrase which is modified by the italicized word. If the italicized word is unsuitable, write a better form.

1. Gladys skipped *nimble* up the steps just ahead of the gorilla.
2. There were just two cookies left on the plate, and so I took the *biggest* one.
3. The creamed spinach made our happiness *complete.*
4. The team felt *unhappily* about losing the swimming meet.
5. Let's all patronize *local* owned stores.
6. Martin certainly looks *nicely* in sideburns.
7. You did *good* to accede to their request.
8. I *sure* would be happier without these snakes.
9. Just then a *beautiful* dressed lady slunk into the room.
10. My classmates tell me that I write *fluent.*

EXERCISE 22

Follow the directions for Exercise 21.

1. Until we get clear of the cobras, Dawson, we had better step extremely *careful.*
2. The trail was *ruggeder* than the ladies thought it would be.
3. Julia will become much more *gracefully* as she gets older.

4. Daisy decided that going to camp was a *real* fine idea.
5. Fearing that he did not smell *well*, Delaney tried another shaving lotion.
6. Mrs. White discovered that the rug spotted very *easy*.
7. Little Edson blinked back the tears and smiled *manly*.
8. We agreed that it was a *most unique* sunset.
9. The rats were still waiting *patient* in the corner of the room.
10. My brother acts much too *cautious*.

EXERCISE 23

Follow the directions for Exercise 21.

1. Rockwell looked *furtive* at the goldfish.
2. To everyone's surprise the play turned out *successful*.
3. Twirling his cane, Wordsworth strolled *slowly* through the meadow.
4. The sign read "Drive *slow*."
5. Gleason applied himself and became an *extreme* successful confidence man.
6. Harvey thinks his car handles *easier* than mine.
7. His leg seems entirely *well* again.
8. When I returned to the house after having shoveled snow for three hours, the hot apple pancakes tasted *good* indeed.
9. Willoughby grows very *dubious* begonias.
10. Dating is a *real* popular leisure-time activity among teen-agers.

20. CONJUNCTIONS

A *conjunction* is a linking word used to connect words or groups of words in a sentence. There are two main kinds of conjunctions: *coordinating*, which join words or groups of words of equal rank, such as *and, but, for, or, nor, either, neither, yet;* and *subordinating*, which join dependent clauses to main clauses, such as *if, since, because, as, while, so that, although, unless.*

Coordinating conjunctions which are used in pairs are called *correlative* conjunctions. Those most frequently used are *both . . . and, either . . . or, neither . . . nor, so . . . as, whether . . . or, not only . . . but also.*

Another kind of conjunction is the *conjunctive adverb*, a type of adverb that can also serve as a conjunction joining two independent clauses. Some conjunctive adverbs are *accordingly, also, anyhow, besides, consequently, furthermore, hence, however, indeed, likewise, moreover, nevertheless, still, then, therefore, thus.*

20a. DISTINGUISH AMONG THE MEANINGS OF CONJUNCTIONS AND CONJUNCTIVE ADVERBS.

Conjunctions, especially those which are to join clauses, must be carefully selected, for they always show logical relationships of ideas. A careless writer will frequently use *and* where the relationship of clauses needs a more accurate expression, probably by use of subordination. In these sentences, compare meaning and emphasis:

The college's drive for new funds has been highly successful *and* further effort on the part of younger alumni will make it even more successful.

Although the college's drive for new funds has been highly successful, further effort on the part of younger alumni will make it even more successful.

Depending upon the writer's expressed purpose, ideas may be coordinated or subordinated in several ways. But unless he knows the meaning or purpose of conjunctions and conjunctive adverbs, the writer will probably have trouble.

1. Purpose: *along the same line or in the same direction of thought*

   and, both . . . and, not only . . . but also, also, besides, furthermore, in addition, indeed, likewise, moreover, similarly, whereby, whereupon

2. Purpose: *contrast*

   although, but, however, instead, nevertheless, not only . . . but also, notwithstanding, still, whereas, yet

3. Purpose: *affirmative alternation*

   anyhow, either . . . or, else, moreover, or, still, whereas, whether

4. Purpose: *negative alternation*

   except that, however, instead, neither, neither . . . nor, nevertheless, nor, only, whereas

5. Purpose: *reason, result, purpose, cause*
accordingly, as, as a result, because, consequently, for, hence, inasmuch as, in order that, since, so, so that, that, thereby, therefore, thus, whereas, why

6. Purpose: *example*
for example, indeed, in fact, namely

7. Purpose: *comparison*
indeed, in fact, moreover, so . . . as, than

8. Purpose: *time*
after, as long as, as soon as, before, henceforth, meanwhile, once, since, then, till, until, when, whenever, while

9. Purpose: *place*
whence, where, wherever, whither

10. Purpose: *condition*
although, as if, as though, if, lest, once, provided, providing, though, unless

11. Purpose: *concession*
although, insofar as, notwithstanding the fact that, though, unless, while

20b. CORRELATIVE CONJUNCTIONS SHOULD CORRELATE ONLY TWO IDEAS.

Doubtful: *Both* her prettiness, charm, wit, *and* talent attracted us. (Delete *both* or two of the four subjects.)

Doubtful: *Neither* noise, a crowded room, *nor* the scorn of his roommate could keep Mark from concentrating on algebra. (Delete one of the three subjects or in another way rephrase the sentence.)

20c. AVOID JOINING WORDS OR PHRASES OR DEPENDENT CLAUSES BY A CONJUNCTIVE ADVERB.

Doubtful: The worst things are poverty, disease, ignorance, *also* prejudice. (. . . ignorance, *and* prejudice.)

Doubtful: John had lost two big contracts; *still* was making money. (. . . *but* he was still making money.)

121

20d. BE CAUTIOUS IN USING *LIKE* AS A SUBORDINATING CONJUNCTION.

The use of *like* in clauses of comparison has increased greatly within the past few years: "It looks *like* I might go." A certain brand of cigarette makes the claim that it "tastes good *like* a cigarette should." We do not avoid the use of *like* "like we once did." However, in standard English *like* is used as a preposition with no following verb: "She looks like an angel." In strictly formal English, use *as* or *as if* for clauses of comparison:

You must march *as* I tell you (not *like* I tell you).

My ankle felt *as if* I had broken it (not *like* I had broken it).

I am being generous to you *as* my brother was generous to me (not *like* my brother was generous to me).

EXERCISE 24

Write on your paper the number of each sentence. If the italicized conjunction is satisfactory, write *S* after the number. If the conjunction is not acceptable, supply a better one next to the number.

1. The suit fitted Henry perfectly, *while* his brother had to shorten the sleeves.
2. Neither the glare, ice *or* the slush caused me to slow down.
3. *Although* some skill is necessary, prowess of Olympic caliber is not required in order to make our swimming team.
4. The fat was Mrs. Spratt's favorite part of the porkchop, *whereas* Jack preferred the lean.
5. *Being as how* Susan loves to sew, she made my evening dress as well as her own.
6. Marvin has measles, *but* he would have joined us today.
7. Henry doubted the wisdom of their action; *however*, he determined not to stand in their way.
8. Both the Monkey *and* the Hitchhiker are variations of the frug.
9. It seems *like* every time I want to visit a foreign country, that country suffers a revolution.
10. My closest friends are Chuck, Bill, Harvey, *also* Mike.

EXERCISE 25

Follow the directions for Exercise 24.

1. The huge boulder looked *like* it would topple over and crush us.

2. Simpson could not make up his mind *if* he would wrestle the crocodile.
3. Bill not only found himself flat broke *but* discovered his friends had vanished completely.
4. The cannibal wanted stew, *and* there was nobody to put into the pot.
5. We had feared that you would give up, *or* you did.
6. Family, *also* friends, are waiting for me in Bridgewater.
7. Entwhistle told her *how that* his heart started pounding when she glanced at him during the concert.
8. She was so wrapped up in her own problems *until* she did not want to listen to mine.
9. I heard on the radio *where* apple pie is losing its eminence as Canada's favorite dessert.
10. I do not care for that expensive blue dress she chose, *and* I will pay for it anyway.

USAGE – GENERAL REVIEW EXERCISES

REVIEW EXERCISE 1

The following sentences contain various faults in usage. On your paper, number each sentence and rewrite it, correcting all errors.

1. For many years our family has went to Florida for their vacation; this is a trip my mother and sister always chose because of her asthma, and my father and me enjoyed the fishing.
2. If he had been given a job, like he was promised before he became desperate, you would never have read of him saying such anti-social things.
3. In today's paper it says as how the earth is gradually growing warmer, the reason being that the sun is getting closer to the earth.
4. The teacher said he was happy that Clifford and myself was doing so good. He thought we would even fuller understand if we applied ourselves.
5. The automobile problem in Canada has went from bad to worse recently, because so many of them are on the road and people will not learn to drive slow.

6. It says in the report that they frequently employ women and children to do this work, which is very dangerous unless carefully regulated.

7. If I was a farmer that lived in some parts of Ontario, I would be real afraid of tornadoes because they strike without warning but do much damage.

8. Robinson informed Jones that his house had been burglarized, that they had stole all they could carry, and that they had wrecked things as if it was a maniac.

9. My Uncle Wren, one of my mother's brothers, have lived at our house until he died last year, which was sure a blow to me.

10. The leader of all seven patrols are to keep contact with headquarters; if any survivors were found, they should report them by messenger.

REVIEW EXERCISE 2

Each of the following sentences contains a form wrongly used. Write each on your paper, underline the faulty expression, and label the error, using the following abbreviations: *Agr*—lack of agreement between subject and predicate; *Mood*—wrong mood; *Tense*—wrong tense; *Verb*—wrong verb form; *Case*—wrong case; *Ant*—lack of agreement between pronoun and antecedent; *Ad*—confusion of adjective and adverb.

1. Clancy sighed disconsolately, wishing he was out of school.

2. My father took it very good when I broke my arm while I was skating.

3. Bartleby hung the cattle rustler, and we cheered at this display of frontier justice.

4. Either my sister or I are going to have to stay home and baby-sit.

5. Nice girls don't kiss whomever asks them.

6. Daisy's father picked her up and swang her into the highchair.

7. The first report, happily erroneous, was that Redblood had hit the referee.

8. Between her and I, we have kept expenses to a bare minimum.

9. The teacher praised the sonnets of Shakespeare, but Thorsby heartily disagrees.

10. When the rudder broke off from the boat, Alvin jumped into the bay and swum to shore for help.

11. I have a cow that gives homogenized milk that might interest you.

12. Martin was so tired from tennis that he laid right down beside the court and took a nap.

13. I'll tell you what I'd do if I was he.
14. I greatly admired Keith giving in to his sister in order to prevent a fight.
15. Sandra whistled lowly, and the others came into the room.
16. How sweetly clover blossoms smell in the early morning air.
17. As it turned out, it was Finxter and myself who were marked tardy.
18. Let's amuse ourselves by making a list of who is taking who to the dance.
19. Gladys dived nimbly under Max's arm and run down the steps.
20. The expression "a rag, a bone, and a hank of hair" are one poet's estimate of woman.
21. A quiet student in the rear responded with a delicate phrased explanation.
22. As soon as he saw Eloise, Martin asked her to the dance, but Edward asked her last week.
23. By the time the horses were lined up at the gate, each spectator has figured the odds and made a bet.
24. Doctor Perkins was persuaded to remove the bullet, but it got him into trouble.
25. Little Edson felt that the insults of his younger tormentor was worse than the torture.

ACHIEVEMENT TESTS IN USAGE

TEST 1

Write on your paper the number of each sentence. Beside the number, write the correction or corrections necessary and give the reason for each correction. If a sentence contains no errors, write C beside the number.

Examples: 1. Jerry went with Bob and I.
2. Each of the students had their own books.

Corrections: 1. me — object of the preposition *with*
2. his — pronoun and antecedent agreement

1. If it had been necessary, George could beat any of the chess players.
2. We did not think that the project would turn out very good.

3. The young girl's eyes mirrored the gratitude that laid in her heart.
4. When I left, after being with the company for ten years, I felt like a piece of my life was gone.
5. He shall not use my money. I will see that he does not.
6. We recommend that there be appointed an experienced parks commissioner.
7. Because of the heat wave, air conditioning sold very satisfactory that month.
8. The firm objects to me studying Spanish because every man and woman in the office have spent a good deal of time on some similar subject that have not helped their work.
9. The beach was so pleasant I could of laid for hours in the sun.
10. If I was him, I'd make a new start.
11. Each of the ten drivers were issued a separate warning.
12. The trophy was to be awarded to whomever made the highest score in the race series, but I never thought it would be me who would win it.
13. A first prize of an expense-paid trip to Mexico will be given to whoever can solve the Spanish riddle.
14. If you won a nomination against Robert Story, you have did very good indeed.
15. I have always felt like I'd like to be a lawyer.
16. Jane has never been strong; so she don't go hiking like the rest of us do.
17. I drunk a huge glass of ice tea when I come home from the movies.
18. Digging a tunnel into the hillside, the boys went away and left it.
19. Headlines in the newspaper is arranged so that it attracts attention.
20. Every evening there has been some sort of meeting; and although I would have liked to have attended all of them, it was physically impossible.

TEST 2

Follow the directions for Test 1.

1. This camp is different than all of the other camps I have attended.
2. The partners wish to express their appreciation for your patronage during the year and welcomes this opportunity to wish you a Merry Christmas.

3. Since one photograph is worth a thousand words, advertisers are turning to them to sell products.
4. It was not prudent of you to have given her your diary.
5. Losing his fortune in a real estate investment, he begun working again at fifty.
6. New cars don't jump direct from the drafting board to the production room like some people think they do.
7. People said he behaved as a fool at the wedding.
8. Since you invited Paul and I for a visit, our mother has been terrible ill; so we will not be able to accept your invitation.
9. The dance will probably last until midnight; so there is no point in you waiting up any longer.
10. A mysterious stranger whom, we discovered later, met Father last winter, crosses the lake and ties up at our dock.
11. When you consider that neither of us have did any water skiing for two years, we are not doing so bad.
12. Neither Mother nor I are surprised to hear that Martha failed; she didn't do her assignments careful at all.
13. I wish I was able to tell Carlton and she the dreadful secret.
14. Since the computer checking system has been used successful, most of our banks have adopted it.
15. He told Mr. Kenworthy that he was sure to be made a director.
16. The lifeguard said that the boys almost drownded because they swum out too far.
17. After we helped sweep out the dining room, we arranged chairs for the meeting.
18. The satellites which we launch makes life more and more complex.
19. I'm afraid his foot is froze.
20. I could have come if I had knew that you were coming.

PUNCTUATION AND MECHANICS

Punctuation is a method or system by which the meaning of written communication is made clear through the use of certain marks.

Mechanics, a rather vague word, applies to the use of capital and small letters, italics (underlining), abbreviations, the representation of numerals in either words or figures, and the spelling of English words and phrases.

The most significant marks of punctuation are:

.	Period	,	Comma
?	Question mark	;	Semicolon
!	Exclamation point	:	Colon
—	Dash	" "	Double quotation marks
-	Hyphen	' '	Single quotation marks
'	Apostrophe	( )	Parentheses

Each of these marks is a sort of shorthand device, or road sign, aimed at assisting the reader along his way. Every mark of punctuation is effective if it helps the reader to understand. The presence, or absence, of every mark is harmful if it impedes the flow of thought from your mind to that of your reader. Punctuation usually serves one of four general purposes:

1. To *end* or *terminate* a statement—use period, question mark, or exclamation point.

> Snow flurries were predicted.
> Have you been home?
> What a surprise!

2. To *introduce*—use comma, colon, or dash.

> He needed only one thing, encouragement.
> My purpose is simple: to succeed in life.
> My goal in life is simple—success.

3. To *separate* parts of a sentence or word—use comma, semicolon, dash, hyphen, or apostrophe.

If you have any influence at all, try to have me excused.

Some people prefer steak for breakfast; others prefer it for dinner.

Sneezing, wheezing, and coughing — these are symptoms of the common cold.

Judy Nash was elected secretary-treasurer.

It will soon be 3 o'clock.

4. To *enclose* parts of a sentence or a whole section — use commas, dashes, quotation marks, single quotation marks, parentheses, brackets. *Enclosure marks are used in pairs, except when the capital letter at the beginning of a sentence takes the place of the first or when a terminating mark at the end takes the place of the second.*

An elderly lady, Miss Elsa Boylen, was my favorite grade school teacher.

Miss Elsa Boylen, an elderly lady, was my favorite grade school teacher.

My favorite grade school teacher was Miss Elsa Boylen, an elderly lady.

You are not — and everyone around here knows it — a very careful driver.

You are not a careful driver — and everyone around here knows it.

"The word 'lousy' is not in reputable use as a term in literary criticism," said the lecturer.

You are referred to Roberts' Rules of Order (see especially Article XII).

The article began: "People these days are to [*sic*] busy to think about problems that arise more than 100 miles from their homes."

21. END STOPS

Punctuation appearing at the end of a sentence is called an *end stop*. Sometimes called *terminal marks*, end stops are periods, question marks, and exclamation points. Approximately 95 percent of all sentences end with a period, regardless of who writes them or for what purposes. Question marks and exclamation points have special, limited uses, but on occasion each can and does add much to the clarity of communication.

A story is told that Victor Hugo, the famous nineteenth-century French writer, wrote the shortest letter on record; wishing to know how his latest novel was selling, he sent a sheet of paper to his publisher on which appeared a single question mark. His publisher, pleased to report good news, replied with a single exclamation point. If you wish to know your standing with an absent sweetheart, you might copy Hugo's letter, but you run the risk of receiving in reply another question mark or, worse luck, a period.

21a. USE A PERIOD AT THE END OF A DECLARATIVE SENTENCE.

School will be dismissed early today.
Ralph prefers driving to flying.

21b. USE A PERIOD AFTER MOST ABBREVIATIONS.

Mr. and Mrs. Robert Manley
Jane L. Freeman, M.D. (b. 1908, d. 1967)
Nov. 5, Alta., St., Ave., A.M., oz., bbl.

21c. USE PERIODS PROPERLY IN AN OUTLINE.

A period should appear after each number or letter symbol in an outline. Use no period at the end of a line in a topic outline, but do place one at the end of each sentence in a sentence or paragraph outline. See Section 93.

21d. USE THREE SPACED PERIODS TO INDICATE AN INTENTIONAL OMISSION.

Such periods, called *ellipses* or *ellipsis periods* or the *ellipsis mark,* indicate an omission of one or more words within a sentence or quotation. If the omission ends with a period use four spaced periods.

"Finds tongues in trees, books . . . in brooks, sermons in stones, . . . good in everything."

The tiger crept stealthily toward its prey. . . .

21e. USE A PERIOD BEFORE A DECIMAL, TO SEPARATE DOLLARS AND CENTS, AND TO PRECEDE CENTS WRITTEN ALONE.

8.43 percent	$5.67	$0.28

21f. USE THE EXCLAMATION POINT TO END A FORCEFUL INTERJECTION OR TO INDICATE SURPRISE OR VIGOROUS EMOTION.

What nerve you have!
I tell you—bluntly!—leave me alone.
So you have changed your mind after all!
So that's what he's after!

21g. USE A QUESTION MARK AT THE END OF EVERY DIRECT QUESTION.

You commented—did I understand you?—that you disliked all TV programs.
Do you really think I am that silly?
Joe asked politely, "May I borrow a dollar?"

21h. USE QUESTION MARKS TO INDICATE A SERIES OF QUERIES IN THE SAME SENTENCE OR PASSAGE.

Are you staying? Is your brother? Carol? Marie?
Do you remember when cars had rumble seats? When boys wore knickers? When grandmothers were elderly?
Who's going to volunteer? John? Andy?

21i. DISTINGUISH CAREFULLY THE PURPOSES OF END STOPS.

1. Use a period, not an exclamation point, after a mildly imperative sentence.

Drive slowly and watch out for falling rock.

2. Use a period, not a question mark, after an indirect question.

Kindly tell me when you will wish this returned to the library.

3. Use a period, not a question mark, after a polite request or only superficially interrogative sentence.

"May I see you to the door" is a remark of courtesy more than of interrogation and does not require a question mark.

21j. DO NOT OVERUSE END STOPS.

1. Do not use a period at the end of a theme title.

2. Do not use end stops (especially the period) to punctuate sentence fragments.

3. Avoid using a question mark enclosed in parentheses to indicate doubt, uncertainty, or a humorous meaning.

4. Use the exclamation point sparingly. The emotion, command, or surprise involved must be strong enough to justify an exclamation point. Writing dotted with exclamation marks all too often lacks genuine thought and frequently suggests immaturity. Avoid using this mark after a long sentence; most of us cannot hold our breath long enough to exclaim more than a few words at a time.

EXERCISE 1

On your paper copy each of the following sentences and supply periods, exclamation points, or question marks where they are needed.

1. Now you never connect a white wire to a black wire except when you are working on the discarded models
2. The Rt Rev Chauncey Chummley will speak at 7:00 P M on Sunday evening, Aug 4, in place of Cecil Bustem, PhD, DD
3. How could a lady answer a question like that before a whole

132

group of strangers Why, the whole situation was ridiculous
Absurd Preposterous

4. On St Sebastian's Day we had cookies, turtle soup, pancakes
Have you ever tried St Sebastian's Day pancakes What a
wonderful day it was

5. The next dance Of course you may have the dance Look who
just asked me for the next dance, Ethel

6. Drop that gun Hold up your hands Who are you, anyway

7. My brother longs to be able to write "BA, MA, and PhD" after
his name, but my sister says "Mrs" before hers is all she wants

8. Look out There's no guard rail Nothing to stop us if we slip off
the road

9. Ours isn't all just run-of-the-mill work; even though our day-to-
day operations are largely routine, we get some fun out of the
ordinary assignments

10. During the summer session, classes are held as early as 7 AM
but never run later than 2 PM

EXERCISE 2

Follow the directions for Exercise 1.

1. That electrician Do you know what he charged Fifty dollars
2. George Harris was graduated from McGill with a BA (1956)
and from Western with an MA (1958)
3. Mr and Mrs Wolverton visited 28 European cities in 23 days
4. Help Help I'm trapped inside of a breadbox Help
5. President and Mrs Zickefoose will address the board of trustees
at 7 PM this evening
6. You take that roast back to the butcher and tell him to trim all of
the fat off Now get going, Sylvia
7. The litter of kittens strolled calmly across the schoolyard
8. I saw him — what's his name — at the movies last Friday night
9. Mr Plunkett, our advisor, ordered six pizzas for the party
10. The plane for Paris is due to depart at 8 PM, not 9 PM

22. THE SEMICOLON

The semicolon (;) is entirely a mark of separation, or
division; that is, it is never used to introduce, enclose, or
terminate a statement. It is a stronger mark than the comma,

signifying a greater break or longer pause between sentence elements. But it is weaker than the period and other terminal marks (question mark, exclamation point) and cannot be used to end a sentence. Its use indicates that two or more statements are not sufficiently related to require commas but are too closely related to justify being put in separate sentences separated by a terminal mark.

22a. USE THE SEMICOLON TO SEPARATE INDEPENDENT CLAUSES NOT JOINED BY A SIMPLE CONJUNCTION.

> Laughter is not at all a bad beginning for a friendship; it is far the best ending for one. (Oscar Wilde)

> Life is very short and very uncertain; let us spend it as well as we can. (James Boswell)

> A little neglect may breed mischief: for want of a nail the shoe was lost; for want of a shoe the horse was lost; for want of a horse the rider was lost. (Benjamin Franklin)

22b. USE THE SEMICOLON TO SEPARATE INDEPENDENT CLAUSES JOINED BY A CONJUNCTIVE ADVERB.

Conjunctive adverbs, special kinds of adverbs which can also be used as conjunctions, include *also, anyhow, as a result, besides, consequently, for example, furthermore, hence, however, in addition, indeed, in fact, instead, likewise, meanwhile, moreover, namely, nevertheless, otherwise, similarly, still, then, therefore, thus.*

> We regret that we have sold all of the shirts in blue; *however,* we have the same style in white.

> Dorothy's brother is a busy boy; *in fact,* he works harder than she does.

> She ran a high fever for three days; *then* she admitted defeat and let her brother summon a doctor.

> He expected a reward for his diligent efforts on behalf of the party, *instead,* he was punished.

22c. USE THE SEMICOLON BETWEEN INDEPENDENT CLAUSES WHICH ARE LENGTHY OR CONTAIN INTERNAL PUNCTUATION.

Many paperback books, especially the cheapest ones, are so hastily and economically thrown together that they soon rip apart; however, with proper care, such as we should give all books, even the cheapest ones can be preserved for a time.

Success in school, so some maintain, requires intelligence, industry, and honesty; but others, somewhat fewer in number, insist that only personality and contacts really count.

22d. USE THE SEMICOLON TO SEPARATE PHRASES AND CLAUSES OF CONSIDERABLE LENGTH AND ALSO SERIES OF WORDS IN WHICH COMPLETE CLARITY IS DESIRED.

The ones chosen to represent the school were Ninki Black, president of the debating society; Jack Smoak, varsity basketball captain; and Gene Toale, active in school dramatics.

22e. DO NOT OVERUSE THE SEMICOLON.

The semicolon has its special uses and should be employed only in the situations described in preceding sections. Like other marks it should not be inserted aimlessly nor should it be overused. Especially avoid using semicolons in the following ways:

1. To set off phrases or independent clauses unless for specific situations mentioned above. The semicolon really has the same function as a period: it indicates a complete break and marks the ending of one thought and the beginning of another. A fairly safe rule: no period, no semicolon. Phrases and dependent clauses cannot be set off by periods and thus cannot be marked by semicolons.

> Faulty: Since Mary wants to go with us; we must revise our plans. (The opening dependent clause should be followed by a comma, not a semicolon.)

> Being aware of the high cost of living; I am sympathetic to your predicament. (The opening participial phrase requires a comma at the end, not a semicolon.)

2. **To introduce statements or lists.** The semicolon is not a mark of introduction, such as are, for example, the colon, dash, and comma, and should never be used for this purpose.

> Faulty: His goal is simple and direct; to make the debating team.
>
> Here is what you need; health, money, and ambition.
>
> Dear Sir; Dear Mrs. Woods; Gentlemen;

Substitute a colon for each semicolon above; however, a dash *could* be used in the first and second illustrations, and a comma could appear in the third group of illustrations.

3. **To indicate a summary.**

> Faulty: Sweeping, dusting, mopping; these were my household chores. (Use a colon or dash, not a semicolon.)

EXERCISE 3

On your paper copy the following sentences and supply semicolons where they are needed.

1. Oscar suddenly found himself eye to eye with a rattler he was unable to move a muscle.
2. The customs inspector looked suspicious as he checked the declaration statement: a camera, complete with flash attachments a portable typewriter, valued at fifty dollars and a machine gun, loaded and ready for use.
3. Mehitabel would not give up easily there was life in the old cat yet.
4. This is the Homecoming weekend, and we have to look our best furthermore, our team must win Saturday's game.
5. The camp nurse told Lulu to open her mouth and stick out her tongue the latter action Lulu performed with extraordinary expertness.
6. Stephanie's Christmas list grew: Owl, a green-and-blue striped tie Pewee, a plaid tie Link, a plain knitted tie.
7. I saw Russ Jackson score three touchdowns against the Toronto Argonauts on the same day, Dave Mann kicked three field goals.
8. When we met Nancy and Gibson, they had just returned from school they greeted us warmly.

9. In spite of the election ratings, Mayor Hinkle remained confident nevertheless, he did not order refreshments for his partisans.
10. We were there when Olga sang in Stratford the appreciative audience would not let her stop singing.

EXERCISE 4

Follow the directions for Exercise 3.

1. Uncle Henry hates to shave he also hates beards.
2. The highest ranking students were Ronald George of Leduc, Alberta Sylvia Marteney of Brandon, Manitoba Mary Jenkins of Kitchener, and I.
3. My Uncle Sherlock lives in a bohemian garret therefore he lacks the room a grand piano requires.
4. All of the Disney pictures are suitable for all members of the family this is but one reason for their great popularity.
5. When they watch television together, they always argue about what programs to see they seem to enjoy these arguments.
6. Fly-fishing has its unique appeal however, I prefer using lures.
7. A rainy spell set in and construction was halted for a week consequently, we were free from Monday through Friday.
8. Three and twenty pigeons were perched upon the ledge therefore, we crossed to the other side of the street.
9. "Let's all go to the art exhibit," she said 15 minutes later, we were on our way and had a wonderful time.
10. Springtime in Vermont is every bit as lovely as the song suggests, all skiers will not agree.

23. THE COLON

The colon (:) is a mark of expectation or addition. Its primary function is to signal the reader to "watch for what's coming." That is, it signals to the reader that the next group of words will fulfill what the last group promised. What does come after the colon is usually explanatory or illustrative material which has been prepared for by a word, or words, preceding the colon.

23a-b-c COLONS

Major uses of the colon are to introduce lists, enumerations, tabulations; to introduce a word, phrase, or even a to-be-emphasized clause; to precede an example or clarification of an idea suggested before the colon; to introduce a restatement of a preceding phrase or clause; to introduce a formal quotation; to spell out details of a generalization.

23a. USE THE COLON TO INTRODUCE A WORD, PHRASE, OR CLAUSE, OR AFTER AN INTRODUCTORY STATEMENT WHICH SHOWS THAT SOMETHING IS TO FOLLOW.

Only one other possibility remains: to travel by bus.
My aim in this course is easily stated: a high grade.
This is my problem: where do I go from here?
Do this before you leave: buy traveler's cheques, check your passport, have your smallpox vaccination.

23b. USE THE COLON TO SEPARATE INTRODUCTORY WORDS FROM A LONG OR FORMAL QUOTATION WHICH FOLLOWS.

Deems Taylor concluded his article on Richard Wagner with these words:
"The miracle is that what he did in the little space of seventy years could have been done at all, even by a great genius. Is it any wonder that he had no time to be a man?"

23c. USE THE COLON AS A SEPARATING MARK IN SPECIAL SITUATIONS.

1. *In business letters*, the salutation is separated from the body of the letter by a colon: Dear Mr. Clark: Dear Sir: Gentlemen: My dear Mr. Swan:.

It is customary to place a comma after the salutation of a friendly or personal letter (Dear Ginny,), but the colon is not so formal a mark as to repulse friendship. Use either a colon or a comma after the salutation in such letters.

2. *Titles and subtitles of books* may be separated by a colon: *Education for College: Improving the High School Curriculum; The English Novel: A Panorama.*

3. *Hour and minute figures* in writing time may be separated by a colon: 8:17 P.M.; 3:26 A.M.

4. *Acts and scenes of plays* may be separated by a colon: Shakespeare's *Twelfth Night*, II:v.

5. *Chapters and verses of the Bible* may be separated by a colon: *James,* 3:16.

6. Volume and page reference may be separated by a colon: *The History of the English Novel*, V:83.

7. *A publisher's location and name* may be separated by a colon: *Toronto: McGraw-Hill Company of Canada Limited.*

8. In stating proportions, both a single colon and double colon may be used: 2:4::4:8 (two is to four as four . . .).

23d. DO NOT OVERUSE THE COLON.

The colon is a useful mark adding clarity to writing, but it should be employed to accomplish only the purposes suggested on p. 138. Used in other constructions, the colon becomes both obstructive and intrusive.

1. Do not place a colon between a preposition and its object:

I am fond of: *Montreal, Ottawa,* and *Banff.* (There is no need for the colon or any other mark of punctuation after *of.*)

2. Do not place a colon between a verb and its object or object complement:

He liked to see: *TV plays, movies,* and *baseball games.* (Use no mark of punctuation after *see.*)

She liked a number of activities, such as: *dancing, cooking,* and *swimming.* (Use no mark of any kind after *such as.*)

EXERCISE 5

On your paper copy the following sentences. Supply colons where they are needed.

1. At 630 the next morning what everyone had been expecting occurred murder.

2. I know only one passage, Martin, that will give you the answer to your question *Exodus*, 614.

3. Of the performance of a celebrated violinist, Dr. Johnson once said "Difficult do you call it, Sir? I wish it were impossible."

4. Donovan refused to economize on the necessities of life, such as good dinner wines, adequate theater seats, and competent valet service.

5. The only magazines she ever reads are *Vogue, Chatelaine,* and *McCall's.*

6. Then from a gloomy corner on the north side of the waiting room came the awful words of the stationmaster "The 945 train for Regina will never leave this station."

7. For Tuesday's assignment we are to read poems by the following Poe, Thoreau, and Melville.

8. My cousin has only one responsibility left to find a home for his aging beagle.

9. Dan chose his car after carefully examining all the convertibles manufactured by the Chrysler Corporation, the Ford Motor Company, and General Motors.

10. The minister took his text from *Psalms,* 133.

24. THE DASH

The dash (−) is an emphatic mark of punctuation most often used to indicate a sudden interruption in thought, a sharp break, or a shift in thought. It has been called "the interruption, the mark of abruptness, the sob, the stammer, and the mark of ignorance." This colorful definition implies that the dash is a vigorous mark which has emotional qualities and which may be misused and overused.

Some other mark of punctuation can always be substituted for a dash. It does have functions roughly equivalent to those of a comma and, moreover, resembles a terminal mark of punctuation (period, exclamation point, question mark) in certain situations. However, a dash lends a certain air of surprise or emotional tone on occasion and, if used sparingly, is a device for adding movement, or a sense of movement, to writing. But it is rightly called a "mark of ignorance," since some writers use it indiscriminately and far too often.

24a. USE A DASH TO INTRODUCE A WORD OR GROUP OF WORDS WHICH YOU WISH TO EMPHASIZE.

> There is only one other possibility—to travel by car.
> There is only one thing he needs for his complete happiness—love.

Either a colon or comma could be used in such constructions as these; the dash adds emphasis, vigor, and a tonal quality of emotion.

24b. USE THE DASH TO INDICATE A BREAK OR SHIFT IN THOUGHT.

> I think—no, I am positive—that you should stay.
> Here is a fuller explanation—but perhaps your students will not be interested.
> She is the most despicable—but I should not say any more.

Breaks or shifts in thought and the use of dashes to indicate them should both be rare.

24c. USE A DASH TO INDICATE OMISSION OF LETTERS AND WORDS AND TO CONNECT COMBINATIONS OF LETTERS AND FIGURES.

> May—August (May to or through August)
> He lived in that city 1962—1967.
> Joe Pear is a pilot on the Toronto — Chicago run.
> The First World War, 1914—1918, was fought to end all wars.
> Selectman B—was an excellent orator.
> We were in one d—of a spot when we landed.

A hyphen (-) might be substituted in typing or handwriting in each of the examples above except the last two, where a double dash could also be used.

Do not use a dash in such expressions as those above when the word *from* or *between* appears:

> From May to (or through) August (not *From May—August*)
> Between 1956 and 1963 (not *Between 1956—1963*)

24d. USE DASHES TO SET OFF STRONGLY DISTINGUISHED PARENTHETICAL MATERIAL.

My advice — if you will pardon my impertinence — is that you apologize to your friend.

My brother is not afraid — he is a surgeon, you know — of performing the most delicate operation.

I was pleased — delighted, I should say — to hear your news.

She was aware — she must have known — that the proposal was hopeless.

EXERCISE 6

Copy the following sentences on your paper and supply dashes when needed in each sentence.

1. No, no, Ed, not that switch, the one with the, for heaven's sake, look out!
2. The stock market crash of 1929, it began on October 24 of that year, brought many a paper millionaire to beggary.
3. The mysterious woman asked Uncle Julian to mind her Pekingese while she, but that's another story.
4. Excuse me, sir, I didn't mean to, why, if it isn't my old friend Glauntz.
5. The lawyer briefly sketched the main facts of his, wait, haven't I said that before?
6. Well, I'll be
7. The coach called the team together, they were in the clubhouse where they had dressed for the game, and reminded them, "This game will decide the league championship. Do your best. That's all I ask."
8. Call Harry, he insists on being involved, and then report back to me.
9. I saw a John Wayne movie, I forget the title of it, in which he didn't win the war single-handedly.
10. Mallard swam the river, believe it or not, wearing sneakers.

25. THE COMMA

Because the comma (,) serves so many different purposes it is the most widely used of all punctuation marks. Its varied and distinct uses make it by far the most troublesome of the marks; in fact, comma usage varies so greatly that only a few rules can be considered unchanging. But this mark of punctuation, more than any others, can and does help to clarify the meaning of writing. Its overuse and misuse also obscure meaning more than the misapplication of any of the other marks. If you can master the uses of the comma—or even the basic ones—no other mark can hold any terrors for you.

As has been noted, the comma is a relatively weak mark as compared with the period, semicolon, etc. It shows a brief pause, less complete separation than other marks. Always used within the sentence, it serves several purposes: to introduce, to separate, to enclose, to show omission.

Commas to Introduce

25a. USE A COMMA TO INTRODUCE A WORD, PHRASE, OR, ON OCCASION, A CLAUSE.

> Only one other possibility remains, to travel by air.
> I had an important decision to make, whether I should drop out of school or borrow the money and continue.
> I have need of only two things, money and more money.

The colon may substitute for the comma in each of the above examples. (See 23a.)

25b. USE A COMMA TO INTRODUCE A STATEMENT OR QUESTION WHICH IS PRECEDED BY A MENTAL QUESTION OR MUSING ALOUD.

> I wondered, should I tell Mother the whole story?
> I thought, you're in real trouble now.
> I told myself, you can do this as well as anyone.

25c. USE A COMMA TO INTRODUCE A SHORT QUOTATION.

> Jack said, "I'll never say that again."

If the "he said" or its equivalent follows the quotation, it is separated from it by a comma, provided a question mark or exclamation point is not demanded.

"I'll never say that again," said Jack.

If the "he said" or its equivalent is inserted between the parts of a quotation, it is enclosed by commas—provided one part is dependent:

"I'll never say that again," said Jack, "unless I lose my temper."

When the quotation being introduced is long or formal, the colon replaces the comma.

Make a careful distinction between quotations which are really quotations of speaking or writing and quoted material which is the subject or object of a verb or material stressed by quotation marks such as titles, slang, and special word use. As examples of such special uses, observe the following:

"Make haste slowly" is the motto that came to my mind.

The usual remark is "May the better man win."

When Patrick Henry thundered "Give me liberty or give me death," he contributed a great catch phrase to the world.

"Itsy-bitsy" is not the exact phrase to use for "very small."

Commas to Separate

25d. USE THE COMMA TO SEPARATE INDEPENDENT CLAUSES JOINED BY SUCH CONJUNCTIONS AS *AND, BUT, YET, NEITHER, NOR, OR.*

This principle is one of the most frequently used and illustrated in English writing. This frequency accounts for considerable flexibility in application, as follows:

If the clauses are short, the comma may be omitted before the conjunction. This brings up the question "How short is short?" If each independent clause consists of only subject and predicate, or of three or four words each, then they are obviously short and the comma may be omitted:

The rains came and the rivers rose.

In the final judging, Mary did not win nor did Jane.

Fairly long clauses are sometimes written without a comma between them if their connection is particularly close or if the subject of both clauses is the same:

Henry read the assignment over hurriedly and then he began a more careful rereading of it.

25e. USE A COMMA TO SEPARATE AN INTRODUCTORY MODIFYING PHRASE OR ADVERBIAL CLAUSE FROM THE INDEPENDENT CLAUSE WHICH FOLLOWS.

>Before John started on his trip, he made a careful plan of his itinerary.
>
>If I arrive first, I'll wait for you in the library.
>
>After thinking about it, he decided to go.

An introductory noun clause is not set off by a comma; an adjective clause follows, not precedes, the noun or pronoun that it modifies.

>That your theme was turned in late is unfortunate.
>
>The man whom you were talking to is my uncle.

Many introductory adverbial clauses are simply transposed elements. Inserted in their natural order, they may or may not have commas, depending upon meaning. Inserted elsewhere, they are enclosed by commas.

>After you arrive on the campus, various meetings will be held to help orient you.
>
>Various meetings, after you arrive on the campus, will be held to help orient you.

When the adverbial clause follows the independent clause, omit the comma if the adverbial clause is necessary to complete the meaning of the sentence.

>Paul works because he has no other way to live.

25f. USE COMMAS TO SEPARATE WORDS, PHRASES, AND CLAUSES IN A SERIES.

>You will find Graham around somewhere: in the living room, in the basement, or out in the garden.
>
>She whispered, she muttered, but finally she shouted.
>
>I have brought my textbook, my notebook, and some theme paper with me.
>
>Stop, look, and listen.

One kind of series is represented by A, B, and C—three or more words, phrases, or clauses, with an appropriate pure conjunction joining the last two members.

Some writers omit the comma before the conjunction and use A, B and C. Since greater clearness is frequently ob-

145

tained by the use of the comma before the conjunction, present practice favors the comma.

Another kind of series is represented by A, B, C — three or more words, phrases, or clauses, with no conjunctions. Commas are used after each member except *after* the last, unless the clauses are all independent.

> This store sells newspapers, magazines, books on weekdays only.

Do not use commas separating members of a series, unless emphasis is desired, when a conjunction is used to join each pair.

> I have read nothing by Swift or Milton or Poe.
>
> I have thought and pondered and reflected and meditated — and I still don't know what to do.

25g. USE A COMMA TO SEPARATE TWO OR MORE ADJECTIVES WHEN THEY EQUALLY MODIFY THE SAME NOUN.

> I bought an old, dilapidated chair and a new, ugly, badly faded rug.

When the adjectives are not coordinate, commas are omitted.

> The old oaken bucket was covered with wet green moss.

Notice that a comma is never used to separate the last adjective from the noun.

Sometimes there may be doubt, as in "an old, dilapidated chair" above. Then you must use your judgment in deciding, for, admittedly, it is sometimes difficult to determine whether the adjectives are coordinate or not. Several tests, although not infallible, may help. One way of testing is to insert the coordinate conjunction *and* between the adjectives; if the *and* fits, use a comma when it is omitted, otherwise not. Another test: if the position of the adjectives can be reversed, the adjectives are coordinate. Another test: does the first adjective modify the idea of the second adjective and the noun? If so, the adjectives are not coordinate. Also, if one of the adjectives describes shape or material or color, the adjectives are probably not coordinate.

25h. USE A COMMA TO SEPARATE CONTRASTED ELEMENTS IN A SENTENCE.

Such contrasted elements may be words, phrases, numbers, letters, or clauses:

Your misspelling is due to carelessness, not to ignorance.
Books should be kept on the table, not on the floor.
My lucky number is 7, not 5.
Psmith begins his name with a *P,* not an *S.*
The harder it snowed, the slower they drove.

25i. USE A COMMA TO SEPARATE WORDS OR OTHER SENTENCE ELEMENTS THAT MIGHT BE MISREAD.

Constructions in which commas are needed to prevent misreading are usually questionable or faulty. If it is possible, rephrase such sentences to eliminate awkwardness and to increase clearness. At times, however, a comma is essential to clarify meaning.

Outside, the house needs a coat of paint; inside, the walls need replastering.
The day after, a salesman called with the same product.
In 1968, 984 freshmen appeared on our campus.
Instead of a hundred, thousands came.
Last week I was in bed with a cold, and my mother took care of me.

25j. USE A COMMA, OR COMMAS, TO SEPARATE THOUSANDS, MILLIONS, ETC., IN WRITING FIGURES.

The government deficit may reach $794,774,669 this year.
In this contest 6,811 entries have been received.

Commas are used with all numbers of four or more digits except years, telephone numbers, and house numbers.

In the fall of 1965 our class numbered exactly 2,302 students.
My number is 255-1229.
The Tomlins have sold their home at 4977 Wood Street.

The comma is usually omitted from certain numbers in specialized use: postal zone number 181; serial number 4589326; motor number 924632; 5/1200 of an inch; 3.0945 inches.

Commas to Enclose

25k. USE COMMAS TO ENCLOSE PARENTHETICAL WORDS, PHRASES, OR CLAUSES.

A fairly adequate test of a parenthetical expression is this: it may be omitted without materially affecting the meaning of the sentence or, frequently, though not always, its position in the sentence may be shifted without any change in meaning.

However, we do not disagree too much.

We do not, *however*, disagree too much.

We do not disagree too much, *however*.

We must, *on the other hand*, discuss every aspect of the problem.

I believe, *if anyone should ask my opinion*, that action should be postponed.

Parenthetic elements vary in intensity, and you show by punctuation their relative strength. Some expressions are so weak that they require no punctuation.

25l. USE COMMAS TO ENCLOSE INSERTED SENTENCE ELEMENTS.

Inserted sentence elements—emphatic, suspending, or transposed expressions—are somewhat similar to parenthetical words, phrases, and clauses. *Emphatic* expressions are set off because the writer indicates that he considers them emphatic. *Suspending* expressions interrupt or retard the movement of the sentence, holding important information until near the end of the sentence. *Transposed* expressions, like *I believe, I think, it seems to me, I suppose, you see*, and, frequently, adjectives following their nouns, are out of their normal order and require punctuation not used in normal word order. Such inserted expressions are frequently more essential to the thought of the sentence than purely parenthetical material, but they are nonrestrictive in function.

He did not make that statement, *as you will see if you read more carefully,* and I am certain that he did not mean it to be misunderstood. (Emphatic)

This is a good novel, *not only because it contains plenty of action,* but because it fully develops three characters. (Suspending)

Action, *I believe,* should be postponed. (Transposed)

25m. USE COMMAS TO ENCLOSE NONRESTRICTIVE PHRASES AND CLAUSES.

Phrases and clauses are *nonrestrictive* when they do not limit or restrict the word or words modified, whereas phrases and clauses are *restrictive* when they limit the word or words modified. Observe what the same clause does in each of the following sentences:

Edmonton, *which is the capital of Alberta,* has a population of 401,299.

The city *which is the capital of Alberta* has a population of 401,299.

In the first sentence, the omission of the italicized clause does not materially change the meaning of the sentence; its purpose is to give added information. In the second sentence, the same clause is necessary; it identifies, it tells which city (the capital of Alberta). The clause in the first sentence is *nonrestrictive,* and it is set off from the remainder of the sentence by commas; the clause in the second sentence is *restrictive* and is not enclosed by commas.

The principle of restrictive and nonrestrictive phrases and clauses should become clear if you will carefully note comma usage in the following sentences:

Chapter 8, *which tells of the rescue,* is well written.

The chapter *which tells of the rescue* is well written.

The car *that you saw* was a sports model.

The books, *those that I own,* are all by Canadian authors.

The man *my brother met in Victoria* has traveled widely.

Engelbert Summerfield, *whom my brother met in Victoria,* has traveled widely.

25n. USE COMMAS TO ENCLOSE ABSOLUTE PHRASES.

An absolute phrase, a group of words having no grammatical relation to any word in the sentence, consists of a noun and a participial modifier, the latter being sometimes omitted but understood.

> *The task having been finished,* we started on our return trip.
> I went to the first desk, *my application (held) in hand,* and asked for Mr. Stump.
> We needed a fourth member for our club, *Ellen having moved to another town.*

25o. USE COMMAS TO ENCLOSE WORDS IN APPOSITION.

A word in apposition is a noun or pronoun (word or phrase) identifying in different words a preceding noun or pronoun. Usually the appositional word or phrase is explanatory and therefore nonrestrictive. When the appositional word or phrase limits or restricts meaning, then the commas are omitted.

> My father, *a physician,* has just retired from active practice.
> This is Mr. Law, *our newly elected president.*
> *Richard the Lion-Hearted* was a famous English king.
> Carl Martin, *our supervisor,* was a considerate man.
> My task, *to compose a short story,* seemed hopeless.
> *The river Seine* is beloved of song writers.

25p. USE COMMAS TO ENCLOSE VOCATIVES.

A vocative is a noun, pronoun, or noun phrase used in direct address. That is, a vocative indicates to whom something is said. A vocative may appear at various positions within a sentence:

> *Mr. Brown,* will you speak next?
> I am proud, *Mother,* of what you have accomplished.
> Will you please, *sir,* speak more distinctly?
> We are assembled, *ladies and gentlemen,* to discuss an important problem.

25q. USE COMMAS TO ENCLOSE INITIALS OR TITLES FOLLOWING A PERSON'S NAME.

Abbett, R. H., Abner, W. G., and Adams, B. R., head the list of names.

John Eddy, M.D., and Robert Morgan, D.D., are the featured speakers on the program.

The son of James Adams, Sr., is listed as James Adams, Jr., on our records.

25r. USE COMMAS TO ENCLOSE PLACES AND DATES WHICH EXPLAIN PRECEDING PLACES AND DATES.

Harry left on May 10, *1964*, to go to Winnipeg, *Manitoba*, for an interview.

He lives in London, *Ontario*, having been transferred there from Truro, *Nova Scotia*.

1. The second comma must be used when the state follows town or city and when the year follows both month and day. When only month and year are used, the use of commas around the year is optional: use two or do not use any.

2. In the date line of a letter punctuation is optional. It was formerly common practice to write *July 7, 1967*; increasingly popular is the form *7 July 1967*. Both are acceptable. For clarity, always separate two numerals; where a word intervenes, the comma may be omitted if you prefer.

Commas to Indicate Omission

25s. OCCASIONALLY, USE A COMMA TO AVOID WORDINESS OR FAULTY REPETITION.

Most sentences which require a comma to make clear that something has been left out are poorly constructed and should be rephrased. In rare instances, however, using a comma to show omission helps to avoid wordiness:

Mary collects stamps; Eliza, coupons; Lois, money.

A decade ago she was young and beautiful; only 6 years later, old and ugly.

In this room are 23 students; in that one are 34.

In this room are 23 students; in that, 34. (The comma replaces the words *one are.)*

He takes himself seriously, others, lightly.

25t. USE NO UNNECESSARY COMMAS.

Modern punctuation usage omits many commas that were formerly used; therefore, be able to account for each comma in your writing. A comma must be *needed* for sense construction, clearness, or effectiveness. Avoid using the comma needlessly to separate closely related sentence elements. Some of the most common misuses or overuses of the comma are discussed in the following "do not use" statements.

1. Do not use a comma to separate a subject from its predicate or a verb from its object or complement. No comma is needed in any of these sentences:

We asked to hear the motion reread.

I found that algebra was not so hard after all.

To do satisfactory work is my aim.

2. Do not use a comma before the indirect part of a quotation. No comma is needed in this sentence:

The speaker asserted that he stood squarely for progress.

3. Do not use a comma indiscriminately to replace a word omitted.

The word *that* in an indirect quotation; the word *that* in introducing other noun clauses as objects, and the relative pronouns *who, whom, which, that* are frequently omitted in informal writing; they should not be replaced by commas. In "Jack replied, he would return next week," the comma is incorrectly used for *that;* in "The man, I met was a friend of a friend of mine," *whom* should replace the comma. "She thought, that man was dead" should be written "She thought that that man was dead." In such constructions both comma and pronoun can be omitted.

4. Do not use a comma before the first or after the last member of a series.

We went swimming in a cool, clear, smooth-flowing, river.

Avoid a mixture of, red, yellow, green, blue, and brown paints.

The red, white, and blue flag waved in the wind.

Omit the last comma in the first sentence, the first comma in the second.

5. Do not use a comma between two independent clauses where a stronger mark of punctuation (semicolon, period) is required.

Confusion is always caused by this misuse, sometimes called the "comma fault" or "comma splice." Use a period or semicolon in place of the comma in such a statement as this:

My mother told me to be home early, I told her I couldn't.

6. Do not use a comma, or pair of commas, with words in apposition which are actually restrictive.

The following italicized words really limit, identify, or define; they should not be enclosed with commas.

Goya's painting *The Shooting* is one of his greatest.

My cousin *Dorothy* is a lovely person.

Zeno *of Elea* was a follower of Parmenides.

7. Do not use a comma in any situation unless it adds to clarity and understanding.

Comma usage is slowly growing more and more "open" and less and less "closed." In the following sentences every comma can be justified, but each could equally well be omitted since clarity is not affected in the slightest degree:

After the movie, Joe and I went home, by taxicab, because we wanted, at all costs, to avoid subway crowds.

Naturally, the last thing you should do, before leaving work, is to punch the time clock.

The most frequently used and most important for clarity of all marks of punctuation are commas. Use them when necessary to make your meaning clear; avoid using them when they slow down thought or interrupt or make your writing look as though you had used a comma shaker.

EXERCISE 7

Supply commas where they are needed in the following sentences.

1. If the culprit does not come forward in the next minute I shall fail the whole class.
2. Apparently Dawson this is the crocodile that ate our guide.
3. On August 12 1952 I happened to be yachting in Prince Rupert British Columbia.
4. The man read the letter looked around furtively tore the paper into sixteen pieces and dropped them into his pocket.

5. A scientist who devotes his life to pure research must not be discouraged by minor setbacks.
6. Girls report two physicians at Montreal Quebec have more birthmarks than boys.
7. We all went to bed happily Monday night for the next day was St. Sebastian's Day.
8. We stopped for the night in Princeton which is a short day's drive from Vancouver.
9. "Frankly I don't care whether you live or die or drown or hang" said Pitman smiling his quiet smile.
10. After all the gifts had been passed around the doorbell rang.
11. Our German shepherd which was kept as a watchdog watched the thief run from the house.
12. If you could see how artfully Martin wields an ax Myrtle you would be proud of him I'm certain.
13. Eric is a fat fluffy beautiful cat with no brains.
14. The Senior Editor who had not seen the manuscript before ground his teeth and swore horribly.
15. Ridgely remarked that *Hamlet Antony and Cleopatra* and *Macbeth* roughly in that order are Shakespeare's greatest plays.
16. Myrtle consumed a bag of peanuts and her roommate drank two bottles of coke.
17. Daisy who finally finished packing was rushed to camp.
18. "This car as you can readily see is the best buy" said the salesman pointing to the sleek expensive-looking Lincoln.
19. The dickcissels alighted in the back yard chirped noisily and gobbled up the suet.
20. The Portland steamer *Bostonia* which foundered in a severe storm thirty years ago was located six miles off the Cape.

EXERCISE 8

Follow the directions for Exercise 7.

1. Little Edson was determined to resist manfully however fiendish the younger tormentor Mario should prove to be.
2. Pansy insisted on taking her faded tattered stuffed elephant to camp with her.
3. The spider which just crawled across this page will not do it again.
4. Suddenly it occurred to me that I the leader of the group was considered an outsider.
5. Life suddenly seemed very bleak to Damon and Pythias could not cheer him up.

6. The next student who throws a piece of chalk will be hurled into the corridor.
7. The train having fallen behind schedule again Gobey a rather quick-tempered man slew the conductor.
8. The menu included pheasant under glass canary tongues in aspic and nectar of rose essence.
9. The man that lives by the side of the road is no friend of mine.
10. Admitting defeat Jay phoned TV Despair Service Inc. but the line was busy.
11. We heard later that he had gone across the river through the tall grass and into the trees.
12. This novel which was written by R. C. Shinningbreek is about turtles.
13. In this town Stevens the custom as I should have told you earlier is to tip the barbers handsomely.
14. Exercise of the legs is important for ballet dancers must have strong leg muscles.
15. Someone proposed a toast to the chairman of the program committee who was asleep in the corner.
16. Finally and this may seem hardest of all we must stand erect and not let our shoulders sag Daisy.
17. Borpmann made money speculating in railroad stocks but he lost it in oils.
18. The contestant who writes the most moving description of the new Winter-Snug Union Suit will receive a cash prize of fifty dollars.
19. Inside two natives were relating humorous anecdotes in Swahili but Klebbers was not amused quite the contrary.
20. Martin bolted his lunch changed into his work clothes sped to Mrs. White's house and arrived fifteen minutes late.

EXERCISE 9

Some commas have been omitted from the following passage. Rewrite the passage in your notebook or on a sheet of paper, supplying commas where they are needed. Be prepared to justify your punctuation.

I wonder if anyone here has ever made a mistake a bad one that neither money nor apologies could correct. I have. My home is in Ontario but the summer that I was sixteen my father and I worked in Alberta on a construction job.

Glacier National Park a famous tourist attraction was only a few hours' drive from where we worked and since Dad and I were both eager to see it we decided that if we had the good luck to get a long weekend off we would spend it there. Sure enough toward the end of the summer a heavy rain stopped construction leaving us free from Friday through Monday.

"This is our chance Son," Dad exclaimed on Thursday when we first heard of the layoff. "Let's plan to leave for Glacier as soon as we finish work this afternoon."

"Gee, Dad" I answered "I've got a big date tonight that I made before the news came. If you don't mind let's go early tomorrow morning instead."

Since he is an understanding father he smiled his assent warning me to get in early. I meant to but you know how dates go; day was dawning when I crawled into bed. An hour later Dad who had heard me come in wakened me to see if I still wanted to go to Glacier. I said "Sure!" and actually managed to stay awake for the few hours that it took us to reach the park entrance. Then I began to drift off. Dad annoyed aroused me several times to look at special points of interest but I couldn't stay awake. The next thing I knew I was stumbling up familiar steps. Dad thoroughly disgusted had driven back to our quarters rather than tour the park with me asleep. Nothing I could say helped.

26. THE APOSTROPHE

The apostrophe ('), a mark of punctuation and a spelling symbol, has three uses: to indicate omission of a letter or letters from words and of a figure or figures from numerals; to form the possessive (genitive) case of nouns and of certain pronouns; to indicate the plural of letters, numerals, symbols, and certain abbreviations.

26a. USE AN APOSTROPHE AND *S* TO FORM THE POSSESSIVE CASE OF A NOUN (SINGULAR OR PLURAL) NOT ENDING IN *S*:

women, women's   office, office's
children, children's   horse, horse's

26b. USE AN APOSTROPHE TO FORM THE POSSESSIVE CASE OF A PLURAL NOUN ENDING IN *S:*

ladies, ladies'	days, days'
boys, boys'	student, students'
heroes, heroes'	horses, horses'

26c. USE AN APOSTROPHE ALONE OR AN APOSTROPHE AND *S* TO FORM THE POSSESSIVE OF SINGULAR NOUNS ENDING IN *S:*

James Jones, James Jones' (*or* Jones's)
Keats, Keats' (*or* Keats's)
She liked Francis' looks and Burns' (*or* Burns's) poems.

26d. IN COMPOUND NOUNS ADD THE APOSTROPHE AND *S* TO THE LAST ELEMENT OF THE EXPRESSION, THE ONE NEAREST THE OBJECT POSSESSED.

somebody else's coat	my mother-in-law's car
Queen Mary's crown	the office manager's chair
Mr. Trudeau's aide	the editor-in-chief's pen

26e. USE AN APOSTROPHE TO SHOW THAT LETTERS OR FIGURES HAVE BEEN OMITTED.

didn't (did not)	wasn't (was not)
isn't (is not)	he's (he is)
can't (can not)	don't (do not)

The most misspelled short and simple word in the English language is reflected in this use of the apostrophe. *It's* means "it is" and can never be used correctly for *its* in the possessive sense. "When a skunk lifts *its* tail, that is a sign *it's* frightened." Before writing *i-t-s* think whether or not you mean "it is."

26f. USE AN APOSTROPHE AND *S* TO INDICATE THE PLURALS OF NUMERALS, LETTERS, AND WORDS CONSIDERED AS WORDS.

Don't overuse *and's*, *but's*, and *for's* in your theme.·
He has trouble making legible *8's*.
My cousin spent the last half of the *1950's* in Korea.

26g. NEVER USE AN APOSTROPHE IN FORMING THE PLURAL OF NOUNS AND THE POSSESSIVE CASE OF PERSONAL AND RELATIVE PRONOUNS.

The Smiths [not *Smith's*] are coming home tomorrow.
Correct: *ours, yours, his, hers, its, theirs, whose*
Incorrect: *our's, ours', your's, yours', his', her's, it's, their's, theirs', who's* (unless you mean *who is*)

EXERCISE 10

Copy the following sentences; insert an apostrophe, or an apostrophe and *s*, where needed in each sentence.

1. Jane sister-in-law visit lasted three days.
2. Its Stewart handwriting, all right.
3. You mustnt spike the counselor orange juice, Daisy.
4. Hers is a sister point of view, not a stranger.
5. The Japanese sometimes pronounce their *ls* like *rs*.
6. The Queen of England aunt was paying us a visit.
7. Isnt it strange that youve heard the same eerie sounds?
8. Both his friends vacations together wont equal his.
9. Plumbers helpers cant help painters.
10. Arent you going to the opening of Smith and Jespers new store?

EXERCISE 11

Follow the directions for Exercise 10.

1. It cant be twelve oclock so soon.
2. Thats Jones business, not mine.
3. The fashions of the 1950s remind me of those of the 1920s.
4. The play is called *Ladies Know*, not *Ladys Nose*.
5. For five hours work Marvin pay was $7.50.
6. Sweeneys term paper was no worse than yours, Iris.
7. The judge decision hasnt been announced.

8. Coach Brown concern was whether the tape would hold Bayard bones together.
9. Marie expects to get mostly As and possibly one or two Bs.
10. Somebody had apparently trimmed the mouse whiskers and brushed its fur.

27. QUOTATION MARKS

Quotation marks, both double (". . .") and single ('. . .'), are marks of enclosure for words, phrases, clauses, sentences, and even paragraphs and groups of paragraphs. By definition, *quotation* means repeating (or copying) what someone has said or written. *Quotation marks* are a device used principally to indicate the beginning and end of material so quoted. These marks, often called *quotes*, consist of two (or one) inverted commas at the beginning *(open-quote)* and two (or one) apostrophes for closing a quotation *(close-quote)*. On a standard typewriter keyboard, single and double quotation marks are the same at beginning and end.

27a. USE QUOTATION MARKS TO ENCLOSE EVERY DIRECT QUOTATION AND EACH PART OF AN INTERRUPTED QUOTATION.

"Dinner will be served at seven," replied Barbara.
"Father," I said, "may I have the car this evening?"

27b. IN DIALOGUE USE A SEPARATE PARAGRAPH FOR EACH CHANGE OF SPEAKER.

Larry was dressing for tennis when Bill walked into the room.
"What's up?" Bill asked. He walked over to the sofa in the corner and sat down leisurely.
"Game with Sue at noon," Larry replied. "But I was up so late last night that I think I'll be awful."
"Well, who was your date?"
"Sue," replied Larry sheepishly.

27c. IF A DIRECT QUOTATION EXTENDS FOR MORE THAN ONE PARAGRAPH, PLACE QUOTATION MARKS AT THE BEGINNING OF EACH PARAGRAPH BUT AT THE END OF ONLY THE LAST.

27d. USE QUOTATION MARKS TO ENCLOSE WORDS WITH A WIDELY DIFFERENT LEVEL OF USAGE.

> The Mayor of our town, in my opinion, is a "stuffed shirt."
> The policeman "lit into" me as if I had committed a major crime; when he finished, I "lit out" in a hurry.
> The person who has "had it" so far as all religion is concerned looks with impatience on the role that religion has played in man's progress toward self-mastery.

27e. USE QUOTATION MARKS TO ENCLOSE CHAPTER HEADINGS AND THE TITLES OF ARTICLES, SHORT STORIES, AND SHORT POEMS.

When both chapter heading and book are mentioned, or title of article (story, poem) and magazine, book and magazine names should be indicated by italics (underlining).

> For such information consult the chapter, "Public Works Mean Taxes," in *Economics in One Lesson.*
> Some humorous theatrical experiences are discussed in Jean Kerr's article, "What Happens Out of Town," in a recent issue of *Harper's Magazine.*
> The book *The Togetherness of Words* has many interesting chapters. The one with the oddest title is called "Varieties of English: Simian, Syntactic, Sensible, and Superb."

27f. USE SINGLE QUOTATION MARKS TO ENCLOSE A QUOTATION WITHIN A QUOTATION.

> "Tell me," Father asked Mother after the wedding, "whether the bride said, 'I promise to obey.' "
> Our teacher said, "When you say, 'I'll bring in my paper tomorrow,' I expect it to be turned in tomorrow, not sometime next week."

On the rare occasions when it is necessary to punctuate a quotation within a quotation within a quotation, the correct order is double marks, single marks, double marks. If you need more than this, rephrase your sentence before you lose your reader entirely.

The teacher next said, "This student asked, 'What did the teacher mean when she said, "Sue, be there on time tonight"?' "

27g. PLACE QUOTATION MARKS CORRECTLY WITH REFERENCE TO OTHER MARKS.

1. The comma and the period *always* come *inside* quotation marks. This rule never varies and applies even when only the last word before the comma or period is enclosed (but not alphabetical letters or numerals).

2. A question mark, exclamation point, or dash comes *outside* quotation marks unless it is part of the quotation. A single question mark comes inside quotation marks when both the nonquoted and quoted elements are questions.

3. The semicolon and colon come *outside* quotation marks.

Are you thoroughly confused by now? Perhaps these illustrations will help:

"I need your help now," she said. "I need it more than ever."

Some praised the performance as "excellent," and others thought it was only "fair."

Did she say, "I have enough money"?

She asked, "Have I enough money?"

"Have I enough money?" she asked.

What is meant by "dog eat dog"?

Our play was obviously a "bust"!

"The play was a 'bust'!" our coach exclaimed.

Read E. B. White's "Walden"; it is, I think, his best essay.

Look up the following in "A Glossary of Famous People": Sir John A. Macdonald, Woodrow Wilson, Charles E. Hughes.

EXERCISE 12

Copy each of the following sentences and supply quotation marks where they are needed.

1. Who said God's in His heaven; all's right with the world?
2. We now have more than 100 guppies in that tank, dear, she noted. Don't you think we have enough?

3. Even Violet was willing to grant that her date was real gone. He thought the same of her, so they made a splendid couple at the senior prom.

4. Waldo, you help your father wash the car; I'm tired, Ralph said. Besides, he hasn't paid me for the last time.

5. Professor White's latest article, How to Be Happy Through Living, has created a stir in the academic world.

6. This is convertible weather, Hugh, she said. Let's take a drive in the country.

7. Did you say you are starting on your diet on Monday?

8. Please, Grandma, begged Susie, show William how you can swallow a cigarette.

9. Well, I must be a-scootin' along, said the little boy as he backed out of the door. And I knew he'd be a-scootin' back again tomorrow.

10. Buster said that he expected everything to turn out all right if we all kept quiet.

EXERCISE 13

Follow the directions for Exercise 12.

1. Don't you want to sit down, Sir? Jay asked his boss. No, no, m'boy, replied his boss. You take this empty chair. I don't object to standing for two hours.

2. Stop! Don't move an inch! Don't you dare touch that cookie jar! Stand right there until I tell you to move.

3. Please pass the ice cubes, murmured Bob White meaningfully. They are exceptionally good today.

4. The word *nip* means father in our language, explained young Bhonggum, laughing.

5. Pointing to an object over the fireplace, Mallard said, There's my last deer head hanging on the wall. I certainly made a honey of a shot that time.

6. This house is queerly constructed remarked Bert; it's plastered with mortgages.

7. The words row, throw, go, tow will help you remember the procedure for life saving from a boat, explained the instructor. Or should it be go, throw, tow, row?

8. I'll never forget what's-her-name. Boy, did she have an appetite, he observed.

9. But what, Daisy inquired, do the whispering pines say?

10. Say ah, said Dr. Goslin, cocking an ear. Now say zoop. Once more. That's fine.

28.   THE HYPHEN

The hyphen (-) is a mark of separation used only between parts of a word. Paradoxically, its most frequent use is unification, bringing together two or more separate words into a compound word which serves the purpose of a single part of speech. The hyphen, therefore, is more a mark of spelling than of punctuation, to indicate that two or more words or two or more parts of one word belong together.

28a.   USE YOUR DICTIONARY TO DETERMINE WHETHER A WORD COMBINATION IS WRITTEN AS A COMPOUND WITH A HYPHEN, AS ONE WORD WRITTEN SOLID, OR AS TWO SEPARATE WORDS.

The general principle of word joining derives from usage. When two or more words first become associated with a single meaning, they are written separately; as they grow to be more of a unit in common thought and writing, they are hyphenated; finally they are written together as one word. This evolution is seen in the following, the third word in each series now being the accepted form: *base ball, base-ball, baseball; basket ball, basket-ball, basketball; rail road, rail-road, railroad; week end, week-end, weekend.*

Many common expressions are still in the first stage: *mother tongue, Boy Scout, Girl Guide, girl friend, high school.* The one-word combination *highschool,* for example, although used by a prominent educational magazine, has not yet been accepted by dictionaries.

28b.   USE A HYPHEN TO SEPARATE (ACTUALLY, JOIN) THE PARTS OF MANY COMPOUND WORDS.

Many compounds are written solid, many are written with a hyphen, and many are written either with a hyphen or as two words, depending upon meaning. However, the present-day tendency is to avoid using hyphens whenever possible. Seven groups, or classes, of words ordinarily require hyphens:

1. Two or more words modifying a substantive and used as a single adjective: *soft-spoken, ocean-blue, wind-blown, trans-Andean, ever-rising.*

2. Words of a compound noun: *mother-in-law, go-between, fellow-citizen.*

3. Compound words, usually, when *self, ex, half,* or *quarter* is the first element: *self-control, ex-president, half-truth, quarter-share.*

4. A single capital letter joined to a noun or participle: *B-flat, H-bomb, S-curve, T-shaped, U-turn.*

5. Elements of an improvised compound: *make-believe, know-it-all, never-say-die.*

6. Compound numerals from *twenty-one* through *ninety-nine.*

7. Compounds formed from the numerator and denominator of fractions: *four-fifths, one-thousandth.*

28c. USE A HYPHEN TO INDICATE THE DIVISION OF A WORD BROKEN AT THE END OF A LINE.

The rambling old house, it is true, would have looked considerably better if it had been freshly painted.

Occasionally, at the end of a longhand or typewritten line, a long word must be divided. Avoid such division if you possibly can, and do not divide the word if it is the last one on the page. When division is necessary, follow these directions:

1. Place the hyphen at the end of the first line, *never at the beginning of the second.*

2. Never divide a monosyllable. Five- to seven-letter one-syllable words like *breath, death, ground, thought,* and *through* cannot be divided. Write the entire monosyllable on the first line; if this is not possible, carry the whole word over to the next line.

3. Divide words of more than one syllable between syllables, but avoid dividing one-letter syllables from the remainder of the word, as well as any unpronounced *ed* in

one- or several-syllable pronunciations. Undesirable: *a-bout;*
i-talics; man-y; ask-ed; dress-ed; attack-ed. Also do not divide words with only four letters. Undesirable: *al-so; in-to;*
on-ly; op-en.

4. When in doubt about correct syllabication, consult your
dictionary in order to divide words properly. Several simple
suggestions, however, apply to many words:

Prefixes and suffixes can be divided from the main words
(but see 3, just above).

Compound words are divided between their main parts.
Two consonants are usually divided.

EXERCISE 14

Copy the following sentences and insert hyphens where
they are needed.

1. Soldiers in war are expected to make all necessary self sac-
   rifices.
2. Four fifths of the students voted for a new social chairman.
3. Is it anti-Canadian to criticize the Prime Minister from time to
   time?
4. According to the X rays, Mr. Whipple, you have a healthy pair
   of lungs.
5. Alphonse's sister in law cleaned all of his pipes with detergent.
6. When Mallard found a lion in his closet, he was wild eyed.
7. Herbie believes that he would make a first rate paratrooper.
8. Callas' A flat in *Medea* was somewhat flat indeed.
9. With a bluish gray sky above us, we sailed out to Saint-Pierre.
10. Because Carol had an I.Q. of 165, she acted like a know it all.

29. PARENTHESES

Parentheses ( ) are curved punctuation marks principally
used to enclose incidental explanatory matter in a sentence.
Such material is important enough to be included but is not
intended to be a part of the main statement and often has no
direct grammatical relationship to the sentence in which it
appears. Marks of parenthesis (or *parentheses*) signal to the
reader what a speaker means when he says "By the way," or
"Incidentally," or something similar.

29a-b-c PARENTHESES

You may set off incidental (parenthetical) material by commas, dashes, or marks of parenthesis. Each of these marks is acceptable for this purpose. Your choice will usually depend upon the closeness of the relationship between the material inserted and the remainder of the sentence. No specific rule can be stated, but commas are ordinarily used to enclose parenthetical material closely related in thought and structure to the sentence in which it occurs. Dashes enclose parenthetical material which more abruptly breaks into the sentence or may be used in a somewhat informal style. Parentheses are used to enclose material more remote in thought and structure or material which runs to some length or may itself contain internal punctuation, such as commas.

29a. USE PARENTHESES TO ENCLOSE MATERIAL ONLY REMOTELY CONNECTED WITH ITS CONTEXT.

These directions (I am certain they are accurate) should be thoroughly studied.

If you find any strawberries (surely they must be plentiful now), please bring me some.

29b. USE PARENTHESES TO ENCLOSE NUMERALS OR LETTERS INDICATING DIVISIONS.

He left hurriedly for several reasons: (a) poor health, (b) lack of money, (c) dull companions, (d) a job in the city.

29c. USE PARENTHESES TO ENCLOSE SUMS OF MONEY WHEN ACCURACY IS ESSENTIAL.

Her grocery bill was fifty-four dollars ($54.00).

The retail price is forty cents (40c) per pound.

Sums of money repeated for accuracy and enclosed in parentheses occur most often in business writing and in legal papers. Ordinarily, you need not resort to this device; either words or numerals will suffice.

29d. AVOID USING PARENTHESES TO ENCLOSE QUESTION MARKS AND EXCLAMATION POINTS TO EXPRESS DOUBT OR IRONY.

Doubt and irony can usually be expressed more forcefully in other ways. Do not use a question mark as a lazy excuse for not finding out exact information.

> Paul is in good shape; he needs to lose only (!) forty pounds.
> This baby was born on June 22 (?) last year.
> The ambitious candidate boasted in a modest (?) way and never raised his voice above a gentle (?) roar.

EXERCISE

Exercises involving parentheses and brackets follow Section 30.

30. BRACKETS

A bracket [or] is one of two marks (brackets are always used in pairs) used primarily for the purpose of enclosing material which is not part of a quoted passage. That is, brackets are editorial marks used to enclose comments, corrections, or additions to quoted material. The mark is often used in professional and academic writing but has limited use elsewhere. Brackets should never be confused with marks of parentheses, which have entirely different uses. Parentheses are used to enclose your own parenthetical material; brackets are used solely to set off matter inserted by you in someone else's writing which you are quoting.

30a. USE BRACKETS TO ENCLOSE A COMMENT INSERTED IN A QUOTED PASSAGE.

> "On the first float rode the Homecoming Queen [Miss Jane Gaston], her attendants, and her escort."
> "In March of that year [1957] Cameron wrote his first book."

30b BRACKETS

If you are quoting a person who has made an error, or what you consider an error, you can add the correction and enclose it in brackets. If you do not wish to make the correction but merely to call attention to it, you may use the Latin word *sic*, which means "thus," and enclose it in brackets:

"Milton portrays Satan as a fallen angle [*sic*] of tremendous size."

30b. USE BRACKETS TO ADD TO A QUOTED PASSAGE.

"He was fined £100 [$240] for the violation."

"Later in the poem," the lecturer continued, "he [Jim Dooley] is killed."

"They [the Indians] were not any more at fault than their adversaries [the cavalry]," the speaker concluded.

The advertisement read: "These sweaters [Fisherman's knit, Scandinavian design] were designed by Ceil Allen."

EXERCISE 15

Copy the following sentences on your paper and add parentheses and brackets where they are needed.

1. In the seventeenth century before your time gentlemen dressed as elaborately as did ladies.
2. Parentheses have three chief uses: 1 to enclose parenthetical remarks; 2 to enclose references and directions; 3 to enclose figures repeated to insure accuracy.
3. A council representing all the Greek-letter organizations both fraternities and sororities met to plan for the annual ball.
4. I'd have the vet take a look at him, if I were you, before it's too late.
5. The first towel is placed on the top of the head see Fig. 16 and is brought down and tied under the chin.
6. Professor McHenry's composition course was very popular, considering that Mr. McHenry taught very little composition in it and customarily failed half the class.
7. The Whites offered a reward of ten dollars and twenty-five cents $10.25 for the return of King, their Chihuahua.
8. The superintendent's directive began as follows: "All teachers should bear in mind that skills in reading and writting *sic* generally accompany successful social development."

9. My brother, an aspiring chemist, is a good mixer.
10. A good dinner will cost you about ten pesos a dollar and a quarter in our money and an ordinary taxi ride three pesos.

EXERCISE 16

Follow the directions for Exercise 15.

1. "Professor Phoebe was born in Cambridge England, but his formative years were spent in the Far East."
2. William's dog largely spaniel I believe accompanied him on all his walks.
3. The Cannonball I think that's the name of the train thunders into town at three o'clock every morning.
4. Wells once wrote: "The land of my birth he was born in Sadler, near Wichita was romantic and picturesque and full of wonderful history."
5. A male lazuli bunting can be identified by 1 the bright turquoise blue on the head, neck, rump, and tail; 2 the rusty band and sides; and 3 the two white wing bars.
6. The shoes will cost eight dollars and a half $8.50, the socks two dollars and seventy cents $2.70.
7. "Professor White's exploits during World War II were recounted in an earlier issue see January 26, 1958."
8. Anyone who tries to understand molecular activity without first mastering Skreek's *Principia* see Chap. II is wasting his time.
9. Note the remark on page 172: "We camped a day's journey from the Divide actually the Divide was five hundred miles farther west and but for our shortage of food might soon have reached the Columbia."
10. If your information comes from *The Third Degree*, the college daily, it must be correct.

31. ITALICS

In longhand and typewritten copy, certain words and groups of words should be underlined to correspond to the conventions of using italic type. These conventions, however, have never been standardized, and the use of italic type varies widely from publication to publication.

31a-b ITALICS

To a printer, italic type means letters with a slope to the right which look quite unlike the so-called roman type ordinarily used. To a reader, italic type indicates that some word or group of words has been singled out for emphasis or other distinction.

As a careful and thoughtful writer, you are urged to employ italics (underlining) in the specific situations cited below and quotation marks (see Section 27) in other constructions.

31a. UNDERLINE THE FOLLOWING GROUPS AND CLASSES OF WORDS.

1. Titles of books and magazines:
   Barometer Rising, The Return of the Native, Harper's Magazine, True
2. Titles of plays, operas, long poems, and motion pictures:
   Oliver (play), *Carmen* (opera), *The Song of Hiawatha* (long poem), *Born Free* (motion picture)
3. Names of ships, trains, and aircraft:
   the *Empress of Scotland* (ship), the *Rapido* (train), the *Spirit of St. Louis* (aircraft)
4. Names of newspapers:
   Toronto Telegram, The Hamilton Spectator

Some teachers and style manuals suggest not italicizing the name of the city or the definite article in the title of a newspaper: the Montreal *Star;* the Vancouver *Sun.* But the actual title itself is always italicized (underlined).

5. Names of legal cases:
   James Smith v. *Mary Smith* or James Smith *v.* Mary Smith
6. Scientific names:
   Haliacetus leucocephalus (bald eagle), *Felis catus* (an ordinary *cat* to you and me)

31b. UNDERLINE FOREIGN WORDS AND PHRASES.

There is a *je ne sais quoi* quality about this painting.
The foreign student in Canada must work out a *modus vivendi.*

Note that thousands of words and phrases have been so thoroughly absorbed into the English language that they need no longer be italicized. Such words as these can safely be written without italics (underlining):

billet doux	mores	alias
et cetera	en route	matinee
delicatessen	carte blanche	bona fide
hors d'oeuvres	gratis	ex officio
vice versa	sauerkraut	prima facie

31c. UNDERLINE ITEMS FOR SPECIFIC REFERENCE OR EMPHASIS.

Never, under any conditions, keep poisonous substances in your medicine cabinets.

You should *always* sign your name to a letter.

EXERCISE

Exercises on the use of italics and capitals appear at the end of Section 32.

32. CAPITALS

It is impossible to state all the rules for employing capital letters in English. The appearance of capitals is widespread; usage is not fixed and unchanging; exceptions occur for almost every "standard" rule of capitalization. *The Canadian Government Style Manual for Writers and Editors* provides a detailed section on the use of capitals. A helpful reference guide, this manual may be purchased at any Queen's Printer Bookshop.

Despite the confusion which exists about capital letters, the basic principles involved are somewhat clearer than they were at the turn of the century. In general, books, magazines, and especially newspapers are employing fewer and fewer capitals than formerly they did. A glance at a book or newspaper of a century or two ago will clearly indicate this trend.

32a. CAPITALIZE THE FIRST WORD OF EVERY SENTENCE, INCLUDING EVERY QUOTED SENTENCE.

> Are you going to the movies tonight?
> Our teacher said, "Don't miss seeing that movie."

When only a part of a direct quotation is included within a sentence, it is usually not begun with a capital letter:

> The accident victim said that he felt "badly shaken," but he refused hospitalization.

32b. CAPITALIZE PROPER NOUNS.

1. Names of people and titles used for specific persons:
   John Diefenbaker, Sir John A. Macdonald, the Senator, the Secretary, the Prime Minister, Mr. Speaker, Mother, Grandfather, the Major

2. Names of countries, states, regions, localities, other geographic areas, and the like:
   Canada, France, Arizona, the Orient, the Torrid Zone, the Midwest, the Blue Ridge Mountains, the Solid South, Painted Desert, the Kanawha River, Lake Erie

3. Names of streets:
   Seventh Avenue, Bronson Road, Cherry Lane

4. Names of the Deity and personal pronouns referring to Him:
   Jesus Christ, the Almighty, God, Heavenly Father, Jehovah, Him, Thy, His

5. Names for the Bible and other sacred writings:
   Book of Psalms, Bible, Gospels, the Scriptures, the Koran

6. Names of religions and religious groups:
   Roman Catholicism, Episcopalian, Moslem, Protestantism, Unitarian

7. Names of the days and the months (but *not* the seasons):
   Sunday, Monday, etc., January, February, etc.; winter, spring, summer, fall, autumn

8. Names of schools, universities, colleges:
   Leaside High School, York University, Ryerson Polytechnical Institute, Bedford College

9. Names of historic events, eras, and holidays:

Civil War, Cenozoic era, Stone Age, Renaissance, Veterans Day, Yom Kippur
10. Names of races, organizations, and members of each:
Eskimo, Negro, Aryan, University Club, Canadian Legion, New York Mets, an Odd Fellow, a Boy Scout
11. Vivid personifications:
Destiny, the Angel of Death, the New Frontier, the Wheat Province, Star of Fortune
12. Trade names:
Pepsi Cola, Bon Ami, Quisp, Mr. Clean, Frigidaire

32c. CAPITALIZE THE FIRST WORD OF EVERY LINE OF POETRY.

"And we are here as on a darkling plain,
Swept with confused alarms of struggle and flight
Where ignorant armies clash by night." (Matthew Arnold)

32d. CAPITALIZE EACH IMPORTANT WORD IN THE TITLE OF A BOOK, PLAY, MAGAZINE, AND MUSICAL COMPOSITION:

Antony and Cleopatra, The Blue Danube Waltz, Better Homes and Gardens, Man Will Prevail, Ten Modern Masters
NOTE: Do not capitalize prepositions, conjunctions, and articles except at the beginning or end of the title or unless they consist of five or more letters:
The Taming of the Shrew, Caught Between Storms, Mr. Pim Passes By

EXERCISE 17

Copy the following sentences and supply italics and capital letters where necessary.

1. Mallard was delighted to learn that his ancestor, elwood p. suggins, had been a major in the war of 1812.
2. Daisy wrote a brilliant analysis of sophocles' concept of fate in oedipus rex.
3. As Henry finally learned through experience, honi soit qui mal y pense.

4. Nathan Cohen was hired by the toronto star to be one of its critics.

5. Thank you, mr. chairman, for that gracious — if misleading — introduction.

6. Bascum was graduated from powder puff junior college last june.

7. Charles leaves copies of saturday night on the coffee table to impress his guests.

8. Did you observe hardy's use of symbolism in chapter seven of tess of the d'urbervilles?

9. Were you there when the ottawa rough riders defeated the saskatchewan rough riders for the grey cup championship?

10. Nietzsche's concept of zeitgeist has influenced several subsequent authors.

EXERCISE 18

In your notebook or on a separate sheet of paper, underline all words or letters in the following passage which need to be italicized. Write in capitals where necessary.

My great-uncle woody was a spinner of yarns in the true maritime tradition. He kept us spellbound with tales of indians who used to creep through the nearby woods; of the sea captain, a descendant of the acadians, who built uncle woody's house on land granted to the family by governor nicholson; and of the captain's wife, primrose, who kept lonely vigils while her husband plied the atlantic in his ship, fid II. Once I even heard him say to his dog, baron, "come on, baron; it's time to turn in. I'll tell you a bedtime story."

Outside uncle woody's house stood a gigantic walnut tree, some of whose branches, uncle woody told us, supplied the wood for the stocks of many guns during the war of 1812. One day, a man who was interested in trees came to the house and asked uncle woody if he knew anything about the old tree. "Do I know anything about it!" said uncle woody. "Why, I know who planted it." "You do!" exclaimed the stranger, and his eyes grew bright. "Sure, it was planted by a viking about 500 years ago." Wishing to terminate this tête-à-tête quickly, the man murmured a hasty "thanks" and departed. "Hasta luego," shouted uncle woody as the man jumped into his plymouth. Several weeks later the roundabout news, the local weekly paper, carried an account of the tree, describing its location and dimensions, and putting its age at about 300 years. Uncle woody fumed. "Dull, that's what it is," he said. "they should have asked me to write the story. I'd have put some life into it."

There were some who branded woody a liar, but he wasn't. He had a joie de vivre that was refreshing. For him life was exciting, and he tried to make it so for everyone he met. But of course there were some who were not simpatico. Anyway, someday someone should write a book about uncle woody and call it woody the wonderful weaver.

33. ABBREVIATIONS

Abbreviations, shortened forms of words and phrases, help save time and space. In addition, proper use of abbreviations avoids the needless spelling out of often repeated phrases and words, a practice which annoys some readers. Coming across spelled-out items such as "Mister Jones" and "Mistress Adams" would be distracting and bothersome to most modern readers.

As a general rule, spell out all words and phrases which would be puzzling if abbreviated and abbreviate correctly all terms which are frequently encountered and readily understood in shortened form.

33a. USE ONLY ACCEPTABLE ABBREVIATIONS IN FORMAL WRITING.

In the following list, some abbreviations are acceptable in any style of writing, some only in informal writing, and some probably should not be used at all because they may cause confusion. For example, the abbreviations *Mr.* and *Mrs.* are acceptable at all times; the abbreviations *c.* and *ct.* (for cent or cents) are suitable only in informal writing; the abbreviation *civ.* probably should not be used on any occasion since it can stand for civics, civilization, civies (civilian clothes), and civil (as in civil engineer).

Names and titles: Capt., Rev., Ph.D., Mr., Mrs.
School subjects: bot., lit., Fr.
Addresses: Ct., Dr., Pl., St., Ter.
Calendar divisions: Wed., Sept., in the '40's
Measurements: A.M., P.M., in., bu., lb.
Money: $, dol., c., ct.
Geographic names: Alta., St. Catharines, B.C., U.S.A.

33b. USE A PERIOD AFTER MOST ABBREVIATIONS.

The rule stated in Section 21b (to use a period after most abbreviations) is clear and normally should be followed. However, you should note exceptions to this rule, as follows:

Specialized forms: CBC, UNICEF, TV, NATO
Shortened forms: phone, ad, lab, exam
Ordinal numbers: 4th, 6th, 9th
Nicknames: Ben, Ted, Ned, Al
Contractions: can't, aren't, doesn't, wasn't

EXERCISE

Exercises in the use of abbreviations and numbers appear at the end of Section 34.

34. NUMBERS

Since exact and unchanging rules for representing numerals cannot be cited, it is preferable to adopt a general system and to use it consistently. In arriving at a formula which will cover most of your uses of numerals, remember these generally accepted principles:

1. Never begin a sentence with an actual numeral.
2. Use words for numbers between one and ninety-nine.
3. Use figures for words above ninety-nine.
4. When a number can be expressed in not more than two words, write it in words.
5. When a number can be expressed in no less than three words, use figures.

6. Arabic numerals are generally preferable to Roman numerals.

Familiarizing yourself with these six principles, which are usually but not always consistent, will save you much trouble.

34a. USE WORDS TO REPRESENT NUMBERS IN SPECIAL USES.

1. Isolated numbers less than 10:
   We can choose one of five magazines to read.
   At least two students should be chosen for alternates.

2. Indefinite expressions or round numbers (figures are also acceptable, however):
   The mid-twenties was a frantic, mad era in this country.
   We have a hundred cows and six hundred pigs on our farm.
   or
   We have 100 cows and 600 pigs on our farm.
   If he lives to be a million, he will still be a bore.
   This stadium will seat ten thousand people.
   or
   This stadium will seat 10,000 people.

3. One number or related numbers at the beginning of a sentence:
   Three of our class officers are from the Faculty of Engineering.
   Four hundred employees were covered by group insurance.

4. Numbers preceding a compound modifier containing a figure:
   Now we need six ¼-inch strips of canvas.
   Our tent is supported by two 8-foot poles.

5. Fractions standing alone:
   This cardboard is one-eighth inch thick.
   I live about one-fourth of a mile from the school.

34b. FIGURES ARE SOMETIMES USED TO REPRESENT NUMBERS IN SPECIAL CASES.

1. Isolated numbers of 10 or more:
   The amount is 10 times what it was in 1964.
   Only 23 students attended the service at the church.

2. Dates, including the day or the day and the year:
   My birth date was July 21, 1953.
   Please report for work on August 1.

3. House, room, telephone, and postal zone numbers:
   I live at 1607 Ravinia Road, Red Deer, Alberta; my telephone
   number is 532-2784.
   Send your request to 3 Park Street, Toronto 18, Ontario.

4. Highway and comparable numbers:
   On this set we cannot get Channel 3.
   We took Ontario Highway 7 to Buttonville.

5. Measurements:
   The white lines on a football field are 5 yards apart.
   The parcel-post package weighed 5 pounds and 10 ounces.
   The rows were planted 3 feet apart.

6. Time:
   9 A.M., 3:46 P.M., half past 6
   10 o'clock (not 10 o'clock A.M. or 10 o'clock *in the morning.*)
   8 years 3 months 25 days; 3 hours 15 minutes 8 seconds.

7. Percentage:
   The interest rate is 5%.
   10 percent, one-half of 1 percent, 4¼ percent bonds

8. Money:
   $4.55, $0.50, 50 cents, $6 per bushel, 35c apiece

9. Chapters and page numbers:
   Chapter 6, p. 483, pp. 20–32, p. 1654

EXERCISE 19

Copy the following sentences and correct each error which
occurs in the use of numbers and abbreviations.

1. They enjoyed a 3 mos. tour of It. and Fr. but did not get to Ger.
2. The contractor ordered ninety one-inch pieces of weather strip-
   ping.
3. The class pres.'s father, who is a prof at the univ., comes home
   at 4 p.m.
4. That minister has a D.D. degree but prefers to be known as Rev.
5. 4 men on our team had scored 4 points by Jan. 3rd, 1968.
6. The banker says that the bond will mature on 1/15/75.
7. It is my painful duty to report that a large % of the juniors failed
   their tests and will be summarily dismissed.
8. Eighty-six fifty a mo. is too much for an apartment on E. 14th
   Street or even on West End Dr.

9. Geo. and Bill were late that day for their psyc. class.
10. The official address is 1620 Lane Street, Moncton, New Brunswick.

EXERCISE 20

Follow the directions for Exercise 19.

1. Mister Jones and Pres. Jones are brothers, and, coincidentally, each makes twelve thousand three hundred dollars a year.
2. N.Y.C. is large; its central boro is Manhattan, which lies s. of the Bx. and e. of the N. Riv.
3. On Ap. twenty-third, 1949, my parents were married at seventeen Lawn Ter., Sydney, Nova Scotia.
4. R. C. Groggins, our grocer, once remarked that he had trusted people for 47 yrs and never been cheated out of a $.
5. The ratio of profits to sales varied during the decade from 4 to nine percent.
6. When Ellen was 5 and Mike 3½, we took them to the zoo in Stanley Pk. to see the otters.
7. Waterloo is the name of a univ. in the prov. of Ont.
8. That famous speech appears in *Hamlet*, Act III, Scene Two.
9. 873-1046 turned out to be the telephone number of an apt. house in Que.
10. Rev. Gilhooley told my brothers Ed and Wm. that the bazaar will be open until 1:30 a.m.

35. SPELLING

Correct spelling is essential for intelligent communication. It is taken for granted and expected at all times. Yet many people realize their writing sometimes contains spelling errors, and they are embarrassed by doubts and fears about the correct spelling of difficult words. Distraction, confusion, and misunderstanding result from errors in spelling. Therefore, no one should be satisfied with anything less than perfection.

If you really have a desire to learn to spell perfectly you can, provided:

1. You can pronounce such words as *affect* and *effect* so that they will not sound exactly alike.

2. You can look at such words as *avenge* and *revenge* and in a single glance, without moving your eyes, detect the difference between them.

3. You can sign your name without looking at the paper on which you are writing and without even consciously thinking about what you are doing.

4. You can tell your friend Jim from your friend Joe by a mere glance.

5. You can learn a simple rhyme, such as "Jack and Jill went up the hill . . . ."

6. You can remember that a compl*i*ment is "what *I* like to get."

7. You can learn the alphabet, if you do not know it already.

8. You can equip yourself with a reliable desk dictionary.

9. You can learn what a syllable is and proofread your writing syllable by syllable.

10. You have normal intelligence, here defined as the ability to read and write simple English and keep out of the way of speeding automobiles.

If you can honestly meet these ten provisions, you can learn to spell *without ever making a mistake*. If you can pass Number 10 and only three or four of the others, you can still double your spelling efficiency. It's worth trying, isn't it?

The first and most important step in correct spelling is to have the desire to learn, really to want to become a competent speller. The second is to devote the necessary time to learning. The third is to use all available means to learn. If you are chronically and consistently a poor speller, your instructor may recommend a special book which deals solely with spelling problems and provides spelling exercises.

In addition to *desire, time,* and *means,* it should be easy to improve if you habitually do these seven things:

1. Pronounce words correctly.

2. Mentally *see* words as well as hear them.

3. Use a dictionary to fix words in your memory.

4. Use memory devices (mnemonics) to help remember troublesome words.

5. Learn a few spelling rules.

6. Write words carefully in order to avoid errors caused not by ignorance but by carelessness.

7. *List* and *study* the words you most frequently misspell.

35a. PRONOUNCE WORDS CORRECTLY.

As is pointed out in Section 114c, a definite relationship exists between pronunciation and spelling. The former is not an infallible guide to the latter nor the latter to the former. Nevertheless, mispronouncing words usually makes them harder to spell because, for many words, pronunciation is closely connected with spelling. Turn to Section 114c and examine the lists of troublesome words which will be easier to spell if correctly pronounced.

Cultivate the habit of spelling troublesome words aloud, syllable by syllable, writing them, and then spelling them aloud again in order to relate the sound to the spelling.

35b. ACTUALLY SEE WORDS AS WELL AS HEAR THEM.

One method of improving spelling is to look at, or repeat, a word until you really *see* it. Correct pronunciation is helpful to an "ear-minded" person in spelling correctly, but to visualize words is also important. Frequently you say of a word you have written, "That doesn't look right." Many students constantly misspell words because they have never learned to observe a printed page; their errors in spelling come from an unwillingness or apparent inability to *see*. Look at the word alone or in its context, pronounce it, study it, write it, see it with your eyes shut, write it again, see whether it is correct, write it again, pronounce it. This method of studying words until you can *see* them anywhere is particularly valuable when dealing with tricky words which for no apparent reason may drop letters; add or transpose letters; change one or two letters for others; or contain unpronounced letters: *proceed* but *procedure; re-*

peat but *repetition; fire* but *fiery; explain* but *explanation; pronounce* but *pronunciation; curious* but *curiosity; maintain* but *maintenance.*

35c. USE THE DICTIONARY TO HELP IN YOUR SPELLING.

When you are suspicious of the spelling of any word, check its spelling immediately in the dictionary. If you cannot find it, look up and down the column, since a silent letter may be causing the trouble: *aghast* will be there, but not *agast.* If the initial letters confuse you, ask someone for suggestions: you will never find *mnemonics* under *n, philosophy* under *f, pneumonia* under *n, psychology* under *s.*

Knowledge of the etymology (origin, derivation) of a word also helps you to spell correctly. For example, if you know that *preparation* is derived from the prefix *prae* plus *parare* (to make ready), you will not spell the word *prepEration.* If you know that *dormir* is the French word for *sleep* (from Latin *dormitorium*), you will not spell *dormitory* with an *a* for the *i.* Sometimes, too, spelling the simpler or root form of the word helps: *finite, definite, infinite,* not *definate, infinate; relate, relative,* not *relitive; contribute, contribution,* not *contrabution; ridicule, ridiculous,* not *rediculous; please, pleasing, pleasant,* not *plesant.* But watch the tricky words that vary from their roots: *fiery, explanation, curiosity, repetition, pronunciation, procedure, maintenance.*

35d. USE MEMORY DEVICES TO HELP YOU REMEMBER TROUBLESOME WORDS.

One kind of memory device has the rather imposing name of *mnemonics.* The word is pronounced "ne-MON-iks" and comes from a Greek word meaning "to remember." A *mnemonic* is a special aid to memory, a memory "trick" based on what psychologists refer to as "association of ideas," remembering something by associating it with something else. You have been using mnemonics most of your life. The term applies to a basic characteristic of the mind—its tendency to associate the newly learned with the already known.

Any mnemonic is a sort of crutch, something you use until you can automatically spell a given word "without even thinking." But so is a rule a crutch, and, in a different sense, a dictionary is too. In time, you can throw away your spelling crutches except on rare occasions; until then you can use them to avoid staggering and falling.

Here are a few examples of mnemonics. They may not help you because they have no personal association, but they will provide ideas for the manufacture of your own:

> *argument*—I lost an *e* in that *argument*.
> *business*—*Business* is no *sin*.
> *corps*—Don't kill a live body of men with an *e* (corpse).
> *dessert*—Strawberry sundae (two *s*'s).
> *potatoes*—*Potatoes* have eyes and *toes*.

35e. LEARN A FEW SIMPLE RULES FOR SPELLING.

Numerous rules for spelling cover certain words and classes of words, but remember that the words came *first*, the rules *second*. These rules are generalized statements applicable to a fairly large number of words, but not all; consequently, every rule has its exceptions.

For words ending in *able* or *ible*, *ant* or *ent*, *ance* or *ence*, *ise*, *ize*, or *yze*, *tion* or *sion*, and for the addition of *s* or *es* to words ending in *o*, no safe guide exists except memory or constant reference to the dictionary.

The rules which follow, with their corollaries, are easily learned; mastering them will eliminate many recurring errors. Memorizing a simple key word or a common example of each rule can help you both to memorize the rule and to recite it from your example.

1. Words containing *ei* or *ie*.
> Write *i* before *e*
> Except after *c*,
> Or when sounded like *a*
> As in *neighbor* and *weigh*.
> *Either, neither, leisure, seize*
> Are exceptions; watch for these.

This rule or principle applies *only* when the pronunciation of *ei* or *ie* is a long *e* as in *he* or the *a* sound as in *pale*. A memory device for remembering whether the *e* or *i* comes after the *c* or *l* is the key word *Celia* (or *police*, or *lice*). Another memory device: *ie* is the usual spelling when an *r* follows: *cashier, fierce, pier.*

If the sound of *ei* or *ie* is other than long *e* or *a*, the principle does not apply: *conscience, foreign, height, their.*

2. Final *y*.

The basic principle of spelling words ending in *y* is this:

a. Words ending in *y* preceded by a consonant usually change *y* to *i* before any suffix except one beginning with *i* (such as *ing, ish, ist*).

activity, activities	copy, copies, copying
library, libraries	beauty, beautiful
carry, carries, carrying	easy, easier
modify, modified, modifying	lucky, luckily
study, studies, studying	lively, livelihood

b. Words ending in *y* preceded by a vowel do not change *y* to *i* before suffixes or other endings.

day, days	annoy, annoyed, annoying
turkey, turkeys	array, arrayed, arraying
valley, valleys	obey, obeyed, obeying
monkey, monkeys	spray, sprayed, spraying

Important exceptions; *day, daily; lay, laid* (but *allay, allayed*); *pay, paid; say, said; slay, slain.*

3. Doubling final consonant.

One-syllable words and words of more than one syllable accented on the last syllable, when ending in a single consonant (except *x*) preceded by a single vowel, double the consonant before adding an ending which begins with a vowel.

Common endings beginning with a vowel are the following: *ed, es, ing, er, est, able, ible, ance, ence, ish*, and *y*.

admit, admitting	forget, forgettable
refer, referring	man, mannish

Important exceptions: *transferable, transference, gases, gaseous, humbugged, humbugging.*

Note, also, if the accent is shifted to an *earlier* syllable when the ending is added, the final consonant is not doubled: *prefer, preferred,* but *preference; refer, referred,* but *reference.*

4. The "one-plus-one" rule.

When the prefix of a word ends in the same letter with which the main part of the word begins, or when the main part of the word ends in the same letter with which the suffix begins, be sure that both letters are included. Otherwise, do not double the letters.

The same rule applies when two main words are combined, the first ending with the same letter with which the second begins.

dissatisfied	overrun	accidentally
dissimilar	unnoticed	coolly
illiterate	underrate	occasionally
bathhouse	bookkeeping	shirttail
irresponsible	misspell	cruelly
brownness	meanness	suddenness

Exception: *eighteen,* not *eightteen.*

Naturally, three identical consonants or vowels are never written solidly together: cliff-face, not clif*fff*ace; shell-like, not she*lll*ike; still-life, not sti*lll*ife; cross-stitch, not cros*ss*titch; sight-seer, not sight-se*eer.*

5. Final silent *e.*

A final silent *e* is an *e* ending a word but not pronounced; its function is to make the vowel of the syllable long; *rate* (but *rat); mete* (but *met); bite* (but *bit); note* (but *not); cute* (but *cut).*

a. Most words ending in silent *e* drop the *e* before a suffix beginning with a vowel but keep the *e* before a suffix beginning with a consonant.

argue, arguing	ice, icy	safe, safety
arrive, arrival	live, livable	sincere, sincerely
believe, believing	true, truism	sure, surely
come, coming	bare, bareness	tire, tiresome
guide, guidance	hope, hopeless	use, useful

Exceptions: When final silent *e* is preceded by another vowel — except *e* — the final *e* is not retained before a suffix beginning with a consonant: *argue, argument; due, duly; true, truly; agree, agreement.*

b. Words which end *ce* or *ge* retain the *e* when *able* and *ous* are added, in order to prevent giving a hard sound to the *c* or *g:*

marriage, marriageable	change, changeable
notice, noticeable	courage, courageous
service, serviceable	outrage, outrageous

c. The few words ending in *ie* (pronounced like long *i*), in which the *e* is also silent, change *ie* to *y* before *ing*, perhaps to prevent two *i*'s from coming together: die, dying; lie, lying; vie, vying.

d. The silent *e* is retained in the *ing* forms of *dye, singe, swinge,* and *tinge* (*dyeing, singeing, swingeing, tingeing*) to distinguish these words from *dying, singing, swinging,* and *tinging.*

35f. DO NOT CARELESSLY MISSPELL WORDS.

Many spelling errors are caused by carelessness, not ignorance. Studies of long lists of misspelled words from students' themes show that two out of every three spelling errors are the result of sheer carelessness and failure to proofread. The careful student, realizing these facts, will proofread his written work once or twice solely for the purpose of finding misspelled words.

The simple, easy words, not the difficult ones, cause most trouble in careless misspelling. The following words, which probably everyone could spell correctly in a test, are among others frequently misspelled in student papers:

> *acquaint, against, all right, amount, appear, arise, around, basis, before, begin, careless, clothes, coming, consider, decide, extremely, field, finish, laid, likely, lonely, mere, noble, paid, passed, past, piece, prefer, prepare, sense, simple, stories, strict, therefore, those, tries, truly, until, whose, woman*

Do not omit letters, or carelessly transpose letters of words, or write two words as one when they should be written separately.

35g. KEEP A LIST OF THE WORDS YOU MOST FREQUENTLY MISSPELL.

Learning to spell correctly seems a hopeless task because so many thousands of words must be mastered. But no one is expected to be able to spell all words, on demand, and only a comparatively few words are the most persistent trouble-makers. Curiously enough, words like *Mississippi, Tennessee, literature,* and *extracurricular* are not frequently misspelled, even when frequently used; rather, words like *too, all right, it's, its, there, their* most often are the offenders.

Keep a list of words which you misspell and study them, perhaps according to Section 35a, b, c, d, e, until you thoroughly learn their spelling.

According to one estimate, a basic list of only 1,000 words appears in 90 percent of all writing. Several of these words appear on the following list of frequently misspelled words. Your own list of misspelled words may not contain all of the words listed here; the listing is prepared from general experience with school students and should be expanded by you to fit your particular needs.

absence	difficulties	ladies	receive
absurd	dining room	laid	repetition
accepted	disabled	library	replied
across	disagree	lightning	representative
afraid	divide	loneliness	respectfully
all right	doesn't	lying	rhyme
already	during	magazine	riding
altogether	easily	marriage	running
always	eighth	mathematics	safety
amateur	embarrass	meant	seize
among	enemies	messenger	sense
anxiety	excellent	minute	sentence
anxious	exercise	misspelled	separate
apartment	existence	mortgage	shepherd
apparatus	experience	mountain	shining
argument	familiar	muscle	shoulder
arithmetic	fierce	mystery	similar
arrival	fiery	necessary	sincerely
assemblies	foreign	neighbor	speech
audience	forty	neither	strength
awkward	fourth	niece	stretch
beginning	friend	nineteen	strictly
believe	frivolous	ninety	studying
biscuit	fulfilled	ninth	summarize
brief	furniture	oblige	superstitious
business	generally	occasionally	surely
buying	governor	occurred	surprise

cafeteria	grammar	offered	thorough
captain	guard	omission	toward
certain	hammer	opportunity	tragedy
cheerful	handkerchief	paid	tries
chief	heroes	parallel	truly
choose	humorous	partner	twelfth
coming	hurried	peculiar	until
copies	imaginary	perhaps	using
courtesy	immediately	pilgrim	usually
cried	independent	pleasant	village
decide	influence	possession	villain
definite	intellectual	potato	Wednesday
descend	invitation	prison	woman
describe	itself	privilege	women
desirable	jewelry	probably	writer
despair	judgment	pronunciation	writing
destroy	knowledge	realize	written
develop	laboratory	really	yacht

EXERCISE 21

Insert *ei* or *ie* in the following:

1. ach____ve
2. bel____f
3. br____f
4. c____ling
5. conc____t
6. dec____ve
7. for____gn
8. financ____r
9. misch____vous
10. n____ghbor
11. n____ther
12. p____ce
13. perc____ve
14. rec____pt
15. rel____ve
16. rev____w
17. sh____ld
18. shr____k
19. v____l
20. y____ld

EXERCISE 22

Add *-ed* and *-ing* to the following:

1. array
2. copy
3. dally
4. delay
5. pry
6. rally
7. rely
8. deny
9. destroy
10. empty
11. imply
12. reply
13. say
14. stay
15. marry
16. pay
17. pity
18. pray
19. toy
20. try

EXERCISE 23

Add -*ing* and -*ment* to each of the following:

1. abridge
2. acknowledge
3. advise
4. amuse
5. atone
6. argue
7. excite
8. judge
9. move
10. settle

EXERCISE 24

Add -*ed* and either -*able* or -*ible* to the following:

1. avail
2. comprehend
3. depend
4. dismiss
5. excite
6. like
7. presume
8. reverse
9. suggest
10. value

EXERCISE 25

From many verbs nouns may be formed which end in -*ance, -ence; -ar, -or, -er; -ary, -ery*. Examples: *contribute, contributor*. Form a noun from each of the following words:

1. act
2. adhere
3. beg
4. carry
5. collect
6. confer
7. counsel
8. defer
9. defy
10. distill (distil)
11. lecture
12. lie
13. occur
14. prefer
15. protect
16. provide
17. repent
18. station
19. subsist
20. visit

EXERCISE 26

Supply the missing letter in each of the following:

1. appar____nt
2. cors____ge
3. crim____nal
4. def____nite
5. friv____lous
6. gramm____r
7. ignor____nt
8. instruct____r
9. irresist____ble
10. livel____hood
11. nes____le
12. priv____lege
13. p____rsue
14. r____diculous
15. sacr____fice
16. su____prise
17. tra____edy
18. tres____le
19. vulg____r
20. We____nesday

EXERCISE 27

Some of the following words are correctly spelled, some incorrectly. If a word is spelled correctly, write "C" next to its number. If it is misspelled, spell it correctly.

1. atheletic
2. competition
3. desireable
4. discipline
5. dissappointed
6. embarassed
7. environment
8. height
9. mischieveous
10. naturally
11. obstacal
12. occassion
13. outragous
14. perseverance
15. reccommend
16. safty
17. suppress
18. vengeance
19. villain
20. sulphur

EXERCISE 28

Consult your dictionary for the preferred or variant spellings of the following words. Write all variant spellings for each word. Underline the preferred spelling.

1. analyze
2. armor
3. canyon
4. catalogue
5. center
6. defense
7. dialogue
8. esthetic
9. fulfil
10. instalment
11. judgment
12. medieval
13. monologue
14. savior
15. sextet
16. sulphur
17. theatre
18. tranquillity
19. traveler
20. vigor

DICTION

When you enter into a conversation, or write a letter or other composition, you *have* to have something to say and *should* have some interest and purpose in expressing that something, whatever it is. Therefore, you call on your word supply, your vocabulary or stock of words, and select those expressions at your command which will communicate to others as best you can what you have in mind. This process of selecting is called *diction:* the choice of a word, or words, or group of words for the expression of ideas. Thus defined, diction applies to both speaking and writing, although "diction" has further meanings when applied to speech, since it involves voice control, voice expression, and even pronunciation and enunciation. The term *diction* comes from the Latin *dictio*, meaning "saying," "word." The root *dict* is familiar to us in words like *dictate*, *Dictaphone*, *dictator*, and *dictionary*.

Our thinking is done in terms of words, of concepts, and since we can't keep our minds still for long at a time, we are constantly using words in thinking and in attempts to express our thinking. Thinking and diction are inseparable for the very good reason that we cannot think without using words. In a real sense, our thinking can be no better than our word supply. There is an almost complete interdependence of thought and language: Oliver Wendell Holmes, the great jurist, once said, "A word is the skin of a living thought."

36. LEVELS OF DICTION

Diction is the basis of all writing. Since diction clearly indicates what we are and what we wish to say, everyone who puts pen to paper, who even starts to speak, should try to improve his choice and use of words, the basic materials he puts into his compositions. There is a constant challenge in the improvement of diction and you, as a student, have a solid opportunity to meet that challenge.

36a. CHOOSE AN APPROPRIATE LEVEL OF USAGE.

Any rule or prescription concerning word usage *must* bend to considerations of time, place, occasion, and circumstances. Word selection is not rigidly "good" or "standard." A word or phrase in correct or suitable usage twenty years or so ago may now be outmoded. A word appropriate in one section of the country ("localisms") or used before a specialized group of listeners (technical expressions, for example) may not be clear, correct, or effective somewhere else.

Moreover, the use of a given word cannot be justified merely because it frequently appears in print. Occasional examples of poor diction may be found in advertisements, newspapers, magazines, and even well-considered books. Repeated examples in print, several misuses by a famous writer or speaker, or recurrent mispronunciations in a television broadcast do not give a word, an expression, a pronunciation general or universal acceptance. If your aim is *general* appropriateness, use words that are understandable in all sections of the country at the present time, words that are used generally by reputable speakers and writers of the past and present. Correct, clear, effective English, therefore, is that which is in *present, national,* and *reputable* use, and employing such English is, generally, our safest course. In the following pages, present usage is discussed in Section 37, national usage in Section 38, and reputable usage in Sections 39-50, inclusive.

The best guide concerning words in present, national, and reputable usage is an adequate dictionary. A reliable dictionary records. It does not dictate. It labels words and expressions for its users. By being attentive to the information provided in a dictionary (see Section 107), you learn what current practice is and can be directed accordingly.

Avoid *substandard* words and expressions, such as strictly local dialect, ungrammatical expressions, mispronunciations, misspellings, illiterate words, excessive and clumsy use of slang, archaic and obsolete words, and unauthorized newly coined words. Assure yourself in every possible way that your diction is *standard* and is understood over a broad area by cultivated people.

Standard diction may be *formal*, i.e., that used for "very proper occasions" such as the writing of letters of application, and serious friendly letters (like condolence), and the preparation of serious speeches, scientific and technical papers, research papers, and some compositions. Or such diction may be *informal*, often termed *colloquial*, i.e., familiar, conversational, the ordinary writing and speaking of most educated people, as in friendly letters, letters home, amicable exchange of ideas, some forms of discussion, much of your conversation, familiar essays, and some of your compositions. Note that *formal* and *informal* apply to both writing and speaking; note also that there are degrees of *formality* and *informality* in language which, as in dress, depend upon the occasion, but that no rigid lines separate these degrees.

EXERCISE 1

Assume that the standard of word choice is that of careful but not affectedly formal Canadian speech and writing. By such a standard, each of the following sentences contains one or more questionable expressions. On your paper, number each sentence; next to the number write the faulty expression and substitute a word or phrase which would be acceptable.

1. I can't hardly understand why Mr. White never graduated high school.
2. I stayed home from school that morning but attended baseball practice latter in the day.
3. Lug in a chair for Lady Percy, Meadowbrook.
4. The manager's attention was arrested by Fillow's ability to fix up any problem that might arise.
5. Why do you reckon she went that way?
6. But I shall not come except we all can come.
7. Martin was acting in his officious capacity as Justice of the Peace.
8. Daisy is the sort of girl with whom one likes to dance with.
9. I see no favorable factors in your case, so I shall have to answer in the negative.
10. The coroner is now examining the corps.

EXERCISE 2

Follow the directions for Exercise 1.

1. We're liable to meet the football captain at Jerry's party on Saturday.
2. The little boats averaged in length a length of eleven feet.
3. Leave go of her this instant.
4. What do you think you are, a television censure?
5. Adele is terribly beautiful, isn't she?
6. Unfortunately, Mother did not put meat enow in the stew.
7. Riding in his car alone by himself, he repeated her name over again and again.
8. He was caught in the immutable web of fate and never reached the goal of his aims.
9. We didn't know it, but this was an exceptionally unique opportunity.
10. Your investigative paper is not exceptable, Mary.

EXERCISE 3

Follow the directions for Exercise 1.

1. The poor loser always gets it in the neck.
2. Although he ordinarily liked the delectable crustacean, he lifted one of the toothsome morsels in a timorous fashion and devoured it with a rueful grimace.
3. I liked her manner but not the way of speaking.
4. We must push on, Dawson, irregardless of the danger.
5. We worked late into the night because we were truly impelled to solve the problem.
6. She took on when she discovered that her diary was missing.
7. It was sure a delicious supper, was it not?
8. I really resent your illusion, Martha.
9. All hands on deck! In this holocaust of misfortune you must not leave a stone unturned.
10. Let us initiate movement toward the portal.

37. PRESENT USE

Good usage requires that words be intelligible to readers and hearers of the present time. Language is constantly changing; words go out of use or are used less frequently.

New words and phrases take the place of old. Except for somewhat doubtful purposes of humor, it is a good practice to avoid using expressions which, though antiquated, may persist in your vocabulary because you have encountered them in books or reprints of books written generations ago.

Outmoded expressions are of two kinds: the actual words themselves which have disappeared from current English, and, more commonly, certain meanings of words which in other meanings are often and acceptably used. (See illustrations in 37a.)

We can also err by using *neologisms,* recently coined words which have not yet been sanctioned by a substantial number of responsible speakers, writers, and editors. Many such coinages are fresh and bright and may work their way into established usage, but they should be avoided if they are not readily understandable to your readers. Obviously, fresh words connected with new discoveries and new inventions are not necessarily incorrect and may even be essential, but they should be used sparingly and probably should be defined if any possible confusion is likely to arise.

37a. DO NOT USE OBSOLETE WORDS.

An *obsolete* word is one which has completely passed out of use, in form or in one or more of its meanings. An *obsolescent* word is one which is becoming obsolete. Because the status of such words is difficult to ascertain, compilers of dictionaries usually label obsolete or obsolescent words "rare" or "archaic." Indeed, dictionaries vary: one may label a word "obsolete," another label the same word "archaic," and a third use no label at all, indicating that the word is in current use. (Look up *murther* and *stound* in several dictionaries.) Consequently, there is a surprisingly small number of word meanings labeled "obsolete" in a dictionary. Examples:

In form:	*egal* for *equal; gaol* for *jail; infortune* for *misfortune; twifallow* (to plow a second time).
In meaning:	*anon* for *coming; and* for *if; garb* for *personal bearing; hold* for *bear, endure; permit* for *give over, commit; prevent* for *precede.*

37b. AVOID THE USE OF ARCHAIC WORDS.

An *archaic* word is old-fashioned, a word which was once common in earlier speaking and writing. In special contexts, such as legal and Biblical expressions, it may be retained, but it has almost entirely disappeared from ordinary language. Like obsolete words, many words labeled archaic are archaic only in one or two meanings and are in current use in others.

Avoid using archaic words except to achieve some particular effect. Even then, be sure that this effect cannot be secured in any other way. A larger number of words are given the dictionary label "archaic" than that of "obsolete" because archaic words are easier to recognize. Thus: *enow* for *enough; eftsoon (eftsoons)* for *again;* to *glister* for to *glisten; gramercy* for *thank you; methinks* for *it seems to me;* to *jape* for to *jest; lief* for *willing; pease* for *pea; whilom* for *formerly; wight* for *person; bedight* for *array; wot* for *know.*

37c. AVOID THE USE OF POETIC WORDS IN PROSE.

Words which have been usually (or are still occasionally) used in poetry but not in prose are known as *poetic diction.* For more than 150 years, much poetic diction has been imaginative combinations of words rather than of particular isolated words themselves.

"Poetic" words, sometimes so designated in dictionaries, are usually archaic words found in poetry composed in or intended to create the aura of a somewhat remote past. Examples of these are certain contractions such as *'tis, 'twas;* the use of *st, est, th, eth* endings on present-tense verbs: *dost would'st, doth, leadeth;* and words like *'neath, oft, ofttimes* and *ope.*

37d. USE NEOLOGISMS SPARINGLY AND ONLY WHEN THEY ARE APPROPRIATE.

Not all neologisms are contrived and artificial, but the majority are. You are advised not to overuse them, but to employ them when no adequate substitutes of older vintage are available. You can add some interesting coinages to your vocabulary by attentive reading, but do not thoughtlessly add them to your vocabulary and carelessly incorporate them in your papers.

Several well-known columnists and broadcasters repeatedly concoct neologisms. So do many sports commentators and advertising writers. Their productions are frequently colorful, attention-getting, and picturesque, but few of them will likely prove permanently valuable.

New words are coined in various ways. Some are adaptations of common words: *millionheiress*. Some, the so-called portmanteau words, are combinations of common words: *brunch* (*br*eakfast and l*unch*), *smog* (*sm*oke and f*og*). Some are formed from the initial letters of common words: *loran* (*lo*ng *ra*nge *n*avigation), *radar* (*ra*dio *d*etecting *a*nd *r*anging). Some are virtually new formations, like *gobbledygook*, modeled on the meaningless sounds of a turkey's gobble. (See Section 52.) And some are comparatively unknown, despite their creation by eminent speakers and writers: *clouderpuffs* (a sky full of round soft clouds), by Conrad Aiken; *popaganda* (Father's Day), by Edward Anthony; *globilliterate* (one ignorant of world affairs), by Norman Corbin.

Discoveries, new inventions, and occupations inspire new coinages: *A-bomb, rhombatron, realtor, beautician*. Registered tradenames or trademarks are in the same classification: *Dacron, Technicolor, Kodak*. Events, like depressions and wars, create words: *jeep, foxhole, blitz*.

New words which appear in dictionaries may have no label or be labeled "slang" or "colloquial." Some neologisms, like *motel*, change to permanent status and become common words.

EXERCISE 4

From your reading, collect as many examples of archaic, obsolete, or poetic expressions as your teacher directs. A suggestion: read several of the older English or Scottish popular ballads and almost any English literature written before 1800 and not "modernized" in the text from which you are reading.

EXERCISE 5

Read or reread one of Shakespeare's plays. From it, compile a list of archaic and obsolete words containing as many items as your teacher directs.

EXERCISE 6

Bring to class a list of as many neologisms as your teacher suggests. Compile the list from reading several newspaper columnists and a few issues of *Time* magazine and by recording coinages which you hear on television and radio.

38. NATIONAL USE

In our writing, it is important that we use words which are generally understood in all parts of the country. Many of us are unaware that words and phrases which are clear and familiar to us may perhaps be strange to the eyes and ears of people who live elsewhere. Also, idiomatic expressions understandable in one section of the nation may be incomprehensible in another. If you customarily use such expressions as the following, try to "lose" them from your vocabulary, unless some specific stylistic effect requires their use: the localisms *calculate, reckon, figure,* and *guess* (for think or suppose); such semi-technical words as *birdie, switch tacks, eagle, double steal* (except in direct reference to various sports); the Anglicisms *bowler* (for derby), *biscuits* (for cookies), *porridge* (for oatmeal), *bonnet* (for hood of a car).

Confucius declared that if he were made Emperor of China his first act would be to "reestablish the precise meaning of words"—an impossible aim then, and today no less impossible in either the Chinese or the English language. Yet if English is to maintain its role as a world language, its words must have not only national, but international, acceptance. It has been noted that we have, among many varieties, what might be called "Oxford English," "Australian English," and "New York English." The difficulty of worldwide acceptance of word meanings in each is pointed up by the following remark: "I was mad about my flat." In England it means "I really liked my apartment." In Canada it would probably mean "I was angry because I had a punctured tire." *Going great guns* is an expression far more picturesque than "progressing satisfactorily," but its meaning might not be clear in South Africa, Kent, or Tasmania. *Jim-dandy* is more colorful than "excellent," but would it be understood in London, Toronto, and Brisbane, Australia? Few Canadians would understand this notice tacked onto a Pennsylvania door: "Button don't bell. Bump." To those who can translate it, the message is quainter and more vivid than "Please knock because the doorbell is out of order." We should not avoid all localisms, Anglicisms, nationalisms, and semi-technical words, but only those which do not effectively convey what we have in mind.

38a. AVOID INAPPROPRIATE PROVINCIALISMS.

A *localism* is a word or phrase used and understood in a particular section or region. It may also be called a *regionalism* or a *provincialism* (apparently because, formerly, English used in London was "good English"; English used outside London in the "provinces" was not good English but "provincial").

The western, southwestern, southern, and northeastern areas of the United States are especially rich in vivid localisms which add flavor to speech but which may not be instantly understandable in other areas. For a person living in one of these areas, such expressions are difficult to detect, for as a writer or speaker he accepts them as reputable and assumes that they are generally understood, since he himself has known and used them from childhood. Although words and combinations of words used locally may not be explained in print anywhere, dictionaries do label or define many words according to the geographical area where they are common. Examples:

> Western: *grubstake* (supplies or funds furnished a prospector), *rustler* (cattle thief), *dogie, dogy* (motherless calf), *sagebrush* (a flower of the aster family). Southwest: *mesa* (flat-topped rocky hill with steeply sloping sides), *mustang* (small, hardy, half-wild horse), *longhorn* (formerly a variety of cattle),

199

mesquite (spiny tree or shrub), *maverick* (an unbranded animal). South: *butternuts* (a kind of brown overalls), *granny* (a nurse), *lightwood* (pitchy pine wood), *corn pone* (corn bread), *hoecake* (a cake of Indian meal). Northeastern: *down-Easter* (a native of New England, especially of Maine).

Should localisms be used? The only satisfactory answer is appropriateness. If you live in an area or address people in an area where localisms are easily understood, they are appropriate in speaking and in informal writing. But in formal writing for such a geographical area, and in formal and informal speaking and writing to be understandable in other sections, avoid localisms in the interests of clarity. To be generally understood, words and phrases must be in national, not merely sectional, use. For example, it is doubtful that many readers, except in a certain locality, know the meaning of *crick, fress, nibby, a scrounge, spritz,* or *any more* (as in "I get tired any more").

Localisms can also include *dialect*—written or spoken expression used in a limited geographical area, or used by a certain social group in a limited area (like French patois), or used by a certain social group on a more extensive geographical scale, like Scotch dialect.

38b. AVOID INAPPROPRIATE NATIONALISMS.

A further extension of localism is *nationalism,* a term here describing expressions common in or limited to English used by one of the English-speaking nations. *Americanism* and *Anglicism* refer to words or word meanings common, respectively, in the United States and in the British Isles; logically, other labels might be, and undoubtedly are, *Canadianisms, Australianisms, New-Zealandisms,* and *South-Africanisms.* All reliable dictionaries label many expressions *U.S., Chiefly U.S., British, Chiefly British* or *Scotch.* Examples:

> Americanisms: *catchup* (tomato sauce); *tote* (carry, or a load); *levee* (an embankment); *calaboose* (prison, jail); *stump* (travel to electioneer); *bellhop; caboose; gangster; haberdasher; gusher.*

Anglicisms: *accumulator* (storage battery); *tube* (subway); *gaol* (jail); *croft* (small enclosed field); *petrol* (gasoline).

Scotch dialect: *bairn* (child); *canty* (cheerful); *auld* (old); *bree* (broth); *awee* (a little while).

Naturally, the advice to avoid inappropriate nationalisms does not apply to Canadian words and phrases but to those of other English-speaking countries when such words and phrases would not be readily understood in your writing.

EXERCISE 7

Make a list of 10 localisms heard in your community. (If you are not certain they *are* localisms, consult your dictionary. Consult it anyway—and your teacher.)

EXERCISE 8

What are Canadian equivalents for the following Anglicisms? (1) *barrister*, (2) *tram*, (3) *treacle*, (4) *lift*, (5) *wireless*, (6) *stay-in strike*, (7) *hire-purchase system*, (8) *lorry*, (9) *chemist*, (10) *black-coat worker*.

39. REPUTABLE AND APPROPRIATE USAGE

A writer's vocabulary is the *number* of words he can command; a writer's diction is the *kind* of words he uses. As is pointed out at several other places in this book, the first, most important, and fairest test of a word is usage. But usage must be "reputable"; that is, in diction one should follow standards set by that large body of accomplished speakers and writers who we have reason to believe know the language best. These standards rule out a number of words which most of us have in our vocabularies, the kinds of expressions discussed in Sections 37-38 and 41-52.

In an endeavor to use reputable language, you need to "lose" from your speech and writing the kinds of expressions mentioned in the following sections, but in compensating for their loss you may fall into other errors. That is, you may substitute reputable expressions for disreputable ones, but in doing so forget that the *primary* purpose of all writing is communication. In short, reputable usage involves appropriateness and can never overlook the basic aim of actually communicating ideas from writer to reader.

This section is designed to warn against certain errors which may creep in as you "lose" parts of your vocabulary and begin to "use" parts of another.

39a. AVOID AFFECTATION IN CHOOSING WORDS.

Affectation is artificial behavior or manners designed to impress others. An affectation is a mannerism for effect which involves some kind of show or pretense. In language, it is especially evident in pronunciation and in the use of words and expressions not customary or appropriate for the speaker or writer employing them. Getting rid of words and expressions that are not reputable and simultaneously trying to increase the vigor and appeal of one's speech and writing are worthwhile endeavors. Deliberately trying to be different or learned or impressive often results in a reader's misinterpretation, confusion, and annoyance. Pretense is a greater sin against expressive English than even "bad grammar."

For example, a recent magazine article contained this paragraph:

> The opportunity for options in life distinguishes the rich from the poor. Perhaps through better motivation, the upper levels of the poor could be tempted onto the option track. It is important to motivate such people close to the breakthrough level in income because they are closest to getting a foot on the option ladder.

What this writer probably meant was "The more money you have, the more choices you have." He used "reputable" expressions, but he fell into the greater error of affectation.

Be on the lookout for examples of "overly refined" English which you may encounter in your reading and listening. Here is a short list of expressions recently noted in magazine and newspaper articles and stories, together with possible translations into useful English:

> preowned car—secondhand car
> senior citizens—old people
> problem skin—acne
> motion discomfort—nausea
> park under construction—town dump
> extrapolation—educated guess
> sanitary engineer — garbageman
> creative conflict—civil rights demonstration
> custodial engineer—janitor
> finalize—end
> experienced tires—retreads or recaps
> collection correspondent—bill collector
> amenity center — village square or public toilet
> mortical surgeon—undertaker
> cardiovascular accident—stroke
> archivist—library worker
> less-privileged, emerging, less-developed, developing, low-income—backward

39b. AVOID USING VAGUE, ABSTRACT WORDS AND EXPRESSIONS.

Although it is impossible always to use concrete words, be certain you mean exactly what you say in writing such generally vague words as *instance, degree, nature, factor, condition, personality, persuasion, character, quality, case, state, asset,* and *thing.* You will probably never really have to make use of these jargonistic expressions: *along the line of, in regard to, according as to whether,* and *in connection with.*

39c. AVOID USING INDIRECT WORDS AND EXPRESSIONS.

The term *jargon* has several meanings, but applied to writing it means the use of "big" words and of circumlocution (an indirect or roundabout manner of expression). Many jargonish terms are reputable enough, but they are never appropriate and often hinder true communication more than would the use of nonstandard words and expressions.

"Short words are words of might." This observation — wise but no truer than most generalizations — does not imply that long words should never be used; it does suggest that long words are more likely than short ones to be artificial, affected, pretentious, and high-flown. The user of jargon will write "The answer is in the negative" rather than "No." For him, "bad weather" is "unfavorable climatic conditions"; "fire" is "devouring element"; "worked hard" is "pursued his tasks with great diligence"; "a meal" becomes "succulent viands" or "a savory repast"; "food" becomes "comestibles." The jargoneer also employs what has been called "the trick of elegant variation": he may call a spade a spade the first time but will then refer to "an agricultural implement." In a paper on Shakespeare, he will use such variations as "the Bard of Avon," "the darling of Renaissance England," "the incomparable master," and "the meteoric Elizabethan." Many of our most prominent sports figures today receive such jargonish names from sportswriters.

39d. AVOID USING EUPHEMISMS IN ALL WRITING.

Effective writers condemn an oblique way of expressing a supposedly vulgar or uncouth idea. If an idea can be discussed at all — admittedly some topics are in debatable taste — it should be treated directly and forthrightly.

Specifically, a *euphemism* is a softened, bland, totally inoffensive expression used instead of one which may suggest something unpleasant. In avoiding the use of such nonreputable words as "croak," "turn up one's toes to the daisies," "kick the bucket," "go West," and "take the last count," you may be tempted to write "pass away" or "depart this life." Unless religious dictates prevent, use the short, direct word *die*. Other examples of euphemisms to be avoided: *perspire* for *sweat*, *prevaricate* for *lie*, *watery plain* for *sea* or *ocean*, *expectorate* for *spit, mortician* for *undertaker, lowing herd* for *cattle, villatic fowl* for *chicken, separate from school* for *expel, intoxicated* for *drunk, abdomen* for *belly, love child* for *illegitimate, obsequies* for *funeral.*

39e. AIM FOR SIMPLICITY IN DICTION.

By *simplicity* is certainly not meant "writing down" to the reader, thus risking insult to his intelligence or his knowledge. Rather, the word means expressing an idea in terms that are clear, logical, and specifically geared to the level (age, education, etc.) of the persons for whom one is writing. A highly technical subject may demand the use of technical terms—but we should define them without using a tone or method insulting to the reader's intelligence. Moreover, the level of the audience for whom we are writing would dictate how many such terms would be defined and in what detail. If we can choose between a polysyllabic and a short word, we should use whichever is clearer and more precise—usually, but not always, the short word. Short words are often more vivid and sharp than polysyllables and, being crisp and to the point, leave as little doubt as possible in the minds of those who are reading or hearing us. But whether we choose long or short words, diction should be as simple and clear as we can make it so that our ideas will flow smoothly.

In school, you hear and read many words previously unknown to you. Like multitudes of your predecessors, you may be tempted to employ such impressive words in your own speaking and writing, not so much for their use in conveying your ideas as to show others how smart you are, how "educated" you are becoming. Enlarging one's vocabulary and using new words to good purpose are praiseworthy activities, but following either pursuit for reasons of vanity, self-esteem, or "culture climbing" is nonsensical. A great book may be called one in which "the words are for children but the meanings are for men." Simplicity without substance is childish; but great thoughts achieve much of their effectiveness and power through simplicity. No great work of literature, nor great scientific discovery, is deliberately and arbitrarily complex and involved. Such a literary work or important scientific discovery may be beyond our understanding, but it is as simple as it can be and still be what it is.

EXERCISE 9

Rewrite each of the following sentences, correcting flaws in diction.

1. Our cooking class serves a luncheon of succulent viands on the first Tuesday of each month.
2. There should be no evidences of expectoration on this doorstep.
3. He plays along the manner of Bob Dylan but, as regards his singing ability, the answer is in the negative.
4. A penny saved is a copper coin received in compensation.
5. A luminous shape, distinctly discernible to the eye, invaded the darkness of the cave.
6. On the regrettable eventuality of the failure of his deterrence policy, General Flap later made little comment.
7. Not until then was Macbeth ready to seize the knife and clobber the sleeping King.
8. We had a groovy time at the hop last Friday night.
9. In the factory, Sotheby pursued his tasks with great diligence and was soon made foreman.
10. The famous actor stepped onstage to give out with the immortal speech.

EXERCISE 10

Follow the directions for Exercise 9.

1. To be elected was indeed a great honor; I would not have swapped it for a king's ransom.
2. Mr. Bloomer told Sam to change his attitude or be separated from school.
3. In my youth I burned the midnight oil, but today I am content to be a vendor of footgear.
4. In my biology class, we discussed the reasons why feathered bipeds of similar plumage will live communally.
5. At the race track, Tom had been given a bum tip about the winning horse.
6. To prevaricate about your marks is useless, Martin.
7. I will make my plans according as to whether Nancy likes dancing better than going to the movies.

8. Jennifer bought some red flannel underwear to keep her limbs warm.
9. Attending the obsequies may delay my departure.
10. After buying some eats at the delicatessen, they drove to the beach.

40. VOCABULARY GROWTH

Each of us has three vocabularies. First, there is our *active,* or *speaking,* vocabulary, a working supply of words which we use daily in our speaking. Second, there is our *writing* vocabulary, which is also active because we have frequent occasion to draw on it in our writing; some of its words we do not habitually use in our speech. In addition to these two active, or productive, vocabularies, each of us has a *potential,* or *recognition,* vocabulary, which is the largest of the three. By means of this potential vocabulary, we can understand speakers and can read with comprehension books, magazines, and newspapers. Still, in our reading and listening we encounter many words which we recognize and partly understand, possibly from the context, but which we would not be able to use in our own speaking and writing. Until we use such words, however—start them working for *us*—they are not really ours.

Consistent effort is needed to move words from our potential to our active vocabulary. It is, however, the logical way to begin vocabulary improvement, for the good reason that words in a recognition vocabulary, having made some impression on our consciousness, are already partly ours.

A reliable scholar has revealed that even Shakespeare, that master of diction, used fewer than 17,000 words in all his plays. And yet the "average Canadian" knows about 10,000 words—words most commonly appearing in newspapers, general magazines, and everyday speech.

Certain quality magazines—*Harper's Magazine,* the *Atlantic, Saturday Review*—assume that their readers possess the vocabulary of the "average" college graduate: 20,000-

25,000 words. Of course, these words are not always the same. An English major and a premedical student at the time of their graduation are bound to have acquired somewhat different vocabularies.

However, we have learned through a number of careful studies that certain basic words are used most frequently in speaking and writing. One such study, Thorndike and Lorge's *The Teacher's Word Book of 30,000 Words,* contains from 10,000 to 15,000 words that are commonly used. It is reasonable to assume, therefore, that you have a vocabulary of at least this size. With such a base, you can begin to build. Try to master the new words you meet not only because doing so will enhance your reading, writing, and speaking but because a good vocabulary will be increasingly important in your life. Johnson O'Connor, a scientific investigator, has stated:

> An extensive knowledge of the exact meanings of English words accompanies outstanding success in this country more often than any other single characteristic which the Human Engineering Laboratory has been able to isolate and measure.

40a. MAKE FRIENDS WITH YOUR DICTIONARY.

The most important element in vocabulary growth is the *will* to learn, and to learn how to use, new words. But wide reading and intelligent listening should lead straight to a good dictionary.

If in reading you dislike to "break the chain of thought" by looking up words in a dictionary (although the very necessity for using a dictionary has already broken that chain!), jot down unfamiliar words and look them up as soon as possible. Keeping a notebook nearby is a good idea. There are wordbooks on the market which are small enough to be carried around in your pocket or purse and which contain headings such as "meaning," "origin," etc. Set down in such a book the unfamiliar words you come across as you read and look them up later, filling out the entries completely. Be sure, after you have thoroughly studied a new word, to use it in speaking and writing until it is yours. Adding words to one's stock can be fascinating, but there must be a systematic and constant exercise of your *will* to study and use·what you have acquired.

40b. STUDY SYNONYMS AND ANTONYMS.

Collecting lists of synonyms and distinguishing their meanings is an effective, and often entertaining, way to enlarge your vocabulary. Your dictionary, if it is a suitable one, includes listings and often brief discussions of hundreds of synonyms. When looking up a word, carefully study the treatment of those synonym entries which sometimes follow the word's definitions. If you do this, you may be able to choose a more exact and effective word for the occasion at hand and also add a useful word to your active vocabulary. See Section 107.

For example, after becoming aware of synonyms, will you necessarily have to write that the girl is *cute*, the game *thrilling*, the idea *interesting*, the dress *glamorous* or *chic*, the play *exciting?* A study of synonyms for *old* might add to your vocabulary these, among other words: *immemorial*, *aged*, *ancient*, *aboriginal*, *decrepit*, *antique*, *hoary*, *elderly*, *patriarchal*, *venerable*, *passé*, *antiquated*, and *antediluvian*.

Similarly, studying antonyms will improve your understanding and also contribute to vocabulary growth. For example, seeking antonyms for *praise* may add to your vocabulary such words as *vilify*, *stigmatize*, *lampoon*, *abuse*, *censure*, *blame*, *deprecate*, *condemn*, *impugn*, *denigrate*, *disparage*, and *inveigh against*. Even such a simple word as *join* has numerous approximate opposites, among them *uncouple*, *separate*, *sunder*, *unyoke*, *cleave*, *disconnect*, and *dissever*. Not all the antonyms you discover will prove directly useful but all will add to the growth of your own word supply.

40c. STUDY PREFIXES AND SUFFIXES.

Another method of adding to your vocabulary is to make a study of *prefixes* and *suffixes*. A prefix is an element placed *before* a word or root to make another word of different function or meaning: (The prefix *pre* means *before:* pre-Canadian premeditate, premature.) A suffix is an element that is placed *after* a word or root to make a word of different meaning or function: tear*ful*, lis*some*. You can add to your vocabulary by learning the meanings of several prefixes and suffixes. Here is a brief list of the most common:

Prefixes

ante- (before)	antedate anteroom	*il-, im-, in-, ir-* (not)	illiterate illogical immature
anti- (against)	antisocial antiwar		impossible inaccurate indefinite
hyper- (beyond the ordinary)	hypercritical hypersensitive		irreligious irresponsible
		poly- (many)	polygon polysyllable
		post- (after)	postseason postwar

Suffixes

-ful (characterized by or as much as will fill)	beautiful spoonful	*-meter* (measure)	speedometer thermometer
		-polis (city or resident of)	Indianapolis metropolis
-hood (state, condition, character)	childhood falsehood likelihood		cosmopolitan
		-ship (condition, character, skill)	friendship statesmanship
-less (without)	faultless hopeless	*-some* (tendency)	loathsome meddlesome
-ly (like)	saintly womanly		

EXERCISE 11

On your paper write the words in the following list. Then write opposite each word the letter of the group of words in the second column that defines it. Use your dictionary early and often.

1. reciprocity	a.	to set apart for a special purpose
2. amphibious	b.	to make payment for expense or loss
3. arbitration	c.	skillful management to get the better of an opponent
4. allocate	d.	decrease in value through use
5. amortization	e.	property or cash possessed by a company
6. reimburse	f.	mutual exchange
7. strategy	g.	having to do with farm matters
8. agrarian	h.	capable of working on both land and water
9. reparations	i.	an addition to a will
10. depreciation	j.	security pledged for payment of a loan
11. codicil	k.	make easier
12. collateral	l.	become worse
13. facilitate	m.	compensation by a defeated nation for damage after a war
14. dilemma	n.	self-governing, independent
15. autonomous	o.	amount subtracted from a bill for prompt payment or other special reason
16. assets	p.	gradual payment of a debt before the due date
17. curtail	q.	to reduce, diminish
18. deteriorate	r.	a difficult or embarrassing situation
19. discount	s.	contact between persons or groups working together
20. liaison	t.	settling a dispute by discussing and coming to an agreement

EXERCISE 12

Follow the directions for Exercise 11.

1. ambidextrous	a.	a hater of mankind
2. assiduous	b.	haughtily disdainful

3. cacophony	c. cowardly
4. elucidate	d. disgrace or reproach incurred by conduct considered shameful
5. grandiose	e. formal expression of praise
6. innocuous	f. logically unsound
7. invective	g. able to use both hands equally well
8. misanthrope	h. constant in application
9. ostentatious	i. false argument
10. supercilious	j. not harmful
11. vicarious	k. affectedly grand
12. encomium	l. make clear
13. concatenation	m. experienced in place of another
14. abscond	n. having one's identity concealed
15. fallacious	o. harsh sound
16. nebulous	p. to run away to avoid legal process
17. pusillanimous	q. vague, hazy, cloudy
18. sophistry	r. an utterance of violent reproach or accusation
19. incognito	s. state of being linked together
20. opprobrium	t. characterized by show

EXERCISE 13

List the synonyms given in your dictionary (or in a thesaurus) for each of the following words. Prepare for class a written or oral presentation (as your teacher assigns) of the likenesses and differences among the synonyms given for *two* of the words:

1. street	6. defame
2. opposite	7. yield
3. frank	8. magic
4. answer	9. tolerant
5. trite	10. effort

EXERCISE 14

Give one or more antonyms for each of the following. Use your dictionary if you think it will help.

1. professional	6. decrease
2. solicitous	7. grave
3. huge	8. sophisticated
4. repudiate	9. fine
5. dark	10. arrogant

EXERCISE 15

Give the meaning of each of the following prefixes and list five words containing each:

1. *mono-*   6. *micro-*
2. *non-*   7. *auto-*
3. *pseudo-*   8. *sub-*
4. *semi-*   9. *bi-*
5. *over-*   10. *multi-*

EXERCISE 16

Give the meaning of each of the following suffixes and list five words containing each:

1. *-est*   6. *-let*
2. *-able*   7. *-ness*
3. *-ment*   8. *-like*
4. *-graph*   9. *-er*
5. *-ish*   10. *-ine*

41. ILLITERACIES

Illiteracies are words and expressions not accepted in either colloquial or formal language. Characteristic of un-educated speech, they are to be avoided in writing except as quotations of people you are characterizing or, on very rare occasions, for purposes of humor. Illiteracies are not neces-sarily vulgar and are often effective; in fact, poorly educated but deeply sincere persons have produced some eloquent writing and speech.

41a. AVOID USING ILLITERATE WORDS AND PHRASES.

Illiterate words and phrases are also referred to as *vulgar-isms* (the language of the uneducated), or *barbarisms*. The latter word, from the Greek word for "barbarian," was once assigned to foreigners not sharing in Greek civilization;

hence, linguistically, a barbarism is a word or expression not included in the language.

In dictionaries some illiteracies are so labeled, but what may be marked *illiterate* in one dictionary may be termed *dialect* or even *colloquial* in another. Because most dictionaries primarily record "standard" usage, few examples may be recorded. When they are, do not assume that you can use them in your writing simply because they appear in the dictionary; be careful to read the label attached to them. The following words and phrases are examples of those which you should guard against: *acrossed, ain't, anywheres, borned, boughten, brung, disremember, drownded, et* (past of *eat*), *excessible, hisself, I been* or *I done, irregardless, kepted, losted, mistakened, nohow, nowheres, ourn, snuck* (past of *sneak*), *vacationize, youse.* Note that a not uncommon illiteracy consists of an *ed* added to past-participle forms of verbs.

EXERCISE 17

As your teacher directs, prepare a short presentation for written or oral delivery that summarizes what your dictionary informs you about these terms: *vulgarism, solecism, impropriety, illiteracy, barbarism.* If available, use dictionary examples of each.

EXERCISE 18

The following paragraph from John Steinbeck's *The Grapes of Wrath* suitably records the remarks of an uneducated person. From Tom's speech, compile a list of words and expressions that are illiterate and a second list which includes words that are informal, dialectal, or colloquial but not outright illiterate.

Tom broke in irritably, "Well, you ain't never gonna know. Casy tries to tell ya an' you jest ast the same thing over. I seen fellas like you before. You ain't askin' nothin'; you're jus' singin' a kinda song. 'What we comin' to?' You don't wanta know. Country's movin' aroun', goin' places. They's folks dyin' all aroun'. Maybe you'll die pretty soon, but you won't know nothin'. I seen too many fellas like you. You don't want to know nothin'. Just sing yourself to sleep with a song— 'What we comin' to?' . . . I didn't mean to sound off at ya, mister. It's the heat. You ain't got nothin'. Pretty soon you'll be on the road yourse'f. And it ain't tractors'll put you there. It's them pretty yella stations in town. Folks is movin'," he said ashamedly. "An' you'll be movin', mister."

42. IMPROPRIETIES

Improprieties, unlike illiterate words, are standard English words which are misused in function or meaning. In an impropriety, the word itself is acceptable; it is the misuse of that word which causes the error in diction.

42a. AVOID IMPROPRIETIES IN GRAMMATICAL FUNCTION.

One classification of improprieties includes words acceptable as one part of speech but unacceptable as another: nouns improperly substituted for verbs, verbs for nouns, adjectives for nouns, adjectives for adverbs, adverbs for adjectives, prepositions for conjunctions. Another includes misuses of principal parts of verbs. Such improprieties have been aptly called "coined grammar."

A word identified as more than one part of speech may be so used without question, but do not remove a word from one part of speech and place it in another until standard usage has sanctioned this new function. Examples of grammatical improprieties:

Nouns used as verbs:	*grassing* a lawn, *suppering*, to *party*, *ambitioned*, *passengered*
Verbs used as nouns:	*eats*, a *repeat*, a *sell*, *advise*
Adjectives used as adverbs:	dances *good*, *awful* short, etc.
Verb forms:	*come* for *came*, *don't* for *doesn't*, *says* for *said*, *done* for *did*, *hadn't ought*, *set* for *sit*, *of* for *have*

Other combinations: *this here, them there, them kind, being that* or *being as* or *being as how* for *because* or *since, except as* for *unless*

For guidance, consult your dictionary, which labels every word according to the part or parts of speech that it is. Note also the "usage" label: *colloquial, dialect, slang,* etc., since the same word may be acceptable as one part of speech but not as another.

42b. AVOID IMPROPRIETIES IN MEANING.

Another classification of improprieties includes words similar or vaguely similar to other words and used inaccurately or wrongly in their place. Such words include homonyms and homographs. *Homonyms* are two words that have the same or almost the same pronunciation, but are different in meaning, in origin, and, frequently, in spelling; for example, *real* and *reel; made* and *maid; hour, our,* and *are; accept, except. Homographs* are two or more words that have the same spelling but are different in meaning, origin, and perhaps pronunciation. Examples: *slaver* (a dealer in slaves) and *slaver* (drool or drivel); *arms* (parts of the body) and *arms* (weapons); *bat* (club, cudgel) and *bat* (flying rodent). Homographs cannot cause misspelling, but they can cause confusion or ambiguity. Words which are near-homonyms may also cause confusion: *farther* for *further, father* for *further, genial* for *general, stationary* for *stationery, morass* for *morose, loose* for *lose, imminent* for *eminent.*

A man of such distinction is certainly one to *immolate.*
The tennis player *lopped* the ball to the back of the court.
To be an engineer, one has to be able to use a *slight* rule.

Such confusions may result from hearing words inexactly rather than seeing them in print and relating their meaning to their appearance as well as their sound.

EXERCISE 19

Use correctly in sentences 10 of the pairs of words listed in Section 59a.

216

EXERCISE 20

Use correctly in sentences 10 of the pairs of words listed in Section 47a.

EXERCISE 21

From your dictionary, find the answers to the following questions. If the answer is "yes," explain. Can the following words be used as indicated?

(1) *Corp* as the singular of *corps?* (2) *Conjugate* as an adjective? (3) *Pshaw* as a verb? An interjection? (4) *Rose* as a verb? (5) *Holp, holpen* as past tense and past participle, respectively, of *help?* (6) *Contrariwise* as an adjective? (7) *Quarry* as a verb? (8) *Throw* as a noun? (9) *Cool* as a noun? (10) *Complected* as a variant for *complexioned?* (11) *Stratums* as a plural? (12) *Ditto* as a verb? (13) *Quail* as a verb? (14) *Manly* as an adjective? (15) *Wrought* as a past participle of *work?* (16) *Hardy* as a noun? (17) *Sure* as an adverb? (18) *Equal* as a noun? (19) *Mimicry* as a verb? (20) *Appropriate* as an adverb?

43. COLLOQUIALISMS

A *colloquialism* is a conversational word (or group of words) which is fully permissible in an easy, informal style of speaking and writing. Indeed, colloquialisms are often indispensable in ordinary conversation. A colloquialism is *not* an illiteracy and therefore is not "vulgar"; it is *not* incorrect, not in bad taste, and not substandard. Colloquialisms *are* expressions more often used in speech than in writing and are more appropriate in informal than in formal speech and writing.

The origin of the word is Latin *colloquium,* for "conversation," from Latin *col* plus *loqui,* "to speak." Our word *colloquy* means "speaking together," a conversation, a conference; the word *loquacious* means "given to talking, fond of talking." In origin, meaning, and use the term colloquialism is associated more with speech than with writing.

Dictionaries mark words and phrases as colloquial *(Colloq.)* when the editors judge them to be more common in speech than in writing or more suitable in informal than formal discourse. Naturally, quite a large number of words and phrases are so labeled. The label "colloquial" applies to many expressions because informal English has a wide range and because editors differ in interpretations of their findings. Certain contractions, such as *don't, shouldn't, won't,* are acceptable colloquialisms; others, however, such as *'tis, 'twas, 'twere,* should be avoided in even very informal writing.

To put it another way, colloquialisms span a range from high, or just below formal written English, to low, or just above dialect, slang, and illiterate English. Content with the general label "colloquial," dictionary editors make no effort to mark differences. As an experiment, you might think of those differences in terms of "high degree," "middle degree," and "low degree."

43a. USE COLLOQUIALISMS APPROPRIATELY AND EFFECTIVELY.

Because colloquial expressions fall within such a wide range, appropriateness and effectiveness are the best tests for their use. No rigid measure or exact rule directs their use at a given time. It is more advisable to use them and make your writing easy and fluent than to avoid them and make your writing stilted and awkward. In the various kinds of informal English, colloquialisms not only are not objectionable but also are positively desirable for smoothness, clarity, ease, and power of communication. Some words are colloquial in all their meanings; others are colloquial only in one or more of several meanings or combinations. Examples (not attempting, as dictionaries and linguists do, to indicate their comparative ranking):

> *brass tacks* (facts), *cute, shape up, nervy, ad, gumption, phone, hasn't got any, enthuse, angel* (financial backer), *take it, fall for, jinx, moxie, come-on, show up, try and, goner* (a person dead, lost, or in deep trouble), *fizzle* (fail), *flabbergast, flop* (to fail or break down), *root for* (cheer).

EXERCISE 22

From any two pages in your dictionary list the words or word meanings labeled "colloquial" or "informal." What general statement can you make about the words on your list?

EXERCISE 23

What are the colloquial (informal) meanings of the following words and expressions?

> *Burg, mum, numbskull, primp, uppish, fizzle, type, catch* (n.), *rambunctious, middy, highfalutin, lab, bossy, grapevine, fluke, preachify, sleuth, buddy, buck fever, pass the buck, pitch in, freeze out, war horse, small potatoes, yes man, yours truly, square shooter, blue streak, rubber stamp, Dutch treat, salt away, close call, play up to, walking papers, make time, sweet tooth, fill the bill, cut a figure.*

44. SLANG

Slang is a label for a particular kind of colloquialism (see Section 43) or illiteracy (see Section 41).

Characteristics of slang include flippant or eccentric humor; forced, fantastic, or grotesque meanings; novelty; attempts to be colorful, fresh, pungent, and vivid. Such expressions may capture the popular fancy or some segment of it (college slang, musical slang, baseball slang), but in the main they are substandard. Even so, slang may for a while be used over a broad area, and a large number of words and phrases bear the "slang" label in our dictionaries. If such expressions survive, they may in time receive the respectable label "colloquial." Some of the following examples appear in dictionaries with the "slang" label; some may appear there eventually; and some will not appear at all, because their vogue is too short-lived.

Slang expressions appear as one of several forms:

1. Neologisms (newly coined words): *scrumptious, wacky, shyster, mooch, beatnik, razz, oops, sockdologer, ixnay,*

hornswoggle, goofy, payola, scram, nix, teenybopper, pizzaz. Not all newly coined words, however, are slang.

2. Words formed from others by abbreviation or by adding endings to change the part of speech: *VIP* or *V.I.P.* (*Very Important Person*), *psych out, C-note, groovy, snafu* (situation *normal; all fouled up*), *copper, prexy, phony, chintzy, nervy, mod.*

3. Words in otherwise acceptable use given extended meanings: *chicken, grind, corny, guts, lousy, swell, buck, bean, jerk, square, dish, guy, grub, sack, blow, grease, tough, cat.*

4. Words formed by compounding or coalescing two or more words: *hepcat, whodunit, stash* (*st*ore and ca*che*), *egghead, sweedle* (*sw*indle and wh*eedle*), *high-hat, slanguage* (*sl*ang and l*anguage*), *attaboy* (that's the boy), *screwball, slithy* (*sli*my and li*the*), *gogo-girl, fly-boy.*

5. Phrases made up of one or more newly coined words (neologisms) or one or more acceptable ones: *goof off, pork barrel, blow one's top, bum steer, shoot the bull, live it up, get in orbit, cut a rug, in cahoots, on the skids, deadbeat, have a ball, off one's rocker, conk out, jam session, cut out, shoot the works, cool it.*

44a. AVOID SLANG IN FORMAL AND INFORMAL WRITING.

Slang, although popular, has little place in formal writing or even in effective informal writing. Sound reasons exist for guarding against it.

First, many slang words and expressions last for a relatively brief time and then pass out of use, becoming unintelligible to many readers and listeners.

Second, using slang expressions keeps you from searching for the exact words you need to convey your meaning. Many slang expressions are only rubber stamps. To refer to a person as a "swell fellow" or a "lemon" hardly expresses exactly or fully any critical judgment or intelligent description.

Third, slang does not serve the primary aim of writing: conveying a clear message from writer to reader.

Finally, slang is not suitable in most formal or competent informal writing because it is not in keeping with the context. Words should be appropriate to the audience, the occasion, and the subject.

However, some do argue in favor of slang in certain places. It does express feeling, although boisterously and sometimes ludicrously. It also makes effective short cuts in expression and often prevents artificiality in writing. Furthermore, it should be used in recording dialogue to convey the flavor of the speech actually used. But for the reasons already set down, an excessive or injudicious use of slang expressions should be carefully avoided.

EXERCISE 24

As your teacher directs, prepare a brief paper or a short talk for class delivery comparing and contrasting the meanings provided by your dictionary for the following terms: *argot, cant, dialect, patois, jargon, lingo, shoptalk, slang, vernacular.*

EXERCISE 25

Look up in your dictionary the meanings of the following slang words and phrases:

1. sound off	11. kibosh
2. on the make	12. pork barrel
3. shyster	13. high-hat
4. cahoot	14. long green
5. get one's goat	15. goo
6. stool pigeon	16. on the loose
7. sad sack	17. jittery
8. hooey	18. stuffed shirt
9. nix	19. mooch
10. tizzy	20. a yard

EXERCISE 26

Provide a slang meaning for each of the following. (If you cannot, your inability to do so will prove the point made about the short life of slang or that the author is "old hat" — another informal expression which may seem "square" to you but does mean "old-fashioned" or "dated.") Then provide a less informal, more acceptable meaning for each expression. Be prepared to discuss in class whatever connection there may be between the slang meaning and the less informal meaning of each word.

1. pinch	11. salted
2. rat	12. plug
3. oyster	13. noodle
4. stall	14. pony
5. stuff	15. ham
6. applesauce	16. sap
7. pad	17. grind
8. green	18. yellow
9. guy	19. flick
10. flame	20. clod

45. TECHNICAL WORDS

Technical words have special meanings for people in particular fields, occupations, and professions. To such words approximately fifty "special subject labels" are attached by dictionary makers: astronomy, engineering, entomology, psychology, and the like.

Examples of technical words are *cuprous* (chemistry), *sidereal* (astronomy), *broadside* (nautical), *lepidopterous* (zoology), *coniferous* (botany), *stratus* (meteorology). Some have crept into popular use: *telescope* (astronomy), *virtuoso* (music and art), *stereo* (sound reproduction), *analog computer* (electronics).

45a. USE TECHNICAL WORDS APPROPRIATELY.

A specialist writing for specialists uses many technical words. If he is writing for others in the same general field, he will use fewer technical terms, or less difficult ones, and will define the more specialized terms. If he is writing for the nonspecialist and the general reader, he will use no technical terms at all or will at least define the ones he does use.

EXERCISE 27

Make a list of 10 technical words or expressions which you know for one reason or another but which you think may mystify some of your classmates and the general public. Provide definitions for each term listed.

EXERCISE 28

With what sports or games are the following associated? (If you do not know from direct experience, consult your dictionary. Consult it anyhow.)

Clay pigeon, strike, Texas leaguer, rabbit punch, fall, K.O., birdie, love, baby split, half nelson, spare, grand slam, ringer, set point, javelin, ace, chucker, double dribble, lateral pass, double fault, frame, bull's-eye, break, mouse trap, deuce, vulnerable, goalie, bank shot, dash, foul, jibe, broad reach, gate, feather, royal coachman.

EXERCISE 29

In literary criticism, what specialized meanings do these terms have?

Essay, meter, verse, setting, theme, accent, climax, novel, tragic hero, stress, plot, style, fatal flaw, character, octave, antihero, archetype, protagonist, trilogy, point of view, stream of consciousness.

46. IDIOMATIC USAGE

English *idiom* or *idiomatic* English concerns words used mainly in combination with others. Of Greek origin, the word meant "a private citizen, something belonging to a private citizen, personal," and, by extension, something individual and peculiar. Idiomatic expressions, then, conform to no laws or principles describing their formation; each idiomatic expression is a law unto itself. It may violate grammar or logic or both and still be acceptable, because the phrase is familiar, deep-rooted, widely used, and easily understandable — for the native born.

Only a few generalized statements may be made about the many idiomatic expressions in our language. One is that several words combined may lose their literal meaning and express something only remotely suggested by any one word: *birds of a feather, black list, lay up, toe the line, make out, bed of roses, dark horse, heavy hand, open house, read between the lines, no axe to grind, hard row to hoe.*

A second statement we can make about idioms is that the parts of the human body and words expressing activity have suggested many of them: *burn one's fingers, all thumbs, fly in the face of, stand on one's own feet, keep body and soul together, make believe, keep one's eyes open, step on someone's toes, rub elbows with, get one's back up, keep one's chin up.*

A third generalization is that hundreds of idiomatic phrases contain adverbs or prepositions with other parts of speech. No "rule" covers their use; yet certain combinations are acceptable and clear while others are not. Here are some examples (see also Section 46a, just below):

> *walk off, walkover, walk-up; run down, run in, run off, run out; get nowhere, get through, get off*

	to a proposal
agree	*on* a plan
	with a person

	for a principle
contend	*with* a person
	against an obstacle

	with a person
differ	*from* something else
	about or *over* a question

	for something desired
impatient	*with* someone else
	of restraint
	at someone's conduct

	for something done
rewarded	*with* a gift
	by a person

46a. USE ACCEPTABLE IDIOMATIC EXPRESSIONS.

Your usage should conform to the idiomatic word combinations generally acceptable. A good dictionary contains explanations of idiomatic usage following key words which need such explanation, even though dictionaries may differ about some expressions. It is important to consult your dictionary when using certain words, i.e., *prepositions* with nouns, adjectives, or verbs. Examples of idiomatic and unidiomatic expressions containing troublesome prepositions are the following:

Idiomatic	*Unidiomatic*
accord with	accord to
according to	according with
acquaint with	acquaint to
adverse to	adverse against
aim to prove	aim at proving
among themselves	among one another
angry with (a person)	angry at (a person)
as regards	as regards to
authority on	authority about
blame me for it	blame it on me
cannot help talking	cannot help but talk
comply with	comply to
conform to, with	conform in
correspond to (a thing)	correspond with (a thing)
desirous of	desirous to
graduated from (high school)	graduated (high school)
identical with	identical to
in accordance with	in accordance to
in search of	in search for
prefer (one) to (another)	prefer (one) over (another)
prior to	prior than
responsible for (to)	responsible on
superior to	superior than
treat of (a subject)	treat on (a subject)
unequal to	unequal for

Collecting idioms can be an enjoyable pastime. Analyzing their structure and meaning can be even more fun. For example, what can you *make* of these idioms?

make a date, make as if, make-up, make a fool of, make heavy weather of, make out, make off, make-ready, make up, make a meal of, make it, make over, make mincemeat of, make do, make merry, make a fuss, make trouble, make a pass

Or of these?

break one's heart, have one's heart in the right place, wear one's heart on one's sleeve, change of heart, after one's own heart, heart and soul, set one's heart on, eat one's heart out, take to heart, cold hands — warm heart, one's head rules one's heart, sick at heart

EXERCISE 30

Use correct prepositions with each of the following verbs to form common idiomatic combinations:

1. acquaint
2. concentrate
3. wait
4. part
5. center

6. acquiesce
7. engage
8. sympathize
9. listen
10. collide

EXERCISE 31

Use correct prepositions with each of the following adjectives to form common idiomatic expressions:

1. independent
2. unmindful
3. adverse
4. identical
5. sick

6. worthy
7. obedient
8. superior
9. angry
10. peculiar

EXERCISE 32

What is the meaning of each of the following idiomatic expressions? Be prepared to discuss in class the difference between the meaning of the idiomatic expression and the individual words considered separately. *petty cash, gentleman's agreement, square dance, pilot plant, oxygen tent, olive branch, king's evil, second fiddle, scorched earth, automatic pilot, salad days, far cry, oak leaf cluster, day letter, pidgin English, round robin, blue laws, match play, rabbit punch, near miss, list price, flying saucer, walking papers, to the ends of the earth.*

EXERCISE 33

Number your paper from 1 to 20. For each sentence, provide a preposition for the blank space.

1. Do not infer ____ my statements that I dislike you, Ted.
2. She was not desirous ____ running afoul of the law.
3. Nightingales think suet superior ____ seeds.
4. Stanley said he was not averse ____ the idea.
5. Gladys was admitted ____ the principal's office.
6. It is difficult to accommodate ourselves ____ that tight schedule.
7. Sweeney is dependent ____ his big brother for dates.
8. I didn't agree ____ any such thing.
9. Contrast this photograph ____ that one.
10. He will never comply ____ your request.
11. Let's not be unmindful ____ the panthers, Dawson.
12. I think pimento farms are peculiar ____ Tasmania.
13. Students often are apprehensive ____ their grades.
14. His mother grew impatient ____ Carter's experiments.
15. I am not capable ____ controlling that horse.
16. What do you imply ____ your remark?
17. Two hours prior ____ leaving, she opened the letter.
18. The difficulty inheres ____ her method of approach.
19. The six characters were in search ____ an author.
20. Marguerite tried to substitute cleverness ____ valid argument.

47. IMPRECISE DICTION

The exact use of words depends upon *clear thinking*. If an idea is only vague, we are prone to express it vaguely, using the first words that come to mind. But if we know *exactly* what we have in mind, we will search for the word or words which will most accurately and clearly express it to others. For example, let us consider one of the most overworked words in the language, *nice*. We speak of a nice trip, a nice person, a nice day, and so on. The word *nice* carries a somewhat general meaning and cannot be called incorrect, but does it express exactly what we want to convey? Perhaps a trip would be more accurately described as *interesting*, or *comfortable*, or *successful*, or *exciting*, or *eventful*, or *pleas-*

ant, or *exhilarating,* or *inspiring,* or *rewarding,* or *well-organized.* These words are not all synonyms for *nice,* but perhaps one of them might more exactly describe our impression than the now somewhat dull and ineffective *nice.* If we will think carefully, draw on the resources of our vocabularies, and use a dictionary or a thesaurus, we will have no great difficulty in finding the right word for the thought.

Since words stand for ideas in our minds and do not stand *directly* for objects or actions, make sure to distinguish the basic elements in words so that you may use them exactly. These elements are: (a) the word itself, which is merely a sign or symbol; (b) the idea in the mind for which the word stands; (c) the real objects which the idea concerns. Misunderstanding results from not recognizing these distinctions. The word as a sign or symbol is mistaken for the idea or for the real thing, or the idea is mistaken for the real object. Not always are these three elements present, and we must be careful that both the transmitter and the receiver of a given communication understand exactly the sense in which a word is used and the meaning which it has. For example, one of the purported ambitions of the explorer Ponce de Leon was to find the "fountain of youth" which was believed to have magic restorative powers. The words "fountain of youth," then, stood for an *idea;* no such *real* fountain was ever found to exist. The trite expression to indicate disapproval of an action, "That's not my idea of fun," illustrates the separation of the second and third elements mentioned above. The person speaking would, perhaps, call the action "a bore" or "hard work" or something similar.

In order to select the exact word for the context, you must become aware of shades of meaning, of distinctions which clarify the idea to be symbolized by the word. When you wish to describe that characteristic of molasses which, particularly in winter, hampers its swift flow from the jug, will you use *thick, viscous, dense, sticky, adhesive, gluey?* Choose always the word which shows most exactly the meaning you intend. Which is most appropriate and exact for your context: *quarrel, altercation, fight, wrangle, brawl, Donnybrook?*

Sometimes the first word which comes to mind is the most

accurate label for the idea you want to express. More often it is not. Also, bear in mind that a word means to the reader what the reader thinks it means, not necessarily what the writer thinks.

47a. DO NOT MISUSE ONE WORD FOR ANOTHER.

It is easy, through ignorance or carelessness, to use a word which "looks like" the one which should be used or which is somewhat related in meaning. Take your time, think, and consult your dictionary. Thus you will avoid using one word in the following pairs when you should use the other:

advise, inform	ingenious, ingenuous
amount, number	lightening, lightning
beside, besides	loose, lose
capital, capitol	marshal, martial
convince, persuade	moral, morale
desert, dessert	personal, personnel
disinterested, uninterested	precede, proceed
expect, suspect	raise, rise
foreword, forward	respectfully, respectively
genius, genus	stimulant, stimulus

47b. USE PRECISE WORDS.

A number of words or phrases may express a particular idea in at least a general and comprehensible way. But after careful thought, you can usually come up with a word which more *precisely fits*. Is *glad* the most precise word you can use in "I was *glad* to be at the party"? How about *overjoyed, exultant, blissful, ecstatic, entranced, jubilant, gratified?*

47c. AVOID EXCESSIVE EXAGGERATION.

To exaggerate is to misrepresent by overstatement. "I thought I'd die of embarrassment"; "That teacher is ten years older than Noah"; "That is a horrible [or ghastly or frightful] tie you are wearing."

Occasionally, exaggeration may be used to good effect, but it is *never* exact and is not intended to be taken literally. It is more often misleading and ludicrous than it is appropriate and picturesque. Be cautious when using such words as *gigantic, tremendous, wonderful, phenomenal, staggering, thrilling, terrible, gorgeous, horrible, marvelous,* and *overwhelming.* These words, and hundreds more like them, characterize what has unkindly been called "schoolgirl style"—a manner of writing noted for its overuse of intensifiers, its exaggeration, and its gushiness.

EXERCISE 34

Rewrite each of the following sentences, substituting more exact and precise words for any which you consider weak. You may rephrase the sentences if you wish, but do not alter the sense.

1. Information letters can notify the same event to many people.
2. I try to put off eating that horrible old cereal until the last minute.
3. The easiest thing in school is Home Economics.
4. By exercising, I reckoned I could pull my weight down.
5. It was a little funny to Jim not to take Diane to the dance.
6. The study of the theories that are attributed to the many flying-saucer sightings is very interesting.
7. During my first term I gained the girls' hockey club and the Graphic Arts Society.
8. Cousins are a wonderful thing, and I am grateful for having such thoughtful cousins.
9. The problem of finding and keeping kitchen help is another obstacle that must be accounted for by the summer camp.
10. One of the greatest things a parent can teach is respect for elderly people.

EXERCISE 35

Follow the directions for Exercise 34.

1. The most important happening to our school was its founding in 1960 by Octavius C. Silversmith.
2. I shall always remember my father informing me to work a little harder.
3. Our new gym is one of the prettiest in the city.

4. At Commencement everyone is obsessed with a wonderful feeling.
5. It's perfectly splendid that you are trying so hard for the job.
6. There have been many boats at the marina which have used sails from Essex.
7. I have trouble with the proper sequence of subjects in my paragraphs.
8. My buddy told me about his first office job and warned me about doing the same.
9. The library provides a numerous amount of information to help students in their homework assignments.
10. Playing that role was my biggest thrill yet, but an even bigger one was coming.

48. MIXED FIGURES OF SPEECH

A figure of speech is a method of using words out of their literal, or ordinary, sense in order to suggest a picture or image. "He is a saint" and "sleeping like a baby" are illustrations of, respectively, the two most common figures of speech: *metaphor* and *simile*. A *metaphor* is a term applied to something to which it is not literally applicable. Associated with *metaphor* in meaning, a *simile* expresses resemblance directly of one thing to another but does so by using the words *like, as,* or *as if.* "She is *like* a china doll." Figurative language, often vivid and imaginative, can add color and clarity to writing. But it can also result in confusion, distraction, or even amusement.

Found occasionally in prose are the following figures of speech, which, like parts of speech, appear in both writing and speaking. In addition to *metaphor* and *simile,* these include:

1. *Synecdoche:* a figure of association: use of a part or an individual for the whole class or group, or the reverse. Part for whole: "We have fifty *head* of cattle on our farm." Whole for part: "Central defeated Gardner High in the homecoming game"; i.e., the two schools did not play, but their football teams did.

2. *Metonymy:* a figure of association, somewhat like synecdoche: use of the name of one thing for that of another suggested by it. "We all agree that the tailor *sews a fine seam*" (i.e., does good tailoring).

3. *Personification:* giving nonhuman objects the characteristics of a human being: "The waves *murmured*, and the moon *wept* silver tears."

4. *Hyperbole* (note suggestion of *effectiveness* in the definition): "exaggeration, or a statement exaggerated imaginatively, for effect; not to be taken literally." Some similes and metaphors express hyperbole: "The young student, innocent *as a newborn babe*, eagerly accepted the bet." "The sweet music *rose and touched the farthest star*."

Because figurative language is colorful and imaginative, it adds vigor and effectiveness to writing. But do not think of figurative language as a mere ornament of style; do not use it too frequently; do not shift abruptly from figurative to literal language; and bear in mind that a direct, simple statement is usually preferable to a series of figures, always preferable when the figures are artificial, trite, or overly elaborate. Many worn-out similes are trite phrases: *happy as a lark, cool as a cucumber, busy as a bee, mad as a wet hen, quick as a wink, smooth as silk, right as rain, quiet as a mouse, hot as blazes, sleeps like a newborn baby.*

48a. AVOID USING MIXED AND INAPPROPRIATE FIGURES OF SPEECH.

Mixed figures are those in which the images suggested by the words and phrases are obviously unrelated. Similes or metaphors are especially likely to become mixed, through inconsistency, over-elaborateness, and incongruity. Here are examples of mixed and inappropriate figures:

1. After football season many a football player who was a tidal wave on the football field has to put his nose to the grindstone and study.

2. Three of us boys were sure the kingpins on the roost in our high school.

3. At any party there is always a rotten apple that throws a monkey wrench in our food and drink.

4. I hope to get to be a big wheel here at high school, but I don't expect to do much trotting around when I get out.

5. When I graduate, I hope to become a well-oiled cog in the beehive of industry.

EXERCISE 36

Point out any inconsistent figurative language in the following, and rewrite the sentences containing it.

1. Some day we will make a start on pruning the vines of bureaucracy, but we must unite, for there are sharks in these waters.
2. There were four of us in the boat; and when we got to shore that night, we were dead.
3. My brother is always on his toes when he is driving a car.
4. I received many valentines, but Harvey's jealousy put a big dent in my enthusiasm.
5. We are going to have to look the situation in the eye with an open mind.
6. Now that I have learned to organize my time, I have attained a foothold by which I can police myself.
7. The spirit of the student body is keyed to only one goal: to cheer their team on to the championship.
8. When you drive a foreign car, you have your feet firmly on the ground.
9. As dishwasher at the cafeteria, I am literally cut to ribbons every day by the great quantities of knives and forks piled in the sink.
10. He was at that awkward age that whenever he opened his mouth, he put his foot in.

49. TRITENESS (FRESHNESS OF DICTION)

Triteness, sometimes referred to as *clichés* or *hackneyed language*, applies to words and expressions which are worn out from overuse.

The words *triteness, hackneyed,* and *cliché* have illuminating origins: the first comes from the Latin word *tritus*, the past participle of *terere*, meaning "to rub, to wear out"; *hack-*

neyed is derived from the idea of a horse, or carriage, let out for hire, devoted to common use, and therefore worn out in service: *cliché* comes from the French word *clicher*, which means "to stereotype."

Trite language is similar to slang in that both are "stereotyped plates" of thought and expression. Clichés may be stampings from common speech, or overworked quotations, or outworn phrases from newspapers. They spare the writer the burden of expressing exactly what he means, but their use results in stale and ineffective writing. Clichés may seem humorous; indeed, they are often used to express humor or irony. When used seriously, however, they indicate that the writer or speaker is naive.

49a. AVOID THE OVERUSE OF TRITE LANGUAGE.

Trite expressions often are expressive and colorful. If they were not, they would never have become hackneyed. But here are examples of colorful expressions now jaded and stale from overuse:

Similes:

brave as a lion	happy as a lark
brown as a berry	like a blundering idiot
clear as mud	like a duck out of water
cold as ice	like a newborn babe
fight like a tiger	pure as new-drifted snow
free as the air	strong as an ox
gentle as a lamb	trees like sentinels
green as grass	wild as a March hare

Other trite words and phrases:

a must	last but not least
all boils down to	last straw
all in all	leaves little to be desired
along this (that) line	live it up
and things like that	mad dash for
any manner or means	main underlying reason
aroused our curiosity	make the world a better
as a matter of fact	place
battle of life	many and varied

beating around the bush
believe me
bigger and better things
bitter end
bright and early
brings to mind
butterflies in my stomach
by leaps and bounds
center of attraction
chills (shivers) up and
  down my spine
come to life
come into the picture
comfortable living
conspicuous by its
  absence
dear old (high school,
  college, Alma Mater)
depths of despair
doomed to dis-
  appointment
dull thud
each and every
every walk of life
fair land of ours
few and far between
fill the shoes of
first and foremost
fond memories
force of circumstances
get our (their) wires
  crossed
give it a try
give out (up)
goes without saying
grand and glorious
great (guy, job, thrill, etc.)
green with envy
hang one on
hapless victim
honest to goodness
if I had it to do over
important day (time,

year) rolled around
in dire straits
in glowing terms
in the best of health
in the long run
in this day and age
interesting (surprising)
  to note
intestinal fortitude
irony of fate
just around the corner
meets the eye
modern world of today
  (our)
more than pleased
Mother Nature
Nature in all her splendor
necessary evil
never a dull moment
nick of time
nipped in the bud
no fooling
no respecter of persons
no thinking men
none the worse for wear
out of this world
packed in like sardines
pounding like a hammer
proud possessor
psychological moment
race, creed, or color (substitute:
  race, belief, or national origin)
raining cats and dogs
real challenge
really a thrill
rise majestically
sad to relate
sadder but wiser
safe to say
setting the scene
shout it from the housetops
sigh of relief
sight to behold

sit up and take notice	wait with bated breath
suffice it to say	wee small hours of the morning
take a back seat for no one	wends his way
take pen in hand	wide open spaces
the time of my life	with a bang
the worse for wear	with fear and trembling
thing of the past	wonderful (time, day, meal, etc.)
this old world of ours	wonders of Nature
through thick and thin	words fail to express
tired but happy	wunderbar
top it off	you can't take it with you

EXERCISE 37

Prepare a comment (written or oral as your teacher directs) on the meanings given in your dictionary for these terms: *trite, stereotyped, hackneyed, commonplace, banal, cliché, platitudinous, bromidic, corny.*

EXERCISE 38

Substitute more effective expressions for those that you consider trite in the following sentences:

1. After all, one does not have to stay out to the wee small hours of the morning simply because it is New Year's Eve.
2. When I applied for my first job, I must admit that I had butter-flies in my stomach.
3. The movie ended with the hero and heroine driving down the highway, like a ribbon winding over the hills, and into the reddening glow of the setting sun.
4. His marks have improved by leaps and bounds. The main underlying reason for it is that he has worked like a dog.
5. At a ripe old age he died, having lived out his life in the wide open spaces.
6. Last but not least, we have scheduled two concerts for our summer schedule.
7. He spent every penny he earned. He saw no sense in putting money aside for a rainy day when he could have been living it up. After all, you can't take it with you.
8. First and foremost, your dinner was wonderful.
9. I can't wait to see my friends again and taste some of that good old home cooking.
10. Suffice it to say, I think it's wacky to worry in this day and age.

50. "FINE WRITING"

"Fine writing" is anything but fine. It is stilted, artificial, overdignified, pompous, insincere, and flowery. Mistakenly, its authors believe they have freed it of all imperfections because they have purified and elevated it. "Fine writing" is characterized by three main faults: overuse of polysyllabic words, overuse of foreign words and Anglicisms, and the use of too many modifiers.

50a. AVOID "FINE WRITING" BY NOT OVERUSING BIG WORDS.

Big, or *polysyllabic*, words are those of more than three syllables. Two of the longest words in the language are *pneumonoultramicroscopicsilicovolcanokoniosis* and *antidisestablishmentarianism*. The word *bafflegab*, coined by Milton A. Smith, Assistant General Counsel of the U.S. Chamber of Commerce, simply means "overuse of polysyllabic words." His definition he satirically illustrates as follows: "Bafflegab —multiloquence characterized by consummate interfusion of circumlocution or periphrasis, inscrutability, incognizability, and other familiar manifestations of abstruse expatiation commonly utilized for promulgations implementing procrustean determinations by governmental bodies."

To avoid this kind of "fine writing," choose the short word instead of the long, if it will serve as well. Short words are usually more understandable, more sincere, and less self-conscious than their polysyllabic counterparts.

50b. AVOID OVERUSING FOREIGN WORDS.

An inexperienced writer, impressed by the seriousness of his purpose and attempting to project it through a pompous style of writing, often makes the mistake of interlarding his work with Anglicisms (British expressions rather than Canadian) or foreign expressions such as these: *à bon marché, à propos de rien, chef d'oeuvre, magnum opus, exempli gratia, robe-de-chambre, dum vivimus vivamus, garçon, morceau, petrol* for *gasoline, perambulator* or *pram* for *baby carriage, lift* for *elevator, barrister* and *solicitor* for *lawyer* (see Section 38).

50c. AVOID THE OVERUSE OF MODIFIERS.

Use necessary words to give your reader a clear, full understanding of your meaning; however, avoid piling on descriptive words for their own sake or for false impressiveness. Be intelligent rather than lavish in your use of adjectives and adverbs. Descriptive writing is particularly liable to be "fine writing":

> A penetratingly loud and constantly insistent buzzer sounded, waking me out of a blissfully pleasant and dream-free sleep. As I rose slowly and regretfully to dress, I could see through the gracefully flowing and swaying open draperies that colorful, Jack-Frost-touched autumn had begun its annual artistic change of dress. The trees with long, yearning, outstretched branches shook violently and fearfully as the caressing gusts of wind nudged their multicolored overcoats of green, brown, red, and yellow.

EXERCISE 39

Following are three statements, as reported by the Associated Press, concerning a promotion refusal. Which is the least and which is the most effective? Why?

1. Verbal contact with Mr. Blank regarding the attached notification of promotion has elicited the attached representations intimating that he prefers to decline the assignment.
2. I have spoken to Mr. Blank about this promotion; he does not wish to accept the post offered.
3. Blank doesn't want the job.

EXERCISE 40

Rewrite this paragraph in simple language:

> Friday at high noon Miss Gloriana Sims-Slocum, the lovely youngest daughter of Mr. and Mrs. Spencer Sims-Slocum, was

given in marriage to her darkly handsome college classmate, Mr. Charles Partridge. The breathtaking, radiant bride was bedecked in shimmering ivory satin decorated with old Alençon lace of surpassing delicacy. Her hands, of sandalwood-fanstick fragility, clasped a white prayer book, symbol of purity, from which cascaded graceful lilies of the valley. As the exquisite bride proceeded toward the sanctum sanctorum, she was followed in close order by three stunning bridesmaids wearing soft pink taffeta. The moving, tender strains of "Oh, Promise Me" were presented by the famous and talented organist, Rudi Apfelbaum.

EXERCISE 41

Sometimes a renowned writer may be accused of "fine writing." In the following paragraph from *The Return of the Native,* do you think Thomas Hardy should be accused of or defended from the charge of "fine writing"?

That night was an eventful one to Eustacia's brain, and one which she hardly ever forgot. She dreamt a dream; and few human beings, from Nebuchadnezzar to the Swaffham tinker, ever dreamed a more remarkable one. Such an elaborately developed, perplexing, exciting dream was certainly never dreamed by a girl in Eustacia's situation before. It had as many ramifications as the Cretan labyrinth, as many fluctuations as the Northern Lights, as much colour as a parterre in June, and was as crowded with figures as a coronation. To Queen Scheherazade the dream might have seemed not far removed from commonplace; and to a girl just returned from all the courts of Europe it might have seemed not more than interesting. But amid the circumstances of Eustacia's life it was as wonderful as a dream could be.

51. EUPHONY

The term *euphony* means "agreeableness of sound," that is, a sound pleasing to the ear. The antonym of euphony is *cacophony,* which means "harsh, ugly sound." Say aloud several times each of these words, euphony and cacophony, and notice how well the words illustrate their definitions.

51a. AVOID AWKWARD AND HARSH COMBINATIONS OF SOUNDS.

Euphony is a largely negative quality in prose; euphonious writing *avoids* unpleasant sounds such as sibilants and gutturals (*flak, clack, hiss, miss, gutter, gaseous,* etc.). It also avoids the overuse of *alliteration* (using in the same sentence or in close succession two or more words beginning with the same sound), as is illustrated in such phrases as "pockets filled with pebbles" and "lean and lithe." Euphonious prose also rarely contains rhyme (the similarity of sound in vowels and consonants) as, for example, in such pairs as "sound, found," "fair, wear," and "trouble, bubble."

51b. AVOID OVERUSE OF THE SAME OR SIMILAR-SOUNDING WORDS.

Overuse of the same or similar-sounding words distracts a hearer's attention and, subconsciously or half-consciously, also distracts the reader. Avoid the following:

1. Overuse of *homographs:* words of the same spelling but of different origin and meaning.

They played a sprightly air from *My Fair Lady* which filled the air with light-hearted melody.

My gossipy aunt's remarks bored me, but I bore with them until she began to bore into my private affairs.

2. Overuse of *homonyms:* words with the same pronunciation but different in origin, meaning, and, very often, spelling.

I wanted to sew a new dress which would resemble Lydia's, but I did not want to sow seeds of bitterness between us.

3. Overuse of a series of words having endings which are alike or nearly alike.

It is forbidden that a horse be ridden after having eaten a given amount of barley and oats.

4. Ending a sentence with a word or phrase and beginning the next sentence with the same word or phrase or nearly the same phrase.

If I go to Europe, I must learn to do without a lot of spare cash this coming Spring term. Doing without a lot of spare cash this Spring term promises to challenge my resourcefulness.

EXERCISE 42

Which of these words are pleasing to your ear? Which are harsh-sounding? *Nevermore, luxuriant, cranberry, shrimp, cuspidor, roundelay, verdant, cacophony, parsnips, lyrical, carcass, murmuring, fisticuffs, lullaby, tintinnabulation, clackety-clack, jazz, autocratic, sap, technocracy, diaphanous, spinach, panic-stricken.*

52. GOBBLEDYGOOK

Gobbledygook (or *gobbledegook)* is a special kind of "fine writing" or jargon; that is, it is wordy, inflated, obscure, and often unintelligible verbiage. The term was coined by a former United States congressman, grown weary of involved government reports, who possibly had in mind the throaty sounds uttered by a male turkey.

The term *gobbledygook* is increasingly being applied to governmental and bureaucratic announcements which have been called "masterpieces of complexity." For example, note this pompous and complex sentence from a recent governmental bureau pamphlet: "Endemic insect populations cause little-realized amounts of damage to forage and timber." This stuffy sentence probably means: "Native insects do more damage to trees and grass than we realize." In another pronouncement, "the chance of war" was referred to, in gobbledygook, as "in the regrettable eventuality of a failure of the deterrence policy."

52a. AVOID THE USE OF GOBBLEDYGOOK.

The use of gobbledygook is not confined to bureaucratic circles, either within or without federal and provincial governments. But pompous and involved language is so prevalent in those areas that two further illustrations may be cited. A recent announcement about Junior Conservation Corps Camps reads as follows:

Section 103 authorizes the Director of the Office of Economic Opportunity to:

(a) enter into agreement with any Federal, State, or local agency or private organization for the establishment and operation, in rural and urban areas, of conservation camps and training centers, and for the provision of necessary facilities and services, including agreements with agencies charged with the responsibility of conserving, developing, and managing the public natural resources of the nation and with protecting the public recreational areas, whereby the Corps enrollees may be utilized by such agencies in carrying out, under the immediate supervision of such agencies, programs planned by such agencies to carry out such responsibilities.

What the writer presumably meant to say in plain English, not gobbledygook, is:

Section 103 authorizes the OEO Director to:

(a) make agreements with any government agency or private group to set up and operate JCC camps and training centers; and make agreements with conservation agencies to use and supervise Corps enrollees on projects these agencies have on public lands.

A plumber, an often-told story goes, wrote to inform an agency of the United States government that he had found hydrochloric acid good for cleaning out pipes. Some bureaucrat responded with this gobbledygook: "The efficiency of hydrochloric acid is indisputable, but the corrosive residue is incompatible with metallic permanence." The plumber responded that he was glad the agency agreed. After several more gobbledygookish letters, an official finally wrote what he should have originally: "Don't use hydrochloric acid. It eats the inside out of pipes."

A recent commentator has suggested that the first duty of schools is to be so soft-minded that children no longer "flunk." Instead, they "experience a temporary lack of success in the daily learning situation." And here is a quotation from a financial adviser concerning shares of stock: "Overall, the underlying pattern, notwithstanding periods of consolidation, remains suggestive of at least further selective improvement over the foreseeable future." Possibly the writer meant to say: "Selected stocks will increase in price." How would you phrase it?

If you are fully aware of gobbledygook and avoid using it at any time, you can have fun by turning good, direct English into wordy, jargonish utterances, a project called for in Exercise 43 at the end of this section. Possibly realizing how absurd gobbledygook is will insure your never using it. Who, for instance, would prefer "Too great a number of culinary assistants may impair the flavor of the consomme" to "Too many cooks spoil the broth"? If you can, laugh at the gobbledygook artist who turned "Birds of a feather flock together" into "Feathered bipeds of similar plumage will live gregariously." Why not try your own hand at turning familiar sayings into gobbledygook?

EXERCISE 43

Rewrite the following sentences in plain, understandable language.

1. You should manufacture desiccated alfalfa during solarized incandescence.
2. A fact is a statement of an empirically verifiable phenomenon within a conceptual scheme.
3. The capital of the Papal States was not constructed during a diurnal revolution of the globe.
4. It has come to our attention that herbage, when observed in that section of enclosed ground being the property of an individual other than oneself, is ever of a more verdant hue.
5. Seeking a suitable place for the purpose of courting a state of dormant quiescence during the first part of the crepuscular period and forsaking said suitable place during the first part of the matinal period results in myriad benefits to *homo sapiens*, among which benefits may be noted a substantial increase in body soundness, monies, and sagacity.

EXERCISE 44

Follow the instructions for Exercise 43.

Much of an organization's effectiveness depends upon the adequacy of the data and information with which its employees work. The multifarious overlapping planning units have produced fragmented data, oriented toward single uses of land, and as these data were used by employees organized into single use office groupings, the problem was exacerbated.

53. FAULTY REPETITION

Effective repetition of entire words and phrases occasionally can be pleasing and useful. We often take pleasure in rediscovering the familiar. In some music, our pleasure comes from a repeated theme. Note how much repetition of both sound (alliteration, assonance) and word add to this beautiful and pleasing passage:

> Vanity of vanities, saith the Preacher; vanity of vanities; all is vanity. What profit hath man of all his labor wherein he laboreth under the sun? One generation goeth, and another generation cometh; but the earth abideth forever. The sun also ariseth, and the sun goeth down, and hasteth to its place where it ariseth. The wind goeth toward the south and turneth about unto the north; it turneth about continually in its course, and the wind returneth again to its circuits. All the rivers run into the sea, yet the sea is not full; unto the place whither the rivers go, thither they go again. All things are full of weariness; man cannot utter it; the eye is not satisfied with seeing, nor the ear filled with hearing. That which hath been is that which shall be; and that which hath been done is that which shall be done: and there is no new thing under the sun.
>
> —Ecclesiastes, 1:2-9

None of us can hope to rival the majestic sound and meaning of this repetitive passage, but at least we can try to avoid faulty and useless repetition which merely annoys or bores our readers.

53a. AVOID THE OVERUSE OF FAVORITE WORDS.

High school classes and homework provide an excellent opportunity for discovering and learning to use words previously unknown. (See Section 40.) In your delight with a new word, you may wish to use it over and over, to the eventual irritation of those who have to listen to you or read what you write. For example, one student discovered the word *nugatory* and used it twelve times in one short composition. It is a good and useful word, and the student objected to his teacher's pointing out that overuse, not use, of "nugatory" reduced its effectiveness. In rewriting his paper, he also used such approximate synonyms as *trifling, worthless, insignificant, frivolous, ineffective, of no real value, trivial,* and *useless* without impairing his idea—and without boring his reader. Almost everyone has a tendency to seize upon some word—a reputable term or a neologism or a slang term—and work it to exhaustion. You probably have your own favorite words and expressions.

53b. AVOID REPETITION OF TOPIC SENTENCES.

The flaw of meaningless, useless repetition of a topic sentence within a paragraph is mentioned also in Section 82d. But the error is so common that it deserves additional mention. Even if you use different words, repetition which adds nothing new is merely thought going around in circles. Aimless repetition of an idea in the same or different words, phrases, or sentences is called *tautology*. Note the inadequacy of this repetitious (tautological) paragraph:

> Some people pay too much attention to their diet. They spend hours every day wondering if they should eat this or that. They are too concerned about their digestive processes. One would think their greatest concern was low-calorie food, and their talk shows that it is. Diet is not nearly so important as these people think it is; it's the amount they eat. Paying so much attention to diet does not warrant so much concern. They just pay too much attention to it.

53c. AVOID OVERUSE OF THE SAME WORD OR PHRASE IN CLOSE SUCCESSION.

This form of repetition is also mentioned in another connection in Section 51b, but it, too, is such a common fault that it requires further comment. The following sentences illustrate repetition which is faulty because of a lack of ideas, or carelessness, or both:

> My coming to college was made possible by some money which was made possible by a job I had last summer.

> His solution involved public support of a mass transit system to move large masses of people.

245

Crop rotation, used on many farms, is the use of a plan by which various fields vary in their crops each successive year.

Organized charitable organizations carry on charitable work in my community.

EXERCISE 45

Rewrite the following sentences, correcting faulty repetition.

1. The ducks were flying well and they were decoying to my decoys.
2. I had never eaten turnips until the summer of 1966. During the summer of 1966, I paid a short visit to an aunt and uncle of mine, and they gave me turnips to eat.
3. The most important decision is deciding what should be one's aim in life.
4. All students in college are required to take placement tests. These placement tests are for the purpose of determining what classes, regular or advanced, the students should be placed in.
5. My final statement relates to a relationship that I have with a relative.
6. After buying our tickets, we came to another waiting line. This line was formed inside the auditorium to await the start of the next show.
7. I got my homework done and got the car out and got off to school.
8. To give you some idea of where I live, I will use the use of Highway 7.
9. I did not enjoy jet flights as much as I enjoyed them in past years, and I enjoyed watching my sister on her first jet flight.
10. I made a B on yesterday's exam. That was my French exam, and that gives me a B average for the year.

54. EMPHATIC DICTION

A word or phrase can be correct and clear and yet be without force, vigor, and strength. Genuinely effective writing and speaking are positive, even dynamic. These qualities depend upon diction more than upon any other single element in speech or written composition.

54a. PREFER CONCRETE TO ABSTRACT WORDS.

An *abstract* word gives no clear picture; it is often a general word. A *concrete* word expresses something tangible, something usually discernible by at least one of the senses: *roses, tap dance, serrated, clove-scented, aquamarine, soft.* Some fine examples of concrete words are onomatopoetic words, words which express or suggest sounds: *crackle, hoot, rustling, murmuring, meow, hiss, singsong, roar, staccato.*

Specific and concrete nouns, colorful and vigorous adjectives and adverbs, verbs which describe action (motion) or relate to the senses (emotion), specific and concrete phrases—all these give force to our writing.

So emphatic and focused is the diction of the following passage that the reader, without the help of further details, can form a satisfactory picture of Ichabod Crane:

> The cognomen of Crane was not inapplicable to his person. He was tall, but exceedingly lank, with narrow shoulders, long arms and legs, hands that dangled a mile out of his sleeves, feet that might have served for shovels, and his whole frame most loosely hung together. His head was small, and flat at the top, with huge ears, large green glassy eyes, and a long snip nose, so that it looked like a weathercock perched upon his spindle neck to tell which way the wind blew. To see him striding along the profile of a hill on a windy day, with his clothes bagging and fluttering about him, one might have mistaken him for the genius of Famine descending upon the earth or some scarecrow eloped from a cornfield.
>
> —Washington Irving, "The Legend of Sleepy Hollow"

54b. PREFER SPECIFIC TO GENERAL WORDS.

Emphatic diction uses expressive nouns, adjectives, verbs, and adverbs. A *general* word names a broad concept: class names of nouns (*flower, food, car*), conventional verbs (*say, come, put*), and vague adjectives and adverbs (*nice, slow, bad, gladly*). Especially dull diction results from overuse of the forms of *to be* (*is, am, are, was, were,* etc.).

A *specific* word names a narrow concept—*lilac, spaghetti, jeep, shout, swoop, cram, captivating, inching, excruciating, jubilantly.* Each of these could be narrowed still further.

Of the following two sentences, why is the second one more emphatic?

There was an old boat moving through the heavy sea.

Like a lady wrestler among thieves, the tanker *Isobel Ann* lunged into each massive green wave and, with a grunt of ancient rage, flung the Arctic-spawned monster over her scaling, brown shoulder.

Other general words are so vague and indefinite that they only approximate an idea. The following ineffective words and phrases can surely be replaced with more specific words: *item, element, case, phase, asset, condition, situation, instance, feature, factor, cute, nature, interesting, quality, nice, persuasion, degree, lot, personality, state, job, thing, along the line of, in respect to, with regard to, according as to whether, in the case of, sort of, on this account.*

Vague and indefinite: a nice person
the time factor
thing used for any idea or object, as "another thing about it"

Specific: a cordial person
timing
another characteristic

EXERCISE 46

With the aid of your dictionary, substitute words or phrases which seem more emphatic (concrete and specific) for the underlined parts of the following phrases. Example: Walking from the room — stalking, trudging, slinking, ambling.

1. a <u>pleasant</u> party
2. a shabby <u>structure</u>
3. a <u>short</u> man
4. a <u>blunt</u> instrument
5. a <u>bright</u> girl

6. he <u>laughed</u> strangely
7. a <u>bad</u> boy
8. a <u>grand</u> day
9. a <u>terrible</u> assignment
10. an <u>anxious</u> moment

EXERCISE 47

Follow the instructions for Exercise 46.

1. a good <u>picture</u>
2. he <u>went</u> home
3. a blunt <u>instrument</u>
4. a <u>sad</u> face
5. a <u>fine</u> thing

6. in the <u>automobile</u>
7. to <u>go</u> away
8. a fine <u>situation</u>
9. a <u>funny</u> lecture
10. a <u>poor</u> cake

55. DENOTATION

The exact, literal meaning of a word is referred to as its *denotation*. Another way of defining the term is to say that denotation means the association that a word or expression usually calls forth for most speakers, writers, and readers of a language as distinguished from those elicited for any individual speaker, writer, or reader because of personal experience. The denotation of *wind* is "air in natural motion," although the word may have individualized, particularized meanings for persons recalling their own experiences with wind. "Labrador retriever" is the denotation of a certain breed of dog, a term generally agreed upon and understood by all users of the English language. "Home" has a denotative meaning of "fixed dwelling place," "house," or "apartment."

55a. USE ONLY DENOTATIVE WORDS WHEN THEY ARE APPROPRIATE.

Denotative words express merely what the definitions say; they are clear and are to be taken in their literal, explicit meaning for neither more nor less than what they say: *wind, Labrador retriever, home, city, man, clothes.*

In writing exposition and argument, you should try to use words as exact, as specific, and as literal in meaning as possible. Clearness should be the basic guiding principle. In all forms of writing, however, even in exposition and argument, it is impossible always to avoid words that express more than their literal meanings. (This problem is treated in Sections 57 and 113.) But we should make the attempt to avoid associated meanings for words unless, of course, we are deliberately trying to appeal to the emotions of readers.

Assume that you see a small four-footed animal on the street and refer to it as a "dog." If your purpose in using the word is to refer to the animal in reasonably exact terminology, you have succeeded in applying a denotative term which is plain, straightforward, and objective. But suppose that one grandparent of the dog was a fox terrier, another was a bulldog, the third was an Irish terrier, and the fourth was a collie. You can denotatively express these facts by referring to the animal you see as "a dog of mixed breed." Here you have continued to use objective phrasing. But if your purpose is to speak exactly and clearly, it would be unwise to call the dog a "mongrel." True, this last term means the same as a dog "of mixed breed," but it is likely to arouse mingled feelings of approval or disapproval toward that dog. In short, when appropriate to do so, use words that do not suggest associated meanings and that do not suggest or imply emotional meanings.

Can you think of other words besides "mongrel" which have either favorable or unfavorable associated meanings?

For further comment on this problem in diction, see Sections 56, 57, and 113.

EXERCISES

See exercises on denotation and connotation at the end of Section 56.

56. CONNOTATION

Nearly all words mean more than they seem to mean; they have associated meanings, a surrounding fringe of suggestive, or connotative, values. The bare, literal meaning of a word is its *denotation*. The *connotation* of a word is the suggestions and associations which attach to its periphery. For example, a dictionary definition of the word *gold* is "A precious yellow metal, highly malleable and ductile, and free from liability to rust." This is its denotation. But with *gold* have long been associated color, riches, power, happiness, evil, unhappiness. Around the core of meaning which the dictionary definition gives are associations, suggestions, implications. These connotations are not always present, but one should be aware of this implicative power in words.

56a. OCCASIONALLY USE WORDS AND PHRASES WHICH PAINT A PICTURE.

We sometimes fail to create with words a feeling which surpasses the power of accepted, denotative meanings. We fail to suggest meanings and associations which will appeal to the experience of our readers. To use words both exactly and effectively, it is necessary to understand their connotations as well as their denotations. Although you must necessarily be cautious in their use, you are urged to avail yourself of the associative powers which nearly all words possess. Only when we wish to express something with literal accuracy do we rely wholly upon the standards set by dictionary definitions.

A writer's obligation is to convey sensible comments clearly. But good writers search for words which suggest more than they say, which stimulate the reader's imagination. These words, having connotative values, suggest associated meanings: *baby sister,* not *girl; enigma,* not *problem; home,* not *house; breechloader,* not *gun; mother,* not *woman.* By exact, or *denotative,* definition, a horse is "a large, solid-hoofed, herbivorous mammal," but to anyone who has ever owned, loved, and cared for a horse, the word suggests many associated meanings. New Orleans is "an industrial and trade center," but its name suggests such images as "Crescent City," "Old French Quarter," "Mardi Gras," "Sugar Bowl," "Mid-Winter Sports Carnival," and "Dixieland Jazz."

Use your imagination in writing, but try not to let it get out of hand. A profusion of connotative words in one short theme will render it less effective.

EXERCISE 48 (Exercises for Sections 55, 56.)

Distinguish carefully the words in the following groups of synonyms or related words:

1. Car, automobile, jalopy, limousine.
2. Dishonor, disgrace, ignominy, shame.
3. Race, folk, people, population, inhabitants.
4. Wealthy, affluent, rich, opulent.
5. School, academy, institute, college, university.
6. Love, affection, friendship, lust, devotion.
7. Fat, portly, stout, obese, corpulent.

8. Goodness, honesty, decency, piety, integrity.
9. Smell, smell bad, reek, stink.
10. Inebriated, intoxicated, tipsy, besotted, crocked.

EXERCISE 49

Do Exercise 36 at the end of Section 113.

EXERCISE 50

For each of the following, provide a word or phrase with about the same denotation but a different connotation. Example: "scholar" for "pedant."

1. sophistication
2. amorous
3. hick
4. eccentric
5. egghead

6. cynic
7. politician
8. mossback
9. beatnik
10. fun-loving

57. EMOTIONAL MEANINGS OF WORDS

All good writers avail themselves of the suggestive power of words, but connotative values are intricate and must be watched carefully.

57a. DISTINGUISH BETWEEN THE OBJECTIVE AND EMOTIONAL MEANINGS OF WORDS AND PHRASES.

As is elsewhere pointed out (in Sections 55, 56, and 113), many words which carry objective meanings also contain powerful suggestions of emotional attitudes. Such words are particularly common in discussing controversial subjects like morals, religion, politics, and human relations. For instance, a well-known saying is that the adjective *firm* can be explained as follows: "I am *firm*, you are *obstinate*, he is *pigheaded*." *Firm, obstinate,* and *pigheaded* have approximately the same denotation, but "firm" conveys an emotional tone, or attitude, of strong approval; "obstinate" suggests mild disapproval; "pigheaded" involves strong disapproval and even distaste and disgust.

Writers of advertising are extraordinarily skillful in using emotionally charged words. The slogan "Pure as the tear that falls upon a sister's grave" pretended, as one writer has pointed out, to describe the quality of an advertised wine. Read literally, the remark is far from complimentary, but the writer was trying to secure a sentimental, buying response to the words "pure," "tear," and "sister."

Many "value" words *are* descriptive, but it is easy to use them carelessly or to employ them with a specific but unfair design. The point is not to refrain from using such words but to use them carefully, thoughtfully, and only in appropriate situations. It is impossible to use only language which neutrally expresses verifiable facts, but we should guard against arousing, directing, or controlling emotions unless we know precisely what we are up to and why we are writing as we are. Even then, we should not forget that both reason and morality ought to enter into our choice of words and their meanings.

EXERCISE 51

For the underlined words in the following phrases substitute words or phrases which convey stronger attitudes of approval.

1. so-and-so's boorishness
2. swilling his coffee
3. a garrulous companion
4. shrewd in his dealings
5. a government spy
6. to speak arrogantly
7. so-and-so's stupidity
8. rather pleasant
9. the children who were flogged
10. a silly girl

EXERCISE 52

For the underlined words in the following phrases substitute words or phrases which convey stronger attitudes of disapproval.

1. the odor of onions
2. a convivial weekend
3. a famous gate-crasher
4. to be excluded
5. careful with his money
6. a corpulent man
7. a precise speaker
8. a strict parent
9. liberal with his money
10. a tolerant attitude

58. CONCISENESS

To be truly effective, diction must be economical. Writing should not be sketchy, nor should necessary words be omitted, but wordiness weakens the force and appeal of expression.

In Shakespeare's *Hamlet,* old Polonius announces:

> Therefore, since brevity is the soul of wit,
> And tediousness the limbs and outward flourishes,
> I will be brief.

Polonius was actually a garrulous, tiresome man but, more importantly, notice that he was not saying that brevity is the soul, the center and heart, of humor. In this context, "wit" means "understanding" or "wisdom." That is, being brief and to the point is the only way effectively to express genuine thought. Conciseness alone does not guarantee good writing, but it is difficult, even impossible, to write forcefully when using three or four words where one would be sufficient. Lincoln's Gettysburg Address contains only 267 words. The Ten Commandments are expressed in 75 words. The Golden Rule contains 11 words.

58a. DO NOT USE TWO OR MORE WORDS WHERE ONE WILL SERVE.

The moral of "few words for many" is in the following: To the simple question of whether rules should be observed, an administrator wrote, "The implementation of sanctions will inevitably eventuate in subsequent repercussions." What he might have said, simply, was "Yes."

Wordy: The teacher stood *in front of* the class.
Concise: The teacher stood *before* the class.

Wordy: Give your instructions *very precisely and carefully*.
Concise: Give *precise* instructions.

Wordy: My flare-up of anger was *due to the fact that* I was fatigued.
Concise: My flare-up of anger was *due to* fatigue.

Other suggestions:

Reduce these	to these
I would appreciate it if	please
in case	if
a certain length of time	a certain time
under date of May 4	of May 4
in the month of June	in June
it has come to our attention that	(begin with the word following *that*)
it is interesting to note that	(begin with the word following *that*)
am, is, are going to	shall, will
before long	soon
in the event that	if
in lieu of	instead
at the present time	now
in so far as	because, since, as
for the amount of	for
on condition that	if
in regard to	about
inasmuch as	since
are of the opinion	believe
in accordance with	by

58b. AVOID OVERUSE OF *THERE IS, THERE ARE, THERE WAS,* ETC.

Usually such "there" beginnings are superfluous words, adding nothing. Occasionally they may be effective, as in "there are four genders in English," and you will find them used by many writers. But each time you see such a beginning, determine whether the writer could have used a more concise way of expressing his ideas.

Wordy: *There were* ten lead soldiers broken in half.
Concise: Ten lead soldiers were broken in half.

Wordy: In the bakery *there are* many cakes awaiting your selection.
Concise: In the bakery, many cakes await your selection.

Wordy: In our apartment building *there* live ten families.
Concise: In our apartment building live ten families.

58c. AVOID ADDING WORDS TO AN IDEA ALREADY EXPRESSED.

When meaning is expressed or implied in a particular word or phrase, repeating the idea by additional words is useless. One word of two or three expresses the idea, and the other words add nothing. Common examples are using *again* with many verbs beginning with *re;* using *more* or *most* with absolute-meaning adjectives; and using *more* or *most* with adjectives and adverbs already ending in *er, est.*

from whence	recur again
separate out	round in form
repeat again	necessary need
more better	first beginnings
long length	each and every one
endorse on the back	cooperate together
completely unanimous	fellow classmates
Christmas Eve evening	more perfect
rise up	resume again
sunset in the west	meet up with
most perpendicular	consensus of opinion
more paramount	return back
connect up with	many in number
loquacious talker	visible to the eye
audible to the ear	final end
more older	revert back
most unkindest	call up on the telephone
descend down	reduce down
individual person	choose up
join together	cover over
complete monopoly	bisect in two
this afternoon at 3 P.M.	back up
this morning at 9 A.M.	around about dinnertime
most unique	extreme prime importance
necessary essential	talented genius

EXERCISE 53

Apply principles of conciseness to the following sentences:

1. There were only about one-third of our platoon who made it back.
2. There should be greater emphasis placed on our tutoring program.

3. Saturdays are the only days I am able to have the car.
4. When I ask for a raise in my allowance, Dad's answer is usually in the negative.
5. In the event that I make the honor roll, I plan to have a party.
6. Some people are resentful with regard to the way the dues have been raised.
7. The story was basically dreary, and it was plain to see that the author had tried to enliven it.
8. I had hoped to become a good student in the field of mathematics.
9. It was at midnight that I awoke to a most astounding sight.
10. It was after the 1966 drought that my father dug himself another well.

EXERCISE 54

Follow the instructions for Exercise 53.

1. In case I am offered the opportunity, I may fly to Winnipeg.
2. We heard that stores would remain open a longer length of time during the Christmas season.
3. I have always shied away from the field of mechanical engineering.
4. About 20 miles north of Gravenhurst is a camp called Rockwood; this is my summer camp.
5. It has been called to my attention by the Secretary that a Board of Directors meeting has been scheduled for June 8.
6. I do not feel the necessity for a conference at the present time.
7. Upon arriving at the Bar-X Ranch, we were assigned horses for the pack trip into the hills.
8. There is still a great deal to be explained in the area of flying saucers.
9. I would like to take this opportunity to introduce myself.
10. I endorsed on the back of a cheque for $10 which my aunt had sent me for expenses.

59. WORDS OFTEN CONFUSED

As is pointed out in Section 47, it is all too easy to use a word which resembles another in some way but actually is chosen because of ignorance, confusion, or carelessness.

59a. DO NOT CONFUSE ONE WORD WITH ANOTHER.

In addition to the list of "confusing pairs" given in Section 47, watch out for the following, which are merely a sampling of the many words in English that can and do cause trouble:

Ability, capacity. *Ability* means the power to do something, mental or physical (*"ability* to manage an office"). *Capacity* is the ability to hold, contain, or absorb ("a suitcase filled to *capacity"*).

Accept, except. *Accept* means "to receive" or "to say yes to"; *except* means "to exclude" or "to exempt." ("I *accept* the terms of this contract." "Jim was *excepted* from the general invitation.") As a preposition, *except* means "other than." ("No one *except* me knew the combination.")

Affect, effect. *Affect,* as a verb, means "to assume," or "to influence." ("Her voice *affected* me strangely.") *Effect,* as a verb, means "to cause"; as a noun, it means "result." ("Being captain *effected* a change in his attitude." "The decision had a profound *effect* on labor relations.")

Among, between. The former indicates a relationship of more than two objects; *between* refers to only two, or to more than two when each object is considered in relation to the others. ("The land was divided *among* seven farmers." "The rivalry *between* Joe and Sam is intense." "Trade *between* nations is desirable.")

Complement, compliment. *Complement* means something which completes. ("This hat will *complement* your wardrobe.") A *compliment* is a flattering comment. ("When she remarked that he was handsome, Ted thanked her for the *compliment."*)

Continual, continuous. In some uses, these words are synonymous. A subtle distinction is that *continual* implies "a close recurrence in time," in "rapid succession"; *continuous* implies "without interruption." ("I objected most to my sisters' *continual* quarreling." "The *continuous* dripping of water from that leaky faucet unnerved me.")

Council, counsel. *Council* means "an assembly," "a group." ("A *council* of labor leaders voted on the proposal.") *Counsel* is both a noun and a verb and means "advice" or "to advise." (" 'Work hard and save your money' is indeed wise *counsel*." "Our minister will *counsel* me whenever problems arise.")

Emigrate, immigrate. The former means "to leave"; the latter means "to enter." ("Our foreman *emigrated* from Russia in 1918." "In the future, a greater number of people from the Latin countries will *immigrate* to Canada.")

Envelop, envelope. The verb *en-vel′ op* (accent on second syllable) means "to cover," "to wrap." ("Fog will soon *envelop* the island.") *En′vel-ope* (accent on first syllable) is a noun meaning "a covering." ("Your invoice is contained in this *envelope*.")

Farther, further. These are interchangeable; however, some writers prefer *farther* to indicate "space," "a measurable distance," and *further* to indicate "greater in quantity, degree, or time," and also "moreover," "in addition to." ("I drove eight miles *farther*." "Let us give the matter *further* consideration.")

Formally, formerly. The first word means "in a formal manner," "precisely," "ceremonially." The latter means "in the past." ("The artist was *formally* introduced to the President." "I was *formerly* treasurer of my class.")

Fort, forte. *Fort* means an "enclosed place," a "fortified building." *Forte* means "special accomplishment or ability." ("The old *fort* has been turned into a museum." "I am not a golfer; tennis is my *forte*.")

Gourmand, gourmet. These words have to do with eating, but they are different in meaning. A *gourmand* is a large eater. ("Teen-age boys are notorious *gourmands*.") A *gourmet* is a fastidious eater, an epicure. ("Les Chevaliers du Tastevin is an association of well-known *gourmets*.")

Hang, hung. The principal parts of *hang* are *hang, hung, hung*. However, when the word refers to the death penalty, the parts are *hang, hanged, hanged*. ("The pictures are *hung*." "The cattle rustler was *hanged*.")

Healthful, healthy. These words are often used interchangeably, but *healthful* precisely means "conducive to health"; *healthy* means "possessing health." In other words, places and foods are *healthful,* people and animals are *healthy.* ("An athlete must be a *healthy* person because of his *healthful* daily workouts.")

Human, humane. The term *human* refers to a person. Some particularly precise writers and speakers do not use the word alone to refer to man as man; they say or write "human being." However, use of the word alone as a noun has a long and respectable background. *Humane* means "tender," "merciful," "considerate." ("The general insisted upon *humane* treatment of all prisoners.")

Impractical, impracticable. Distinctions in the meanings of these words have broken down somewhat, but the former means "speculative" or "theoretical." *Impracticable* means "not capable of being used," "unmanageable." ("His plan is *impractical* and his instructions are *impracticable.*")

Jealous, zealous. The former means "resentful" or "envious"; idiom decrees that *jealous* should be followed by *of,* not *for.* ("Ingrid is *jealous* of Margaret's ring.") *Zealous* means "diligent," "devoted." ("They were *zealous* workers on behalf of their candidate.")

Later, latter. The spelling of these words is often confused. They also have different meanings. *Later* refers to time. ("The train arrived five minutes *later* than usual.") For *latter,* see *Former, latter,* Section 60.

Lead, led. These words show the confusion that our language suffers because of using different symbols to represent one sound. *Lead* (pronounced *lēd)* is the present tense of the verb and causes little or no difficulty. *Led* (pronounced like the name of the metal) is the past tense and is often misspelled with *ea.* ("*Lead* the horse around the paddock." "He *led* the horse around the paddock yesterday.")

Least, lest. The former means "smallest," "slightest." The latter means "for fear that." ("It was the very *least* I could do." "Close the door *lest* our secret be overheard.")

Leave, let. Both words are common in several idiomatic expressions implying permission, but *let* is standard whereas *leave* is not. (*"Let* [not leave] me help you wash the dishes."*)

Loan, lend. Many careful writers and speakers use *loan* only as a noun ("to make a *loan*") and *lend* as a verb ("to *lend* money"). Because of constant and widespread usage, *loan* is now considered a legitimate verb to be avoided only in strictly formal English.

Luxuriant, luxurious. The former term refers to abundant growth; *luxurious* pertains to luxury. ("The blooms in her garden were *luxuriant*." "Silk curtains gave the simple room a *luxurious* touch.")

Maybe, may be. The first means "perhaps." (*"Maybe* I will go bowling today.") *May be* (two words) is used to express possibility. ("There *may be* some food in the refrigerator.")

Most, almost. *Most* is the superlative of *many* and *much* and means "greatest in amount, quality, or degree." *Almost* indicates "very nearly," "all but." *Most* is colloquial when used for *almost*. ("He has *almost* [not most] come to a decision.")

O, oh. The former is usually part of a vocative (direct address), is normally capitalized, and is rarely followed by any mark of punctuation. *Oh* is an interjection, may be followed by a comma or exclamation point, and is capitalized according to the usual rules. (*"O* Dawson! Stop your clowning." "Yet, *oh*, what a happy ending!" *"Oh*, what gorgeous eyes!")

Passed, past. The first word is the past tense of the verb *to pass;* in its use as a verb, the latter is the past participle. ("He *passed* quietly by the open doorway." "The years of struggle are now *past*.") *Pass* is not only a verb; it is also a noun. In one or the other of these two categories, it appears in many expressions which are either colloquial or slangy, among them *pass the buck, make a pass at, a pretty pass, pass up, pass out.*

Principal, principle. *Principal* is a noun indicating "sum of money" or "a chief person," and an adjective meaning "chief" or "main." *Principle* is a noun only, meaning "a rule of conduct," "a doctrine," "a governing rule or truth." ("Both *principals* endorsed the request for funds, less for the the money itself than for the *principles* which were involved.")

Quiet, quit, quite. *Quiet* means "still" or "calm." ("Later, at a *quiet* meeting in the board room, he announced his resignation.") *Quit* means "to stop," "to desist." ("He *quit* his complaining.") *Quite* means "positively," "entirely." ("You are *quite* sure of your facts?")

Rabbit, rarebit. A *rabbit* is a rodent of the hare family. In standard English there is no such word as *rarebit*. It frequently appears in the phrase *Welsh rarebit* (a dish of melted cheese on toast) but only because of faulty etymology; the correct phrase is *Welsh rabbit*. However, *rare* and *bit* can be correctly used as two words. ("I have a *rare bit* of inside information for you: Tesoro Oil Corporation is going to double in price.")

Rang, wrung. *Rang* is the past tense of the verb *ring*, meaning "to give forth a sound." ("I *rang* the bell and then entered.") *Wrung* is the past tense of the verb *wring*, "to press or squeeze." (I *wrung* the water from my socks.")

Regard, regards. The latter is used with *as* to mean "consider" or "think." ("He *regards* me as a sister.") *In regard to* and *with regard to* are idiomatically sound, but both phrases are wordy and jargonistic. In these same phrases, *regards* is nonstandard. Limit your use of *regards* to the plural form of the noun *regard* and the singular form of the verb. ("Please give your aunt my *regards*.")

Sensual, sensuous. The first refers to gratification of the more gross bodily pleasures or appetites. *Sensuous* suggests the appeal of that which is pleasing to the senses. ("The movie served no purpose other than to arouse *sensual* desires." "The velvet had a *sensuous* softness.")

Stationary, stationery. The former means "having a fixed or unmoving position." ("Prices remained stationary for six months.") *Stationery* means "paper for writing." ("My name and address are printed on my *stationery*.")

Statue, stature, statute. A *statue* is a sculptured likeness. ("A *statue* of Jacques Cartier may be found in the park.") *Stature* is often used figuratively. ("He has great political *stature.*") A *statute* is a law. ("This *statute* is un-enforceable and should be stricken from the book.")

Tasteful, tasty. The former means "having or showing good taste, sense, or judgment." *Tasty* means "flavorful," "savory," "having the quality of tasting good." ("She made a *tasteful* arrangement of linen, china, and silverware. It was her *tasty* casserole of veal, however, that won first prize.") *Tasteful* for *tasty* is in rare or archaic use; *tasty* for *tasteful* is colloquial.

Then, than. These words are often confused in writing and sometimes in pronunciation. *Than* is a conjunction used in clauses of comparison. ("I made a better score *than* Harvey did.") *Then* is an adverb of time. ("You may *then* proceed to clean up.")

To, too, two. Correct use of these words is largely a matter of careful spelling. *To* is a preposition ("*to* the gate") and the sign of an infinitive ("*to* hurry"). *Too* is an adverb meaning "also" or "overabundance of." ("I *too* am impressed, but Mary is *too* sophisticated *to* show surprise.") *Two* is the number after one. ("The *two* soldiers were *too* exhausted *to* run.")

Unmoral, amoral, immoral. *Unmoral* means "having no morality," "non-moral," "unable to distinguish right from wrong." Thus we may say that an infant or a mentally disordered person is *unmoral. Amoral* means "not concerned with moral standards," "not to be judged by criteria or standards of morality." Morons and animals for example, may be called *amoral. Immoral* means "wicked," "contrary to accepted principles of right and wrong." The acts of thieves, murderers, and embezzlers may be called *immoral.*

Unpractical, impractical, impracticable. The first two of these terms are interchangeable, although *impractical* is considered slightly more formal and refined. Each means "not practical," "lacking practical usefulness or wisdom." *Impracticable* means "not capable of being carried out, used, or managed." ("It is *impractical* to suggest that a boy be sent on a man's errand." "Because of the high wind, our leaf-raking methods were *impracticable.*") (See *Impractical, impracticable.*)

60. GLOSSARY OF MISUSED WORDS

The following glossary, alphabetically arranged for easy reference, contains words and expressions often misused. The list, not all-inclusive, is a capsule discussion of some of the most common violations of good usage. If the material given below does not apply to your problem, if you want more detailed information, or if you do not find listed the word or phrase you are seeking, consult your dictionary.

A few of these expressions are always to be avoided, but many are unacceptable only in formal English. Apply the advice of Section 36 as you interpret the comments provided for these words and phrases. Remember especially that no stigma attaches to the label "colloquial"; it indicates that a given expression is generally more appropriate in conversation and in informal discourse than it is in formal writing.

Usage is so constantly changing that expressions now restricted in some way may later be considered standard. Furthermore, because no dictionary or grammar is a final authority, some usages are disputed. Probably no two linguists would agree on all the comments which follow. But this illustrative list should be serviceable as a starter; to it you may add from time to time other words and expressions.

A, an. *An* should be used before an initial vowel sound, *a* before a word which begins with a consonant sound: *an* answer, *a* battery; *an* honor, *a* hotel.

Absolutely. This word means "perfectly," "wholly," "completely." Besides being greatly overused as an intensifier, it is both wordy and faulty in an expression such as "*absolutely* complete." Never use *absolutely* or any other such modifier with words like *complete, perfect, unique.* (See *Unique.*)

Accidently. This "word" is an illiteracy. The word should be *accidentally.*

Ad. A colloquial abbreviation, much used, for *advertisement.* In strictly formal writing, avoid such abbreviations as *ad, auto* for *automobile, phone* for *telephone, exam* for *examination.*

Ad lib. This verb, meaning "to improvise," "to extemporize," is both overused and colloquial. It is derived from the Latin phrase *ad libitum*, meaning "at pleasure," and is appropriately used in music to mean "freely." Avoid using *ad lib* to mean adding words and gestures not in the script or not intended to be said or otherwise expressed.

Advise. This word, meaning "to counsel," "to give advice to," is overused in business letters and other forms of communication for "tell," "inform." ("I am pleased to *inform* [not *advise*] you that the check has been received.")

Ain't. This contraction is considered illiterate, dialectal, or colloquial and is cautioned against in standard English, both written and spoken. The word, which stands for *am not,* is often informally used even by educated people, but it has not been accepted in the sense that *isn't* (for *is not), aren't* (for *are not),* and *weren't* (for *were not*) have been.

Alibi. Used colloquially to mean "an excuse or any kind of defense," the word precisely and correctly should be used to mean "a plea or fact of having been elsewhere when an offense was committed." *Alibi* is often used in the loose sense mentioned above and is now a trite and jaded expression.

All right, alright. The former expression is correct but has been overworked to mean "satisfactory" or "very well." *Alright* is analogous to *altogether* and *already* (both standard words) but is not yet an acceptable word in standard usage.

Already, all ready. The former means "earlier," "previously." ("When she arrived, her friend had *already* left.") *All ready* means "all are ready." ("They will leave when they are *all ready*.")

Altogether, all together. *Altogether* means "wholly," "completely." ("He was not *altogether* pleased with his purchase.") *All together* means "all in company" or "everybody in one place." ("The family was *all together* for the holidays.")

And etc. A redundant expression. *Etc.* is an abbreviation for the Latin phrase *et cetera,* meaning "and so forth." Omit the *and* in "and etc." (See *Etc.*)

And how! A slang expression indicating strong feeling or approval. Avoid its use in standard English; it is both informal and trite.

And/or. Primarily a business and legal expression, *and/or* is objected to by purists and other especially fastidious users of English. It is somewhat vague and also has business connotations objectionable to some people. Although it is a useful time-saver, in formal English you should avoid using it.

And which, and who, but which, but who. Correct sentence structure provides that these phrases should appear in clauses only if preceded by clauses which also contain *which* or *who*. ("This is the first book *which* I bought *and which* I treasure," not "This is the first book I bought *and which* . . .")

Anyway, anyways. *Anyway* means "in any case," "anyhow." ("She was planning to go *anyway.*") *Anyways* has the same meaning as *anyway,* but it is considered either dialectal or colloquial when used to mean "in any case." ("*Anyway* [not anyways], I want to go too.")

Apt, liable, likely. *Apt* suggests fitness or tendency. ("She is *apt* in arithmetic.") *Liable* implies exposure to something burdensome or disadvantageous. ("You are *liable* for damages.") *Likely* means "expected," "probable." ("We are *likely* to have snow next month.") *Likely* is the most commonly used of the three terms. Distinction in meaning has broken down somewhat, but *apt* and *liable* used in the sense of "probable" are sometimes considered colloquial or dialectal.

As. One of the most overworked words in the English language. It is a perfectly good word, but *since, because,* and *when* are more exact and effective conjunctions. ("*Since* [not *As*] we were alone, we could speak frankly.") *As* is also often misused in place of *that* or *whether.* ("I felt *that* [not *as*] I was right.") In negative comparisons some writers prefer *so . . . as . . .* to *as . . . as.* ("She is not *so* graceful *as* her cousin.") In general, use *as* sparingly; nearly always a more exact and effective word can be found.

As good as, if not better than. A correctly phrased but awkward and mixed comparison. A statement will be more effective when "if not better" is put at the end. (*Awkward:* "His style is *as good as, if not better than,* your style." *Improved:* "His style is *as good as yours, if not better.*")

Awful, awfully, abominably. These and such other expressions as *terrible, ghastly,* and *horrible* are loose, overworked intensifiers. If you really need an intensifier, use *very* (which see).

Bad, badly, ill. *Bad* is an adjective meaning "not good," "not as it should be." *Badly* is an adverb meaning "harmfully," "wickedly," "unpleasantly," "inefficiently." *Ill* is both an adjective and an adverb and means "sick," "tending to cause harm or evil," or "in a malevolent manner," "wrongly." ("He was very *ill.*") *Bad* and *badly* are often incorrectly used with the verb *feel.* ("I feel *bad* today" — not *badly,* unless you mean that your sense of touch is impaired.)

Balance, remainder. The latter term means "what is left over." *Balance* has many meanings, but its use as "remainder" is considered colloquial. ("She finished the *remainder* [not *balance*] of her chemistry homework.")

Being as. A colloquial or illiterate substitute for *since, because, inasmuch as,* etc. ("*Since* [not *Being as*] I have a cold, I'll stay indoors.")

Beside, besides. *Beside* is normally a preposition meaning "by the side of." *Besides* is an adverb meaning "moreover," and, infrequently, is a preposition meaning "except." ("The young mother sat *beside* the cradle." "I am angry because he left suddenly, and *besides,* he owes me money.")

Be sure and. This expression is considered both colloquial and unidiomatic. ("When you reach Windsor, *be sure to* [not *sure and*] telephone us.")

Blame me for it, blame it on me. Both of these expressions are in everyday use, but only the former is considered idiomatically correct and proper. *Blame it on me* is either dialectal or colloquial.

Broke. This word has standard uses, but it is a colloquialism or slang when used to mean "out of money." To *go broke* (become penniless) and *go for broke* (dare or risk everything) are slangy expressions.

Bunch. A colloquialism for "a group of people," "crowd," or "set." ("Our *crowd*—or *group* or *set* or *gang*—attended every dance.") A "bunch of bananas" is correct.

Calculate, reckon, guess. These words are *localisms* for "think," "suppose," and "expect." Each of the words has standard and acceptable meanings, but in the senses indicated here they should always be avoided except in informal conversation.

Can, may, might. *Can* suggests "ability," physical and mental. ("She *can* sing beautifully when she wants to.") *May* implies permission or sanction. ("You *may* borrow my suitcase.") The distinction between *can* and *may* (ability *vs.* permission) is illustrated in this sentence: "I *can* swim, but Mother says I *may* not." *May* also expresses possibility and wish (desire): "It *may* turn cold this evening" (possibility); "*May* you have a safe journey" (wish, desire). *Might* is used after a governing verb in the past tense, *may* after a governing verb in the present tense: "She *says* that we *may* proceed"; "She *said* that we *might* proceed."

Cancel out. Omit the *out*. This wordy expression is often used, perhaps by analogy with *cross out* or *strike out*.

Cannot help, cannot help but. The first of these expressions is preferable in such statements as "He *cannot help* mentioning . . ." The *but* should be omitted since its addition results in a double negative: *cannot help* and *can but*.

Can't hardly. Omit the *not* in the contraction. ("I *can* hardly hear you.") *Can't hardly* is a double negative.

Common, mutual. The former means "belonging to many or to all." *Mutual* means "reciprocal." ("Airplanes are *common* carriers." "Our respect and love were *mutual*.") Avoid the redundancy of such a statement as "He and I entered into a mutual agreement."

Compare, contrast. *Compare* is used to point out likenesses, similarities (used with the preposition *to*), and to examine two or more objects to find likenesses or differences (used with the preposition *with*). *Contrast* always points out differences. ("The poet *compared* his lady *to* a wood thrush." "The teacher *compared* my paper *with* Henry's and found no signs of copying." "In *contrast* to your work, mine is poor.")

Complected. This may be considered an illiteracy or a dialectal expression. The standard word is "complexioned." ("Janet was dark-*complexioned.*")

Contact, contacted. Each of these words has perfectly proper uses, but as business terms they have been overworked. Possible substitutes are *communicate with, call, call upon, telephone.*

Continue on. This is a wordy phrase. *Continue* means "to endure," "to last." Hence *on* is unnecessary to convey full meaning.

Cool. In the sense of "lacking warmth," "moderately cold," and several other meanings, *cool* is a useful and correct word. But it is informal or slangy when used to mean "actual" ("a *cool* million dollars"), "great," and "excellent." It is also highly informal in such debatable expressions as "cool jazz," "cool cat," and "cool customer."

Could of. An illiteracy. Probably because of its sound, it is sometimes written for *could have.* ("The rusty nail *could have* [not *could of*] hurt you.") (See *Would of, etc.*)

Cute. This is an overworked and somewhat vague word which generally expresses approval. Probably *charming, clever, attractive, winsome, piquant, pleasant, vivacious,* or one of a dozen other adjectives would come nearer the meaning you have in mind.

Data. This word was originally the plural of the Latin *datum* and means "facts and figures from which conclusions may be drawn." Purists consider the word to be plural and use it with a plural verb, but its use with a singular verb is becoming more widespread. (*"These* data *are* not reliable." *"This* data *is* not reliable.")

Different from, than, to. *Different than* and *different to* are considered colloquial by some authorities, improper and incorrect by others. Even so, these idioms have long literary usage to support them and certainly they are widely used. No one ever objects on any grounds to *different from.* Use *different from* and be safe.

Disinterested, uninterested. The former means "unbiased," "not influenced by personal reasons." *Uninterested* means "having no interest in," "not paying attention." ("The minister's opinion was *disinterested*." "I was completely *uninterested* in the play.") As a colloquialism, a somewhat inexact one, *disinterested* is often used in the sense of "uninterested," "indifferent."

Disregardless. See *Irregardless, disregardless.*

Disremember. An illiteracy. Never use this word in standard English.

Done, don't. The principal parts of this verb are *do, did, done. Done* is frequently used incorrectly as the past tense of *do.* ("We *did* [not *done*] our work early today.") *Don't* is often used incorrectly for *doesn't.* ("It *doesn't* [not *don't*] make much difference to me.")

Due to. Some authorities label this phrase "colloquial" when it is used to mean "because of." Nevertheless, it is widely used in this sense by capable speakers and writers. Purists prefer such expressions as *owing to, caused by, on account of,* and *because of.* If you wish your English to be above any possible criticism, avoid using *due to* as a preposition. ("Tension there was *caused by* [not *due to*] racial unrest which had been building for decades.") Most importantly, remember that *due to the fact that* is a wordy way of saying the short and simple word *since.* (See *Fact that.*)

Each . . . are. *Each,* even if not followed by *one,* implies "one." Any plural words used in modifying phrases do not change the number. ("Each *is* [not *are*] expected to contribute *his* time." "*Each one* of you *is* a fraud.")

Either . . . or, neither . . . nor. The former means "one of two." *Neither* means "not one of two." *Or* is used with *either, nor* with *neither.* The use of *either . . . or* and *neither . . . nor* in coordinating more than two words, phrases, or clauses is sanctioned by some dictionaries but not by others. ("*Either* of you *is* satisfactory for the role." "*Neither* the boys *nor* the girls wished to dance.")

Enthuse. This word is a formation derived from "enthusiasm." Most dictionaries label *enthuse* as colloquial, although it is shorter and more direct than preferred locutions such as *be enthusiastic about* or *become enthusiastic over.* Even so, the word is greatly overused and somewhat "gushy"; do not use it in formal English.

Etc. *Etc.* is an abbreviation of the Latin *et cetera* and means "and so forth." It looks somewhat out of place in formal writing and tends to be overused. Furthermore, it cannot be pronounced in speech without sounding individual letters or giving the entire phrase. Sometimes we use *etc.* at the end of a list to suggest that much more could be added. But do we really have anything in mind? (See *And etc.*)

Fact that, the fact remains that. Roundabout, wordy substitutes for *that* and *the fact is,* respectively (see *Due to*).

Faze. The word, which means "to disturb" or "to agitate," is considered informal (colloquial) in this spelling by some authorities. Other spellings are *fease, feaze,* and *feeze.* The word *phase* has entirely different meanings.

Feature. As both verb and noun, *feature* is an overworked colloquialism in the sense of "emphasize" or "emphasis." *Feature* is slang in the expression "Can you *feature* that?" meaning, presumably, "Can you imagine that?"

Fed up. An expressive but slangy term meaning "to become disgusted, bored." Don't use it when you're trying to impress an intellectual.

Feel. This useful word appears in several expressions which are colloquial or dialectal. In standard English avoid using *feel of* (for *feel*), *feel like* (for *wish to, desire*), *feel up to* (for *feel capable of*).

Female. Fastidious usage restricts *female* to designations of sex in scientific contexts. If *female* is considered colloquial, and it is, then what word can we use to express "female human being of whatever age"? "Correct" usage can indeed be a nuisance at times.

Fewer, less. Both of these words imply a comparison with something larger in number or amount. Although *less* is widely used in place of *fewer,* particularly in informal writing and in speech, the distinction between them seems useful. *Fewer* applies to number. ("*Fewer* horses are seen on the streets these days.") *Less* is used in several ways; *less* material in the dress, *less* coverage, *less* than a dollar. ("The *less* money we have the *fewer* purchases we can make.")

Fine. The word is much overused in the general sense of approval. It is colloquial when used as an adverb: "Mona sang *well* [not *fine* or *just fine*]."

Firstly, secondly. These words are acceptable, but most skilled users of the language prefer *first* and *second* because they are just as accurate and are shorter. *First of all* is a wordy expression.

First-rate, second-rate. These words suggesting rank or degree of excellence are vastly overused. *First-rate* is colloquial in the sense of "very good" or "excellent" or "very well."

Fix. This is a word of many meanings. In standard English it means "to make fast." As a verb, it is informal (colloquial) when used to mean "to arrange matters," "to get revenge on," "to repair." As a noun, it is used colloquially for "difficulty," "predicament."

Folks. This word is colloquial when used to refer to "relatives" and "family." Both dialectal and colloquial is the expression *just folks*, meaning "simple and unassuming people." *Folksy* is a colloquial word for "sociable."

Former, latter. *Former* and *latter* refer to only two units. To refer to a group of more than two items, use *first* and *last* to indicate order.

Free from, free of. The former is idiomatically correct. *Free of* is considered either colloquial or dialectal.

Free gratis. *Gratis* means "without payment," "free." Use either *free* or *gratis*, not both.

Funny. A common and useful word but one that is vastly overworked. Its use to mean "strange," "queer," "odd," "remarkable" is considered colloquial. Its primary meaning is "humorous" or "comical."

Good, well. The former is an adjective with many meanings: a *good* time, *good* advice, *good* Liberal, *good* humor. *Well* functions as both adjective and adverb. As an adjective it means "in good health," and as an adverb it means "ably" or "efficiently." ("I feel *well* once again." "The sales force worked *well* in this campaign.")

Got, gotten. The principal parts of *get* are *get, got, got* (or *gotten*). Both *got* and *gotten* are acceptable words. Your choice will depend upon your speech habits or on the rhythm of the sentence you are writing or speaking. *Got* is colloquial when used to mean "must," "ought," "own," "possess," and many other terms. ("I *ought* [not *got*] to go.") (See *Have got to.*)

Graduate. This word has several meanings, all of which are in some way related to marking in steps, measuring. Idiom decrees that one *graduate from* (not *graduate*) a school.

Grand. This word means "imposing," "magnificent," "noble." It is overused as a vague counter word meaning "delightful" or "admirable." *Grand* is colloquial in such expressions as *look grand, a grand time, feel grand.*

Guy. This word has several meanings but we most often use it colloquially to refer to a man, boy, or individual generally. Some experts regard this use of the word as slang; it should be avoided in standard English. To *guy* someone is a highly informal way to express the sense of teasing or joshing.

Gyp. This word, which probably derives from *gypsy,* is a slang term which refers to a swindler, a cheat, and to cheating or swindling. It is expressive enough but hardly dignified or tasteful; omit it from standard English.

Have got to. A colloquial and redundant expression for "must," etc. ("I *must* [not *have got to*] do my laundry today.") (See *Got, gotten.*) *Have* is a useful verb and appears in many expressions we use constantly. In standard English we should avoid using such expressions as *have a cheque bounce, have cold feet, have a lot on the ball, have it in for someone.* In these expressions the *have* is only partly responsible for the colloquialism.

Heap, heaps. *Heap* means a "mass," a "mound." Both *heap* and *heaps* are colloquial when used to mean "a great deal," "a large amount." ("He owns much [not *a heap of* or *heaps of*] real estate.")

Home, homey. Do not loosely use *home* for *house.* Do not omit the preposition in such an expression as I *am at home.* Most importantly, remember that *homey* is a colloquial word for *homelike.*

Hunch. This word has acceptable meanings as both verb and noun. In the sense of "a premonition or feeling that something is going to happen," it is informal and should be avoided in standard English.

If, whether. In standard English, *if* is used to express condition; *whether*, usually with *or*, is used in expressions of doubt and in indirect questions expressing condition. ("*If* it isn't raining, we'll be in the garden." [simple condition] "I am wondering *whether* he can do it." [doubt] "He asked *whether* the car had stopped." [indirect question]) In standard English *if* is not used with *or*. ("I do not know *whether* [not *if*] I am rich or poor.")

Imply, infer. To *imply* is to suggest a meaning hinted at but not explicitly stated. ("Do you *imply* that the cashier is dishonest?") To *infer* is to draw a conclusion from statements, circumstances, or evidence. ("From your reply I *infer* that you would rather stay at home.") Do not confuse these two words in use.

In, into. The former is used to indicate motion within relatively narrow or well-defined limits. ("The prisoner paced back and forth *in* his cell.") *In* is also used when a place is not mentioned. ("The skaters came *in* for some hot coffee.") *Into* usually follows a verb indicating motion to a place. ("When Sue tiptoed *into* the kitchen, the kitten mewed softly.")

In accordance to, with. *In accordance with* is the preferred idiom. However, the phrase is wordy and trite.

In back of. This phrase is colloquial for "behind." However, *in the back of* and *in front of* are considered standard terms, although both are wordy. *Behind* and *before* are shorter and nearly always will suffice. ("*Behind* [not *in back of*] the counter were six crates." "*Before* [or *in front of*] the mirror stood a beautiful girl.")

Individual. See *Party, person, individual.*

Inferior than, to. The former is not standard idiom; the latter is. ("This brand of chocolate is *inferior to* [not *than*] that.")

In line, on line. The first of these idiomatic terms is more widely used than the second throughout Canada. ("Joe waited *in line* with the other cadets.") However, *on line* may be used if doing so causes no confusion to your reader or listener. The word *line* appears in several expressions which are considered colloquial or dialectal: *come into line* (meaning "to correspond" or "agree"), *get a line on* (meaning "to find out about").

In regards to. Omit the *s* in *regards*. Better yet, substitute *concerning* or *about* for the entire phrase; one word is usually more effective than three. (See *Regard, regards* in Section 59.)

Inside of, off of, outside of. The *of* in each of these expressions is superfluous. ("*Inside* [not *Inside of*] the barn the horses are eating hay." "The girl fell *off* [not *off of*] her tricycle." "Will you travel *outside* [not *outside of*] the province?") When these expressions are not prepositional, the *of* should be included: the *outside of* the house, the *inside of* the tent.

Irregardless, disregardless. Each of these words is an illiteracy. That is, neither is a standard word and neither should be used under any circumstances, formal or informal. The prefixes *ir-* and *dis-* are both incorrect and superfluous in these constructions. Use *regardless*.

Is, was, were. These are parts of the verb *to be*. It may help you to remember that *is* is singular in number, third person, present tense. ("*He* [or *She* or *It*] *is* in the room.") *Was* is singular, first or third person, past tense. ("*I* [or *He* or *She* or *It*] *was* in the room.") *Were* can be either singular or plural, second person in the singular and all three persons in the plural, and is in the past tense. ("*You* [both singular and plural] *were* in the room." "*We* [or *You* or *They*] *were* in the room.") The two most frequent errors in using *to be* are employing *was* for *were*, and vice versa, and using *is* in the first or second person instead of in the third, where it belongs.

Is when, is where. These terms are frequently misused, especially in giving definitions. Grammatically, the fault may be described as using an adverbial clause in place of the noun phrase or clause which is called for. "A subway *is where* you ride under the ground" can be improved to "A subway *is* [or *involves*] an electric railroad beneath the surface of the streets." "Walking *is when* you move about on foot" can be improved to "Walking *is the act of* [or *consists of*] moving about on foot."

It stands to reason. A cliché.

Its, it's, its'. This little three-letter combination causes more errors than any other grouping of letters in the English language. However, the distinctions among them are simple and easily learned. *Its* is the possessive form of *it*. ("The dress has lost *its* shape.") *It's* is a contraction of *it is* and should never be used unless it means precisely this. ("I think *it's* [*it is*] going to rain.") *Its'*? There is no such form or word in the language.

Job. This word is frequently and inexactly used in the sense of "achievement." The chief objection to it is its overuse to cover many general and vague meanings. Furthermore, *job* is colloquial when used to mean "affair" and slang when applied to a robbery. In short, *job* is a useful word, but it should be employed carefully and sparingly. Consult your dictionary.

Kid. This word means "a young goat," in which sense it is rarely used. But *kid* in two other senses is one of the most ubiquitous words in the language. We use it to refer to a "child or young person" and we use *to kid* when we mean "to tease, banter, jest with." In both uses the word is dubious in standard English.

Kind of a, sort of a. In these phrases the *a* is superfluous. Logically, the main word (which can be *kind, sort,* or *type)* should indicate a class, not one thing. ("*What kind of* [not *what kind of a*] party is this?") Although *kind of* and *sort of* are preferred in this construction, these same phrases are often used colloquially to mean "almost," "rather," "somewhat." ("She was *rather* [not *kind of*] weary." "Martha was *almost* [not *sort of*] resigned to his leaving.")

Knock. In the primary sense of "strike" and in several other meanings, *knock* is a legitimate word on any level of usage. We should avoid its use in such phrases and terms as *to knock* (colloquial for "to criticize"), *to knock about* (colloquial for "to wander"), and *to knock down* (colloquial in the sense of "to embezzle" or "to steal"). *Knock off,* meaning "to stop," as in "to knock off work," is ever more frequently heard, but it is still considered colloquial by most authorities.

Learn, teach. Standard English requires a distinction in

meaning between these words. ("I'll *learn* the language if you will *teach* me.") *To learn* someone something is an illiteracy.

Legible, readable. These terms are synonymous in the meaning of "capable of being deciphered or read with ease." *Readable* has the additional meaning of "interesting or easy to read." ("Your handwriting is *legible*." "This book is *readable*.")

Let. This word, with a primary meaning of "allow," "permit," has many legitimate uses. Such phrases involving *let* as the following, however, are colloquial and should not be used in standard English: *let on* (in the sense of "pretend"), *let out* (as in "school let out"), *let up* (meaning "cease"). *To let one's hair down* is both colloquial and trite. (See also *Leave, let* in Section 59.)

Liable. See *Apt, liable, likely.*

Lie, lay, lye. The first of these words is the present tense (infinitive) of a verb meaning "to be in a recumbent or prostrate position." As a noun, it means "falsehood." ("Please *lie* down." "Never tell a *lie*.") *Lay* has several meanings, but it is most often used as the past tense of *lie*. ("He *lay* down for a nap.") *Lye* is an alkaline substance. ("Some soaps contain *lye*.")

Line. This standard word has several nonstandard uses. It is considered slang in such expressions as *come into line* (meaning both "agree" and "behave properly"); *get a line on; he gave* [or *fed*] *her a line*.

Literally. This word not only is overused but also is confused with *figuratively*. It is an antonym of the latter and really means "not imaginatively," "actually."

Loose, lose, loss. *Loose* means "not fastened tightly." ("This is a *loose* connection.") *Lose* means "to suffer the loss of." ("Don't *lose* your hard-earned money.") *Loss* means "a deprivation," "a defeat," "a reverse." ("The coach blamed me for the *loss* of the ball.")

Lots of, a lot of, a whole lot. These terms are colloquial for "many," "much," "a great deal." The chief objection to their use is that each is a vague, general expression.

Lousy. This word actually means "infested with lice." It is constantly used as a slang expression, however, to mean "dirty," "disgusting," "contemptible," "poor," "inferior," and "well supplied with" (as in "*lousy* with money"). Use it in only the most informal of informal conversations. You can startle or impress your friends by using *pediculous.*

Mad. This short and useful word has many acceptable meanings such as "insane," "frantic," and "frenzied." Most authorities consider *mad* to be colloquial when it is used to mean "angry" or "furious." ("I was *angry with*—or *furious with*— [not *mad at*] him.")

May. See *Can, may, might.*

Might of. An illiteracy. ("If you had asked, I *might have* [not *might of*] accompanied you.") (See *Would of,* etc.)

Mighty. This word means "strong" or "powerful." When it is used to mean "very" or "extremely," it is considered a colloquialism. ("Tom was a *very* [not *mighty*] lucky boy.") (But see *Very.*)

Muchly. An illiteracy. Despite the fact that you may often hear the word, it really doesn't exist—at least not in standard English. Use *much* instead.

Must. As a noun, this word is no longer considered slang by most authorities, but it is tiresomely overused to mean something essential or necessary, as in "This movie is a *must.*"

Neither . . . nor. See *Either . . . or, neither . . . nor.*

No place, nowhere. The former is a perfectly sound phrase ("There's *no place* like home"), but in standard English it cannot be a synonym for *nowhere.* ("She could find her purse *nowhere* [not *no place*].") Be certain to spell *nowhere* correctly; *nowheres* is as dialectal as *no place.*

Of. *Of* is an exceedingly common word with a variety of standard uses. However, it is not an allowable substitute for *have* after auxiliary verbs in such expressions as *could of, would of, might of, should of.* ("You *should have* [not *should of*] been here yesterday.")

Off of. See *Inside of,* etc.

O.K. This everyday term is colloquial or business English for "all right," "correct," "approved." It is occasionally spelled *OK, okay, okeh.* The terms *oke* and *okeydoke* are slang. For the debatable origin of *O.K.,* see any standard dictionary.

Once-over. A slang term meaning "a swiftly appraising glance," or what boys and girls, men and women, quite often give each other.

Oral, aural, verbal. *Oral* means "spoken." ("The order was *oral*, not written.") *Aural* means "received through the ear," or "pertaining to the sense of hearing." ("After the concussion, Jane's *aural* sense was below normal.") *Verbal* means "of, in, or by means of words." In such a sentence as "Our contract was *verbal*," it means "unwritten." *Oral* and *verbal* are thus often confused in everyday use.

Out loud. *Aloud* is considered more nearly standard English. *Out loud* is colloquial and not entirely idiomatic.

Outside of. See *Inside of*, etc.

Overuse of "so." *So* is correctly used as a conjunctive adverb with a semicolon preceding, and it is frequently used between independent clauses with only a comma before it. The chief objection to *so* in such constructions is simply *overuse*. In constructions like those below, *so* can often be replaced by *therefore, thus, accordingly,* and the like, or predication may be reduced.

Ineffective: The jazz concert was canceled, *so* we took our dates to the movies.

Improved: *Since* the jazz concert was canceled, we took our dates to the movies.

In correcting the overuse of *so*, guard against a worse error, that of using another conjunctive adverb with a comma before it and thus writing an unjustifiable comma splice:

Wrong: The jazz concert was canceled, *therefore* we took our dates to the movies. [Use a semicolon or a period.]

Sometimes *so* is misused when the writer means *so that* or *in order that*:

Ineffective: Is it possible to buy potatoes in quantity *so* each potato may cost us less?

Improved: Is it possible to buy potatoes in quantity *in order that* each potato may cost us less?

Paid, payed. *Paid* is the past tense and past participle of the verb *pay*. ("He *paid* his bookkeeper's expenses.") *Payed* is used only in the sense of to *pay* out a cable or line. ("He *payed* out line as soon as the fish struck.")

Party, person, individual. Except in telephone and legal language, *party* implies a group and should not be used to refer to one person except in a colloquial sense. *Individual* refers to a single, particular person. As nouns, *individual* and *person* are synonymous. As an adjective, *individual* means "single," "separate," and is therefore unnecessary and repetitious when used to modify *person* or when "each" has been used. Both *individual person* and *each individual member* are wordy phrases.

Pass out. In the sense of "to faint" or "to become unconscious," *pass out* is a useful term but, as slang, should not appear in standard English.

Pep, peppy. The former is an informal expression as both noun and verb. *Peppy*, an adjective, is fully as colloquial. Use some such standard word as *energy, briskness, spirit, vigor*. Corresponding adjectives would be *energetic, brisk, spirited, vigorous*.

Percent, per cent. This word (from Latin *per centum*, meaning "by the hundred") may be spelled as either one or two words. *Percent* is colloquial when used as a substitute for *percentage* (the noun). *Percentage* is colloquial when used in the meaning of "profit" or "advantage," as in "What's the *percentage* in hard work?"

Phony. As both adjective and noun, this word is slang. As a quick and easy substitute for "not genuine," "fake," *phony* is so often used that, presumably, it will in time be acceptable in standard English. Until then, no.

Plan on going, plan to go. Both of these expressions are in everyday use, but the former is considered colloquial and idiomatically not so sound as *plan to go*.

Plenty. This word is colloquial when used to mean "very," "fully." ("The water is *very* [not *plenty*] hot today.") But see *Very*.

Prior than, prior to. Both terms are in common use but only the latter has the sanction of accepted idiom.

Quite a. This phrase is colloquial when used to mean "more than." In standard English avoid using such phrases as *quite a few, quite a bit*, and *quite a party*.

Real. In the sense of "really" or "very," *real* is an impropriety. ("Are you *really*—or *very*—[not *real*] certain of your figures?") Adverbial use of *real* is increasing.

Reason is because. In standard English, the construction beginning "The reason . . ." is followed by a noun or a noun clause usually introduced by *that*. Yet we often hear such a sentence as "I couldn't go; the *reason was because* I had to work." In spite of its form, the construction introduced by *reason was* is a noun clause rather than an adverbial one. But such a use should appear only in colloquial speech. Standard writing requires "I couldn't go; the *reason was that* I had to work."

Reason why. A redundant expression. Omit *why* and, in most constructions, also omit *reason*. "The *reason why* I like this job is the salary I get" can be improved by writing "I like this job because of the salary."

Receipt, recipe. Both words mean "a formula" or "directions for making or preparing something." Fastidious users of the language prefer *recipe*, but in this meaning the terms are interchangeable. *Receipt* also means "a written acknowledgment of something received." It is considered badly overworked business jargon in such an expression as "We are in *receipt* of . . ."

Refer, refer back. *Refer* means "to direct attention" or "to make reference"; therefore, *back* is superfluous. ("Please *refer* [not *refer back*] again to my statement.") The same faulty diction occurs in *repeat again* and *return back*.

Remainder. See *Balance, remainder*.

Repeat again. See *Refer, refer back*.

Return back. See *Refer, refer back*.

Said, same, such. As an adjective, *said* is used in legal writing but is considered to be jargon in standard English. Avoid such expressions as *said party, said person*, and *said proposal*. *Same* as a pronoun is also characteristic of legal and business use. Lawyers may insist upon its retention, but businessmen in general and you in particular should avoid such expressions as "cheque enclosed in payment for *same*." *Such* may be an adjective, an adverb, and a pronoun—all with standard uses. It is considered colloquial, however, when used in place of a demonstrative. ("I could not tolerate *that* [not *such*].") *Such* is also colloquial when used as an intensifier. ("She is *a very* [not *such a*] charming person.")

Saw, seen. The principal parts of *to see* are *see, saw, seen.* *Seen* is improperly used as the past tense; *saw* is incorrect as the past participle. ("I *saw* [not *seen*] my lawyer this morning." "I *have seen* [not *have saw*] my lawyer every morning this week.")

Setup. In the sense of "an easy victory," this term is slang. More importantly, *setup* is now being used widely to refer to anything related to organization, conditions, or circumstances. ("He's got a great *setup*.") The term is vague, at best. Try to find something less used and more exact.

Shall, will. Distinctions in the use of *shall* and *will* have largely broken down, but a few careful speakers and writers still observe them.

1. Use *shall* in the first person and *will* in the second and third persons to express simple futurity. ("I *shall* arrive." "You [or He] *will* arrive.")

2. For *emphasis,* to express *determination, command, intention,* or *promise,* use *will* in the first person and *shall* in the second and third persons. ("I *will* pay him back, no matter how long it takes." "You *shall* pay him back," meaning "You must pay him back.")

Should of. See *Of.*

Should, would. In general, use *should* and *would* according to the rules for *shall* and *will* (which see). The following may be helpful:

1. *Should*

   Obligation—"I *should* exercise regularly."

   Expectation (a corollary of obligation)—"They *should* be on the next train."

   Condition—"If he *should* be late, telephone his assistant."

   Simple future (first person only)—"I *should* feel sorry to hear it."

2. *Would*

   Habitual action—"He *would* walk in the garden during lunch hour.

   Condition (*after* a conditional clause)—"If it weren't raining, he *would* walk in the garden."

   Determination—"He *would* do it, even if we objected."

Wish or desire—"*Would* that I had accompanied him!"

Simple future (second and third persons only)— "He said that he *would* go." (If the governing verb is in the past tense, use *would* to express futurity, as above. If the governing verb is in the present tense, use *will:* "He *states* that he *will* come with us.")

Sit, set. *Sit,* predominantly an intransitive verb, not requiring an object, has the meaning of "to place oneself." *Set,* predominantly a transitive verb, requiring an object, means "to put" or "to place." ("*Set* the lamp by the fireplace and come *sit* by me.") *Set* used for *sit* in the meaning shown is dialectal or an impropriety. However, both words have several special meanings. For example, *set* has an intransitive use, as in "The sun *sets* in the west."

So. See *Overuse of "so."*

Sort of a. See *Kind of a, sort of a.*

Sure. This word is used as adjective or adverb, but it is colloquial in the sense of "surely," "certainly," "indeed." ("She was *certainly* [not *sure*] sad to see him go.") *Sure* is also colloquial in such expressions as *sure enough* (meaning both "certainly" and "real") and *sure-fire* (meaning "certain to be successful"). See *Be sure and.*

Sure thing, a. A slang expression.

Swell. This word is not acceptable in standard English as a modifier. It is colloquial when used to mean "stylish," "fashionable," and it is slang when used as a general term of approval meaning "excellent." ("He gave *an excellent* [not *a swell*] lecture.") In the meaning of "conceited," *swelled head* is considered colloquial or slangy.

Take. *Take* is a good, simple, useful word, but it appears in many expressions which are substandard. For example, *take and* is a colloquial and wordy expression. In the sentence, "He *took and* beat the horse unmercifully," *took and* should be omitted entirely. *Take* is colloquial or dialectal in *he took sick, she takes well* (she photographs well), *the days's take* (money or profit received), *take someone for* (cheat), *take it* (withstand difficulty, hardship), *take it lying down* (submit without protest), *take it on the chin* (undergo punishment or pain), *take it out of* (tire, exhaust), *take it out on* (make another suffer), *take-on* (show emotion such as sorrow or anger), *take-in* (trickery), *take-off* (an amusing or mocking imitation), *taking* (contagious, said of a disease).

Take it easy. A trite expression which is used *ad nauseam.* So, also, is *take my word for it.*

Their, there, they're. These simple and common words cause much difficulty, but they are easy to keep straight. *Their* is a possessive pronoun. ("This is *their* house.") *There* means "in or at that place." ("Were you *there* when she arrived?") *They're* is a contraction of *they are.* ("We are disappointed because *they're* not coming.")

These kind, those kind, these sort, those sort. *Kind* and *sort* are singular nouns; *these* and *those* are plural modifiers. Say and write *this kind, those kinds, this sort, those sorts.* (See *Kind of a, sort of a.*)

Thusly. An illiteracy. Use *thus.*

Till, until, 'til. Each of these words means "up to the time of." *Till* and *'til* (a shortened form of *until*) have the same pronunciation and are more often used within a sentence than at the beginning. *Until* more often appears at the beginnings of sentences and is sometimes considered somewhat more formal than its two synonyms. All three terms are correct in standard English.

Try and, try to. The correct idiom is *try to.* However, *try and* is in everyday use and has been for a century. Standard English would have you write "*Try to* [not *try and*] finish your work early."

Uninterested. See *Disinterested, uninterested.*

Unique. This word means "having no like or equal" and expresses absoluteness as do words such as *round, square, perpendicular.* Logically, therefore, the word *unique* cannot be compared; something cannot be "more unique," "less unique," "more round," "less round." If a qualifying word such as *nearly* is used, the illogicality is removed. "This is the *most unique* statue in the park" is not standard, but "This is the *most nearly unique* statue . . ." is.

Up. This useful little word appears in many verb-adverb combinations (*grow up, give up, take up, use up*). In other phrases it adds nothing to the meaning of the verb; *up* is colloquial in such expressions as *choose up, divide up, finish up, increase up, wait up. On the up and up* is slang. *Up against* (meaning "face to face with") and *up against it* (meaning "in difficulty") are colloquial. *Up on* (meaning "informed about") and *up to* (meaning "scheming" or "plotting") are colloquial. *Up-and-coming* and *up one's alley* are other phrases to avoid in standard English. *Open up* is wordy in the sense of "give access to" and is colloquial when used to mean "speak freely."

Used to, used to could. In the phrase *used to,* the *d* is often elided in speaking so that it sounds like *use to.* In writing, the *d* must be included. *Used to could* is an illiteracy; write *used to be able to.*

Very. *Very,* like *so, surely, too, extremely, indeed,* has been so overused that it has lost some of its value as an intensifier. Use these words sparingly and thoughtfully; consider whether your meaning isn't just as emphatic without them: "You are [very] certain of your position." *Very* is used colloquially to qualify participles; formal use has adverbs like *much* or *greatly.*

    Colloquial: I was *very irritated* by his comments.
       Formal: I was *greatly irritated* by his comments.
    Colloquial: I am *very obliged* to you for giving me the benefit of the doubt.
       Formal: I am *much obliged* to you for giving me the benefit of the doubt.

Video. This word referring to the transmission of television images is rapidly growing in popularity. Purists insist that it is still colloquial, but general usage has decreed otherwise.

Wait on. In the sense of "serve," this is an acceptable phrase. ("I have to *wait on* the office-workers before I serve the shoppers.") In the sense of "await" or "wait for," the phrase is dialectal or colloquial. ("Hurry up; I can't *wait for* [not *wait on*] stragglers.")

Want for, want in, want out. The *for* in *want for* is dialectal. ("She *wants* [not *wants for*] to buy groceries.") Neither *want in* nor *want out* is acceptable in formal English. ("The prisoner *wants to get out* [not *wants out*].")

Way, ways. The former is colloquial when used to mean "away." ("The school is *away* [not *way*] across town.") The following phrases involving *way* are also colloquial: *in a bad way, come my way* (achieve success), *act the way he does. Ways* is a dialectal substitute for *way* in such an expression as *a long ways to the mountain.*

Where. This is a useful word but it should not be substituted for *that* in standard English. ("We saw *that* [not *where*] another dishwasher was needed.")

Where at. As two words this phrase is redundant for *where.* In standard English avoid such a statement as "Steuben couldn't say *where* he was *at.*"

Whether. See *If, whether.*

Who, whom. The former is the nominative case, the latter the objective. When in doubt, try as a memory device the substitution of *he* for *who* and *him* for *whom*, since the proper use of *he* and *him* is more easily recognized: "I am wondering *who* [or *whom?*] we should hire." "We should hire *him.*" Therefore: "I wonder *whom* we should hire."

Who's, whose. The former is a shortened form of *who is.* ("*Who's* ahead in the race?") *Whose* is the possessive case of *who.* ("*Whose* toes did I step on?")

Wire. This word (derived from *wireless*) is considered informal when used as a substitute for *telegram* or *telegraph.*

Wise. This word is an acceptable adjective but is nonstandard in such expressions as a *wise guy, get wise to, get wise, put wise to, wise up, wisecrack.*

Worst kind, worst sort, worst way. Slang terms for *very much, greatly, intensely,* and the like.

Would of, could of, might of, should of. These terms are all illiteracies probably resulting from attempts to represent what is pronounced. In rapid and informal speech, that is, *would have (would've)* has the sound of *would of.* In each phrase, *have* should replace *of.*

You all. In the sense of "all of you," this phrase has a recognized and standard plural meaning. When used to refer to one person, it may be considered either dialectal or an illiteracy.

THE SENTENCE

All writing of whatever kind—answers to many examination questions, personal and business letters, reports, research papers, paragraphs, and English compositions—is dependent upon that basic unit of composition called the *sentence*. It is not entirely correct to say that we think in terms of words, phrase our thoughts in terms of sentences, and write in terms of paragraphs. And yet it is largely true that everyone uses concepts (words) to form sentences which are then tied together in paragraphs. A sentence is a link between a thought and the full expression of that thought in a paragraph or group of paragraphs. Like all links, the sentence is important. If it is true—and it is—that good sentences derive at least in part from good diction, it is equally true that effective paragraphs and compositions stem from effective sentences.

You cannot shingle a house or paint a roof before you have laid a foundation and built a framework. You cannot write a satisfactory composition unless its sentences (its foundation, framework, *and* roof) are correct, clear, effective, and appropriate. Thoreau once said: "A sentence should read as if its author, had he held a plough instead of a pen, could have drawn a furrow deep and straight to the end." As a literary carpenter, you should both learn and understand the grammatical structures and functions of a sentence; upon that foundation and framework of knowledge you should then, as a literary farmer, cultivate your own sentences in correct, clear, and expressive form.

You would be helped in learning to write effective sentences if you could be provided with a positive, no-nonsense statement of what a sentence is. But as is pointed out in Section 9a, no fully satisfactory definition is possible. A usable opinion is this: a sentence consists of one or more words conveying to the reader (or listener) a sense of complete meaning. Another traditional definition is that a sentence is a group of words containing a subject and a predicate and expressing a complete thought. But problems immediately arise with both definitions: sentences do not always contain expressed subjects and predicates and, more significantly, do not invariably express complete thoughts. When we say that a sentence conveys a "complete meaning" or "complete thought," we cannot thereby dispense with the context of the sentence, the words which precede or follow it.

Normally, we cannot express or receive a complete thought until we have written (spoken) or read (heard) a series of sentences. A pronoun in one sentence may take its meaning from an antecedent in another. Such words as *again*, *thus*, and *these*, and such phrases as *on the other hand* and *for example* reveal that the thought in one sentence is related to the thought in another. This interrelationship and interdependence of sentences provide further proof of their importance in building larger units of composition—the paragraph and the theme.

A sentence should indeed contain a group of words that is grammatically self-sufficient as, for example: "She was one of the great romantic figures of history." This sentence has a subject, *she*, and a predicate, *was*; it begins with a capital letter and ends with a period. But its "complete" meaning depends upon other sentences that tell us that *she* refers to Cleopatra and that Cleopatra was a "great romantic figure" because she was a queen of Egypt, because she led a revolt supported by Julius Caesar, because she married two of her own brothers and was mistress to Caesar, to whom she bore a son, because she had a love affair with Marc Antony, because she died from the bite of an asp, and because she was acknowledged to be a fabulously alluring woman.

To be able to quote from memory "A sentence is a group of words containing a single, complete thought, or a group of closely related thoughts" is valueless in itself. The shortcomings of this definition must be kept in mind; its terms must be fully understood. To learn the meanings of parts of speech, to distinguish the varied kinds, uses, and patterns of sentences—such additions to knowledge represent wasted effort until we see that knowledge operating upon the sentences that we write or speak. Sections 9 and 61-80 are designed to help you write sentences that are grammatically correct and rhetorically effective and to enable you to see *why* and *how* you do so.

Commenting on the qualities and characteristics of sentences is a necessary but somewhat artificial activity. Truly, good sentences are as much a matter of personality and judgment as of rules and requirements. Good sentences will come — perhaps not easily, but they will come eventually — when you know what you want to say, have some interest in what you know or think, and wish to share that knowledge and understanding and point of view with your readers.

Learning to write effective sentences is a central goal of high school education. In fact, this art, or technique, is paramount in nearly all learning processes, on whatever level. It has been said that the simple declarative sentence is the greatest invention of the human intellect.

61. INCOMPLETENESS

A definition of the word *sentence* can be "a stated thought." Accordingly, all words, or groups of words, which "make sense" to the reader or hearer can be called sentences. However, to be fully coherent, a sentence must be *complete:* it must contain both a subject and a predicate (verb) which are expressed or clearly implied, and it must not begin with a connecting word such as *because, before, as, although,* and *while* unless an independent clause follows immediately in the same construction.

For example, the statement "Susan has cut her hair" is a coherent and complete sentence which would be unable to stand by itself if the subject, *Susan,* were omitted or if the verb, *has cut,* were replaced by a compound participle such as *having cut.* Moreover, the use of some connecting word such as *because* before *Susan* will render the sentence incomplete: "Because Susan has cut her hair" requires the support of some other statement. The fully coherent sentence could be: "Because Susan has cut her hair, she no longer resembles my sister." Or, "Because Susan has cut her hair, her mother won't let her go to the party."

61a. AVOID SETTING OFF A PHRASE AS A SENTENCE.

A phrase is only a portion or fragment of a full sentence. It should be attached to or incorporated in the sentence with which it belongs. Or it should be made to stand by itself through the addition of a subject, or a predicate, or both.

Incorrect: *Spring having come late that year.* The lilacs were not yet in bloom.

Correct: Spring having come late that year, the lilacs were not yet in bloom.

Spring came late that year, and the lilacs were not yet in bloom.

Incorrect: Mary constantly talks about clothes. *Without regard for other people's interests.*

Correct: Mary constantly talks about clothes, without regard for other people's interests.

Incorrect: I have two purposes in dieting. *To trim my waistline and to save money.*

Correct: I have two purposes in dieting. I wish to trim my waistline and to save money.

I have two purposes in dieting: to trim my waistline and to save money.

61b. AVOID SETTING OFF A DEPENDENT CLAUSE AS A SENTENCE.

Adjective and adverbial clauses are frequently mistaken for sentences. The adjective clause may be wrongly set apart when it properly should be at the end of an independent clause. The adverbial clause may be wrongly set apart when it properly should be at the beginning or end of an independent clause. A dependent-clause fragment may often be corrected, with no change in wording, by substituting a small for a capital letter and replacing a period with a comma or no mark at all. Or a dependent adjective clause may be made independent by changing the relative pronoun into a personal pronoun, and an adverbial clause be made independent by omitting the subordinating conjunction.

Incorrect: We have talked with a marine biologist. *Who is convinced that the seas can feed the world.* (Adjective)

The desk had a secret drawer. *Into which I stuffed the muddy bills.* (Adjective)

Wadsworth gave up hope. *When suddenly a ship appeared on the horizon.* (Adverbial)

Unless all planes are grounded. We shall take off for Ottawa in less than an hour. (Adverbial)

Correct: We have talked with a marine biologist who is convinced that the seas can feed the world.

We have talked with a marine biologist. He is convinced . . .

The desk had a secret drawer, into which I stuffed the muddy bills.

Wadsworth gave up hope. Suddenly a ship appeared on the horizon.

Unless all planes are grounded, we shall take off for Ottawa in less than an hour.

61c. AVOID STARTING A STATEMENT WITH ONE CONSTRUCTION AND THEN STOPPING OR SHIFTING TO ANOTHER.

An unfinished or incomplete sentence results when a writer begins a statement and then shifts his thought and construction, keeps adding words, yet stops before he has given meaning to his opening words. Or the writer may start with an independent clause but then add an unfinished statement which he forgets to coordinate with his first independent statement. In correcting such unfinished constructions, the writer should determine carefully what is missing and then supply it, in proper grammatical elements:

Incomplete: An old woman in the apartment, who, because she had become progressively more lame, was forced to use a cane and then to be confined to a wheelchair.

Improved: An old woman in the apartment, who, because she had become progressively more lame, was forced to use a cane and then to be confined to a wheelchair, ordered the landlord to install a telephone in her kitchen.

Incomplete: I thought that preparing dinner for eight guests would be a simple matter, but after deciding on a menu and shopping for the food, being very careful to stay within my budget, and then spending hours over a hot stove that burned the lima beans and three of my fingers.

Improved: I thought that preparing dinner for eight guests would be a simple matter, but after deciding on a menu and shopping for the food, being very careful to stay within my budget, and then spending hours over a hot stove that burned the lima beans and three of my fingers, I realized that a dinner party is a formidable undertaking.

61d. USE ONLY JUSTIFIABLE SENTENCE FRAGMENTS.

Although a sentence, when defined grammatically, consists of a subject and predicate and expresses a complete thought, various statements without an actual or implied subject and verb may also express a full thought. Expressions such as *Hello, What a day, Sure, Ouch, Enough for now, To summarize* are grammatically only sentence fragments; otherwise they are clear and forceful. They are often found in dialogue because they represent normal conversation. Put in context, they amply serve to answer questions and to give details after general statements. Sentence fragments in the following piece of dialogue, for example, are fully justifiable:

"Where are you going tonight?"
"To the Spring Dance."
"With Tom?"
"Not a chance."
"Because he lied to you?"
"But of course."
"Smart girl."
"Just lucky, I guess."

EXERCISE 1

Correct the unjustifiable sentence fragments in the following by attaching them logically to materials with which they belong.

1. There are many words that he uses incorrectly. Such as *have went* for *have gone*, *I seen* instead of *I saw*, and many, many others.
2. Since school afforded few extracurricular activities of any kind. I participated in all those that were offered.
3. Senior week we shall never forget. The magnificent prom, a great picnic, and much fun.
4. Winter does something to me. When the snow leaves a white blanket over the ground.
5. My clothing bill for this summer was $415. This being more than double what I expected to spend.
6. Then Mother begins preparing Thanksgiving dinner. Roast turkey and dressing, mashed potatoes and gravy, baked beans, coleslaw, pickles, radishes, and carrots.
7. I slid through high school as an otter slides down a snowy hill. Free and easy without a care in the world. Not caring about anything.
8. The next experience that I recall happened to my mother and me. Mother being the driver, of course.
9. The plane rose higher and higher. Its wings swept back and its nose piercing the air.
10. Magazine rates for three-year subscriptions are cheaper. Thereby saving the subscriber a considerable sum of money.

EXERCISE 2

Expand into sentences the unjustifiable sentence fragments in the following statements.

1. I wish I could go back to the time I was a freshman in high school. With the knowledge I have now about how important study is and the importance of good study habits.
2. New York City—a place everyone would like to visit.
3. A man of average height and rugged build, with silvery gray hair, his hair indicating that he was in his fifties.
4. In college there is nobody to tell you to get up in the morning. Nobody to make you study.
5. The whine continued and the old man got more and more nervous. If only he could stop the noise.

6. The name of our farm is The Oaks. Named thus because of the abundant growth of oak trees.

7. Fraternities want you to be a "big activities" man on the campus. Get you into all the activities they can load you down with and then they wonder why your grades in school are so low.

8. Experience is a good but expensive teacher. Although after having a costly experience, one usually never lets it take place again.

9. The card catalog has three divisions. The first of which contains the author cards.

10. Some thoughtless, self-centered driver can cause an accident. Where if he had yielded the right of way, a life could have been saved.

62. COMMA SPLICE

When our thoughts stray from or dart ahead of our writing, we may find that, instead of setting down full sentences one at a time, we are joining, or splicing, with a comma statements which should be separated by a period or should be linked by a semicolon, a colon, or a conjunction *and* a comma. Such comma splices, considered faulty in both punctuation and in sentence construction, are serious flaws because the reader cannot determine where one sentence ends and the next one begins.

62a. AVOID UNJUSTIFIABLE COMMA SPLICES.

Comma splices, or "comma faults," occur in several forms:

1. Two statements which are not grammatically related but which are related by content.

2. Two related statements, the second of which begins with a personal pronoun whose antecedent is in the first.

3. Two related statements, the second of which begins with a demonstrative pronoun or adjective (*that, this, those, these, such*).

4. Two statements, the second of which begins with or contains a conjunctive adverb (*nevertheless, however, then,* etc.).

Following are illustrations of these forms of comma splice, in the order set forth above:

    1. Our alumni dinner will be held on Friday evening, the new dean of freshmen will be introduced.

    2. The sentry bent over the crumpled form, he let out a low, soft whistle.

    3. Make use of the suggestions on the label, these are very helpful.

    4. I made the four-o'clock train, however, my brother couldn't meet me.

There are several ways to correct a comma splice error:

1. Use a period after the first statement and capitalize the first letter of the second.

2. Use a semicolon between the statements.

3. Place a conjunction between the statements, or as a substitute for the conjunctive adverb, and retain the comma.

4. Subordinate one of the statements and retain the comma.

One or more of these methods may be used to correct the comma splices illustrated above. Be careful to avoid a succession of short, choppy sentences, and do not attempt to show a causal relationship where in fact it does not exist without proper subordination.

62b. USE A JUSTIFIABLE COMMA SPLICE WHEN IT IS EFFECTIVE AND APPROPRIATE.

Many writers and editors carefully avoid all comma splices on the grounds that a comma splice is a serious error which always confuses the reader. However, occasional examples of such faults have been deemed justifiable because they are stylistically effective in certain constructions. Consider, for example, the following:

    It bubbled, it welled, it shot into the air.

    You do not show courage, you show recklessness.

    That is the library, this is the Town Hall.

    Philosophy comes from two Greek words: *philos* means "loving," *sophia* means "wisdom."

EXERCISE 3

Correct all the comma faults in the following sentences. If possible, correct each one by all the methods suggested above. Arrange corrected versions in the order of most effective to least effective.

1. Our farm is not too large, it consists of 200 acres.
2. One defect is incorrect spelling, the other is the occasional use of faulty diction.
3. Hockey would probably die out if the people in Canada didn't like to criticize, thus when they attend a game, they can really blow off their steam.
4. Let's share our vacation experiences, here are mine.
5. The streets are not clean, the buildings lining the streets are old, dirty, and broken down.
6. The students and the teacher did not get along properly, therefore, about all I remember was a riot each day.
7. The average student does not find the subject matter too hard, instead he finds it hard to adjust himself to the new way of college life.
8. "We do not have a thirteenth floor," he explained, "it is a superstition of the hotel."
9. A city that should be interesting to you is Victoria, it is the capital of British Columbia.
10. It seemed to me that the day nursery school would be much more suitable to me than teaching, consequently I changed my course of study.

63. FUSED (OR BLENDED) SENTENCES

An error even more serious than the comma splice is the fused sentence; whereas in the former at least some indication of separation between statements is given, in the latter two complete sentences are fused or pushed together with no punctuation at all. The reader is therefore unable to distinguish where one full thought ends and another full thought begins.

63a. DO NOT WRITE TWO SENTENCES WITH NO PUNCTUATION BETWEEN THEM.

A sentence is a meaningful and coherent statement and should always be followed by a terminal mark, that is, a full stop: period, question mark, exclamation point.

Incorrect: The Depression deepened its hold on Canadian business thousands of men lost their jobs and breadlines became a common sight.

When he left the Army, Herbert took up horseracing this activity is often called the Sport of Kings.

Judged by grammatical standards, each of these "sentences" contains two independent and distinct statements which can be written separately. If the writer decides that the two statements are sufficiently related in thought, he may choose to connect them more closely with punctuation which is not terminal.

Correct: The Depression deepened its hold on Canadian business. Thousands of men lost their jobs and breadlines became a common sight.

When he left the Army, Herbert took up horseracing. This activity is often called the Sport of Kings.

When he left the Army, Herbert took up horseracing, often called the Sport of Kings.

63b. AVOID CORRECTING A FUSED SENTENCE BY PLACING A COMMA BETWEEN ITS PARTS.

Two complete sentences should never be fused together, or blended. However, to separate them with a comma would result in another violation of unity: the comma splice. A comma splice is almost as grave an offense as the fused sentence. A comma is not adequate in a sentence such as this: "We lived in Springdale two years ago our house was in the center of town." Using a comma after the word *ago* is not permissible. One of the four methods by which a comma splice may be corrected should therefore be applied to the correction of a fused sentence.

We lived in Springdale two years ago. Our house was in the center of town.

We lived in Springdale two years ago; our house was in the center of town.

We lived in Springdale two years ago, and our house was in the center of town.

When we lived in Springdale two years ago, our house was in the center of town.

EXERCISE 4

Correct the following by using terminal marks of punctuation or by subordination:

1. Then suddenly we knew what was wrong the man in the middle had no face.
2. He is an excellent performer, one of the best in the province, I think do you think so, too?
3. I'm afraid dinner will be delayed, the French fried potatoes are acting up again.
4. Curtis was too shy to play the piano before so many strangers moreover he had no piano.
5. He remained in Germany for two years when he returned to enter college.
6. "Help Help" the man cried I hurried to the edge of the river, but I could see that he was only playing.
7. He was garrulous I did not pay any attention to his harangue.
8. I'll tell you one thing it surely is hard to eat peas in a small airplane.
9. But how could Stephenson get into the laboratory to release the mice with whose connivance could he have entered the building?
10. I'll show you how to do it just break off the neck of the bottle and jump back.

64. RELATED IDEAS (UNITY)

Unity, which means "singleness of purpose, harmony," demands that a sentence express a single thought or group of closely related thoughts. Sentence unity has little to do with sentence length. A long sentence may contain several references to people, places, things, or ideas and still be unified, whereas a short sentence may refer to one person only and yet be ununified. This extended sentence shows unity of thought: "Although his friends claimed that George made the Honor Roll without effort, often at midnight he could be found at his desk, nibbling on a favorite snack of peanut-butter crackers as he painstakingly reread all of his written homework." But this sentence, only a fraction as long, lacks unity: "George was a good student, and he liked peanut-butter crackers."

64a. AVOID RAMBLING SENTENCES WHICH CONTAIN TOO MANY DETAILS.

Faulty: As I grew older, my desire to play basketball grew also, and when I entered high school I was too small to play my first two years of school, being only five feet tall, so I had to sit on the bench, but later in high school I began to grow, and before I graduated my senior year I was playing center on the first team, for I had grown 13 inches in two years.

Improved: Although my interest in basketball had grown with the years, I discovered upon entering high school that my physical growth had not kept pace with my desire to play. For two years my five-foot frame glumly occupied the bench. That before I graduated I was playing center on the first team I contend is due to a genuine, if familiar, miracle: in the years between I had grown 13 inches.

64b. AVOID PLACING UNRELATED IDEAS IN THE SAME SENTENCE.

When unrelated ideas occur in the same sentence, unity can sometimes be achieved by showing some evidence of relationship or by subordinating one idea to another. If the ideas are not closely related and cannot be made to link, use separate sentences. If no relationship whatever exists, one of the ideas should be omitted.

Faulty: His brother was a tall man, and he was a good fisherman.

Improved: His brother, a tall man who loved the sea, was a good fisherman.

His brother was a tall man. He was also a good fisherman.

EXERCISE 5

Rewrite the following sentences, making one idea subordinate to the other in sentences where the parts are sufficiently related. If the parts are not sufficiently related, divide them into two sentences.

1. My cousin was given a handsome watch for graduation, and he has gone to Vancouver on the Senior trip.
2. I want to get a good liberal education, and history, which is a required course, is difficult for me.
3. Martin's roommate is the most absent-minded boy I have ever known, and he comes from San Francisco.
4. We paid a guide ten dollars for taking us across the island-studded bay, and the scenery was very beautiful.
5. The asphalt highway was slippery when it was wet, and it led from Guelph to Brampton.
6. Toronto is a city with a famous meat-packing industry, and it is located on Lake Ontario.
7. My brother is an excellent swimmer and was born on Christmas Day.
8. Last summer my family and I went on a long trip through the West, and I have always liked to drive.
9. Martin said to Myrtle, "I love you; will you please lend me five dollars until tomorrow?"
10. July 1 is Dominion Day in Canada, and large uranium discoveries have been made there.

EXERCISE 6

Divide the following into unified sentences, supplying or deleting words where necessary.

1. The band was astonished to learn that it was to play an engagement in Plevna, a whistle stop a day's drive from Toronto with no suitable hotel accommodations, and they blamed their manager, Freddie Swange, a fellow with a good business head but little interest in music, for booking them where they couldn't even get a decent meal.

2. From the service head the wires run through the meter and into the switch box or circuit breaker, which should by all means provide for six branch circuits in addition to a 220 circuit for the electric range, which many wives find much more convenient than gas, especially in view of recent improvements in such features as quick heating which have been provided by highly skilled electrical engineers determined to give the public the full benefits of electricity, one of the greatest marvels of our times.

3. The job was a good one for Crubfield, who couldn't get around very well because of his foot trouble, a recurrent tendonitis which had not responded very well to the treatment prescribed by Dr. Goslin, who had been trained at the Mayo Clinic and who should have been able to cure tendonitis if anyone could.

65. MISUSED DEPENDENT CLAUSES

All dependent clauses have the functions of separate parts of speech—noun, adjective, adverb. To substitute one such clause for another is as serious an error as misusing an adjective for an adverb. The most common misuses are an adverbial clause used for a noun clause, an adverbial clause used as a substitute for a noun, and a full sentence used for either a noun clause or a noun.

65a. DO NOT USE AN ADVERBIAL CLAUSE AS A NOUN CLAUSE.

A noun clause is properly the subject of a verb, the object of a verb, or a predicate nominative; an adverbial clause is not. To correct a misused adverbial clause, substitute for it a noun clause, or supply a verb which the adverbial clause may modify.

> Dubious: George remembered *where the radio said* the stock market is dropping.
> *Because there was no use in his staying* was the reason Bob left the meeting.

Correct: George remembered *that the radio said* the stock market is dropping.

Bob left the meeting *because there was no use in his staying.*

That there was no use in his staying was the reason Bob left the meeting.

65b. DO NOT USE AN ADVERBIAL CLAUSE IN PLACE OF A SINGLE NOUN OR NOUN PHRASE.

For reasons similar to those which apply above, avoid using adverbial clauses for single nouns or noun phrases. *When, where, because* clauses are frequent offenders.

Dubious: False flattery is *when* you pay a lot of compliments that are not sincere.

My sailing trophy was *because* I won three races out of four.

Clear: False flattery is paying a lot of insincere compliments.

False flattery is the payment of a lot of compliments which are not sincere.

Winning three races out of four gained me the sailing trophy.

I earned the sailing trophy by winning three races out of four.

65c. USE A NOUN CLAUSE, NOT A SENTENCE, AS THE SUBJECT OR COMPLEMENT OF *IS* AND *WAS*.

The use of a quoted sentence is generally accepted as a subject or complement:

"When I consider how my light is spent" is a line from John Milton's famous poem, "On His Blindness."

In general, however, a sentence cannot be suitably used as a subject or complement of *is* and *was*. To correct the illogical construction, change the sentence, or independent clause, into an adverbial clause, reduce the independent clause to a phrase, or make the sentence into a dependent clause by using the proper subordinating conjunction, usually *that.*

Dubious: I had broken my leg was the reason I resigned from the team.

Bill's only virtue is he never is rude to his mother.

Improved: The reason that I resigned from the team was that I had broken my leg.

I resigned from the team because I had broken my leg.

Bill's only virtue is that he is never rude to his mother.

Bill has only one virtue: never being rude to his mother.

EXERCISE 7

Correct the following sentences:

1. His home is where you can always have a good time.
2. A state of rebellion is when armed forces seize control of the government.
3. The reason the mower did not cut the grass was because its blades were dull.
4. I see in the paper where the weather has been unusually cold this winter.
5. The seat of the chair has been stood on so often by you children is the cause for its giving way under Mrs. Smith.
6. Only because they have formal clothes is why the dance is being held.
7. His definition of freedom is when you can look any man squarely in the eye.
8. Perjury is where a man swears to tell the truth and then tells a lie.
9. Her father pointed out where she had been making the same mistakes for years.
10. The thing that upset our chickens was a skunk came into the henhouse looking for eggs.

66. MISPLACED MODIFIER

Some languages are highly inflected; that is, the endings of their nouns, adjectives, adverbs, and verbs are varied and it is relatively easy to identify their relationships to other

words in a sentence. The English language is not highly inflected. Relationships between words in an English sentence
depend largely upon the *order* in which those words occur.
Consider how the meaning of the following sentence
changes as the position of the adjective is shifted:

> My *first* husband's job was in market research.
> My husband's *first* job was in market research.

Related words should be kept together so that their connection may be clearly seen. Modifiers, especially, should be
placed close to the words or phrases they are intended to
modify.

66a. AVOID A "SQUINTING MODIFIER."

When a modifier is placed so that it could as readily
modify the word or phrase preceding it as the word or phrase
immediately following, it is said to "look two ways" or to be
a "squinting" modifier. In the sentence "The boy who is
delivering our mail *currently* needs a haircut," there is
ambiguity: is the boy who needs a haircut in current possession of the delivery chore, or is the official delivery boy in
current tonsorial distress?

To clear up the confusion, you should revise. One way to
do this is to add *certainly* after *currently*. In this way, you
indicate that the adverb *currently* modifies *is delivering,* and
the adverb *certainly* applies to *needs.* Another method is to
move the modifier and include it with the material it modifies, i.e., transfer *currently* to a position between *who* and *is,*
or (if such is the writer's intention), to a position following
haircut. If the resulting sentence is still awkward, rewrite it.
Punctuation may also help in this instance, but it is not
always a reliable guide.

66b. PROPERLY POSITION SUCH WORDS AS *EVEN, HARDLY, NOT, ONLY, SCARCELY.*

These words, as well as others like correlative conjunctions, *both—and, either—or, not only—but also,* can cause
confusion to the reader unless they are placed precisely.

Note the difference in meaning of the following:

I will ask Bill to the dance tomorrow.

I will tomorrow ask Bill to the dance.

Note further how the position of *only* affects the following sentence in eight different ways:

Only my sister asked me to lend her a few dollars.

My *only* sister asked me to lend her a few dollars.

My sister *only* asked me to lend her a few dollars.

My sister asked *only* me to lend her a few dollars.

My sister asked me *only* to lend her a few dollars.

My sister asked me to lend *only* her a few dollars.

My sister asked me to lend her *only* a few dollars.

My sister asked me to lend her a few dollars *only*.

Such words as *only* are generally associated with the word or phrase immediately following or preceding. Thus:

Ineffective:	I *only* have one more lawn to mow.
	They *scarcely* have enough food to sustain them.
More effective:	I have *only* one more lawn to mow.
	They have *scarcely* enough food to sustain them.

66c. PROPERLY POSITION PHRASES AND CLAUSES.

Modifying phrases and clauses, like modifying words, should be so placed that their meaning is entirely clear. Writers of the following could not have meant what their sentences say:

We put the cake in the refrigerator, which we would eat the next day.

I gave a jar of cucumbers to the vicar freshly pickled.

WANTED: Asst. Supervisor for kindergarten children with college degree.

EXERCISE 8

Revise the following sentences by repositioning misplaced modifiers.

1. Sweeney was singing as he walked home at the top of his voice.
2. Last summer Mrs. Wiggans almost killed thirty chickens a week.

3. We only bought small souvenirs to take home to our family and friends.
4. He first met the woman who was to become his wife on a crowded bus.
5. Shirley dumped the food right into the garbage can that she had on her tray.
6. A man who tries to please his wife frequently may be henpecked.
7. McMasters kept the skin of the tiger he had shot in his den.
8. Until recently, hay has either been taken from the field loose or in bales.
9. She asked him to meet her when night fell in front of the house.
10. At birth we all know that an infant is incapable of taking care of itself.

EXERCISE 9

Follow the directions for Exercise 8.

1. Unsatisfied creditors go away seldom happily.
2. Violet says that she remembers Christmases spent as a little girl well.
3. I hardly ever think that Morton and his wife go to the movies.
4. A coffee table stood before the fireplace with carved legs and a glass top.
5. The week Jerry made twenty dollars it almost seemed like a million.
6. We decided entirely to trust Kenneth.
7. It was a beautiful sunny morning, such as you can only find in the North Woods.
8. Never give fruit to a baby that hasn't been strained.
9. The teacher picked up the essay Franklin had written with a sigh.
10. The college that Carson chose after deliberation rejected his application.

67. DANGLING MODIFIER

Modifiers which do not correctly and clearly depend upon the right words are called "dangling modifiers" because they hang loosely within the sentence and produce confusion, ambiguity, and even ludicrousness. Verb phrases and elliptical clauses are said to "dangle" when the words with which they should be associated are incorrectly placed or not expressed.

67a. AVOID DANGLING VERBAL PHRASES.

Three methods may be used to correct sentences containing dangling verbal phrases: (1) by making the verbal phrase a dependent clause; (2) by expressing the noun or pronoun (substantive) to which the phrase applies; (3) by placing the phrase so close to the substantive that no confusion is possible.

Questionable: *Standing at the station,* the train hurtled by. (Participial phrase)

To drive safely, a good set of tires is needed. (Infinitive phrase)

In typing a theme, it is advisable to use wide margins. (Gerund phrase)

Improved: While I was standing at the station, the train hurtled by.

Standing at the station, I saw the train hurtle by.

We, standing at the station, saw the train hurtle by. (Because the subject and verb are placed so far apart, this sentence ideally should be rephrased.)

To drive safely, you need a good set of tires.

When you are typing a theme, it is advisable to use wide margins.

Participial phrases tacked on to the end of a statement with *thereby, thus,* and *therefore* are also dangling because they have no substantive to modify. Sentences containing such constructions may be corrected by rephrasing or by including the participle in a compound predicate.

Questionable: I was taken aside by Roger, thus causing me to lose my place in line.

Improved: I was taken aside by Roger and thus lost my place in line.

Being taken aside by Roger caused me to lose my place in line.

307

When a verbal phrase is used to express a general action rather than a specific one, it is *not* held to be a dangling modifier:

Generally speaking, tennis is a strenuous sport.

Words or phrases such as *according to, concerning, considering, owing to,* etc., are used prepositionally, not as verbals. "*Considering the circumstances,* he is not to be blamed" is a clear and proper sentence.

67b. AVOID DANGLING ELLIPTICAL CLAUSES.

An *ellipsis* is an omission. An elliptical clause is one from which the subject or verb, or both, have been left out. Such a clause dangles unless the omitted subject or predicate, intended to be understood, is in fact the same as that of the main clause.

Incorrect: Though crying for attention, my aunt ignored the baby.

When thirty-two, his third son was born.

Before completely adjusted, you should not use this compass.

To correct such unclear sentences you should insert in the dependent clause the needed subject and verb, or change the subject or subject-verb in the main clause.

Correct: Though he was crying for attention, my aunt ignored the baby.

Though crying for attention, the baby was ignored by my aunt.

When he was thirty-two, his third son was born.

When thirty-two, he rejoiced at the birth of his third son.

Before it is completely adjusted, you should not use this compass.

You should completely adjust this compass before you use it.

EXERCISE 10

Rewrite the following sentences so that they contain no dangling modifiers.

1. While lecturing to the class, a fly lit on Professor Moriarty's nose.

2. To understand the Middle Ages, Dante should be read with great care.
3. Being the oldest child of the family, Mother made an example of me in front of my brothers and sisters.
4. At the age of eleven, Myrtle's father remarried.
5. If held correctly, one can get much pleasure from a kaleidoscope.
6. Looking over my right shoulder, Mount Robson was very impressive.
7. Stepping inside the huge building, a jet airplane is seen.
8. Being a small town in a farming community, the stores are open only on Saturday nights.
9. Just before slithering through a tiny hole in the wall, Morris caught the weasel.
10. Having never before been in Alberta, Banff was a pleasant surprise.

EXERCISE 11

Follow the directions for Exercise 10.

1. A good dictionary should be at hand when writing themes.
2. Fish are easy to catch in these waters when using the right bait.
3. Falling softly past the window, we watched the first snow of the winter.
4. Having lost consciousness, the coach sent in a substitute for Simpson.
5. Looking to the left and to the right, the water could be seen.
6. To punish me for misbehaving, I was forbidden use of the car for a full month.
7. Rose-colored glasses should always be worn when going on a blind date.
8. Not much interested in poetry, *Hamlet* was lost on Harvey.
9. To make a good cake, fresh eggs are always required.
10. The hat should always be held in the hand when chatting with a lady.

68. SPLIT CONSTRUCTION

Nothing is actually incorrect about separating or "splitting" related elements in a sentence. However, in the interests of clarity, one should strive to keep related materials as closely together as possible. Awkwardness often results from splitting such elements as verbs in a verb phrase, the parts of an infinitive, a preposition and its object, and other word combinations which logically belong together.

68a. AVOID SPLITTING AN INFINITIVE.

A *split infinitive* occurs when words, phrases, or clauses are inserted between the infinitive sign *to* and the verb. Split infinitives have been used by reputable writers; on rare occasions their use is even required. For example, in the sentence, "Mary wants *to actually remake* her dress," *actually* modifies the verb *remake* and is effectively and properly placed next to it.

Usually, however, putting an adverb or phrase or other group of words between *to* and a verb serves only to weaken a sentence. "We were ordered to *as quietly as possible* leave the classroom" would be less awkward if the italicized phrase were placed at the end of the sentence.

68b. AVOID SEPARATING THE PARTS OF A VERB PHRASE.

Splitting an auxiliary verb and a main verb is rarely effective or natural. Consider the following sentences:

The instructor *has*, although one would hardly believe it, *been* lecturing for over an hour.

This was the recording we *had* before we left Toronto *heard* so often in discotheques.

He *has*, to my great surprise, *sung* very well.

By bringing together the words in italics, the sentences become more clear and direct:

Although one would hardly believe it, the instructor *has been* lecturing for over an hour.

This was the recording we *had heard* so often in discotheques before we left Toronto.

To my great surprise, he *has sung* very well.

68c. AVOID THE UNNECESSARY SEPARATION OF SUBJECT AND VERB, PREPOSITION AND OBJECT, AND OTHER CLOSELY RELATED SENTENCE ELEMENTS.

On occasion, separation of such elements achieves special clarity. In general, however, the italicized elements in the sentences below should be written together:

The king *summoned*, as soon as I had made my proposal, *his councillors*.

John, upon hearing the remark, *reached for the telephone*.
Reuben walked *under*, although he was superstitious, *the ladder*.

68d. PLACE COORDINATE ELEMENTS TOGETHER.

Two coordinate phrases or two coordinate dependent clauses should not be widely separated. Because of their approximately equal weight, they should be brought together and their relationship indicated by the appropriate coordinating conjunction:

Ineffective: *Although he was conscientious on the job,* he could not win a promotion, *although he performed many extra duties.*

Effective: *Although he was conscientious on the job* and *although he performed many extra duties,* he could not win a promotion.

Ineffective: *Unless the blizzard lets up,* we cannot make it to the mountain lodge, *unless the roads are passable.*

Effective: *Unless the blizzard lets up,* and *unless the roads are passable,* we cannot make it to the mountain lodge.

EXERCISE 12

Find and correct all faulty split constructions in the following sentences.

1. Because it was raining, I did not like to go fishing, because the fish would not bite well.

2. I have found that it is sometimes possible to without much planning and with some haste in the writing compose a good essay.

3. If the coach gives his permission, we can play three sets of tennis today, if it does not rain.

4. I would like to merely and in simple words make a few statements about my trip to Mexico.

5. No one in my community has ever in all these years known such a dry spring.

6. We, during the last three years, have shared the rent.

7. Then the painstaking task of salvaging the rare books which have been buried in mud and the priceless paintings which have been stained by the rising flood begins.

8. During our visit to Mexico, we discovered that when the sun sets, people stroll around the town squares, when the evening breeze blows.

9. My sister, after a summer at camp, had, in many different ways, improved.

10. Martha did all she could to subtly and without showing any intention of doing so, thwart, harass, and disparage her rival for the starring role.

69. FAULTY COORDINATION

The ideas expressed within a sentence have degrees of importance, or rank, which should be shown by their constructions. Elements of equal rank are *coordinate;* those of lesser importance are *subordinate* to first-rank thoughts.

An effective writer will avoid too much coordination because it is monotonous and frequently childish. Furthermore, he will carefully distinguish between major or minor elements so as not to convey hazy impressions or weaken the significance of his main statement.

69a. AVOID STRINGY, "RUN-ON" SENTENCES.

The compound sentence should not be overworked. Obviously, a long series of short independent clauses joined by conjunctions has the effect of running on and on, much as the strung-out speech of a child: "We bought a beautiful car, and it has wire wheels, and it goes very fast, and we drive it every day." The best way to correct such a run-on sentence is to reduce predication: change an independent clause into a dependent one, a dependent clause into a phrase, a phrase into a single word.

> Immature: Yesterday it snowed, and we went sledding, and we went tobogganing, and we went skiing, but we didn't go skating and we didn't go ice-boating.
>
> Improved: When it snowed yesterday we went sledding, tobogganing and skiing, but we didn't go skating or ice-boating.
>
> Yesterday in the snow we went . . .

69b. AVOID "SEESAW" SENTENCES.

Compound sentences containing two independent clauses of nearly equal length occasionally may be effective. Such balanced sentences, however, have a monotonous, seesaw quality when they appear in steady succession. The following would be improved by reducing predication:

> I did not have too good a time between Dominion Day and Labor Day, but I managed to see a number of good friends during the summer. I met a nice girl named Sarajean at a beach picnic, and we went to a couple of movies together. She was quite interested in tennis and golf, and active sports like that, but I never was too much of an athlete. Most of the gang liked her a lot, and they say they will miss her when she flies to Nova Scotia next week. All in all, it was a pretty quiet two months, but I certainly shouldn't complain about the lack of excitement.

69c. AVOID INACCURATE COORDINATION.

Two sentence elements should be related by the correct coordinating conjunction. Do not use *but* if *or* is the exact connective, *and* for *but,* etc.

> I needed a haircut, *but* [not *and*] the barbershop was closed.
> John suffered a setback, *or* [not *but*] he would have finished first.

69d. AVOID FALSE COORDINATION: DO NOT JOIN A RELATIVE CLAUSE TO ITS PRINCIPAL CLAUSE BY *AND, BUT,* OR *OR.*

Since *coordinate* signifies "of equal rank," a dependent clause may not be connected to an independent clause by a coordinating conjunction. This principle is most often violated by the so-called "and which" construction. Never use *and which, but which, and who, but who,* etc., unless this expression follows a coordinate "which clause" or "who clause."

> She showed much enthusiasm at first, *but which* soon melted away.

This sentence can be corrected by omitting *but* and retaining the comma, since the clause is nonrestrictive. Another way is by providing a preceding "which clause": "She at first showed much enthusiasm which was praised by her teacher but which soon melted away." Still another method is cutting away some of the deadwood: "Her great initial enthusiasm soon melted away."

69e. AVOID OVERUSING *SO* AS A CONJUNCTION.

So is correctly used as a conjunctive adverb following a semicolon, and it is often used between independent clauses with only a comma before it. Nevertheless, there are three objections to *so* in such constructions: ineffectiveness through overuse, a juvenile effect in many instances, and a sense of inappropriateness in formal use. Overuse of *so* can be remedied by replacing that conjunction with *therefore, accordingly, thus, so that,* and like expressions. Remember, however, to avoid the error of the comma splice (see Section 62).

> Ineffective: He had to earn money for tuition, so he planned his leisure time carefully.
>
> Twenty boys wanted to go, so we hired a bus.
>
> Our school cafeteria has been completely redesigned so it can better accommodate the students.

Improved: He had to earn money for tuition; therefore he planned his leisure time carefully.

Having to earn money for tuition, he planned his leisure time carefully.

Since twenty boys wanted to go, we hired a bus.

Our school cafeteria has been completely redesigned so that it can better accommodate the students.

EXERCISE 13

Rewrite the following sentences in order to eliminate improper coordination.

1. My brother and I have eye trouble, but we both wear glasses.
2. The train home was crowded, and we stood all the way.
3. There are many art courses offered so I shall have a wide choice.
4. I can be around a golf course and continue to play golf and there will be many chances for me to go to different towns and states to play in tournaments.
5. They walked for miles and miles but finally they were arrested and Tess was taken to jail, and she was tried, and then she was finally executed.
6. We had a flat tire, but we should have been here an hour ago.
7. The students choose their own subjects, or they report on things they are interested in.
8. There was a good movie at one of the theaters so we decided to go.
9. In 1801 Springfield was planned, and in 1818 Clark County was created, and in 1827 Springfield was incorporated.
10. The clambake turned out to be a success even though it was undercooked a little, and the camping trip ended the day after the clambake.
11. We must learn to speak German fluently so we can transmit our ideas to businessmen in Berlin.
12. Mr. Harrison had been in the Army and he sometimes addressed us as if he were still a top sergeant.
13. I went on a tour of the submarine base and it proved to be very inspiring.
14. I have a brother who is 19 years old and he is in the Army.
15. We told our scoutmaster that we did a passable job, but we were weary and our joints ached, and we told him we would turn in a full report tomorrow.

70.   FAULTY SUBORDINATION

A good writer, recognizing that not all of his ideas merit equal rank, will carefully select some of them for his prime statements and subordinate minor thoughts to selected major ones. As with proper and appropriate coordination, good subordination produces clear, effective, and mature writing.

For the same reasons that he avoids excessive and faulty coordination, a careful writer avoids excessive and faulty subordination. In reducing predication, he determines exactly what the relationships of his ideas are to be and he expresses them in constructions that assure his readers a clear understanding of those precise relationships.

70a.   AVOID PUTTING A COORDINATE IDEA IN A SUBORDINATE FORM.

Inaccurate: He was lean and energetic, *while* his brother was fat and lethargic.

Educated in Switzerland, he received his college degree in Canada.

I asked Nan to the game; *though,* she turned me down.

Improved: He was lean and energetic, *but* his brother was fat and lethargic.

He was lean and energetic, *whereas* his brother was fat and lethargic.

He was lean and energetic; his brother was fat and lethargic.

He was educated in Switzerland, *but* he received his college degree in Canada.

He was educated in Switzerland; *however,* he received his college degree in Canada.

I asked Nan to the game, *but* she turned me down.

I asked Nan to the game; *however,* she turned me down.

70b. AVOID PUTTING THE MAIN IDEA OF A SENTENCE IN A SUBORDINATE FORM; AVOID PUTTING A SUBORDINATE IDEA IN A MAIN CLAUSE.

If an idea of less importance is put into an independent clause and an important idea is put in a dependent clause, the result, although grammatically correct, is an *upside-down subordination* of content. Determining the relative importance of ideas is sometimes difficult; usually, however, the most dramatic incident and the effect comprise major elements, whereas preliminaries, such as time, place, and circumstances, form minor and subordinate elements.

Ineffective: John was nearly out of breath when he spied a light in the distance.

I was halfway across the field when the bull suddenly charged.

Improved: When John was nearly out of breath, he spied a light in the distance.

Just as (when) I was halfway across the field, the bull suddenly charged.

70c. AVOID EXCESSIVE SUBORDINATION.

Subordinate statements which overlap each other in a mounting series are not effective. Clauses and phrases should be properly linked, but the finished structure should not resemble a staircase.

Ineffective: These are lobsters which were caught off the coast of Nova Scotia, where the water is cold, and which were flown in today.

I liked to watch the children who fed the elephants the peanuts which were peddled at the circus wagon that was near the main tent.

Improved: These lobsters, caught off the Nova Scotia coast where the water is cold, were flown in today.

These lobsters, caught in Nova Scotia's cold coastal waters, were flown in today.

I liked to watch the children feeding peanuts to the elephants. The nuts were peddled at the circus wagon near the main tent.

Rewrite the following sentences, correcting the faulty subordination.

1. As the lightning struck the house, Dad was watching TV.
2. Port Credit is seven miles north of Oakville, having a population of 14,000.
3. One of my fondest memories is the old Pierce-Arrow which I bought for $30.00 from the man who owns a delicatessen near Hague where I took the train that took me to work.
4. Father had little resistance to disease, because when he contracted pneumonia he spent over four weeks in the hospital.
5. I saw him frequently, when he looked at me queerly, and with his eyes blinking.
6. I was not driving fast through the intersection when a policeman shouted "Stop!"
7. During my year abroad I am living with a family which is headed by an elderly man whose brother was a college professor for some fifty years at l'Academie Industrielle, which is the other college in the city supported by public funds.
8. I was six years old when I was given my first pair of ice skates.
9. It was so noisy that I had to shut the door to hear the radio in the den that leads out to the terrace which is on the west side of the house that faces the pond which is covered with lily pads.
10. This unforgettable character was usually desperate, being out of work, and he had no money.

71.   FAULTY PARALLELISM

In mathematics, *parallel* refers to two lines extending in the same direction and having an equal distance between them at every point. In writing, *parallel* means "similar, having close resemblance." When two or more ideas in a sentence are alike in form and purpose, they can and should be expressed in the same grammatical forms:

Words: Carey is *big* but *graceful.*
Midge wants to *hop, skip,* and *jump.*
His manner is *high, wide,* and *handsome.*

Phrases: *At work* and *at play,* Henry always pushed himself hard.

> *Over the river* and *through the woods,* to Grand-
> father's house we go.

Clauses: My spirits rose *when I arrived in Puerto Rico* and
when I saw my roommate in the airport lobby.

I cannot drive in this province *until I am 16 and
until I pass my driver's test.*

One of the tersest reports in naval history is this:
"*Sighted sub. Sank same.*"

71a.   SENTENCE ELEMENTS THAT ARE COORDINATE IN RANK SHOULD BE PARALLEL IN STRUCTURE.

A prepositional phrase should be coordinate with a prepositional phrase, an infinitive phrase with an infinitive phrase,
a dependent clause with a dependent clause, and so on.

Wrong: This book is out of stock and not being printed.

Our band plays at many school dances, town parades, and concert tours.

My ambition is to win an Atkinson scholarship and
that I might graduate from York.

Right: This book is out of stock and out of print.

Our band plays at many school dances, marches in
town parades, and makes several concert tours.

My ambition is to win an Atkinson scholarship and to
graduate from York. (Or: I have two ambitions:
to win an Atkinson scholarship and to graduate
from York.)

Absolute parallelism is not always required. In the following sentences, the functions are parallel even though the
form is not strictly so:

She dressed *flamboyantly* and *with a distinct flair.*

We saw *Carol, Helen,* and *a girl whom we did not recognize.*

71b.   AVOID MISLEADING PARALLELISM.

If ideas are arranged in parallel form but are neither
parallel nor coordinate in content, they are only *apparently*
parallel and thus will mislead the reader.

Wrong: We bought that refrigerator from a discount store
and with a four-year guarantee.

> The chemist pointed out that non-smokers have longer lives, enjoy better health, and can be more accurately tested in an experiment of this sort than smokers.

> Better: We bought that refrigerator from a discount store; it carries a four-year guarantee.

> The chemist pointed out that non-smokers have longer lives and enjoy better health than smokers; besides, they can be more accurately tested in an experiment of this sort.

A writer should be particularly cautious in handling a series of elements which, though appearing to modify the same element, are not actually parallel.

> Wrong: In your behalf in effect I will be bringing suit against the firm for $20,000.

> Better: In effect I will be bringing suit in your behalf against the firm for $20,000.

71c. AVOID PARTIAL PARALLELISM.

In arranging a parallel series, make sure that each element is similar in form and structure to every other element in the series:

> Wrong: Corinne has served our local Red Cross as typist, ambulance driver, and has worked as an aide in the nursery room.

> The movie is well directed, nicely choreographed, and the scoring is beautiful.

> Better: Corinne has served our local Red Cross as typist, ambulance driver, and nursery-room aide.

> The movie is well directed, nicely choreographed, and beautifully scored.

71d. SENTENCE ELEMENTS FOLLOWING CORRELATIVE CONJUNCTIONS SHOULD BE PARALLEL IN FORM.

The four common pairs of correlative conjunctions are *both—and, either—or, neither—nor,* and *not only—but also.* Each part of the pair should be followed immediately by the same grammatical form, two similar words, two similar phrases, or two similar clauses.

Wrong: You can *either* take the high road *or* the low road.

She *not only* is quite rich *but also* quite stingy.

The admissions director requests that you be *either* prepared to take the examination on Friday *or* that you submit another application in August.

Better: You can take *either* the high road *or* the low road.

She is *not only* quite rich *but also* quite stingy.

The admissions director requests *either* that you be prepared to take the examination on Friday *or* that you submit another application in August.

EXERCISE 15

Rewrite the following sentences, making the coordinate elements parallel in form.

1. Not only was she noisy and rude but also rather stupid.
2. Marvin didn't like Conservatives and especially to have one in the family.
3. I spend too much time both playing bridge and on bull sessions.
4. Jay is a man whom people respect but is not very approachable.
5. At about noon every day the siren blows and warning the residents of another big blast at the quarry.
6. The constant nibbling away of the rats and to hear them running across the foot of the bed undermined little Edson's confidence.
7. Later that year, having lost his job and unable to find another, he had to sell his car.
8. My Uncle Julian wrote his autobiography but which was uninteresting because nothing had ever happened to him.
9. Students too often come to class with pencil and paper, carrying notebooks and texts, and a torpid mind.
10. The Admiral was told he was either a liar or he was a fool.

EXERCISE 16

Follow the directions for Exercise 15.

1. It is well to invest in a variety of enterprises rather than putting all your eggs in one basket.
2. Professor Higgins assigned an article in Spanish and had to be read by Thursday.
3. Martin has a great sense of humor and who likes to play jokes on his friends.

4. What a joy it is to find a woman who is attractive, modest, and knows how to treat a man!
5. The old house needed painting, to be papered, and a patch job.
6. To the yolks of three dozen eggs add a pint of goat's milk, three tablespoons of sunflower seed, a head of lettuce, and then you should stir briskly for forty-five minutes.
7. After you've been there a while and beginning to know your way around, look up Charley.
8. My grandfather always voted Conservative and being a conservative in every way.
9. Daisy stumbled, fell, and the counselor reluctantly helped her to her feet.
10. Going rapidly and on only one water ski, Al came to grief.

72. POINT OF VIEW (CONSISTENCY)

A good writer maintains a consistent point of view. The principle of consistency applies not only to a theme (see Section 100) but also to the construction of sentences. To be consistent, two or more elements in a sentence must agree and remain similar until a good reason exists for shifting them. To write appropriately, be consistent in tense, voice, mood, pronoun reference, and figures of speech.

72a. BE CONSISTENT IN THE USE OF SUBJECT AND VOICE IN A SENTENCE.

Voice is a term in grammar which indicates whether the subject is acting (active) or being acted upon (passive). In general, the active voice is more effective than the passive; however, adhering to the use of either one removes a major cause of shifts in subject. Ordinarily, one should have a single subject in a sentence and should use only one voice.

Faulty: The diesel engine burns little kerosene, and Ed says it is completely reliable.

As you sail across the harbor, channel markers can be seen.

Improved: Ed says that the diesel engine burns little kerosene and is completely reliable.

As you sail across the harbor, you can see channel markers.

72b. BE CONSISTENT IN THE USE OF NUMBER.

Frequent mistakes in the use of number are careless switchings from plural nouns to singular nouns, or singular to plural, or failing to make pronouns agree in number with their antecedents.

Faulty: I enjoy an ice cream soda, but *they* tend to make me fat.

If boys treated Grandmother with respect, she would surely respect *him*.

Improved: I enjoy an ice cream soda, but *it* tends to make me fat.

If boys treated Grandmother with respect, she would surely respect *them*.

72c. BE CONSISTENT IN THE USE OF TENSE.

Tense, meaning the time of the verb (present, past, future, present perfect, etc.), may be a pitfall to writers of narrative and narrative exposition, who often shift unnecessarily from present to past, or from past to present, or back and forth between the two. Note the switches in tense in the faulty example below.

Faulty: Claire *was walking* briskly along the sidewalk when suddenly a riderless horse *came charging* around the corner. At a full gallop, it *races* down the middle of the street, then *veers* abruptly and *heads* directly for her. In panic, Claire *leaped* to the nearest doorway.

Improved: Claire was walking briskly along the sidewalk when suddenly a riderless horse came charging around the corner. At a full gallop, it raced down the middle of the street, then veered abruptly and headed directly for her. In panic, Claire leaped to the nearest doorway.

72d. BE CONSISTENT IN THE USE OF THE CLASS OR PERSON OF PRONOUNS.

Pronouns and antecedents should agree in person; commonly, however, a careless writer will violate this principle by thoughtlessly shifting from the third person to the second:
If one practices scales on the piano for one hour each day, *you are* bound to improve *your* finger dexterity.

72e. BE CONSISTENT IN THE USE OF MOOD OR MODE.

Mood or *mode* in grammar indicates the "style" or "fashion" of the verb. (See Section 18.) A good writer will not unnecessarily swing back and forth between the indicative and subjunctive or imperative:

Faulty: Last year at school I would play hockey on Thursday afternoons and edited the yearbook on Thursday evenings.

Improved: Last year at school I would play hockey on Thursday afternoons and would edit the yearbook on Thursday evenings.

Last year at school I played hockey on Thursday afternoons and edited the yearbook on Thursday evenings.

72f. BE CONSISTENT IN THE USE OF FIGURES OF SPEECH.

Figures of speech, that is, words used not in their literal sense but for the images they suggest, are occasionally effective and vivid. However, guard against sudden switches from literal to figurative speech and switches from one figure to another:

That foreman is a cold fish who always has an axe to grind.

Before we pass judgment on the unfortunate foreman, we must answer a question: what use has a fish for an axe? Perhaps this might be a clearer statement:

That disdainful foreman always has a selfish motive.

EXERCISE 17

Improve the following sentences by eliminating the structural inconsistencies.

1. One can accomplish a great deal more in a day if you get up early in the morning.
2. Whenever a paper is written, you should use good English.
3. Mr. Throop was idly watching the monkey when suddenly it jumps into his lap.
4. When tyranny threatens your country, a man should resist it, even though resistance means jail.
5. When you make sukiyaki, you must arrange the ingredients attractively, and it is cooked at the table.
6. My room at the dormitory has a large bookcase where you can keep your books.
7. Ingrid's father handed me my hat, and I was told by her mother not to return.
8. Just when Toro was on the ropes, Larkin's manager throws in the towel.
9. When my brother bought the *Encyclopaedia Britannica*, I was promised a quarter by him for every volume I read.
10. One who travels abroad ought always to keep his passport where you can get to it easily.

EXERCISE 18

Follow the directions for Exercise 17.

1. The whole family was sitting around discussing their financial situation.
2. Cousin Milton was apprehended by the local police, and the RCMP seized Uncle Henry.
3. In strumming a guitar, you should not strike the strings vigorously, but they should be stroked with a sweeping motion.
4. What a nuisance a little brother can be when they are in a mischievous mood!
5. When one is tired and dispirited after a hard day at the office or in school, try a Whammo Atomic-Action Vitamin Capsule.
6. You kill the buffalo, Dawson, and the lions will be taken care of by me.
7. My big brother came coasting down the hill on a bicycle and yells, "Look, Ma, no feet!"
8. The tourist can now cross the Straits in a few minutes by bridge, whereas they often used to wait hours for a ferry.

9. By making that statement, Claghorn really put his foot in his mouth, but there is no use in crying over spilled milk.
10. He bids a dramatic farewell to the world and its troubles and leaps into the river, only to discover that it had been dry since early June.

73. CHOPPINESS

An occasional short sentence is effective and appropriate. A number of short sentences in succession is not appropriate; the effect is choppy, jerky, or "hiccupping." Such a series also gives emphasis to relatively unimportant ideas which should be subordinated to primary statements.

73a. AVOID WRITING A SERIES OF SHORT, CHOPPY SENTENCES.

Evaluate the ideas in short, jerky sentences and then coordinate them or subordinate them in a longer, unified sentence.

Faulty: She waded into the stream. She was determined to save the kitten. The current clutched at her knees. It almost pulled her under. Steadily she gained on the terrified animal. She seized it in both hands.

Improved: Determined to save the kitten, she waded into the stream. The current which clutched at her knees almost pulled her under, but steadily she gained on the terrified animal. Then she seized it in both hands.

Faulty: We have an eighty-acre farm located in southern Ontario. Besides the eighty acres, we rent a neighbor's farm of fifty acres. Our farm is in the rolling country. We have to terrace our land. On our farm we have a small wood. This wood has a creek running through it. There

are two hills on both sides of our farm. We
therefore call our farm "Green Valley Farm."
Our farm is shaped like the province of British
Columbia. The creek we call the Little Fraser.

Improved: In southern Ontario we have an eighty-acre
farm, to which we have added fifty more acres
rented from a neighbor. The rolling land,
which we have to terrace, is flanked by two
hills; hence the name "Green Valley Farm."
Running through a small wood on our property is a creek which, because the farm is
shaped like the province of British Columbia,
we call the Little Fraser.

73b. AVOID WRITING A SERIES OF SENTENCES CONTAINING SHORT, JERKY INDEPENDENT CLAUSES.

Compound sentences containing short, choppy clauses are
just as monotonous as a series of short sentences. To improve
them, apply the principles of coordination and subordination.

Faulty: I work in a rock-and-roll group and I play lead
guitar. I admire the other members of the
group, but perhaps the one I admire most is
John Curtis. He has a genuine musical talent,
which I don't.

Improved: I play lead guitar in a rock-and-roll group. Of
the other members, John Curtis, who has the
genuine musical talent I lack, is the one I
admire most.

Faulty: There were two ways to reach the cone: one was
by cable car, the other was by car and foot.
Mother and I chose the latter. The road was
under construction; once we had to wait
for a load of stone to be unloaded before
we could pass.

Improved: Of the two ways to reach the cone, one by cable
car and the other by car and foot, Mother and
I chose the latter. The road was under construction, and once we had to wait for a load of
stone to be unloaded before we could pass.

EXERCISE 19

By subordinating and by supplying connectives build up the following choppy sentences into larger units.

1. Martin's reform is miraculous. He gets to his classes on time. He arrives at work on time. He drives no more than ten miles over the speed limit. He lives within his allowance. He saves what he earns. He even studies sometimes. His fraternity brothers are watching him with interest.

2. He looked at the sun. He saw that it was within a few minutes of setting. There was just time to fix the barn. That was done and then he put his mackinaw on the old couch. He put his plaid cap on the couch. He dropped his boots on the floor near the potbellied stove. He noticed that the fire was out. There was no wood in the woodbox, either.

3. Bridge is a popular game among students. Many people play bridge after they leave school. Women frequently belong to Thursday afternoon bridge clubs. Playing bridge is also a good way for men and women to spend sociable evenings. Some people become expert at the game. They travel all over the country playing in tournaments. It is important to remember that bridge is only a game.

EXERCISE 20

Follow the directions for Exercise 19.

1. Through the wilderness of rugged mountain ranges a long file of Indians made its way. All of the Indians were on snowshoes. Each man, woman, and child was bent under a heavy load. They carried their wealth with them. The dogs alone were unburdened.

2. I remember one family in particular. Mother, Dad, and I used to visit them often. There were two boys and three girls in the family. One of the girls was my age. Her name was Susan. We were in the same grade all through school. I usually managed to sit behind Susan. Susan had long blonde pigtails. This was a great temptation. I was sent to the corner almost every day for pulling Susan's pigtails.

3. He was occupied in his favorite diversion. This was a puzzle made from two nails. Then an automobile stopped near the door. Afterwards there was a loud knock. But that was no business of Manuel's. The person at the door could not want to see him. So Manuel continued with his puzzle. He knew there was no one else in the house.

74. COMPARISONS

Comparisons, necessary and effective in good writing, should be so constructed that their meaning is logical and clear.

74a. MAKE CLEAR WHETHER AN OBJECT OR TERM BEING COMPARED IS OR IS NOT PART OF A CLASS OR GROUP.

A confusing comparison occurs when a part or a member of a class or group is also treated as a unique member. Avoid including within the class or group the object or term being compared, if it is part of the group. This may be done by inserting the excluding word *other*.

 Illogical: Henry is noisier than any boy in the bus.

     Sharon has a higher scholastic average than any student in the Junior Class.

 Clear: Henry is noisier than any *other* boy in the bus.

    Sharon has a higher scholastic average than any *other* student in the Junior Class.

However, a part or a member of a class or group may illogically be excluded from the class or group to which it belongs. In comparison, when the superlative degree indicates that the object being compared belongs within the group, do not use the word *other*.

 Illogical: Henry is the noisiest of all the *other* boys in the bus.

     Sharon has the highest scholastic average of any *other* student in the Junior Class.

 Clear: Henry is the noisiest of all the boys in the bus.

    Sharon has the highest scholastic average of all the students in the Junior Class.

74b. AVOID A MIXED OR DOUBLE COMPARISON.

When a writer tries to include two comparisons in the same statement, a confused construction often results. A double comparison in the same sentence is acceptable, but only when the second is presented after the first has been completed.

Wrong: He is *as* sorry, if not sorrier, *than* Polly.

For a small man, Mike can wrestle *as* well, if not better, *than* Bob.

Improved: He is *as* sorry *as*, if not sorrier *than*, Polly.

For a small man, Mike can wrestle *as* well *as*, if not better *than*, Bob.

Preferable: He is *as* sorry *as* Polly, if not sorrier.

For a small man, Mike can wrestle *as* well *as* Bob, if not better.

Wrong: My brother is *one of the tallest, if not the tallest, man* on the swim team.

The Flag Debate was *one of the longest, if not the longest, debate in Canadian history.*
ican history.

Preferable: My brother is *one of the tallest men on the swim team, if not the tallest.*

The Flag Debate was *one of the longest debates in Canadian history, if not the longest.*
the greatest.

74c. DO NOT OMIT WORDS NECESSARY IN A COMPARISON.

When a comparison is begun or implied, supply the words necessary to complete it and to make it clear. Never omit the standard of comparison.

Doubtful: He is so clever.

Improved: He is so clever that some of his disguises have never been penetrated.

He is really clever.

Doubtful: Your play has been the greatest triumph.

Improved: Your play has been the greatest triumph of any presented in this theater.

Your play has been a great triumph.

Doubtful: Science interested Marvin more than Marianne.

Improved: Science interested Marvin more than it did Marianne.

Science interested Marvin more than Marianne did.

EXERCISE 21

Correct errors in comparison in the following sentences.

1. Our school has one of the best gymnasiums.
2. Our region is rural, and the farmers, therefore, are more dependent upon one another.
3. He is one of my favorite and definitely my most skillful cousin.
4. Jet planes in the future will be safer and more advanced in their performance and engineering.
5. The tourists cheer as loud, if not louder, than the rest of the bullfight aficionados.
6. This is one of the most, if not the most, important conferences of the fiscal year.
7. Rembrandt was the greatest influence on my painting than any other artist.
8. I enjoyed this kind of companionship with my white mice, and even wondered if they were more intelligent.
9. Our highways are very good in comparison with other countries.
10. He is one of the most talked about, but the man on the street knows less about, than anyone else.

75. CONCISENESS

Concise means "brief and to the point." Although conciseness is primarily a concern of diction, it is also a problem in writing sentences.

A sentence may be fairly well constructed and still be ineffective because it is loaded with nonessential words. Furthermore, a sentence of 100 words may be economical, whereas a sentence of 20 words may be verbose. The true test of conciseness in a sentence is effectiveness: are there so many superfluous words that the meaning is lost, or so few words that the meaning is not fully conveyed?

75a. REDUCE PREDICATION.

By reducing predication, one may improve the conciseness of a sentence. The method involves reducing the number of words to make a statement, cutting out all unnecessary words by making one word serve the purpose of two or more. To reduce predication, you can use one or more of the following shortcuts:

1. Combine two short sentences into one. (See Section 73.)

From: She was a seamstress in a tailor shop. She specialized in buttons and hems.

To: She was a seamstress in a tailor shop, specializing in buttons and hems.

2. Reduce a clause to a phrase.

From: A fog which resembled the color of cotton.

To: A fog the color of cotton.

3. Reduce a phrase to a single word.

From: A fog the color of cotton.

To: A cotton-colored fog.

4. Reduce two or more words to one.

From: . . . a man on the police force.

To: . . . a policeman.

5. Reduce a compound or complex sentence to a simple sentence.

From: Apple pie for years has been a favorite Canadian dessert, and there isn't anybody in the world who doesn't like apple pie.

To: Everybody in the world likes apple pie, which for years has been a favorite Canadian dessert.

Or: Everybody in the world likes apple pie, for years a favorite Canadian desert.

75b. AVOID WRITING SENTENCES CONTAINING UNNECESSARY DETAILS.

A sentence which carries an excess of details is a prolix sentence. It is ineffective because its longwindedness obscures or dilutes the main idea.

Wordy: Last winter the intramural squash tournament was won by Central High's Barry Stebbins with a racquet he had purchased two months before from a friend of his who had bought a new one made of catgut and who sold Barry his old one for $8.50.

Improved:	Last winter the intramural squash tournament was won by Central High's Barry Stebbins with a racquet he had bought from a friend for $8.50.
Still Better:	Last winter Central High's Barry Stebbins won the intramural squash tournament with a second-hand racquet.

75c. AVOID THE USELESS REPETITION OF AN IDEA.

Useless repetition of an idea, or *tautology*, can weaken the impact of the sentence:

This entirely new and novel innovation in our program will delight our TV viewing audience; it has just been introduced for the first time and will cause pleasure to many people who will be watching.

EXERCISE 22

Improve the following sentences by eliminating superfluous words and phrases.

1. I have four good tires on my car, but in addition I always carry a spare tire besides.
2. Every student should know the correct procedure for successful theme writing in composition.
3. Since Jensen was illiterate and couldn't read, he was generally pitied by most people.
4. The houses were mostly well built in construction, but the interior furnishings within the houses left much to be desired.
5. I reflectively contemplated the fact that the machine was manually controlled and had to be operated by hand and not by another machine.
6. In the words of W.K., and I quote, "We're off to the drugstore to whistle at girls."
7. On Christmas Eve in December last winter, Uncle Toohey got stuck in the chimney.
8. Beeblemoth knew only that Shakespeare was an ancient dramatist who wrote plays in the olden time.
9. Daisy is an only child, as she has no brothers or sisters.
10. As a result of its feline nature, our cat Eric doesn't like to walk in the rain and get wet.

EXERCISE 23

Reduce predication in the following:

1. There are two basic forms of communication which man uses. These two forms of communication are writing and speaking.
2. Las Vegas is a resort which is well known for gambling, and people who like to gamble often go to Las Vegas to pursue that activity.
3. In the distance we could see the peak of Mt. Columbia, which was covered by snow.
4. There, in the back hallway, I detected a smell which resembled the odor of gasoline.
5. Mr. Ames, an instructor in the Department of Naval Science, gave a lecture on celestial navigation.

EXERCISE 24

Improve the following sentences by eliminating unnecessary details.

1. In reply to your letter of March 16, just a week ago, we are compelled to advise you that there has not yet been allowed to us a sufficient amount of time to prepare a compilation of the data which is to be encompassed by the Adams Report.
2. Last summer a weekend journey was made to Cultus Lake, where the water is very cold, by five of us who were majoring in physics and who had borrowed a royal blue 1936 Pierce-Arrow from a car dealer in Toronto, where these cars are no more common than elsewhere.
3. All that one needs to do in the process of boiling an egg is to lower a fresh egg, preferably a white one, into a pot containing water which has just begun to boil, and to keep the egg in the water for three minutes and then to lift it out gently with a spoon that is slotted.
4. A lot of time is required by many students in order to study the daily assignments in Canadian history, which covers the entire period from the first sighting of the east coast in 986 to the recent Federal election during which, as you know, a lot of fierce campaigning went on, including upright formal debating and downright mudslinging.
5. Mary went to a dance, a New Year's Eve dance it was, and there met the man who was tall, dark, handsome, and rich from all the gilt-edge securities and blue-chip stocks he owned, whom she would marry.

76. EMPHASIS

Not every sentence is meant to be emphatic, nor should it be. A series of hard-hitting, hammering sentences will pall on the reader almost as quickly as a group of flabby, namby-pamby ones. A writer should learn to judge the tone and appeal of his composition and emphasize precisely that material which he wishes to have stand out in the mind of his reader. As a consequence of this purpose, he should arrange minor thoughts as background material.

Three specific methods of securing emphasis in sentences that involve the positioning and arranging of words are discussed and illustrated in Section 79. Three other methods — one of which partially depends upon position and arrangement — are developed somewhat briefly in the paragraphs which follow.

76a. REPEAT IMPORTANT WORDS TO GAIN SENTENCE EMPHASIS.

Although faulty repetition should be avoided (see Section 53), you may heighten the effectiveness of your message by repeating key words in a series of sentences. All of us enjoy encountering the familiar; for example, much of our appreciation of music stems from our recognition of a reiterated theme. When we come across certain words and phrases in a written passage, or hear them in speech, we find that they have a special impressiveness and appeal. But repetition is a device, perhaps merely an artificial device, and should be used sparingly and only for a specific effect. It seems pleasing in the first of the illustrations which follow, but it may be grating in the second:

> *Give! Give* money when you see that women and children are hungry. *Give* sympathy when you can cheer a beaten man. *Give* time to study conditions in your own community. *Give* your whole self in an attempt to change and better the life of all humanity.

Do you want luxury? Buy a home in Oakdale. Do you want good schools for your children? Buy in Oakdale. Do you want compatible neighbors? Buy in Oakdale. Do you want room and freedom to move around? Buy in Oakdale. Oakdale will satisfy every need and every want of every discriminating buyer.

76b. USE PERIODIC SENTENCES TO SECURE EMPHASIS.

Most of the sentences we speak and write are *loose* sentences in that they achieve some completeness of meaning before they reach their actual ends. An effective departure from this predominant pattern is the *periodic* sentence, one in which elements are transposed or inverted so that full meaning is not apparent until the period is reached. When meaning is thus withheld, the reader continues in a state of suspense until the sentence terminates.

Only if, which heaven forbid, we extend our present tribal conflicts to the other planets will the Moon become of military importance. (Arthur C. Clarke)

And pulseless and cold, with a Derringer by his side and a bullet in his heart, though still calm as in life, beneath the snow lay he who was at once the strongest and yet the weakest of the outcasts of Poker Flat. (Bret Harte)

Tired, wet, and hunched against the cold, the passengers from the stalled bus stumbled the last hundred feet to the warm and brightly lit diner. At first slowly, then eagerly, then almost fiercely, each seized and drank a mugful of steaming coffee.

76c. GAIN EMPHASIS BY USING THE ACTIVE VOICE.

Use of the active voice usually provides greater force than use of the passive for the sound reason that a subject being acted upon is rarely as effective as a subject acting. Agents and doers are normally more interesting than those who sit still and do nothing. Your choice of active or passive voice depends upon context, upon the relative importance of the doer and the recipient of the action. Use the active voice whenever you desire to state or imply action, either mental or physical; use the passive voice in impersonal writing and as little elsewhere as possible. Your reader will react more strongly to "Buck *swept* Ninki into his arms" than to "Ninki *was swept* by Buck into his arms." Buck and Ninki probably do not care what voice you use and may be sorry that you mentioned them at all. Also, it is possible that Ninki was as active in "being swept" as Buck was in "sweeping." But your reader is your concern here, not the embracing lovers. Use the active voice.

EXERCISE 25

Rewrite the following sentences, making them more emphatic.

1. Martin made a favorable impression upon Myrtle's father, although he was uneasy most of the time.
2. The talk by Renfrew on spinning reels was the high spot in some respects.
3. I could just grasp the furry body of a baby chinchilla by reaching down into the burrow to the point where it widened out into the nest.
4. After eating the spoiled custard, one child was rushed to the hospital and several were slightly ill.
5. Simpson will lose consciousness if the coach doesn't take him out of the game.
6. Mallard's mountain-climbing companion fell and broke his leg because he wouldn't watch where he was going.
7. A battered old portable was the machine on which Shillingbreek's early novels were written.
8. The misery of the stranded group reached a climax in some ways with the coming of the first freezing weather.
9. We thought more and more of Sue Jenkins as time went on.
10. Thousands of valuable trees throughout the province were uprooted by the savage hurricane.

77. TRANSITION

Correct, clear, effective individual sentences, when set forth in a paragraph, may appear neither clear nor effective to the reader. If their order within the paragraph is logical, lack of clearness is most likely the result of faulty *transition*. *Transition* means passing from one state or position to another; in writing, evidence of transition is comprised of links and bridges connecting related units. If the links are weak, the reader will not be able to pass smoothly from one thought to another.

77a. MAKE SENTENCE TRANSITIONS CLEAR BY USING TRANSITIONAL WORDS AND PHRASES.

Not all sentences require within or between them transitional words or phrases. However, the writer constantly should ask himself: have I made the relationship between statements clear to the reader? If not, an inconspicuous and usually brief transitional device may indicate more clearly the association.

Evidence of relationship between dependent and independent clauses is shown by (a) subordinating conjunctions such as *because, for, after, as soon as, in order that, if, unless, since, lest, until, whereupon, where, when*, etc., and (b) relative pronouns: *who, whose, whom, which, that*.

Evidence of relationship between independent clauses or between sentences is shown by (a) personal pronouns: *I, my, me, we, our, us, you, your, he, his, him, she, her, it, its, they, their, theirs, them;* (b) demonstrative pronouns: *this, that, these, those, such;* (c) simple conjunctions: *and, but, or, neither, nor, yet;* (d) correlative conjunctions: *either . . . or, neither . . . nor, not only . . . but also, both . . . and;* (e) conjunctive or parenthetic adverbs: *besides, consequently, hence, however, instead, meanwhile, moreover, nevertheless, still, therefore,* etc.

Many other words and phrases may be used for transitional signals: *afterward, as a result, as an illustration, as I said, for example, hopefully, fortunately, from what has been said, by way of comparison, in addition, in fact, in short, in the next place, indeed, most of all, namely, naturally, now, of course, on the contrary, soon, temporarily, too, truly, on the other hand, correspondingly.*

Transitional devices are especially necessary when the writer moves from his own writing to the quotation or phrasing of another's work. Consider the following:

As Pierre Elliott Trudeau said, in his Acceptance Speech, "..." His words well illustrate . . .

Before passing judgment on this unfortunate man, we should reflect on the statement in Shakespeare's *The Merchant of Venice* concerning the quality of mercy.

77b. AVOID INEXACT TRANSITION.

Transitional words and phrases should be carefully selected in order to show the relationship of ideas correctly.

Inexact:
    I cannot take time to buy a ticket *but* I shall miss my train.

    I wanted to go to Toronto, *and* my parents wanted me to come home to Keswick.

    I know I forgot to pay the bill *whereupon* I have the money in my pocket.

    Hank wants to take Martha to the dance; *on the other hand,* Martha wants the same thing.

Better:
    I cannot take time to buy a ticket *or* I shall miss my train.

    I wanted to go to Toronto, *but* my parents wanted me to come home to Keswick.

    I know I forgot to pay the bill *for* I *still* have the money in my pocket.

    Hank wants to take Martha to the dance; *happily,* Martha wants the same thing.

77c. MAKE SENTENCE TRANSITIONS CLEAR BY REPETITION OF NOUNS AND BY USE OF PRONOUNS.

Pronouns which refer to preceding nouns and pronouns constitute an effective kind of repetition for showing sentence transition. The use of synonyms is also helpful. On occasion, important or pivotal words may be repeated in several sentences; they are, however, generally more effective when repeated between paragraphs.

In the following, taken from Arnold Bennett's "Why a Classic Is a Classic," the various transitional devices which have been discussed above are italicized:

What causes the passionate few to make such a fuss about *literature?* There can be only one reply. *They* find a keen and lasting *pleasure* in *literature*. *They enjoy literature* as some men *enjoy* beer. The recurrence of *this pleasure* naturally keeps *their* interest in *literature* very much alive. *They* are *forever* making new researches, *forever* practicing on *themselves*. *They learn* to *understand themselves*. *They learn* to *know what they want. Their* taste becomes surer and surer as *their* experience lengthens. *They* do not *enjoy* today what will seem *tedious* to *them* tomorrow. When *they find* a book *tedious, no* amount of popular clatter will persuade *them* that *it* is *pleasurable;* and when *they find it pleasurable* no chill silence of the street-crowds will *affect their conviction* that the book is good and permanent.

77d. AVOID LABORED AND ARTIFICIAL TRANSITION IN SENTENCES.

It is important to show relationship and the direction of relationship; the transition which serves this purpose should be effected smoothly, deftly, and inconspicuously.

Inadequate: Television viewing is said to be the national pastime; I do not like it. If it is the national pastime, hundreds of thousands must enjoy it constantly, or occasionally. I know people who do not ever watch a TV show; I know people who view 25 shows over a weekend. I should not make a dogmatic statement about the appeal of the activity; I have never owned a set.

Clumsy
transition: Television viewing is said to be the national pastime; *however,* I do not like it. *Yet* if it is the national pastime, hundreds of thousands must enjoy it constantly, or occasionally. *To be sure,* I know people who do not ever watch a TV show; *on the other hand,* I know people who view 25 shows over a weekend. *Perhaps* I should not make a dogmatic state-

ment about the appeal of the activity; *you see,* I have never owned a set.

Smoother
transition: *Although* television viewing is said to be Canada's national pastime, I do not like *it*. *Yet* if *it* is the *national pastime,* hundreds of thousands must enjoy *it* constantly and millions more must enjoy *it* occasionally. I know people who do not ever watch a TV *show* and *couldn't* be persuaded to see *one; on the other hand,* I know people who view 25 *shows* in the course of a weekend and *couldn't* be dragged away from *them. Perhaps* it is all a matter of taste, *and perhaps* I shouldn't make a dogmatic statement about the appeal of television viewing. *You see,* I have never owned a set, *and* I *prefer* a pastime that I can take part in, *one* that demands response. I *prefer* conversation.

EXERCISE 26

Use better connectives for the inexact ones in the following sentences.

1. Dinosaurs once roamed this area, because their bones are still to be found.
2. Martin wonders if he should go to summer school this year or get a job.
3. I had a wonderful time at the county fair, but so did Lemuel, my favorite cousin.
4. Mallard likes to scale mountains, and Jay prefers to scale fish.
5. We were all having a good time and didn't want to go home; nevertheless, the party lasted till dawn.
6. Wild strawberries grow on the island; on the other hand, blueberries are prolific, too.
7. Father lost his job in the fall of 1957; however, Mother was taken ill the same year.
8. Myrtle's great-aunt Petunia admires Martin, although he is fond of the old lady.
9. Wesley and his aunts had barely got settled than the curtain rose.
10. As I was going to St. James anyway, I offered to take the things to the cleaner's.

EXERCISE 27

Supply correct transitional words and phrases where they are needed within and between the sentences in the following paragraph.

It seems to be a cold day; the temperature was only 30°. I had risen early; my alarm clock went off too soon. John was still asleep. I shook and shook him; he did not move. I left him behind, hurried to George's house. He was asleep. He got up, dressed himself; we set out on our long-anticipated hike. Both George and I like to walk; we had a good time. The winter day was too short; we had to return in a few hours. John had stayed indoors all day.

78. VARIETY

There are many different kinds of sentences, each of which may be good in itself. "Too much of a good thing" is, however, a bad thing in theme composition. A series of similarly constructed sentences quickly becomes monotonous and ineffective.

The reader tires when he encounters a succession of short, simple sentences; a series of compound sentences; a series of sentences beginning with the same word or similar phrasing, or the same kind of dependent clause; a series of "look-alike" complex sentences; or a series of sentences nearly identical in length.

No definite rule can be set down about how much variety sentences should have. Indeed, good professional writers neither count the number of words in their sentences nor consciously intersperse simple and compound sentences with complex. But they do achieve variety in sentence structure. They vary length and, occasionally, word order. They use declarative, imperative, interrogative, and exclamatory sentences, periodic as well as loose sentences. They refresh a series of simple sentences by using various kinds of words, phrases, and clauses as beginnings or endings.

78a. DO NOT BEGIN SUCCESSIVE SENTENCES WITH THE SAME WORD OR PHRASE OR DEPENDENT CLAUSE.

Avoid beginning a sentence with the same words that end the sentence before it, or beginning sentences with such shopworn words and phrases as *there is, there are, there was, it was, it, this, that, I, we, she, and these.*

Awkward: There was a house at the top of the hill. There was a sinister look about the house because there was a tree in front of it covered with Spanish moss. There was a pair of tombstones close beside the tree, and to add to the gloomy effect there was a black cat sitting on what looked like a new grave.

Improved: There was a house at the top of the hill. A tree in front of it, covered with Spanish moss, gave the surroundings a sinister look. A pair of tombstones close beside it, and a black cat sitting on what appeared to be a new grave, added to the gloomy effect.

Awkward: Celestial navigation is very confusing. Celestial navigation involves many facts and figures which one must look up. Celestial navigation encompasses many different fields of science, requiring knowledge of astronomy, mathematics, physics, and electronics.

Improved: Celestial navigation is confusing to the beginning student, involving as it does many facts and figures which he is required to look up. The study, which encompasses many different fields, requires some knowledge of astronomy, mathematics, physics, and electronics.

Avoid beginning every sentence with a phrase and avoid overusing the same kind of phrases (participial, prepositional, prepositional-gerund, absolute, adverbial) as a beginning. Consider the monotony of the following paragraph:

Having decided to take a summer job, I wrote to various firms about available jobs. Receiving several replies, I gave them careful study. Deciding that a job in an oyster hatchery would be most interesting, I made an appointment to interview the manager of the Pine Island Marine Station. Being hired, I made plans to start work on June 29th. Having carried out these plans, I am now here, starting a new page in my personal journal.

Avoid, too, beginning every sentence with a dependent clause, and avoid especially beginning a series of dependent clauses with the same subordinating conjunction.

78b. VARY THE FORM OF SUCCESSIVE SENTENCES.

A succession of sentences should not be exclusively simple, complex, compound, compound-complex, periodic, or loose. The inexperienced writer will produce predominantly simple or compound sentences, whereas the skilled craftsman will vary his forms of expression and provide an interesting mixture of sentences containing ideas well coordinated and subordinated.

78c. VARY THE LENGTH OF SUCCESSIVE SENTENCES.

Whether long, medium-long, or short, sentences made up of the same number of words, or approximately the same number, should not appear in sequence. Most sentences contain from ten to two dozen words; vary this length on occasion with a 3- or 4-word, or a 30- or 40-word construction.

78d. DO NOT PLACE THE SUBJECT AT THE BEGINNING OF EVERY SENTENCE.

In ordinary speech, it is natural to start sentences with the subject. In writing, a series of subject + verb + complement structures is monotonous. Occasional deviation from this order is emphatic and refreshing.

Usual order: I met those singers when I was in Montreal.
He who can sing with an octet is fortunate.

Varied: Those singers I met when I was in Montreal.

Fortunate is he who can sing with an octet.

EXERCISE 28

Rewrite the following sentences, eliminating whatever is monotonous. Rephrase and add words if necessary, but preserve the original meaning.

1. My buddy and I once went on a camping trip through the provincial parks. First we visited Wasaga, on Georgian Bay. Then we drove north to Misty Lake. Then we went to Canoe Lake. Then we went to Bancroft, where an old pioneer home has been restored. Next we went to Fenelon Falls on the Burnt River, and finally to Pontypool.
2. Jensen was forty-two years old. But he had never learned to read. He was very industrious, and his intelligence was only a little below average. But educational opportunities had never come his way. He had left school at an early age.
3. After the ingredients required for making bread have been combined, the resulting dough should be kneaded. After it has been kneaded, it should be put in a warm place to rise. When it has doubled its size, it should be kneaded again, shaped into loaves, and allowed to rise a second time. When it has once more doubled in bulk, it is ready to bake.
4. I was born on a farm, and I have lived on farms all my life. I like country life—the clean air, the animals, even the work, though I admit I sometimes wish I didn't have to do quite so much work. I should also like it if I weren't quite so far away from town and social life.
5. Jay wants to go to New York City for his vacation, but Rose wants to visit her cousin in Alberta. His idea of a good time is to hear topflight jazz bands, but she prefers to visit with relatives and old friends. My guess is that they will go to New York.

79.   POSITION AND ARRANGEMENT

By applying suggestions for emphatic diction, for effective word arrangement, and for proper coordination and subordination, writers often attain correctness and clarity in their sentences only to find that those sentences do not really "get across" to the reader. To achieve desired impressiveness, words should be so selected and arranged that secondary items will form a background against which primary items prominently stand out.

79a. PLACE STRONG AND RELATIVELY IMPORTANT WORDS AND THOUGHTS AT THE BEGINNING OR END OF A SENTENCE.

First and last impressions are usually strongest; in sentences, and in independent clauses, the beginning and end are the most emphatic and memorable parts. In these places the most important ideas should be put, so that they will claim attention where attention is sharpest. Transitional words and phrases, though less vivid, are important and often deserve near-beginning positions; however, pure conjunctions, prepositions, and a number of other parenthetical expressions are usually not focal and normally should not start a sentence.

Unimpressive: This is the cafeteria which the students eat in.

Mother is the only person I haven't yet written to.

X-rays show that Martin suffered a broken neck. However, the boy will live, the doctor says.

Improved: This is the cafeteria in which the students eat.

The only person I haven't yet written to is Mother.

or

The only person to whom I haven't yet written is Mother.

X-rays show that Martin suffered a broken neck; however, the doctor says that the boy will live.

Prepositions at the ends of sentences are neither grammatically incorrect nor unclear. They are merely ineffective — weak words which have been put in strong positions.

79b. ARRANGE IDEAS IN THE ORDER OF THEIR IMPORTANCE SO AS TO SECURE CLIMAX.

Ideas in a sentence should be arranged so that in force and importance they build up to the highest point, or *climax*. The initial idea would then be entitled to least, and the final idea entitled to most, of the reader's attention.

Unemphatic: In this derailment, some died horrible deaths, some suffered serious injuries, and a few escaped with minor scratches.

Better: A few escaped from this derailment with minor scratches; but some suffered serious injuries; and some died horrible deaths.

Unemphatic: Some of my instructors have been bad, some excellent, some indifferent, some fair.

Better: Some of my instructors have been bad, some indifferent, some fair, and some excellent.

79c. USE WORDS OUT OF THEIR NATURAL ORDER, ONCE IN A WHILE, AS A METHOD OF EMPHASIS.

Since the usual word order of most sentences is subject and modifiers, predicate and modifiers, object or complement and modifiers, the reader expects to encounter it. What he does *not* expect to encounter, therefore, is more likely to capture his attention. By putting the predicate or the object or the complement or an adverbial modifier first, as an *occasional* change of pace, the writer will impart emphasis to his statement.

Usual: The mighty and wicked are fallen.
Seven little dwarfs lived here in the center of the dark forest.
If any, speak; for I have offended him.

Inverted and
effective: Fallen are the mighty and wicked.
Here, in the center of the dark forest, lived seven little dwarfs.
If any, speak; for him I have offended.
(Shakespeare, *Julius Caesar*)

Increase the effectiveness of the following sentences:

1. He started out to take a walk because he was desperate, unable to sleep, and tired of hearing the radio.
2. At first, she did not love him, but she came to like him as time went on.
3. This is not good soil to plant flowers in.
4. In short, both candidates promised to help the farmer out.
5. John's fender was bent when he did not have enough room to turn the station wagon around in.
6. You know that your bill will be paid by me as soon as I am able.
7. In order to accomplish this, you should be willing to give up honor, family, friends, and acquaintances, I think.
8. He became better liked as more people came to know him and gradually his circle of acquaintances widened.
9. The days when our hearts were young and gay are gone.
10. He came here to recuperate from a serious illness, play bridge, and have the sun brown him, I suppose.

80. GLOSSARY OF SENTENCE ERRORS

Sections 61-79 discuss and illustrate many kinds of errors in sentence structure. These faults are of unequal significance, although none should be left unstudied and neglected.

The following alphabetically-arranged survey of errors which teachers and writers consider most important may serve you as a quick reference guide.

"And which, but which, and who, but who." Joining relative clauses to independent clauses by using a conjunction (making dependent and independent clauses coordinate). Section 69d.

Choppy sentences. A series of short, perhaps simple, sentences, the result being jerky and monotonous reading— analogous to riding a boat on choppy waves. Section 73.

Climax, faulty. In a series of ideas, failure to arrange their order so that the weakest is put first, the next stronger, next, etc. Section 79c.

Comma splice (comma fault). Using a comma between two independent clauses not joined by a conjunction (splicing two complete sentences with a comma if the second sentence does not begin with a conjunction). Section 62a.

Comparisons, mixed, double, confusing. Using illogically the positive and comparative degree of adjectives or adverbs in one single statement, and including a member in a class or group and yet as a single member, or excluding a member from a class or group in which it belongs. Section 74.

Conciseness, lack of. See *Wordiness,* below.

Consistency, lack of. Unjustifiable shifting of tense, mood, voice, number, or the class or person of pronouns. Section 72.

Dangling elliptical clause. A dependent clause with its subject or predicate omitted, the omitted part not the same as that expressed in the independent clause. Section 67b.

Dangling verbal phrase. A phrase which should clearly modify a specific noun or pronoun and does not. Section 67a.

Dependent clauses, illogical. The use of noun or adverbial clauses to serve as parts of speech which they cannot correctly or effectively serve. Section 65.

Fused sentences. Two sentences in succession with no mark of punctuation between. Section 63.

Misplaced modifier. A word, phrase, or clause so placed that it modifies words other than those it should clearly modify. Section 66.

Mixed and illogical construction. Starting a sentence and shifting to a different construction. Section 61c.

Parallelism, faulty. Not using the same grammatical constructions for sentence elements equal in rank. Section 71.

Period fault. A word or group of words not conveying complete sense but punctuated as a sentence. Section 61a, b.

Point of view, inconsistent. See *Consistency,* above.

Position and arrangement, ineffective. Failure to order words in their maximum effectiveness. Section 79.

Rambling sentences. Sentences having grammatical completeness but violating unity. Section 64.

Seesaw sentences. An ineffective series of compound sentences. Section 69b.

Separation of parts, needless. Unnecessary or ineffective separation of closely related sentence elements. Section 68b, c, d.

"So" overused. Monotonous, overfrequent, and therefore ineffective joining of independent clauses with the conjunctive adverb *so*. Section 69e.

Split infinitive. Needlessly separating the sign of the infinitive *to* and the infinitive verb. Section 68a.

Squinting modifier. A word or word group which can look in two directions at once. Section 66a.

Stringy sentences. A series of short, independent clauses combined, or knotted, into a string. Section 69a.

Subordination, faulty. Confusing the structure of primary and subordinate ideas; employing excessive subordination. Section 70.

Transition, faulty, or lack of. Failure to make evident the relationship between clauses and sentences by means of transitional expressions. Section 77.

Unity, lack of. Inclusion of excessive detail or of unrelated ideas in the same sentence. Section 64.

Upside-down subordination. A structure in which the more important idea appears in a dependent clause or the less important in an independent clause. Section 70a, b.

Variety, lack of. An ineffective series of sentences monotonous in structure for various reasons. See Section 78.

Wordiness. Using too many, or unnecessary, words to express ideas; primarily, failure to reduce predication. Section 75.

THE SENTENCE—*GENERAL REVIEW EXERCISES*

REVIEW EXERCISE 1

The following sentences contain errors in sentence structure. Copy and correct them.

1. Assignments which are handed in later than Friday of this week, you might as well not hand it in at all.

2. We approached the city with great interest, it was not a small city with narrow streets, as we had expected, but a large city with towering skyscrapers.

3. Being only four years old, the nose specialist found it hard to examine Sammy.

4. Stooping to pick up a dime, the old man's galluses broke.

5. Fred thought that Lee was smart, pretty, but was too eager for money and social position.

6. Because it was after midnight, we decided to excuse ourselves, because we were tired.

7. Although man has been able to invent such destructive forces as the atomic bomb, he has also found some new drugs which are very effective and some instruments that helped greatly in wartime to reduce the danger of death or disease from injuries or wounds received in wartime.

8. Gleason's assets were his ready wit, a fast talker, and seemed to inspire confidence in people.

9. Jay was approached by a man with a wife and a baby daughter who was looking for work.

10. My companions, who refused to stop talking, the people to the rear in back of them could not hear.

REVIEW EXERCISE 2

Follow the directions for Review Exercise 1.

1. I agree to drive with Walter to Oshawa and then that I should return alone by train.

2. His sources of income consist of the following: owner of a small vegetable market, and for the past four years he has been manager of a produce department.

3. As he listened to the symphony, Roley was suddenly conscious and disturbed by a certain giddiness among the first violins.

4. My next job was a bill collector for a doctor but which did not pay enough money.

5. If I have enough money left, I am going to fly there for Christmas, if my father will let me.

6. When Daisy returned home from camp, she finds a baby brother.

7. Because Martin has reformed is why Myrtle is so proud of him.

8. This teacher often quotes himself he thinks it adds flavor to his conversation.

9. The mechanic located the cause of our trouble in a flash.

10. At Central High they devote two weeks at the close of each semester to final examinations.

REVIEW EXERCISE 3

Follow the directions for Review Exercise 1.

1. The furniture was dusted and the ornaments washed in preparation for the party to be given tomorrow and which will celebrate the fiftieth wedding anniversary of my grandparents.

2. The salesman told Mrs. Banks that the factory could not make the pair of shoes that she wanted and would she consider buying another type?

3. Instead of campaigns, bazaars, tag days, and other energy-wasting drives which often did not produce even minimum funds for welfare work.

4. The hostile attitude of one of the adversaries who opposed us had in its character something that was rather belligerent in nature.

5. Carter had to see his dentist about a small cavity, which terrified him.

6. I can understand why Florida is a popular vacation spot: it has so many bathing beauties.

7. It is my duty to clearly and emphatically say that football today is both war and sport.

8. Referring to the views of various experts, the fall was given by the majority as the best time for that kind of planting.

9. If one likes good French food, you should go to Paris or New Orleans.

10. Holly thinks that if one has a chance to get a man like Mallard they should not let it slip.

THE PARAGRAPH

When you write, you are in effect a builder engaging in a construction project. You are building letters into words, words into sentences, sentences into paragraphs, and paragraphs into a composition. A building needs a firm foundation and a sound superstructure. A composition needs firmly-shaped sentences and soundly-formed paragraphs. Only a jerry-built house will result from flimsy materials, and only a jerry-built paper will result from vague, inept, haphazard paragraphs.

The sentence is the unit of writing, but the paragraph may be termed the *basic unit of thought*. That is, the very heart of learning to write effectively lies in paragraph development. If the successful writer has a secret, it is his ability to form a thought —almost any thought—and then develop this idea, however vague and fragmentary it may be, so that it becomes clear and interesting to his readers. Hasn't everyone had the experience of writing a sentence or making a statement and then halting, aware that it needs expansion, certain that the idea standing alone seems bare and incomplete but unsure about how to "flesh it out"? This problem, and only this problem, stands at the center of the problem of writing, all writing you are likely to do both in school and out.

The method of putting flesh on the bare bones, the skeletons of ideas, is known as paragraph development. That is, a paragraph is a group of statements, of sentences, developing an idea or topic. This idea may be independent or it may be one part of a larger topic. In other words, a paragraph that develops one topic may be part of a composition or a short composition in itself. Single paragraphs appear frequently in print, such as, for example, short items in newspapers and magazines or the pithy sayings of certain columnists and wits. Sometimes, when the occasion requires, a paragraph may consist of a single sentence. Far more often, however, paragraphs depend for their development and meaning on their role as units of a larger topic. The wording of each paragraph is then dependent on the paragraph just before or after; it is not an independent unit but part of an organic whole.

Clear paragraphing is essential to both writer and reader. By properly separating his sentences into groups, a writer controls his subject and plots his course as he proceeds from point to point. For the reader, clearly formed paragraphs are signposts by which he follows the path of the writer's thought. By understanding the parts, he reaches an understanding of the whole.

Good paragraphs are also mechanically correct. They are properly indented. They contain no blank spaces except when part of a line is left blank at the end. If a writer uses dialogue, each paragraph should correctly indicate each change of speaker. See Section 90.

81. THE TOPIC SENTENCE

The topic sentence is the statement in a paragraph that tells the reader which topic or which aspect of a larger topic the paragraph is intended to develop. It states, suggests, or in some other way indicates the heart, the core, of the idea which is to be, is being, or has been developed.

Generally, the topic sentence comes first. Occasionally, as has been suggested, it may appear somewhere toward the middle or at the end of the paragraph, depending upon content and the writer's method of organizing it. Sometimes the topic sentence is not expressed at all but is implied by the paragraph as a whole.

81a. USE THE TOPIC SENTENCE AS A GUIDE FOR THE PARAGRAPH.

When you begin a paragraph with a topic sentence, you make a definite commitment on what you are about to discuss and you arouse the reader's expectation. If your paragraph is successful, it will fulfill the promise in your initial sentence and satisfy the reader. Consider how the following paragraph achieves both objectives. The topic sentence is shown in italics.

> *With his telescope Galileo made some important astronomical discoveries.* For instance, he discovered that there are satellites around the planet Jupiter. He saw that the moon was not flat, as people commonly believe, but that it had high and low areas, and he even calculated the height of some of its mountains. The Milky Way revealed itself to him as a vast collection of stars, and by studying sunspots he reached the conclusion that the sun rotates.

81b. VARY THE POSITION OF THE TOPIC SENTENCE.

The most common position of the topic sentence, as in the foregoing example, is at the beginning of the paragraph. In a short paper of three or four paragraphs, each could begin with a topic sentence. But in a longer paper of, let us say, eight or more paragraphs, placing the topic sentence at the beginning of every paragraph might make the writing seem both mechanical and monotonous. It is then better to change the position of the topic sentence occasionally. It would not be difficult, for instance, to put the topic sentence about Galileo's telescope at the end of the paragraph:

> Galileo was the first man to discover that there are satellites around the planet Jupiter. He saw that the moon was not flat, as people commonly believed, but that it had high and low areas, and he even calculated the height of some of its mountains. He perceived the Milky Way as a vast collection of stars, and by studying sunspots he reached the conclusion that the sun rotates. *Thus with his telescope Galileo was able to make some important contributions to astronomy.*

Notice that here the topic sentence is used to sum up the paragraph instead of to introduce it.

When the topic sentence is placed within the paragraph, the sentence or sentences before it are usually introductory:

> Many people have heard about the famous Leaning Tower of Pisa, but few know that Pisa also has a university of ancient origin. In about the year 1580 its most illustrious student was a mathematical genius named Galileo Galilei, who was soon to invent the hydrostatic balance, a thermometer, and a propor-

tional compass. *But Galileo's greatest invention was his telescope, which enabled him to make some significant contributions to astronomy.* It was this instrument that made it possible for Galileo to discover satellites around Jupiter, the unevenness of the moon's surface, the fact that the Milky Way is a vast collection of stars, and, by studying sunspots, to infer the rotation of the sun.

Sometimes the topic sentence is not stated at all, is merely implied, but every good paragraph is so well knit that any reasonably thoughtful reader can sum up the central thought of the paragraph in his own "topic sentence." A paragraph of this kind, however, should focus on one subject, like any other paragraph.

Among the great men of the Renaissance, many were artists, like Raphael, Titian, Michelangelo, Van Dyke, and Rembrandt. Others were poets, such as Spenser, Shakespeare, Tasso, and Ronsard. Still others were pioneers in science: Galileo and Kepler in astronomy, for instance, and Vesalius and Harvey in medicine.

The implied topic sentence here is, "The Renaissance produced many creative men."

EXERCISE 1

Copy out the topic sentence in each paragraph below. If you think the topic sentence is merely implied, state what it would be.

1. Cowardice generally invites attacks. A dog may chase a man who turns and runs, whereas if the man holds his ground the dog will do him no harm and even let itself be patted. A boy who runs away at the first sight of a neighborhood gang will only attract pursuit. Had the boy just continued on his way, the gang might not have paid the least attention to him.

2. A robin or an oriole or any other bird will always build its nest in the same way. So will a beaver or a mole. Animals go by instinct. They have no need for invention. Man, on the other hand, needs to invent in order to adapt himself to climatic or geographical conditions. In the Southwest, he builds adobe houses; on the narrow island of Montreal, he constructs skyscrapers; in the far North, he fashions igloos.

3. One of Benjamin Franklin's rules was "Never ask another to do what you can do for yourself." It is a good rule. The student

who depends on another to do his math problem or Spanish translation for him not only runs the risk of getting the wrong answers but also is not acquiring self-reliance. There is no substitute for self-reliance. Nobody, unless he has a serious physical handicap, can expect to go through life depending on others to do his thinking or to solve his personal problems.

EXERCISE 2

Write two paragraphs of between 75 and 100 words each, choosing any *one* of these topic sentences. In your first paragraph place the topic sentence at the beginning, in the second either toward the middle or at the end. Underline the topic sentence in each paragraph you write.

1. Practical jokes can be painful.
2. Going steady has its disadvantages (advantages).
3. Don't be a back-seat driver.
4. Our student government could be improved.
5. A teen-ager is seldom understood by his family.

82. SUBSTANCE

A composition may contain several good ideas as expressed in topic sentences but still be weakly written because its paragraphs are undeveloped or are padded with hazy generalizations. Such paragraphs are only the skeletons of what they should and could be. You would not care to be served only the bare bones of Thanksgiving turkey. "Where's the meat?" you would ask. A paragraph too needs fleshing out.

"Everyone should learn to swim" is a good enough topic sentence, but if all you say about it is that the ability to swim may on some occasion save one from drowning, you have hardly begun. If you really start thinking your subject through, you can find some other things to say about it. For one thing, you might point out that swimming is a beneficial exercise that engages many of the body muscles. You might think of swimming at beaches and pools as a source of recreation. You could enumerate some enjoyable water sports for which knowing how to swim is a requisite, such as skin-diving, water-skiing, or riding the breakers on a surf board. And do not overlook your own experience as material, something relevant to swimming that you yourself have seen or learned or done.

82a. DRAW ON YOUR OWN EXPERIENCE FOR MATERIAL.

Your own experience can often supply details you can use in developing your paragraphs. Your total experience lies not only in what you have done but also in what you have seen, heard, thought, felt, and learned. What you can find in your own experience, if only you look for it, will yield details that are alive and meaningful for the very reason that they are yours.

Such details are not the secondhand impressions and comments of someone else but are really a part of the essential you. Only you know precisely what you mean when you say, "Robin is fun-loving and good-natured." Your observations of Robin in action, your thoughts about her, can and will help you develop this remark by methods suggested in Section 83. For one example, you can relate how Robin revived a dull party that seemed to be dying, how through sheer good spirits she got everyone into a lively mood, ready and eager to enter into the spirit of a "fun" evening. Or you can contrast the good-natured reaction of Robin when made the butt of a practical joke with the sour or angry reaction of Dee in a similar situation. Or you can define what you mean by "fun-loving" or "good-natured" or both, making specific references from your own experience about Robin's personality and mannerisms.

Let us suppose that you are writing about swimming. Presumably you know how to swim. How and when did you first learn? Have you or someone you know had any narrow escapes from drowning? Were you ever in a canoe or other craft that might easily have capsized? Where do you go swimming, and what gives you the most pleasure from this activity? If you really dig into your own experience, you might build your whole paragraph from it alone, as this beginning-writer did:

"Everyone should learn how to swim," my father used to tell us. When I was seven and my brother Tommy five, we lived not far from a small lake. Every Saturday afternoon that first summer my father waded out with us, while he showed us the first stroke we were to use. After about the fourth time, my brother Tommy could swim well enough to be allowed to go into water above his head, but try as I might, I could not get the hang of it. Whenever Father took us out in the rowboat, it was I who had to wear a life-preserver and endure the superior smirk of my little brother, who didn't have to wear one. But one weekday, when Father was away, I happened to go down to the lake with a couple of boys a year or two older than I was. They were soon in the water, swimming about and diving under and coming up sputtering and having a fine time, while I was watching on shore. Then, on a sudden impulse, I jumped in among them, and all at once, to my own amazement, I was swimming! That evening at supper I turned to my father. "Everybody should learn to swim," I said, "like me."

82b. DRAW UPON THE EXPERIENCES OF OTHERS FOR MATERIAL.

It is probable that you will sometimes be called upon to write about a topic that lies outside the range of your experience. Then your own thought and knowledge will not suffice; you will have to turn for material to the thoughts and experiences of others. You may obtain some material from conversations, but your chief sources will be books and works of reference, as well as newspapers and magazines. Radio and TV programs, even motion pictures, are other possibilities. Yet nothing you learn will become part of your knowledge unless you first assimilate it so that you can put it in your own words.

82c. AVOID STATEMENTS ALREADY OBVIOUS.

To tell your reader what he and everybody else already knows will accomplish no more than boring him. One student, asked to write about the newspaper he read regularly, wrote this:

> The newspaper has several kinds of headlines. Among them are the main headings and subheads. The main headlines are found at the top of the page.

Instead of interesting the class, he evoked yawns.

82d. AVOID NEEDLESS REPETITION OF THE TOPIC SENTENCE.

Keep your topic sentence clearly in mind and use the remainder of the paragraph to develop the topic. Simply repeating what the topic sentence has already made plain is to mark time and get nowhere. Consider this example:

> I think a person makes a great mistake to drop out of school. Boys and girls should not leave school before they graduate. Students who stay long enough to get their diplomas get better jobs than the drop-outs do.

EXERCISE 3

Point out the main weakness in each paragraph below. Tell how you might revise it to give it more substance and interest.

1. Firemen are brave men. They often risk their lives to save people from burning houses. They have to be ready to go out in all kinds of weather. At any time of year, even in zero weather, a fireman has to be prepared to answer an alarm.

2. Once I had a very embarrassing experience. My older sister was getting married, and I was to be an usher at the wedding. I had on a pair of new shoes, and all during the first part of the wedding my shoes squeaked. This was very embarrassing for me, and I guess for some of the other people too.

3. The Government ought to help every boy or girl who wants to go to college and can't afford it. The Government should give them money for tuition and books and also for board if they go to a college away from home. By helping them go through college, the Government would benefit because it would have more educated people to run the Government in the future. This is a great advantage. Therefore the Government ought to help them get a college education.

4. Termites are small insects. They can do a great deal of damage. They damaged our house so badly that we had to call an exterminator. He did a lot of things around the house and charged a lot of money, but he did not get rid of all of them.

5. My favorite relative is my Uncle Fred. When he came on visits he always used to bring something for me. He also took me to a number of places of interest. Once he took me to a big league ball game. No wonder he is my favorite relative.

EXERCISE 4

Develop *one* of the following topic sentences into a substantial paragraph based wholly on your own experience. Supply specific details.

1. Once I scored a minor triumph.
2. Punishment is often deserved (unjust).
3. A little sister (brother) can be a nuisance.
4. Not only cats can be too curious.
5. Some people say that I am accident-prone.
6. My room is my castle.
7. Anyone can learn to dance.
8. Even two can sometimes be a crowd.
9. Some people think they are always right.
10. One can (cannot) always trust a friend.

83. METHODS OF DEVELOPMENT

Paragraphs may be developed in a number of ways. No one way is necessarily better than another. All can be said to have one purpose in common: to make the reader see exactly and fully the point specifically made in the topic sentence or implied by the paragraph as a whole. Often a writer can achieve this purpose best by a combination of methods. When he begins a paragraph, he does not deliberately say to himself that he will now use this or that method but lets his central idea determine the best way to make the reader visualize and understand it.

The different names which label material in the sections which follow are of little importance and frequently are of even less help. The only sure test of the substance of a paragraph is that of communication. *Define,* if the terms you use are not clear; give *instances and examples* of the concept you have in mind which will relate to your reader's experience and understanding; *compare or contrast* the idea expressed in your topic sentence with something which you can be reasonably sure the reader already comprehends; *explain in detail* if the idea is difficult to understand.

An illustration: a student was recently reading about attempts of American and Russian scientists to land men on the moon. Plans and preliminary steps to this end were being ridiculed by the author of the article, and it occurred to the student that, throughout history, daring thinkers and discoverers have been laughed at or disregarded by their contemporaries. He also recalled that many of those who have been ridiculed have later come to be accepted as great men because of their eventual success. Such reflection enabled him to come up with a topic sentence: Shortsighted people ridicule what they cannot understand. After further thought and much reading, he developed the following paragraph. It uses several methods of paragraph development, but the thing to keep in mind is that it clearly communicates to the reader the basic idea of the writer's topic sentence:

> *History follows a pattern of first denouncing great discoveries only to honor them after the discoverers themselves are destroyed or ridiculed by their detractors.* For centuries, men have honored the teachings of Socrates as preserved in the *Dialogues* of Plato, but the man himself was condemned to death for corrupting youth with his novel ideas. Lee de Forest was prosecuted for using the mails to defraud because he wrote that his vacuum tube "would transmit the human voice across the Atlantic." And this was as recent as 1913! Daguerre, the creator of photography, was committed to an insane asylum for insisting that he could transfer a likeness to a tin plate. The automobile was opposed because agriculture was felt to be doomed by a vehicle that ate neither oats nor hay. Stephenson's locomotive was denounced on the grounds that its speed would shatter men's minds and bodies. The eminent Sir Walter Scott called William Murdoch a madman for proposing to light the streets of London with coal gas, and the great Emperor Napoleon laughed off the idea as a "crazy notion." Some churchmen argued against the plan as being blasphemous, since God had

divided the light from darkness. And some physicians insisted coal-gas lights would induce people to stay out late and catch cold. Who are the heretics and madmen of the 1960's who will be honored and acclaimed a decade or century from now?

83a. DEVELOP A PARAGRAPH WITH PARTICULARS AND DETAILS.

Topic sentences may often be clarified and developed by the use of specific details and concrete particulars. This method involves expansion of the basic idea with separate items arranged in some logical order. This method employs ideas related to or suggested by preceding ideas. This type of development is illustrated by the paragraph quoted above and by this one, which has only an implied topic sentence:

The loft itself must have measured fifty feet, with dirty windows stretched along two sides; the floors were rotten, hairy as coconut shells, patched here and there with squares of tin. Half a dozen cumbersome etching presses with their great splaying wheels, shelves, benches cluttered with gear, and a flock of high stools left only narrow channels for locomotion. Half-way down the room stood the huge pot-bellied coal stove —red-hot this morning in early December—a stove that seemed to operate selfishly, refusing to communicate its warmth save to the big iron kettle whispering above. Beside the stove was an old-fashioned cane rocking chair with a greasy little cushion tied on its back. This was where Mr. Biggs always ate his lunch —in a picturesque oasis at the heart of the machine age.

—From "Etcher's Heaven," by Peggy Bacon

83b. DEVELOP A PARAGRAPH BY INSTANCES OR EXAMPLES.

This method of development uses a series of sentences which furnish an illustration representative of the more general statement in the topic sentence. The instance may be only partly specific, such as "Here is a man who is overly ambitious." Or it may be more definite: "Consider Shakespeare's Macbeth, who was overly ambitious."

Following are paragraphs developed by instances or examples. In each, the topic statement is italicized.

The story of the Arizona rancher who made out a $500 check on a six-by-three-foot cowhide recalls the *many curious surfaces on which checks have legally been written through the years:* in lipstick on handkerchiefs, on cigarette paper, on calling cards, fragile valentines, on whisky labels, Christmas cards, envelopes, newspapers, cigar-box tops, paper bags, laundry bills. A check written on a hard-boiled egg was cashed without trouble at the Victoria branch of the Canadian Bank of Commerce. A Midwestern lumberman made out so many checks on his own brand of shingle that his bank had to construct a special type of file cabinet for them. A contractor in Memphis once settled his weekly payroll by drawing on the bank with slabs of wood. A businessman eager to pay for a newly arrived television set recently pried off the side of the packing case and wrote his check on it.

—From "Topics," *The New York Times*, September 20, 1960

It is important to remember that, in the strict sense, there is no such thing as an uneducated man. Take an extreme case. Suppose that an adult man, in the full vigor of his faculties, could be suddenly placed in the world, as Adam is said to have been, and then left to do as he best might. How long would he be left uneducated? Not five minutes. Nature would begin to teach him, through the eye, the ear, the touch, the properties of objects. Pain and pleasure would be at his elbow, telling him to do this and avoid that: and by slow degrees the man would receive an education which, if narrow, would be thorough, real, and adequate to his circumstances, though there would be no extras and very few accomplishments.

—Thomas Henry Huxley

On the morning of December 7, 1951, in the General Sessions Court in New York City, fourteen tall young men stood before Judge Saul S. Streit. The scene was the climax of the notorious basketball scandals in which players had been convicted of receiving bribes from professional gamblers for throwing basketball games in Madison Square Garden. The judge was stern, but for the culprits he tempered justice. Jail sentences and fines were few and light. Judge Streit then looked over the heads of the defendants and hurled angry words at the colleges and universities they represented. *He charged that these institutions had so far forgotten their educational mission and had so over-emphasized athletics that they themselves had made this scene in his courtroom all but inevitable.*

—From "Education or Show Business," by Harold W. Stoke

83c. DEVELOP A PARAGRAPH BY COMPARISON OR CONTRAST.

A topic may be made clear by means of comparison or contrast or by the two methods either combined in one paragraph or in successive paragraphs. Comparison shows the likeness between the topic and some idea or object familiar to the reader; contrast reveals differences.

The oblique band of sunlight which followed her through the door became the young wife well. It illuminated her as her presence illuminated the heath. *In her movements, in her gaze, she reminded the beholder of the feathered creatures who lived around her home.* All similes and allegories concerning her began and ended with birds. There was as much variety in her motions as in their flight. When she was musing, she was a kestrel, which hangs in the air by an invisible motion of its wings. When she was in a high wind, her light body was blown against trees and banks' like a heron's. When she was frightened, she darted noiselessly like a kingfisher. When she was serene, she skimmed like a swallow, and that is how she was moving now.

—From *The Return of the Native*, by Thomas Hardy

The bumblebee is a more casual pollen gatherer than the honey-bee. Her pollen baskets consist of irregular rows of feathery hairs with which she may carry a pollen ball or dust off the pollen from an anther, while the honey-bee always works hard all day to build up one enormous ball of moist pollen after another to carry back to the hive. The bumblebee appears to be more interested in nectar—she's a comparatively lazy fat mechanic possessed of a wondrous long proboscis with which she is able to set off the mechanisms of flowers with deeply concealed nectar that the honey-bee can't reach.

—From *This Green World*, by Rutherford Platt

83d. DEVELOP A PARAGRAPH BY DIVISION.

Developing a topic by division means that the writer calls attention to two or more parts of the topic and discusses each briefly. Obviously, if each portion deserves extended treatment, separate paragraphs would be indicated and required.

There are three kinds of book owners. The first has all the standard sets and best-sellers—unread, untouched. (This deluded individual owns pulp and ink, not books.) The second has a great many books—a few of them read through, most of them dipped into, but all of them as clean and shiny as the day they were bought. (This person would probably like to make books his own, but is restrained by a false respect for their physical appearance.) The third has a few books or many— every one of them dog-eared and dilapidated, shaken and loosened by continual use, marked and scribbled in from front to back. (This man owns books.)

—From *How to Read a Book*, by Mortimer J. Adler

The question—*"Which is the happiest season of life?"*—being referred to an aged man, he replied: "When spring comes, and in the soft air the buds are breaking on the trees, and they are covered with blossoms, I think 'How beautiful is Spring!' And when the summer comes, and covers the trees with its heavy foliage, and singing birds are among the branches, I think 'How beautiful is Summer!' When autumn loads them with golden fruit, and their leaves bear the gorgeous tint of frost, I think 'How beautiful is Autumn!' And when it is sere winter, and there is neither foliage nor fruit, then I look up through the leafless branches, as I never could until now, and see the stars shine."

—From *Cheer*, April, 1960. Author unknown.

83e. DEVELOP A PARAGRAPH BY DEFINITION.

This method of paragraph development involves answering the implied question of the reader, "What do you mean by this?" Sometimes, this method is called for when an unfamiliar term is used or when you employ a term in an unusual way. Ordinarily, this method involves the use of still other kinds of paragraph development, but here are two examples of straightforward definition:

Science is a method of knowledge that arose and first proved its usefulness within the realms of mechanics, physics, and chemistry. In essence it is remarkably simple. The first step is to discover the pertinent facts. Next, you make a guess as to the law which accounts for these facts. And finally, you test the correctness of this guess by experiment. If your experiments do not verify the first guess, you admit that you were wrong, and make another guess. And so on, until you have found a piece of demonstrable knowledge, or demonstrated that the truth with regard to that particular matter is so far unknown.

—From "The Pretensions of Science,"
by Hugh Stevenson Tigner

Let me define my terms. By social ethic I mean that contemporary body of thought which makes morally legitimate the pressures of society against the individual. Its major propositions are three: a belief in the group as the source of creativity; a belief in "belongingness" as the ultimate need of the individual; and a belief in the application of science to achieve the belongingness.

—From *The Organization Man*, by William H. Whyte

83f. DEVELOP A PARAGRAPH BY REASONS OR INFERENCES.

When the topic sentence states a general opinion, especially a debatable one, the writer must support his point of view. He can do so either (1) by giving reasons for his assertion or (2) by drawing inferences from certain facts he has presented.

Our citizens will have to learn at least one foreign language. The reason is not so they can sell things to the Brazilians, or study German medical books, or appreciate those beauties of Homer which are lost in translation. Nor is it because they will gain satisfaction in recognizing the Latin root of the word *satisfaction*. It is not even because grubbing for roots is good discipline. It is because they cannot understand their own language unless they have studied another. The native of any country is immersed in his own language and never sees it as a linguistic structure. He cannot learn what he ought to know about language from talking about his own.

From "Education and Freedom,"
by Robert Maynard Hutchins

The questions, "Is that enough? Is that all?" began to plague me. Or "This may be art, but is it my art?" And then I began to realize that however professional my work might appear, even how original it might be, it still did not contain the central person, which, for good or ill, was myself. The whole stream of events and of thinking and changing of thinking; the childhood influences that were still strong in me; my rigorous training as a lithographer with its emphasis on craft; my several college years with the strong intention to become a biologist; summers at Woods Hole, the probing of the wonders of marine forms; all my views and notions of life and politics, all this material and much more which must constitute the substance of whatever person I was, lay outside the scope of my own paintings. *Yes, it was art that I was producing, perfectly competent, but foreign to me, and the inner critic was rising up against it.*

— From "The Shape of Content," by Ben Shahn

83g. DEVELOP A PARAGRAPH BY CAUSE OR EFFECT.

In this type of paragraph development, the topic sentence makes a generalized statement or provides a conclusion drawn from data. These data make up the supporting material of the paragraph, the cause or reasons. Or the supporting material suggests what the various results or effects are of the general statement provided in the topic sentence.

The birth of a volcanic island is an event marked by prolonged and violent travail: the forces of the earth striving to create, and all the forces of the sea opposing. The sea floor, where an island begins, is probably nowhere more than fifty miles thick—a thin covering over the vast bulk of the earth. In it are deep cracks and fissures, the results of unequal cooling and shrinkage in past ages. Along such lines of weakness the molten lava from the earth's interior presses up and finally bursts forth into the sea. But a submarine volcano is different from a terrestrial eruption, where the lava, molten rocks, gases, and other ejecta are hurled into the air through an open crater. Here on the bottom of the ocean the volcano has resisting it all the weight of the ocean water above it. Despite the immense pressure of, it may be, two or three miles of sea water, the new volcanic cone builds upward toward the surface, in flow after flow of lava. Once within reach of the waves, its soft ash and tuff are violently attacked, and for a long period the potential island may remain a shoal, unable to emerge. But, eventually, in new eruptions, the cone is pushed up into the air and a rampart against the attacks of the waves is built of hardened lava.

— From *The Sea Around Us,* by Rachel Carson

To most participating nations, *a modern war brings complex economic results.* Science and industry are occasionally advanced by researches derived from the stimulus and energy of war. Life and property are destroyed; vast sums are consumed in armament; impossible debts accumulate. Repudiation in some form becomes inevitable; currencies are depreciated or annulled, inflation relieves debtor governments and individuals, savings and investments are wiped out, and men patiently begin to save and lend again. Over-expansion in war is followed by a major depression in peace. International trade is disrupted by intensified nationalism, exalted tariffs, and the desire to develop at home all industries requisite in war. The vanquished are enslaved—physically, as in antiquity, financially and by due process of law today. The victorious masses gain little except in self-conceit; the ruling minority among the victors may gain much in conquered lands, markets, spheres of influence, supplies, and taxable population.

—From "Why Men Fight," by Will Durant

83h. DEVELOP A PARAGRAPH BY A COMBINATION OF METHODS.

Each of the methods so far explained is useful, and examples of several of them can be found in every published essay or article. Many paragraphs, however, do not follow a single method but use a combination of methods. The following is one example of methods in combination. For the sake of reference, a number is assigned to each sentence. (1) Topic sentence. (2) Amplification by contrasting statement. (3) Cause. (4) Effect, again contrasting statement. (5) Illustration. As a whole, the paragraph supplies reasons to support the topic statement, but, as you can see below, it does so in more than one way.

(1) The people have no tradition of outsiders and no procedures for handling them. (2) They are not hostile, but they are suspicious and afraid of them. (3) History has proved that to talk to strangers sooner or later leads to trouble or ends up costing money, and so history has rendered them incapable of telling truths to outsiders. (4) They don't lie, but they never of their own will provide the truth. (5) There are people in Santa Vittoria who are capable of denying knowledge of the town fountain when it can be heard bubbling behind their backs.

—From *The Secret of Santa Vittoria*, by Robert Crichton

EXERCISE 5

By means of one of the eight methods of paragraph development discussed and illustrated in Section 83, develop one or more of the following topic sentences (as your teacher suggests):

1. Sending a man to the moon is (is not) lunacy.
2. Movies are (are not) "better than ever."
3. Here is one way to "win friends and influence people."
4. A pretty girl is like a _____.
5. Yes, there is a Santa Claus.

EXERCISE 6

Follow the instructions for Exercise 5.

1. My favorite spectator sport is _____.
2. What is a good student?
3. The greatest need of this town is _____.
4. Atomic energy is changing our lives in many ways.
5. School is a poor place in which to get an education.

EXERCISE 7

The following paragraph, from "The Reading Machine," by Morris Bishop, is developed by an example (Section 83b).

> "Think of the efficiency of the thing!" Professor Entwhistle was really warming up. "Think of the time saved! You assign a student a bibliography of fifty books. He runs them through the machine comfortably in a weekend. And on Monday morning he turns in a certificate from the machine. Everything has been conscientiously read!"

Write a paragraph developing Bishop's idea with a different method (or combination of methods).

EXERCISE 8

The following paragraph, from "Such, Such Were the Joys . . . ," by George Orwell, is developed by cause or effect (Section 83g).

> But this sense of guilt and inevitable failure was balanced by something else: that is, the instinct to survive. Even a creature that is weak, ugly, cowardly, smelly, and in no way justifiable still wants to stay alive and be happy after its own fashion. I

could not invert the existing scale of values, or turn myself into a success, but I could accept my failure and make the best of it. I could resign myself to being what I was, and then endeavour to survive on those terms.

Write a paragraph developing Orwell's thought with a different method.

84. UNITY

No matter by which method or combination of methods a paragraph is constructed, every sentence should contribute to the central thought. In other words, a paragraph should have unity, or oneness, a singleness of focus.

The key to paragraph unity is the topic sentence. Therefore, when you develop a paragraph, concentrate on the topic in hand and do not let it slip away. However enticing a momentary thought may seem, if it leads you into any sentence, even so much as a phrase, which has nothing directly to do with your topic, put it out of mind or save it for a different paragraph.

84a. OMIT MATERIAL UNRELATED TO THE MAIN THOUGHT OF THE PARAGRAPH.

Lack of unity is ineffective. A reader who has been following you down one line of thought would not only be puzzled but understandably annoyed if he came abruptly upon a statement that has no relation to what the paragraph has thus far been treating. Here are two sound tests for unity, whether the writing be a composition, a paragraph, or even just a sentence: (1) *omit* all material which is not an essential, logical part; (2) *include* all material which is an essential, logical part and do not place it in another sentence or paragraph where it does not belong.

The italicized sentences and parts of sentences that violate unity are shown in italics in the following paragraph:

Tennis has certain other advantages over golf. It is a less time-consuming activity. In most communities tennis courts are more easily accessible than golf courses. *In my town, real estate taxes are high, and housing developments are springing up all over nowadays.* A pair of tennis players will often be on their second or third set while the golfing twosome is still on its way to the course or waiting for its turn to tee off. In a couple of hours or so, the tennis pair will have had its fill of fun and exercise, while the golfers will take the better part of a day to play their eighteen holes, *although older men, like my grandfather and his partner, play only nine holes.*

By mentioning real estate, the writer veers away from his topic. Since he has been comparing tennis players and golfers in general, his remarks about elderly golf players are irrelevant. Omitting both comments would have insured a unified paragraph.

EXERCISE 9

Point out the lack of unity in each of the following paragraphs:

Lake-of-the-Woods is an excellent place for the sportsman to spend the summer. If you like to fish, there are all kinds of freshwater fish to be found, the most common of which is the pike. A few miles away, up in the mountains, the streams are filled with brook trout. For people who like to winter-fish, there is ice-fishing nearly every day. People who are fishing there for the first time can obtain guides, leaving the town early in the morning before the weather gets hot and returning in the cool of the evening.

Thanksgiving is always a happy time at my home. This is the time of year to be thankful for all the things we have in this country. Thanksgiving was first started by the Pilgrims during the time of the foundation of the United States of America. The Pilgrims left England in September, 1620, and arrived at Plymouth in November. They had a long, hard winter; many died. But the following year was prosperous, and in gratitude to God they celebrated the first Thanksgiving with prayers and a bountiful feast. They invited many Indians to the feast. At Thanksgiving our family is always together for at least one time during the year. Sometimes we have friends in for dinner; at other times we have a large family reunion. When all of the relatives are present, everyone has a wonderful time.

There are many superstitions all over the world. In some foreign countries like New Guinea, superstitions have more meaning to the people than they do here in Canada. Many people believe in superstitions to the extent that they would stake their lives on them. However, the other group of people disbelieve in superstitions. I am one of these people who disbelieve them, and I am proceeding to tell why I do.

85. ORDER

A paragraph can have fully developed, interesting, and unified content and still be unsuccessful unless its sentences are correctly and logically arranged. If a book you were reading began with chapter 5, followed by chapters 2, 4, 1, and 3, you would be baffled, confused, and out of patience with the author. So would the reader of a paragraph in which the sentences follow one another in helter-skelter fashion because the writer has not kept related parts of his topic together, has shuttled back and forth between ideas, or has set down afterthoughts that should have been stated earlier.

85a. ARRANGE SENTENCES IN A CLEAR, ORDERLY SEQUENCE.

The sentences in a paragraph, like the chapters of a book, should show clear progress or readily understandable forward movement. But since the ideas that pop into our minds do not automatically shape themselves into paragraphs, we first have to arrange them properly. Anyone who has tried to tell a story or who has heard one told knows how easy it is to present ideas in the wrong order.

Several kinds of arrangement may be used. Which of these is best depends upon the subject matter of the paragraph and the effect desired. All arrangements, however, have one end in view: the thought in the paragraph must move forward in some way, must *progress*. The three principal types of arrangement are these:

85a ORDER

1. Arrangement by chronology (progress through time). Sentences follow one another in the order of the events narrated, the steps of a process being explained, or the description of something that involves passage of time, as, for instance, a sunrise or the approach of a storm.

2. Arrangement by physical point of view (progress through space). Details are arranged from near to far, left to right, inside to outside, top to bottom, etc., or the reverse, as in describing a landscape, a building, a painting, and countless other objects.

3. Arrangement by logical reasoning (mental progress). The writer makes a general statement and follows it with details, or states an effect and then cites causes, or names a term and then explains it.

EXERCISE 10

Rearrange the sentences of these paragraphs in an orderly sequence. Write the numbers of the sentences in the order in which you feel they should appear.

(1) The view at Lookout Point was spectacular. (2) As far as one could see were mountains. (3) Closer by, off to our right, rose enormous cliffs, from one of which cascaded a waterfall that disappeared into the chasm below. (4) It was amazing to think that we had driven up so high along that winding road. (5) It was so quiet that we could hear the roar of the water. (6) To our left was a deep, wooded gorge. (7) Way down below we could see the roof of the hotel we had left that morning. (8) As it was mid-summer, I was surprised to see there was still snow on some of the highest peaks.

(1) A hot rod can also be called a custom-made car. (2) It has a custom-made engine and a special body. (3) Most hot rods are built around stock parts from standard model cars. (4) Hot rods can do 90 to 100 miles an hour and get 20 or more miles on a gallon. (5) The car which holds the speed record can go 189 miles an hour. (6) Some of the parts used are found in auto graveyards. (7) Souping up the engine is the most important step. (8) This means tearing down the engine and adjusting the block for an easier flow of gas to the combustion chamber.

(1) Teston is a very small village in southern Ontario. (2) A few years ago my parents and I visited my grandfather, who

has lived there ever since he was born. (3) It has a population of only 127. (4) In such a small place there wasn't much for a boy to do but swing in the hammock or go fishing and swimming in the creek. (5) People have to go two miles to Maple to shop. (6) Teston has a small church but no post office or general store. (7) Once I rode a borrowed bicycle all the way to Maple just for an ice cream soda.

86. TRANSITION

A well-written paragraph depends not only on a writer's control of what he wants to say but also on the ease and smoothness with which his thought moves from sentence to sentence. Ease of movement between sentences is aided by a skillful use of transitional devices. Lack of them, or of effective use of them, often accounts for awkwardness in writing. It is important to know what different kinds of transitional devices are available and to what uses you can put them.

Transition means "passage or change from one position, place, or stage to another." In writing, transition involves *showing* evidence of the links, the bridges, between related units (sentences and paragraphs).

Even though a paragraph contains ample substance, with its sentences logically and clearly arranged, it will not make sense to a reader if the sentences appear to be loosely joined or even disconnected. It is easy to assume that a reader should readily understand our shifts in thought, whereas we ought to be aware that if we fail to express the hidden connectives that appear in our private thinking we are causing reader confusion. The relationship of one sentence to another in a paragraph often *requires* the use of transitional words. Haven't you noticed that some teacher or other speaker is particularly easy to understand because he or she constantly relates one thought to another by using such transitional devices as *however, on the other hand, for example, similarly, conversely,* and the like?

Transitions resemble highway signs: "Detour: 100 Yards"; "Slow Down: End of Pavement"; "Form Single Lane"; "End of Construction." Such signs prepare a motorist for changing conditions. Transitional expressions have precisely the same effect upon the reader. For example, when you complete a paragraph, you can then let the reader know what is coming next. When you finish a group of paragraphs dealing with one phase of a topic, you can let the reader know that another topic is being taken up. Sometimes, you can sum up what has been written; more often you may point out the road ahead, a continuation in the same direction.

86a. USE TRANSITIONAL EXPRESSIONS WITHIN THE SENTENCE, BETWEEN SENTENCES, AND BETWEEN PARAGRAPHS.

The transitional expressions listed below are all useful, but be sparing in employing them. Transitions should be unobtrusive and not weigh down the paragraph. Rarely if ever use the same transitional expression more than once in the same paragraph.

To add an idea:	besides, also, moreover, in addition, another way, a second method, furthermore, similarly.
To contrast ideas:	but, yet, nevertheless, still, however, in contrast, on the contrary, instead, otherwise, on the other hand, whereas, unlike, yet.
To compare ideas:	like, similarly, equally, correspondingly, in like manner.
To show result:	therefore, thus, consequently, as a result, hence.
To show time:	then, afterwards, later, meanwhile, now, earlier, immediately, henceforth, before.
To show frequency:	often, frequently, sometimes, now and then.

86b. REPEAT A KEY WORD OR A VARIATION OF A KEY WORD.

Simple repetition of a key word in successive sentences, sometimes even in the same sentence, is frequently effective for emphasis. When emphasis is not a primary consideration, an unobtrusive and more subtle transitional device is using a different form of the same word the second time.

One of the greatest disappointments of *childhood* is a *broken* promise. An adult who *breaks* his word never fully regains a *child's* confidence.

They knew it would take a long time for the *dust* to settle out of the air. In the morning the *dust* hung like fog, and the sun was as red as ripe new blood. All the day the *dust sifted* down from the sky, and the next day it *sifted* down.

— From *The Grapes of Wrath*, by John Steinbeck

86c. USE DEMONSTRATIVE ADJECTIVES *THIS* AND *THAT*, AND PRONOUNS *HE, SHE, IT, THEY* TO REFER TO NOUNS IN THE PRECEDING SENTENCE.

The demonstratives *this* and *that* are effective transitional words but should not be used to excess. Be especially careful in your use of *this* and do not use it by itself to refer to a general statement. It should refer to a specific noun, and then only if the reference is entirely clear.

A rumor was recently circulated that Easter vacation would be shortened to three days. *This* rumor is false.

Pronouns are common transitional aids. No narrative could dispense with them, and they occur frequently in all other types of writing.

Live-oaks are so called because *they* do not lose *their* leaves. *They* also differ from other oaks in that *they* have relatively short trunks out of which spring heavy curved or crooked limbs. Because of *their* shape and because *their* wood is tough and durable, *they* were once much sought after by shipbuilders. Today, in certain areas, many of *them* are being killed by infestations of Spanish moss.

EXERCISE 11

Each of the two original paragraphs below contains seven incomplete sentences. The sentence subjects (topics) are numbered in proper order. Reconstruct each paragraph, making each statement into a sentence and supplying whatever transitions you consider necessary.

1. Little security for musicians, even if famous. 2. Uncertain today whether job tomorrow. 3. Most well paid, seldom save money, travel town to town expensive. 4. Leader of orchestra paid much more, works harder for money. 5. Many responsibilities, orchestra successful, leader's name famous. 6. Always in music feeling of beauty, makes people happy. 7. Musician's life rough, many compensations.

1. Fire warden hard work. 2. Area to patrol, no fires except at designated camp grounds. 3. Visits lumber camps, no smoking permitted. 4. Much walking, patrolling of lakes in outboard boat. 5. If fire, must organize firefighters. 6. Observe game laws, helps game warden. 7. Cooperate together in searching lost persons.

EXERCISE 12

The following underdeveloped paragraphs lack proper transitional aids. Rewrite each.

1. "Never cross a bridge till you come to it" is a wise saying. Many people worry too much. W. H. Auden says we live in an "Age of Anxiety."

2. In most European countries students are taught to speak English the way it is pronounced in England. I know a man from Canada whose speech is hard to tell from American.

3. Most boys do not like girls to use too much make-up. Some girls use too much eye-shadow. There are many rinses on the market that a girl can use to make her hair any color she likes.

87.   PROPORTION

Proportion is a matter of the relative importance of paragraphs in a composition. A paragraph should be developed according to the value of the point it has to make, its relative idea value. If that point is the main topic, the paragraph should be fuller in detail or analysis than one which serves an introductory or transitional function. Readers are likely to attribute importance to ideas on the basis of the length of paragraphs in which they are discussed. Often such emphasis is unwarranted and causes distortion. Nevertheless, one should not expand ideas that are comparatively subordinate or treat sketchily those that are of basic importance.

87a. MAKE SURE THAT YOUR PARAGRAPHS ARE CORRECTLY PROPORTIONED.

Proportioning paragraphs depends upon analysis and judgment of the ideas which are to be used in developing a theme. That is, you should plan and outline a paper in advance and then, after it is completed, carefully weigh the separate paragraphs to make certain that each contributes its share, and no more than its share, to the development of the paper as a whole. These suggestions may help you to proportion your paragraphs effectively.

1. Consider the whole subject before you start to write. What is your central purpose? What effect upon the reader are you aiming for?

2. Always keep your reader in mind. Does each paragraph have a central idea worth communicating to him? What, to your reader, is the value, the weight, of each paragraph?

3. If your assignment calls for a certain number of words, make a tentative allotment for each paragraph before you begin to write. Alter this plan if you need to.

4. Shorten any paragraph that does not carry its weight, even though you like its details and must sacrifice valued wordage in cutting it down.

5. Lengthen a paragraph if its central topic or thought seems to deserve further development by detail, illustration, definition, or any other means necessary to communicate to a reader.

EXERCISE 13

Study one of the essays in an anthology or a magazine. Does each paragraph seem to make a point the relative importance of which is proportionate to its length?

EXERCISE 14

Indicate the number of words proportionately correct for each paragraph of a 400-word composition devoted to the explanation of a process: learning to dance, or play bridge, or give a party, or play tennis, or some comparable activity, sport, or recreation. Select *one* subject and adapt or alter the following plan, as necessary:

Learning to Swim

A. Correct mental attitude for the beginner
B. Correct body position
C. How to breathe
D. How to handle the arms
E. How to handle the feet and legs
F. Fears to overcome
G. Errors to be avoided
H. Summary

In a 400-word theme, is each of the eight paragraphs worth exactly fifty words? Why? Why not? (Your answer will depend more upon the needs and attitudes of a beginning dancer or tennis player or what not than upon your particular interests, knowledge, or enthusiasms.)

88. LENGTH

The length of a paragraph, like its proportion, depends on the weight and value of its controlling idea in relation to other paragraphs in the same paper. No definite rule for paragraph length can be given. About the *average* length, however, something can be said. This varies with an author's subject and the demands he makes upon his readers. If his subject is analytical and literary, philosophical, or scientific, one demanding full concentration from readers, a writer's paragraphs will tend to be longer than if he were writing an article for a popular magazine, for instance, designed to be read rapidly. In the former, the average length of paragraphs might be 400 words; in the latter, the longest would rarely exceed 150 words.

Great variety in length of paragraphs appears in narrative writing. For example, Mark Twain's *Life on the Mississippi* contains numerous paragraphs running to 600 words but also many (exclusive of dialogue) that consist of one or two sentences. Here are two consecutive Twain paragraphs, one consisting of a single sentence, the other of two sentences connected by a semicolon:

> An article in the New Orleans *Times-Democrat*, based upon reports of able engineers, states that the river annually empties four hundred and six million tons of mud into the Gulf of Mexico — which brings to mind Captain Marryat's rude name for the Mississippi — "the Great Sewer."

> This mud deposit gradually extends the land — but only gradually; it has extended it not quite a third of a mile in the two hundred years which have elapsed since the river took its place in history.

Short paragraphs such as these can be effective. These examples from *Life on the Mississippi* are preceded and followed by longer paragraphs. A succession of short paragraphs, as Mark Twain well knew, would lessen the emphasis he wanted to give to each of these stated facts. When too many ideas are emphasized, nothing is emphasized.

88a. AVOID SHORT, UNDERDEVELOPED PARAGRAPHS.

Although an occasional short paragraph is effective for emphasis and variety, especially in a long paper, it must always be a complete unit of thought. If it is short simply because the writer has not thought out his topic, it will leave the reader stranded, for he has been led to expect something that the topic statement indicates but never supplies. In the following examples, in which the key statements are italicized, the writer was evidently careless and too easily satisfied.

As an attendant at a filling station last summer, *I met some strange people*. One car even had an Alaska license plate.

What about those "strange people" he was to tell about?

An interesting program of arts and crafts has been started at our Civic Center. Wood-carving was canceled for lack of interest.

Specifically, why was the program interesting? Was wood-carving canceled because it was an uninteresting course or because not enough people registered for it?

88b. AVOID A SERIES OF SHORT, CHOPPY PARAGRAPHS.

Sentences so closely related in thought that they belong together should not be split into a series of separate short paragraphs under the impression that such an arrangement creates variety or achieves emphasis. The effect will only be distracting to the reader, who has to assemble piecemeal what a connected paragraph would have told him quickly. Notice the ineffectiveness and monotony of short paragraphs such as these:

Having never been on a hayride before, I had no idea what fun it could be.

The wagon we rode on was big and piled up with hay about three feet thick.

There were more girls than boys, it turned out. Every boy sat next to a girl, and some boys sat next to two.

I sat next to Alice Dewar, who sings in the choir in our church.

We sang all the way out to the picnic grounds. After we had eaten our lunches, we played baseball and other games.

On the way home we were all too tired to sing.

88c. AVOID A SERIES OF LONG, CUMBERSOME PARAGRAPHS.

Just as a succession of short paragraphs is unsatisfying because they splinter the writer's thought, so two or three very long paragraphs following one another probably indicate that the writer has overloaded them. A sequence of long, heavy paragraphs may also tax a reader's patience. Like everyone else, he prefers variety to monotony. Make it a point, therefore, to vary the length of the paragraphs in your compositions. If you have written two or more long paragraphs in a row, examine them carefully to see whether you can break one or two of them into shorter units or can condense them if they contain excess detail or have been over-elaborated in any other way.

In present-day writing, paragraphs tend to grow shorter and shorter, perhaps through the influence of advertising materials, news stories, business letters, and talks on TV and radio programs. Such influences are powerful, although not always helpful; but it is true that the eye, the ear, and the mind can "take in" relatively short units of thought more readily than they can absorb extended passages. Also, it is true that most beginning writers find it difficult to write unified paragraphs in excess of about 200 words (see Section 84). No standard rule about paragraph length can be helpfully stated, but comparatively short paragraphs which are adequately developed are usually more effective than a series of overextended ones.

EXERCISE 15

Count the number of words in five consecutive paragraphs of some essay in an anthology or magazine. How many words does the longest contain? The shortest? What is the average? Repeat this exercise for another article by another writer on a different subject. Make a comparison of the two.

EXERCISE 16

Compare the average length of paragraphs in an article in *The Atlantic* or *Harper's Magazine* with the average length of an article in *Time, Maclean's, Life, Newsweek,* or *Reader's Digest.*

EXERCISE 17

Count the number of words in the paragraphs of a paper which you have written. Write a paragraph commenting on your findings about their average length and their proportion to each other.

89. VARIETY

No paragraph is ever more effective than its sentences. If its component sentences have a monotonous sameness, the paragraph itself will be monotonous. Avoid, therefore, using the same sentence form consecutively and do not begin consecutive sentences with the same type of phrase or clause. For a detailed discussion of sentence elements that make for monotony, see Section 78.

Sentences also involve sound and rhythm. Make a practice of reading your paragraphs aloud to yourself. Often the ear will detect what the eye has passed over. How do your sentences *sound?* If some of them seem halting and jerky, perhaps you have broken your thought into several short sentences that need revising or combining. On the other hand, if the pace seems slow and lumbering and you have to take several breaths between the periods, your sentences may have combined ideas which should be expressed in shorter units. Your ear may also detect awkward or jarring sound-combinations which the eye has failed to observe.

89a. AVOID USING TOO MANY SHORT SENTENCES IN SUCCESSION.

In the paragraph below, the first two brief sentences are effective because they engage our attention at once. But thereafter, short sentences which lack variety beat upon us like hailstones, the monotony of which is not relieved even by transitional devices.

> An exciting thing has happened in our town. A circus has set up winter quarters. Animals are being trained for the spring shows. The circus owners also saw a chance to make some extra money. They put some of their animals on television. A young girl put the elephants through their paces. She is said to be the youngest elephant trainer in the world. After the TV program, many people rushed to the winter quarters. Again the owners made extra money. They charged 25 cents admission. So far I have gone three times. Each performance was different. At the first, they were training seals. At the second, the bareback riders were practicing. The third, however, was best. A pan-

ther was being taught to roll over and to jump through a hoop. I will be sorry to see the circus leave.

This paragraph has other flaws (improper order of sentences and lack of unity), but its greatest fault is lack of sentence variety.

89b. AVOID USING TOO MANY LENGTHY SENTENCES IN SUCCESSION.

A sequence of overloaded sentences makes heavy reading. Besides crowding together unrelated ideas, prolonged sentences tend to be unemphatic and pompous. If the following paragraph were read aloud, some of the sentences would require several intakes of breath.

Because little of note ever happens in our town, considerable excitement was generated when a circus established its winter quarters in our midst. During the winter, circus people occupy themselves primarily with rehearsing and improving their acts and training animals for performances to be given in the spring. The circus owners, seizing the opportunity to earn some extra money, exhibited some of their animals on a television program, which also showed a young girl, said to be the youngest elephant-trainer in the world, putting the pachyderms through various stunts. As a result of this publicity, many people hastened to the winter quarters, where the shrewd owners again netted a profit, this time by charging an admission fee of 25 cents, which, however, was well worth paying, for each performance was different from the one before. I first witnessed the training of seals, next some bareback riders practicing, and last, the best exhibition thus far, a panther being taught to lie down and turn over, and also to jump through a hoop. I doubt whether anyone will be more regretful than I to see the circus depart.

89c. AVOID REPEATING THE SAME SOUND WITHIN A SENTENCE OR IN SUCCESSIVE SENTENCES.

Harsh-sounding word combinations, unnecessary repetitions of the same sounds, or unconscious rhyming will repel the reader or divert his attention from the main idea.

<table>
<tr><td>Unpleasant:</td><td>Some countries are becoming *impatient* with the *deliberations* of the United *Nations*. The *fact* is that there are many *factions* and that the *organization lacks* the force to *back* its decisions.</td></tr>
<tr><td>Improved:</td><td>Some countries are becoming disillusioned about the United Nations. Such nations claim that there is too much factionalism and not enough power to enforce decisions.</td></tr>
</table>

EXERCISE 18

Rewrite each of the following paragraphs so that the sentences will exhibit greater variety in structure and length:

Thanksgiving originated in New England. The first one was in 1623. There had been a bad drought. The colonists had a day for fasting and prayer. While they were praying, rain began to fall. The prayer was changed to giving thanks. For years Thanksgiving was a harvest celebration. Finally President Lincoln made it a national holiday. He set it as the last Thursday in November. He did that in 1864.

When my father bought the encyclopedia set and the bookcase to hold it, I was disappointed because it meant that I would not get the new bicycle I wanted. When I first showed my father the picture of the bicycle in the mail-order catalogue, he said I could have it, as my old one, which I had bought second-hand, had a wobbly front wheel, rusty handlebars, and most of the paint chipped off the frame, but after he paid for the encyclopedia he said he couldn't afford to buy me a new bicycle and that I had to make out as best I could with the old one. When I saw my father and my older sister taking volumes of the encyclopedia out of the bookcase and looking up different things in them, I was still annoyed about the bicycle, but after a while my curiosity got the best of me and I began to look up some things I'd wanted to know, like where Hong Kong is and why Louis Riel became an American citizen. When I later got my newspaper route, I saved up enough money to buy the new bicycle anyway, and I was never sorry again that we had a good encyclopedia, because I get a lot of use out of it in my school assignments.

Having received a stiff lecture from their coach, the team, promising to do its best, went out for the second half. Receiving the kickoff, Jim Matthews, dodging the first two tacklers, carried the ball to the 35-yard line, before being downed. Making three first-downs in succession, the team reached the opponents' 30. Fading back, Dave Prokowski heaved a pass to Stan Graminian in the end zone. Matthews' kick, sailing neatly between the crossbars, brought loud cheering from our side in the stands, the score now being in our favor 7 to 6.

EXERCISE 19

Copy a paragraph from a book or magazine which seems to you to indicate especially good variety of sentences. Write a brief analysis of the length and structure of the sentences.

90. MECHANICS

The few rules for mechanical correctness in paragraphs are easy to learn. The following are the principal ones.

90a. INDENT THE FIRST LINE OF EVERY PARAGRAPH.

The break of distinct paragraph indentation is a clear and effective help to both writer and reader in recognizing the divisions of thought within a composition. When you are writing in longhand, indent (set in) the first line of each paragraph about three quarters of an inch. Keep your indentations the same throughout so that they line up neatly and evenly. If you typewrite, indent five spaces each time. (Business letters are sometimes typed without indentations.)

90b. DO NOT LEAVE PART OF A LINE BLANK WITHIN A PARAGRAPH.

It is difficult in writing or typing to keep right-hand margins even, but try to keep them as even as you can. Gaps at the end of lines not only produce a jagged appearance but also are a hindrance to the reader, who is accustomed to seeing spaces at the ends of paragraphs and whose eye must make constant readjustments when the spaces occur earlier.

90c. WHEN WRITING DIALOGUE, USE A NEW PARAGRAPH FOR EACH NEW SPEAKER.

In recording conversation and writing dialogue, use a separate paragraph for each speaker's words. Most of these paragraphs will be short, sometimes very short, but starting a new paragraph for each change of speaker enables the reader to keep track of who is talking to whom. When only two persons are speaking, the routine speaker-identifications, such as *James said, Joan asked, Bill replied,* etc., can also be reduced to a minimum.

Mr. Stilby had always had us recite in alphabetical order. He had called on me yesterday, as I had known he would, and I had taken care to be prepared. As my name was next to last in Mr. Stilby's roll book and there were twenty-two names ahead of mine, I hadn't done today's reading assignment. At the moment, I was pondering the problem of which of several girls I'd ask to next Friday's dance, and the teacher's voice seemed only a sort of background static. Suddenly I had the strange notion that someone was calling me by name. Then I heard it again. It was really a voice—the voice of Mr. Stilby. I rose to my feet.

"Yates!"

"Sir?" My heart was pounding like a pile-driver.

"I assume you have normal hearing, Yates?"

"Yes, sir." What did he want of me? Today wasn't my turn.

"Then how do you explain that I had to call your name *three* times?"

An explanation would have been complicated. Besides, I didn't think it would interest Mr. Stilby very much. All I could do was to say I was sorry, and I did.

"Very well. But don't let it happen again, Yates. Now suppose you tell the class why knocking on the gate in *Macbeth* is so dramatically effective."

"I don't know, sir." I remembered that we were supposed to have read some essay about that. I was going to read it, too, sometime.

"Oh, you don't know, sir." He was mimicking me. Someone giggled. I knew it was Lucy Chapman. "Then sit down, Yates!"

I knew Mr. Stilby was putting a neat zero in his roll book, but I didn't care. All I cared about just then was to cross Lucy's name off my list.

THE LONGER PAPER

In writing a composition, all the knowledge and skills required of you at the end of an English course are needed at the beginning. In your very first paper, you must hit upon a subject, limit it to manageable size, find material to develop it, outline and plan this material, and write sentences and paragraphs which are correct, clear, and effective. That is, you are expected to master in advance all those involved problems you have not yet had a chance to study.

Unfair? Yes, to some degree. But you *have* been using the English language since infancy and you do know more than you perhaps realize about its structure and usage.

Are teachers who set such assignments thoughtless and cruel? Consider this: laboratory work is the method a physical scientist employs to turn theory into fact. Field work is the most significant means by which a social scientist translates theories into techniques and tools. Chemists, biologists, physicists, social scientists, engineers, and home economists use test-tubes, microscopes, case studies, testing machines, and demonstration homes to relate theory to actuality. For those who wish to learn to use English efficiently, the prescribed laboratory work is composition writing.

In any case, the only way to learn to write is to write; the sooner the process is started, the quicker the complete design of theme writing becomes clear. Mere knowledge of words and their ways is worth little until it is applied, precisely as worthless as facts gleaned from a biology textbook until they are demonstrated, proved, and observed in the laboratory. The word, the sentence, the paragraph are only the bricks that make up a house. One can never be said to write competently until he can achieve a completed whole, an entire composition.

If you think of writing a theme as a single operation, or process, you *will* be faced with a challenging task that may be overly difficult at the beginning. But if you think, instead, of composition writing as a series of steps, your task will be easier. Each step is dependent upon others, but the separate stages involved are considerably less intricate and more manageable than the complete operation.

The first step may be called *planning*, or *prewriting*. This stage involves selecting something to write about and narrowing this subject into one phase or segment which becomes a manageable *topic*. Next, consider *whom* you intend to write for and what *purpose* you hope to achieve. (If you blithely respond that you are writing for your teacher and your purpose is to get a passing grade, you may have given an honest answer but you have also missed the real point at issue.) Also a part of the planning, or "before writing," stage is gathering material to develop your topic. This substance, or content, comes from varied sources, yourself not least important among them. Then comes the matter of shaping, designing (actually, outlining) the material you have collected. This stage completed, you are now ready for the second step, *writing*. Remember that the prewriting step in composition work bears a relationship to the final two steps involved as the part of an iceberg under water does to that above the surface. Seven-eighths or eight-ninths of the chances for success in composition writing lies in the planning stages.

When the basic decisions involved in this first stage are out of the way, you can then concentrate on what might be called the actual writing. This second step really consists of carrying out pre-planned decisions through a complete draft. Here you can focus on those numerous and perplexing details discussed below in Sections 95-101, but you can do so secure in the knowledge that your task is already largely determined (or should be) and with a mind free to concentrate on specific but limited writing problems and requirements.

Your first draft completed, you are then ready for the third step. This involves *revision*, correction, and—where necessary—some rewriting. In this phase you can concentrate on matters taken up in Sections 104, 105.

Separating the task into parts will make the operation simpler and easier to perform. True, these stages sometimes overlap. Each of these stages of composition is detailed in sections which follow.

91. CHOOSING A TOPIC

When your teacher leaves the choice of a theme topic to you, and you can think of nothing much, refer to the sources mentioned for paragraph substance (Sections 82a, b). Consider the following paragraphs before you finally decide on your subject.

91a. CHOOSE A TOPIC OF INTEREST TO YOURSELF.

First, you should have a genuine interest in the subject. If you choose it largely because you are expected to write a certain number of words, you will probably produce no more than a perfunctory piece of writing that is padded with generalities, uninspired, and dull. Your writing has a chance to be lively and sincere if you can exhibit some enthusiasm for your topic.

You could give a more interesting account, for example, of how to build a tree-house you once constructed yourself than you could of one you saw in a Tarzan film. Or again, you may never have given any particular thought to labor relations. But if someone in your family or in that of a close friend joined a picket line, or felt himself a victim of an unjust strike, labor relations might come alive as a potential subject for writing.

Sometimes, your instructor may assign topics which seem to leave no room for originality. But if you consider them carefully, you can usually find some approach to the subject or some limited part of it that you can take genuine interest in developing. Until you do find some topic of direct interest to you, you should keep turning the subject over and over in your mind until you hit upon some phase or angle that directly appeals to you. Almost always, you will be able to write with confidence and vitality when your interest is immediately involved. When it is not, it is almost a waste of your time and that of your readers to bother writing at all.

91b. CHOOSE A TOPIC OF INTEREST TO YOUR READERS.

When you decide upon your subject and begin examining its possibilities, you must consider the reader you intend to address. Your potential readers fall into two groups. In the first are your actual readers: your instructor, your classmates (who may hear your composition read to them), someone in your family, a friend, or anyone else to whom you may show it.

Also, you will be writing for readers in another category, readers who you imagine would be interested in your theme if they saw it in print. Suppose, for instance, you had chosen hitch-hiking as your subject, a means of travel in which you have had considerable experience. If your intention is to provide helpful pointers on how to get lifts from passing motorists, your imagined readers would be those who had never thumbed a ride or who had gone about it in the wrong way. If one point you are making suggests an amusing hitch-hiking incident you want to tell about, you would be writing for all readers in both categories who relish a funny story.

Psychologists, sociologists, and other experts in human behavior contend that each of us is first of all interested in himself. They point out that your reader, *any* reader, is constantly searching for information which will benefit him in some way, that he is always interested in material to which he can relate and by which he can measure himself. If we possibly can, we identify with ourselves nearly everything that we see or hear. What do you look for first in a group photograph of a meeting you have attended? In reading advertisements for a dress or suit, does not each of us think "How will that look on me?" "Will I like it?" "Can I afford it?"

In addition to oneself, nearly everyone is also likely to be interested in:

1. *Other people:* unique, prominent, well-known, unforgettable.

2. *Personal reminiscences:* especially recollections told in the form of dialogue, incident, or anecdote (that is, in story form) and making a point with which the reader can easily identify.

3. *Places:* historical, scenic, unusual (or uncommon features of common places, unfamiliar features of familiar places) which the reader would like to visit or which he can visualize or recollect in terms of his own interests, desires, and memories.

4. *Life, property, welfare:* important matters involving other people which have direct relationship to the reader's own welfare and ideas: money, health, self-improvement, etc.

5. *Conflict:* contests between people, between man and nature, man and space, within the individual. (Conflict is the basis of all narrative writing: plays, short stories, narrative poems, and novels.)

6. *Amusements, hobbies, recreation:* television, movies, radio, recordings; spectator and participation sports; growth of, development of, interest in, and profit from hobbies.

Also could be mentioned such subjects as the varied ways in which people earn their living (occupations), religion (both formal and informal) and the lack of it, relationships of the sexes, nature, and dozens of other topics.

91c. CHOOSE A TOPIC ABOUT WHICH YOU KNOW SOMETHING.

Most magazine articles and nearly all books, both nonfiction and fiction, are based on many months or years of direct observation, study, and personal familiarity with the materials involved. Every good writer goes to his own experience —to those things he knows or has thought or seen or heard. But every good writer also remembers that his experiences are quickly exhausted as writing materials unless he develops from them some new insights, novel conclusions, or fresh judgments and aspects of thought. Any one of your well-recollected experiences will become boring to your reader (see Section 91b) unless you use it to develop some new relationship or idea which has a meaning to the reader above and beyond the experience itself.

Some topics you can develop by relying entirely on what you already know. But some topics for papers that will be assigned, or which may occur to you, will send you on a search for information. For example, if you need to know whether the First Quebec Conference applied to Canada, you should spend some time in the library (see Section 108). It would be both foolish and vain for you to write on such a topic without exact and concrete information secured from sources other than yourself. If in a paper on television, you need to know how many minutes of commercials interrupt an average-length motion picture showing, you should be willing to sit at your set with a watch, pencil, and paper. Or, of course, you may be able to find out this item of information from a magazine article or book (see Sections 108c, 108d). In getting to know your subject intimately, you are merely doing what good writers take for granted as a necessary task. Besides, learning about a subject which really interests you can provide a lot of rewarding and even exciting fun.

91d. CHOOSE A TOPIC WHICH YOU CAN TREAT ADEQUATELY.

In selecting a topic, keep in mind the approximate length of the paper you plan to write. It is impossible to write an adequate theme of 500 words on a subject that would require 5000. The shorter a composition is, the more limited its subject should be. A thorough discussion of the topic "Social Injustice" would require a book or a number of books. But limiting your subject to "A Case of Social Injustice" which you have observed in your own neighborhood or by which you yourself have been affected could be treated in a short theme. The American Automobile Association has discussed "Safe Driving" in a series of pamphlets, but you can write a short theme on "An Error in Driving" or on "Elementary Courtesy for Drivers."

The word *theme* implies a single, well-defined *phase* of a subject. Consequently, you must limit a broad subject or general topic so that your composition can deal with it with reasonable thoroughness in the space at your command. A short composition on a large and lengthy subject is necessarily fragmentary, disconnected, and generally ineffective. When you restrict a subject, you narrow the range of investigation and thus increase your chances of finding out what it is you really want to say to your reader. Your success with a pinpointed topic is much more likely than with a broad subject, no matter how great your interest in it or that of your reader.

EXERCISE 1

List five incidents in your life which you think might be developed into compositions interesting to other members of your class. Include an explanatory (topic) sentence for each incident.

EXERCISE 2

From the following general subjects, select four about which you have information perhaps not shared by possible readers: Animals, Athletics, Childhood, Dancing, Food, Friends, Illness, Memories, Men, Music, Reading, Recreation, Relatives, Sorrow, Sports, Success, Superstition, Vacations, Wearing Apparel, Women. Restrict each of these four chosen subjects to a *specific, limited topic* which you think might interest readers whom you designate.

EXERCISE 3

From the following list of Canadian holidays and special occasions, select four about which you have, or can find out from other sources, detailed information probably not shared by your classmates or other readers *whom you specify.* For each of the four selected holidays or special events, write two limited topics which interest you and possibly will appeal to designated readers: New Year's Eve, New Year's Day, Valentine's Day, Easter, April Fool's Day, Mother's Day, Dominion Day, Labor Day, Halloween, Thanksgiving Day, Christmas Eve, Christmas Day, My Birthday, My Girlfriend's (or Boyfriend's) Birthday, a Family Anniversary. For each of the limited topics (eight in all) write an explanatory (topic) sentence.

EXERCISE 4

Apply the four tests (Sections 91a, b, c, d) to the following suggestions for compositions and suggest what readers you have in mind.

1. The greatest personal disaster I can imagine.
2. Favorite TV programs.
3. My criticism of a motion picture recently seen.
4. The school cafeteria at the luncheon hour.
5. Our family doctor.
6. Dating customs now and fifty years ago.
7. Fighting the school bully.
8. My ideas about friendship.
9. Why I can't understand people over thirty.
10. My greatest fault.

92. ANALYZING A TOPIC

Assume that you have chosen or been assigned a subject and have limited it in accordance with the approximate length of the paper you plan to write. What you should do next is to analyze the topic carefully so that you will fully understand what it involves and how you can most effectively develop it.

As is pointed out in Section 91, a theme must have a specific purpose. You will be writing for a particular reader or group of readers, either actual or imagined, and your purpose should be to produce a specific and named effect on your reader(s). Consequently, you must know clearly just what you are setting out to do. Begin the analysis of your subject by asking these basic questions:

1. Specifically, what reader or readers will my topic interest?

2. For what purpose am I writing? What do I want to say about my subject?

3. Can I accomplish my purpose best by narration, description, explanation, or persuasion? Perhaps by a combination of two or three of these methods?

4. Do I know my material well enough, or do I need to find out more about it?

5. Can I summarize the gist or substance of my paper in a single sentence?

92a. HAVE A CENTRAL PURPOSE CLEARLY IN MIND.

If you have thought out your subject so that you know what you intend to do with it, you ought to be able to state the central purpose of your theme in a single summarizing sentence. To illustrate, suppose your first general idea for a subject is "Summer Jobs for Students," too broad for a 600-word paper you intend to write. It needs limiting. Suppose further that you have held two summer jobs: once as a file clerk and once as a waiter in a summer resort. You choose the second as more interesting. You might then jot down the following items on a work sheet:

Limited subject:	"My Experiences as a Summer Waiter."
Possible Title:	"Tips on Summer Tables"
Reader:	Student contemplating a job for his or her next summer vacation.
Short Summary (thesis sentence):	Waiting on tables at a summer resort combines profit and recreation.
Fuller summary:	As a waiter in a summer resort you can make a sizable sum on tips by giving good service and learning the individual preferences of finicky guests, and you will have enough leisure time for an afternoon dip in the pool and for evening entertainments and dances.
Probable method:	Mostly explanation, with some narrative and descriptive details, all of which are designed to persuade your reader that your thesis sentence is both sensible and correct.

92b. MAKE A LIST OF POINTS TO BE INCLUDED.

To clarify your purpose further, make an inventory of details that might be covered. Jot them down on a work sheet just as they spring to mind; you can rearrange them later. You may then want to eliminate some of them in view of the limited length of your theme, or you may discover a few points about which you need to know more.

1. Experience unnecessary.
2. Neat appearance essential.
3. Apply early in spring.
   Query: I used Carter's Employment Agency. Do some of the other agencies also list resort jobs? Will check by telephone.
4. Instructions from headwaiter.
5. Annoyances: cranky and fussy guests; children spilling milk.
6. Clothes to bring: 2 pairs of dark slacks to wear with waiter's jacket, lightweight suit (preferably dark) for evenings.
7. Early rising (6 A.M.)
8. Hours for work, for recreation.
9. Be pleasant, cheerful. Sometimes hard to do.
10. Cooks. Irritable when diners send back overdone eggs or meat.
11. Tips: good if you're attentive. Men give more than women as a rule.
12. Student waiters and waitresses permitted to mingle with guests in off hours and evenings.
    Query: Is my experience typical of what one would encounter at most resorts? Check with Jim Gaines and Rhoda McKay on their experiences. Also, find out how they applied for and got jobs.

Now review your summarizing sentence and rearrange your list to place items in the order in which you want to treat them. Should any be omitted? What should be added? Which points need the fullest development? Which should be mentioned only briefly?

Arranging the items to be finally included in the form of an outline will provide you a clearer view of how to proceed. (See Section 93.)

92c. MAINTAIN A CONSISTENT TONE.

When you have worked out the central purpose of your theme and how you propose to develop it, consider what *feeling* you have toward the material and your prospective reader. In other words, in what *tone* are you going to write? A paper about waiting on tables at a resort might adopt an informal, even intimate, approach. You might choose to be candid about the advantages and disadvantages of such a job, with perhaps an occasional touch of humor from your own encounters with eccentric guests or irate cooks. Your purpose here would be to let your reader know what situations, favorable and unfavorable, he might encounter at any summer resort where he worked as a waiter.

On the other hand, if you were attempting to persuade readers in general to accept your point of view for or against a more serious subject, such as, for example, capital punishment, your tone should be formal and serious, since any humor or levity would be decidedly out of place. You might, however, use an ironical or satirical tone in writing about some aspect of society that strikes you as absurd and which you want to persuade your readers to view in the same light. But whatever tone you adopt in a composition, make sure it is appropriate to your purpose, your material, and your reader.

You should choose and maintain a consistent method of development. When you have finished writing, check to see that you have not, for example, used a light, bantering tone in one paragraph and a solemn, dignified approach in the next. Every good theme possesses unity of tone and purpose.

EXERCISE 5

Examine the following possible audiences of papers written for high school English classes. Which seem appropriate or inappropriate? Which seem too general? Too specific?

    A. Anyone who has a younger brother or sister.
    B. Anyone not from the province of Quebec.
    C. My boyfriend.
    D. People who live in large cities.
    E. Everyone who hates to eat breakfast.

EXERCISE 6

For *one* of the following broad subjects, list ten to fifteen points or items which might be used in its development:

    A. School Politics.
    B. Socialism in Canada — Past and Present.
    C. Dating Customs in This Town.

D. Weekend Fun.

E. Provincial Parks.

F. Vocational Experiences My Friends Have Had.

G. Driver Education.

H. My Philosophy of Life.

I. Peaceful Uses of Atomic Energy.

J. The Value of a Time Budget.

EXERCISE 7

For three of the subjects listed in Exercise 2, briefly discuss two or more tones (attitudes) which might be used in the development of each.

93. OUTLINING

After you have analyzed a topic and jotted down the points you want to make, you must then determine in what order to present them to carry out a stated purpose. If you have only two or three points to cover for a short paper of 200 or 300 words, your problem is rather simple. But if you have several or a dozen ideas to arrange for a longer theme, putting them in effective order amounts to making an outline. For that is what outlining really is—arranging clusters of related ideas in a sequence which will efficiently carry out the purpose of a composition as expressed in a summarizing sentence. An outline need not be complicated, nor need it be followed exactly. You can revise it, if need be, as you proceed with writing. An outline is not a strait jacket. It is rather a guide of one's own choosing.

Frequently, teachers, who have had to read many poorly organized papers, will ask students to submit outlines before beginning to write. Students have been known to argue that an outline hampers their spontaneity and that they can write better without one. Sometimes they confess privately to having written their compositions first and their outlines afterward. This is a topsy-turvy procedure. It is much as though a contractor built a house without a plan. Afterwards, he might discover that he had omitted some of the beams. When he made his after-the-fact blueprint, he drew in the beams as if they were actually there. Often an outline written from a theme is a better indication of the structure the theme *should* have than it has in reality.

When time is short, as in writing an impromptu theme in class or answering a discussion question on an examination, a very brief "scratch" outline, consisting of jotted down ideas, will serve the purpose. More detailed, and far more efficient, outlines are of three types: the topic outline, the sentence outline, and the paragraph outline. Your teacher will usually state which type he prefers. Sometimes, he may leave the choice to you. You should therefore be familiar with all three forms discussed and illustrated in the following sections.

93a. FOLLOW A SUMMARIZING SENTENCE IN CONSTRUCTING AN OUTLINE.

As pointed out in Section 92a, a summarizing sentence suggests the material to be developed. It will not include everything you may wish to include, but it should serve as advance notice of what is to come. The clearer a summarizing sentence is, the easier the preparation of an outline will be. A summarizing sentence serves as a check against the unity and coherence of an outline and the theme written from it.

93b. USE A TOPIC OUTLINE TO MAKE CLEAR THE ARRANGEMENT OF IDEAS.

A topic outline uses words and phrases, but no complete sentences. It may be quite simple:

Tips on Summer Tables

I. How to apply
II. Learning the job
III. Problems with people
IV. Monetary rewards
V. Leisure-time activities

This is basically a sketch outline suggesting only major divisions of a proposed theme. It can be made more elaborate by enumerating some of the details you intend to discuss under the major headings above, as in the following example:

Tips on Summer Tables

I. How to apply
    A. At employment agencies
    B. By writing to resorts
II. Learning the job
    A. Mechanical aspects
       1. Setting tables
       2. Taking diners' orders
       3. Carrying trays
    B. Problems with people
       1. Dealing with fussy guests
       2. Soothing irate cooks
III. Monetary rewards
    A. Free room and board
    B. Substantial tips
IV. Leisure
    A. Short periods between meals
       1. For letter-writing
       2. For swimming
       3. For walks
    B. Evenings
       1. Public (guest) entertainments
       2. Dances
       3. Trips to nearby town
       4. Dates

93c. USE A SENTENCE OUTLINE TO MAKE CLEAR TO YOURSELF OR OTHERS THE ARRANGEMENT OF IDEAS.

As the term implies, a sentence outline consists of complete sentences for main divisions and all subordinate sections. Since the items in a sentence outline are fully stated, they are likely to be clearer to the writer than a topic outline and more informative to a teacher or other reader who may wish to offer helpful suggestions.

Tips on Summer Tables

I. Summer jobs of waiting on tables are not hard to obtain.
    A. Some agencies list such openings.
    B. Application can be made direct to resorts.
II. You will learn the mechanics of the job from the head-waiter.
    A. You must know how to set a table and clear away.
    B. You must master the art of balancing loaded trays.
    C. You must learn how to remember what each guest orders.
III. You will learn a lot about human nature, including your own.
    A. You must not show annoyance at difficult guests.
    B. You must be patient with undisciplined children.
    C. You must be diplomatic in dealing with temperamental chefs.
IV. If you are good at your job, your rewards can be high.
    A. You will have only minor expenses.
    B. You will take home a substantial sum from tips.
    C. You will be asked to come back next summer if you wish.
V. Your job will not be all work.
    A. You will have some leisure hours between serving meals.
    B. Your evenings will be free for entertainments, dances, and dates.

93d. USE A PARAGRAPH OUTLINE MAINLY FOR SUMMARIZING THE WORK OF OTHERS.

A paragraph outline is composed of a series of sentences, each of which gives the gist of an entire paragraph. Sometimes the topic sentence of a paragraph will serve the purpose. The sentences of a paragraph outline are numbered in the order in which the paragraphs themselves follow one another.

This method can be helpful in planning the successive paragraphs of your own theme, but it is especially useful as a means of taking notes on the content of paragraphs in a selection to be studied. Efficiently summarizing successive paragraphs in an essay or a chapter of a book involves reading them with attention and understanding.

For example, assume that each of the thirteen subheads in the sentence outline shown in Section 93c is to be developed in a paragraph. The first five items in a paragraph outline based on this topic might be as follows:

1. Numerous employment agencies list summer job openings and welcome applications from interested and qualified persons.
2. If one wishes, he may bypass employment agencies and write direct to resort hotels and restaurants of which he knows or has seen advertised.
3. The headwaiter or one of his assistants will provide thorough training in place and table settings and in the removal of silver, cutlery, china, and glassware.
4. You will need instruction and practice in the difficult art of loading trays fully and balancing them comfortably and safely.
5. Learning to remember which guest ordered what is a fundamental requirement for every waiter.

And here is how a paragraph outline might be prepared from (and for) a chapter in a book:

The First Railroads

1. Neither roads nor canals provided a fully satisfactory method for transporting individual goods.
2. The first roadbeds, built in Germany in the fifteenth century, were tramways made by laying heavy timbers in parallel rows to bear the wheels of heavy wagons drawn by horses or oxen.
3. Tramways later introduced into England were made of iron, were either privately owned by miners, manufacturers, and merchants or were open to the public at a toll charge.
4. The modern railroad was at first little more than an attempt to substitute the steam engine for the horse.
5. When in 1825 England built the first railroad, trains were run at a speed of 10 to 15 miles per hour.
6. The early English railroads, like the turnpikes and tramways, were rented to any person who wished to pay the tolls, but this process grew so complicated that commercial companies took them over.
7. American engineers made many improvements in order

for trains to make the steeper grades and longer distances in North America.

8. Americans also found a way of getting around sharp curves by putting swivel axles on the cars and built more flexible roadbeds than the British, whose tracks were rigidly mounted on piles driven into the ground.

9. Most English railroad lines were short, averaging only 14 miles.

10. The need for government regulation of the railroads in England gradually grew, and in 1893 the maximum rates they could charge were fixed by statute.

11. England's experiments with railroads showed the way to the rest of Europe with respect to engineering and social problems.

—Harry Elmer Barnes, *The History of Western Civilization*

93e. MAKE OUTLINES CORRECT IN FORM.

If you prepare an outline only for personal use, the main requirement is a logical arrangement of major and minor divisions so that the theme will be sensibly constructed. But an outline to be submitted to your teacher should also conform to certain conventions of long standing which you should fully understand.

When constructing a *topic outline,* follow these suggestions:

1. For major divisions, use Roman numerals I, II, III, IV, etc., placing them flush with the margin.

2. For subdividing major divisions, use the capital letters A, B, C, etc., indenting them evenly.

3. Indent again if you have a subdivision under any of these letters and use the Arabic numerals 1, 2, 3, etc.

4. In the remote event that you want to subdivide still more, use another indentation and the lower case letters a, b, c, etc.

5. Follow each number or letter with a period. The use of a period after each topic is optional, but be consistent in whichever practice you follow.

When constructing a *sentence outline,* follow the same procedure as for the topic outline with one exception: place an end-stop—a period, question mark, or exclamation point—after each sentence.

The following skeleton indicates correct form for either a topic or a sentence outline:

I.
    A.
        1.
        2.
            a.
            b.
    B.
        1.
        2.
            a.
            b.
                (1)
                (2)
II.
    A.
    B.
    C.

In a paragraph outline the sentences are indicated by Arabic numerals and must also have end-stops. As in the other outlines, a period follows each number. The beginning of each sentence may be flush with the margin and the run-over sentences indented, or the beginnings may be indented, with the run-over sentences coming out flush with the numbers.

Any outline which clearly reveals the structure of a theme is effective, so that "correctness" in form is more often a matter of convention and practice than of logic. Writers, however, have tended to follow certain conventions with which you should be familiar:

(1) Outlining is division; subdivision means division into at least two parts. If a single minor topic (subhead) must be mentioned, express it in its major heading or add another subhead.

(2) Use parallel phrasing. Do not use a word or phrase for one topic, a sentence for another. Topic, sentence, and paragraph outlines should be consistent in structure throughout.

(3) Avoid meaningless headings such as *Introduction,*

Conclusion, Reasons, and Effects. If you feel they must appear, add specific explanatory subheads.

(4) The first main heading of the outline should not repeat the title of the theme. If the idea expressed in the title logically should appear in the outline, at least rephrase it.

(5) Avoid putting into a subhead any matter that should appear in a larger division; even more importantly, do not list in a main heading material belonging in a subdivision.

EXERCISE 8

Revise the following outline so that items will follow a correct, logical form:

How Drivers Cause Accidents

I. By violating traffic regulations
   A. Passing a halted school bus
   B. Going through a stop light
   C. Turning a corner without flashing a signal
II. By being selfish
   A. Not moving over for a passing car
   B. Blocking another car when parking
   C. Failing to dim lights when meeting another car
III. By being unfit to drive
   A. Driving while intoxicated
   B. Driving in wrong direction on one-way street
   C. Being too young or too old to drive
   D. Having poor vision
   E. Driving an unreliable car

EXERCISE 9

Make the following into a consistent topic or sentence outline:

My First Day at Work

I. Prework jitters
   A. The night before
      1. I set the alarm for 6 A.M.
      2. I could not sleep
      3. Fear of failing
   B. The next morning at home
      4. Dressed hurriedly
      5. Bolted my breakfast

II. The Workday
    A. My first hour
        1. I meet the foreman
        2. Friendliness of other workers
        3. My tension gradually eases
    B. How the day went
        1. Slow passage of time
        2. Lunch hour
        3. Afternoon weariness
        4. Quitting time
        5. I feel satisfied and ready for tomorrow.
            a. I get to sleep quickly, tired but relaxed

EXERCISE 10

Criticize these outlines. State how each could be improved.

(A) Meet My Best Friend

    I. Physical appearance
        A. Height and weight
        B. Complexion
    II. Chief character trait
        A. Good-natured

(B) My Favorite Restaurant

    I. It serves two kinds of food.
    II. It serves Italian dishes
    III. It serves Canadian dishes
    IV. Its service is excellent
        A. The waiters are courteous
        B. They are also very efficient

EXERCISE 11

Rewrite the following outlines, eliminating all errors.

(A) Why Accidents Happen

    I. Major reason for accidents
        A. Drivers at fault
    II. Minor reason for accidents
        A. Roads and highways at fault
    III. Proposed solution
        A. Better driver training

(B)   Three Boy Scout Activities

     I   Junior leadership
          a)   age
          b)   experience
          C)   girls' and boys' projects
    II   Clothing
          a)   Age
          B)   experience
          C)   Time
          D)   Cost
   III Crafts
          a)   materials
          B)   Cost

94.   DEVELOPING A TOPIC

Choosing, analyzing, and outlining a topic (Sections 91, 92, 93) are important basic steps in composition writing. Overlooking or slighting them will invariably cause you to produce weak and generally unsatisfactory themes. But even if these three essential elements of writing are handled carefully, you are faced with yet another major problem: what do I have in mind to say about my selected, analyzed, outlined topic?

A good rule to follow is this: sit down to write what you have thought; don't sit down to write what you will write. In other words, think hard about your topic before trying to develop it. The following suggestions will help you once you start putting your ideas down on paper. But remember: think first, write afterwards.

94a.   START WITH A CORE SENTENCE.

As repeatedly mentioned in this book, you should *never*, repeat *never*, start writing a composition of any length without taking an essential first step: state in a single sentence your central purpose, the dominating idea of what you propose to say. To play on words, what is the *theme* of your theme? A *thesis* statement, a summarizing, guiding, or topic sentence, will define your purpose and help you to gather supporting material that bears directly on the topic in hand.

Assume, for example, that you have recently visited a planetarium and had an absorbing, even exciting, series of glimpses into the heavens. You have never been particularly interested in any science — certainly not astronomy — but, to your amazement, what began as a project to kill a few hours turned into a fascinating experience. You believe that certain of your classmates might similarly enjoy a planetarium visit if only you can convince them that the trip will be both educational and exciting. So you phrase a title "I Saw Stars!" and a thesis sentence: "A trip to a planetarium can be an informational, thrilling, and humbling experience."

With this general plan in mind, you list several items that might be usable. Some of these will come from your own experience, some will require the thoughts and knowledge of others, to be secured from conversation and reading. Such a list might begin like this:

1. What a planetarium is.
2. What one looks like.
3. History of the planetarium I visited.
4. My talk with a planetarium guard.
5. Location.
6. Cost of operation.
7. Special exhibits.
8. Special lectures.
9. Mechanics of the projecting machine.
10. My recommendations and suggestions about a planetarium visit.
11. Best days to go to avoid crowds and admission fees.
12. My outstanding experiences there.

Each of these items is generally applicable to your topic, but in view of the core (or thesis) sentence, several should be eliminated and others added. A summary sentence will save you far more time and effort in gathering material than its phrasing will require. In addition, it will force you to stick to one central purpose and thus have a more direct, immediate, and forceful appeal to your readers.

94b. SELECT MATERIAL WITH A SPECIFIC READER, OR READERS, IN MIND.

Usually, your readers will be your teacher and classmates, but on occasion you may wish, or be asked, to write for someone else. Whoever your reader, remember that he is limited to the written word and cannot ask questions of a writer who is normally not present. How much does he already know about the topic? What do you think a reader may not know that will be interesting to him and will coincide with your underlying purpose in writing? If you are writing on a topic the prospective reader likely knows little or nothing about, what background information should you supply? What terms need defining? (After all, your reader ordinarily cannot ask "Just what do you mean? In what sense are you using this term? This expression? This technical detail?") What kinds of examples, illustrations, and descriptive details will make the topic as clear and interesting to your reader as it is to you? Consider a reader, or readers, objectively. Do not write down to readers; superfluous definitions and unneeded explanations are irksome and insulting. Remember, however, never to underestimate the intelligence of your readers or to overestimate their information.

94c. BE HONEST ABOUT THE MATERIAL YOU GATHER.

Taking the ideas and words of another and stating them as your own is *plagiarism.* In a short, ugly word, it is stealing.

When you use an idea new to you, whether you express it in your own or in quoted words, state your indebtedness. Sometimes, you can acknowledge a source with a mere phrase, "as Salinger suggests in *The Catcher in the Rye*," or "These writers, Joseph Warren Beach says in *American Fiction*, were influenced by social conditions." Occasionally you will need to make fuller acknowledgment in a footnote (see Section 103f) or in a general statement preceding, following, or attached to your composition.

In general, it is permissible and even necessary to borrow, but always indicate who the lender is. In gathering material from others, think about it, try to absorb it, and attempt to state in your own words what you learned, unless you are quoting directly. But whether quoting or paraphrasing, do not attempt to pass off as your own what you have appropriated from others.

It is instructive to note that the word *plagiarism* comes from a Latin term meaning "kidnapper." Kidnapping is a criminal offense and so should be plagiarism. It might also be well to remember that "copying from one source is plagiarism, copying from two or more is research" is a dishonest and inaccurate statement. See Section 103.

EXERCISE 12

Consider each of the following as a core (thesis) sentence. Select one of them. With a specific, named reader in mind, list five items from your own experience (observation, imagination, reflection) which could be used as developing material for a composition of 300-400 words.

A. Movies are (or are not) better than ever.
B. Television programming does (does not) accurately reflect our cultural tastes and levels.
C. All forms of dancing are (are not) a waste of time.
D. Beauty is (is not) in the eyes of the beholder.
E. Interscholastic sports should (should not) be abolished.

EXERCISE 13

Follow directions given for Exercise 12, except for item sources. For *one* of the five topics listed, write five sentences indicating material to be based on other than your own resources.

EXERCISE 14

For the topic selected in Exercises 12 and 13, indicate how items of developing material would differ for each of the following imagined readers:

1. My English teacher.
2. My best friend.
3. My parents.
4. A "pen pal" in some named European country.
5. My Aunt Tillie.

95. CHOOSING A TITLE

You have learned that a well-phrased topic sentence can help you to keep on the track within a paragraph (Section 81). Similarly, an effective thesis sentence aids in selecting materials for developing a theme (Section 94). An almost equally useful device, this time for maintaining the steady focus of an entire composition, is a suitably chosen title.

A good title will serve as a constant reminder that all material included in a theme should bear upon the subject. But since a really effective title often can be hit upon only after a composition is completed, start with at least a tentative one that will unify a treatment while it is developing.

In addition to its unifying effect, a title can secure the attention of a reader. Most of us have been drawn to a particular motion picture, television program, book, magazine article, or short story because of its attractive title. Giving a composition a good title is an important step in making an entire paper effective.

95a. DISTINGUISH BETWEEN A SUBJECT AND A TITLE.

The term *subject* is broader and more inclusive than the word *title*. If your teacher suggests a composition on "Eating Habits," he is referring to a subject and neither a specific *topic* nor a title. But if a limited topic or actual title is assigned, then you must find out what subject is referred to. The most effective titles of papers indicate not a general subject but a specific topic with a stated *theme*.

95b. WORD THE TITLE CLEARLY AND EFFECTIVELY.

A title cannot mention everything a composition contains, but it should provide at least a hint of the contents. Most effective titles provide a clear suggestion of what is to follow and are also catchy. If you cannot phrase a title that is both descriptive and arresting, settle for the former quality. These titles are effective, even though not unusually imaginative or intriguing: "Why a Classic Is a Classic," "How to Find Time to Read," "The Case for Greater Clarity in Writing," "Canadians on Campus," "College Athletics: Education or Show Business?" "A Windstorm in the Forest," "An Apology for Idlers," "How Canadians Choose Their Heroes." As a working title for your first draft, try to come up with something accurate and clear; later you may be able to add appeal to accuracy.

Here are three simple suggestions for phrasing effective titles:

1. *Avoid long titles.* The most memorable titles usually, but not always, do not exceed six to eight words. "My Interview with Mr. Bixler" is not as attention-getting as "The Time My Teacher in Seventh Grade Sent Me to the Principal's Office," but it is preferable because of its comparative brevity. Students of Wordsworth's poetry refer to a familiar poem as "Tintern Abbey" rather than by the title the poet gave it: "Lines Composed a Few Miles Above Tintern Abbey, on Revisiting the Banks of the Wye During a Tour, July 13, 1798."

2. *Avoid misleading or confusing titles.* A title such as "Watch the Birdie" might refer to a paper on photography, or bird-watching, or golf, or badminton. Examine a title from a reader's viewpoint. Will it mean to him what it does to you?

3. *Avoid vague and commonplace titles.* Many a good composition has gotten off to a poor start because of an unclear, dull, or uninteresting title. A trite title such as "An Embarrassing Experience" can be altered to "My Face Was Red"; "A Trip to Ottawa" can be called "A Capital Journey"; "How to Paint a Room" might become "Goodbye, Old Paint"; "My Operation" is duller than "Proudly I Wear a Scar."

95c. PLACE AND PUNCTUATE THE TITLE CORRECTLY.

A title should be centered on the page, on the first line of ruled paper or two inches from the top of unruled paper.

Leave a space between the title and the first line of the theme.

Capitalize important words (see Section 33). Do not underline (italicize) a title or enclose it in quotation marks unless it is itself a quotation or unless you quote it in the theme. If the title is a question or exclamation, use a question mark or exclamation point, but never place a period at the end.

EXERCISE 15

Consult three or four copies of widely circulated magazines such as *Esquire, The Reader's Digest, Life, Maclean's, The Atlantic.* Examine the titles of articles; then skim the articles enough to decide whether the titles are (1) both descriptive and arresting, (2) neither of these, (3) one of these, (4) too novel or contrived.

EXERCISE 16

Apply the directions of Exercise 15 to the titles of five essays or articles in your literature anthology.

EXERCISE 17

One of the most famous articles ever written was a study of automobile accidents and fatalities. It was called "— And Sudden Death." Can you phrase more effective titles for articles on the following subjects?

A. Why an airplane flies.
B. Advertisements designed to appeal to women.
C. A study of Canadian cowboys
D. A criticism of Canadian sports.
E. How statistics can tell lies.
F. Why money isn't everything in life.
G. The story of Fort Garry.
H. The fun of being lazy.
I. The best way to get good marks in school.
J. How to get a bid to a school prom.

EXERCISE 18

What title (or titles) would you suggest to writers of papers on these topics?

1. Whether a boy wants to grow a beard and wear his hair long is his own business and should not be regulated by school authorities.

2. Young men and women are disillusioned about politics and politicians, and only a few of them want to make a career in government.

3. For a boy and girl to "go steady" in school may be convenient and economical, but how can they be sure they are meant for each other if neither ever goes out with anyone else?

96. BEGINNING A THEME

Having completed the planning stages of your theme, you must now start to write it. Although the body, or middle, will naturally be the main part, both the beginning and ending are important because they are the first and last impressions your reader will have of your paper. They should be written with care and forethought. Neither should be abrupt nor mechanical; neither should be so lengthy as to throw your theme out of proportion. (Proportion is developed more fully in Section 98.)

96a. AVOID HAVING AN OPENING SENTENCE DEPEND ON THE TITLE FOR ITS MEANING.

Title and theme are independent. A first sentence should be self-explanatory without indirect or vague reference to the title. Avoid reference words like *this, that, such* in beginning sentences.

Faulty beginnings:

1. Someday I hope to follow my father's footsteps in this profession.

2. Raising these has fascinated me since childhood.

3. I once endured the discipline of such an academy for a year.

4. In professional football this is the man to watch.

416

Improved beginnings: 1. Someday I hope to follow my father's footsteps in the practice of law.
2. Raising tropical fish has fascinated me since childhood.
3. I once endured the discipline of a military academy for a year.
4. In professional football the linebacker is the man to watch.

96b. AVOID UNNECESSARY FORMAL INTRODUCTIONS.

Write an introduction only if your theme needs one. Introductions are usually needed only in long papers beginning with a definition of terms, a history of the subject, or an explanation of reasons for the study of a problem. The shorter your composition is, the shorter your introduction should be.

96c. AVOID WORDY BEGINNINGS.

Students frequently use up space in preliminary sparring with a subject before facing up to it. Examine your second and third paragraphs. If your theme really begins there, throw away everything preceding it. Otherwise, you are writing a theme which will be mostly beginning, with little between it and the ending.

Unless you are dealing with a controversial subject, avoid beginning with expressions such as "I think," "In my opinion," "It seems to me." Since you are the person writing the paper, it can be taken for granted that the thoughts and opinions are yours unless you state otherwise.

96d. AVOID BEGINNINGS THAT ARE ABRUPT.

A beginning should permit a reader to find his bearings. Instead of starting a theme with "The first step in building a bookcase is . . ." or "We must have better laboratory equipment because . . .", the writer should begin with at least a brief paragraph to prepare the reader for the process or argument to follow.

An abrupt opening with a quotation, however, can sometimes be effective. Such a device should be used sparingly and with skill. It should also be followed immediately by an explanatory passage to make the situation clear to the reader, as in this example:

"Hey you, Slim!"

The boss at the cement plant, where I worked last summer, had given me the nickname my first day on the job. Now he was calling me to drive a truckload of bags to the freight yard.

96e. MAKE BEGINNINGS CLEAR AND PURPOSEFUL.

A firmly-composed beginning which leads directly toward the topic will engage the reader's attention and induce him to read on. Here are some types of beginnings.

1. *Beginning by repeating or paraphrasing the title.*

This is a song of the once open road. Is there as much as five miles of highway left in the United States today without ten filling stations and at least one farmhouse called "Ye Willowe Inne"?

—Charles Merz, "The Once Open Road"

The principle of liberty, as we Americans interpret it, forbids interference with certain of our activities.

—Alexander Meiklejohn, "Liberty—for What?"

2. *Beginning with a question.*

What is this democracy for which we fight?

—Geoffrey Crowther, "The Citizen's Charter"

What is success? And how is it gained?

—Johnson O'Connor, "Vocabulary and Success"

3. *Beginning with an exclamation.*

Something is wrong somewhere! That is the obvious thing to say about poetry in America today.

—Earl Daniels, "Outline for a Defense of Poetry"

4. *Beginning with a quotation.*

"None can love freedom heartily but good men; the rest love not freedom, but license." That was Milton's opinion, and he had thought much about freedom and goodness.

—Elizabeth Jackson, "Of Goodness"

5. *Beginning by showing the divisions of the topic to be discussed.*

Two things become increasingly evident as the sickness of our American democracy approaches its inevitable crisis: one is the surpassing genius of the founders of this Republic; the other is the transience of even the greatest of political resolutions.

—Archibald MacLeish, "Loyalty and Freedom"

6. *Beginning with a framework or setting for the topic.*

The two greatest nations in the world are now preparing to land on the Moon within the next decade. This will be one of the central facts of political life in the years to come; indeed, it may soon dominate human affairs. It is essential, therefore, that we understand the importance of the Moon in our future; if we do not, we will be going there for the wrong reasons and will not know what to do when we arrive.

—Arthur C. Clarke, "The Uses of the Moon"

7. *Beginning with a general misconception which the writer intends to correct.*

Science is often defined inadequately as "an organized body of knowledge." This would make cookbooks, Sears, Roebuck catalogues, and telephone books science, which they are not.

—Ralph Ross and Ernest Van den Haag,
"The Nature of Science"

Many people, if not most, look on literary taste as an elegant accomplishment, by acquiring which they will complete themselves, and make themselves finally fit as members of a correct society.

—Arnold Bennett, "Literary Taste; How to Form It"

8. *Beginning by directly addressing the reader.*

If you are an average reader you can read an average book at the rate of 300 words a minute. You cannot maintain that average, however, unless you read regularly every day. Nor can you attain that speed with hard books in science, mathematics, agriculture, business, or any subject that is new and unfamiliar to you.

—Louis Shores, "How to Find Time to Read"

Let's say you're in the business of making automobile tires. Tests on a type you've been making tell you it is good, on the average, for 20,000 miles.

—Darrell Huff, "How to Look at a Statistic"

EXERCISES   (See end of Section 97)

97. ENDING A THEME

To come to a sudden stop because you have reached your quota of words is not to end a paper but to abandon it. Obviously, a theme must have an ending as well as a beginning, preferably an effective one. A proper ending gives the reader a sense of completeness. It does not leave him stranded, expecting the writer to go on. You should foresee your ending by the time you begin developing the last item in your outline, if not before. A good ending should emerge naturally from what precedes and not be tacked on as an afterthought.

97a. USE A SHORT, COMPACT ENDING.

What has been said about avoiding abruptness, wordiness, and formality in beginnings (Sections 96b,c,d) applies equally to endings. An abrupt ending brings a reader up short; a rambling one strains his patience. An effective ending is a happy medium between these extremes.

In a theme of normal length, the ending should be compact. As a general rule, you should manage it in no more than two or three sentences; often a single sentence which summarizes or rounds off the content is sufficient. You may make your ending the closing words of your last paragraph or, if you wish to give it more emphasis, set it apart.

In ending, avoid expressions such as "thus we see," "to sum up my conclusions," "in closing, let me state," etc. Even in argumentative writing, where there is some excuse for them, such phrases are overworked.

97b. USE AN APPROPRIATE ENDING.

An ending may be brief, but it must be appropriate.
I. Appropriate use of pronouns.
    . . . Since in *our* society all men are politically equal, since all men are ruler and ruled, *they* must be educated to be ruler

and ruled. If *we* cannot give *them* all this education *we* may as well drop the pretense of democracy. *We* may as well admit that, though *it* was a good idea, *it* would not work.

—Robert M. Hutchins, "Education and Freedom"

. . . *You* have known complete exertion, *you* have answered every trouble of mind, spirit, and being with skilled violence and guided unrestraint, a complete happiness with eight other men over a short stretch of water has brought *you* catharsis.

—Oliver La Farge, "Rowing"

II. Appropriate varieties of endings.

1. *Ending with a question.*

Or shall we really get down to the roots of good and evil and wrestle with our theories until we bring them into some kind of working conformity, not only with one another but with fact?

—Elizabeth Jackson, "Of Goodness"

The miracle is that what he did in the little space of seventy years could have been done at all, even by a great genius. Is it any wonder that he had no time to be a man?

—Deems Taylor, "The Monster" (Richard Wagner)

2. *Ending with an exclamation.*

If present-day Louisiana has any claim to individuality, a color, a note of her own, it is lodged unmistakably in this sport-loving, sun-loving, unquenchable spirit which was and is New Orleans. Mistress of chivalry, cuisine, and the dance; cosmopolis of legend, caprice, and motley; the Columbine of the cities—New Orleans!

—Basil Thompson, "Louisiana"

3. *Ending with a direct or indirect quotation.*

. . . But if he does remember poems pleasantly, no matter how few; even if there be only one, among those quoted here, which he has in the slightest degree liked, he is invited to continue in our common adventure after the peculiar pleasure of poetry, assured, in advance, of fun, and, I hope, of discovering in his experience

life and food
For future years.

—Earl Daniels, "Outline for A Defense of Poetry"

. . . The elder Dumas enunciated a great principle when he said that to make a drama, a man needed one passion, and four walls.

—Willa Cather, "The Novel Démeublé"

4. *Ending by bringing up and stressing a final important point.*

I will close with one last point. Science is fun, even for the amateur. Every scientist is himself an amateur in another field of science which is not his specialty, but the spirit is the same. Science is a game that is inspiring and refreshing. The playing field is the universe itself. The stakes are high because you must put down all your preconceived ideas and habits of thought. The rewards are great because you find a home in the world, a home you have made for yourself.

— I. I. Rabi, "Faith in Science"

Finally, it is a spirit of leadership seeking both courage and tolerance: the courage to search for truth and speak it even when, especially when, it pains; and the tolerance to understand that good and evil in human relationships, from the personal to the international, are not absolutes.

— G. Gaddis Smith, "Lo, the Old College Spirit"

5. *Ending by summarizing the central thought or point of the theme or essay.*

... Thus it is no mere transcript of life at a certain time and place that Hardy has given us. It is a vision of the world and of man's lot as they revealed themselves to a powerful imagination, a profound and poetic genius, a gentle and humane soul.

— Virginia Woolf, "The Novels of Thomas Hardy"

6. *Ending with a prediction or a warning.*

... A less commercial, more responsible America, perhaps a less prosperous and more spiritual America, will hold fast to its sentiment, but be weaned from its sentimentality.

— H. S. Canby, "Sentimental America"

... Comfort is a means to an end. The modern world seems to regard it as an end in itself, an absolute good. One day, perhaps, the earth will have been turned into one vast feather-bed, with man's body dozing on top of it and his mind underneath, like Desdemona, smothered.

— Aldous Huxley, "Comfort"

The important thing to remember in ending themes is this: When you have said all you intended to say, *stop.* Do you remember the story of the guest who lingered at the door mumbling, "There was something else I wanted to say"? To this the hostess made a wise response, "Perhaps it was *goodbye.*"

EXERCISE 19 (Exercises for Sections 96, 97)

Choose five articles or essays from your literature anthology and study their beginnings and endings. Is each effective and appropriate? Does any one of them seem unnecessary or unnecessarily long?

EXERCISE 20

Apply the directions given in Exercise I to five articles selected from one issue of a magazine such as *The Atlantic, Holiday, Maclean's, The National Geographic Magazine, Scientific American.*

EXERCISE 21

Which of the following beginnings are clear and effective and which are not? State reasons for your answers.

1. Have you ever thought what life was like five million years ago?
2. The title of this theme suggests a number of important questions.
3. Three important steps toward effective studying are selecting a definite place to study, planning ahead, and concentrating.
4. A manned rocket to the moon was a dream of yesterday, it is a possibility today, and it will be a reality tomorrow.
5. I think this is the most important question a high school student can ask. (Theme title: "Am I Going To Be Ready for College?")

EXERCISE 22

Which of the following endings are clear and effective and which are not? State reasons for your answers.

1. These facilities and many more like them make Oakdale a wonderful place in which to live.
2. Experiments in teaching tricks to animals are enjoyable for me. Why don't you try them? You might enjoy them, too.
3. Then the band began to play the recessional and the line of graduates began to move. I smiled as we walked forward to meet tomorrow. (Theme title: "Graduation Day at Junior High")
4. From recent experiments in rocketry, we realize that a dream of yesterday is a possibility of today and will be a reality of tomorrow.
5. I have known her for only three weeks, but I wish I had never met her at all.

98. PROPORTION

Proportion requires that you develop each section of your theme according to its relative importance. For instance, you may have disposed of an introduction in a short paragraph, then devoted a longer paragraph to the next item (not one of major import), developed the most important item in three paragraphs, given two paragraphs to the next (of secondary importance), and used a brief paragraph for the ending. This could represent a well-proportioned theme. Yet a theme could have more or fewer divisions and be arranged in different order. Proportion is always *relative* and so is importance; neither is *absolute*. In determining what to expand and what to contract in writing a theme, keep in mind not only the subject you are writing about, but also your purpose and your reader.

A well-planned outline (Section 93) helps in proportioning. The discussion in Section 87 is also pertinent to theme proportion.

98a. GIVE ADEQUATE ATTENTION TO THE CENTRAL THOUGHT OF YOUR THEME.

Avoid elaborating minor details either in the beginning or later in your theme. Doing so may throw your theme out of proportion, obscure main points, and distract the reader.

For example, your purpose in writing a theme may be to persuade fellow students to "Support the Debating Team!" Your reasons are that debating is a more important activity than they believe, that debating deals with significant issues of the day, and that debating is better preparation for adult life than are team sports. Proceed quickly to the heart of your argument. You need no long introduction about famous debates of the past, such as the Pipeline or Flag Debates. Nor need you provide a long list of issues which might be worth debating; two or three good examples will suffice.

98b. AVOID DEVELOPING DETAILS FAMILIAR TO YOUR READERS.

Do not waste time and space defining common terms or describing objects which you can presume your readers to know as well as you do.

Suppose your hobby is photography and that your purpose is to tell your readers "How to Enlarge Snapshots for Framing." Your title presupposes that you are addressing yourself to readers who own cameras of one kind or another. You would be wasting their time and your own by explaining the difference between a positive print and a negative, by describing a flash bulb, and by defining *time exposure.* You can safely assume that your readers know such facts. What they do want to learn from your theme is how to use an enlarger, how much one costs, whether it is timesaving and money-saving to do one's own enlargements or advantageous to have them done commercially. Proceed to these points immediately and stress them throughout your paper.

The basic principle of proportion is that of giving any part of a composition the space and attention which are appropriate to your purpose, your topic, and your reader. In other words, "Render unto Caesar the things which are Caesar's."

EXERCISE 23

Count the number of words in each paragraph of *two* of your most recent compositions. Write a paragraph commenting on the proportion used, giving consideration to the topic, your reader(s), and your purpose.

99. UNITY

Unity means *oneness, singleness of purpose,* or as the *Standard College Dictionary* defines it, "The arrangement of parts into a homogeneous whole exhibiting oneness of purpose, thought, spirit, and style; the subordination of all parts to the general effect." The principle of unity applies to the whole composition, to the sentence (Section 64), and to the paragraph (Section 84).

A theme is a short paper dealing with a single phase of a subject. Constantly keep in mind "the *theme* within the *theme.*" If every paragraph bears upon this phase or develops it in some way, the entire paper has unity. But if even so much as one sentence introduces an unrelated or irrelevant idea or detail, the unity of the theme is impaired. In all writing, keep your eye steadily on the track along which you have elected to move your topic so that no derailment or detour can occur even momentarily.

99a. DEVELOP IN A THEME ONLY ONE PHASE OF A SUBJECT.

Beginning writers frequently assume that certain details are pertinent to the topic they are discussing when in fact these are irrelevant or, at best, only loosely connected with it. Several misjudgments are responsible for such assumptions:

1. Not being sufficiently thoughtful or self-critical to eliminate irrelevant items from a guiding outline or having prepared no outline at all.

2. Tacking on useless preliminary matter to a beginning or ending in order to pad out a theme to the required number of words. An example would be to begin a book review by stating the facts of the author's life or to end a theme on target-shooting with comment on the history of the rifle since the flintlock.

3. Including material which has some possible relation to the central idea but which makes no real connection to the purpose of the theme. For instance, if your purpose is to give an account of an original experiment in chemistry, it would break the unity of the theme to describe the supply room or cabinet from which you selected chemicals or reports.

99b. GIVE YOUR THEME UNITY OF TONE.

Whether your purpose is to inform, to persuade, to satirize, to ridicule, or whatever, be consistent. The tendency of basketball coaches to give preference to candidates according to height could be treated seriously as a questionable trend, or it could be treated humorously by speculating how some major schools might compete for a player who happened to be seven feet three inches tall. But to mix the two in the same theme would be equivalent to offering your reader oatmeal and dill pickles in the same dish.

In short, avoid mixing comedy and tragedy, satire and pathos, humor and stateliness, reverence and irreverence, absurdity and dignity in the same composition. A solemn paper on the assassination of D'Arcy McGee should not refer to humorous anecdotes of which McGee was fond — even though one such anecdote might have a general bearing on the subject and would enable you to fill out the word quota needed. For another illustration, it would be difficult to maintain unity of tone in a serious paper on international relations if you decided to add a comical or satirical story about any particular race, nation, or creed.

EXERCISE 24

Discuss violations of unity in the following plan (sketch outline) for a theme:

My Best Friend's Father

I. My friend's father is an excellent lawyer.
II. He studied hard when he was in college and law school and received many honors.
III. His parents died during his last year at law school.
IV. My friend is not a good student; he is more interested in dancing, girls, and hot rods than he is in school subjects.
V. After he was graduated, my friend's father had a financial struggle for ten years.
VI. He now has a large practice and substantial income.
VII. He is getting older, is in poor health, and has hired a young lawyer as an assistant.
VIII. My friend and his father have many personality traits in common.

EXERCISE 25

Indicate how the following composition lacks unity. If your teacher requests, rewrite the paper by removing irrelevant ideas and adding material which seems appropriate.

The Inventor of the Automobile

Credit is usually given to a group of men who were said to have invented the automobile. These fifteen or twenty inventors each contributed something toward the invention of the automobile. The period of years for the contributions of these inventors fell between the years of 1880 and 1903. These inventors gained significance by the invention of a horseless carriage or a motor-driven vehicle. However, the latest facts prove that a man named Siegfried Marcus should receive full credit for the invention. In 1861, the first automobile chugged down the street in a small town in Germany. This information has been presented quite recently, and has startled many automobile fans.

In the first years of automobiles, people were decidedly against them. Automobiles were declared a menace to humanity. Farmers were constantly suing drivers for scaring their chickens and horses. A few states tried to obtain laws against automobiles but did not succeed.

As time went by, the public was gradually realizing that automobiles were becoming more useful. Roads and other conditions were now in favor of the automobile instead of against it.

100. CONSISTENCY

To be consistent, a theme must maintain a uniform point of view, mood, and tone. Unity is primarily concerned with content, consistency with the writer's point of view and feeling toward subject matter.

Point of view has several different meanings. Physical point of view has to do with the position in time and space from which one approaches or views material. Personal point of view concerns the relationship through which you narrate or discuss a subject, whether first, second, or third person. Mental point of view involves attitude and feeling toward a subject.

100a. BE CONSISTENT IN THE PHYSICAL POINT OF VIEW.

Whenever you write a paper involving physical point of view, choose some point in space or time (day, season, decade, century, etc.) from which to consider your subject. If you wish to describe a lake, for instance, choose a particular season of the year (obviously this makes considerable difference) and a specific spot from which you view it. Then use a consistent method of depicting scenic details. You could proceed clockwise or counter-clockwise around the lake, from the nearby to the distant, or the reverse. Always let your reader know if and when you shift your point of view. He will be confused if you veer suddenly from the far shore of the lake to comment on the dock upon which you stand.

Unless you know your material at first-hand, your account of it may exhibit inconsistency in facts, such as describing a garden with lilacs and roses in full bloom at the same time.

Aimless or abrupt shifts in time are also bewildering. Do not jump suddenly from one period in history to another or give the impression that it is morning and then unaccountably mention that it is after eight in the evening.

Both space and time were ignored in the following; a thousand miles disappeared between the two sentences:

> Not long after dawn the four survivors were picked up by a French naval ship some thousand miles off shore. To their surprise, they were immediately seized by port authorities and clapped in jail.

100b. BE CONSISTENT IN THE PERSONAL POINT OF VIEW.

In most themes, you will choose one of four personal points of view. Which choice you make depends on your subject, your reader, and appropriateness in general. In relating a firsthand experience or in taking the reader into your confidence in a discussion, use the *first person: I, my, mine, me, we, our, ours, us.* In addressing the reader directly, use the *second person: you, your, yours.* When speaking about someone or about some group, use the *third person: he, his, him, she, her, hers, they, their, theirs, them.* In writing explanatory or argumentative papers, you may have occasion to use the *impersonal: one, anyone, everybody,* etc., or nouns such as *a person, a student, a writer,* etc.

Combinations of personal points of view (*I* and *you, we* and *they*) are frequently used by writers. But do not carelessly or thoughtlessly shift the point of view from *I* to *we* or *you* to *one,* or from any one of these to another. If such a shift is necessary or advantageous, as may happen, make sure that the reader will be prepared for the shift and will readily understand what you are doing.

100c. BE CONSISTENT IN THE MENTAL POINT OF VIEW.

Mental point of view may be considered in two ways. The first is the objective attitude taken in discussing or arguing an issue. You may weigh pros and cons, but it should be clear that you are consistently upholding a position, not changing it in mid-theme or being so ambiguous that the reader is confused about where you stand. For example, much can be said in favor of learning about science in a laboratory and learning about it in a "general science" course. You could be consistent in pointing out the merits of each, or you could argue in favor of one or the other, but you should make clear to the reader at the outset what your point of view is and should uphold it throughout.

Another aspect of the mental point of view is the subjective response to writing, the frame of mind or mood in which a writer approaches a given subject. Going fishing on a fresh spring morning might evoke a light-hearted mood. A rainswept, overcast day at the beach might occasion gloom. An expected failure on an upcoming examination would engender pessimism. But if you merely told your reader "I felt light-hearted," or "I was deeply pessimistic," you would be making an observation but not creating a mood. Establishing a mood requires choosing and accentuating details consistent with it. Observe in the following example how the italicized words build up a scene of dreary solemnity.

In outward appearance, the whole of the court-room scene was *drab, ordinary*. There was the *stuffy* rectangle of a room, *half dark* in the *January dusk*. The electric lights glowed with *meager* incandescence. There was the judge, in his *robe*, at the desk of the court. There were the jurymen, *solemn* as in church. There were the men of the daily journals, more *aloof*, more *judicial* than the judge. There were the policemen and court attendants, relaxed of body, concentrated of eye, jealous of the dignity of the court as a house-dog of its master's room. Through the windows could be seen the *bulk of the Tombs, heavy, hopeless, horrible* as the things whence it takes its *chilly* name.

100d. MAKE YOUR WRITING CONSISTENT IN PHYSICAL IMPRESSION.

In addition to maintaining a unified point of view, you may wish to create for your reader a distinct physical impression, a sense of being on the spot, present where the action is. To do so, try appealing to one or more of his senses: sight, sound, smell, touch, taste. The impression you create may be favorable, positive, and pleasant or it may be unfavorable, negative, and unpleasant. Whatever it is, the impression should be consistently developed.

In the following paragraph, the dominant physical impression is one of *smell*. Notice that the italicized words consistently appeal to that sense:

Of all hours of the day there is none like the early morning for *downright good odours* — the morning before eating. Fresh from sleep and unclogged with food a man's senses cut like knives. The whole world comes in upon him. A still morning is best, for the *mists* and the *moisture* seem to retain the *odours* which they have *distilled* through the night. Upon a *breezy* morning one is likely to get a *single predominant odour* as of *clover* when the wind blows across a *hay field* or of *apple blossoms* when the wind comes through the orchard, but upon a perfectly still morning, it is wonderful how the *odours* arrange themselves in upright strata, so that one walking passes through them as from room to room in a *marvellous temple of fragrance*. (I should have said, I think, if I had not been on my way to dig a ditch, that it was like turning the leaves of some *delicate* volume of lyrics!)

— David Grayson, *Adventures in Contentment*

EXERCISE 26

What is the *physical* point of view (place, time) of some short story or other narrative that you have read? Does this point of view shift?

EXERCISE 27

What is the *personal* point of view in one of the essays or short stories in your literature anthology?

EXERCISE 28

What is the *mental* point of view in one of the essays in your literature anthology?

EXERCISE 29

What is the *physical impression* created in one or more pieces of description which you have read?

EXERCISE 30

The Declaration of Independence is an outstanding example of effective, consistent prose. Below are reprinted the closing paragraph of the original and a version written by H. L. Mencken in what he called "American." Discuss the difference in tone between the two versions. Is each thoroughly consistent in its style and development?

> We, therefore, the representatives of the United States of America, in general Congress assembled, appealing to the Supreme Judge of the world for the rectitude of our intentions, do, in the name and by the authority of the good people of these colonies, solemnly publish and declare that these united colonies are, and of right ought to be, free and independent states; that they are absolved from all allegiance to the British crown, and that all political connection between them and the State of Great Britain is, and ought to be, totally dissolved; and that, as free and independent states, they have full power to levy war, conclude peace, contract alliances, establish commerce, and to do all other acts and things which independent states may of right do. And for the support of this declaration, with a firm reliance on the protection of Divine Providence, we mutually pledge to each other our lives, our fortunes and our sacred honor.

Therefore be it resolved, That we, the representatives of the people of the United States of America, in Congress assembled, hereby declare as follows: That the United States, which was the United Colonies in former times, is now a free country, and ought to be; that we have throwed out the English King and don't want to have nothing to do with him no more, and are not taking no more English orders no more; and that, being as we are now a free country, we can do anything that free countries can do, especially declare war, make peace, sign treaties, go into business, etc. And we swear on the Bible on this proposition, one and all, and agree to stick to it no matter what happens, whether we win or we lose, and whether we get away with it or get the worst of it, no matter whether we lose all our property by it or even get hung for it.

—H. L. Mencken, *A Mencken Chrestomathy*

101. COHERENCE AND TRANSITION

Coherence as applied to themes means a "holding together" of parts, so that the relationship of ideas is immediately clear to the reader. In writing a theme, you are actually trying to *transfer* thoughts from your own mind to the reader's mind and at the same time trying to show clear and orderly progress from start to finish. In a coherent composition, each paragraph grows out of the preceding one and each group of paragraphs dealing with one section of a theme is closely related to other paragraph groups. A composition is coherent when its parts have been so carefully woven together that the reader is never confused about the relationships of ideas.

101a. LEAVE NO MISSING LINKS IN THOUGHT.

Connections between ideas which you may believe sufficiently clear and established because they seem plain to you do not always strike the reader the same way. The fault may be that you have used an ambiguous reference word (*it* or *they*, for instance) which has one meaning to you, a different one for the reader. Or perhaps you have confused the reader by omitting some pertinent connective detail either through oversight or because it seemed unimportant to you at the time.

For example, in one paragraph you write that you are at an airport intending to fly to Vancouver, but fog has grounded all planes. In the next paragraph you describe having dinner at a Vancouver restaurant with a friend. "How did you get there?" your reader wants to know. "Did the fog lift? Did you hitchhike? Go by train?" Only you know the answer, and it could have been easily supplied in a single sentence: "There was nothing to do but to wait for the fog to lift (or resign myself to going by train), (or undertake the hazards and uncertainties of getting a lift in such weather)."

101b. ATTAIN COHERENCE BY USING TRANSITION.

Transition is defined as "a word, phrase, sentence, or group of sentences that relates a preceding topic with a succeeding one." It is thus an important means of achieving coherence in a theme. A writer who builds transitional bridges between paragraphs or groups of paragraphs is likely to see and to correct any missing links in his discussion.

Each new paragraph indentation is a signal to the reader to expect a changeover, a movement of some kind, in the writer's thought. The opening sentence of the paragraph must make this movement clear by transition—by the use of a transitional word, phrase, dependent clause, or sentence. Transitional expressions and devices are discussed in some detail in Section 86.

Here is an example showing the opening sentences of five successive paragraphs concerning the early history of science, with transitions italicized:

1. There is no doubt whatever that our earliest scientific knowledge is of Oriental origin.
2. *For example*, as early as the middle of the fourth millenium, the Egyptians were already acquainted with a decimal system of numbers. (The writer then gives some additional examples.)

3. *These examples* will convince you that a considerable body of systematized knowledge was far anterior to Greek science.

4. *At any rate,* in the present state of our knowledge there is a gap of more than a thousand years between the golden age of Egyptian science and the golden age of Greek science.

5. *The spirit of Greek science,* which accomplished such wonders within a period of about five centuries, was essentially the Western spirit, whose triumphs are the boast of modern scientists.

EXERCISE 31

In your literature anthology or in a current magazine, select an essay and study its transitional devices. Limit your study to transitions between paragraphs. Prepare for class a brief discussion of your findings.

EXERCISE 32

For another selected essay, list the transitional devices mentioned in Section 86a which occur both within and between paragraphs.

102. REPORT WRITING

A *report* is an account or statement describing in adequate detail an event, situation, or circumstance, usually as the result of observation or inquiry. As a verb, *report* means literally to "carry back" and more generally means to "relate what has been learned by seeing and investigating."

As someone has observed, if you witness a person entering a thicket where you have noticed a reptile and cry "Look out for the snake," you have produced an efficient report. That is, you have clearly, briefly, and effectively conveyed important and useful information on a single topic about which you have become knowledgeable.

Report writing, however, is usually less simple and informal than this warning about a snake. It may involve two or three pages of expository writing or, possibly, many pages bound in a folder containing pictures, diagrams, and charts. Regardless of length or form, report writing and letter writing are likely to be the two forms most frequently used and most important to your success in adult life.

A report can appear in the form of a research paper (Section 103) or a letter (Section 109) or even a précis (Section 110), but usually comprises a piece of writing based on an experiment or an investigation that results in a summary of activity or a series of recommendations. For example, class activities in most schools require reports from a secretary, committee chairman, treasurer, or other class officer. Learning to write reports of this sort will help you in later life when you are an officer in a civic group, chairman of a union committee, or a supervisory employee in a business firm.

102a. PLAN AND OUTLINE THE REPORT CAREFULLY.

A good report is one which contains enough accurate and pertinent information to accomplish the job designed — and not one bit more. In order to ensure adequate but not excess coverage, outline the report before you begin or frame one as you proceed (Section 93). No satisfactory report was ever written without an outline prepared in advance or developed as the writing progressed.

Such a plan for an informal report might cover these questions:

1. Who asked you to study the problem? When? Why?
2. Precisely what is the subject to be reported on?
3. How was the investigation made? (Authorities consulted, people interviewed, places visited, tests made, reading done.)
4. What are the specific results or recommendations?

In a formal or lengthy report, a summary of methods used to obtain information and of results or recommendations comes first. This summary is followed by the main body of the report which discusses these summary points in detail. A list of topics on "Club Conditions in This School" might resemble this:

1. Summary
2. Members of the investigating committee
3. Methods of conducting the survey
4. Number and kinds of clubs investigated
5. Means of selecting club members
6. Activities of the clubs involved in this study
7. Club contributions to the school
8. Clubs and school elections
9. Clubs and the community
10. Effects of clubs on the student body

Not every report must contain mention of each of these items, nor need those points which appear be handled in the exact order indicated. The plan of an effective report is usually dictated by the opening summary, an illustration of which follows:

The purpose of this report is to determine (1) whether the program designed to give new employees an understanding of the products and social significance of the company has actually justified its cost in time and money; and (2) whether changes are needed to improve the program if it is retained.

The investigation has been based on four sources of information: (1) interviews with employees who have completed the program; (2) interviews with supervisory personnel; (3) statistical comparisons of work efficiency between those who have and have not taken the program; (4) published reports on related programs at four other industrial centers.

The report establishes the value of the program and recommends its continuation. Suggestions for improvement: (1) Top-level executives should contribute more actively to the program through individual interviews with employees and by lectures to groups; (2) greater use of visual-aid material is needed to explain certain complex company operations; (3) the orientation course should be extended by two weeks.

102b. THE REPORT SHOULD BE SELECTIVE BUT COMPREHENSIVE.

No report reveals everything known about any subject; a good report writer indicates ability as much by what he omits as by what he includes. Nevertheless, no competent reporter regrets collecting more material than he can use;

only if he collects more than he needs can he "write from strength" by appearing to have in reserve more than he actually needs.

102c. A REPORT SHOULD BE OBJECTIVE.

An investigator who knows in advance what answers he wishes to get and uses data to support his predetermined point of view is neither a competent nor fair reporter. A report should be approached without personal prejudice; results and recommendations should be based on materials collected and assembled with an open mind. An effective report contains no exaggerations and few superlatives. The reliable report writer presents facts as clearly as possible and phrases recommendations without resort to argument and appeals to emotion.

102d. A REPORT SHOULD BE DIRECT.

Each paragraph in a report should begin with a topic sentence. A reader who, after absorbing the opening summary, wishes to examine in detail a particular part of the report should be able to locate that part at once by glancing at topic sentences only. The writer of a good report comes to each point at once and adds no unnecessary details.

EXERCISE 33

As your teacher directs, prepare an informal or formal report on one of the following topics:

A. Student control in study halls
B. Furnishing a recreation room
C. How cafeteria officers are chosen
D. Safety programs in this school
E. Student transportation to school

EXERCISE 34

Follow the directions for Exercise 33.

A. A plan for handling school social functions
B. Treatment of athletes injured in school games
C. School-sponsored community activities
D. Discipline in this school
E. Curricula offered in this school

103. THE RESEARCH PAPER

Research is a word which came into English from an Old French word, *cercher*, meaning to seek or search, and the prefix *re* (again). Research may be defined as intensive search with the purpose of becoming certain.

Actually, the essentials of research procedure are almost as natural as eating and sleeping. On your own, you have gone from one store to another to locate the suit or dress or hat which best became both your appearance and your pocketbook. You have tried out various restaurants, diners, soft drinks, and amusement places in what are actually research projects. What, actually, is the activity of dating but a problem in research?

After you have had some practice in theme writing, you may be assigned a *research paper* (also called a *term paper* or *library paper* or *investigative theme*). This will be somewhere between 1500 and 6000 words, depending on the subject and the limit set by your teacher. Your purpose should be to make a careful search for information about a particular subject and then to present and interpret what you have found out. A research paper should not be a mere reading report or a hodgepodge of quotations and summaries. An effective paper is an orderly, systematic study undertaken for a specific purpose.

To turn out a good investigative theme takes time. It constitutes a task you cannot do hastily or postpone until the last moment. It means choosing a suitable subject and knowing how and where to inform yourself about it. It means knowing how to take efficient notes on your reading and having a clear conception of what is relevant to your subject and what is not. Further, preparing a good paper requires knowing the mechanics of research and having the patience and will to write and rewrite.

As overwhelming as this task may appear to you, your labors will seem less burdensome if you have a genuine interest in your subject and the curiosity to get at the facts behind it. You will not be the first to discover that researching a subject and coming upon a missing fact you have been hunting for has the fascination of detective work. Students who approach a research assignment with reluctance often become engrossed in their subject once they begin gathering information.

An increasing number of students enter colleges where professors take for granted that term papers will be the result of original research and will be correctly written and documented. Even in business and community life, the writing of reports and preparation of speeches involve basic principles of gathering information and presenting it.

103a. SELECT AND ANALYZE YOUR SUBJECT CAREFULLY.

1. Choose a subject which already interests you or conceivably can engage your interest. But avoid selecting one which is overly technical or too specialized to be of interest to your readers.

2. Choose a subject which you can treat adequately in the space assigned. A topic suitable for a paper of 1000 words could be spun out to 5000 only by padding, repetition, and irrelevancies.

3. Select a subject about which enough has been written for you to obtain pertinent information. Consider the resources of the library where you intend to do your investigating.

4. Have a clear purpose in view as you start gathering material. Formulate some idea of what you intend to demonstrate or prove by investigating your subject, what conclusions you expect to draw from it. (See Section 92a.)

103b. BE THOROUGH IN INVESTIGATING YOUR SUBJECT.

Many scholars, as well as authors of historical novels, often spend months and even years in the world's greatest libraries. You have only a matter of days or weeks to gather your material. No one expects you to learn *all* about a subject in so brief a time. But you ought to make as thorough an investigation as you can by making use of reference books, periodicals, newspapers, and books from the general collection of the library. Learn how to make efficient use of books of reference, periodical indexes, and the general card catalog. From these, make out a preliminary list of books and articles which seem *likely* to contribute to your subject. Write each item on a 3 x 5 inch card. Be careful to put down *full* information. This will save you time in two ways: (1) you will have detailed facts about it if you use the information in the bibliography of your paper; (2) you need not repeat these facts on note cards. How a bibliography card can be made is shown on page 442. Observe that the material is arranged as it will appear in the bibliography, except that you may not need to include the publisher's name. Note also that the card lists a library call number. This number can also save time if you have to put in a second request for the book to check it again, as happens even to experienced researchers.

The number shown for the biographies of Conrad illustrates a common way of cataloging biographies. Many biographies have call numbers that consist of the letter *B* (for *biography*), the first letter of the person's last name (in this case, *C*), a special number representing the person (in this case 754 represents Conrad, so that all biographies with C 754 are biographies of Conrad), and the first letter of the author's first name (in this case, *J*). The card for Conrad's novel, *The Shadow Line*, illustrates a common way of cataloging fiction: *F* stands for fiction and *C* for the author — in this case, Conrad. A novel by Charles Dickens would be catalogued *FD* and one by Herman Melville would be catalogued *FM*.

Jean-Aubry, Georges.

Joseph Conrad: Life and Letters.

2 vols. New York: Doubleday,
Page and Company, 1927.

B
C 754 J

Otago   (Joseph Conrad)

Conrad outwardly calm on appointment
to command, which is an abstract idea
to him. He suddenly realizes it involves
the concrete existence of a ship.
"A ship! My ship! It was mine, more
absolutely mine for possession and
care than anything in the world; an
object of responsibility and devotion."
p. 40
Joseph Conrad, The Shadow Line, (New
York: Doubleday, Page and Company, 1926).
F
C

Small 3″ x 5″ cards are useful for bibliographical information. Larger cards, 4″ x 6″ preferably, are more useful for extended note-taking. An explanation of the call numbers (*FC* and *B/C 754 J*) is given on page 441.

Citizen and Master

August 19, 1886, Joseph Conrad Korzeniowski, "subject of the Russian Empire, of the age of twenty-nine years, mariner, unmarried," was given a certificate of British naturalization.

November 11, 1886, awarded "Certificate of Competency as Master." p. 111.

Jean-Aubry, Georges, *The Sea Dreamer: A Definitive Biography of Joseph Conrad*, New York, 1926, 1957

B/C 754 J

Having filled out bibliography cards for as many books and articles as you believe you will need, begin examining the items themselves, retaining those which contain information pertinent to the phase of the subject you are concerned with and rejecting those that do not. You reach this decision by glancing through articles and studying the prefaces, tables of contents, and indexes of books. When you are fairly certain which of this material you will need for your paper, you are ready to start taking notes.

103c. TAKE CAREFUL NOTES FROM YOUR READING.

The most efficient way to take notes is on 4 x 6 inch cards, one note to each card. Note cards should be larger than bibliography cards because they will need to hold more information. Sheets of paper of about this size, or larger, or pages from a loose-leaf notebook will also answer your purpose, but cards seem preferable because they are easier to sort and rearrange, an important step preparatory to writing your paper.

Before you take notes on a book, examine the preface and table of contents to learn the scope and purpose of the book. If the volume has an index, save time by looking there for your particular subject or material related to it. In reading a magazine article or a chapter of a book, glance through it first, then begin reading carefully and taking notes.

Keep your notes compact. You will only waste time by taking down whole pages. You can often condense a paragraph, sometimes even a page, to a single summarizing sentence. Other shortcuts can be made by omitting minor words and using abbreviations for names and words which occur frequently. (But do not use so many shortcuts that you cannot decipher what you have written.)

Unless you are quoting exactly, always take notes *in your own words*. You can then use material from your note cards when you are writing the paper without having to reword it. You are entitled to borrow information from an author and are required to acknowledge your debt in a footnote. You are *not* entitled to use an author's sentences except as direct and acknowledged quotation. When you find something you wish to quote in your paper, copy it carefully and accurately and surround it with quotation marks for later use. But keep in mind that a research paper should not consist of only a string of quotations.

Also, try to judge the reliability of your sources. If the material is controversial, consider the possible bias of an author. If your subject is largely factual, how recently was a particular item of information published? Is there a later book on the subject that is more accurate and up-to-date?

For an efficient method of note taking examine the sample note cards shown on pages 442-443. Note the bibliographical information, with the author's name in its normal order as it would be given in a footnote. (This information need appear only on the first note card on each book or article. Thereafter you can use abbreviations for the same source. If your source is a book of two or more volumes, include the volume number on the card.)

As your notes accumulate, regroup them so that those dealing with the same aspect of your subject are together. In this way you can more readily see which topics you have dealt with sufficiently and which require more information. This grouping will also help to shape a preliminary outline for your paper.

103d. PREPARE AN ADEQUATE OUTLINE FOR YOUR PAPER.

While taking notes, presumably you had in mind a controlling purpose (Section 103a). You should therefore be able to arrange your grouped notes to form a tentative sentence or topic outline for your paper (Section 93). You will, however, probably want to make changes before deciding on a final outline. For example, you may want to shift a note or group of notes to achieve a more effective beginning or ending.

A tentative outline, suitable for some subjects, might cover these major points:

I. Purpose of the paper

II. Value of the subject (importance, significance)

III. Background or history of the subject

IV. Nature of the investigation (its substance)

V. Conclusions (generalized statements based on the investigation)

Do not begin writing your paper until you have worked out an outline in its final form. This is essential to assure a well-structured whole. A meandering discussion unfortunately implies that the writer's research was equally haphazard.

103e. WRITE A FIRST DRAFT OF YOUR RESEARCH PAPER.

Your paper is the end result of all your reading and note taking. If the final outline is well designed and sufficiently detailed, and if your notes are arranged to follow its divisions, you should be able to write the paper with only normal difficulty. You should, however, write a first draft as a working copy to get material down on paper to see how it looks and sounds. Leave one or two spaces between the lines for revisions. You can then make changes in sequence, strengthen your beginning, eliminate overlapping details, or make your discussion more effective in any other needed way. Determine which facts require acknowledgment and write out proper footnotes for them. Prepare your bibliography from your 3 x 5 cards, putting them in alphabetical order according to the authors' names. In short, the greater likeness of first draft to final one, the easier the last stage of your writing will be.

A research paper is an objective presentation of the facts about a subject. Its point of view is *impersonal*. Ordinarily, do not refer to yourself as "I" or to the reader as "you." If you refer to either—and you should rarely do so—speak of "the present writer" and "the reader."

Write in as clear and straightforward a manner as you can. A research paper need not be stiff, overformal, or pedantic. It can be enlivened by touches of irony, humor, or a well-turned phrase. Most research papers are duller than they need be. A good research paper is a living, tangible accomplishment. You may be delightfully surprised at your success in mastering one phase of a subject and communicating it with clarity, vigor, and appeal.

103f. USE FOOTNOTES TO INDICATE SOURCES OF INFORMATION.

In addition to writing as clearly and correctly as possible, you must also document the borrowed materials you use. Documentation involves the use of both footnotes and a bibliography.

The purpose of a footnote is to mention the authority for some fact stated or to develop some point referred to in the body of a paper.

Commonly known facts or quotations do not require footnotes, but you must avoid *plagiarism*. Unless the idea and the phrasing are your own, refer the reader to some source for your statement. To be completely honest, acknowledge every source of indebtedness even when no direct quotation is used.

Occasionally you may wish to develop, interpret, or refute some idea but not want an extended comment to clutter up the body of your paper. Use a footnote.

How many footnotes should appear in a research paper? One investigation may call for twice the number of entries as another. Some pages of your paper may call for a half-dozen or more footnotes; others may need only one or two or none at all. Acknowledge credit where it is due and provide discussion footnotes where they are required for understanding.

Systems of footnoting are numerous, but whatever method you choose should be used consistently throughout your paper and be immediately clear to any intelligent reader.

For books, standard usage favors this form: (1) author's first name or initials followed by surname; (2) title of book (in italics) and number of edition; (3) place of publication; (4) name of publisher (optional); (5) date of publication; (6) volume and page reference.

In listing information about periodical material, place the title of the article or story after the author's name and before the name of the periodical. The title is put in quotation marks, the name of the magazine is italicized (underlined). Place the volume number, in Roman numerals, immediately after the name of the magazine or journal. By using Roman numerals for the volume number and Arabic for the page numbers, you avoid the necessity for volume and page abbreviations. Examine the correct forms for entering the following kinds of information:

BOOKS

[1] James Truslow Adams, *History of the United States* (New York, 1933), IV, 147.

[1] *The Great West*, ed. Charles Neider (New York, 1958), p. 168.

[1] Henry B. Culver and Gordon Grant, *The Book of Old Ships* (New York, 1935), p. 225.

[1] Marcel Proust, *Remembrance of Things Past*, trans. C. K. Scott Moncrieff (New York, 1935), I, 31.

ARTICLES (ESSAYS, STORIES)

[1] Foster Nostrand, "Out of a Clear Blue Sky," *Yachting*, CXXII (October, 1967), 42.

[1] "The Chameleon Chemical," *Life*, LXIV (January 12, 1968), 41.

[1] Edith Wharton, "Xingu," *Short Stories*, ed. Edwin H. Sauer and Howard Mumford Jones (New York: Holt, Rinehart and Winston, Inc., 1963), p. 204.

Your teacher may prefer a shorter form or one in which the information is arranged differently. For example, he may require you to omit the author's first name, the place of publication, or the name of the publisher. After the form has been decided upon, be consistent in its use.

In documenting your research paper, you may be urged by your teacher to use abbreviations wherever possible for increased efficiency. The main, or primary, forms shown above may well be used less often than short-cut versions. For example:

ibid.: The same. If a footnote refers to the same source as the one referred to in the footnote *immediately* preceding, the abbreviation *ibid.* (from the Latin *ibidem,* meaning "in the same place") may be used. If the volume, page, title, and author are the same, use *ibid.* alone. If the volume and page differ, use, for example, *"Ibid.,* III, 206." *Ibid.* usually comes at the beginning of a footnote and is capitalized for that reason only.

op. cit.: The work cited. After the first full reference to a given work, provided no other work by the same author is mentioned in the paper, succeeding references may be indicated by the author's surname followed by *op. cit.* (from the Latin *opere citato,* meaning "in the work cited") and the volume and page:

> Corwin, *op. cit.,* V, 41.
> Parsons, *op. cit.,* p. 12.

However, *op. cit.* does no real work and its use is being abandoned in favor of an entry containing only the author's last name and the page number involved: "Smith, p. 320."

passim: "Everywhere," "throughout." It is used when no specific page reference can be given.

loc. cit.: The place cited. If the reference is to the exact passage covered by an earlier, but not immediately preceding, reference, use *loc. cit.* (from the Latin *loco citato,* meaning "in the place cited"). Like *op. cit., loc. cit.* seems wordy and is gradually being discarded in research writing. Actually, *ibid.* can do anything which *loc. cit.* can.

p. *(plural,* pp.): page (pages)
l. *(plural,* ll.): line (lines)
vol.: volume
ch. *(plural,* chs.): chapter (chapters)
ff.: following (e.g., pages 424 ff.)
v.: verse
ante: before
art.: article
sec. *(plural,* secs.): section (sections)
n. *(plural,* nn.): note (notes)

A footnote is indicated by an Arabic numeral placed above and to the right of the word requiring comment. If the reference is to a quotation, place the numeral at the end of the passage. In front of the actual footnote at the bottom of the page repeat the number used in the text. Asterisks or other symbols should not be used in place of Arabic numerals.

Footnotes may be numbered consecutively throughout the manuscript or separately for each page. Follow the directions given by your teacher.

Footnotes may appear at the bottoms of pages, between lines in the text proper, or all together at the end of the manuscript. Most teachers prefer the first of these methods. If footnotes are to be placed at the bottom of the page, care should be taken not to crowd them. Always leave a clearly defined space between the text and the footnotes.

103g. USE A BIBLIOGRAPHY TO DOCUMENT YOUR RESEARCH PAPER.

In a research paper, a bibliography is an alphabetical, sometimes classified, list containing the names of all works quoted from or generally used in the preparation of the paper. Every formally prepared research paper should include a bibliography begun on a separate page and placed at the end of the theme.

Bibliographical items should be arranged correctly and consistently. Usage may vary, but unless your teacher rules otherwise, follow these suggestions:

1. Arrange items alphabetically by last names of the authors. Each surname is followed by a comma, then by the author's given name(s) or initials.

2. If the author's name is not given and not known, list the item by the first word (except *a, an, the*) in the title. List titles by the same author alphabetically, using a blank line about three-fourths of an inch long in place of the author's name after its first appearance.

3. The author's complete name is followed by a period.

4. A period follows the title of a book. Citing the publisher's name is optional.

5. Place and date of publication are separated by a comma and are not put in parentheses.

The following are examples of citations of books and of articles from periodicals.

BIBLIOGRAPHY

BOOKS

Dee, P. Christopher. *The Togetherness of Words: Composition in the Classroom.* New York: Harper & Row, 1970.

Mitchell, Carleton. *Summer of the Twelves.* New York: Charles Scribner's Sons, 1959.

Morison, Samuel Eliot. *Spring Tides* (pp. 62-80). Boston: Houghton Mifflin Company, 1965.

Spectorsky, A. C., ed. *The Book of the Sea* (pp. 124-126). New York: Grosset & Dunlap, 1954.

ARTICLES

Alpert, Hollis. "How Useful Are Film Festivals?" *Saturday Review* (July 8, 1967), pp. 56-58.

Bolling, Richard. "What the New Congress Needs Most," *Harper's Magazine*, CCXXXIV (January, 1967), 79-81.

Childs, John W. "A Set of Procedures for the Planning of Instruction," *Educational Technology*, Vol. 8, No. 16 (August 30, 1968), 7-14.

Chorover, Stephan L. "The Psychophysiology of Memory," *Technology Review*, LXIX (December, 1966), 17-23.

103h. MAKE YOUR FINAL DRAFT CORRECT AND ACCURATE.

The final version of your paper must be carefully prepared. Except for minor changes, it will be essentially a transcription of your first draft. It should be as nearly letter-perfect as possible. To make sure of this, first read slowly through the text with an eye to spelling and punctuation. Corrections in these can usually be made without blemishing your manuscript. Larger errors involving revision of a sentence or the addition of one should necessitate rewriting a whole page.

Next, check your footnotes. Are they correct in form and complete in detail? Last, ask yourself the same questions about the bibliography. Then lay the paper aside, preferably for several days, but at least for one day. Then look over your paper once more with fresh eyes. If you discover no other lapses, probably you have done the best you can. No one can ask more than that.

JOSEPH CONRAD AS A COMMANDER

For fourteen months of his twenty years as a mariner, Joseph Conrad Korzeniowski, as he was then known, held command of a ship, the 350-ton barque _Otago_, owned by an Australian company.[1] The command ended with his abrupt resignation. What kind of master did he prove to be? What were his strengths and his shortcomings? We have no profile on him in this capacity. If no complete one is possible, some of the line-aments may be sketched in from evidences in Conrad's own writings, the recollections of persons who knew him at this time, and the accounts of his biographers.

In 1886, First Officer Korzeniowski was awarded two certificates in London. The first granted him British citizenship, the second qualified him as Master.[2] Since there were no vacancies for captains, and he had to support

---

[1] Jean—Aubry, Georges, _The Sea Dreamer: A Definitive Biography of Joseph Conrad_ (New York, 1957) p. 132.
[2] _Ibid._, p. 111.

himself, he had to be content to serve under other commanders. When two years later he obtained a ship of his own, it was through pure coincidence.

Conrad himself tells us about it.[3] Having left his last ship at Singapore, he was staying at the Sailors Home waiting for passage to Europe, when he was summoned by the harbor master and offered command of the Otago. The barque was currently at Bangkok, her former master having died near that port. Outwardly calm, the newly appointed captain was understandably elated:

> A ship! My ship! She was mine, more absolutely mine for possession and care than anything in the world; an object of responsibility and devotion.[4]

Before he was long aboard the Otago, his responsibilities grew to staggering proportions and his devotion underwent a serious test. Mr. Burns, the mate, several years the captain's senior, was resentful and taciturn.

---

[3] In The Shadow Line (New York: Doubleday, Page & Company, 1926). The book is a reminiscence of Conrad's first command for the first two months. The account begins with his arrival at Singapore and ends with his return on the Otago.
[4] Ibid., p. 40.

Having been acting—commander after the death
of the former master, he had expected to be
named as successor. The new captain met the
issue head—on:

> ''Look here, Mr. Burns,'' I began, very
> firmly. ''You may as well understand that I
> did not run after this command. It was
> pushed my way. I am here to take the ship
> home, and you may be sure that I shall see
> to it that every one of you on board here
> does his duty to that end. That is all I
> have to say at present.''[5]

But at present few of the men were able to
to do their duty. All were feverish and weak to
the point of helplessness. The steward was
taken ashore, where he died. A Chinese, hired
to replace him, stayed aboard just long enough
to run off with the captain's hard—earned
savings of thirty—three gold sovereigns.[6] Mr.
Burns, a victim of the contagion, was carried
off, delirious, on a stretcher.

The captain was beginning to discover that
''even the command of a nice little barque may
be a delusion and a snare for the unwary spirit

[5] Ibid., pp. 63—64. Actually, in real life the
acting commander was named Born as is pointed
out in Jocelyn Baines, Joseph Conrad: A Critical
Biography (New York, 1960), p. 93.
[6] Jean—Aubry, The Sea Dreamer, p. 133. In his
earlier book, Life and Letters, Jean—Aubry
gives the sum as ''thirty—two pounds.'' 1, 107.

of pride in men.''[7] He needed Mr. Burns. The mate knew the ship and the adjacent waters. The enforced delay had already lasted two weeks. But he would not leave port without his first officer. Captain Korzeniowski's orders were to bring his ship to her home port as soon as possible, and he would brook no further delay.

Feverish and raving as he still was, Burns was brought aboard at the captain's orders and put to bed. Ransome, the cook, already doubling as steward and suffering from a heart ailment, also now served as nurse. Only he and the captain escaped contagion.

[7] Joseph Conrad, Falk, A Reminiscence (New York: Doubleday, Page & Company, 1920), p. 20.

104. REVISION AND PROOFREADING

"There is no such thing as good writing; there is only good rewriting." Many students have objected to this statement. They will mention an occasion when they really "got going" and turned out an effective first, last, and only draft. Or they will say, "I wrote this paper in an hour and got a C grade on it; here's one which took some four hours and was marked D." Or they will recall that Shakespeare never "blotted a line" or that Sir Walter Scott or O. Henry or this and that writer never rewrote his material.

And yet the fact is that the writer of a good "hour" theme probably had composed it in his mind many times before setting it down on paper. He had thought it through; he had written "on the hoof," while walking, eating, dressing, even bathing. His "quickly written" paper was not quickly written at all, even though he thought it was rapidly put on paper.

Not even a professional writer can plan, write, and proofread all at one time. A naive and inexperienced person tends to think that a writer just writes, the words pouring out. And yet most skilled writers have testified that writing is laborious, time-consuming labor. If an experienced professional can get only a few hundred words on paper during a full working day, he feels encouraged and happy. Consider this comment from John Steinbeck, a Nobel Prize winher:

> Many years of preparation preceded the writing of *Grapes of Wrath*. I wrote it in one hundred days, but the preparation, false starts, and wasted motion took two and a half years. The actual writing is the last process.

104a. CAREFULLY REVISE EVERY COMPOSITION.

Three kinds of alteration are possible when you revise a paper. You can *substitute,* you can *delete,* and you can *add.* When your reasons for making such changes are considered, certain subdivisions appear.

One such subdivision consists of asking and answering these twelve "mopping up" questions:

1. Have I chosen a suitable subject and narrowed it so that in the number of words I have at my disposal I can provide a clear and reasonably complete account of what my reader expects or has a right to expect?

2. Have I followed an orderly plan in writing, working from either a mental or written outline? Have I divided the treatment into related parts and written at least one paragraph on each?

3. Is each of my paragraphs adequate in material, unified in substance, correctly proportioned?

4. Does my theme contain any unjustified sentence fragments?

5. Does my theme contain any fused sentences?

6. Have I avoided all comma splices?

7. Is all of the punctuation in my theme logical, necessary, and a clear aid to communication?

8. Have I checked to make sure that my theme contains no glaring errors in grammar — agreement, reference of pronouns, correct verb forms, correct case of pronouns, etc.?

9. Is the sentence construction accurate and clear — no misplaced or dangling modifiers, split constructions, faulty parallelism, faulty coordination or subordination, illogical constructions, inconsistencies in tense, choppiness, etc.?

10. Is the diction as correct, clear, and effective as I can make it?

11. Have I checked the spelling of all words?

12. Have I proofread the theme carefully, checking painstakingly to eliminate all careless errors?

Another group of alterations consists of efforts to achieve greater accuracy of expression, or more clarity, so as to drive home more forcefully to a reader a particular point, idea, mood, or impression. In this sort of revision, you check and recheck your choice of words; you revise the word order and structure of a sentence or group of sentences; you alter a figure of speech to make an image sharper or clearer; you add a bit of dialogue or an incident or anecdote to reinforce an idea; you remove a section which seems stale and ineffective; you alter the position of sentences within paragraphs or the order of paragraphs in the entire paper.

104b. THOROUGHLY PROOFREAD EVERY THEME YOU WRITE.

In proofreading we narrow our range of vision and thereby pick up mistakes hitherto unnoticed by the writer. In other words, we spot errors not by reading but by *proofreading*.

The following triangle will show you how wide your vision (sight spread) is. Look at the top of the triangle and then down. How far down can you go and still identify each letter in each line at a *single* glance? Your central vision is as wide as the line above the one where you cannot identify each letter *without moving your eyes at all.*

o

or

ord

ordc

ordcf

ordcfe

ordcfeg

ordcfegh

ordcfeghi

ordcfeghia

ordcfeghiar

The range of vision differs in people as does nearly everything else. Still, many people have trouble identifying more than six letters at a single glance, and some have a span limited only to three or four letters. Whatever your span, you should not try to exceed it when you are carefully checking for mistakes. To do so would be reading—perhaps with effective comprehension—but it would not be *proofreading*. And it is proofreading alone which enables one to catch and eliminate errors caused not by ignorance or stupidity but by carelessness.

EXERCISE 35

Make an honest analysis of the time spent on three of your compositions written outside class. Estimate the amount of time spent on preparation for writing, actual time spent in writing, and the time spent on revision and proofreading.

EXERCISE 36

Write a paragraph or short paper developing this summary sentence: "Careless errors in writing hinder communication as much as stammering does in conversation."

105. MANUSCRIPT FORM

When you prepare the final draft of a composition, remember that yours is but one of a large number of papers your teacher will be reading. As interesting and well planned as your paper may be, it is unlikely to win approval if it is untidy and illegible. Your handwriting need not be a model for a copybook, but neither should it be a scrawl decipherable only by yourself. With some care and effort, even the most eccentric handwriting can be made readable to others. If neatness alone will not redeem a composition poor in substance and organization, it will assure an unusually favorable reception for one that is at least passable on both counts.

Teachers are only human: many of them are likely to give a low grade to a paper which is slovenly written or typed. Try to give to your ideas the outward appearance which will guarantee ready communication. At a party or dance, your body may be clean, your mind witty, your disposition genial and outgoing. But what if your clothes need cleaning, your fingernails and shoes need cleaning, your hair needs combing?

105a. CONFORM TO STANDARDS IN PREPARING MANUSCRIPT.

If your class has been given instructions for preparing manuscript, follow those directions. If not, use the following suggestions as a guide.

1. *Paper.* Use prescribed paper or standard-sized sheets, 8½ by 11 inches, with lines of handwriting or typing ⅓ to ½ inch apart. (Avoid ordinary notebook paper, because the narrow spaces between lines crowd the writing and leave no room for corrections.) For typing, use regular typewriter paper, which is also 8½ by 11 inches. Write on only one side of the sheet.

2. *Ink.* Use black or blue-black ink. Ballpoint pens should be of good quality to write legibly on the prescribed or suggested paper.

3. *Typing.* Use black ribbon and be certain that the type is clean. Submit typewritten compositions only if you typewrite them yourself.

4. *Margins.* Leave a frame of white space all *around* each page—about 1½ inch at top and left, an inch at right and bottom.

5. *Indentation.* Indent each paragraph equally, almost an inch in longhand, five spaces when typewriting.

6. *Paging.* Mark each page after the first by placing an Arabic numeral in the upper right-hand corner. Arrange the pages in proper order.

7. *Title.* Center the title on the first line or about two inches from the top of the page. See Section 95c.

8. *Insertions.* Use a caret (∧) when inserting something omitted. Preferably, recopy the page.

9. *Cancellation.* Draw a neat line through material you wish to omit. (Do not use brackets or parentheses.) Preferably, recopy the entire page.

105b. AVOID NUMEROUS CORRECTIONS IN YOUR FINAL DRAFT.

We are all prone to make errors even in the final drafts of our writing. Sometimes the errors are few and can be corrected without numerous erasures and canceled words. It is better, however, to rewrite a whole page than to submit a manuscript with several erasures, blurs, and canceled or inserted words.

105c. MAKE YOUR HANDWRITING LEGIBLE.

1. Use a good pen with black or blue-black ink.

2. Do not crowd your writing by running words together; do not write consecutive lines too closely together; leave ample margins.

3. The consecutive letters in a word should be joined.

4. Take your time.

105d. IF POSSIBLE, TYPE YOUR THEMES AND OTHER WRITTEN WORK.

Typescript is more legible than handwriting and, with rare exceptions, neater. In addition, you can detect mistakes in typescript more easily than in handwriting. If you do not know how to type, learning might be an excellent investment of time and money. If you do type, be certain to double-space all lines; quotations of more than four lines, however, should be single-spaced.

105e. PROOFREAD A THEME CAREFULLY BEFORE SUBMITTING IT.

When you have made the final corrections on the paper you are going to submit, put it aside for at least an hour before you reread it for the last time. If you read it over immediately after you have written it, your mind will still be so full of what you intended to say that you will not notice the imperfections you can detect if you approach it with a fresh mind. Even professional writers have to check their final drafts for oversights. See Section 104.

SPECIAL PURPOSES
AND PROBLEMS

Mastering an effective use of English is not an impossible task by any means, but it is surely an exasperating and complex one. As you write papers and study Sections 1-105 of this handbook, it probably will occur to you that the problem of writing good English is somewhat like that of repairing a worn bicycle or automobile tire: you repair one leak only to have air escape through other holes. Despite all attempts that have been made to cover all conceivable approaches to ordinary writing and to pigeonhole them in conveniently studied sections, some problems will be seen to overlap and others will remain unattended. For example, a flaw in diction may involve pronunciation or mechanics or grammar or sentence structure, or all four simultaneously. In addition, what is studied about diction in one section might not apply with full meaning if your purpose in writing were different or if your task were the preparation of a quite distinct form of paper or report. Even if you were able to master every problem involving grammar, punctuation, mechanics, diction, sentence structure, and paragraph development in all specific and interrelated aspects, your task would not be completed.

What you and your teacher are striving for is your application of individual principles of writing, "rules" about what to do and what not to do, in such ways as to achieve completed wholes: effective paragraphs and entire papers of varied sorts. Such an accomplishment depends upon far more than mere "rules" and routine attention to specific *do's* and *don't's*. Several closely related but nonetheless distinct aims, patterns, ideas, and forms applying to writing can be neither forced into pigeonholes nor neglected because they fit no particular mold. Such purposes and problems are briefly discussed in Sections 106-120.

Possibly you will have little interest in, nor will your teacher necessarily care to assign, sections dealing with letter-

462

writing, the précis, the paraphrase, diagraming, semantics, linguistics, or the history of our language. Yet each has a distinct contribution to make to the study of composition and each is worth some attention. Several of the sections that follow, however, treat topics indispensable to all school work, not English alone: thinking, using a dictionary and a library, reading, listening, speaking, pronunciation, and taking tests. All, moreover, are important, not only for now, but for the future.

106. THINKING

"We do not think enough about thinking, and much of our confusion is the result of current illusions in regard to it." This is the first sentence in a justly famous essay entitled "On Various Kinds of Thinking," by James Harvey Robinson. Perhaps we do not think enough about thinking because thinking is hard work, because we seem to get along fairly well without doing much of it, possibly because we think we are thinking when actually we are doing nothing of the sort. "If you make people think they're thinking," once wrote Don Marquis, an American humorist, "they'll love you. If you make them think, they'll hate you."

106a. INDUCTION AND DEDUCTION

Two common methods of thinking, used and abused every day, are *induction* and *deduction*. The former seeks to establish a general truth, an all embracing principle or conclusion. The inductive process begins by using observation or specific facts; it classifies these facts, looks for similarities among them, and from what may be considered a sufficient number of these facts or particulars draws a conclusion or "leads into" a principle. Movement of thought is always from the particular to the general.

Deduction seeks to establish a specific conclusion by showing that it conforms to or "leads down from" a general truth or principle. Movement of thought, expressed or implied, is from the general to the particular.

In other words, induction is the process of thinking by which one generalizes from particulars; deduction is that form of reasoning wherein we put ideas together to see what can be inferred from them. In induction, one reasons from facts to generalizations; in deduction, one reasons from premises (propositions, assumptions) to conclusions. The premises involved in deduction may be the product of inductive reasoning and therefore rooted in fact, but investigation of fact is not part of the deductive process itself.

Processes of thought such as these may seem different from any thinking of which you consider yourself capable, but look at this example. Early in history, men became convinced that no one lives forever, that sooner or later all men die. Through inductive thinking, mankind arrived at a general conclusion, "All men are mortal." A generalization as well established as this, one which needs neither reexamination nor further testing, may be used as a starting point, that is, a *premise* in deductive thinking. In light of the general truth that all men are mortal, we examine the future of a man named George White. In the form of a *syllogism,* this deductive process may be expressed:

> Major premise: All men are mortal.
> Minor premise: George White is a man.
> Conclusion: George White is mortal.

Although we do not formally arrange our thoughts in syllogisms such as the one just illustrated, we reason in much the same way. For example, we regularly assume that events encountered in the future will be like those met with in the past. What, indeed, is the real meaning of the saying, "A burnt child dreads the fire"?

In induction, the possibility of exceptions always exists, but those general conclusions reached by inductive processes are usually acceptable. When you write, "Most honor graduates of high school do well in college," you cannot be absolutely certain because you cannot possibly have examined all records of past and present students and cannot be positive about the future. But the statement is sufficiently probable. So is the inductive conclusion that no two people have identical fingerprints, although this statement, too, is only theoretically capable of being positively proved.

Through inductive reasoning, the laws (that is, the principles, the generalized and descriptive statements) of any science, such as biology, chemistry, and physics, have been arrived at. Through deductive reasoning they are applied in particular situations: the launching of a space rocket, the manufacture of a computer, the development of a vaccine. In pure and applied science, such reasoning is virtually foolproof. But loopholes do occur where human beings and human behavior are directly concerned.

106b. LOGICAL LOOPHOLES

Here is brief comment on the most common everyday offenses against straight and clear thinking:

1. *Hasty generalization.* The most prevalent error in inductive reasoning is observing only a few instances and then jumping to an unwarranted conclusion. For instance, you know a few athletes whom you consider stupid; does it follow that all, or even most, athletes are mentally deficient? What is the inductive evidence for labeling certain groups "teen-age gangsters," "irresponsible women drivers," "absent-minded professors," "dumb blondes"? What is the evidence for "Every schoolboy knows..." or "All good Canadians realize . . . " or "Statistics show . . . "? Fundamental honesty and your own personal responsibility should prevent loose and unwarranted conclusions.

2. *Non sequitur.* The major error in deductive thinking is the "it does not follow" assumption. *Non sequitur* is an inference or conclusion that does not proceed from the premises or materials upon which it is apparently based. This fallacy can be caused by a false major premise and by a minor premise which is only apparently related to the major premise. For example, some good professional writers admit to being poor spellers. Are you justified in concluding that you, too, also a poor speller, are destined to be a good professional writer? These syllogisms illustrate the *non sequitur* flaw in thinking:

All members of X club are conceited.
Frances is not a member of X club.
Therefore, Frances is not conceited.

and

Some members of X club are conceited.
Frances is a member of X club.
Therefore, Frances is conceited.

3. *Post hoc, ergo propter hoc.* This term, a name applied to a variation of *hasty generalization,* means in English "after this, therefore on account of this." It involves a mistake in thinking which holds that a happening which precedes another must naturally or necessarily be its cause or that when one event follows another the latter event is the result of the first. "I have a cold today because I got my feet wet yesterday." "No wonder I had bad luck today; I walked under a ladder yesterday." The Roman Empire fell after the birth and spread of Christianity. Would anyone seriously argue that Christianity *alone* directly *caused* the fall of Rome? Those who do—and many have—make the *post hoc, ergo propter hoc* error in reasoning.

4. *Biased or suppressed evidence.* Facts which furnish ground for belief and which help to prove an assumption or proposition constitute evidence. An obvious and serious flaw in reasoning (and in basic honesty) is selecting evidence from questionable sources or omitting evidence that runs contrary to the point you wish to make. The testimony of dedicated club members is in itself not sufficient to prove that club membership promotes good scholarship or happy social life. What do non-club students think? What do teachers think? Other school authorities? Parents?

Figures and statistics themselves can be made to lie if evidence is biased or suppressed. Many of the so-called truths we hear and read have been prepared by paid propagandists and directly interested individuals or groups. Biased and suppressed evidence has caused everyone to recognize that "figures don't lie, but liars figure."

5. *Distinguishing fact from opinion.* A fact is based on actuality of some sort, a *verifiable* event or statement, whereas opinion is an inference which may be mingled with

a supposed fact. That Farley Mowat was "a Canadian author" is a statement based on actuality which can be positively proved. That Mowat was "the greatest Canadian writer of the twentieth century" is only an opinion of those who hold it. That William Lyon Mackenzie King was Prime Minister from 1935 until Louis St. Laurent took office in 1948 is a fact; that King was our "greatest Prime Minister" is a matter of opinion. A favorite device of many writers and speakers is to mingle opinions with facts and thus obscure the difference between them.

6. *Begging the question.* This flaw in thinking consists of taking a conclusion for granted before it is proved or assuming in the propositions (premises) that which is to be proved in the conclusion. A question such as "Should a vicious man like C. Melvin Jones be allowed to hold office?" is "loaded" because it assumes what needs to be proved.

Common forms of "begging the question" are *slanting, name calling*, and *shifting the meaning of a word.*

Using unfairly suggestive words to create an emotional attitude (as in the application of "vicious" to C. Melvin Jones, above) is a form of slanting. It is also a form of *argumentum ad hominem,* a Latin phrase meaning "argument against the person." That is, it is an argument against the person who may hold an opinion rather than against the opinion itself: "Only an idiot would believe that."

Guard against using or fully believing such suggestive words and phrases as "bigoted," "saintly," "progressive," "reactionary," "undemocratic ideas," "dangerous proposal." Use them if you have supporting evidence; accept them if the proof offered seems valid and thorough. Otherwise, avoid slanting in writing and be on your guard when reading and listening.

Name calling is closely allied to slanting. It appeals to prejudice and emotion rather than to the intellect. It employs "good" words to approve and accept, "bad" words to condemn and reject. In writing and reading, be cautious in using such terms as "wolf in sheep's clothing," "angel in disguise," "rabble rouser," "benefactor," etc.

Shifting the meaning of a word consists of using the same word several times with a shift in meaning designed to confuse the reader or listener. A *conservative* disposed to preserve existing conditions and to agree with gradual rather than abrupt changes is one thing; a *conservative* against all progress, a thorough reactionary and mossback, is another. Student *unions* are one thing; labor *unions* are another.

7. *Evading the issue.* This error in logic is common everywhere but most of all in heated arguments. It consists of ignoring the point under discussion and making a statement that really has no bearing on the argument. If you tell a friend that he drives too fast and he responds that you are a poor driver yourself, he has evaded the issue. He may be right, but he has neither met your objection nor won the argument. (Actually, he has employed the *ad hominem* argument mentioned above.) Such argument is especially common in political campaigns, both those in school and out. It is only too easy to sidestep an issue and launch a counterattack.

8. *Faulty analogy.* Because two objects or ideas are alike in one or more respects, they are not necessarily similar in some further way. Analogy (partial similarity) can be both accurate and effective; otherwise we could not employ either similes or metaphors. But when we use figurative-language analogy, we do not expect such a figure of speech to *prove* anything. In much of our own writing, we *are* trying to be clear and trying either to develop an idea or defend a position.

In the kind of writing most of us do most of the time, an analogy is chiefly useful as an illustration. In many analogies, differences outweigh similarities. "Why do we need pension plans? Do we help trees when they lose their leaves in autumn winds? Do we provide assistance to dogs and horses in their old age? Don't some tribes kill people when they are too old to be useful?" Such false analogy as this is obviously absurd, but even more literal analogies than this can be ridiculous. You may, for example, reason that since the honor system has worked well in several small schools you have attended, it will work equally well in the high school in which you are now a student. Are the similarities between the schools either superficial or less important than the differences? The whipping post was a deterrent to crime in seventeenth-century New England. Is it false analogy to suggest that similar punishment should be inflicted on twentieth-century criminals, dope addicts, "hippies," or "squares"?

9. *Testimonials.* Citing statements from historical personages or well-known contemporaries is not necessarily straight thinking. In an attempt to bolster an argument, we are quick to employ such terms as "authorities have concluded," "Science proves," "Doctors say," "Laboratory tests reveal . . . " Sir John A. Macdonald, Karl Marx, and Friedrich Nietzsche — justly renowned as they are — might not have held economic, social, and political views necessarily valid in the twentieth century. Andrew McNaughton was a great military strategist, but something he said about combustion engines may be less convincing than the words of a good local mechanic. Is an authority in one field an oracle of wisdom about any subject on which he speaks or writes? As a witness for or against an important interscholastic policy, how effective would an eminent surgeon be? A football hero? A TV personality? If you were writing an attack on vaccination, would you reasonably expect the cited opposition of George Bernard Shaw to outweigh the pronouncements of the entire medical profession? Thomas A. Edison was a great inventor, but you would be ill-advised to cite his odd notions about gravity. Henry Ford would not be a wise choice for you to quote in some argument about history.

But even where there is little question of the validity of authority, be careful, as has been suggested, to see that neither bias nor the time element weakens your presentation. Some businessmen and labor leaders are experts on economic problems, but their particular interests might prevent their having the impartiality, the objectivity, of a disinterested observer, such as a professor of economics. And even a professor might be biased in favor of some specific school of economic thought.

As for timing, remember that in many fields of human activity and knowledge, authorities soon become obsolete. Charles Darwin no longer has the last word on evolution; Sigmund Freud is not universally considered the final authority in psychoanalysis.

In conclusion, logic may be called the rule by which we

evaluate the statements and arguments of others, particularly when our skeptical minds and common sense have already made us suspicious. Logic should also be the rule by which we measure our own thinking in order that it will produce the effects we wish. Actually, if we do think soundly, we always approximate the processes of logic. It requires only small effort to convert unconscious thinking or common sense to conscious reasoning. This effort, small though it be, is perhaps the most important one any student can make in any school.

EXERCISE 1

In your own compositions, those of your classmates, and newspaper articles, try to locate statements which can be criticized according to the following list of suggestions prepared by Professor Macklin Thomas of Chicago State College:

1. The statement needs qualification; it is too sweeping or dogmatic. (This comment refers to assertions which are *not* altogether false or irresponsible but simply cover too much ground too positively and need to be guarded with a limiting phrase or clause specifying the degree of certainty warranted, taking account of possible exceptions, or confining the generalization to what the writer is reasonably sure of.)
2. The facts cited are not such as are likely to be accepted on the writer's bare assertion. He should supply informally in the current of his development some authority, occupational experience, or other reason why he should be believed.
3. The writer's argument is good so far as it goes, but it is unconvincing because he has failed to dispose of some obvious and overriding argument that can be made on the other side. His case is strengthened when he evaluates his own argument and shows that he has disposed of possible alternatives.
4. The evidence supplied is pertinent but falls far short of proof. One good reason does not build a case.
5. There is such a thing as being too specific, if the writer does not make clear what generalization is supported by the instances given. A well-developed train of thought works back and forth between the general and the specific, showing the connections and applications intended at each point.
6. The writer's treatment here is obviously marked by particular bias and prior emotional commitment. This does not neces-

sarily make his conclusions false, but it does make them all suspect.

7. The writer's approach here is essentially moralistic and directive rather than analytical. No law exists against preaching, but one should distinguish preaching from investigation, analysis, and reasoning.

8. Here the writer is exploring religious or philosophical questions which have been canvassed for thousands of years by serious thinkers without being brought to an issue. He of course has a right to try his hand at them, but he shouldn't expect an easy success and must remember that no certain conclusions are possible when the assumptions with which he starts out are untestable.

EXERCISE 2

On a separate sheet of paper identify the logical fallacy in each of the following statements, using these letters: A: hasty generalization; B: *non sequitur;* C: *post hoc, ergo propter hoc;* D: biased or suppressed evidence; E: fact from opinion; F: begging the question; G: evading the issue; H: faulty analogy; I: testimonials.

1. In reply to Mr. Marsh's claim that his administration is prepared to help the poor, I wish to point out that he has never been hungry in his entire life, that he has inherited a vast fortune, and that his children attend exclusive private schools.

2. Courses in marriage and the family cannot prepare men and women for marriage. To try to educate them for marriage is like trying to teach them to swim without letting them go into the water. It just can't be done!

3. "Chuck Steak—star of stage, screen, and television—says, 'I smoke Summit cigarettes. They contain a balanced mixture of carbon and hydro-syntheme.'"

4. Oliver Wendell Holmes, Jr., the Supreme Court Justice, was a greater American than his father, the poet, essayist, and doctor.

5. Ladies and gentlemen of the jury, the prosecution is prepared to prove to you that this wretched murderer who sits before you is guilty as charged.

6. There are three Norwegians in my math class. They invariably get the highest scores on exams. Obviously, Norwegians are mathematically inclined.

7. Lazy students often flunk out of school. My neighbor is one of the laziest students I have ever met. Therefore, he is flunking because of his laziness.

8. Uncle Charlie suffered from rheumatism all last summer. His illness disappeared, however, when he began drinking German beer. Therefore, we are all convinced that German beer is a remedy for rheumatism.

9. Dissecting animals is an evil, wicked practice. How would you like it if someone snipped off your arm, leg, or finger?

10. I refuse to vote for a divorced man, for how could John Wilbur, a home wrecker, be trusted to lead this nation?

EXERCISE 3

In a biography entitled *Napoleon,* Emil Ludwig shows how Paris newspapers changed their tunes from the time the deposed emperor escaped from the island of Elba on March 1, 1815, until he arrived in Paris three weeks later. Write a composition of 300-400 words as a commentary on this kind of name calling and on the weaknesses of human nature thus exhibited:

* The monster has escaped from his place of exile.
* The Corsican werewolf has landed at Cannes.
* The tiger appeared at Gap, troops were sent against him, the wretched adventurer ended his career in the mountains.
* The fiend has actually, thanks to treachery, been able to get as far as Grenoble.
* The tyrant has reached Lyons, where horror paralyzed all attempts at resistance.
* The usurper has dared to advance within a hundred and fifty miles of the capital.
* Bonaparte moves northward with rapid strides, but he will never reach Paris.
* Tomorrow Napoleon will be at our gates.
* His Majesty is at Fontainebleau.
* The Emperor has reassumed his imperial duties in Paris.

EXERCISE 4

Without paying much attention to exact names for the flaws in thinking involved, comment on and explain errors in the following sentences:

1. Today's society has changed considerably in the past century.

2. A good student is always working ahead and preparing himself in advance.

3. The interior of the car showed that it had been driven many miles.

4. Teaching me good English makes about as much sense as teaching a cat to fight an elephant.

5. In commenting on the fire, the Chief explained that Mr. Smithers, in whose apartment the blaze had started, had a habit of smoking in bed.

6. The folder mentions how many people this medicine has helped. I am going to get some.

7. He is an attractive person and has many friends; therefore, he deserves your vote as class president.

8. Because some people choose to read obscene books and go to sexy movies, all books and movies should be censored to protect the public.

9. The way to prevent war is to be fully prepared for war.

10. Students who do more work than is assigned make it hard for the rest of us to get good grades. If it weren't for such people, I'd be getting an A instead of a D.

107. USING A DICTIONARY

To speak and write competently, everyone needs as a guide a reliable dictionary. No speaker or writer of English knows all the words in the language. Often or occasionally, every user of language needs help with the meaning, spelling, pronunciation, and specific use of a particular word.

If you have not done so yet, make the acquaintance of your dictionary *now*. Better still, make it your friend and constant companion.

The following dictionaries are highly recommended:

The American College Dictionary (New York: Random House)

Funk & Wagnalls Standard College Dictionary (New York: Funk & Wagnalls; Text edition, Harcourt, Brace & World)

The Random House Dictionary of the English Language, College Edition (New York: Random House)

Thorndike-Barnhart Comprehensive Dictionary (Chicago: Scott, Foresman & Company)

Webster's Seventh New Collegiate Dictionary (Springfield, Massachusetts: G. & C. Merriam Company)

Webster's New World Dictionary of the American Language (Cleveland: World Publishing Company)

Any one of these six dictionaries would represent an excellent investment in a practical, constantly useful, and reliable aid in speaking and writing.

Excellent larger dictionaries are available also. Each of them contains at least three times as much information as those listed above. Entries are not only more numerous but are frequently more detailed and often provide finer shades of meaning. Such dictionaries are called "unabridged" because they are not cut-down, like "abridged" versions. However, unabridged dictionaries are more expensive than the works suggested above, are usually more awkward to handle, and are difficult to carry around. Such sizable and valuable dictionaries are often placed in classrooms, in school libraries, and in teachers' offices and staffrooms. The best known and most available of the unabridged dictionaries are:

Funk & Wagnalls' New Standard Dictionary of the English Language (New York: Funk & Wagnalls)

New English (Oxford) Dictionary (New York: Oxford University Press. *The Shorter Oxford Dictionary* appears in both one- or two-volume editions; the larger work is in twelve volumes and a supplement.)

The Random House Dictionary of the English Language (New York: Random House)

Webster's Third New International Dictionary (Springfield, Massachusetts: G. & C. Merriam Company)

107a. LEARN HOW TO USE AND INTERPRET A DICTIONARY.

Many persons consult a dictionary to find the spelling or meaning or pronunciation of a word, or all three of these bits of information, but using it for no more than this is to ignore many other kinds of valuable and useful material that it provides.

Dictionaries differ somewhat in their presentation of material. If you have never done so before, examine your dictionary carefully and critically. Read its table of contents; examine the material given on the inside of front and back covers. Read, or at least skim, some of the prefatory pages as well as supplementary material at the back. After you have done this, you should read carefully and attentively articles headed "General Introduction," "Guide to the Use of This Dictionary," "Guide to Pronunciation," "Etymology Key," "Explanatory Notes," "Symbols and Abbreviations Used." Your dictionary may not have sections entitled precisely thus, but it will contain equivalent material. You really cannot use your dictionary with full effectiveness until you are acquainted with its plan and method of presentation.

Although dictionaries differ in methods of listing entries and citing information, all reliable dictionaries have a common purpose: they report on the way language currently is used and, occasionally, on how it has been used in the past. The skilled persons who make dictionaries, called lexicographers, do not themselves decide what words mean or even how they should be spelled and pronounced. A good dictionary is the product of careful study and research, a report on what is known as *standard English*, that is, the practice of those socially accepted and relatively well educated people who may be said to carry on the important affairs of English-speaking persons.

A dictionary is not an "authority" in any exact meaning of the word. Nor, as is pointed out in Section 114, does it even pretend to be. It does not dictate or prescribe except in the sense that it records and usually interprets the status of English words and phrases. It indicates what is general language practice; only in this way can it be said to constitute authority. When you have a specific problem about usage, apply in your own writing and speaking the information recorded and interpreted in your dictionary. But do not think of your dictionary as a final arbiter of what is right and what is wrong. To do so is to act as illogically as to say "That must be right, I saw it in print."

107b. MASTER THE VARIETY OF INFORMATION GIVEN FOR WORD ENTRIES.

As an attentive reader, writer, and speaker you should actually *study* each word you look up. Take your time. It requires only a moment to learn the spelling, pronunciation, or one meaning of a word. But hasty examination will prevent your mastering the word and making it a part of your active vocabulary, will thwart any hope of your greeting the word as a familiar friend when next you meet it in an unfamiliar context. Time spent in learning words thoroughly will save time, errors, and annoyance later.

For any word listed in an adequate dictionary, each of the first five of the following items is given. For many words, some of the next five kinds of information are provided:

1. Spelling
2. Syllabication
3. Pronunciation
4. Part(s) of speech
5. Meaning(s)

6. Level(s) of meaning
7. Derivation (origin)
8. Synonyms
9. Antonyms
10. Other information

abridge \ə-'brij\ *vt* ME *abregen,* fr. MF *abregier,* fr. LL *abbreviare,* fr. L *ad-* + *brevis* short - more at BRIEF **1 a** *archaic* : DEPRIVE **b** : DIMINISH, CURTAIL **2** : to shorten in duration of extent **3** : to shorten by omission of words without sacrifice of sense : CONDENSE syn see SHORTEN - **abridg·er** *n*
abridg·ment *or* **abridge·ment** \ə-brij-mənt\ *n* **1 a** : the action of abridging **b** : the state of being abridged **2** : a shortened form of a work retaining the general sense and unity of the original
syn ABRIDGMENT, ABSTRACT, SYNOPSIS, CONSPECTUS, EPITOME mean a condensed treatment. ABRIDGMENT suggests a reduction in compass with retention of relative completeness; ABSTRACT applies to a summary of points of a treatise, document, or proposed treatment and usu. has no independent worth; SYNOPSIS implies a skeletal presentation of an argument or a narrative suitable for rapid examination; CONSPECTUS implies a quick overall view of a large detailed subject; EPITOME suggests the briefest possible presentation of a complex whole that still has independent value

By permission. From *Webster's Seventh New Collegiate Dictionary,* copyright 1965 by G. & C. Merriam Company, Publishers of the Merriam-Webster Dictionaries.

1. *Spelling.* The basic or "entry" word is ordinarily given in black (boldface) type. Associated with the main entry may be other words in black type indicating run-on entries (endings such as *er, like* may be added—*begin, beginner; clerk, clerklike)* and alternative entries of variant forms *(Bern,*

Berne; diagram, -gramed, -graming or *-grammed, -gram-ming).* Note especially that:

a. The plurals of nouns are given if a noun forms its plural other than by adding *s* or *es.*

b. The comparative and superlative degrees of adjectives and adverbs are given if a spelling change is made in the addition of *er, est.*

c. The past tense, past participle, and present participle of verbs are given if these forms differ from the present-tense form or if the spelling changes in the addition of an ending.

d. Many compound words spelled with a hyphen or as one word or as two words are so indicated.

When a word has two or more spellings, the preferred spelling form is usually given first. Sometimes the variant spelling is also placed separately as a vocabulary entry.

The spelling of proper names (people, places, etc.) is given either in the regular place in the alphabetical listing or in a special section or sections at the back of the dictionary, depending upon the dictionary.

2. *Syllabication.* Learn to distinguish between the light mark or dot (·) used to separate syllables (ri·dic·u·lous — so labeled in the dictionary but in use written solid) and the hyphen (-) used to show that the word is a compound *(hard-fisted).* All reliable dictionaries use the dot system of indicating syllabication; some substitute for the dot in the vocabulary entry an accent mark after the stressed syllable.

Knowledge of syllabication is important in two ways: it helps in the pronunciation of words, which in turn helps in correct spelling, and it shows where to divide words, between syllables, if division is necessary at ends of lines (Section 28).

3. *Pronunciation.* Pronunciation is based upon accent or emphasized syllables and upon the sound given to alphabetical letters or letter combinations.

Both accent marks and syllabication dots are included in the entry word by some dictionaries; other dictionaries carry only the syllabication dots in the entry word and include the accent marks in the "pronunciation" word.

Learn to distinguish the accent marks: primary or heavy stress is shown by a heavy mark (′) and secondary or less heavy stress by a light (′) or double (″) mark: *com′pass′*, *com′pass″*, *dif′fer′*, *dif′fer″*; *spell′ing′*, *spell′ing″*; *pro′ nounce′*, *pro″nounce′*.

Pronunciation of sounds is more complicated than accent. The fact that 26 alphabetical letters are used in 250 common spellings of sounds is evidence that you need considerable help. Linguists have successfully developed systems whereby 40 to 60 symbols, depending upon the dictionary, are adequate to solve most pronunciation problems. The common method is the use of a "pronunciation" word which is usually found in parentheses just after the entry word. It is a respelling of the word, giving the sounds of vowels and consonants by syllables and according to the pronouncing key which the dictionary has adopted. Familiarize yourself with this pronouncing key in your dictionary; it may be included at the bottom of each page or alternate pages, or it may be inside the front or back cover or both.

Learn to interpret diacritical marks. These marks (¨) placed over the second of two consecutive vowels are used when each vowel is pronounced separately. As a variant method hyphens may be used instead. Examples: *naïve*, *reënforce* or *re-enforce*, *preëminence* or *pre-eminence*. As such words become common, diacritical marks or the hyphen may be left out, as in *preeminence*.

For foreign words or those newly adopted from a foreign language, your dictionary may include a separate "foreign sounds" key.

Generally, when two or more pronunciations of a word are included, the one more commonly used is given first. A variant pronunciation may occasionally be labelled *British* or *Chiefly British, Brit.* or *Chiefly Brit.*, to show that this pronunciation is the common one in Great Britain.

4. *Part(s) of speech.* Since all English words are "parts of speech," the part of speech of every entry is generally given. If the word is used as more than one part of speech, such information is provided, with the particular meaning or meanings under each explained. Also shown are the singular or plural forms of many nouns, the comparative and superlative degrees of many adjectives and adverbs, and the correct use of verbs as transitive, or intransitive, or both.

Study the following excerpt:

sweet (swēt), *adj.* 1. pleasing to the taste, esp., having the pleasant taste or flavor characteristic of sugar, honey, etc. 2. not rancid, or stale; fresh. 3. fresh as opposed to salt, as water. 4. pleasing to the ear; making a pleasant or agreeable sound; musical; 5. pleasing to the smell; fragrant; perfumed. 6. pleasing or agreeable; yielding pleasure or enjoyment; delightful. 7. pleasant in disposition or manners; amiable; kind or gracious, as a person, action, etc. 8. dear; beloved; precious. 9. easily managed; done or effected without effort. 10. (of wine) sweet-tasting (opposed to dry). 11. free from sourness or acidity, as soil. 12. *Chem.* a. devoid of corrosive or acidic substances. b. (of substances such as gasoline) containing no sulphur compounds. 13. *Jazz.* in a straight or sentimental style (contrasted with the hot or improvisatory style of performance). —*adv.* 14. in a sweet manner; sweetly. —*n.* 15. sweet taste or flavor; sweet smell; sweetness. 16. that which is sweet. 17. *Chiefly Brit.* candy; a sweetmeat or bonbon. 18. *Brit.* a sweet dish, as a pudding or tart. 19. something pleasant to the mind or feelings. 20. a beloved person; darling; sweetheart. [ME and OE *swēte,* c. D *zoet,* G *süss,* Icel. *saetr.,* akin to Goth. *sūts,* L *suāvis*] sweet′ly, *adv.*—sweet′ness, *n.*—Syn. 1. sugary, honeyed. 4. melodious, mellifluous, harmonious. 7. winning, lovable, charming.

Sweet (swēt), *n.* Henry, 1845-1912, British philologist and linguist.

sweet alyssum, a cruciferous garden plant, *Lobularia maritima,* with small white or violet flowers.

sweet basil, a plant of the mint family, *Ocimum Basilicum,* whose leaves are used in cookery.

sweet bay, 1. the bay, or European laurel. 2. an American magnolia, *Magnolia virginiana,* with fragrant, white, globular flowers, common on the Atlantic coast.

sweet·bread (swēt′ brĕd′), *n.* 1. the pancreas (stomach sweetbread) of an animal, esp. a calf or a lamb, used for food. 2. the thymus gland (neck sweetbread or throat sweetbread), likewise so used.

sweet·bri·er (swēt′ brī′ ər), *n.* a rose, *Rosa Eglanteria,* a native of Europe and central Asia, with a tall stem, stout, hooked prickles often mixed with bristles, and single pink flowers; the eglantine. Also, sweet′ bri′ ar.

This reprint from the ACD (*American College Dictionary*) provides substantial information about *sweet* as an adjective, adverb, and noun. Additional entries reveal how the word *sweet* appears in other words and word combinations. If you were to keep reading, you would come across entries for *sweet cicely, sweet cider, sweet clover, sweet corn, sweeten, sweetening, sweet fern, sweet flag, sweet gale, sweet gum, sweetheart, sweetie, sweeting, sweetish, sweet marjoram, sweetmeat, sweet oil, sweet pea, sweet pepper, sweet potato, sweet shop, sweetsop, sweet spirit of niter, sweet-tempered, sweet tooth,* and *sweet william.* Such a collection of word entries should indicate the vast amount of information which a good dictionary provides not only about parts of speech but other important matters as well.

Teach yourself the more common abbreviations from the table of abbreviations or elsewhere in your dictionary: *act.* for *active, adj.* for *adjective, adv.* for *adverb, art.* for *article, auxil.* for *auxiliary, compar.* for *comparative, conj.* for *conjunction,* **def.** for *definite, fem.* for *feminine, fut.* for *future, indef.* for *indefinite, indic.* for *indicative, inf.* for *infinitive, intens.* for *intensive, interj.* for *interjection, masc.* for *masculine, n.* for *noun, neut.* for *neuter, nom.* for *nominative, obj.* for *objective, part.* for *participle, pass.* for *passive, perf.* for *perfect, pers.* for *person* or *personal, pl.* for *plural, poss.* for *possessive, pp.* for *past participle, pred.* for *predicate, prep.* for *preposition, pres.* for *present, prin. pts.* for *principal parts, pron.* for *pronoun, refl.* for *reflexive, rel.* for *relative, sing.* for *singular, subj.* for *subjunctive, superl.* for *superlative, v.* for *verb, v. i.* for *verb intransitive, v. imp.* for *verb impersonal, v. t.* for *verb transitive.*

This list is a reminder that some knowledge of grammar and grammatical terms is necessary for intelligent and successful use of the dictionary (see sections on "Grammar," especially Section 10).

5. *Meanings.* Words may have one or more of the following meanings: a traditional meaning, a historical meaning, a figurative meaning, a special meaning, or a new meaning. Note the various definitions giving both usual and specialized meanings. Learn the method used in the order of definitions—for example, by parts of speech, by historical development of meanings, by frequency of occurrence, or by general to specialized meanings. Master, too, the significance of definitions preceded by Arabic numbers (1, 2, 3, etc.) or by letters of the alphabet (a, b, c, etc.). Note the method of entry for capitalized and small-letter words, for words known as homographs and homonyms, and for words having a superficial resemblance. Although all these may have similar spellings, or pronunciations, their meanings are quite different. Place the meaning of the word into the context of your encounter with it in reading and listening.

Hyphenated words and two or more words forming phrases which have idiomatic, specialized, or figurative meaning are explained in the regular alphabetical listing, either entered separately or put under the main word. Abbreviations and foreign words or phrases are in most dictionaries included in their alphabetical position.

6. *Level(s) of meaning.* Entry in a dictionary is not a guarantee that a word is in good use or that its special meanings are suitable in current English. Your dictionary enables you to weigh the appropriateness of a word by the absence or presence of a "restrictive label." Some words have no labels, and others have labels for certain meanings or for use as a certain part of speech. Any word not given a restrictive label is acceptable in formal and informal English. Any word labeled "colloquial" is usually suitable in *all* informal speech and writing. All other labels are guides to special appropriateness of word use.

Four classifications of restrictive labels are common:

a. *Geographical,* indicating a country or region of a country where the word is in general use: *Chiefly U.S., British, Scotch, New England, Southwest, Western U.S., dialect,* etc. The necessity for geographical labels is not surprising in view of the fact that 300,000,000 people in various parts of the world share English as their native language and that even more people use it as a second language.

b. *Time,* indicating that the word is no longer used, or is disappearing from use, or is still used but has a quaint form or meaning: *obsolete, obsolescent, archaic.* However, words with these labels are no longer common, and when words are no longer used, dictionaries seldom record them. Words having no time label are in current use.

c. *Subject,* showing that a specialized word or word meaning belongs to a limited area of knowledge such as science, technology, craft, sport, and the like. As many as 100 of these labels are used, including astronomy, biology, electrical engineering, architecture, dentistry, painting, football.

d. *Cultural,* indicating whether the word or a special meaning is substandard or suitable as informal English: *illiterate, slang, dialect* (which may be geographical also), *colloquial, poetic, literary.* Absence of any such label signifies that the word is acceptable in formal and informal writing and speaking.

NOTE: There is no Supreme Court in language to which a final appeal can be made. Lexicographers can only use their best judgment in collecting and interpreting data on language. Dictionaries may therefore differ in the labels they give to certain words or certain meanings. For example, the same word in several dictionaries may carry the label "obsolete," "archaic," "dialect," or even no qualifying label whatever.

Some dictionaries carry brief comments on levels of meaning and the usage problems involved. Here, for example, is such an entry:

> ◄ **like, as, as if**   In formal American English, *like* is not considered acceptable as a conjunction (that is, when followed by a clause containing a verb), although this use has been defended or permitted by some grammarians. The preferred forms are: a *As* to introduce factual clauses of comparison: He sings *as* (not *like*) Caruso sang. b *As if* with the subjunctive to introduce contrary-to-fact clauses: He sings *as if* (not *like*) he were Caruso. c *As if* with the indicative in noncomparative factual clauses: It looks *as if* (not *like*) he means to stay. When no verb is expressed, however, *like* functions in its accepted role as a preposition: He sings *like* Caruso. *Like* is acceptable in place of *as if* when followed by a short verbless expression: It looks *like* new.

Quoted by permission. From *Funk & Wagnalls Standard College Dictionary*. Copyright 1963 by Funk & Wagnalls Company, Inc.

7. *Origin.* The origin of a word—in linguistics, its etymology—may be twofold: (a) less commonly, a narrative account of how a word was formed or was given its meaning (see in your dictionary, for example, *derrick, burke, macadam, radar*), or (b) whenever known, the ancestral or foreign languages through or from which the word evolved to its English form. Old English, Latin, Greek, German, and French have heavily contributed, but several other languages have had a part: Italian, Spanish, Scandinavian, etc.

Such derivations, generally entered between brackets, may come near the beginning or at the end of the vocabulary entry. They help to fix the meaning and spelling of words in your mind. Learn the more common abbreviations with which your dictionary indicates them: *OE (Old English), L.*

(Latin), Gk. (Greek), Sp. (Spanish), etc. Learn also the space-saving short cuts: *b. (blended of); f. (formed from); t. (taken from); < (derived from);* etc. A table or tables of such abbreviations is contained in every dictionary.

8. *Synonyms.* Words that in one or more of their definitions have the same or similar meanings as other words are called synonyms. Make a study of synonyms; often these approximate equivalents have significant differences in meaning which enable you to choose exact and emphatic words (see Sections 47, 54). So important is this study that whole books have been compiled for the benefit of writers and speakers, such as *Webster's Dictionary of Synonyms, Crabb's English Synonyms,* and *Roget's International Thesaurus of English Words.*

Dictionaries include the listings and often brief discussions of hundreds of synonyms, indicating differences in meaning of apparently similar words and signifying by a number which usage is part of synonymous meaning.

9. *Antonyms.* Antonyms are pairs of words that have opposite or negative meanings: *man — woman, man — boy, man — beast, man — God, holy — unholy,* etc. These opposite meanings are not all-inclusive: a word may be an antonym of another only in a certain restricted meaning. One antonym of *man* concerns sex; another, age; another, biology; another, religion. Dictionaries suggest antonyms for many words.

10. *Other information.* Other information which may be carried as part of an entry or as separate entries in the main part of your dictionary includes abbreviations; biographical names; capitalized words and words spelled with both capitals and small letters; cross references to words listed elsewhere; examples of word use in phrases and sentences; foreign words and phrases (usually labeled as such or given a special symbol); geographical names; homographs and homonyms (the former, words spelled alike but having different meanings, and the latter, words spelled differently but pronounced alike); meaning of idiomatic phrases; prefixes, suffixes, and other combining word-elements; and, for some words, graphic or pictorial illustrations.

As an instance of the wealth of material contained in every good dictionary, assume that you need to refer to the entry for the word *look*. Having mastered the main entry, let your eye wander on; here is some, and only some, of what you might find later along:

it looks like. 1. it seems that there will be. 2. [Colloq.] it seems as if.

look after, to take care of; watch over.

look alive [Colloq.], to be alert; act or move quickly: usually in the imperative.

look back, to recall the past; recollect.

look daggers, to look with anger; glare.

look down on (or upon), 1. to regard as an inferior. 2. to regard with contempt; despise.

look for, 1. to search or hunt for. 2. to expect; anticipate.

look forward to, to anticipate, especially eagerly.

look in (on), to pay a brief visit (to).

look into, to examine carefully; investigate.

look on, 1. to be an observer or spectator. 2. to consider; regard.

look oneself, to seem in normal health, spirits, etc.

look out, to be on the watch; be careful.

look over, to examine; inspect.

look to, 1. to take care of; give attention to. 2. to rely upon; resort to. 3. to look forward to; expect.

look up, 1. to search for in a book of reference, etc. 2. [Colloq.] to pay a visit to; call on. 3. [Colloq.] to get better; improve.

look up and down, 1. to search everywhere. 2. to examine with an appraising eye; scrutinize.

look up to, to regard with great respect; admire.

SYN.—**look** is the general term meaning to direct the eyes in order to see (don't *look* now); **gaze** implies a looking intently and steadily, as in wonder, delight, or interest (to *gaze* at the stars); to **stare** is to look fixedly with wide-open eyes, as in surprise, curiosity, abstraction, etc. (it is rude to *stare* at people); to **gape** is to stare with the mouth open in ignorant or naive wonder or curiosity (the child stood *gaping* at the elephant); to **glare** is to stare fiercely or angrily (he *glared* at her for talking); to **peek** is to take a quick, furtive look, as through a hole or from behind a barrier, at something not supposed to be seen; to **peer** is to look searchingly with the eyes narrowed (she *peered* down the well). See also **appearance**.

From *Webster's New World Dictionary of the American Language*. College Edition. Copyright 1964 by the World Publishing Company.

In addition to the wealth of information included under each vocabulary entry, good dictionaries offer other materials in the front or back pages. Familiarize yourself with this material. Besides a discussion of spelling (orthography), pronunciation, usage levels, etc., sections may give guidance on punctuation, grammar, letter writing, proofreading, and rhyming; a list of colleges and universities; and other helpful and interesting information.

107c. USE A DICTIONARY TO IMPROVE AND INCREASE YOUR VOCABULARY.

The kind and number of English words you know and are able to use and understand will be important throughout your life. As is pointed out in Section 40, building and using a vocabulary is a lengthy process which requires years and, indeed, is never completed. But you can make genuine and even rapid progress in vocabulary growth through intelligent use of a good dictionary. Study of this never-failing companion and tool can helpfully supplement the growth in vocabulary which you can also accomplish through listening to good speakers in person and on television and radio and through careful reading of proficient writers.

EXERCISE 5

Read carefully every word on *one* page of your dictionary. Write a paper of 300-400 words mentioning and developing three or four of the interesting items you have found.

EXERCISE 6

What restrictive label, if any, is attached in your dictionary to each of the following words?

baloney, benison, boughten, caboose, cocky, colleen, dight, disremember, dogie, eld, jiffy, larrup, lulu, mavourneen, nohow, nubbin, pectin, pesky, renege, sashay.

EXERCISE 7

What is the total number of meanings listed in your dictionary for each of the following words?

about, appeal, belt, direct, field, fix, free, give, go, it, place, play, point, protest, set, spring, stay, strike, walk, work.

Prepare for class an oral or written discussion of *one* of these words; develop your report around these questions: Which meanings are the most common? Which meanings seem most unusual? What idiomatic phrases does the word appear in? To how many parts of speech does it belong?

EXERCISE 8

Give the derivation (origin) of these words:

agnostic, agriculture, April, bazooka, biped, boondoggle, cape, Christian, football, magenta, marathon, meander, microscope, nicotine, pastor, policeman, professor, sadism, Thursday, traitor.

EXERCISE 9

With the aid of your dictionary, list three or more synonyms for each of the following:

bad, building, defend, enthusiasm, faithful, greedy, heavy, play, strength.

(If your dictionary does not carry a list of synonyms for each of these words, ask your teacher about other source-books you can use.)

EXERCISE 10

List one or more antonyms for each of the following:

chaotic, fabulous, fair, free, huge, lean, obscure, pleasant, refined, slow.

(See the note about consulting your teacher in Exercise 9.)

EXERCISE 11

When the following words begin with a capital letter, they mean one thing; when they begin with a small letter, they mean another. For each of the following, distinguish both meanings:

chinook, derby, husky, polish, revere, sac, scotch, seine, utopia, warren.

EXERCISE 12

With the aid of your dictionary, answer the following questions:

A. *Bomb* may be used as what parts of speech?
B. What is the meaning of *S.P.Q.R.?*
C. Can *cabbage* be used as a verb?
D. What is the meaning of the phrase *in status quo?*
E. What was O. Henry's real name?
F. Can *how* be a noun?

G. Can *dieing* ever be a correct spelling?

H. Where was ancient Ilium?

I. What is minestrone?

J. What is the meaning of the mathematical symbol $<$?

108. USING A LIBRARY

The word "library" comes from the Latin *liber*, meaning "book." The heart of any library, great or small, is its collection of books and bound magazines, but a library is more than merely a static collection of volumes. Any library is a depository, a treasury of the written word and the dynamic, graphic portrayal of thought preserved in print, pictures, and manuscript.

If you are a normally alert and curious person who wishes to become better informed about one or a thousand different subjects, the library should be the first stop in your quest for knowledge. It may not be the last or only stop, but millions of library users and book lovers insist that no other source can provide greater riches. Learning to use a library intelligently can lead to a less monotonous, more exciting, far richer life for everyone. Libraries are truly a symbol of civilization. Thanks to them, we can stand on the shoulders of giant thinkers of the past and present.

One primary reason for attending school, according to many students, is to make friends. If you will learn to use them sensibly and resourcefully, the best and longest-lasting friends you or anyone else is ever likely to make in school are the library and a good dictionary. (See Section 107.) Both library and dictionary are open doors to an enormous amount of personal satisfaction while you are in school and all through later life.

But the resources and genuine pleasures of neither a library nor a dictionary can be yours until you learn how to use them intelligently, sensibly, and without waste of time and motion. Libraries differ greatly in actual content and physical arrangement, yet the basic principles which determine library organization have been sufficiently standardized to enable you to use *any* library intelligently provided you understand the following:

1. The physical arrangement of a library
2. The card catalog and its uses
3. The uses of periodical indexes
4. Reference books and their resources

108a. PHYSICAL ARRANGEMENT.

Before losing time through a trial-and-error method of discovering the resources of the school or public library you use, devote a free hour (or several of them) to a tour of its physical arrangement. Your use of a library, any library, will be far more efficient if you know the location of the main items you may wish to use. Furthermore, a tour of the library will uncover exciting stores of information which you may wish to investigate later.

Examine the main reading room, reserved-book room, study alcoves, reference section, and periodical room. Your particular library may not be arranged to include such divisions, but it will have an equivalent organization, on either a smaller or larger scale. You should find out where the desk is located at which books are charged out for home or classroom use, where the card catalog is located, where current magazines and newspapers are filed or racked. Books of fiction (novels and stories) are arranged in most libraries in sections to themselves, shelved alphabetically by authors; find out if your library employs this system. Stroll in the room or section where reference books are located and discover the kind and location of books there. In short, "case the joint" thoroughly. Doing so will save time, trouble, annoyance, and disappointment for you, your teacher, and the library staff.

A large school or public library may have available a guide, handbook, or pamphlet which explains and interprets the organization of the library and which sets forth regulations for its use. If so, examine this publication carefully. In addition, both your teacher and the librarian of the library you frequent will be equipped and eager to answer any reasonable questions you may have about the physical arrangements of the library and the most efficient means of using its resources.

108b. THE CARD CATALOG.

A large library contains a vast amount of material of varied kinds. Even a small library has a wealth of resources which will bewilder one unaccustomed to them. The key which will open this treasure (or at least its collection of books and bound magazines) is the card catalog. (The word may be spelled "catalog" or "catalogue," but the former is preferred by most professional librarians and library associations and is also shorter.)

This index to a library consists of 3-by-5 cards filed alphabetically in long trays or drawers and located in a series of filing cabinets. Book information may be found in a card catalog in three ways: (1) by author, (2) by title, (3) by subject.

In most libraries, every nonfiction book is represented by at least three cards, identical except that certain lines giving subject headings and joint author may be typed across the top. If you know the author or the title of a book, you will most easily get needed information from an author or title card. If you know the name of neither, consult the subject cards for books dealing with the subject about which you are seeking information.

In addition to unlocking the resources of a library, the card catalog provides the call number by means of which each book is located on the shelves. Many libraries are arranged so that all (or some) of its books are placed on open shelves easily accessible to readers. If this is the system used in your library, then the call number will help you quickly locate the volume you are seeking. In other libraries, the main collection of books is shelved in closed stacks; in order to get a book, you must fill out a "call slip" furnished by the library and present it at the Circulation or Loan desk. A copy of the book you wish will be located by a library worker through the use of its call number and then made available to you.

In every library, books are arranged according to a definite

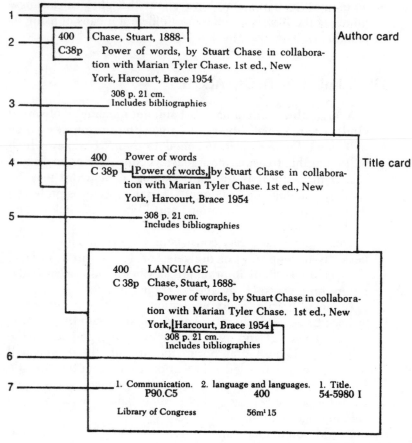

Author card

| 400 | Chase, Stuart, 1888- |
| C38p | Power of words, by Stuart Chase in collaboration with Marian Tyler Chase. 1st ed., New York, Harcourt, Brace 1954 |

308 p. 21 cm.
Includes bibliographies

Title card

| 400 | Power of words |
| C 38p | Power of words, by Stuart Chase in collaboration with Marian Tyler Chase. 1st ed., New York, Harcourt, Brace 1954 |

308 p. 21 cm.
Includes bibliographies

400	LANGUAGE
C 38p	Chase, Stuart, 1688-
	Power of words, by Stuart Chase in collaboration with Marian Tyler Chase. 1st ed., New York, Harcourt, Brace 1954

308 p. 21 cm.
Includes bibliographies

1. Communication. 2. language and languages. 1. Title.
        P90.C5   400   54-5980 I

Library of Congress   56m¹ 15

Subject card

1. Author and date of his birth
2. Call number
3. A bibliography is included
4. Title
5. Number of pages
6. Publisher and date of publication
7. Other headings under which the book is listed

system, the notational expression of which is the first part of the call number. The two classification systems most commonly used in the United States are the Dewey Decimal Classification and the Library of Congress Classification. The former, named for its developer, Melvil Dewey, an American librarian, is more often found in high school libraries than the latter, but some knowledge of each is helpful because you may find occasion to study in different libraries at different times.

In the Dewey Decimal system, fields of knowledge are arranged in ten groups, including one group for reference or general books. Each major class and each subclass is represented by a three-digit number. Further subdivisions are indicated by numbers actually following a decimal point. On a separate line beneath the Dewey number will be found the author and book number. Books are classified in the Dewey Decimal system as follows:

000-099   General works (encyclopedias, periodicals, etc.)

100-199   Philosophy (psychology, etc.)

200-299   Religion (mythology)

300-399   Social sciences (economics, government, etc.)

400-499   Language (linguistics, dictionaries, etc.)

500-599   Pure science (mathematics, chemistry, etc.)

600-699   Applied science (engineering, aviation, etc.)

700-799   Arts and recreation (painting, music, etc.)

800-899   Literature (poetry, plays, etc.)

900-999   History (Travel, 910-919; Biography, 920-929)

In the Dewey Decimal system, every book has its individual call number. An illustration: Canadian literature has the subclassification 819. An edition of E. J. Pratt's *Collected Poems* has the call number 819.12 and beneath this the author and book number, P668. The 819.12 is the Dewey Decimal classification; the P668 is the author and book number: *P* is the first letter of the author's name, and 668 the book number. With this explanation in mind, you can see now why the Stuart Chase title noted on p 490 has the call number it does.

The Library of Congress Classification uses letters of the alphabet followed by other letters or by Arabic numerals.

Its main classes are:

A. General works	K. Law
B. Philosophy, religion	L. Education
	M. Music
C. History, auxiliary sciences	N. Fine arts
	P. Language and literature
D. History, topography (except American)	Q. Science
	R. Medicine
E,F. American history	S. Agriculture, husbandry
G. Geography, anthropology	T. Technology
	U. Military science
H. Social sciences	V. Naval science
J. Political science	Z. Bibliography, library science

In this system, PR 9249-9263 and PR 9161-9181 are devoted to Canadian poetry; PR 6031.R3, to E. J. Pratt. Pratt's *Here the Tides Flow* has the call number PR 6031.R3.H4.

Those confused and bewildered by innumerable trays of cards filed in the card catalog see no sense in the filing system. Some libraries use a strictly alphabetical order, but most of them follow the rules outlined below.

All libraries file by entry, that is, according to what appears first on the card, whether author, subject, or title. Articles which comprise the first word of a title are ignored; most libraries file letter-by-letter to the end of the word. This means that the title card, *The American way,* would be filed in front of the subject card, AMERICANISMS, just as all cards beginning with "New York" would be filed in front of cards with "Newark" as the entry word. Libraries which use a system of strictly alphabetical order would, of course, file *-isms* before *way* and *-ark* before *York.* It may be noted that encyclopedias, as well as library catalogs, differ in this fundamental rule.

Books which are *about* an author (considered subject entries and typed in red or in black capitals) are filed after books which are *by* that author.

Author cards having the same surname as the entry word are filed according to the given name; always note carefully the first name, or at least the initials, of an author and the *exact* title of the book you wish.

Abbreviations and numerals are filed just as they would be if the words they represent were spelled out.

When an entry name is the same, all authors by that name precede all subjects, and all subjects come before all titles. Hence, King, William Lyon Mackenzie (books by), KING, WILLIAM LYON MACKENZIE (books about), *King Cohn* (title) are filed in that order.

108c.   PERIODICAL INDEXES.

Most libraries display current and sometimes recent issues of magazines on racks or in a special periodical room. Older issues of many magazines and of some newspapers are bound in book form; if your library has such volumes, you will find what you need from them by consulting *periodical indexes*. These are helpful guides to articles and other material which might lie buried except for the ready aid provided by indexes.

When you consult a periodical index, turn first to the front. Here you will find full, helpful instructions for use of the volume and also a list of the periodicals indexed.

For example, here are two entries from *Readers' Guide to Periodical Literature* and their meaning:

Author entry:

> MANCHESTER, Harland
> What you should know about flammable fab-
> rics. Read Digest 90:37-8+ My '67

This entry means that Harland Manchester published an article entitled "What You Should Know About Flammable Fabrics" in the *Reader's Digest* for May, 1967. The volume number is 90. The article begins on page 37 and continues on page 38 and later pages.

Subject entry:

> MARINE painting
> Frederick Waugh. America's most popular
> marine painter. G. R. Havens, IL Am Artist
> 31:30-7+ Ja '67

An illustrated article on the subject MARINE painting en-titled "Frederick Waugh, America's Most Popular Marine Painter," by G. R. Havens, will be found in volume 31 of

American Artist, pages 30-37 (continued on later pages of the same issue) the January, 1967, number.

Indexes are of two kinds. *General indexes* list the contents of magazines and a few newspapers of widespread circulation and interest. Unless you are working on some highly specialized and rather unusual subject, a general index, such as *The Readers' Guide to Periodical Literature, Facts on File, The New York Times Index,* or *Social Sciences and Humanities Index,* probably will meet your needs. *Special indexes,* occasionally more helpful than general ones, restrict themselves to coverage of one particular area. *Agricultural Index, Applied Science and Technology Index, Art Index, Chemical Abstracts, Engineering Index,* and *Psychological Abstracts* are examples of special indexes.

Here is brief comment on the ten periodical indexes likely to be of most use to you. (If your library does not subscribe to them, consult the librarian about your specific needs and interests. The librarian may be able to make other suggestions or provide adequate substitute material.)

1. *Annual Magazine Subject-Index,* 1907-1949. (A subject index, until discontinued, to a selected list—dealing mainly with history, travel, and art—of American and British periodicals and professional or cultural society publications.)

2. *Bibliographic Index, A Cumulative Bibliography of Bibliographies,* 1937—. (A subject index to separately published bibliographies, and to bibliographies included each year in several hundred books and approximately 1,500 periodicals.)

3. *Public Affairs Information Service Bulletin,* 1915—. (A cumulative subject index to current books, pamphlets, periodicals, government documents, and other library material in the fields of economics and public affairs.)

4. *Facts on File,* 1940—. (A weekly world news digest with cumulative index, including world, national, and foreign affairs, Latin America, finance and economics, art and science, education and religion, sports, obituaries, and other miscellany.)

5. *Index to Legal Periodicals,* 1908—. (A cumulative subject and author index to articles in law journals.)

6. The *Social Sciences and Humanities Index,* formerly the *International Index to Periodicals,* 1907—. (A cumulative author and subject index to articles in domestic and foreign periodicals dealing with literature, history, social science, religion, drama, and pure science. It is really a supplement to *Readers' Guide,* below.)

7. *The New York Times Index,* 1913—. (A cumulative guide to events of national importance by reference to day, page, and column of *The New York Times.* Material is entered by subjects, persons, and organizations. The only index to an American newspaper, it is an indirect guide to events in other newspapers.)

8. *Nineteenth Century Readers' Guide to Periodical Literature,* 1890-1899, with supplementary indexing, 1900-1922, 2 vols.

9. *Poole's Index to Periodical Literature.* 7 vols. (An index of articles, by subject only, in American and British periodicals from 1802 to 1906.)

10. *Readers' Guide to Periodical Literature,* 1900—. (A cumulative index, most useful to the general reader, to over 100 popular and semipopular magazines. Entries are according to author, subject, and fiction title.)

108d.   REFERENCE BOOKS.

Any book can be used for reference, but those which really merit the name are condensed, authoritative, conveniently arranged, and up to date. (You should remember, however, that because the preparation of a genuine reference book is expensive in time, money, and effort, it cannot be revised and reprinted very often.)

In many libraries, reference books are available on shelves open to students or on tables in a special reference section. Your teacher, or the school or reference librarian, can tell you which of the scores of reference books at hand are likely to be most helpful with a particular subject. In addition, if your library has a copy of any of the following titles, examine it carefully for useful, timesaving hints on using reference books:

American Library Association. *Ready Reference Collection.* Chicago: American Library Association, 1962.

Barton, Mary Neill. *Reference Books: A Brief Guide for Students and Other Users of the Library,* 6th ed. Baltimore: Enoch Pratt Free Library, 1966.

Hoffman, Hester R. *Reader's Adviser and Bookman's Manual,* 10th ed. New York: R. R. Bowker Co., 1964.

Murphey, Robert W. *How and Where To Look It Up.* New York: McGraw-Hill Book Co., 1958.

Winchell, Constance M. *Guide to Reference Books,* 8th ed. Chicago: American Library Association, 1967. Supplements.

Reference works are so numerous and so varied in content and quality that no fully adequate discussion can be provided here. But you should become acquainted with at least such important works as these:

A. GENERAL ENCYCLOPEDIAS

Collier's Encyclopedia. 20 vols. (Kept up to date with an annual volume, *Collier's Year Book Covering National and International Events.*)

Columbia Encyclopedia, 2nd ed.

Columbia-Viking Desk Encyclopedia, 2nd ed.

Encyclopaedia Britannica. 24 vols. (Kept up to date with an annual volume, *Britannica Book of the Year, a Record of the March of Events.*)

Encyclopedia Americana. 30 vols. (Kept up to date with an annual volume, *The Americana Annual, an Encyclopedia of Current Events.*)

New International Encyclopaedia. 25 vols. (Kept up to date with an annual volume, *New International Year Book, a Compendium of the World's Progress.*)

Seligman, Edwin R. A., and Alvin Johnson, eds. *Encyclopaedia of the Social Sciences* (commonly known as E.S.S.). 15 vols. (Less comprehensive than the volumes listed above, it deals with many subjects directly and indirectly related to the social sciences.)

B. GENERAL DICTIONARIES (See Section 107.)

Funk and Wagnalls New Standard Dictionary of the English Language.

Murray, Sir James A. H., and others, eds. *A New English Dictionary on Historical Principles*, reissued as *The Oxford English Dictionary*. 13 vols. (Commonly referred to as the NED, N.E.D., OED, or O.E.D.)

The Random House Dictionary of the English Language.

Webster's New International Dictionary of the English Language.

C. YEARBOOKS, in addition to the annual yearbooks of the various encyclopedias (see A, above)

Annual Register: A Review of Public Events at Home and Abroad (British).

Canada Year Book. (Official statistical annual of the resources, history, institutions and social and economic conditions of Canada.)

Europa Yearbook. 2 vols. (Vol. I, Europe, Vol. II, Africa, The Americas, Asia, Australasia.)

International Yearbook and Statesmen's Who's Who. (Data on countries and political leaders.)

Statesman's Year-book: Statistical and Historical Annual of the States of the World. (Over 100 annual volumes have been published.)

United Nations Yearbook.

World Almanac and Book of Facts. (Miscellaneous information.)

In addition, your library probably has many other encyclopedias, handbooks, and dictionaries. Special reference works are available dealing with subjects such as biography, business and economics, education, drama and the theater, history, language, literature, music and the dance, painting and architecture, philosophy and psychology, religion, and science. Some of these special subject reference books will be useful and helpful. Ferret them out. Once again, a good reference book is the place where you should start—but only *start*—any research project you have.

EXERCISE 13

After you have become familiar with your library, choose three of the following sentences. Use each as the first (topic) sentence for a paragraph. Develop each idea into a paragraph of about 100-150 words.

A. Several things impressed me about our library.
B. The _____ room in the library is an interesting place.
C. Here are directions for borrowing books from the library.
D. The library has a _____ room.
E. A library is a busy place.
F. You can even have dates in the library.

EXERCISE 14

Make a floor plan of the main reading room of your school library, showing the location of shelves, tables, and any special sections devoted to particular kinds of books or periodicals.

EXERCISE 15

In your library, what is the (a) most recent book by William Faulkner, (b) most recent book about Faulkner, (c) most recent magazine story or article by Faulkner, (d) most recent article about Faulkner, (e) most recent review of a book by Faulkner, (f) most interesting account of his death?

EXERCISE 16

How many books does your library have about Alexander Graham Bell, Charles Dickens, Sir John A. Macdonald, Winston Churchill? Copy the title and author of one book about each person named.

EXERCISE 17

Who are the authors of the following:

1. *An American Tragedy*
2. *Leaves of Grass*
3. *Dombey and Son*
4. *Henry Esmond*
5. *The Call of the Wild*
6. *Lie Down in Darkness*
7. *Robinson Crusoe*
8. *Madame Bovary*
9. *War and Peace*
10. *Outward Bound*

EXERCISE 18

Who were the following? What did they do? When did they live? When did they die? (1) Thomas à Becket; (2) Thomas à Kempis; (3) Thomas Aquinas; (4) Thomas Browne; (5) Thomas Hardy; (6) Thomas Henry Huxley; (7) Thomas Woodrow Wilson; (8) Thomas Carlyle; (9) Thomas A. Edison; (10) Thomas C. Haliburton.

EXERCISE 19

List sources which you think would be best to find:

1. A brief biography of a Canadian cabinet minister.
2. A quotation from Shakespeare when you remember only one key word.
3. The total number of baseball records broken in the 1966 World Series.
4. A synopsis and analysis of Arthur Miller's play, *Death of a Salesman*.
5. A recent biographical sketch of the concert pianist Rudolf Serkin.
6. A list of essays and articles about Leonard Cohen which have appeared in books and magazines.
7. The origin of the English wo.d *barrister*.
8. Whether the "Garrick Club" was an organization, a golf club, or a weapon.
9. A good general discussion of jazz.
10. A recent magazine article on succession duties.

EXERCISE 20

What references would you consult in order to locate the following:

1. An account of the origins and customs of St. Valentine's Day.
2. A summary of the history of the French in Canadian theater.
3. An evaluation of the work of the German composer, Ludwig van Beethoven.
4. A report of recent developments in undersea exploration.
5. A brief discussion of the career of Pierre Elliotte Trudeau which would include his present position.
6. Information about religion, culture, and ethnic distribution of Manitoba.

7. A scholarly discussion of "lobbying" followed by a bibliography.

8. A list of magazine articles concerning the relationship of smoking to cancer.

9. The date of the birth and death of the Russian novelist, Boris Pasternak — without using a book.

10. The source of the following quotation: "Laughter is a proper function of man."

109. WRITING LETTERS

Throughout your high school years, you will probably write more letters than all other types of composition combined: reports, résumés, themes, and examinations. After you leave school, the bulk of your letter correspondence may increase rather than diminish, for in social, business, and professional life no other form of written communication is so widely used. Therefore, time and attention directed to a study of writing good letters — their purposes, their method of presentation, and their content — are well worthwhile.

Letters are, and should be, a reflection of their writer. Just as a speaker's facial expressions, gestures, and voice project his personality and attitude, so does the message in a letter, the quality of paper which bears it, the typing or penmanship producing it, even the way it is folded and sealed. Furthermore, the message of a letter is, in effect, a *theme*, and as such it must be governed by the requirements of good theme writing: clarity and force, correctness and appropriateness. A hasty or cursory letter is seldom worth even the short time needed to dash it off, for effective communication in letters, as in all kinds of composition, depends upon careful planning and writing.

Two main kinds of letters are informal (or friendly) and business letters. A third category, formal letters, includes elaborate invitations and their replies, the patterns for which are standardized and may be found in a reference book on etiquette.

109a. INFORMAL LETTERS.

Informal letters constitute perhaps the greater part of your correspondence. Everyone likes to receive personal letters; at the same time, few of us prefer writing to receiving them. But since "the best way to have a friend is to be one," we should try to cultivate in our letters the art of communicating friendship. This obligation requires thoughtfulness and takes time, but the result, in letters that are neither labored and artificial nor slipshod and disconnected, will be worth the price paid. Here are some suggestions that will improve your technique in friendly letter writing:

1. *Write legibly.* A letter must be capable of being deciphered. Moveover, the appearance of your writing or typing must convey respect for your reader, no matter how close a friend he may be. Letters which by general sloppiness or careless scrawl proclaim "I haven't the time or inclination to take pains, you can take this or leave it," are neither courteous nor effective. A friendly letter is, and should be, more personal and intimate than a business letter, but informality is no excuse for inconsiderateness.

2. *Think about your reader, not only about yourself.* Your correspondent will, of course, be interested in your activities and affairs, and one of your purposes in writing is to report on them; however, no one should risk boring a listener by talking only about himself. An excessive number of *I's*, *me's,* and *myself's* in a letter is equivalent, in writing, to taking that same risk. Show sincere interest in your reader's concerns and activities and offer, too, accounts of other events, persons, and places in which you are not necessarily the sole actor.

3. *Take your time.* Many friendships are kept alive through the medium of letter-writing, but *all* letters to friends should suggest that the writing of them is a pleasurable and rewarding undertaking. Five or six letters dashed off in thirty minutes, each beginning with "I am in a hurry," or signed "Yours on the run," merely imply that the writer finds the task tiresome and his friends not worth much trouble. A good correspondent makes mental or written notes about people,

ideas, and events which he knows will interest his reader and then sits down to describe or narrate them with thoughtfulness, freshness, and liveliness. A good informal letter takes more time than a ten-minute note, but it is an investment in friendship which possibly you cannot afford to overlook. It is time well spent.

4. *Give details.* A clear, detailed description of one person or one place will likely be more interesting to read than a series of random and terse notes on many persons or places. An account of a single experience in vivid terms is more engaging than snippets of several incidents. Full particulars of one conversation you have had will be more entertaining than fragmentary comments from several unconnected sources. Disjointed notes are really topic sentences only, each of which needs enlargement. A good letter expresses or implies a central theme inspired by one primary incident, conversation, description of a person or place, or expression of thought. Such a letter may contain more than one topic, but all topics should be clearly related and adequately developed.

5. *Make your letters appropriate.* The activities and tastes of individual friends differ, and so should the individual letters you devote to them. Identical birthday gifts would not suit all recipients; similarly, an account of an incident written for one friend might not particularly interest another. Always keep your reader in mind and tailor the content of a letter to his specific interests. Keep in mind also, of course, the age levels of the people you write to. Your nine-year-old nephew and your forty-year-old aunt would not find the same things interesting—or even understandable.

Although long letters that give information are most commonly exchanged among friends and relatives, brief, sincere notes are sometimes called for in special circumstances. Thanks for hospitality (sometimes known as a bread-and-butter letter) or for a gift, appreciation of a favor, a bon-voyage message, or written congratulations are examples of such notes. These are so personalized and varied that no one suggestion can cover them all. Here is an example of a short bread-and-butter letter:

Dear Mrs. Curtis:

Friday evening was clear and crisp. I was enjoying a delicious supper, and I was with old friends who are dear to me. Tonight it is raining; we have just finished some tasteless stew, and I am alone in my room except for a buzzing insect which may be old but certainly is not dear. I wish that favorite and well-remembered evenings were like lucky pennies, to spend at will and find again in our pockets.

The Swiss have really made a happening of cheese fondue. Amy has often spoken about her mother's favorite recipe, but I was unprepared for the delicious meal you served. The ritual of eating was fun, too—spearing cubes of bread with a fork and swirling them in bubbling cheese, trying to be careful not to lose a cube in the fondue lest we ''owe the master a glass of wine.'' Both the food and the ceremony were unforgettable.

Now it's back to the books for me. We will see you again soon, because our families will be together on New Year's Day. And don't forget

that you and Mr. Curtis are invited to our

school performance of <u>Macbeth</u> on February 10.

Remember, I am to be ''a most believably

hideous witch.''

    Thank you again for a most delightful

evening.

                      Affectionately,

                      Sue

If this letter does not appeal or provide many ideas for your own correspondence, consider the following from the pen of a famous writer somewhat more skilled than Sue. On October 4, 1875, Mark Twain had occasion to write a "bread-and-butter" letter to his friend and editor, William Dean Howells, himself a noted writer and critic. Notice that Twain writes humorously and informally but note particularly that he develops one theme, the well-known troubles he had with behaving as his wife thought that he should:

My dear Howells,

    We had a royal good time at your house and have had a royal good time ever since, talking about it, both privately and with neighbors. Mrs. Clemens's bodily strength came up handsomely under that cheery respite from household and nursery cares. I do hope that Mrs. Howells's didn't go correspondingly down, under the added burden to her cares and responsibilities. Of course I didn't expect to get through without committing some crimes and hearing of them afterwards.

    So I have taken the inevitable lashings and been able to hum a tune while the punishment went on. I caught it for interrupting Mrs. C. at the last moment and losing her the opportunity to urge you to send her that MS. when the printers are done with it. I caught it once more for impersonating that drunken Colonel James. I caught it for mentioning that Mr. Longfellow's picture was slightly damaged; and when, after a lull in the storm, I confessed, shamefacedly, that I had privately suggested to you that we hadn't any frames, and that if you wouldn't mind hinting to Mr. Houghton, etc., etc., the Madam was simply speechless for the space of a minute. Then she said:

"How could you, youth? The idea of sending Mr. Howells, with his sensitive nature, upon such a repulsive er-"

"Oh, Howells won't mind it. You don't know Howells. Howells is a man who—"

She was gone. But George was the first person she stumbled on in the hall, so she took it out on George. I was glad of that, because it saved the babies.

I've got another rattling good character for my novel. That great work is mulling itself into shape gradually.

Mrs. Clemens sends her love to Mrs. Howells and meantime is diligently laying up material for a letter to her.

Yours ever,
Mark

109b. BUSINESS LETTERS.

The purpose of a business letter is largely utilitarian: to convey a message clearly. Your primary concern as a writer of business letters is with *presentation* and *content*, that is, with the order and expression of your material and with the subject matter itself. There are many kinds of business letters, the most common of which are order letters, inquiries, sales letters, adjustment letters, credit letters, collection letters, letters of recommendation, and letters of application. All of these kinds of business letters are written to a form now standardized in six parts:

1. *The Heading.* This contains the sender's *full* address and the date, usually placed in the upper right-hand of the sheet, an inch or more below the top edge and flush with the

right margin, and typed or written single space. On station-ery with a letterhead, only the date is entered, either flush with the right-hand margin or centered under the letterhead.

2. *The Inside Address.* The name, preceded by a proper title, and the address of the person or company written to should appear flush with the left-hand margin of the paper, usually two or four spaces below the heading but sometimes farther, depending upon the length of the letter. If only the last name of the person written to is known, the letter is directed to the firm and an attention line, consisting of *Attention: Mr. —* or *Attention of Mr. —*, is inserted two lines below the address and two lines above the greeting. It has no bear-ing on the greeting, which is indicated by the first line of the inside address.

3. *The Greeting or Salutation.* This comes two spaces be-low the inside address, is flush with the left-hand margin, and is usually punctuated with a colon only. It should be in harmony with the first line of the inside address and the gen-eral tone of the letter: for example, when writing to a man, correct forms would be *Dear Sir; My dear M. —;* or, prefer-ably, *Dear Mr. —.*

4. *The Body.* Beginning two spaces below the greeting, the body is the message. It is commonly single-spaced (al-though short messages on a large sheet may be double-spaced) and has two spaces between paragraphs, which may be in block form or indented. Long messages are never con-tinued on the back of a sheet but are carried over to a second sheet which should contain at least two lines in addition to the complimentary close and signature and which should carry in a top line some sort of identification such as the addressee's initials, page number, and the date.

5. *The Complimentary Close.* Usually placed at the mid-dle or slightly to the right of the middle of the page, two or three lines below the last line of the letter's body, the close harmonizes with the formality or semi-formality of the greeting. Correct forms, capitalized in the first word only and usually followed by a comma, include *Yours truly, Very truly yours, Yours sincerely, Cordially yours, Cordially,* etc. (*Cordially yours* is often used among business friends and by older people writing to younger.) Independent of the

last paragraph, the close should not be linked to it by participial phrases such as *"Thanking you in advance, I am,"* etc.

6. *The Signature.* Unless a letter is mimeographed or is plainly a circular, it should have a handwritten signature placed directly below the complimentary close. If the name is typed in, four spaces should be allowed for signature. An unmarried woman places *Miss* in parentheses before her name; a married woman signs her full name, which is followed by her married name. A man places no title before his written or typed name, but often his business title is placed after it: *General Manager, Superintendent,* etc.

A good business letter, correct and attractive in form, reflects a courteous attitude toward the reader. Unruled, white paper of good quality and standard size (8½ x 11 inch) or half-size (8½ x 5½ inch) contributes to this impression of courtesy, as does neat typing with fresh black ribbon, or legible longhand in black or blue-black ink. Materials of unusual size and color are a distraction to the reader. The layout of the letter should be balanced on the page, with margins at least an inch wide and with the right-hand margin as even as possible.

In writing a business letter, you may arrange the lines of the heading and of the inside address according to the *full block* or the *modified block* system. In both, the second and third lines of the heading and of the inside address, respectively, begin directly underneath the beginning of the first line. In the full block form, all the parts of the letter, including the heading, complimentary close, and signature, begin at the left-hand margin. In the modified block form, the heading, complimentary close, and signature are in their conventional place, on the right side of the letter.

Rarely seen in a present-day business letter is the formerly popular *indented* system, in which each line of the heading and of the inside address was indented a few spaces to the right of the line preceding it.

Heading and inside and outside addresses should be punctuated consistently according to the *open* or the *closed* system. In the open system, no commas or final periods, except after abbreviations, are used after the separate lines, and some letterwriters prefer, also, to omit the colon after the salutation and the comma after the complimentary close. In the closed system, commas are placed after each line of the heading and inside address, except the last, at the end of which a period is used. Open punctuation is most frequently used today because it is convenient and saves time.

Finally, as a business correspondent you should observe convention in folding the letter and inserting it in its envelope: for the standard large envelope, fold the lower third of the letter over the message and fold the top third to within a half-inch of the creased edge; for the standard small envelope, fold the lower part of the page to within a half-inch of the upper edge, fold from the right slightly more than one third so that the left folded portion will come slightly short of the right creased edge. Attention to such details may seem tedious and unnecessary, but it has a valid purpose: to make opening and reading your letter as easy as possible, so that your reader may focus his entire attention on what you have to say.

Since a business letter seeks to convey information by precise exposition, you should apply to its composition the general rules of effective writing. Starting with the opening sentence, your letter should show careful planning: a statement of your subject or purpose and inclusion in the first paragraph of any pertinent background information which will clarify your message. After making your purpose evident, your letter should reveal your thoughts in logical, easily followed units, with short, separate paragraphs for separate ideas. The letter should close strongly and effectively with a complete sentence — a direct question, an invitation, a restatement of the subject, or an important comment. A cogent business letter contains no hackneyed, worn-out "business" expressions such as these, sometimes referred to as "letter-killers": *am pleased to advise, beg to acknowledge, contents noted, enclosed please find, in receipt of, thank you in advance, under separate cover, wish to advise,* and many others. Instead, it is written in an informal, soundly idiomatic style, using much the same language that is used in a business conversation over the telephone.

In composing a business letter, whether your subject is a one-sentence request, a multiple-item order, a detailed inquiry, or a job application with a request for an interview, you should be brief, clear, and exact. Here is an example of a letter of application. Note how the writer comes to the point as quickly as possible and how he then proceeds without delay to describe himself and his qualifications.

135 Summerville Road

Richmond Hill, Ontario

February 15, 19--

Mr. Ralph Knox, President

Knox Sporting Equipment, Inc.

1403 Sullivan Avenue,

Montreal, Quebec

Dear Mr. Knox:

Mr. Gary Foster, coach of the Arcadian High School football team, has informed me that your firm intends to open a branch store in Toronto late this coming spring and that you will need a additional salesman during the summer. I should like to apply for that position.

A resident of suburban Toronto, I am a junior

at Arcadia High, where I have been a member of the
football, swimming, and baseball teams. In junior
high I played baseball and soccer. In addition, I
have had five years of tennis instruction and
competition, under the joint auspices of the
Arcadia Field Club and our local Y.M.C.A.

My age is 17. I am in excellent health, am
5'10" tall, and weigh 160 lbs. I have maintained a
B-plus average in grades in high school.

We shall have our mid-winter recess during the
week of February 27. I shall be staying with my
uncle in nearby Dorval, and can drive to Montreal
for an interview at any time convenient to you.
What day and hour would be most agreeable?

                                    Very truly yours,

                              Hennis R. Hughes

                              Hennis R. Hughes

Note how the above applicant has presented his case
effectively, briefly, and precisely. He has also suggested an
interview in a way that would be hard to turn down. He will
probably get his interview — and perhaps the job.

Here are examples of an *order* letter and of one requesting an *adjustment*. Both of these letters are brief, precise, and to the point. And both will probably get prompt attention.

240 Mill Road

Hamilton, Ontario   305

May 6, 19--

T. Eaton Co.

Queen and Yonge

Toronto, Ontario

Gentlemen:

Please send me, by return parcel post, six pairs of ladies' nylon hose, 15 Denier, size 9, medium length, suntan color. In payment, I enclose a money order for nine dollars ($9.00).

Yours very truly,

Beulah H. Smith

(Miss) Beulah H. Smith

240 Mill Road

Hamilton, Ontario

June 24, 19--

T. Eaton Co.

Queen and Yonge

Toronto, Ontario

Gentlemen:

On May 6, I ordered from you six pairs of ladies' nylon hose, 15 Denier, size 9, medium length, suntan color, total price $9.00.

The hose arrived on June 22, too late for me to give them as a high school graduation present, as planned. In addition, the hose were size 11 and gunmetal in color.

Since it is too late to have the order corrected, I am returning the hose by parcel post and am asking that you return to me the purchase money of $9.00. Thank you for your prompt attention to this refund.

Yours very truly,

Beulah H. Smith

(Miss) Beulah H. Smith

EXERCISE 21

Answer the following "Want Ad": WANTED: Counselors and aides for boys' and girls' camps, June through August. Children are from 8 to 13. Give full details concerning qualifications. Apex Summer Camps, Lake Simcoe, Ontario.

EXERCISE 22

Answer the following "Want Ad": WANTED: Student to be waitress and cashier in local tea room. Hours 3 to 6. Time for study during work. Give age, references, and previous experience, if any. Dept. S-7, *Progress,* Chilliwack, B.C.

EXERCISE 23

Write an informal invitation to a friend asking him to join you and your family on a week's camping trip.

EXERCISE 24

Write a letter to a friend who is in the hospital for a long stay following a serious operation.

EXERCISE 25

Collect and bring to class at least eight examples of business letters. (Perhaps a relative or business acquaintance may lend you some letters from his files.) Study the letter-heads used; note especially both the usual and unusual features about the six parts of the letters (heading, inside address, greeting, body, complimentary close, signature). Notice the quality of paper used, the spacing and length of the paragraphs, the tone of the letters.

EXERCISE 26

Write a "bread-and-butter" note to a friend who has given you a surprise birthday party.

EXERCISE 27

Write a letter of sympathy to a friend who has just lost a close relative due to an automobile accident.

EXERCISE 28

Write a letter of inquiry to your provincial historical society concerning some old industries in your town.

EXERCISE 29

Write a request for a refund on an unused bus ticket.

EXERCISE 30

From a magazine advertisement, write a letter ordering the item or items advertised.

110. PRÉCIS

A *précis* (pronounced "pray-see"; the form is both singular and plural) is a short summary of the essential ideas of a longer composition. In a précis, the basic thought of a passage is reproduced in miniature, retaining the mood and tone of the original. No interpretation or comment should be interjected; it is the author's exact meaning which should be scaled down, without omitting any important details.

The material to be reduced must be carefully chosen. Some choices readily lend themselves to condensation, but others are so compactly written that further reduction is almost impossible. Loosely-knit selections such as most novels, stories, speeches, and essays are suitable for the making of précis, whereas very taut and epigrammatic material such as some poems, prayers, and inscriptions are not. Avoid writings which have already been summarized, abridged, or edited; the essential thought of the original becomes distorted through constant "boiling down."

110a. READ THE SELECTION CAREFULLY.

Since a précis must be brief, clear, but, above all, faithful to the original, you must read through the chosen material analytically and reflectively. After reading the whole selection to determine its central ideas, reread it paragraph by paragraph, noting as you do the topic of each one and searching for key expressions which you can use to project in your summary the flavor of the original. See how the author has organized his material, what devices he has employed, and what kinds of illustrations support his thesis. Before writing a précis you must, to use Sir Francis Bacon's phrase, "chew and digest" your selection through reading; neither nibbling nor gulping will suffice.

110b. USE YOUR OWN WORDS.

Though you must master and present the major thought of the selection, the précis itself should be your own composition. Some quoting of sentences from the original may be appropriate, but by and large the author's phrasing cannot readily be adopted; furthermore, quoting sentences, perhaps topic sentences, from each paragraph will produce a sentence outline, not a précis. The author's wording and order may serve as a guide, but the summary statement produced must be yours.

110c. SET LIMITS TO THE NUMBER OF WORDS YOU USE.

Précis are condensations, and although their length cannot be arbitrarily set, they can be used to reduce most prose by two-thirds to three-quarters. Some poetry is so tightly written that reduction is virtually impossible; other verse can be pared even more than prose. Leave out nothing of importance, but limit your summary to one-fourth or one-third of the original.

110d. FOLLOW THE PLAN OF THE ORIGINAL.

In order to be faithful to your selection, you must preserve its proportion. Changing the author's logical plan would distort its essence. Refrain from rearranging facts and thoughts, and try to preserve the original mood and tone.

110e. WRITE A PRÉCIS IN EFFECTIVE ENGLISH.

A précis is not likely to be so well written as the selection itself, but it must possess clear, emphatic diction and effective sentence construction. Its unity and coherence should be emphasized through smooth, unobtrusive transitions. Your summary must be intelligible to a reader who has not seen the original and should therefore have solid compositional worth.

EXERCISE 31

In the light of the comments above, analyze each of the following student précis. What suggestions can you make to improve each one? Write your own précis of either the excerpt from Robinson or that from Fielding.

A. ORIGINAL

A third kind of thinking is stimulated when anyone questions our beliefs and opinions. We sometimes find ourselves changing our minds without any resistance or heavy emotion, but if we are told that we are wrong we resent the imputation and harden our hearts. We are incredibly heedless in the formation of our beliefs, but find ourselves filled with an illicit passion for them when anyone proposes to rob us of their companionship. It is obviously not the ideas themselves that are dear to us, but our self-esteem, which is threatened. We are by nature stubbornly pledged to defend our own from attack, whether it be our person, our family, our property, or our opinion. A United States Senator once remarked to a friend of mine that God Almighty could not make him change his mind on our Latin-America policy. We may surrender, but rarely confess ourselves vanquished. In the intellectual world at least, peace is without victory.

Few of us take the pains to study the origin of our cherished convictions; indeed, we have a natural repugnance to so doing. We like to continue to believe what we have been accustomed to accept as true, and the resentment aroused when doubt is cast upon any of our assumptions leads us to seek every manner of excuse for clinging to them. *The result is that most of our so-called reasoning consists in finding arguments for going on believing as we already do.* [242 words]

—James Harvey Robinson, "On Various Kinds of Thinking"

PRÉCIS

A third kind of thinking occurs when we are told that our beliefs and opinions are wrong. We may have been heedless in their formation, but our self-esteem will not permit us to change. We may have to give up, but we are not convinced. We do not study the origin of our beliefs; we believe as we have been accustomed to believe, and we seek arguments for continuing to believe as we already do. [75 words]

B. ORIGINAL

But as for the bulk of mankind, they are clearly devoid of any degree of taste. It is a quality in which they advance very little beyond a state of infancy. The first thing a child is fond of in a book is a picture, the second is a story, and the third a jest. Here then is the true Pons Asinorum, which very few readers ever get over. [69 words]

—Henry Fielding

PRÉCIS

Most people lack taste; they remain childlike. Readers, like children, rarely ever get over the "bridge of asses" constituted by pictures, stories, and jokes. [24 words]

EXERCISE 32

Write several précis of selections from your literature anthology. Choose not more than three paragraphs from an essay or article. Or perhaps your teacher will prefer to make a uniform assignment.

EXERCISE 33

Choose an article in a current magazine and condense it as you think *The Reader's Digest* would.

111. PARAPHRASE

Much of what we learn in high school comes from writings that contain timeless ideas and concepts expressed in unique ways. Moreover, the process of learning demands that at least temporarily we make the ideas of these writers *our* ideas, their statements *our* statements, their thoughts *our* thoughts. To do so, a form of translation is often required. Just as the French phrase "chacun à son goût" has little meaning to an English-speaking person until he has turned it into its English equivalent, "each to his own taste," so must language and imagery written in other times and other circumstances usually be given equivalent expression in our own words. Restating the sense of a passage through the use of different words is called paraphrasing.

111a. PARAPHRASING AND CLARIFICATION.

Frequently we have encountered prose and poetry which seems unfamiliar, obscure, or difficult to comprehend. Before a passage can fully "come through" to us, we must put the sense of it into words of our own. Our aim should not be to compress the author's statements (as is done when making a précis) but rather to reset or rephrase those statements in their full proportion, preserving original thought and detail, so that the message is fully clear. We may agree or disagree with that message, accept or reject it; either way, the author's thinking has been translated into our own thought processes. A paraphrase of a good poem or essay cannot rival the original. It should, however, be a faithful rewording of all that the original contains in its meaning, organization, details, proportion, and even tone. Achieving a successful paraphrase calls for careful reading and reflection, for disciplined interpretation, for precise writing. Consider the following suggestions:

1. Read and reread carefully the original passage until its full meaning is clear. Sometimes a statement will have exact and implied meanings; both must be understood. Determine the central idea and study its method of presentation, how subordinate thoughts are arranged, what purposes they serve. Weigh individual words and phrases and consider the author's reasons for selecting them. If doubts arise over archaic words or obscure allusions, consult a dictionary or other reference book for their meanings.

2. Use your own words. Reshape phrases in familiar terms. If

an original word or phrase is exact and understandable, do not change it; on the other hand, *do* change words and phrases which are unfamiliar, even if such recasting is difficult, so that their meaning will be clear.

3. Restate the entire passage in its original proportion. You must be objective in order to paraphrase well: subtracting part of a passage because you think it extraneous, or do not agree with it, will upset the balance which the author set; adding interpretations or personal ideas will do the same. A paraphraser's thinking should be directed solely toward a faithful recreation of the author's statement.

4. Preserve the tone and form of the original. The qualities in a great speech or in a poem such as Rudyard Kipling's "*If,*" are unique, and their duplication in a paraphrase is impossible. However, try to retain as much of the tone and form of the original as clarity permits.

5. Use good English. The quality of a jewel cannot be matched in paste, and the sense of a good author's work cannot be captured exactly in even a good paraphrase. Restatement of an original passage deserves and demands the best writing of which the paraphraser is capable. Careful and sensitive reading, constructive thought, and precise interpretation will result in paraphrasing which most nearly matches the original.

EXERCISE 34

From your book of readings, select five short poems or five paragraphs from an essay. With the advice of your teacher, select *one* of these poems or paragraphs and write a paraphrase of it.

EXERCISE 35

Criticize the following student paraphrases in the light of suggestions given in Section 111:

CXVI

Let me not to the marriage of true minds
Admit impediments. Love is not love
Which alters when it alteration finds,
Or bends with the remover to remove:
O, no! it is an ever-fixed mark
That looks on tempests and is never shaken;
It is the star to every wandering bark,

Whose worth's unknown, although his height be taken.
Love's not Time's fool, though rosy lips and cheeks
Within his bending sickle's compass come;
Love alters not with his brief hours and weeks,
But bears it out even to the edge of doom.
 If this be error and upon me proved,
 I never writ, nor no man ever loved.

—William Shakespeare

Paraphrase

I do not acknowledge any real obstacles to true love. Love is counterfeit when it changes because of problems or wavers if one of the lovers tries to alter the relationship. On the contrary, true love is steadfast. Just as we cannot know what a star's true value is, although we can measure its altitude and navigate by it, just so we cannot know what love is really worth despite its guidance. Love is no jesting servant of Time, even though lovers do wither and die; true love lasts to the brink of eternity. If what I say is wrong, and can be proved wrong, then I have never made a valid statement and no one has ever loved.

ON FIRST LOOKING INTO CHAPMAN'S HOMER

Much have I travell'd in the realms of gold,
And many goodly states and kingdoms seen;
Round many western islands have I been
Which bards in fealty to Apollo hold.
Oft of one wide expanse had I been told
That deep-brow'd Homer ruled as his demesne:
Yet did I never breathe its pure serene
Till I heard Chapman speak out loud and bold:
Then felt I like some watcher of the skies
When a new planet swims into his ken;
Or like stout Cortez, when with eagle eyes
He stared at the Pacific—and all his men
Look'd at each other with a wild surmise—
Silent, upon a peak in Darien.

—John Keats

Paraphrase

I have read widely in the great classics of literature and have noted many examples of great poetry. I had often been told of the work of Homer and the poetry which he had created, but I never really understood or appreciated its great beauty and power until I read Chapman's translation. Then I felt as awed as some astronomer who unexpectedly discovers a new planet, or as surprised and speechless as Cortez (Balboa) and his followers were when they saw the Pacific Ocean for the first time, from Panama.

112. DIAGRAMING

Each of us learned to speak without any conscious knowledge of how our language works. To write with competence and assurance, however, we need to be able to analyze sentences and identify their parts. Consider this sentence:

The perplexed student is diligently studying his notes.

We should be able to analyze this sentence both by individual words and by word groups:

The is a definite article modifying the noun *student. Perplexed* is an adjective modifying *student. Student* is a noun used as the subject of the sentence. *The perplexed student* is the complete subject of *is studying.*

Is is an auxiliary verb which with the present participle *studying* forms the present progressive tense, active voice, and is the predicate of the sentence. *Diligently* is an adverb modifying the verb phrase *is studying.*

His is a possessive pronoun, third person singular masculine; it refers to *the perplexed student* and modifies the noun *notes. Notes* is the object of the verb phrase *is studying.*

112a. THE DEVICE OF DIAGRAMING.

A mechanical method to aid in identifying words and phrases (as is done above) is called diagraming. The placing of sentence elements in a largely arbitrary graphic organization to disclose their functions in a sentence is a kind of game. Some experts consider diagraming of questionable value, whereas others think it a legitimate and useful device. Both advocates and attackers of diagraming agree that it is only a means to an end. Proponents of diagraming insist that both means and end are sensible and worthwhile; some of its detractors claim that neither the method of analysis nor analysis itself is of much value.

In conventional, or traditional, diagraming, it is understood that every simple sentence and complete clause is made up of two elements, a subject part and a predicate part. The latter is present in every sentence and clause; the former is, too, except in imperative sentences when it is implicit (understood). Traditional diagraming indicates (shows) relationships in *linear* fashion.

Other methods of diagraming consist of placing each word in a sentence in a box. This plan results in a set of boxes, each enclosed in another box except the last, which encloses the entire sentence. Still another method of diagraming is accomplished by the use of lines branching like the limbs of trees. The first branching is from the sentence (S) to the subject (noun or noun phrase, N or NP) and the predicate (verb or verb phrase, V or VP). Further branchings reveal as many levels and varieties of structural relationships as the sentence to be diagramed involves.

Both traditional and "tree" diagraming are briefly illustrated in this section.

The purposes of traditional diagraming are accomplished through the use of lines: horizontal, perpendicular, slanting, curved, and dotted. The parts of a sentence are put on lines in the positions indicated in the following skeleton diagram. The three most important sentence elements (subject, predicate, object) are usually put on a horizontal line; any modifiers are placed on lines underneath.

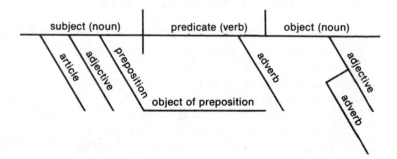

Filled in, such a diagramed sentence might read:

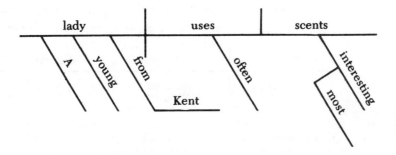

A young lady from Kent often uses most interesting scents.
The simple subject, the simple predicate, the direct object (as above) and, when they appear, the object complement, the predicate noun or pronoun, and the predicate adjective are written on the main horizontal line. (If you have forgotten the meanings of these terms, look up each at its appropriate place in this handbook.) The subject and predicate are separated by a perpendicular line intersecting the horizontal line. A direct object is separated from its verb by a short perpendicular line extending up from a horizontal line. The object complement, the predicate noun or pronoun, and the predicate adjective are set off by short slanting lines extending up to the left from the horizontal line. When conjunctions appear, dotted lines are used to join.

The following diagrams illustrate these principles and directions:

The class	has elected	Tom	president
subject	predicate verb phrase	direct object	object complement

That	is	she
subject	predicate (linking verb)	predicate pronoun

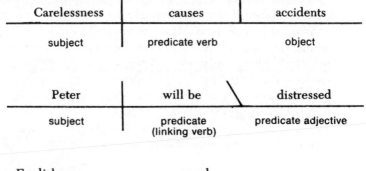

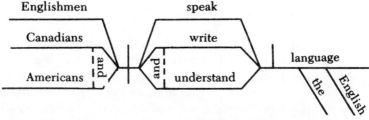

Several other types of sentences (compound, complex, compound-complex) and structures containing absolute phrases, expletives, infinitive phrases used as predicate nouns, etc., are not shown for two reasons: (1) fundamental principles remain identical with those shown and can be easily adapted; (2) diagraming is a game — useful or not — and should be kept no more involved than an individual or a particular class wishes it to become.

For a study of "tree" diagraming, you may need first to refer to Section 120b in which certain terms are defined and explained by means of "scientific" grammar.

The simplest tree diagram is obviously of a two-word sentence such as "Children play." A "tree" diagram of this sentence is as follows:

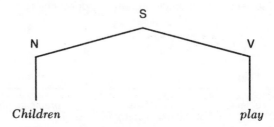

If the sentence were "The small children play quietly," then the label N (for noun) would become NP (noun phrase) and would represent "the small children." Similarly, V would become VP (verb phrase) and would stand for "play quietly." The words are written out in their usual order below each final branch; their grammatical construction (or part of speech) is labeled at the point at which branching occurs. This point is called a *node*.

In tree diagraming, the sentence on p. 524, "The class has elected Tom president," would appear like this:

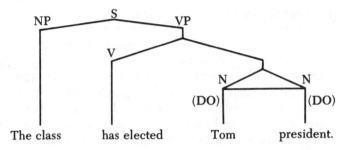

In this diagram, the sentence consists of a noun phrase (NP) and a verb phrase (VP). The latter contains both a direct object (DO) and an object complement (also DO), both referring to the same person. Thus the two are joined by a horizontal line.

Like traditional diagraming, the use of "trees" is a kind of game. If you play the game of diagraming by either method, you may learn much about the structure of sentences of varied sorts. But "fun and games" should not take precedence over the primary purpose of this or any other course in writing: learning to write and rewrite with clearness, effectiveness, and appropriateness.

113. SEMANTICS

Semantics is the study of word meanings and changes of meaning. Specifically, semantics refers to that branch of linguistics which deals with word meanings and historical changes in meaning and that also involves a study of the relations among signs (words, symbols), their meanings, and the mental or physical actions called forth by them. As the science of meanings, semantics (which comes from the Greek *semainein,* "to know," "to signify") is contrasted with *phonetics,* the science of speech sounds and their production. A form of semantics concerning only the relationship between symbols and human behavior is known as *general semantics.*

113a. WORDS AS SYMBOLS.

Words are actually signs, that is, items or objects the value of which lies in the fact that they single out or point to something else; words are a particular kind of sign called a symbol. Certain words (such as conjunctions and prepositions) are symbolic only in a special or limited way. Also, the things symbolized vary widely: words may stand for concrete objects such as *house* or *horse;* for imagined objects such as *elves* and *pixies;* for nonphysical things such as *honor* or *horror;* and for varied other states, feelings, abstractions, and concepts. Sometimes, the thing represented is involved and complex; what, for example, is the thing to which "Canada" corresponds — an area of earth, a people, a culture, a form of government?

A word has three relationships: (1) with other words with which it is used, (2) with the persons who speak, write, and hear it, (3) with the thing it represents, the *referent.*

The relationship of words with each other is a matter of *grammar* — a set of observations and rules for combining different classes of words into understandable sequences. The relationships between words and people is the primary concern of *general semanticists.* The relationships of words to the things they represent, their referents, is the basic concern of *semantics.*

Semantics and general semantics, which are discussed in the two sections that follow, have been the subjects of increasing attention in the last few decades. Some understanding of them is an important part of a well-rounded education.

113b. THE SCIENCE OF SEMANTICS.

Strictly speaking, no word has a meaning as exact as, for example, the measurements of a physical object. That is, words exist in people's minds and, since all minds are dissimilar, no word can have a meaning that it precisely and inevitably calls up in everyone. When Humpty Dumpty said to Alice, "When I use a word, it means just what I choose it to mean — neither more nor less," he was not speaking complete nonsense. But it is true that people do commonly agree on the association of certain words with certain thoughts; if a given word did not generally symbolize a given idea, we could hardly communicate with each other in speech or writing.

You can use the word *peach* as a symbol to express your thought about a particular fruit, "a subacid, juicy, drupaceous" food; the fruit is the *referent* of peach. By general agreement, those who use English employ this symbol when they think of a specific kind of fruit. And yet the symbol would not work if the writer or speaker were thinking of the peach tree itself, or of a certain color, or of something made or cooked with peaches or with a flavor like that of a peach. And the symbol would be far afield if the writer used it to express his opinion of someone he especially admired or enjoyed or employed it in the sense of informing against someone or of "giving away" a companion or secret.

It may be helpful to recall that the meanings of many words have two overlapping aspects. A word has its *denotation*, a certain set of things which it stands for and points to and about which most people generally agree. It also has its *connotation*, a set of feelings and associations which it arouses in the people who use it and who hear or read it.

Words are symbols whose arbitrary relationships to the things they represent must always be kept in mind. Again, this relationship is the concern of semantics.

113c. GENERAL SEMANTICS.

So far as we now know, man is the only animal capable of inventing symbol systems, such as mathematics and the

English language, with which to record his past, evaluate his present, and plan his future. The systematic study of the role of human symbols in the lives of individuals and groups is called *general semantics*. This branch of semantics is concerned with meanings in more than just their "dictionary sense"; it involves several kinds of verbal and nonverbal meanings and the importance of those meanings in our private lives and public affairs.

General semanticists recognize that, like words, sentences and paragraphs, chapters, essays, songs, plays, poems, and books have meaning. You cannot find the meaning of a sentence, a paragraph, or a poem by "looking up" in a dictionary each of its words. Nor will you, as a general semanticist, the late Wendell Johnson, remarked, find the meaning of a particular sunset in a dictionary. You will find its meaning only in yourself, in your thoughts and feelings, in what you say and do. The meanings of words are no more in the words than is the meaning of a maple tree in a maple. The meanings of words, claim general semanticists, are in the person who uses them or responds to them, just as the meanings of "a green meadow are the children who chase butterflies across it, the artist who paints it, the cows which graze upon it, or the old soldier who remembers the battle that once was fought across its green slope" (Johnson).

To the general semanticist, a study of words is not merely the study of words, or paintings, or musical scores. To him, the study of words includes a study of people and what words and paintings and musical scores mean to them. To discover what such things mean to people is to observe what people do to, with, and about them. General semantics deals with symbolic behavior, its patterns, its principles, its effects on man and his world, and with the conditions of its changes from time to time in the lives of men and their societies.

In summary, general semantics is concerned not only with word meanings but also with a consideration of human beings and what words mean to them at different times and under different circumstances. In these respects, semantics tends to overlap *rhetoric*, the art of persuasion. But whereas the set of devices known as rhetoric enables us to affect the emotions of others, general semanticists are most concerned that we understand the emotional effects of words so that we can resist appeals which may be faulty, illogical, or deliberately propagandistic. A knowledge of semantics can help us to control emotional language when we employ or hear it but can hardly prevent its use entirely.

EXERCISE 36

Discuss the connotation and, where possible, the denotation of each of the following:

1. reactionary
2. extremist
3. bureaucrat
4. bleeding heart
5. brainwashing

6. vested interests
7. thought control
8. do-gooder
9. senior citizen
10. welfarism

EXERCISE 37

Write a paragraph of 50-75 words using as many of the terms in Exercise 36 as you sensibly can.

EXERCISE 38

Comment on the use (meaning) of words in the following sentences. Point out any shifts in meaning or emotionally-toned words which you find.

1. No race is inferior; in fact, some are superior.
2. "A pickpocket is obviously a champion of private enterprise." (G. K. Chesterton)
3. Of course, I am not a liar; I'm only a prevaricator.
4. Canada must be a welfare state because the Constitution requires the government to promote the general welfare.
5. "The movie is the diversion of slaves, the pastime of illiterate wretches harried by wants and worries, the astutely seasoned pabulum of a multitude condemned by the forces of Moloch to this vile degradation." (Georges Duhamel)

114. PRONUNCIATION

For nearly everyone, words actually *live* in oral rather than in written form, because we spoke before we learned to write and continue to speak many times more often than we write. This handbook deals primarily with writing, but we should not overlook the central importance of spoken language in our daily lives. An important phase of speaking is pronunciation.

Pronunciation may be defined as the act, or result, of producing the sounds of speech. Pronunciation is complex and many-faceted; it involves, among other matters, levels of pronunciation, spelling, punctuation, tone of voice, and dialect. The brief comment which follows is designed to call attention to those phases of pronunciation which have direct bearing upon a few aspects of the use of English in spoken and written form.

None of us speaks "language" but rather *a particular language.* And the language which each of us speaks is made up of a variety of what may be called dialects that are not necessarily deviations from "standard language." That is, each of us speaks a language with characteristics peculiar to a language in a particular social group or specific locality. In addition, each of us retains certain speech patterns (variations in pronunciation, vocabulary, even in syntax) which are uniquely our own. These characteristics are called an *idiolect.* Everyone possesses his own idiolect despite apparent conformity to group or social usage. With so many millions of idiolects in use, no one dialect may arbitrarily be termed "better than" or "preferable to" another, except to the degree of its success or failure in communicating meaning with ease, appropriateness, and effectiveness in the speech situation in which it is used.

An English scholar, H. W. Fowler, has neatly stated a good rule: "Pronounce as your neighbors do, not better." The artificiality and elaborateness of "stage" pronunciation, so carefully taught by some dramatic coaches, seems out of place in most everyday speech situations, no matter how "cultivated" or "educated" the conversationalists involved. Careful attention to pronunciation is worthwhile; elaborate and overly conscious concern handicaps a speaker and often annoys his listeners.

In Canada, there is no single pronunciation standard. English is made up of a number of local and regional types of speech, but the differences among them are relatively minor and usually do not interfere with communication. No one dialect has become dominant. Cultivated speech exists in every part of the country.

114a. LEVELS OF PRONUNCIATION.

In determining what speech patterns are acceptable, observers often use the terms *standard* and *nonstandard.* To those varieties of speech employed by the educated, or cultivated, people of any given community is applied the term "standard." To departures from this speech pattern is given the designation "nonstandard." But not even these labels are concerned with perhaps ninety percent of the total vocabulary, since most Canadians pronounce most words about the same way. To the question about remaining words, "What is the *correct* pronunciation?" the answer is that the pronunciation of any word or phrase is acceptable or "correct" if it is one used by a majority of educated speakers under a similar set of circumstances in a given Canadian major speech area.

Such an answer may seem to lack the "final authority" being sought, but it is the only defensible and honest reply that can be made to the question. This answer also suggests an obvious truth: every person, on occasion, uses different styles of speech. The two most commonly identified styles are "formal" and "informal." For example, one who habitually employs "cultivated" speech would pronounce words in a *cultivated formal* style in making a public speech or careful report and in conversation on what might be called "business suit" or "black tie" occasions. At other times and in other places, the same speaker might use *cultivated informal* speech which conceivably could be careless, casual, and even filled with slang, language shortcuts, possibly even "grammatical" inaccuracies and such normally indefensible elements of language as vulgarities and profanity. That is, cultivated informal pronunciation often verges on substandard usage but is usually the result of planned casualness rather than ignorance. It is more important to avoid nonstandard pronunciation than the informal pronunciations of educated people, but the language of the classroom usually should be formal rather than informal.

In recent years, scholars have painstakingly identified many major speech areas. For example, in the eastern part of the United States and Canada, three regional areas have been isolated: Northern, Middle Atlantic (Midland), and Southern. These areas, in turn, embrace distinct subareas such as Eastern New England, Western New England, New York City, etc. Allowing for the discovery and identification of far more than the major speech areas referred to below, the following comment is useful:

> Correct pronunciation is the pronunciation of educated, careful speakers of the general region in which one happens to have formed his speech habits. This definition allows for the differences in pronunciation which we hear in different regions of the English-speaking world. If one has grown up, for example, in the southern part of the United States, he is entirely justified in using the speech of the educated, cultured speakers of the South, which we call "southern speech." One whose linguistic background lies along the northern Atlantic coast may reasonably be expected to use the type of speech characteristic of that section, which we call "eastern speech." And one reared in any part of the remaining area of the United States may properly use the speech of his educated and cultured fellows, which we call "general American speech."
>
> —G. S. Gray and C. M. Wise,
> *The Bases of Speech* (New York, 1934)

114b. PRONUNCIATION AND THE USE OF A DICTIONARY.

It is incorrect to assume that "the dictionary," *any* dictionary, is a never-failing guide in determining what pronunciation is acceptable at any given time. No good dictionary makes any such claim for itself. In different words, every reliable dictionary now available states approximately what is here quoted from Webster's *Third New International Dictionary,* p. 41a:

> The standard of English pronunciation, . . . so far as a standard may be said to exist, is the usage that now prevails among

the educated and cultured people to whom the language is vernacular [native]; but . . . since somewhat different pronunciations are used by the cultivated in different regions too large to be ignored, we must admit the fact that uniformity of expression is not to be found throughout the English-speaking world, though there is a very large percentage of practical uniformity.

Although a reputable dictionary neither claims to be, nor is, an infallible guide to pronunciation, you should not ignore its findings nor fail to study it carefully and intelligently. At the very least, you should learn to distinguish accent marks which indicate heavy and secondary stress as well as diacritical marks that indicate a specific sound value, stress, or pitch. Actually, pronunciation largely depends upon accent (emphasized syllables) and upon the sound given to alphabetical letters or letter combinations. Learn the exact pronunciation system which your dictionary uses; for example, some dictionaries include both accent marks and syllabication dots in entry words; other dictionaries include only syllabication dots in entry words and place accent marks in the "pronunciation" word.

114c. PRONUNCIATION AND SPELLING.

Pronunciation is not a safe guide to spelling, but properly pronouncing certain words will help in spelling them correctly, whereas mispronouncing them will cause spelling difficulty for nearly everyone. Spelling may, or may not, be considered a major problem in writing, but correct spelling has a direct connection with the pronunciation of many words.

Scholars generally agree that about fifty speech sounds in the English language must be represented in writing by twenty-six letters of the alphabet. These fifty speech sounds appear in some 250 spelling combinations. For example, consider the sound of long *e*, the sound we have in *equal:*

1. *eve*	5. p*eo*ple	9. p*ie*ce
2. s*ee*d	6. k*ey*	10. am*oe*ba
3. r*ea*d	7. qu*ay*	11. C*ae*sar
4. rec*ei*ve	8. pol*i*ce	

Despite such an illogical and apparently hopeless situation, some relationship often exists between sound and spelling. Proper or suitable pronunciations will enable you to avoid many errors in spelling which result from confusion in pronunciation. For example, if you "correctly" pronounce *carton* (box, receptacle) and *cartoon* (drawing, sketch) you will not mistakenly spell them for each other.

Misspellings caused by mispronunciation are of many kinds. Here are examples of common errors:

1. Misspellings due to incorrect prefixes — *perform*, not *preform; perspiration*, not *prespiration; professor*, not *perfessor; proposal*, not *preposal* or *porposal*.

2. Misspellings due to added vowels: *athletics*, not *athaletics* or *atheletics; partner*, not *partener; remembrance*, not *rememberance; umbrella*, not *umberella*.

3. Misspellings due to dropped vowels: *accidentally*, not *accidently; civilian*, not *civilan; familiar*, not *familar; laboratory*, not *labortory*.

4. Misspellings due to dropped consonants: *arctic*, not *artic; awkward*, not *awkard; February*, not *Febuary; surprised*, not *suprised*.

5. Misspellings due to unstressed vowels: *grammar*, not *grammer; murmur*, not *murmer; sponsor*, not *sponser; dollar*, not *doller*.

6. Misspellings due to silent letters: *align; comb; crumb; fourth; gnaw; knit; knuckle; plumber; pneumonia; raspberry; psychology; write*.

114d. PRONUNCIATION AND PUNCTUATION.

When we talk we do not depend upon words alone to tell our listener what we mean. The tone and stress of voice can and do influence the meaning of spoken words. We yell or whisper, speak calmly or angrily. We raise or lower our voices at the end of a statement or a question. That is, rising inflection in one's voice when he asks a question indicates the same thing as a question mark at the end of a sentence. An exclamation point conveys an idea of surprise or determination or command which would be indicated by a strongly emotional tone in speaking.

Facial and bodily gestures add much meaning to spoken words themselves: we clasp hands, shrug a shoulder, raise an eyebrow, grin or grimace, wiggle a finger, stamp a foot, wink, bend forward or backward, and nod or shake the head. Again, meaning in talk is affected by pauses and halts which often are as significant as words themselves. Each of us has seen a skilled actor convey ideas and moods without using any words at all. The inflections, pauses, and stresses which occur in speech that we call pronunciation are represented in writing by various marks and devices which we call punctuation.

Pronunciation is important because it makes clear to others the meanings of spoken words. Punctuation came into existence solely for the purpose of making clear the meaning of written words and their interrelationship. Pronunciation has a clear relationship to punctuation; one is as essential to spoken communication as the other is to written.

EXERCISE 39

Words in this list are often mispronounced. Consult your dictionary for recommended pronunciations, that is, those recorded as being standard on all levels throughout the country. Practice saying these words to yourself and use them in your own conversation when they are appropriate.

adult	escape	length
amateur	experiment	mischievous
attacked	film	perspiration
candidate	genuine	pianist
caramel	government	positively
column	height	preferable
corps	hostile	strength
data	humble	subtle
drowned	imperturbable	superfluous
egotist	indefatigable	victuals

EXERCISE 40

Find out what seems to be the standard pronunciation of the following words: *acumen, advertisement, au gratin, beret, chiropodist, combatant, conversant, coupon, culinary, drastically, forehead, gnome, grimace, impugn, incompar-*

able, lingerie, maraschino, modern, often, quay, suite, surprise, ultimatum, valet, verbatim.

EXERCISE 41

Each of the following has more than one pronunciation. What does each pronunciation indicate about the part of speech and the meaning? *address, appropriate, compound, contest, contrast, increase, insert, insult, minute, moderate, object, present, produce, progress, protest, rebel, record, refuse, subject, transfer.*

EXERCISE 42

What is the standard pronunciation of each of these proper names? *Assisi, Audubon, Austerlitz, Avalon, Daguerre, Damocles, Eire, Euripides, Icarus, Liszt, Monaco, Oahu, Okinawa, Riviera, Rosicrucian, Sault Sainte Marie, Thames, Tschaikovsky, Valkyrie, Van Gogh.*

115. READING

Writing and reading are two closely linked parts of one process: the communication of moods, thoughts, and emotions. When you write effectively you convey ideas and feelings to others; when you read well you receive from others their ideas and feelings. In learning to improve our writing it will help also to improve our reading.

It has not been fully proved that all good writers have been efficient readers, but generations of high school students and their teachers have discovered a striking parallelism between efficient reading and effective writing. The powerful influence of television, radio, motion pictures, and varied audio-visual devices may eventually alter the situation, but at least for now a good general education cannot be acquired by anyone who cannot read both accurately and thoughtfully. The famous English writer, Thomas Carlyle, once said: "If we think of it, all that a university can do for us is still what the first school began doing—teach us to read."

Learning to read efficiently is a long and sometimes difficult task. Perhaps it should be both time-consuming and occasionally arduous, because reading is almost miraculous when we stop to think that through it we have at our command and for our daily use much of the best that has been thought and written by the greatest minds of many centuries. But remarks here should not be considered as overly stressing the dullness and difficulty of reading at the expense of the pleasure and excitement which it affords many millions of readers. After all, reading is one of the few pure pleasures—some say the only one—known to mankind. Reading can be a delight, a pastime which in the words of another great English writer, Sir Philip Sidney, "holdeth children from play and old men from the chimney corner." Although you may not be among their number, many persons actually read for enjoyment and sheer pleasure "heavy" works dealing with science, biography, history, and the like. One's active sympathies and intellectual curiosity strongly affect what and how one reads.

115a. READING TO COMPREHEND.

Much of our reading is neither accurate nor thoughtful. When we read a newspaper, a light short story, a mystery, or a comic book, we are usually seeking relaxation and naturally skip and skim. Ordinarily, such reading fare as this neither deserves nor receives careful attention and subsequent reflection. But all too often we attempt similarly to read meaty fiction and drama, closely reasoned essays, carefully wrought poems, and fact-packed textbooks. When we do, we receive all too little of the meaning intended and thus grow bored or discouraged. Reading to understand does not necessarily mean reading with speed and never involves reading with inattention and lack of concentration. The reading of genuinely important material must be painstakingly careful. In *Translating Literature into Life*, a famed author, Arnold Bennett, wrote:

> What is the matter with our reading is casualness, languor, preoccupation. We don't give the book a chance. We don't put ourselves at the disposal of the book. It is impossible to read

properly without using all one's engine-power. If we are not tired after reading, common sense is not in us. How should one grapple with a superior mind and not be out of breath?

But even if we read with the whole force of our brain, and do nothing else, common sense is still not in us, while sublime conceit is. For we are assuming that, without further trouble, we can possess, coordinate, and assimilate all the ideas and sensations rapidly offered to us by a mind greater than our own. The assumption has only to be stated in order to appear in its monstrous absurdity. Hence it follows that something remains to be done. This something is the act of reflection. Reading without subsequent reflection is ridiculous; it is equally a proof of folly and of vanity.

Bennett here used the word *reflection* to mean "evaluation," analysis, thinking through and putting the author's words into one's way of saying things.

In reading to understand, to comprehend, one should keep in mind that every student ought to learn to read well enough to

1. Gain and understand accurate information and ideas.

2. Recognize the organization and style of what he is reading.

3. Interpret what he is reading in terms of his own experience.

4. Analyze and evaluate what he is reading.

Whether we read for relaxation, information, or both, our aim should be to use our time intelligently. More than three centuries ago, Francis Bacon wrote as wisely as anyone ever has on the relationship of reading and writing:

Read not to contradict and confute; nor to believe and take for granted; nor to find talk and discourse; but to weigh and consider. Some books are to be tasted, others to be swallowed, and some few to be chewed and digested; that is, some books are to be read only in parts; others to be read, but not curiously; and some few to be read wholly, and with diligence and attention. Some books also may be read by deputy, and extracts made of them by others; but that would be only in the less important arguments, and the meaner sort of books; else distilled books are like common distilled waters, flashy things. Reading maketh a full man; conference a ready man; and writing an exact man. And therefore, if a man write little, he had need have a great memory; if he confer little, he had need have a present wit; and if he read little, he had need have much cunning, to seem to know what he doth not.

115b. SPEED IN READING.

Reading effectively is reading with both comprehension and speed. By a conspiracy of silence in high schools, until recently little attention was given to rapid reading. But the necessity for reading with reasonable rapidity has finally been recognized, and numerous steps have been taken to achieve this end. The necessity for learning to skip and scan certain kinds of material is now considered as important as learning to read other kinds of material with care and concentration.

An efficient reader reads thought units, not word-by-word. The technique involved is connected with the number of fixations the eyes make as they move across a page. Our aim should be to reduce the number of fixations, to lengthen the span of our eye movements. Our reading rate will increase as we learn to do this efficiently, and so will our comprehension. A skillful reader does not work with isolated units but with context—what precedes and follows the particular material he is looking at. A good reader rarely loses time by having to refer to the beginning of a sentence or paragraph he has finished. Rather he will have carried the thought through in one series of lengthened glances.

The best advice in learning to read with speed as well as comprehension is to "read with your head, not with your eyes." Doing this will enlarge comprehension by reducing the number of fixations and increasing concentration. Practice finding main thoughts in a passage and separating them from subordinate thoughts; learn to find key words and key sentences and to distinguish them from purely illustrative material. These steps will greatly increase reading speed without reducing the even more important matter of comprehension. Your school may maintain a special reading class or laboratory designed solely for the purpose of helping you learn to read with greater speed and understanding; if so, consult your teacher about it.

The reading rate of the general literate population of this country is about 250 words a minute with an attained comprehension of about 70%. This may seem a rapid rate, but actually it is about the sixth-grade level for elementary school. As a high school student, you should be able to read much more rapidly than this, although one must never forget that different kinds of material require different reading speeds.

115c. READING DIFFICULTIES.

Certain hindrances to effective reading exist for some people. For example, if, after concentrated reading for a short time, your eyes feel tired or begin to smart, or your head begins to ache, you should arrange to visit an ophthalmologist or oculist. Again, good body posture while reading will help to prevent muscular weariness and incorrect breathing; you won't need to consult a physician in order to correct this problem. Nor will you necessarily need to consult a lighting engineer to provide for yourself a good light for reading which illuminates the pages without glare and does not shine directly into your eyes.

You may have fallen into the bad habit of pronouncing words as you read silently. Few, if any, "lip movers" can read with either comprehension or speed. If you suspect yourself of this acquired fault, have someone observe you and try to break this bad habit.

Daydreaming, napping, and just plain letting your mind "wander from the reservation" are enemies of reading with either speed or comprehension. Good reading is as much a matter of concentrated attention as it is anything else.

115d. READING AS A READER.

When you read as a *reader*, your purposes should be to acquire information, to form opinions, to draw conclusions. You try to stock your mind with ideas for use in thinking, discussion, and writing. You consider new problems, answers to questions, visual details which widen your experience and understanding. Careful reading of any selection should help you to partial understanding of an author's background and sometimes of his actual life, to a statement of central theme and purpose, to an understanding of the organization of main divisions and supporting material. Efficient reading of a selection will also enable you to answer these questions:

What is the author attempting to do?
How well does he succeed in his attempt?
What value has the attempt?
Has the author affected me personally?

115e. READING AS A WRITER.

When you read as a *writer*, you should focus not only on the approaches mentioned above but also upon the author's technique, his methods of manipulating material. It should become habitual for you to study a writer's choice and use of words, his sentence and paragraph development and structure, even such relatively minor matters as punctuation and mechanics. Look deliberately and carefully for the methods by which an author secures interest and attention: humor, irony, anecdote, reports of conversation, appeals to emotions, and the like. Reading as a writer involves reading thoroughly, imaginatively, creatively. It implies consideration of subject matter, style (the imprint of an author's personality on subject matter), and technique.

116. LISTENING

You do a lot of reading and writing in school, but you listen much more often than you do either. It may be fair to say that school essentially provides an opportunity to listen. Certainly, much of what we know — including the prime ability to speak our language — has come through our ears.

Listening is a learning tool, perhaps the most significant one available to us whether in school or out. When we understand this fact, we discover that nearly everyone within hearing distance becomes a potential source of information.

Many friends have large stores of knowledge to offer, if we will only listen. The person who sits next to you on a bus may be an authority on some subject; give him or her your attention and you may receive a wealth of information about something interesting and even important. The staff at your school, teachers and others, is composed of persons expert in many fields; most of them will take time outside of class to pass on what they know to an interested listener. A willingness of people to talk about what they know does not necessarily spring from a generous nature; people are often flattered and eager to share their knowledge. A good listener is not only a welcome conversationalist; actually he is in a position to learn far more than the person who pays little attention to what he hears or who talks incessantly.

116a.   BEING A GOOD LISTENER.

Ability to listen is directly related to how much opportunity we have to learn by ear. When a person talks to you, he is usually affected by how you listen. If you are attentive, you help the speaker to say exactly what he has in mind. Inattentiveness acts as a brake on the person speaking; he will sometimes falter, stop, or lose interest in continuing. (Ask any teacher why he or she feels more effective in certain classes than in others.)

Try an experiment. In an empty room, talk out loud to yourself about some simple fact or happening. Your words may not flow smoothly, you may become confused, bored, or listless. Ask someone, a friend or member of your family, into the room and explain the same fact or happening to him. Probably you will find doing so far less difficult. We all *need* listeners, good listeners; without them, we are mentally lost as we talk. Consequently, when we are on the receiving end of oral information, we have an obligation to help produce effective communication by being attentive and receptive. And remember that good listening is not easily faked. Facial expressions, body posture, eye movements, and gestures betray the poor listener and support the good one.

116b. TAKING NOTES ON LECTURES.

Some students fail to take good notes because of inattentiveness, but perhaps even more fail because they attempt to write down too much of what is being said. Many students feel that they should transcribe as many of the lecturer's words as possible. Actually, the efficient notetaker spends most of his time listening and a minor amount in writing. He listens carefully and *thinks* about what he is hearing, with comparatively little emphasis on the mechanical process of writing. He knows that neither food nor ideas can be nourishing unless they are digested.

Properly proportioning time between listening and writing is found in the *précis* system of notetaking (see Section 110). That is, you listen for the period of time it takes a speaker to make a point and then you write down that point in a one-sentence summary. A classroom talk, for example, is usually organized so that the teacher makes a series of points (comparable to the topic sentences of written paragraphs; see Section 81) which support a main idea. Catch these points and summarize them.

This kind of notetaking requires practice, but actually the amount of time to listen and time to write will become more obvious as you gather experience in learning how talks, lectures, sermons, or what not are organized. When you become more skilled at précis-writing, you will find your notes more useful not only because they lead to central ideas but also help you to remember through mental association the figures and facts which should be in your mind because you were listening and not writing constantly during the lectures.

Here are two worthwhile suggestions: (1) Leave ample space around each sentence that you write in your notebook; (2) As soon as possible after a talk, review your précis notes and, where possible, expand them with whatever they bring to mind about the lecture. In this way you will produce a more effective set of notes depending less on memory, yet your notetaking will not have interfered with attentive and creative listening.

116c. LEARNING TO LISTEN WHILE LISTENING TO LEARN.

Compared to reading, listening is sometimes a faster and even more efficient means of gathering information. If you need to learn something about a subject quickly, you can often find an authority who is likely to speak in terms you can understand. Depending upon your interest and attentiveness, this expert may select and consolidate information from his wide field of knowledge to give you an accurate view of the subject which might require many hours of reading to acquire. Furthermore, if you don't understand something he says, you can ask a question and get immediate clarification. Listening is no substitute for reading but on occasion is surely a complementary learning tool.

Again, writing that may seem difficult and even dull can often be understood and appreciated when it is also listened to. The plays of Shakespeare are a good example. They were written to be heard and are at some disadvantage when presented simply as words on a page. However, if you first hear one of the plays and then read it carefully, the visual experience is increased and your chances of really appreciating Shakespeare are greatly enhanced. It is rarely difficult to find a friend who will join you in reading aloud. Also, if you have access to a record player, investigate the spoken-word records now produced in quantity and available in many school and public libraries. On such records accomplished speakers and actors read classical literature and famous authors read their own writings. They truly bring alive our literary heritage.

Finally, good listening is one of the best-known ways for improving language facility. This fact probably stems from early childhood when we learned to talk by listening to and imitating our elders. The principle remains at work regardless of how old we are. Otherwise, how can one explain the large amounts of time and money wisely expended, for example, on language laboratories? In school, you have many opportunities to listen to accomplished speakers in public-speaking situations, in classrooms, and in conversation. Use them.

116d. LISTENING OUTSIDE OF SCHOOL.

When you leave school, your ability to listen may become more important than ever. An adult spends at least half of his communication time in listening. That poor listeners are expensive and expendable employees is being increasingly recognized in the business world. Indeed, many of our most important affairs depend on listening. What does a jury do? It listens, sometimes to millions of words of testimony, and then makes up its mind about the case on trial. The way one votes in an election depends to a large extent upon his ability to listen. Listening situations and opportunities confront us many times every day. What else can and should one expect in a nation that has millions of television sets, more radios than bathtubs, and several million *new* telephone installations every year?

EXERCISE 43

You may have acquired some bad listening habits which thwart your attempts in learning to listen while listening to learn. These habits will be less difficult to overcome if you are aware of them. Honestly consider the following faulty listening habits. Do you recognize any of them in yourself? Write a paragraph analyzing your problems with *one* of these patterns of listening:

1. *Supersensitive listening.* Some persons refuse to listen to anything which does not agree with their own private thoughts. Hearing statements that they do not like, they immediately plan a rebuttal and stop listening to what the speaker has to say. Perhaps they should make it a policy to hear the speaker out. When he has finished, they can make final judgments.
2. *Avoiding difficult explanations.* If something is difficult to understand, many listeners tend to give up too easily. They blame the speaker for not making his points clearer. The remedy: go out of your way to hear material which is hard to grasp; stick with the subject from beginning to end and make a concerted effort to force yourself to listen. Listening requires practice just as writing does.
3. *Premature dismissal of a subject as uninteresting.* If a speaker's material seems dry, some of us use that impression as rational-

ization for not listening. We feel that if a speaker's material is not stimulating, he must not have anything worth hearing. Such an opinion is not always correct. Someone once remarked that there are no uninteresting subjects, only uninterested people. When one forms the habit of listening attentively, many previously dull subjects seem to take on new life. Have you never become friends with, or even fallen in love with, someone whom you used to consider dull and uninteresting?

4. *Finding fault with a speaker's delivery or appearance.* Sometimes we become so deeply involved in a speaker's delivery or appearance that we cannot concentrate on what he or she is saying. If his manner or appearance creates an unfavorable impression, we lose interest. Conversely, a speaker's looks or manner may cause romantic or other dreams which distract us with equal loss of comprehension. The most important task in listening is to learn what the speaker says, not how he says it or how he looks when saying it.

117. SPEAKING

This handbook emphasizes writing, an important and involved series of processes which requires close attention and intelligent, hard work. Problems in writing effectively are sufficiently numerous and complex to permit little space in this book for consideration of other types of mental activity. And yet it is obvious that nearly everybody speaks a thousand words for every one that he writes. It is also true that writing and speaking share one common goal: *communication.*

Consequently, some consideration of speaking should shed light on the aims and purposes of communicating orally as well as in writing. The two processes possess likenesses and dissimilarities. In addition, the activities of speaking and listening are important sources of material for writing. Also, learning to converse well and to participate effectively in group discussion contributes much to the problems of learning to write correctly and clearly.

117a. DIFFERENCES BETWEEN ORAL AND WRITTEN COMPOSITION.

We are normally more relaxed in speaking than writing, less concerned with "rules" and "errors." But just because speaking comes easily and more naturally to us than writing does not mean that speech has no requirements, no aims, no goals. In fact, the circumstances of speaking impose conditions that are sometimes more difficult than those of writing.

For example, a spoken message usually has only one hearing. The speaker who does not immediately gain the attention and interest of his listener has lost them forever; a reader can always go back and reread. Again, one's hearer cannot usually meditate upon something a speaker has said because if he does he is sure to lose what follows. For these two reasons, oral style markedly differs from written style.

As a speaker, your sentences are properly shorter than most of those you use in writing. Language is usually more direct and simpler in speech than in writing. A reader and writer are normally separated, but in most instances a speaker and listener are thrown into close association. The reader is usually alone or in a quiet room free from distractions. The listener, conversely, is normally surrounded by others and is sometimes distracted by them. Even when a listener is at home, following a speech over TV or the radio, his mind tends to wander and he cannot recapture what he has missed as he can by rereading something written. Most people are more eye-minded than ear-minded. Finally, the speaker's voice, gestures, and use of his body are important considerations that influence oral communication but which have no exact counterparts in writing. In short, speaking is more widespread than writing can ever be, is faced with more problems of delivery, and needs to be worked at to be genuinely effective. A speech has been called "an essay on its hind legs," but all speeches and all speaking are much more than just that.

There is a final critical difference between writing and speaking. You can rewrite endlessly until your thoughts are clear, well-organized, and effective. But you can't talk endlessly!

117b. CONVERSATION.

The most universal form of social activity and our most important means of communicating with others is conversation. The good conversationalist — one who listens courteously and attentively to others and also has something interesting to say to his listeners — is welcomed everywhere. A lack of opportunities for exchange of talk can produce irritation, boredom, and even serious mental disorders. One of the most severe of all prison punishments is solitary confinement.

Good conversation — a genuine meeting of minds — has nothing to do with mere talkativeness, such as chatter about dates, games, clothes, food, and the weather. Conversation is a stimulating pastime when it represents an honest interchange of facts and opinions. Glibness and superficiality may save one the trouble of clarifying or defending his position in a conversation, but they actually waste the time of both speaker and hearer.

How can one become a good conversationalist? Here are a few suggestions:

1. Be sincere and straightforward but also tactful, courteous, and friendly. A spirited discussion may be argumentative — a group of people will seldom agree about any matter of real consequence — but one can state his opinions firmly and frankly without hurting the feelings of others, without being rude and brusque.

2. Try to find out as much as you tactfully can about the person to whom you are talking. For example, if you are left with the guest of honor at a reception, a stranger at a party, an older person at a dance, a teacher at a school function, do not try to interest him in yourself and your problems but try to draw him out. You probably will learn some highly interesting facts; even if you don't, your listener will not fail to be flattered by your interest and will consider you an excellent conversationalist. A good conversationalist, as a matter of fact, is a good listener.

3. Study every conversation you have an opportunity to overhear or engage in. Analysis of such conversations will indicate that the best talkers are those with the largest fund of interesting experiences, or, better yet, the most familiarity with subjects of greatest interest to the people in the circle. You

will also observe that the best conversationalists do not talk constantly and are fully capable of quiet listening.

4. Try to get and keep informed about subjects of timely interest: current events, political affairs, personalities in the limelight, music, sporting events, art, and literature. Read as much as you can: books, worthwhile magazines, a daily newspaper. Try to remember good stories you hear or read, funny or interesting incidents which happen to you or your friends, amusing or significant happenings you see or read about.

5. Practice conversation. Join in good talk whenever you can. Listen in on good conversations when you have the opportunity to do so without being a pest or an eavesdropper.

117c. GROUP DISCUSSION.

Various types of public discussion are in general use today, but all have basically the same purpose: to pool the information of a group and try to find a satisfactory approach to the problem under discussion. Hundreds of thousands of people have had an opportunity to speak in public through discussion groups; millions have heard group discussions on TV and radio programs.

1. The single-leader type.

This kind of program often follows a speech and provides an open forum period during which members of the audience may address questions or remarks to the speaker. The speaker may preside, or a chairman may act as moderator and direct questions to the speaker. If no formal speech is involved, a leader may recognize speakers from the audience, guide the discussion, and summarize remarks at the end of the session. Most assemblies and parliamentary bodies follow a system of this type and are governed by specific rules of conduct and order.

2. The panel, or round-table, type.

A group of experts or well-informed people, literally sitting around a table, discusses various aspects of a selected topic. The discussion, usually informal, resembles a spirited conversation. The function of the chairman is to keep the talk going, to sift out agreements where possible, to summarize the argument for the audience at the end. Panel discussions occur frequently on TV and radio programs.

3. The "town meeting" type.

A group of experts — usually four — discusses opposing attitudes toward some important public question. Each speaker is given at least one opportunity to reply to another's argument. The audience is provided chances to enter the discussion and ask questions of the speakers. A moderator presides over the meeting, introduces the speakers, and controls audience participation.

4. The debate.

Formal debate has characteristics in common with more informal discussions, but it is closely controlled by rules. This form of intellectual sport is far less popular now than in previous years, but it continues to crop up in political campaigns and is still encouraged by debating coaches at numerous schools and colleges. In formal debates, the proposition to be argued is carefully formulated so as to avoid ambiguity and to insure direct clash of opinion. Opposing members are organized into teams, each with a captain. Each speaker is usually allowed to speak twice in a prescribed order; a rigid time limit is imposed. A judge, or board of judges, awards a decision to the team which has played this intellectual game more skillfully.

EXERCISE 44

Write a 300-word description of the best conversationalist you know.

EXERCISE 45

Listen to what you consider a typical conversation between two friends or schoolmates. Summarize it for the class, using direct quotations if you can. Criticize the conversation from the point of view of Section 117b.

EXERCISE 46

Find an example of an interesting conversation in one short story from your book of readings. Read it to the class and tell why you think it is interesting and effective.

EXERCISE 47

Listen to a television or radio speaker who interests you. Prepare a report, oral or written as your teacher directs, which analyzes this speaker's performance in the light of comments made in Section 117.

EXERCISE 48

Find an interesting modern speech in a collection. Prepare a detailed outline of it, including purposes and central theme, and list the rhetorical devices which the speaker used.

EXERCISE 49

Prepare a three-minute speech to be delivered to class on a subject which you have previously used for a theme. Hand in in advance an outline of the speech and a summary of the differences between speech and theme.

118. TAKING TESTS

Tests have become a part of your life. There is no escaping them. As a student, you face a test of one sort or another nearly all the time, whether it be ten brief questions intended to check on a reading assignment or a two-hour essay examination designed to evaluate a semester's work. But tests are not confined to course work. Some of you, for example, will take college entrance examinations. The results of these tests will be used to determine readiness for college, admission to the school of your choice, scholarship eligibility, and advance standing. Others will take tests used by employers to evaluate skills necessary for various types of jobs. Most of you, no matter what you do, will continue to take tests for a long time to come.

It is obvious that study is the best preparation for most tests. Tests used for college admission and for employment evaluation, however, attempt mainly to determine general knowledge and ability. Detailed study of specific subject matter is impossible. But you can prepare for these tests by acquainting yourself with the kinds of questions which are asked. This section explains the kinds of language questions which frequently appear on various tests of general knowledge. It also contains advice on approaching tests of several other types. The accompanying exercises are designed to give you practice answering the kinds of questions which you frequently encounter.

118a. VOCABULARY QUESTIONS

As a general rule, the larger an individual's vocabulary, the greater his knowledge. There is a direct relationship between the size of your vocabulary and the amount of knowledge you possess. Consequently, questions dealing with vocabulary are commonly used on tests of general ability.

Matching Words with Definitions

In this type of question, a column of definitions is presented opposite a column of words to be defined. You are asked to match each word with its definition.

The best way to answer such a question is to consider, one at a time, the words to be defined. Search the opposite column for the definition which seems best. If more than one definition seems possible, go on to the next word. Narrow down the field of choices by first selecting only those which you are sure of.

EXERCISE 50

Number your paper from 1 to 20. Write opposite each number the letter of the group of words in the second column which best defines it. (The directions, of course, might vary depending upon the test.)

1. PENURY	a.	marked by shrewdness
2. DETER	b.	express indirectly
3. ANTICIPATE	c.	utter and total confusion
4. PROFICIENT	d.	open to view
5. INSTIGATE	e.	extreme poverty
6. REBATE	f.	take away
7. COMPOSITE	g.	a return of a portion of a payment
8. WRATH	h.	prevent from acting

9. DIRE	i. noisy in an offensive manner
10. JOCULAR	j. urge forward
11. ADROIT	k. showing reverence or devotion
12. IMPLY	l. deserving imitation
13. VULNERABLE	m. violent anger
14. EXEMPLARY	n. given to jesting
15. PIOUS	o. a false idea
16. BLATANT	p. foresee
17. RESCIND	q. made up of distinct parts
18. OVERT	r. desperately urgent
19. CHAOS	s. open to attack
20. FALLACY	t. well advanced in an art or occupation

Choosing from Several Definitions

In this type of question, a word to be defined is followed by four or five definitions. You are asked to select the one which offers the best definition. The usual procedure is to place the letter preceding your choice in the space provided on the answer sheet or to blacken the area corresponding to the letter on a specially prepared answer sheet.

EXERCISE 51

On your paper write the number of each sentence. Next to each number, write the letter corresponding to your choice of definitions.

EXAMPLE: *Sinister* means most nearly
a) serious b) threatening evil c) gloomy d) sorrowful e) difficult
ANSWER: b

1. *Tepid* means most nearly a) foreign b) precise c) moderately warm d) intensely interesting e) hopeless.
2. *Profane* means most nearly a) skillful b) irreverent c) competent d) profound e) pleasant.
3. *Relinquish* means most nearly a) abandon b) remain c) control d) construct e) modify.
4. *Contrite* means most nearly a) opposed b) foolish c) furious d) decisive e) sorry.
5. *Hypothesis* means most nearly a) complexity b) theory c) feeling d) fascination e) indication.
6. *Garnish* means most nearly a) direct b) cover c) frequent d) embellish e) complete.

553

7. *Garrulous* means most nearly a) dangerous b) angry c) talkative d) loud e) persistent.

8. *Patent* means most nearly a) defective b) exact c) quiet d) careful e) obvious.

9. *Impeccable* means most nearly a) flawless b) imperfect c) inconsiderate d) competent e) workable.

10. *Fallacious* means most nearly a) incomplete b) faltering c) deceptive d) resolute e) aggravating.

11. *Nurture* means most nearly a) object b) confess c) foster d) separate e) fail.

12. *Repugnant* means most nearly a) acceptable b) modern c) adequate d) dreary e) repellent.

13. *Replica* means most nearly a) substitute b) reproduction c) remembrance d) movement e) strategy.

14. *Contrived* means most nearly a) controlled b) destroyed c) artificial d) incomplete e) convincing.

15. *Remunerate* means most nearly a) pay b) enumerate c) repair d) rebuild e) copy.

16. *Germane* means most nearly a) fertile b) pertinent c) possible d) sufficient e) desirable.

17. *Subterfuge* means most nearly a) deception b) alliance c) scandal d) plan e) escape.

18. *Dire* means most nearly a) enough b) pleasant c) formidable d) significant e) extreme.

19. *Diminutive* means most nearly a) positive b) intelligent c) small d) direct e) helpful.

20. *Arcane* means most nearly a) distant b) usual c) conceited d) mysterious e) comprehensive.

Choosing Synonyms

The English language is rich in vocabulary. The richness is due in part to the fact that many words have a number of synonyms, words which have basically—but not exactly—the same meanings. Questions which require you to identify a word's synonym appear frequently on tests of general ability. Such questions effectively measure your ability to exploit the resources of language to the fullest.

EXERCISE 52

On your paper write the number of each item. From the choice given, select the word or group of words which most nearly means the same as the italicized word. Write the letter of your choice next to the appropriate number.

1. *Sanguine.* a) thorough b) special c) optimistic d) particular e) bright.
2. *Precarious.* a) dangerous b) stable c) preventable d) helpful e) satisfying.
3. *Intermittent.* a) frequent b) regular c) unusual d) creative e) periodic.
4. *Appease.* a) create b) decorate c) calm d) distribute e) repeat.
5. *Maelstrom.* a) congregation b) turmoil c) thunder d) miracle e) steadiness.
6. *Mercurial.* a) changeable b) balanced c) inquiring d) new e) daily.
7. *Dissipate.* a) disperse b) brusque c) happy d) organized e) beautiful.
8. *Curt.* a) talented b) brusque c) happy d) organized e) courteous.
9. *Interdict.* a) please b) intertwine c) remove d) frequent e) prohibit.
10. *Indigent.* a) poor b) indecent c) dependent d) unhappy e) composed.
11. *Altercation.* a) movement b) perfection c) beginning d) quarrel e) reparation.
12. *Proffer.* a) offer b) exit c) return d) proceed e) spread.
13. *Transient.* a) perpetual b) changeable c) short-lived d) different e) automatic.
14. *Incessant.* a) irritating b) secret c) scarce d) doubtful e) unceasing.
15. *Dogmatic.* a) animal-like b) dictatorial c) automatic d) religious e) efficient.
16. *Obtuse.* a) dull b) characteristic c) fortunate d) trustworthy e) enthusiastic.
17. *Stoic.* a) experienced b) excited c) average d) impassive e) perfect.
18. *Vivid.* a) muddled b) comparative c) graphic d) ancient e) intelligent.
19. *Voluble.* a) expectant b) glib c) domestic d) enlightened e) unstable.
20. *Prosaic.* a) unimaginative b) tragic c) devoted d) possible e) ineffective.

Choosing Antonyms

An antonym is a word of opposite meaning. You will frequently encounter questions which require you to choose the antonym of a given word. A word is followed by several choices, one of which is its exact opposite. At the outset, it is a good practice to search the choices for synonyms, which are commonly included among the choices. The immediate elimination of synonyms enables you to focus your attention upon the remaining choices.

EXERCISE 53

Each of the words given below is followed by five lettered choices. Number your paper from one to twenty. Choose the lettered word which is most nearly *opposite* in meaning to the capitalized word. Write the letter representing your choice next to the appropriate number.

1. *Punctual.* a) precise b) dilatory c) rare d) concise e) succinct.
2. *Subsequent.* a) eventual b) comparative c) prior d) subservient e) succeeding.
3. *Apropos.* a) pertinent b) contrite c) sensible d) ancient e) irrelevant.
4. *Infringe.* a) respect b) perceive c) bestow d) encircle e) violate.
5. *Succor.* a) neglect b) arrange c) administer d) fragment e) help.
6. *Transitory.* a) temporary b) bearable c) permanent d) troublesome e) numerous.
7. *Culpable.* a) responsible b) obedient c) innocent d) immoral e) anticipated.
8. *Dogmatic.* a) reasonable b) militant c) expectant d) rigorous e) constrained.
9. *Intrinsic.* a) necessary b) basic c) extraneous d) magnificent e) furtive.
10. *Clandestine.* a) overt b) secret c) shadowy d) brilliant e) mellow.
11. *Abridge.* a) offset b) build c) condense d) discard e) expand.
12. *Restive.* a) simple b) comfortable c) reticent d) hardy e) patient.
13. *Voluble.* a) large b) fluent c) reticent d) complete e) vexing.
14. *Lachrymose.* a) happy b) tearful c) laden d) brown e) latent.
15. *Migratory.* a) moveable b) subversive c) subtle d) satisfied e) stationary.
16. *Orthodox.* a) sound b) plentiful c) usual d) heretical e) reactionary.
17. *Prodigious.* a) abundant b) minute c) slow d) deadly e) amateurish.

18. *Ingenuous.* a) real b) rustic c) everlasting d) clever e) flexible.

19. *Capricious.* a) entertaining b) steady c) erratic d) splendid e) jovial.

20. *Obfuscate.* a) aver b) estrange c) clarify d) confuse e) assemble.

Choosing Words in Context

Words do not appear in a vacuum. They appear in context, surrounded by other words. Words typically have more than one meaning. Context determines the particular meaning which a word has. Your ability to use a word in context indicates your control over the various meanings of words.

In tests designed to evaluate your ability to use a word in context, blank spaces are usually provided in sentences. From a number of choices given, you are to select the one word which best fits the context.

EXERCISE 54

Each of the following sentences contains a blank space where a word has been omitted. From the choices following each sentence, select the one word which best fits the context. Number your paper from one to ten and write the letters corresponding to your choices next to the appropriate numbers. (All of the sentences in this exercise are taken from the works of practiced writers.)

1. They (the Custodians of Language) hold that there is a right and a wrong way of expressing yourself, and that the right way should be ____ by works of a certain description, chief among them the dictionaries of the language. (Mario Pei)
   a) suggested b) prescribed c) counterbalanced d) eradicated e) replaced

2. The first of all the challengers, in point of time, bulk of literature and noise, number and ingenuity of supporters, is Francis Bacon, whose claim, first advanced in 1785, rests fundamentally on the assumptions that the author of the plays was ____ and that Bacon not only knew everything but had practically a monopoly on information. (Bergen Evans)
   a) daring b) omnipotent c) academic d) omniscient e) attentive

3. In the middle of 1964—a year otherwise marked in Russia by

attempts to ___ the ordinary citizens—the Soviet Government announced a new drive to wipe out religious influences among its people. (Barbara Ward)

a) conciliate b) arouse c) insult d) aggravate e) compromise

4. Knowledge then is the ___ condition of expansion of mind, and the instrument of attaining to it; this can not be denied; it is ever to be insisted on; I begin with it as a first principle; however, the very truth of it carries men too far and confirms to them the notion that it is the whole of the matter. (John Henry Newman)

a) casual b) impractical c) destructive d) indispensable e) original

5. In Europe the frontier is stationary and presumably permanent; in America it was ___ and temporal. (Walter Prescott Webb)

a) ugly b) primitive c) transient d) routine e) false

6. His face wore a leaden hue; the eyes were utterly lusterless; and the ___ was so extreme that the skin had been broken through by the cheek-bones. (Edgar Allan Poe)

a) expectation b) inability c) anticipation d) recreation e) emaciation

7. Every spring in the wet meadows and ditches I hear a little shrilling chorus which sounds for all the world like an endlessly ___ "We're here, we're here, we're here." (Loren Eiseley)

a) confused b) stubborn c) reiterated d) remote e) disguised

8. The world is very different now. For man holds in his mortal hands the power to ___ all forms of human poverty and all forms of human life. (John F. Kennedy)

a) alter b) abolish c) justify d) renew e) balance

9. In the opening scene of the movie *Scarface*, we are shown a successful man; we know he is successful because he has just given a party of ___ proportions and because he is called Big Louie. (Robert Warshow)

a) clever b) opulent c) standard d) satisfactory e) lasting

10. It is curious that fire, the most impermanent of all phenomena, is precisely that which (like the sea) shows no change, but is itself an endless thread of ___ through the years. (John Lafarge)

a) continuity b) amusement c) absurdity d) performance e) courtesy

Completing Analogies

Verbal analogies appear frequently on tests of general knowledge. In a verbal analogy, you are asked to select, from a number of choices, the one pair of words which is related to each other in the same way as a given pair of words. Since such a question demands that you be able to analyze and identify basic relationships, it is thought to provide a good measurement of mental ability.

Every analogy begins with a pair of words written as follows: BASKET: STRAW. The symbol (:) stands for "is related to" or simply "is to." The base pair is followed by several choices and the whole question is written as follows: BASKET: STRAW: : a) dress: stitch b) house: room c) table: leg d) desk: write e) blanket: wool. The symbol (::) stands for "in the same way as" or simply "as."

In working out an analogy, you must begin by determining the nature of the relationship which exists between the two words in the base pair. In our example, analysis indicates that *straw* is a material from which a *basket* might be made.

The next step is to study the relationships existing between the words in the pairs which make up the choices. In our example, a study of the first pair indicates that a *stitch* is that which holds the parts of a *dress* together. But a dress is not made of a stitch. In the second choice, *room* is related to *house* in that a room is a part of a house. A room, however, is not the material from which a house is made. Similarly, a *leg* is a part of a *table* in the third choice, but the basic material of a table is not a leg. In the fourth choice, *write* refers to the type of activity which often takes place at a *desk*. In the final pair, *wool* is a type of material from which a *blanket* might be made. Of all the choices given, the words in the final pair match most closely the relationship expressed in the base pair. Consequently, choice *e* provides the best answer.

In working out analogies, you should keep in mind that the pair of words which comprises the correct answer must match the base pair in *form* as well as relationship. If, for example, the base pair illustrates a relationship between two nouns, the correct answer will also consist of two nouns. If, moreover, the base pair is made up of two plurals, the correct answer will be made up of two plurals. Sometimes even a quick examination of the choices will enable you to reject immediately choices which do not have the same form as the base pair. In the example you have just studied, choice *d* could be eliminated immediately because it is made up of a noun and a verb, whereas the base pair consists of two nouns.

Verbal analogies frequently illustrate common relationships. The following are worth noting:

1. *A part is to a whole.* COUNTY: PROVINCE
2. *A member is to a class.* GOLD: METAL
3. *A word means the same as another word.* HARD: DIFFICULT
4. *A word means the opposite of another word.* SIMPLE: COMPLICATED
5. *A quality is to a possessor.* BRAVERY: SOLDIER
6. *A person is to an activity.* PILOT: FLY

There are, of course, other types of relationships which can best be understood through close study of the base pair.

EXERCISE 55

Each of the following questions consists of two italicized words which have a certain relationship to each other, followed by five lettered pairs of related words. Select the lettered pair of words related to each other in the *same* way as the original words are related to each other. Number your paper from one to twenty-five. Write the letters corresponding to your choices next to the appropriate numbers.

1. *Cow: Milk* :: (a) bird: nest (b) tree: sap (c) street: curb (d) water: river (e) plum: tree.
2. *Transparent: Translucent* :: (a) clear: foggy (b) night: day (c) black: white (d) frog: water (e) intelligent: dull.
3. *Saki: Japan* :: (a) grain: Iowa (b) water: ocean (c) politics: Washington (d) Chianti: Italy (e) beer: Milwaukee.
4. *Contemplation: Monk* :: (a) quiet: noise (b) desk: chair (c) model: beauty (d) activity: salesman (e) reader: magazine.
5. *Sand: Beach* :: (a) paint: wall (b) water: ocean (c) farm: soil (d) gems: bracelet (e) salt: pepper.
6. *Munificent: Philanthropist* :: (a) inventive: scientist (b) searching: astronomer (c) competent: doctor (d) parsimonious: miser (e) circumspect: race car driver.
7. *Ham: Eggs* :: (a) blue: turquoise (b) meat ball: spaghetti (c) wheel: rim (d) cloud: sky (e) bacon: bread.
8. *Abhor: Love* :: (a) hope: despair (b) happiness: sorrow (c) like: enjoy (d) hate: disgust (e) fear: terror.
9. *Homer: Greece* :: (a) Frost: America (b) Naples: Italy (c) Virgil: Rome (d) Poland: Russia (e) Wordsworth: England.
10. *Elegy: Poetry* :: (a) sing: bird (b) wheat: harvest (c) bread: flour (d) corn: grain (e) tractor: farm.

11. *Vaccination: Smallpox* : : (a) doctor: disease (b) antibiotic: flu (c) caution: carelessness (d) activity: fatigue (e) condition: accident.

12. *Fraternity: Boy* : : (a) congress: representative (b) sorority: girl (c) voter: electorate (d) light: electricity (e) class: student.

13. *Nocturnal: Diurnal* : : (a) annual: perennial (b) dark: light (c) pope: church (d) outside: inside (e) midnight: noon.

14. *Grass: Seed* :: (a) map: territory (b) idea: invention (c) plant: flower (d) wall: room (e) book: reader.

15. *Obese: Emaciated* : : (a) thin: slender (b) cavity: tooth (c) obsolete: new (d) lead: silver (e) twenty dollars: fifty dollars.

16. *She: Her* : : (a) man: men (b) boy: boy's (c) yours: ours (d) boy: boys' (e) theirs: they.

17. *Lighthouse: Danger* : : (a) cold: snow (b) foundation: house (c) symptom: disease (d) deadline: work (e) ship: channel.

18. *Gold: Ore* : : (a) dear: cheap (b) iron: steel (c) pearls: oysters (d) steel: iron (e) intelligence: astuteness.

19. *Steak: Steer* : : (a) boat: sail (b) grass: green (c) flour: wheat (d) street: curb (e) wool: sheep.

20. *Ship: Harbor::* (a) mountain: rock (b) house: roof (c) chrome: bumper (d) sole: shoe (e) car: garage.

21. *Brake: Automobile* : : (a) stop: red (b) conscience: man (c) current: canoe (d) saw: tree (e) thinking: doing.

22. *Alps: Europe* :: (a) Pyrenees: France (b) Mt. McKinley: Alaska (c) Rockies: Canada (d) Andes: South America (e) Sierras: California.

23. *Carefulness: Safety* : : (a) tires: automobile (b) siren: police car (c) frugality: security (d) binding: book (e) planning: success.

24. *B: Two* :: (a) C: six (b) F: nine (c) X: fourteen (d) A: ten (e) M: thirteen.

25. *Aviary: Peacock* :: (a) kennel: dog (b) fish: aquarium (c) warren: rabbit (d) covey: quail (e) cage: parrot.

118b. READING COMPREHENSION.

Numerous quizzes, tests, and examinations are designed to find out how well and how rapidly you can read material of normal difficulty. Such tests usually seek to discover whether you can understand what you read, whether you can draw conclusions from your reading—that is, make judgments and inferences—and whether you can do all of this within specified and reasonable time limits. Here is an example of such a test of reading comprehension:

Those who take honors in Nature's university, who learn the laws which govern men and things and obey them, are the really great and successful men in this world. The great mass of mankind are the "Poll" [mob], who pick up just enough to get through without much discredit. Those who won't learn at all are plucked [dropped]; and then you can't come up again. Nature's pluck means extermination.

Thus the question of compulsory education is settled so far as Nature is concerned. Her bill on that question was framed and passed long ago. But, like all compulsory legislation, that of Nature is harsh and wasteful in its operation. Ignorance is visited as sharply as willful disobedience—incapacity meets with the same punishment as crime. Nature's discipline is not even a word and a blow, and the blow first; but the blow without the word. It is left to you to find out why your ears are boxed.

The object of what we commonly call education—that education in which man intervenes and which I shall distinguish as artificial education—is to make good these defects in Nature's methods; to prepare the child to receive Nature's education, neither incapably nor ignorantly, nor with willful disobedience; and to understand the preliminary symptoms of her pleasure, without waiting for the box on the ear. In short, all artificial education ought to be an anticipation of natural education. And a liberal education is an artificial education which has not only prepared a man to escape the great evils of disobedience to natural laws, but has trained him to appreciate and to seize upon the rewards, which Nature scatters with as free a hand as her penalties.

That man, I think, has had a liberal education who has been so trained in youth that his body is the ready servant of his will, and does with ease and pleasure all the work that, as a mechanism, it is capable of; whose intellect is a clear, cold, logic engine, with all its parts of equal strength, and in smooth working order; ready, like a steam engine, to be turned to any kind of work, and spin the gossamers as well as forge the anchors of the mind; whose mind is stored with a knowledge of the great and fundamental truths of Nature and of the laws of her operations; one who, no stunted ascetic, is full of life and fire, but whose passions are trained to come to heel by a vigorous will, the servant of a tender conscience; who has learned to love all beauty, whether of Nature or of art, to hate all vileness, and to respect others as himself.

— "A Liberal Education," by Thomas Henry Huxley

EXERCISE 56

1. Distinguish between "Nature's university" and artificial education.
2. What is the primary object of "artificial" education?
3. A liberal education has what effects upon the body?
4. A liberal education has what effects upon the intellect?
5. A liberal education has what effects upon the mind?
6. A liberal education has what effects upon moral and social conduct?
7. Your evaluation: What do you think is meant by Nature's discipline?
8. Your evaluation: Can one attain the liberal education described here or is this a "counsel of perfection" and therefore impossible to achieve?

118c. ESSAY QUESTIONS.

Probably no type of test question frightens students so much as an essay question. Most students would rather submit to objective tests than be faced with questions which demand somewhat lengthy answers in intelligible prose.

Essay questions, however, are necessary because they test for the type of information which objective questions tend to ignore. An essay question enables the tester to determine a student's ability to put facts into perspective, to generalize from the data that he has assembled, and to draw subjective conclusions from the content of his study. The essay question may also be used to measure how well a student is able to communicate in writing.

You should approach an essay question with the same care as you would any formal written assignment. A careful reading of the question is indispensable. You must determine exactly what it is the question seeks to discover and the general type of information which the answer requires. It is also good practice to sketch out an outline before you begin to write. The preliminary steps in answering an essay question are as important as they are in planning a formal composition.

Perhaps the most difficult step in an essay answer is the framing of the first sentence of the first paragraph. It is frequently possible to restate the central part of the question as the opening sentence. Note the following question:

In a famous definition of the tragic hero, Aristotle pointed out that he was a man who was not preeminently virtuous or just, but one who came to his tragic end not through some essential lack of goodness but through some error of judgment. How well do you feel that Macbeth measures up or fails to measure up to Aristotle's definition? Use incidents from the play to support your judgment.

Depending upon your judgment, the central part of the question might be expressed as the first sentence of your answer as follows: *Macbeth fits (or does not fit) perfectly Aristotle's definition of the tragic hero.*

Some essay questions merely require you to provide factual data. Most, however, demand that you come to a conclusion or formulate a judgment based upon your study; you must see to it that your conclusions are concretely supported by pertinent facts and examples. Moreover, the relationship between your supporting facts and your conclusion must be evident. Note that the sample question above directs the student to support his answer by citing incidents from *Macbeth.*

For example, you may write that Macbeth's judgment was affected by his impatience and rashness. In an essay answer, such a statement should be supported by mention of Macbeth's determined disregard of consequences in seeing the Witches again. Or you might refer to his blotting out a former nobility because of a wild recklessness which caused him to take further bloody, cruel, and useless action in the massacre of Lady Macduff, her children, and the servants. On the other hand, if you feel that his judgment was distorted more by his fear than his rashness, you might refer to the stark terror and sense of guilt which overcame his momentary desire to spare Macduff's life. Again, you may wish to write that Macbeth's judgment was affected by weakness, or his sense of pity for others; if so, you should refer to the conflict by which he is torn between a need to rely on his wife and his own protective love of her. Whatever your approach, your answer should consist of a conclusion, or series of conclusions, based on specific examples and citations that exactly set forth what you are trying to communicate.

The body of an essay answer should illustrate the same attention to the techniques, conventions, and mechanics of writing as a formal composition assignment. Paragraphs should be unified, coherent, and amply developed. Care should be taken in spelling and punctuation. If time permits, it is a good idea to set down a rough draft before writing your final copy.

There is very little correlation between length and impressiveness. Common sense indicates that there is merit in brevity. Many students have a tendency to expand their essay answers, believing that those who evaluate them will be favorably disposed by bulk. On the contrary, those who must read essay answers are much more impressed by pertinent material economically expressed.

EXERCISE 57

The following essay questions are representative of the type that you might encounter on semester or year-end examinations. Choose one and answer it as best you can, paying particular attention to the structure of your answer. Keep in mind that you would be graded for both content and the quality of the writing.

1. Plot has been defined as a series of causally related events working up to a conclusion. A distinction may then be drawn between story and plot. Events which are chronologically related to each other comprise what we call "story." "The king died and then the queen died" constitutes the essentials of "story." "The king died and then the queen died because of grief" constitutes "plot." By referring to a short story or novel which you have read recently, isolate at least five events which constitute plot, indicating how each is causally related. Explain each relationship in some detail.

2. Many literary works express a theme which the author wishes the reader to understand. Identify the theme presented in a recent work which you have read. Support your judgment by referring to specific incidents in the work.

3. Relate the following quotation to one of the works you have read recently.

> Every man who knows how to read has it in his power to magnify himself, to multiply the ways in which he exists, to make his life full, significant, and interesting.
>
> (Aldous Huxley)

118d. THE COLLEGE ENTRANCE EXAMINATION

If you plan to go to an American college, you will probably have to take the entrance examination developed and administered by the College Entrance Examination Board. This examination is required for admission by a great number of American colleges and universities.

The College Entrance Examination Board administers a three-hour examination called the Scholastic Aptitude Test (SAT). The SAT examination is designed to measure your ability to handle college-level work. It is a test of general ability, consisting of both verbal and mathematical questions. The verbal questions are, for the most part, of the type presented in this section. Questions which measure reading comprehension are also included. The mathematical section tests your ability to understand number concepts. Your score on this test is forwarded to the college which you specify when you take the test.

The SAT is a test of general ability. Consequently, it is impossible to prepare for it by mastering specific material. Familiarizing yourself with the type of questions presented in this section and in the Bulletin of Information published by the College Entrance Examination Board will provide the best preparation. You might also wish to obtain one of the many review books available which provide additional exercises of the type presented here.

It is also a good idea to take the Preliminary Scholastic Aptitude Test which is given in October of each year. Since this test consists of questions identical to the type presented on the SAT, it provides an excellent indication of how well you might do. Your score on this test is reported only to you.

The College Examination Board also provides Achievement Tests in specific subject areas which are required by some colleges. These tests are offered in English, social studies, mathematics, German, Latin, Spanish, French, biology, chemistry, physics, Hebrew, and Russian. Each test is of an hour's duration. These tests are sometimes used by colleges to verify the student's high school record.

Since 1960, some colleges have required a writing sample of all applicants. An essay of between 350-450 words is required to be written in one hour. The College Examination Board does not grade this writing sample. It merely forwards it to the college of your choice.

A Bulletin of Information concerning the Scholastic Aptitude Test, The Achievement Tests, and the Writing Sample is available upon request from the College Entrance Examination Board, P. O. Box 592, Princeton, New Jersey.

119. A BRIEF HISTORY OF THE ENGLISH LANGUAGE

Because the English language is our rightful heritage, one handed down to us by the English, Scotch, and Irish colonists who settled our country in the seventeenth century, we often take it for granted. And yet the origins and development of our language comprise an interesting story with which everyone who uses English should become at least slightly acquainted. Our language is a priceless legacy that, in a continuous process of growth and change, has come down to us from beyond antiquity.

119a. ORIGINS OF ENGLISH

Although our interest in the language we have inherited may be slight, and our concern about the origins of language itself even less than that, thousands of scholars have excitedly debated for centuries about the beginnings of speech. As of now, no one yet knows who "invented" language or when and how it came into existence. Arguments about the birth of speech have been so varied, so vigorous, and so fruitless

567

that scholars today hold that language was never *invented* at all. They contend that language is apparently so native to man that it began to spring up in many ways and many forms when vertebrates attempted to become human and that, indeed, man has had language of one sort or another ever since he could really be called human. Humanity and language may be only two aspects of the same thing. If so, language may be considered one way of defining man.

Ancient Greeks studied their own language and wrote useful and sound grammars of it during the five centuries immediately preceding the Christian era. (These Greek grammarians gave us the eight parts of speech which we still study.) But they had no better idea than we do today where language actually originated and, furthermore, knew little about languages other than their own which had sprung up in centuries before them. The Old Testament indicates that God and Adam began talking as soon as Adam was created, but the Bible does not suggest what language they used. Later in the Bible, we are informed that the Lord "confounded" the languages of certain people so as to prevent their erecting a building into the sky (the Tower of Babel), but most linguists feel that this account has more theological than philological meaning.

And yet a few actual facts about language were positively known for many years before the Christian era. It was clear to students that Latin was a different language from Greek. It was later recognized that Latin had changed from Classical times to such an extent that the tongue had become Italian in its native peninsula, French as it had been spoken in what was then known as Gaul, and Spanish and Portuguese as it was used on the Iberian peninsula. Learned scholars argued that if these languages shared Latin as a father, it was reasonable to assume that Latin, too, must have had a father at some time and in some place. In fact, reasoned some scholars, might not all languages have descended from a single parent language as all men are said to descend from Adam and his spouse? Precisely this assumption by philologists has led to the conviction that indeed there was at one time a vast system of tongues known as Indo-European, a complex language family in which grammatical structures and vocabularies of the various branches basically corresponded.

This Indo-European family of languages flourished on the plains of eastern Europe north of the Black Sea several thousand years before the Christian era. The group includes many culturally and politically important tongues, especially those of the Italic, Hellenic, Slavic, Indo-Iranian, and Germanic branches. (It is from the last-named that English has directly descended.) Scholars can only guess at the exact makeup of this ancient progenitor-language, but when some of the cuneiform writings of Sanskrit, a member tongue, were uncovered, diligent students found valuable leads to the nature of Indo-European which point to the fact that English, if not a direct lineal descendant, is undeniably related to it through its connection with Germanic dialects.

It should be remembered that "Indo-European" probably never existed as a specific spoken and written language and that it is a fabrication of linguistic scholars. Furthermore, scholars are uncertain about the peoples who have been labeled "Indo-Europeans"; even their name has been coined for them. Apparently, these vaguely-referred-to persons were a semi-nomadic people who lived in what we would call an almost barbaric state. And yet the highly inflected tongue which they are reputed to have used has accounted for most of the languages of Europe and many of the most important in North and South America, Asia, and Australia.

It should also be remembered that the figure of speech, "language family," is an approximate description of linguistic relationships and not an exact reference. A parent language, such as Indo-European, does not produce an offspring at a specific time and place in the manner that a mother bears a child.

When history dawned over western and northwestern Europe, the territory we now know as England, Scotland, and Ireland was inhabited by tribes of fishermen and hunters known as Celts. Invading Romans succeeded in conquering most of these tribes, but the Roman Empire began to decline after several centuries. When the last of the Romans left the islands during the fifth century A.D., Germanic peoples began to move west to take over the forsaken areas.

Before they invaded Britain, these Germanic tribes, from one of whose dialects our English language was derived, had lived mainly along the shores of the Baltic Sea in northern Germany. They were a fierce and nomadic people, savage in their ways, who at least ten centuries before the birth of Christ had been roaming the fields and forests of northern Europe. Three of these tribes—the Angles, Saxons, and Jutes —spoke dialects which differed from each other but were related. Furthermore, in the course of their later wanderings over the European continent, the Germani, as they were called, encountered traders and soldiers from then-dominant Rome, from whom they borrowed and incorporated into their own speech such practical words as *wine, cheap, cook,* and *anchor.* These early Latin borrowings began a process of continuous word adoption which is still a characteristic of English today.

119b. OLD ENGLISH

The Angles, Saxons, and Jutes who began their invasion of the lowlands of Britain in the fifth century were Germanic tribes from northwest Germany and Denmark: the Saxons came from the Holstein district of Germany, the Jutes from Jutland (a part of Denmark), and the Angles from Schleswig, also a German state at the base of the Danish peninsula. The Angles, called "Angli" in Latin and Germanic, gave the name "Engla-land" to the new country; by 1000 A.D., the name was acknowledged by all the Germanic peoples who had settled there. It was from the mixing and mingling of Germanic dialects, after the occupation was complete and intercourse with the continent was largely discontinued, that English sprang. After the year 600, when St. Augustine introduced Christianity, and the islands now known as Great Britain had undergone at least partial Christian conversion, a superstructure of adopted Latin words began to give the language a new dimension.

Contrary to what one might expect from relatively primitive and nomadic tribes, Old English comprised a remarkably large vocabulary, estimated by scholars to have amounted to almost 50,000 words. This "word hoard," as some Anglo-Saxons picturesquely called it, was partly attributable to a talent for modifying and joining two base words to form a new one; thus, Anglo-Saxons were able to express new, occasionally even sophisticated, concepts through the use of familiar material. For example, a native word, *God*, was combined with *spell*, meaning "message," to make *Godspell*, "message of God," or, in modern English, *Gospel*. Other related words were *godcund*, "divine"; *godferht*, "pious,"; *godspellian*, "preach the gospel"; *godsunu*, "godson." The words *gospel* and *godson* are found in modern English, whereas other secondary words have been supplanted.

If an Anglo-Saxon were heard speaking his native tongue today, he might be dimly understood; however, because of different spellings, heavy inflections, and the use of symbols no longer in existence, written Old English appears at least as foreign as do French and Latin. Even so, many words are recognizable: hete (hate); weorc (work); sāwol (soul); fȳr (fire); heofan (heaven). A noun, *gelīca*, whose modern counterpart is *like,* was inflected, that is, given numerous changes to denote its use as an adjective, a verb, an adverb, or a preposition. Today's English depends more heavily upon word order than inflection to convey meaning, but our word *like* nevertheless has the same functional versatility: "I won't deal with his *like*" (noun); "as *like* as two peas" (adjective); "we *like* her" (verb); "more *like* forty than thirty" (adverb); "cry *like* a baby" (preposition).

The Lord's prayer, here given in the dialect spoken about the time of King Alfred (ninth century), is largely foreign-appearing:

Fæder ūre þū þe eart on heofonum, sī þin nama gehalgod.
Father our thou that art on heavens, be thy name hallowed.

Tobecume þīn rīce. Gewurþe þīn willa on eorþan swā swā on
Come thy kingdom. Be done thy will on earth just as on

heofonum. Ūrne gedæghwāmlīcan hlāf syle ūs tō dæg. And forgyf
heavens. Our daily bread give us to-day. And forgive

ūs ūre gyltas, swā swā wē forgyfaþ ūram gyltendum. And ne
us our guilts, just as we forgive those guilty to us. And do not

gelæd þū ūs on costnunge, ac ālȳs ūs of yfele. Sō þlīce.
lead thou us into temptation, but unloose us from evil. Verily.

NOTES:

1. The character þ, called a "thorn," has the sound of modern *th*.

2. Despite differences in spelling (and thus in pronunciation) several of the words are easily recognizable: *Fæder*, *forgyf*, etc.

3. Inflectional endings are frequent. *Heofonum*, for example, is a plural dative.

4. Old English contains few words borrowed from Latin or any other source. For example, *costnunge* was a native word which, of course, has been replaced by a later borrowing from Latin, "temptation."

119c. MIDDLE ENGLISH

Old English survived an invasion of Scandinavians occurring in the ninth century, but it was very nearly swallowed up by the great Norman Conquest in 1066. This was an onslaught by people militarily and politically superior to the defenders. The eventual result was a vast change in the character of English, a change so profound that the language of the Old English period, which may be said to have ended about 1100, resembled the language at the end of the Middle English period (about 1475) far less than Middle English resembles our own.

About the time that Anglo-Saxons were settling in England, similar Northmen were migrating to Normandy, on the northern coast of France. In a century and a half, they succeeded not only in absorbing some elements of French civilization but also in adopting the French language. After their victory in the Battle of Hastings (1066), these Normans sought not to dispossess the English, as earlier Scandinavians had done, but rather to become their masters. Feudalism was imposed, a French aristocracy largely replaced the English nobility, and a new judicial system was established. Because it was the tongue of the ruling class, French was the only acceptable language for affairs of the church, government, society, and education. "Common" people continued to speak English, but their dialect underwent dramatic changes as it gradually dropped inflections and became more and more simplified. By about 1500, the end of the period known as Middle English, many thousands of French words and French-modified Latin words had been assimilated into native speech. An educated guess is that half the vocabulary used by Geoffrey Chaucer (c. 1340-1400) consisted of Old French and Anglo-French words.

Though more familiar to our eyes than the version quoted from King Alfred's time, the Lord's Prayer as John Wycliffe (c. 1320-1384) set it down in the first translation into English of the entire Bible is still difficult to read:

> Oure fadir that art in heuenes, halwid be thi name; thi kyngdom cumme to; be thi wille don as in heuen and in erthe; ȝif to vs this day ouer breed oure other substaunce; and forȝeue to vs oure dettis as we forȝeue to oure dettours; and leede vs nat in to temptacioun, but delyuere vs fro yuel. Amen.

By way of contrast, here is the Lord's Prayer as it appeared in Matthew VI:9-13 of the King James or Authorized Version of the Bible, published in 1611:

9. After this manner therefore pray ye: Our Father which art in heaven, Hallowed be thy name.
10. Thy kingdom come. Thy will be done on earth, as it *is* in heaven.
11. Give us this day our daily bread.
12. And forgive us our debts, as we forgive our debtors.
13. And lead us not into temptation, but deliver us from evil: For thine is the kingdom, and the power, and the glory, for ever. Amen.

Here the wording approaches present-day English.

119d. MODERN ENGLISH

English evolved to its present state through processes of growth and decay, of expansion and simplification. As with human beings, the growth did not come smoothly but in spurts, sometimes dramatic, interspersed with calm periods in which changes were barely perceptible. Such a "spurt" in the development of English followed the innovation of printing from movable type, introduced into England in 1476 by William Caxton. So rapid was the effect of this method of producing books that in less than two centuries there were over 20,000 titles in English, and when Shakespeare wrote his plays, between a third and a half of the population could read. Cheaper books, more available education for the middle classes, and trade with new lands caused a deep change in linguistic development: the language became more uniform and was thus enabled to spread.

In the Middle English period, the most drastic changes in English had been grammatical: complex inflections and systems of conjugations and declensions had been pared away, and the language had moved toward clearer, more direct expression heavily based upon word order and intonation. True, remnants of the old structure can be found even today: the plural endings shown by *foot, feet; tooth, teeth; ox, oxen; mouse, mice;* and the tense formation shown by *shake, shook, shaken.* But if some examples like these may be cited, many thousands more attest to an evolved regularity, simplification, and standardization.

Unlike Middle English, however, which had survived a relatively massive injection of French import-words, modern English drastically changed in vocabulary. Increased trade, popular education, and above all the effects of the Renaissance gave the language an enormous appetite.

Our modern English vocabulary is roughly half Germanic (English and Scandinavian) and half Romance (Latin and French). The Scandinavians gave us such common words as *awkward, egg, bread, kid, crook, scare, ugly, ill, call, scrub,* and *want.* Words from the French are so numerous as to be virtually uncountable, but include *city, charity, interior, action, grace, dinner, merge, price, spouse,* and *residence. Acrobat, catarrh,* and *magic* are Greek; so are *arithmetic, astronomy, rhetoric, music, theater, drama,* and *scene —* words which acknowledge ancient Greece as the cradle of liberal arts. Latin, the language of scholars and churchmen, supplied our earliest loan words, and today the language abounds with them as well as a Latin terminology for such sciences as biology, botany, chemistry, engineering, medicine, and others. But English has ranged even wider for loans; we are sometimes surprised to find that the words *cruller, golf,* and *wagon* are Dutch; that *chess, lemon,* and *shawl* are Persian; that *piano, balcony,* and *granite* come from Italy; and that *cork, mosquito,* and *vanilla* were imported from Spain. The Australians have given us *boomerang,* the Mexicans *chocolate,* the Malaysians *bamboo* and *gingham,* and American Indians *chipmunk, moccasin, hominy,* and *moose.* The list is virtually endless.

English-speaking people have never attempted to keep their language pure. Some critics attribute this tendency to linguistic laziness, to a preference for adopting scraps of other languages rather than for designing new words from native material. Others say that modern English simply grew faster than English resources could nourish. Because of this, our English possesses extraordinary richness, clarity, and flexibility. It lends itself to continuous simplification and at the same time welcomes terms from any language which will enhance the expression of an idea. It is a truly cosmopolitan tongue. One day, perhaps, and perhaps not, it may become a universal world language.

120. LINGUISTICS

Linguistics is a term derived from a Latin word meaning "tongue" or "language" — *lingua.* Thus the very origin of the word indicates that linguistics and those who study and practice it, *linguists,* are more concerned with language as speech and its sounds than with writing and its meaning. A basic assumption of linguists is that language is primarily a matter of speech.

For each of us, language is largely an unconscious process. Since infancy, we have automatically been uttering words and relating them to each other without conscious thought or concern, without even knowing or caring what structures are involved. And yet without a substantial knowledge of grammar we would never have been able to phrase even the simple words and short sentences of late infancy and early childhood. As a two-year-old throwing a toy from your playpen, you may have exclaimed "Me no want," a statement not so "correct" as "I do not want it," but fully grammatical in the sense that a foreigner's "No me want" would not be. The ordinary user of English, whether two or twenty years of age, knows much about his language which he cannot state in "rules." He may be unable to formulate the principles that enable him to make a sensible, understandable statement, but he has no more difficulty expressing thoughts than he does in recognizing a physical object such as a rubber ball and determining its size, appearance, and distance from him. The basic principles of grammar are few and not difficult to "pick up" from one's infancy, but the English language is complicated, as are all languages. Understanding its grammar in every detail requires long study — a task more exacting and less revealing than high school writing itself requires or can profit by.

Linguists attempt to present and explain in fairly exact form primarily those facts about language that all of its speakers and writers know intuitively. They also try to account for a native speaker's ability to understand almost any sentence of his language and to make sentences of his own which are understandable to others. That is, they make clear why "Me no want" is an understandable English sentence, however "incorrect," and why "No me want" is not. In sum, linguists have sought to find out how people actually do speak, to distinguish speech characteristics from those of writing, and usually to avoid judgments about how people *should* speak and write their language.

Linguistics has been defined as the scientific study of language, but it more accurately may be called a *systematic* study. Its methods are objective, but since speech is a uniquely human characteristic, linguistics is really a more humanistic than scientific discipline. In fact, linguistics is an investigation of human behavior and thus is scientific to the extent that certain branches of psychology and sociology are. Language is sequences of sounds. Sound is invisible, and no one can "see" its structure as, for example, one can see the structure of a cell or of the human body. And yet linguistics is objective rather than subjective in its methods; it has borrowed techniques from both the social and natural sciences; and it may fairly be called a branch of anthropology.

The word *anthropology,* which means "the science of man and his works," is made up of *anthro-,* a borrowing from Greek meaning "human," and *-logy,* a combining form used in naming bodies of knowledge as, for instance, biology, theology, psychology, and geology. (The relationship of linguistics to anthropology is suggested by the strongly held belief that language ability is the single most important characteristic of human beings.) The division of anthropology known as English linguistics involves examination and analysis of the structure and development of the English language, a study of how those who speak English actually form sentences.

In high school English classes, a branch of anthropology can hardly be expected to receive the rigorous study it requires for adequate understanding and application. The direct relationship of composition and the science of linguistics becomes even more strained when it is recognized that although speech is primary and basic, nevertheless it does differ in many ways from writing which, after all, is the primary concern of the course you are now taking. (See Section 117a.)

The connection becomes yet more tenuous when it is realized that linguistics is logically seen to be a division of still other sciences than anthropology. Linguistics is linked with physiology and physics in its concern with the production, transmission, and reception of the sounds of speech. It is related to psychology in its approach to the origin and meaningfulness of speech forms. Both linguistics and sociology are involved in study of the origin, development, and functioning of human society; without language, there could be no human society, and thus no sociology. In fact, linguistics is even linked with the humanities in the sense that both are concerned with the expression of human thought in language.

In short, linguistics is a deliberate, conscious, purposeful activity of the whole mind and its means of communication by speech.

This systematic study involves numerous technical and sophisticated areas:

1. *Etymology,* a study of historical linguistic change,

especially as applied to individual words and the history of a particular word or phrase.

2. *Phonology*, a description of the primary sound units of speech. *Phonetics* may be defined as the science or study of speech sounds and their production, relaying, and reception —analysis, classification, and transcription.

3. *Morphology*, the patterns of word formation in a given language, the primary meaningful units of speech and their derivation, inflection (changes in form), and composition. A *morpheme* is a linguistic term for the smallest grammatically meaningful unit in a language.

4. *Syntax*, a study of the rules for forming grammatical sentences in a language, the arrangement of morphemes, words, and phrases in meaningful utterances.

5. *Semantics*, the study of linguistic development through classifying and examining changes in word meaning and form (see Section 113).

Involved as this sketchy explanation is, still further detail is needed fully to define linguistics. This highly technical field involves *juncture* (a distinctive sound feature marking the phonological—sound—boundary of a word, phrase, clause, or sentence). Also involved are *phonemes*, a class or set of closely related sounds considered as a single sound. *Pitch* (the degree of height or depth of a tone or sound) is a concern of linguistics because a set of voice signals indicates emphasis which, for example, distinguishes a statement from a question. Still other phases of linguistics would be mentioned in a thorough definition.

Faced by such a formidable body of technical material, you may wish to retreat to a study of whatever minimum "grammar" you need for successfully completing writing assignments. But a "new look" at grammar may help you in writing. Certainly some understanding of the paragraphs which follow will not impede your writing and may, indeed, prove interesting and rewarding.

The development of a systematic description of language has produced several approaches. The two thus far most widely accepted are called *structural linguistics* and *transformational grammar*. The first may be said to describe what a language system is; the second explains how a particular language system is formed. In other words, structural linguistics deals with the grammar of a sentence already written; transformational grammar is the grammar of a sentence being written.

120a. STRUCTURAL LINGUISTICS.

Structural linguistics is a somewhat incongruous term because all linguistics is necessarily concerned with structure (form, system) and because anyone who pursues the study of language is to some extent a linguist. But structural linguistics, or *structural grammar,* or *structural analysis,* is a common label for that kind of linguistic study which began with anthropologists in the United States about the turn of the century, thrived during the 1940's, and has since somewhat altered its focus and direction.

Structural grammarians say that language is first of all a structure, a system, an involved set of patterns. Any such system, or set of patterns, they logically assert, can be explained systematically; that is, a series of patterns in spoken language can be isolated and described. Structural linguists claim that older, or "traditional," grammar has explained the language only in bits and pieces and has dealt insufficiently with the ways in which words are formed and the methods by which they are chosen and arranged in phrases, clauses, and sentences.

Second, structural grammarians contend that in describing a language one must actually explain its *forms* and not merely label them. They object to traditional definitions of grammatical classes ("A noun denotes or names a person, place, or thing, a quality, idea, or action"). Such definitions, according to the doctrine of structural grammar, are logically indefensible and useless in practice. Structural grammarians insist that all such "semantic" or "notional" definitions are inadequate and that only linguistic forms can be made the subjects of precise statements.

All words, and combinations of words, give signals, each of which has a function. In structural grammar, focus is primarily on the *form* of the signals (system) and secondarily on meaning. To a structuralist, words and their functions are classified by formal and structural means (changes in the form of a word, the various ways it can be used in a sentence) with no particular attention paid to the meanings involved. That is, in structural grammar, "the cat's whiskers" and "the jat's whiskers" would receive equal attention because of the form and function of *cat* and *jat*, even though the latter is meaningless.

Form Classes

Using the principle that words with the same inflectional characteristics and the same positions in sentences should be grouped together, structuralists have come to recognize four *form classes* of words which correspond approximately to the parts of speech traditionally known as nouns, verbs, adjectives, and adverbs. The class of a given word may be determined by trying the word out in test frames typical of the noun, verb, adjective, and adverb forms:

Noun	She was making ____ (s).
Adjective	He feels ____.
Adverb	They have done it ____.
Verb	He can ____ (it).

Structure Words

All other words—a few hundred as compared to many thousands of form class words—are called *function* or *structure* words and consist mainly of pronouns, prepositions, and conjunctions. Their job is to provide information about the relationships of parts of a sentence made up of form classes of words. Being function words (for example, *a, about, by, everyone, through, unless,* and *what*), they mean little by themselves but they do supply clues to the structure of a sentence; they make a framework into which "form class" words can be fitted.

A ____ can ____ unless the ____ seems ____.

In the above sentence, the blanks can be filled by thousands of different words and word combinations, yet structurally the sentence remains the same.

A *flight* can *proceed* unless the *weather* seems *inclement*.
A *musician* can *perform* unless the *audience* seems *hostile*.

Structures and Functions

Combinations of form class words and function words produce various kinds of structures: noun, verb, and modifier structures. Noun and verb structures are named after the form class words that usually are found in them, but it is as *structures* — composed of single words or groups of words — that they are used like nouns or like verbs. All substantives — nouns, pronouns, verbal nouns, or phrases and clauses used like nouns — are noun structures. In the sentence, "Snow is falling," the single word *snow* is a noun structure. In the sentence, "Every skier hopes that snow is falling," *every skier* and *that snow is falling* are both noun structures.

Verb structures consist of words of the verb form class together with such function words as linking verbs:

Couples *dance.*

Diana *has been dancing.*

Sometimes a structure word may be the entire verb structure:

They *are* dancers.

Modifier structures are words from adjective or adverb form classes or groups of words used as adjectives and adverbs are used:

His sister is married *too.*

He quit *our* firm *at the peak of success.*

People *who like reading* are *seldom* bored.

Patterns

Structural linguists normally classify sentences according to the structures they contain and the arrangement of these structures. Different kinds of *patterns* are the result of such classification:

Noun-verb (subject-verb):

"Swimmers compete."

Noun-verb-essential modifier (subject-verb-predicate adjective):

"Swimmers are healthy."

"That water looks cold."

Noun-verb-noun (subject-verb-subjective complement):

"Mary and Tom are newlyweds."

"They were students."

"Cutting the grass qualifies as gardening."

Noun-verb-noun (subject-verb-object):

"Children make noise."

"Girls want boyfriends."

Noun-verb-noun-noun (subject-verb-indirect object-direct object)

"Mary got Jim a date."

Noun-verb-noun-noun (subject-verb-direct object-object complement)

"The boys elected Bill captain."

Noun-verb-noun-adjective (subject-verb-direct object-adjective complement)

"The woman considered politicians foolish."

From such basic patterns, more complicated sentences may be evolved by using structures within structures; that is, by expanding through the insertion of modifiers or through substitution of more complex structures for simple ones.

Parts of Patterns

Structural grammar has provided an objective test for breaking a sentence into the structures it contains so that the grammatical relationship of words may be revealed. Because a sentence may hold structures which themselves are parts of larger structures, the test assumes that any sentence, simple or compound or complex, consists mainly of two parts having a clear grammatical relationship to each other, and that these parts also have parts in relation, and so on until the sentence is broken down to its individual words. When a structuralist makes his first cut, he divides a sentence into the two conventional parts of subject and predicate. These are the first elements, called *Immediate Constituents*, in structural analysis. Here is a complex sentence:

The puppy who slept in our basement found its owner.

Division of the sentence into two main parts would show a cut between the words *basement* and *found*, indicating the grammatical relationship of actor to action. This relationship may be further clarified by substituting a single word on each side of the divisional cut:

The puppy who slept in our basement/found his owner.

He   did

This test may be applied to breakdowns into smaller and smaller parts of the two main structures:

The puppy / who slept in our basement // found / his owner.

Here, the clause *who slept in our basement* works as a modifier structure related to *the puppy;* the verb *found* is complemented by the noun structure, *his owner.*

In further dividing the structures noted above, one may use the same rule of direct grammatical relationship:

The / puppy (modifier and noun structure)

who / slept in our basement (subject and predicate of subordinate clause)

found / his owner (verb and noun structure)

his / owner (modifier and noun structure)

The prepositional phrase *in our basement* in the subordinate clause may also be divided:

in / our basement (subordinator and noun structure).

In summary, structural linguistics seeks (1) to classify most words by their formal characteristics and their positions in sentences, not by semantic definitions; (2) to show that words appear in sentences as structures; (3) to show that a structure functions as a unit and that one structure can, and often does, contain another.

120b. TRANSFORMATIONAL GRAMMAR

Another school of linguists gradually became as dissatisfied with what they considered the deficiencies of structural grammar as they had been with the shortcomings of traditional grammar. In 1957, Professor Noam Chomsky, of the Massachusetts Institute of Technology, published *Syntactic Structures*, a work which raised many questions about language and language learning that Chomsky felt no previous "school of grammar" had successfully answered. His contention, eagerly embraced by the group which became his followers, is that when one learns a language he learns a sentence-making mechanism. This doctrine, which has become known as *transformational grammar* or *generative grammar* or *transformational generative grammar*, differs markedly from its predecessors—in some respects more widely from structural grammar than from traditional.

It should be noted, however, that the new term has been widely misused: to Chomsky and most of his disciples, the term *generative* reflects a view of the purpose and function of a study of grammar; *transformation* refers to a device for indicating certain relationships between structures in a grammar. Although the terms are freely interchanged and combined, they are not entirely synonymous.

Whereas traditional grammar explains the way a language works, and structural grammar sets forth a language system, *transformational* grammar explains the *processes* by which sentences are formed. Much as carpentry instructions can explain what a bench is by directing the making of one, transformational grammar seeks to provide an understanding of English sentence construction through step-by-step directions. Transformational grammar begins by assuming that a few basic sentence patterns, similar to the patterns for structural grammar, may be called *kernel sentences*. These, when combined or added to or changed according to set rules, become *transformed sentences*, or *transforms*, and, again through single steps, are made into "pronounceable" English sentences.

Kernel Sentences

Beginning with kernel sentences, the first forming rule in transformational grammar reads like this:

$$S \rightarrow NP + VP$$

The S stands for sentence, NP stands for noun phrase, and VP stands for verb phrase. The arrow (an arrow is used in every transformational grammar rule) indicates that the part of the formula on the right of the arrow is a fuller description of the part on the left. Thus $S \rightarrow NP + VP$ means "Sentence should be a noun phrase plus a verb phrase" and is an instruction to rewrite S as NP + VP.

The second rule, also written as a formula with an arrow, then explains what NP should be; it is devised so that the first instruction may be carried out.

$$NP \rightarrow (D) + N.$$

Here NP must be rewritten as a D plus N, terms which themselves need covering rules:

$D \rightarrow$ a, the

$N \rightarrow$ bag, mouse, poet, pencil, etc.

NP, therefore can be rewritten as *a* or *the* plus *bag* or *pencil* or any other noun. Or, because D is surrounded by parentheses which indicate that D may, but need not, be present, NP may be rewritten in three ways:

> the mouse (D: the)
> a poet (D: a)
> physics (D: not used)

The preceding rules tell us how to make half the rewrite for S. For the other half, verb phrase, more rules are given:

> VP → verb + NP
>
> verb → ran, used, wrote, bulged, etc.

With the elements of NP already known, the instructions for rewriting S are complete. Following the successive steps set forth, a kernel sentence can be formed, as illustrated below:

Sentence

NP	VP
(D) N	VP
the N	VP
the poet	VP
the poet	verb (NP)
the poet	used (NP)
the poet	used (D) N
the poet	used a N
the poet	used a pencil

Omitting the use of NP in parentheses will result in another kind of sentence:

Sentence

NP	VP
(D) N	VP
the N	VP
the poet	VP
the poet	verb (NP)
the poet	wrote

Many sentences may be produced from these simple rules, although many more rules are needed for certain refinements.

Transformed Sentences

Kernel sentences are made by single-step rules; another set of rules governs combining, adding to, and switching around the elements of kernel sentences in order to produce new, or "transformed," sentences. These rules, presented in formulas, cover such transformations as the kernel sentence "They are here" into "Are they here?"; "Where are they?"; "They are here, aren't they?"; "Who are here?" The rules also cover the combining of kernel sentences to produce such sentences as "The brave boy rescued the swimmer." Because an adjective standing before the noun it modifies is considered as a predicate adjective from one kernel sentence incorporated into another kernel sentence, this sentence is a combination of two kernels:

> The boy rescued the swimmer.)
> The boy was brave.   ) The brave boy rescued the
>   ) swimmer.

Likewise, rules cover substituting a *who* or *that* for the subject of one kernel sentence and then combining the results to effect a more complex sentence:

> The barber was promoted.   )
> The barber clipped the poodle.) The barber who clipped the
>   )   poodle was promoted.

Rules exist for such transforms as passive, emphatic sentences, other kinds of questions, and more complex forms. Here, for example, are some transforms derived from "Judy put the cans in the closet":

1. The cans were put in the closet by Judy.
2. What was put in the closet by Judy?
3. What did Judy put in the closet?
4. Did Judy put the cans in the closet?
5. Where did Judy put the cans?

Pronunciation

The third major set of rules in transformational grammar applies to changing the results of transformations into pronounceable (sense-making) English sentences. For example, the appropriate pronunciation rules for the sentence: *The + chorus + have + present + be + en + sing + ing + in + the + cathedral* would read: *have + present = has*; *be + -en = been*; and *sing + -ing = singing*. Using these rules, the sentence would become *The chorus has been singing in the cathedral.*

INDEX